Praise for

Ronald C. White, Jr., and *A. Lincoln*

"If you read one book about Lincoln, make it *A. Lincoln*."   —*USA Today*

"Does the world really need another Lincoln bio? White's exhaustive yet accessible work tips the scales to yes."   —*People*

"This thoroughly researched book belongs on the A-list of major biographies of the tall Illinoisian; it's a worthy companion for all who admire Lincoln's prose and his ability to see into, and explain, America's greatest crisis."   —*The Washington Post Book World*

"While this is a serious, weighty book, it's also enormously readable, illuminating Lincoln's intellectual prowess and personal magnetism in a way we've rarely seen before."
—*Chicago Tribune* (10 Top Books About Lincoln)

"The torrent of Lincoln books past and present . . . means that the bar is necessarily set high. *A. Lincoln: A Biography,* by Ronald White, Jr., an academic and established Lincoln historian, [is] among the most substantial new entrants."   —*The Economist*

"Distinctive and winning . . . [A] lively biography."   —*The Boston Globe*

"Impressive."   —*U.S. News & World Report*

"Comprehensive . . . Taking advantage of newly available resources, such as the recent publication of the voluminous Lincoln Legal Papers, Mr. White delivers a strong narrative . . . [aimed] at the general reader."   —*The Wall Street Journal*

"Comprehensive . . . an admirable account of the life in full."
—*Los Angeles Times Book Review*

"This brilliant account of the man and his times will be the standard for biographers."
—*San Francisco Chronicle*

"A sure-footed and richly detailed biography."   —New York *Daily News*

"A vivid and readable narrative . . . [White] is that rarity: a scholar who can tell a good story."   —*The Miami Herald*

"Sympathetic and encyclopedic . . . thorough and lively."   —*Pittsburgh Post-Gazette*

"Engaging from beginning to end, a worthy memorial to its subject in this bicentennial year."   —*St. Louis Post-Dispatch*

"One of 2009's best bets."   —*Lexington Herald-Leader*

"Towering . . . a work of such depth, care, and craft that it stands alone as the most important single biography of Lincoln."   —*The Courier-Journal* (Louisville, KY)

"Ron White's *A. Lincoln* is a superb biography of America's greatest leader. It is fully fleshed, thoughtful, provocative, and scholarly. Lincoln is never out of fashion. After a generation during which three comprehensive one-volume Lincoln biographies appeared—Benjamin P. Thomas's *Abraham Lincoln: A Biography* in 1952; Stephen B. Oates's *With Malice Toward None: A Life of Abraham Lincoln* in 1977; and David Herbert Donald's *Lincoln* in 1995—*A. Lincoln: A Biography,* with its rich detail, will be the standard text for years to come. The author includes the religious connections to his subject like no other biographer. This is a remarkable Lincoln biography by an outstanding writer."

—FRANK J. WILLIAMS, founding chair of the Lincoln Forum
and chief justice of the Rhode Island Supreme Court

"Lincoln's bicentennial will bring a flood of books about the sixteenth president. Anyone seeking an expansive, thoroughly engaging biography should turn to Ronald C. White's gracefully written narrative. It does full justice to the complexity and drama of the era and allows readers to understand how Lincoln ultimately triumphed in guiding the nation through its greatest trial."

—GARY W. GALLAGHER, John L. Nau III Professor of History, University of Virginia

"Ronald C. White's *A. Lincoln* is the best biography of Lincoln since David Herbert Donald's *Lincoln*. In many respects it is better than Donald's biography, because it has incorporated the scholarship of the past fourteen years and is written in a fluent style that will appeal to a large range of general readers as well as Lincoln aficionados. The special strengths that lift this work above other biographies include a brilliant analysis of Lincoln's principal speeches and writings, which were an important weapon in his political leadership and statesmanship, and on which Ronald C. White is the foremost expert. Another strength is White's analysis of Lincoln's evolving religious convictions, which shaped the core of his effective leadership, his moral integrity. White's discussion of Lincoln's changing attitudes and policies with respect to slavery and race is also a key aspect of this biography. Amid all the books on Lincoln that will be published during the coming year, this one will stand out as one of the best."

—JAMES M. MCPHERSON, Pulitzer Prize–winning author of *Battle Cry of Freedom*

"A beautifully written, deeply personal story of Lincoln's life and service to his country. Ronald C. White's moving account is particularly strong in its analyses of Lincoln's rhetoric and the process by which the president reached decisions."

—DANIEL WALKER HOWE, Pulitzer Prize–winning author of
What Hath God Wrought: The Transformation of America, 1815–1848

"Each generation requires—and seems to inspire—its own masterly one-volume Lincoln biography, and scholar Ronald C. White has crowned the bicentennial year with an instant classic for the twenty-first century. Wise, scholarly, evenhanded, and elegant, the book at once informs and inspires, with a rewarding new emphasis on the complex meaning and timeless importance of Lincoln's great words. Brimming with new anecdotes and informed interpretations, White's superb study brings vivid new life to an American immortal."

—HAROLD HOLZER, author of *Lincoln: President-Elect,* and
co-chairman, Abraham Lincoln Bicentennial Commission

A. LINCOLN

A. LINCOLN

A Biography

. . . .

RONALD C. WHITE, JR.

RANDOM HOUSE

TRADE PAPERBACKS

NEW YORK

For my wife,
Cynthia Conger White

2010 Random House Trade Paperback Edition

Copyright © 2009 by Ronald C. White, Jr.
Maps copyright © 2009 by David Lindroth

Published in the United States by Random House Trade
Paperbacks, an imprint of The Random House Publishing
Group, a division of Random House, Inc., New York.

RANDOM HOUSE TRADE PAPERBACKS and colophon are
trademarks of Random House, Inc.

Originally published in hardcover in the United States
by Random House, an imprint of The Random House
Publishing Group, a division of Random House, Inc.,
in 2009.

LIBRARY OF CONGRESS CATALOGING-IN-
PUBLICATION DATA
White, Ronald C. (Ronald Cedric).
A. Lincoln: a biography / Ronald C. White, Jr.
p. cm.
Includes bibliographical references and index.
ISBN 978-0-8129-7570-3
1. Lincoln, Abraham, 1809–1865.   2. Presidents—United
States—Biography.   3. United States—Politics and
government—1861–1865.   I. Title.
II. Title: Abraham Lincoln.
E457.W597 2009 973.7092—dc22 2008028840
[B]
Printed in the United States of America

www.atrandom.com

4 6 8 9 7 5

Book design by Barbara M. Bachman

CONTENTS

...

LIST OF MAPS

...

CAST OF CHARACTERS

...

EDWARD DICKINSON BAKER (1811–61) A close friend, Baker served with Lincoln in the Illinois legislature. Lincoln named his second son, Edward, after Baker. Elected U.S. senator from Oregon, he raised the California Regiment at the outbreak of the Civil War.

EDWARD BATES (1793–1869) Missouri lawyer and conservative Whig politician who took his time in entering the Republican Party. Vied with Lincoln for the Republican nomination in 1860 and then served as attorney general during the Civil War.

MONTGOMERY BLAIR (1813–83) Member of a distinguished Democratic family who became a Republican over the slavery issue. Served as counsel for Dred Scott. Controversial postmaster general in Lincoln's cabinet.

NOAH BROOKS (1830–1903) Correspondent for the *Sacramento Daily Union* who became a close friend of both Abraham and Mary Lincoln. He reported on life inside Lincoln's White House, and was slated to become Lincoln's secretary in his second term.

ORVILLE HICKMAN BROWNING (1806–81) Conservative Illinois Republican who supported Edward Bates at the Republican convention. After the death of Stephen Douglas in 1861, Browning was appointed to complete his term. His diary is a source of information on Lincoln.

AMBROSE EVERETT BURNSIDE (1824–1881) A likeable and self-effacing West Pointer, Burnside and Lincoln struggled to find the right strategy for the Army of the Potomac's advance south and the curtailment of the Copperhead movement in the Midwest.

SIMON CAMERON (1799–1889) As a senator from Pennsylvania, he became a candidate for the Republican nomination for president in 1860. With some misgivings, Lincoln appointed him secretary of war in his cabinet.

PETER CARTWRIGHT (1785–1872) A Methodist circuit-riding evangelist who, as the Democratic candidate, ran against Lincoln in the 1846 congressional election.

SALMON P. CHASE (1808–73) Ohio senator and governor, and an anti-slavery leader in politics, Chase became a candidate for the Republican nomination for president in 1860. Chase served as secretary of the treasury in Lincoln's cabinet. He tried to outflank Lincoln for the Republican nomination in 1864. Despite all their differences, Lincoln appointed Chase chief justice of the United States.

HENRY CLAY (1777–1852) Lincoln admired Clay, a fellow Kentuckian, who three times ran unsuccessfully for president. He advocated Clay's "American System" of strong government support for economic growth. Lincoln called Clay his "beau ideal of a statesman."

JAMES C. CONKLING (1816–99) Lincoln's neighbor and fellow lawyer; when Lincoln decided he could not return to speak to a Union rally in Springfield in September 1863, he sent Conkling his speech to read at the meeting.

DAVID DAVIS (1815–86) Illinois lawyer and judge and a close friend of Lincoln when they traveled together across the Eighth Judicial Circuit in the 1850s. He served as Lincoln's campaign manager at the Republican convention in Chicago in 1860.

STEPHEN A. DOUGLAS (1813–61) Illinois Democratic rival, sponsored the Kansas-Nebraska Act in 1854 whose language about the extension of slavery into the territories helped prompt Lincoln's return to politics. Their debates in 1858 brought Lincoln national attention even though he lost to Douglas in a contest for the Senate. Douglas ran against Lincoln in the presidential contest of 1860.

FREDERICK DOUGLASS (1818–95) Editor and abolitionist, Douglass watched Lincoln from a distance starting in 1858, and then met him twice at the White House during the Civil War. A former slave, Douglass formed a distinctive relationship with Lincoln, culminating in Douglass's presence at Lincoln's second inauguration.

JOHN C. FRÉMONT (1813–90) The first Republican candidate for president, he lost to James Buchanan in 1856. Lincoln appointed him commander of the Department of the West in July 1861, but the president, Frémont, and Frémont's wife, Jessie, soon differed over government policy, including slavery.

ULYSSES S. GRANT (1822–85) Having failed in several civilian jobs in the 1850s, Grant rose through the Union army to become general in chief by the end of the Civil War. As Lincoln went through general after general in the first years of the war, Grant gained the president's admiration, which was returned in kind.

HORACE GREELEY (1811–72) Founding editor of the *New York Tribune* and powerful opinion maker, Greeley changed his opinion of Lincoln often. Lincoln's reply to Greeley's plea for him to move faster on emancipation marked the beginning of a series of public letters to present his views to a wider public.

PHINEAS DENSMORE GURLEY (1816–68) Lincoln appreciated the sermons of this learned minister of the New York Avenue Presbyterian Church in Washington, D.C. Lincoln met Gurley in the years he was rethinking the meaning of faith and God's activity in history.

JOHN J. HARDIN (1810–47) A friend, lawyer, and Whig politician from Jacksonville, Illinois, Hardin opposed Lincoln on internal improvements in the Illinois legislature and defeated him for the Whig nomination for Congress in 1843.

JOHN HAY (1838–1905) Young John Hay, a graduate of Brown, served as one of Lincoln's secretaries. With a literary flair, he and Lincoln read to each other. Hay's diary is one of the most insightful guides to the inner history of the Lincoln administration.

WILLIAM H. HERNDON (1818–91) Lincoln's surprise choice as law partner in 1844. Herndon, so unlike his senior partner in temperament and more radical in his political views, actively supported Lincoln's rise in Illinois politics.

JOSEPH HOOKER (1814–1879) He earned the nickname "Fighting Joe" for his courage under fire in the Virginia Peninsula campaign in the spring of 1862. Lincoln appointed him commander of the army of the Potomac in January 1863, and watched, with both admiration and alarm, Hooker's military leadership unfold at a critical time in the war.

NORMAN B. JUDD (1815–78) As an anti-Nebraska Democrat, he voted against Lincoln in the legislative vote for the Senate in 1855. Judd became a prominent Republican, chaired the state committee, and became a voice for Lincoln in northern Illinois and at the Republican convention in Chicago in 1860.

GEORGE B. MCCLELLAN (1826–85) Lincoln named McClellan, who received the nickname "Young Napoleon," commander of the Army of the Potomac in July 1861, and then general in chief of the Union army. Excellent at organizing and preparing his men to fight, he nonetheless shrank from fighting, often exaggerating the strength of enemy forces.

JOHN G. NICOLAY (1832–1901) Lincoln's loyal secretary, he admired the president in all ways. His notes about life in the White House would become source material for a biography of Lincoln he would write with John Hay.

WILLIAM H. SEWARD (1801–72) Lincoln's chief opponent for the Republican nomination for president in 1860; Lincoln asked him to become secretary of state. Disliked and criticized by many, Seward would become Lincoln's best friend in his cabinet.

WILLIAM TECUMSEH SHERMAN (1820–1891) After a struggling start at West Point, in business, and in the first years of the Civil War, Sherman rose to become a much-loved and criticized Union general who won victories at Atlanta and across the South in his controversial march to the sea.

JOSHUA F. SPEED (1814–82) A fellow Kentuckian, Speed became Lincoln's only truly close friend. They met when Lincoln moved to Springfield in 1837 and remained friends even when Speed moved back to Kentucky in 1841.

EDWIN M. STANTON (1814–69) A renowned lawyer, Stanton first met Lincoln in the "Reaper Case" in Cincinnati in 1855. Lincoln invited Stanton, a Democrat, to become his second secretary of war in January 1862.

CHARLES SUMNER (1811–74) Antislavery Republican senator from Massachusetts. Early in the war he believed Lincoln moved too slowly in his aid for African-Americans. As chairman of the Senate Committee on Foreign Relations, he proved enormously helpful to Lincoln.

LEONARD SWETT (1825–89) A lawyer who met Lincoln in 1849 on the Eighth Judicial Circuit, he told Lincoln in 1854, "Use me in any way you may think you can." Swett supported all of Lincoln's subsequent political campaigns and traveled to the White House from Illinois because Lincoln so valued his counsel.

LYMAN TRUMBULL (1813–96) A lawyer and Illinois Democrat, he ran against Lincoln for the 1855 Illinois Senate seat. He supported the founding of the Republican Party in Illinois in 1856 and thereafter became a critical ally of Lincoln.

ELIHU B. WASHBURNE (1816–1887) An antislavery Republican congressman from northern Illinois, he supported Lincoln in his 1855 and 1858 Senate races. Washburne became Lincoln's eyes and ears in Washington during the long secession winter before his inauguration in March 1861.

GIDEON WELLES (1802–78) As secretary of the navy in Lincoln's cabinet, he became one of the president's most sympathetic supporters. His diary is an invaluable source for understanding the Lincoln presidency.

A. LINCOLN

*The best-known sculpture of Abraham Lincoln is in the templed space of
the Lincoln Memorial. Daniel C. French sculpted this working model in 1916.
His final rendering of the huge statue was dedicated in 1922.*

CHAPTER I

A. Lincoln and the Promise of America

. . . .

E SIGNED HIS NAME "A. LINCOLN." A VISITOR TO ABRAHAM LINCOLN'S
Springfield, Illinois, home at Eighth and Jackson would find "A. Lincoln" in silvered Roman characters affixed to an octagonal black plate
on the front door. All through his life, people sought to complete the
A—to define Lincoln, to label or libel him. Immediately after his death
and continuing to the present, Americans have tried to explain the
nation's most revered president. A. Lincoln continues to fascinate us
because he eludes simple definitions and final judgments.

Tall, raw boned, and with an unruly shock of black hair, his appearance could not have been more different from that of George Washington and the other founding fathers. Walt Whitman, who saw the
president regularly in Washington, D.C., wrote that Lincoln's face was
"so awful ugly it becomes beautiful." But when Lincoln spoke, audiences forgot his appearance as they listened to his inspiring words.

He is one of the few Americans whose life and words bridge time.
Illinois senator Everett Dirksen said fifty years ago, "The first task of
every politician is to get right with Lincoln." At critical moments in our
nation's history, his eloquent words become contemporary.

As a young man, he won the nickname "Honest Abe" when his store
in New Salem, Illinois, "winked out." Rather than cut and run from his
debts in the middle of the night, as was common on the frontier, he
stayed and paid back what he called his "National Debt." His political
opponents invented a long list of denunciations, ranging from "the
Black Republican" to "the original gorilla" to "the dictator." His supporters crafted monikers of admiration: "Old Abe," affectionately
attached to him while he was still a relatively young man, and the "Rail
Splitter," to remind voters in the 1860 presidential campaign of his roots

in what was then the Western frontier. During the Civil War, admiration became endearment when the soldiers he led as commander in chief called him "Father Abraham." After his controversial decision to sign the Emancipation Proclamation on New Year's Day 1863, grateful Americans, black and white, honored him with the title "the Great Emancipator."

Each name became a signpost pointing to the ways Lincoln grew and changed through critical episodes in his life. Each was an attempt to define him, whether by characterization or caricature.

Yet how did Lincoln define himself? He never kept a diary. He wrote three brief autobiographical statements, one pointedly in the third person. As the Lincolns prepared to leave for Washington in the winter of 1861, Mary Lincoln, to protect her privacy, burned her correspondence with her husband in the alley behind their Springfield home. In an age when one did not tell all, Lincoln seldom shared his innermost feelings in public. Lincoln's law partner, William Herndon, summed it up "He was the most . . . shut-mouthed man that ever existed." Yet when Lincoln spoke, he offered some of the most inspiring words ever uttered on the meaning of America.

Each generation of Americans rightfully demands a new engagement with the past. Fresh questions are raised out of contemporary experiences. Does he deserve the title "the Great Emancipator"? Was Lincoln a racist? Did he invent, as some have charged, the authoritarian, imperial presidency? How did Lincoln reshape the modern role of commander in chief? How are we to understand Mary Lincoln and their marriage? What were Lincoln's religious beliefs? How did he connect religion to politics? As we peel back each layer of Lincoln's life, these questions foster only more questions.

Actually, Lincoln did keep a journal, but he never wrote in a single record book. What I call Lincoln's "diary" consists of hundreds of notes he composed for himself over his adult life. He recorded his ideas on scraps of paper, filing them in his top hat or his bottom desk drawer. He wrote them for his eyes only. These reflections bring into view a private Lincoln. They reveal a man of intellectual curiosity who was testing a wide range of ideas, puzzling out problems, constructing philosophical syllogisms, and sometimes disclosing his personal feelings. In these notes we find his evolving thoughts on slavery, his envy at the soaring career of Stephen Douglas, and the intellectual foundations of his Second Inaugural Address.

Lincoln's moral integrity is the strong trunk from which all the branches of his life grew. His integrity has many roots—in the soil, in Shakespeare, and in the Bible. Ambition was present almost from the beginning, and he had to learn to prune this branch that it not grow out of proportion in his life. Often, when contemporary Americans try to trace an inspired idea or a shimmering truth about our national identity, again and again we find Lincoln's initials carved on some tree—AL—for he was there before us.

Lincoln was always comfortable with ambiguity. In a private musing, he prefaced an affirmation, "I am almost ready to say this is probably true." The lawyer in Lincoln delighted in approaching a question or problem from as many sides as possible, helping him appreciate the views of others, even when those opinions opposed his own.

In an alternative life, Lincoln might have enjoyed a career as an actor in the Shakespearean plays he loved. As a lawyer, he became a lead actor on the stages of the courthouses of the Eighth Judicial Circuit of central Illinois. As president, he was a skillful director of a diverse cast of characters, civilian and military, many of whom often tried to upstage him. Although his military experience was limited to a few months in the Black Hawk War of 1832, Lincoln would become the nation's first true commander in chief, defining and shaping that position into what it is today.

Lincoln is the president who laughs with us. His winsome personality reveals itself in his self-deprecating humor. As a young lawyer and congressman, his satire could sting and hurt political foes, but later in life he demonstrated a more gentle sense of humor that traded on his keen sense of irony and paradox. During the Civil War, some politicians wondered how Lincoln could still laugh, but he appreciated that humor and tragedy, as portrayed in Shakespeare's plays, are always close companions.

Recently, the question has been asked with renewed intensity: What did Lincoln really believe about slavery? Born in Kentucky, raised in Indiana, and becoming a politician in Illinois, Lincoln answered this question differently in his developing engagement with slavery throughout his life. One of the reasons he hated slavery was that it denied the American right to rise to African-Americans. In debates with Stephen Douglas and conversations with African-American leader Frederick Douglass, Lincoln understood that in doing battle with slavery, he was wrestling with the soul of America.

Lincoln has often been portrayed as not religious, in part because he never joined a church. How to reconcile this, then, with the deep religious insights of his second inaugural address, given only weeks before his death? Where are the missing pieces in his spiritual odyssey? One clue is a private musing on the question of the activity of God in the Civil War found after his death by his young secretary, John Hay, in a bottom drawer of his desk. A second is a religious mentor in Washington who played a largely overlooked role in the story of Lincoln's evolving religious beliefs.

Lincoln would have relished each new advance in the information revolution. Before the modern press conference, he became skilled at shaping public opinion by courting powerful newspaper editors. During the Civil War he learned how to reach a large audience through the writing of "public letters." He understood the potential of the chattering new magnetic telegraph, which allowed him to instantly communicate with generals in the field and become a hands-on commander in chief. In the last year and a half of his life, he surprised members of his cabinet by accepting a clearly secondary role in the dedication at Gettysburg, only to deliver a mere 272 words that stirred a nation.

Even though we have no audio record of Lincoln's words, he still speaks to us through his expressive letters and his eloquent speeches. Lincoln may not have read the ancient Greek philosopher Aristotle's *Treatise on Rhetoric,* but he embodied his definition that ethos, or "integrity," is the key to persuasion. Even when Lincoln disappears in his speeches—as he does in the Gettysburg Address, never using the word "I"—they reveal the moral center of the man.

Lincoln was conservative in temperament. As a young man he believed that the role of his generation was simply to "transmit" the values of the nation's founders. Over time he came to believe that each generation must redefine America in relation to the problems of its time. By the end of 1862, Lincoln would declare, "The dogmas of the quiet past are inadequate for the stormy present." In the last two and a half years of his life, Lincoln began to think in the future tense: "We must think anew, and act anew." However one decides to define Lincoln, whatever questions one brings to his story, his life and ideas are a prism to America's past as well as to her future.

CHAPTER 2

Undistinguished Families
1809–16

IT IS A GREAT PIECE OF FOLLY TO ATTEMPT TO
MAKE ANYTHING OUT OF MY EARLY LIFE.

ABRAHAM LINCOLN
Autobiography written for John L. Scripps,
Chicago Press and Tribune, *June 1860*

IN MAY 1860, ABRAHAM LINCOLN BECAME THE SURPRISE NOMINEE OF
the Republican Party for president. The selection catapulted the little-
known lawyer from Springfield, Illinois, onto the center stage of American life. Ordinary citizens were both curious and anxious about this
lanky Westerner with a meager education and limited political experience. He quickly became courted by journalistic suitors wanting to
write his campaign biography. While candidate Lincoln was busy thinking about the nation's future, the public was eager to learn more about
his past.

John Locke Scripps, a senior editor of the *Chicago Press and Tribune,*
managed to convince Lincoln to write an autobiographical account that
would serve as the basis for a campaign biography. This essay of just
over three thousand words would prove to be Lincoln's longest work of
autobiography. His description of his early education is typical of the
essay's unusual third-person style: "A. now thinks that the agregate of
all his schooling did not amount to one year. He was never in a college
or Academy as a student; and never inside of a college or academy building till since he had a law-license. What he has in the way of education,
he has picked up."

Lincoln began his autobiography referring to himself as "A" and pro-
gressed to "Mr. L." Remarkably brief about certain periods of his life,

the essay stops in 1856 and does not include the 1858 debates with Stephen A. Douglas that first brought him to national attention. Lincoln's spare account tells us as much as he wanted the public to know.

Scripps would recall the difficulty he encountered "to induce [Lincoln] to communicate the homely facts and incidents of his early life." Plainly uncomfortable talking about his childhood in Kentucky and Indiana, Lincoln told Scripps, "It is a great piece of folly to attempt to make anything out of my early life."

AMERICANS HAVE LONG HEARD that Lincoln was little interested in his forebears. This viewpoint misses the paradox of his persistent curiosity about his family history. As he matured, Lincoln explored his family background, writing to rumored relatives in Massachusetts and Virginia, but as the 1860 presidential election approached he wished to focus the portrait of himself as a self-made man. In the nineteenth-century world of public politics, where it was an advantage to exemplify the heroic ideal of a self-constructed individual, Lincoln inquired about his family in private. In December 1859, he responded to a request for autobiographical information from a Bloomington, Illinois, newspaper editor. Lincoln said tersely, "My parents were both born in Virginia, of undistinguished families."

Lincoln became discouraged that he could not trace his lineage back definitively beyond his paternal grandfather. Yet the story of Lincoln's ancestry is much more complex, and certainly more geographically diverse, than Lincoln could ever have suspected. He knew almost nothing about the generations of Lincolns that stretched all the way back to the early seventeenth century when they migrated with some of the first colonists from England to the New World.

ON A BLUSTERY MORNING, April 8, 1637, young Samuel Lincoln boarded the *Rose* at the port of Great Yarmouth in the county of Norfolk, England, for the arduous transatlantic crossing to New England. Two years after the *Mayflower* had landed at Plymouth, Samuel was baptized in St. Andrews Church near Norwich on August 24, 1622. At age fifteen he decided to leave behind his village of Hingham in the east of England and journey to a new life in a New England.

Samuel Lincoln was one of thousands of English men and women who were pushed as well as pulled from their island home during the politically tumultuous decade of the 1630s. With the flag of England, an upright dark red cross of St. George on a white background, flapping in the breeze, young Samuel became part of "the Great Migration" of nearly two hundred ships and more than thirteen thousand people who set their course for the so-called New World between 1630 and 1640.

Derisively called "Puritans" by their opponents, these emigrants had given up hope of purifying England from the twin tyrannies of state and church. Between 1629 and 1640, King Charles I attempted to rule absolutely without Parliament. At the same time, Archbishop William Laud sought to rid the Church of England of its Puritan members while they sought to further purify it according to the beliefs and practices of the new Protestant churches of Europe. These dissenters were prepared to cross the ocean so they could practice their faith freely.

Like many of his fellow immigrants, Samuel Lincoln may have sailed to New England for both religious and economic reasons. He was coming of age as an apprentice linen weaver just when an economic depression was hitting East Anglia. He had heard stories of higher wages in the New World, but he knew that life there could also be harder.

After a journey of more than two months, Samuel Lincoln landed in Salem, in the Massachusetts Bay Colony, on June 20, 1637. He settled in the new village of Hingham fifteen miles south of Boston. Because of an abundance of weavers, Samuel initially turned to farming. In time he would pursue business ventures earning him enough wealth to build a substantial house. He became a member of the Old Ship Church, which he helped build and which still stands today. For the Puritans, church membership provided not only an individual pathway to God but a community that transcended economic distinctions. Samuel Lincoln, Abraham Lincoln's first American ancestor, lived a long life by the standards of the time, dying in 1690 at the age of sixty-seven.

THE NEXT GENERATIONS of American Lincolns carried Samuel's sense of wanderlust. They successively traveled farther and farther from their homes in search of new lands and opportunities on the frontier. The adventures of the Lincoln family's succeeding generations offer a portrait of the shaping of the American character.

Samuel's son, Mordecai Lincoln, moved twice, to Hull and Scituate, both within the Massachusetts Bay Colony. Mordecai Lincoln, Jr., Samuel's grandson, ventured nearly three hundred miles south early in the eighteenth century to the market town of Freehold, the seat of Monmouth County, in what would become New Jersey. There he married Hannah Salter, daughter and niece of two New Jersey assembly-men. Mordecai, Jr., became a successful landowner and businessman. Eventually he moved his family west along the Burlington Road into southeastern Pennsylvania. He enlarged his land holdings and became prosperous in the newly developing iron industry. He erected a forge where the French Creek flowed into the Schuylkill River at Phoenixville, about thirty miles west of Philadelphia. In 1733, he built a spacious steep-roofed brick house nestled into the side of a hill a few miles east of Reading, Pennsylvania. It still stands today. Mordecai Lincoln, Jr., the great-great-grandfather of Abraham Lincoln, lived in three different colonies before he died in 1735 at age forty-nine. He left behind a substantial estate, including more than one thousand acres of land, plus his iron business.

His eldest son, John Lincoln, inherited lands in New Jersey but decided to continue to reside in Pennsylvania. There he married Rebecca Flower, who came from a prosperous Quaker family. In 1768, John, who headed the fourth generation of American Lincolns, traveled along the Great Philadelphia Wagon Road that ran down through Lancaster, York, and Gettysburg. He continued south, eventually reaching the Virginia Road in the Shenandoah Valley. "Virginia John" Lincoln settled on Linville Creek, a tributary of the Shenandoah River, in Rockingham County, near the site of present-day Harrisonburg. At the time, Virginians called these migrating Pennsylvanians "northern men," a designation that meant this part of northern Virginia was becoming a southern extension of Pennsylvania. John Lincoln settled in a part of the Shenandoah Valley where Europeans had begun to live only in the 1730s. They developed small farmsteads, quite different from the large tobacco plantations of the older regions of Virginia. Many of these new immigrants were Quaker farmers who would have nothing to do with slavery.

JOHN'S SON, ABRAHAM LINCOLN, the grandfather of Abraham Lincoln, was born in Pennsylvania in 1744. He would be the last ancestor that Abraham Lincoln could learn much about. In 1770, Abraham married Bathsheba Herring, the daughter of one of the leading families of Rockingham County. He joined the Virginia Militia, becoming a captain in 1776, just as the colonies were declaring their independence. Captain Lincoln, as everyone called him, made a distinguished name for himself in his community.

John Lincoln

During this time, Daniel Boone was busy exploring the western part of Virginia, a region called by the Cherokee *"Ken-tah-the."* Reports of Kentucky as a new "Eden of the West" sparked great interest, especially in Pennsylvania, Virginia, and North Carolina. In March 1775, Boone and his crew of frontiersmen started constructing the "Wilderness Road" into Kentucky. Nineteenth-century Western artist George Caleb Bingham's painting *Daniel Boone Escorting a Band of Pioneers into the Western Country* depicts a strapping Daniel Boone marching through the Cumberland Gap, traversing the Appalachian Mountains just north of where the states of Virginia, Tennessee, and Kentucky meet. This image helped mythologize the great adventure of opening up the Kentucky frontier.

The stories of Daniel Boone's explorations into Kentucky, the "Eden of the West," may have inspired Lincoln's grandfather, Abraham Lincoln, to take his family through the Cumberland Gap into Kentucky.

Grandfather Abraham Lincoln's decision to continue the family pattern of migration may have come from Boone's descriptions of Kentucky. In Virginia, it was common to respond to queries regarding the whereabouts of a person by replying, "He's gone to hell or to Kentucky." In 1782, while peace talks to end the Revolutionary War started in Paris, Abraham and Bathsheba Lincoln and their family left the Shenandoah Valley on a two-hundred-mile journey through difficult terrain to Kentucky. Traversing the Wilderness Road, the Lincolns carried their household goods and farm tools, as well as their Bible and a flintlock rifle.

If wanderlust was romantic, it could also be perilous. After the French and Indian War ended in 1763, Native Americans were surprised when American settlers pushed into their territories. Even after the Continental Congress established the Ohio River as a dividing line between American Indians and the settlers, colonists continued to attack tribes north of the Ohio in their relentless search for more land. The Indians retaliated with raids into Kentucky. Living at the edge of the constantly moving frontier, the settlers learned to build their homes in or near fortified stockades.

Captain Abraham Lincoln built his family a log cabin on land near Hughes Station, probably just east of what is today Louisville. On a May afternoon in 1786, while Captain Abraham Lincoln and his three sons were out planting corn, a Native American, probably a Shawnee, shot Abraham from the nearby woods. Terrified, his sons Mordecai, fourteen, and John, twelve, ran for the safety of the stockade, leaving their brother Thomas, age six, sobbing beside his dying father. The warrior dashed from the woods, descending upon the younger brother who could be killed or taken away. Young Mordecai turned, steadied his flintlock rifle, and fired at the silver crescent suspended from the neck of the Shawnee warrior, killing his father's assailant.

Abraham Lincoln, the future president's grandfather, was buried in deerskins near Hughes Station. Although only forty-two, he had followed the wealth-building pattern of his father and grandfather in Pennsylvania and Virginia, amassing more than five thousand acres of

Kentucky land. Sixty-eight years later, at age forty-five, his grandson, Abraham, would recall to a newly discovered relative the story of his grandfather's death, this "legend more strongly than all others imprinted upon my mind and memory."

IN A FRONTIER SOCIETY, the death of a father turned everything upside down. Abraham left his wife, Bathsheba, and their five children ample property, but his sons were too young to carry on the necessary clearing and cultivation of the land.

Thomas Lincoln, the future president's father, was only six years old when his father died before his eyes. His life without a father and with his oldest brother, Mordecai, managing their father's estate, would now be lived out in different conditions from his forebears.

Abraham Lincoln would say of his father's youth, "Even in childhood [he] was a wandering, laboring boy." This brief comment might suggest that Thomas Lincoln from a very young age had no home or support. In truth, relatives of Bathsheba Lincoln reached out to help after her husband's death. Hannaniah Lincoln, a cousin who had served as a captain in the Revolutionary War, welcomed Bathsheba and her five children into his home forty miles to the south near Springfield, Kentucky.

Within a few years of his father's death, young Thomas Lincoln was sent out to work. He labored on neighboring farms, earned three shillings a day at a mill, and worked one year for his uncle Isaac on his farm in the Watauga River Valley in Tennessee. Returning to Kentucky, Thomas apprenticed as a carpenter and cabinetmaker in a shop in Elizabethtown.

The lens of history has often filtered Thomas Lincoln in dark and disapproving colors, detractors framing him as lacking in initiative and economic accomplishment. Part of this portrait comes from a son who would say his father "grew up literally without education," the very value Abraham Lincoln would come to prize the most.

The filter should be removed in order to color in a more accurate picture. Reminiscences about Abraham Lincoln's father offer an ambiguous report on what kind of man he truly was. Thomas Lincoln was a sturdy man, about five feet ten inches tall, with dark hazel eyes, black hair, and high cheekbones. Although he lacked formal education, this was not unusual on the early American frontier. He served in the local militia, on juries, and became an active member of the Baptist church.

Dennis Hanks, a cousin of Abraham Lincoln's mother, said of Thomas, "He was a man who took the world Easy—did not possess much Envy," observing that Thomas "never thought that gold was God." One neighbor remembered him as a "plain unpretending plodding man." Another called him a "good quiet citizen," and a third said he told stories with a wry sense of humor, a trait his son would inherit.

One neighbor recalled that Thomas "accumulated considerable property which he always managed to make way with about as fast as he made it." Like the Lincolns before him, Thomas Lincoln had a hunger for land. At the age of twenty-five, in 1803, he purchased a 238-acre farm on Mill Creek, a tributary of the Salt River, for 118 pounds in cash. At about the same time, he bought two lots in Elizabethtown. Thomas Lincoln's accumulation of property was such that within a decade he would rank fifteenth of ninety-eight property owners listed in Hardin County in 1814. For a long time in American presidential history, the demeaning of Thomas Lincoln became a means to set up a contrast with the accomplishments of his supposedly self-made son. The truth, as always, is much more complex.

Thomas Lincoln

ON JUNE 12, 1806, Thomas Lincoln married Nancy Hanks. How and when Thomas and Nancy first met and courted has unfortunately disappeared into the mists of time.

Nancy Hanks's ancestry is also shrouded in mystery. Her forebears may well have traveled the same route as John Lincoln and his family from Pennsylvania to Virginia, also settling in Rockingham County around 1770. Nancy was born in Virginia, probably in 1784, and as a young child traveled to Kentucky in the late 1780s.

Her father, whom Lincoln believed to be a Virginia farmer, died when Nancy was a young girl, and her mother, Lucy Shipley Hanks, died soon thereafter. The family of eight children were scattered among various relatives. Her aunt, Rachel Shipley Berry, and her husband, Richard, took Nancy into their family on their farm near Springfield, Kentucky.

Although we don't know when, Thomas Lincoln and Nancy Hanks probably met at the Berrys' two-story log home. Their marriage, presided over by Jesse Head, a well-known Methodist minister, took

Thomas Lincoln lived nearly his whole life as a farmer in Kentucky and Indiana.
His relationship with his son has been the subject of much speculation.

place at sunset on an early summer evening. Weddings were grand social occasions for people who lived great distances from one another on the frontier. Friends of Thomas and Nancy enjoyed the wedding feast, a barbecue, accompanied by the singing of the good old tunes "The Girl I Left Behind" and "Turkey in the Straw." On their wedding night, Thomas was twenty-eight and Nancy was twenty-two.

The young couple moved to Elizabethtown shortly after their wedding. Etown, as it was called, was a raw frontier settlement made up of mainly log cabins. It boasted a few frame houses, a new courthouse made with brick from the local brickyard, and a debating society. Thomas built a log cabin on one of the two lots he owned.

Thomas and Nancy's first child, Sarah, was born on February 10, 1807. The biblical name for their daughter had appeared often in the previous generations of Lincolns. Sarah had dark hair and gray eyes. As she grew, many neighbors remarked that she resembled her father.

In December 1808, Thomas sold his first farm and purchased a second farm on the Big South Fork of Nolin Creek, twelve miles southeast of Elizabethtown. The Sinking Spring farm took its name from its freshwater spring at the foot of a deep cave. Thomas built a one-room rude cabin on a knoll above the farm's spring. The sixteen-by-eighteen-foot cabin's simple construction consisted of logs lined with clay. It had a dirt floor and a stone fireplace, standard for the day. The cabin may have had a window, without glass, covered by greased paper. Nancy gave birth to her second child, Abraham, in this new log cabin on February 12, 1809. He was named for his assassinated grandfather.

AT THE TIME OF LINCOLN's birth, Kentucky embodied all that was new in a region people called "the West." Like Abraham's parents, most settlers had come from someplace else. Life was difficult on the frontier, but letters to relatives on the Atlantic seaboard told stories of people choosing pioneering life, hard though it might be, over the more settled lives they left behind.

George Washington, the nation's first president, died in 1799, ten years before Lincoln's birth. Such was Washington's stature that the new nation was still mourning his passing, observing in elaborate ceremonies the dates of his birth and death. Within a month of Lincoln's birth, Thomas Jefferson, author of the Declaration of Independence, would complete his second term as the third president of the United States. When Jefferson articulated his vision of an America of small farmers, he was thinking of people like the Lincolns.

In later years, Lincoln would say that he could remember nothing of his birthplace and the log cabin at the Sinking Spring farm. As a toddler, he may have wandered the hillsides or explored the cave by the spring. There is little reason to think it was an unhappy place to be born.

In 1811, when Abraham was two, Thomas and Nancy Lincoln moved again, their third move in five years. Drawn by more fertile land, they relocated six miles north to a farm in the Knob Creek Valley. Thomas could now work the long tongues of level land made rich by Knob Creek. Heavily wooded steep limestone bluffs, marked by deep gullies and small knob-like hills, from which the valley and creek derived their names, bounded the farm. The creek, piercing its way through the limestone rock, was adorned with sycamore and elms, their branches hanging in a protective pattern over the waters. Thomas Lincoln's chief crop was corn, but he also planted beans. Abraham, like his father and grandfather before him, grew up a farmer's son.

Young Abraham lived near the old Cumberland Trail, the road for travelers on their way from Nashville to Louisville. On many days the boy could watch and wonder at all kinds of people passing by: soldiers on their way home from the War of 1812, evangelists taking part in the religious revival called the Second Great Awakening, peddlers selling goods procured from a larger world, promoters of land schemes, and— every once in a while—a coffle of slaves plodding behind a slave trader.

ABRAHAM LINCOLN came of age amid a growing controversy over slavery in Kentucky. David Rice, a Presbyterian minister, had delivered an address before the Kentucky Constitutional Convention of 1792 calling "Slavery Inconsistent with Justice and Good Policy." Rice argued that slavery was "a standing monument of the tyranny and inconsistency of human governments." He declared slavery to be not only bad for blacks, but corrosive of the values of whites as well.

Both Thomas and Nancy Lincoln experienced slavery everywhere they lived. The Berrys, with whom Nancy lived before her marriage, owned five slaves. When Thomas worked for a year in Tennessee, he came to know his uncle Isaac's six slaves. In 1811, two years after Abraham Lincoln was born, the tax list for Hardin County listed 1,007 slaves for taxation, whereas the white male population over the age of sixteen was 1,627.

The churches in Kentucky became central players in the debate over slavery. The Baptists, Methodists, and Presbyterians—the largest Protestant churches in the early settlement in Kentucky—were torn and sometimes divided by the controversy. Jesse Head, the Methodist minister who married Thomas and Nancy, had a reputation for speaking boldly against slavery; it is likely they heard him preach on the subject.

Thomas and Nancy Lincoln attended the South Fork Baptist Church, a Separate Baptist congregation two miles from their Sinking Spring farm. At the time, Baptists in Kentucky were divided into three main varieties. General Baptists emphasized free will, believing that salvation was open to anyone who desired it. Particular Baptists were more exclusive, believing in a strict Calvinism emphasizing God's providential initiative in salvation rather than human free will. Separate Baptists, by far the largest group of the Kentucky Baptists, were more experiential and thus emotional in their worship.

In the year before Abraham Lincoln's birth, the South Fork Baptist Church burst apart in a debate over slavery. In December 1807, the minister, William Whitman, had declared himself to be an "amansapater" (emancipator). In August 1808, fifteen members "went out of the church on account of slavery."

Thomas and Nancy Lincoln decided to join those helping to found the new Little Mount Baptist Church located three miles northeast of the Sinking Spring farm. William Downs, the organizing pastor, was recognized as one of the "brilliant and fascinating orators" among the Kentucky Baptists. The Lincolns, sitting through Downs's emotional antislavery sermons, surely brought this into family conversations with young Abraham and Sarah.

"MY EARLIEST RECOLLECTION is of the Knob Creek place," Lincoln would tell a friend many years later. "I remember that old home very well." Lincoln recalled that one Saturday afternoon when "the other boys planted the corn in what we called the big field; it contained seven acres—and I dropped the pumpkin seeds. I dropped two seeds every other hill and every other row." He never forgot what happened next. "There came a big rain in the hills; it did not rain a drop in the valley, but the water coming through the gorges washed ground, corn, pumpkin seeds and all clear off the field." He was eight years old.

Abraham also remembered his brother, Thomas, Jr., born in 1812. Abraham must have hoped he would have a playmate, but Thomas died within several days, the exact date unknown.

Lincoln's campaign autobiography of 1860 included little mention of his mother. In a section describing his father, he wrote, "He married Nancy Hanks, mother of the present subject." Neighbors remembered she had a fair complexion, with light hair and blue eyes. Friends and neighbors called her "quiet and amiable," of "a Kind disposition," as "Vy affectionate in her family" and with neighbors. She was illiterate. Nancy Hanks Lincoln died before the invention of photography in 1839. Yet Lincoln's best friend, Joshua Speed, recalled that he spoke of her as his "angel mother."

———

ABRAHAM ATTENDED THE ONE-ROOM log school two miles north of the Sinking Spring farm for only short periods of time, no more than three or four months total in his five years at the farm. The terms of these subscription schools were erratic, in large measure because the settlers had to provide a stipend and sometimes room and board for the teacher.

10   A NEW GUIDE

Box fox. The. Who. Cry dry fly fry pry shy sly sty thy try why. Act, all, and, apt, ark, arm, art, ash, ask, asp, ass. Ebb, egg, ell, elm, end. Ill, ink. Odd, off, oft, old.

TABLE III.

Words of three letters, viz. one consonant and two vowels, or a diphthong.

PEA sea tea yea. Bee fee see. Die fie lie. Doe foe roe toe. Due rue sue. Awe daw jaw law maw paw raw saw. Dew few hew mew new pew (sew.) Bow low mow row sow tow.

Cow how mow now sow vow. Coo too woo. Bay day gay hay jay lay may nay pay ray say way. (Key) (eye.) Boy coy joy toy. Ace, age, ape, are, aid, aim. Ear, eat. Ice, Oak, oil, oar, oat, one, our, out, owl, own. Use, (use.) You.

Some easy lessons on the foregoing Tables, consisting of words not exceeding three letters.

LESSON I.

NO man may put off the law of God. The way of God is no ill way. My joy is in God all the day. A bad man is a foe to God.

LESSON II.

To God do I cry all the day. Who is God, but our God. All men go out of the way of thy law. In God do I put my joy, O let me not sin.

LESSON III.

Pay to God his due. Go not in the way of bad men. No man can see God. Our God is the God of all men.

LESSON IV.

Who can say he has no sin? The way of man is ill, but not the way of God.

This page from Thomas Dilworth's New Guide to the English Tongue *shows what young Abraham Lincoln first learned in school. Dilworth, an eighteenth-century minister, used the Psalms to teach spelling.*

Zachariah Riney, a Catholic born in Maryland, was Abraham's first teacher. A piece of roughly dressed timber, placed entirely across the room, served as a writing desk for the students.

These early schools were called "blab" schools. Teachers encouraged students to employ the two senses of seeing and hearing. Abraham learned his lessons by reading and reciting aloud, repeating the lessons over and over. For the rest of his life, he always read aloud.

Spelling occupied a central place in the curriculum. Thomas Dilworth's *New Guide to the English Tongue* served as the main textbook. Dilworth started with one-syllable words of three letters and proceeded to one-syllable words with four, five, and six letters. Lincoln first encountered one-syllable words with three letters in verse:

> *No Man may put off the Law of God.*
> *The Way of God is no ill Way.*
> *My Joy is in God all the Day.*
> *A bad man is a Foe to God.*

Dilworth, an eighteenth-century English minister, taught moral education while teaching vocabulary and grammar. Lincoln read and memorized words from the Old and New Testaments, especially Psalms and Proverbs. Dilworth used the Psalms for students to learn rhyme and cadence.

Caleb Hazel, Lincoln's second part-time teacher, a farmer and surveyor, lived on a neighboring farm. He "could perhaps teach spelling reading & indifferent writing & perhaps could Cipher to the rule of three." The quality for which many remembered him was his "large size & bodily Strength to thrash any boy or youth that came to School."

A trustees' book for Hardin County included instructions for teachers to maintain order: restrain card playing and gambling, and suppress "cussing." Abraham Lincoln and other students were not allowed to shoot pop guns, pin guns, or bows and arrows, nor could they throw stones or use other dangerous weapons.

IN 1816, WHEN Abraham Lincoln turned seven, the Lincoln family moved again. After living in Kentucky for thirty-four years, Thomas Lincoln repeated the Lincoln family pattern of picking up and moving in search of better lands. Forty-four years later, Abraham Lincoln would write in his 1860 campaign biography that his father left Kentucky "partly on account of slavery; but chiefly on account of the difficulty of land titles in Ky."

A joke made the rounds in early Kentucky: "Who [ever] buys land in Kentucky, buys a lawsuit." Thomas Lincoln purchased a farm stated to be 230 acres, but the boundaries were uneven. The Kentucky territory was originally the western part of Virginia, and Virginia did not supply surveys of its public lands. This neglect resulted in settlers purchasing "shingled" properties, lands that overlapped one another.

Thomas Lincoln had run afoul of surveying methods and land titles with all three of his farms. Nearly half of the early settlers in Kentucky lost part or all of their lands due to legal irregularities. Some settlers had to buy their land three or four times in an attempt to gain a clear title. Thomas found himself caught up in a land title struggle on the Knob Creek farm. Ten farm families, including the Lincolns, had purchased parts of the ten-thousand-acre Middleton tract. Heirs of Thomas Middleton now sought the land. Lincoln was to be the test case of the ten, but before the case could be decided, Thomas made his decision to move.

The Lincolns and their neighbors were well aware that slavery would never cross north of the Ohio River. The Northwest Ordinance of 1787, the charter for organizing the Northwest Territory, stated in article 6, "There shall be neither slavery nor involuntary servitude in the said territory." The area defined in the ordinance referred to territories and new states that would be "northwest" of the "River Ohio." Even while fighting the court case, Thomas Lincoln decided to do what many of his friends and neighbors were doing: seek a better opportunity for his family and find a new farm north of the Ohio in the free state of Indiana.

ACROSS SEVEN GENERATIONS, the American Lincolns migrated in search of new lands and fresh opportunities. After Samuel and Mordecai Lincoln, each succeeding forebear of Abraham Lincoln lived in at least three different colonies or states. Lincoln's cultural heritage was Puritan, Yankee, Middle Atlantic, and Upland South. One by one, all of the sons of John Lincoln who made the trek from Virginia to Kentucky would continue their migration to the free states of either Indiana or Illinois. Several of the daughters married Kentucky men and would continue to live in the South.

Abraham Lincoln thought his family background was "undistinguished." He made this judgment primarily on the basis of what he believed was the lack of achievement of his father. Had he been able to see farther into history, he might have changed his mind. The previous generations of American Lincolns included Puritan courage, adventurous migration, bold commercial ventures, proud military service, and political office holding. Rather than being "undistinguished," many of the qualities that Abraham Lincoln would come to prize in his own life were present in the ancestry of his long, distinguished family.

CHAPTER 3

Persistent in Learning
1816—30

YOUNG ABE WAS DILIGENT FOR KNOWLEDGE—WISHED TO KNOW &
IF PAINS AND LABOR WOULD GET IT HE WAS SURE TO GET IT.

SARAH BUSH LINCOLN
Interview with William Herndon, September 8, 1865

"HERE I GREW UP" IS THE UNDERSTATED WAY ABRAHAM LINCOLN
described his fourteen years in Indiana in his 1860 campaign autobiographical statement. Arriving with his family in the late fall of 1816 at
the age of seven, Lincoln would grow from a boy to a youth to a young
man who would prove different from any young man in the world
around him.

The formative years from seven to twenty-one are critical for every
person, and especially for Lincoln. In Indiana, the young Lincoln would
grow physically, so that by the time he was twenty-one he was six feet
four inches tall and weighed more than two hundred pounds, his physical strength setting him apart early in the frontier's masculine culture.
Lincoln would also grow intellectually on the small but steady diet of
books he mastered. Early on, no matter how bleak and limiting life on
his family's farm became, he learned to rely on his books and his imagination to satisfy his curiosity and intellect. Finally, in Indiana, Lincoln
would develop the interior moral compass that enabled him to navigate
not simply the forests and streams of the state, but the more difficult terrain of ethical decisions in a young America on the rise.

IN THE FALL OF 1816, Thomas Lincoln began the first of two journeys
to move his young family across the Ohio River from Kentucky to Indiana, which was about to become the newest free state. On a flatboat of

yellow cedar, Thomas floated down Knob Creek into the Rolling Fork, steered his boat into the Beach Fork, and finally moved west on the broad Ohio River.

Coming ashore in Indiana at a gentle bend in the Ohio, Thomas cut his own trail through sixteen miles of dense wilderness. Only eight months later, in July 1817, Elias Pym Fordham, a young English farmer, would describe Indiana as "a vast forest, larger than England." In the midst of this huge forest Thomas selected a quarter section, or forty acres. He marked his claim by stacking brush at the corners of his property. Thomas had purchased "Congress land," which had been surveyed by the government; the title would be indisputable.

After many weeks on his new property, Thomas Lincoln returned to his wife, Nancy, and Sarah and Abraham at their Knob Creek farm in Kentucky. The family enjoyed reports of good land with deep, rich soil. At age seven, Abraham joined in the family preparations to move for the third time in his young life.

Thomas and Nancy had been married for ten years and had accrued a good deal of household possessions. They decided to leave their furniture behind because Thomas, a skilled carpenter, could make furniture for their new home. They packed their wagons with their featherbed, a spinning wheel, cooking utensils, and many tools, including an ax to clear their new land.

In the late fall of 1816, the Lincoln family began their trek to Indiana. Just before departing they walked to the cemetery on the top of a hill to pause at a small field stone marked with the initials T.L., the grave of little Thomas Lincoln, Jr., who had died four years before.

The Lincolns made stops to say their good-byes to friends in Elizabethtown and at various farms along the way. As they journeyed, Abraham and Sarah were excited to see who would be the first to catch a view of the mighty Ohio River. The 981-mile winding river had become the major interstate highway carrying settlers to new lands and adventures.

After several days, the Lincolns reached a ferry about two and a half miles west of Troy, Indiana. Fees to cross the river were one dollar for horse and wagon, twelve and a half cents per adult, and free for children under ten years, which included Abraham and Sarah. As they crossed, the children were on the lookout for flatboats and barges. Thomas Lincoln told Abraham and Sarah that they might see a steamboat, maybe the *Washington* or the *Pike,* descending the Ohio River on its way to faraway New Orleans.

———

AFTER STEPPING ONTO Indiana soil, the family had to "pack through" sixteen miles of almost impenetrable forest and underbrush. Dense fog could darken the forest in the middle of the day. With his ax and hunting knife, Thomas cut his way to the farm, felling oak, hickory, beech, maple, and walnut trees entangled with grapevines. No wonder the early pioneers called these forest thickets the "roughs."

Arriving in the region near Pigeon Creek, the Lincolns immediately set about to build a "half-faced camp," a rough log shelter enclosed on three sides with a blazing fire on the fourth. After a few days they began erecting a cabin on a knoll overlooking their land.

Learning to use the ax, Abraham helped his father build the cabin and establish the farming. Thomas constructed a pole bedstead in a corner opposite the fireplace where Abraham could climb up to sleep. Young Abraham learned from his carpenter father to build a three-legged stool, which, though small, rested sturdily because of its precise balance. Photographs from later in the century often pictured old, run-down cabins on the frontier, but the Lincoln cabin was new and smelled of fresh-cut timber.

The memory of clearing the Indiana land with his ax became part of Lincoln's campaign biography thirty-four years later: "A., though very young, was large of his age, and had an axe put into his hands at once; and from that till within his twenty-third year, he was almost constantly handling that most useful instrument."

An ax in Lincoln's day would have been hand forged of bar iron and cast steel, giving it its proper shape in relation to its weight. It took up to two days to make such an ax. The price would have been an enormous three to five dollars. Many woodsmen chose to split and finish their own handles from second-growth hickory. Men in frontier Kentucky and Indiana would ride a hundred miles on horseback to purchase such an ax, or to have their favorite ax resteeled. Pioneers often discussed the proper weight of an ax and the best kind of handle as much as they discussed politics.

Abraham helped his father clear the land, chop wood, and split fence rails. Early on, he developed the muscle coordination necessary for a powerful swing. As he grew in size and coordination, young Abe could fell trees of four to six feet in diameter. Handling an ax with such skill was a sign that a boy was becoming a man.

Wild animals flourished in the forest around Pigeon Creek. Deer, wolves, panthers, wildcats, bears, turkeys, quail, and grouse were all plentiful. During the Lincolns' first winter in Indiana, before they were able to plant vegetables, the family lived on forest game.

More than two decades later, Lincoln returned to Indiana and wrote a poem describing the scene of his youth:

> When first my father settled here,
>   'Twas then the frontier line:
> The panther's scream filled night with fear
>   And bears preyed on the swine.

THE LINCOLNS' FIRST YEAR in Indiana, 1817, was lonely. Their nearest neighbors with children near Abraham's age lived several miles away— through the forest. In winter, the encirclement by the never-ending trees increased the sense of darkness and isolation.

A few months after their arrival, "a few days before the completion of [my] eighth year, in the absence of [my] father," Abraham asked his mother's permission to borrow his father's gun because he had spied a flock of wild turkeys flying overhead. In a frontier household, guns were a regular part of daily life, and their use became a central part of a boy's rite of passage. In his campaign statement, he described what happened next. "A., standing inside, shot through a crack, and killed one of them."

Lincoln surprised himself with his response to his accurate marksmanship. Upon examining the beautiful dead bird, he found himself filled not with pride but sorrow. At that moment, young Abraham made an unexpected choice: "[I have] never since pulled a trigger on any larger game." Even more unexpected, he decided to include this admission in his presidential campaign autobiography.

In the fall of 1817, a break in the loneliness came with the arrival of Nancy's aunt, Elizabeth Sparrow; her husband, Thomas; and Dennis Hanks, Lincoln's mother's cousin. The Sparrows had come from Kentucky, the victims of an "ejectment" suit like the one that had helped persuade Thomas Lincoln to relocate to Indiana the year before. Abraham was especially pleased to welcome Dennis Hanks, who, at eighteen, exuded good fun. Abe came to enjoy him as an older friend.

———

IN THE LATE SUMMER of 1818, a ravaging illness spread through southern Indiana, a mysterious disease that infected whole communities. No one could anticipate its coming or fathom its cure. Later, it was discovered that one contracted the disease by drinking milk from a cow who had ingested a poisonous white snakeroot plant while grazing.

In September, the "milk sick" struck the Lincoln family. It claimed first the life of Thomas Sparrow, and shortly thereafter his wife, Elizabeth.

By the end of September, Nancy, Abraham's mother, began to experience the "trembles," symptoms of the dreaded disease. She died seven days later, the saddest day in Abraham's young life. He watched as his father, who had made coffins for others, wielded a whipsaw to construct a green pine coffin for his wife of twelve years. On October 5, 1818, Abraham stood in a densely wooded grove of persimmon trees while his mother, age thirty-four, was buried about one-fourth of a mile from the family log cabin. He was only nine. Abraham never mentioned her in any of his autobiographical writings. That she was a loving, nurturing presence we hear from others. Nathaniel Grigsby, Lincoln's boyhood

The death of Nancy Hanks Lincoln, who died of "milk sick" at the age of thirty-four on October 5, 1818, left a huge hole in the heart of nine-year-old Abraham Lincoln.

Indiana friend, said of Nancy Hanks Lincoln, "Her good humored laugh I can see now—is as fresh in my mind as if it were yesterday."

On February 12, 1819, Abraham marked his tenth birthday in a home that had little cause for celebration. With the death of the Sparrows and Nancy Hanks Lincoln, the family life of Thomas, Abraham, Sarah, and Dennis Hanks was sliding into disarray. In the fall, thirteen months after his wife's death, Thomas decided to return to Kentucky to seek a new wife and mother for his children. In Elizabethtown he called upon Sarah Bush Johnston, a widow. Thomas had known Sarah for many years and may have courted her before he married Nancy. Sarah had been married to Daniel Johnson, the town jailer, who had died in 1816. She had to provide for her three children, Elizabeth, John, and Matilda, and was left with the considerable debts of her husband.

Thomas arrived unannounced at Sarah's door. Whatever romantic feelings they may have experienced, they had urgent practical needs to be met. Each had lost a spouse. Thomas and his children needed a wife and mother. Sarah and her children needed a husband and father. Part of Thomas's proposal to Sarah was his commitment to pay off her debts. They married in Elizabethtown on December 2, 1819. Thomas was now forty-one and Sarah thirty-one. A second Lincoln procession set out for Indiana three years after the first.

Upon her arrival at Pigeon Creek, Sarah discovered how much work there was to do. She took charge and directed all hands to attack the dirty, disheveled cabin. No more hunting for Thomas Lincoln and Dennis Hanks, she said, until they had constructed a floor, put in a door, and made some proper furniture.

She found Abraham clad only in buckskins. "She Soaped—rubbed and washed the Children so that they look pretty neat—well & clean," Dennis described. She then dressed Abraham and his sister in some of her own clothing.

The real mending that Sarah brought was the healing of two broken families. Her impact was enormous. She brought order to a household; more important, she brought love and concern for young Abraham. Years later, in his campaign autobiography, he remarked, "She proved a good and kind mother to A."

Going to the mill was an indispensable part of the pioneer routine. When Abraham was ten, his father let him go to the mill alone, toting a heavy sack of corn and a bag of meal. He rode a mile and a half to Noah Gordon's mill, then waited his turn as the horses went around a circle

Sarah Bush Lincoln, Abraham Lincoln's stepmother, came into his life when he was ten years old. She loved him and consistently encouraged his education. This photograph was taken much later, when she lived in Illinois.

supplying the power for grinding the corn. When it was his turn, he hitched his mare to the arm of the mill. With the impatience of youth, Abraham hit the mare with a switch to move her along. The horse responded with a prompt kick that sent young Abe slumping to the ground. He lay unconscious and bleeding until Gordon picked him up. In 1860, he remembered this incident. "In [my] tenth year [I] was kicked by a horse, and apparently killed for a time."

BY AGE TEN, LINCOLN'S attention and affections would have typically begun to flow from his mother to his father, but the Lincoln family didn't always follow typical patterns. Even as Sarah Bush Johnston became a binding force in the family, an unbinding was occurring between father and son.

Cousin Dennis Hanks, who continued to live with the Lincolns, later offered contradictory reminiscences on Thomas and Abraham's relationship. On the one hand, Dennis stated, "I have Seen his father Nock him Down," but on the other hand he recalled, "the Old Man

Loved his Children." Years later, Dennis doubted whether "Abe Loved his father Very well or Not." Augustus H. Chapman, son-in-law of Dennis Hanks, added his perspective. "Thos. Lincoln never showed by his actions that he thought much of his son Abraham when a boy."

Many years later, when Lincoln served in Congress, he responded to a query from Solomon Lincoln of Massachusetts about his family history. "Owing to my father being left an orphan at the age of six years, in poverty, and in a new country, he became a wholly uneducated man; which I supposed is why I know so little of our family history." How does one interpret Lincoln's comments? Are his words descriptive—is this simply how he remembered his father? Or prescriptive—is he judging his father? As an adult who made it on his own, Abraham showed little empathy for his father, who as a boy found himself suddenly bereft of a father, and as a young farmer struggled against lawsuits that challenged parts or all of three farms.

At the same time, Abraham's stepmother's love and encouragement became critical to his development. Sarah Bush Lincoln believed that what she gave was returned in kind. "I can say what scarcely one woman—a mother—can say in a thousand and it is this—Abe never gave me a cross word or look and never refused . . . to do anything I requested him."

Decades later, when Lincoln was traveling the judicial circuit in Illinois, he told his law partner William Herndon, "God bless my mother; all that I am or ever hope to be I owe to her." There is some dispute as to whether Lincoln was referring to his birth mother or stepmother, but the larger point is that the praise of his mother only emphasized his silence about his feelings for his father.

IF THE PREVIOUS GENERATIONS of American Lincolns had a hunger for the land, Abraham was developing an insatiable hunger for learning. His stepmother said that young Abe "didn't like physical labor—was diligent for Knowledge—wished to Know & if pains & Labor would get it he was sure to get it." His youngest stepsister, Matilda Johnston, recalled, "Abe was not Energetic Except in one thing—he was active & persistent in learning." From an early age this yearning to learn directed the way young Abraham spent his free time.

At the age of ten, Lincoln attended school for the first time in Indiana. In the winter of 1818–19, he and his sister attended a school in a cabin of rough-hewn logs on the Noah Gordon farm. The term of the early subscription schools in Spencer County was usually only one to three months, from December into early March, before the boys returned to work in the fields. In remote districts like Pigeon Creek, school was often held only every two years.

Abraham's first teacher in Indiana was Andrew Crawford. In addition to teaching spelling and grammar, he instructed the children in courtesy and manners, including the art of introducing and receiving guests. A student would leave the schoolhouse, and as he or she reentered another student would introduce the guest to all the children in the room.

Lincoln would look back on his part-time studies in the rustic Indiana schoolhouses with a mixture of affirmation, amusement, and regret. In a brief autobiographical statement written in 1859, Lincoln recalled, "There were some schools, so called; but no qualification was ever required of a teacher, beyond 'readin, writin, and cipherin' to the Rule of Three. If a straggler supposed to understand latin, happened to sojourn in the neighborhood, he would be looked upon as a wizard." His regret about what he missed is caught in his observation "There was absolutely nothing to excite ambition for education." The "nothing" Lincoln spoke of included the lack of real encouragement from his father. Lincoln's motivation would have to come from within.

Nathaniel Grigsby and Abraham Lincoln went to school together in Indiana. Grigsby remembered that "Whilst other boys were idling away their time Lincoln was at home studying hard." Grigsby said that Lincoln liked to "cipher on the boards [calculate numbers]." His persistence struck Grigsby. "Abe woulde set up late reading & rise Early doing the Same." David Turnham, a neighbor and friend, remembered that "What Lincoln read he read and re-read."

Lincoln's hunger for learning could never be satiated by part-time teachers and two-month school terms. Years later, he would say in his autobiographical third-person voice, "What he has in the way of education, he has picked up." Young Abe begged, borrowed, and then devoured a small library of books. Each book that Lincoln read by the fireplace in Indiana became a log in the foundation of the schoolhouse of his mind.

Dennis Hanks recalled that "Abe was getting hungry for books, reading Evry thing he could lay his hands on." These books included classics such as *Aesop's Fables, Robinson Crusoe, The Arabian Nights,* as well as William Scott's *Lessons in Elocution* and Noah Webster's *American*

Eastman Johnson's appealing painting The Boyhood of Lincoln *portrays the young Lincoln reading by the light of a fire in his log cabin home. The painting suggests that, regardless of social station, learning is Lincoln's key to a life of purpose and meaning.*

Spelling Book. Hanks added, "He was a Constant and I may Say Stubborn reader."

Lincoln read the King James Version of the Bible, which in the early nineteenth century often functioned as a textbook for its readers. Lincoln did not simply read the Bible. In Indiana, he began his lifelong practice of memorizing whole sections. One of his favorite portions to memorize was the Psalms.

When Lincoln read *Aesop's Fables*, he was not just reading ancient tales; through the editor's foreword he learned lessons for American young people. An edition that Lincoln may well have read bemoaned the religious and political teachings put before European children. American editions of *Aesop's Fables* featured exhortations at the end of each tale. Young Lincoln may well have been drawn to the moral added to the conclusion of "The Crow and the Pitcher." Through the ages young people have responded to the story of the thirsty crow who, flying over a farm, sees a pitcher with a small amount of water in it sitting on a picnic table. The crow attempts to drink the water but cannot reach it. At last he collects stones and drops them one by one into the pitcher until he can drink.

The traditional moral of the story is that necessity is the mother of invention. The American editor enhanced the moral by telling his young readers that when meeting "a difficulty," the person "of sagacity" should be ready to employ "his wit and ingenuity . . . to avoid or get over an impediment" and "makes no scruple of stepping out of the path of his forefathers."

Lincoln also likely read the tale of "The Lion and the Four Bulls." The lion cannot attack the four bulls as long as they stand together in the pasture. But once they separate, they become easy prey. The moral of this fable is "A kingdom divided against itself cannot stand"—words that would go on to have profound meaning in Lincoln's life.

According to Grigsby and Turnham, Lincoln also enjoyed Starke Dupuy's *Hymns and Spiritual Songs*. Dupuy, of French Huguenot background, was the son of a Baptist minister of Woodford County, Kentucky. Published in Louisville in 1818, his hymnbook became popular in Kentucky and Tennessee. In addition to traditional hymns focusing on God, the book's "Spiritual Songs" focused on the experience of life with God and were sung to popular tunes of the day. Although young Abraham did not have a voice for singing, he enjoyed the practice of reading hymns aloud.

Lincoln also reportedly read John Bunyan's *Pilgrim's Progress,* which appealed to both children and adults in a culture where religious questions permeated everyday conversations. If a pioneer family had only a few books in their home, it was likely that two would be the Bible and *Pilgrim's Progress*. The prefaces to American editions of *Pilgrim's Progress* in the early nineteenth century encouraged readers to read Bunyan's stories aloud on "the Lord's day evening" as well as on weekday evenings. The tales of Mr. Worldly Wiseman, Obstinate, Goodwill, and Patience inspired men and women whose daily lives were interspersed regularly with fire and flood, sickness and death; many saw the stories as a map toward a better life.

According to his stepsister Matilda Johnston, Lincoln read William Grimshaw's *History of the United States,* published in 1820. Grimshaw, who emigrated from Ireland, where he experienced intolerance, made no excuses for the colonists' turning a blind eye to slavery. "What a climax of human cupidity and turpitude! The colonists . . . place the last rivet in the chain." In the last paragraph of his history, Grimshaw, at the time a resident of Philadelphia, told the reader: "Let us not only declare by words, but demonstrate by our actions, that 'all men are created equal.' "

Abraham's stepmother, Sarah Bush Lincoln, remembered that when Abraham came across a passage that particularly struck him, "he would write it down on boards if he had no paper & keep it there till he did get paper—then he would re-write it—look at it repeat it." She reported that her stepson "had a copy book—a kind of scrap book in which he put down all things and thus preserved them."

Abraham's copy book served several purposes. He used it as an aid in his memorization of poetry and prose. He also wrote his own verse. The copy book that he started in 1826, at age seventeen, began:

> Abraham Lincoln is my nam
> And with my pen I wrote the same
> I wrote in both hast and speed
> And left it here for fools to read.

Although other young people used copy books in their schooling, Lincoln's copy book also became a forerunner of the reflections he wrote out on odd pieces of paper as an adult.

The books young Lincoln read tell us he was drawn to morality tales of the triumph of good over evil. Above all, what tied his books together was the possibility that ordinary people could do extraordinary things.

AT SOME POINT IN INDIANA, Abraham realized that he was different from the other boys he knew. He delighted in listening in to adult conversations, often turning the ideas he heard over and over in his mind as he fell asleep. Although thoroughly taking part in the young masculine world of wrestling, running, and jumping, he was also carving out an interior world of intellectual curiosity, reading and memorization, and imagination. What could be better than traveling with Shakespeare and Bunyan to England, with Robert Burns to Scotland, and Lord Byron to Italy?

"He was different from those around him," Nathaniel Grigsby remembered. "His mind soared above us." Grigsby, who knew Lincoln well in Indiana, summed up the feelings of Abraham's young friends: "He naturally assumed the leadership of the boys."

—

IN THESE INDIANA YEARS, Lincoln read books laden with moral fruit—fruit he readily picked and consumed. One evening when Lincoln was a little older, he and his friend David Turnham were returning home from Gentryville. "We saw something laying near or in a mud hole," recalled Turnham, "and Saw that it was a man: we rolled him over and over—waked up the man—he was dead drunk—night was cold—nearly frozen." Who we are can be defined by our ethical actions when there is no time to think. Turnham did not give himself high marks in describing what happened next. "We took him up—rather Abe did—Carried him to Dennis Hanks—built up a fire and got him warm. —I left—Abe staid all night—we had been threshing wheat—had passed Lincoln's house—Lincoln stopt & took Care of the poor fellow." Turnham never forgot the Good Samaritan encounter. It was the kind of moral action Lincoln had learned from his early reading.

"A DEVOUT CHRISTIAN of the baptist order"—so Thomas Lincoln was regarded by Nathaniel Grigsby. In 1821, the Little Pigeon Baptist Church asked Thomas Lincoln to oversee the building of their new meetinghouse. His selection spoke both of his standing within the church and the community as well as of an appreciation for his skills in construction and woodworking. Thomas also built the pulpit and did the cabinet work inside the meetinghouse. Abraham, now twelve, worked alongside his father.

Thomas and Sarah Bush Lincoln became members of the Little Pigeon Baptist Church on June 7, 1823. Since Thomas had been a member of the Little Mount Baptist Church in Kentucky, why did he not join a Baptist church when he first settled in Indiana? In the nineteenth century, with stricter standards for membership, it was not at all unusual for people to attend a church regularly but not become members. Perhaps Thomas Lincoln had waited because he had been part of a Separate Baptist congregation in Kentucky, whereas the Little Pigeon Baptist Church was Regular Baptist. A unity movement among Baptists had spread to Indiana just as Thomas enrolled in the Little Pigeon Baptist Church. He became a member by letter of transfer from Little Mount Baptist, indicating he was a member in good standing in another congregation. Sarah evidently had not been a member of a church before; she was enrolled "by Experience." Abraham's sister, Sarah, joined the Little Pigeon Baptist Church on April 8, 1826, by "Experience of grace."

Abraham, however, did not become a member of the Little Pigeon Baptist Church. He never said why he did not join. In a family-oriented society, the fact that he did not join would have struck others in the community as unusual. According to his stepmother, "He sometimes attended Church." Young Abraham, with his early attraction to words, did become fascinated by the language of the preachers. Lincoln's stepmother recalled, "He would hear sermons preached—come home—take the children out—get on a stump or log and almost repeat it word for word." Lincoln's stepsister Matilda also remembered how Abe would "call the children and friends around him" and "get up on a stump and repeat almost word for word the sermon he had heard the Sunday before." She recalled that Thomas Lincoln did not approve of Abraham's preaching and "would come and make him quit—send him to work."

WHEN ABRAHAM WAS thirteen or fourteen, he began to work for other farmers. It was the custom that money earned by youths be given to the father for family expenses, but a small amount be returned to the youthful laborer. Hiring himself out to harvest corn or split rails brought him into contact for the first time with a wider circle of people than his immediate family and neighbors. In working for neighboring men, Abraham encountered the personalities and habits of other fathers, especially in relation to their sons.

As the pioneers moved west and cultivated the land, the need for fences grew. Fences protected settlers from attack, preserved gardens and food supplies, and acted as lines of demarcation between neighbors. They became higher as dangers from attack grew on the frontier, and as boundary lines became disputed because of inadequate titles to land. The pioneers had a rule that a rail fence should be horse high, bull strong, and pig tight—high enough that a horse could not jump over it, strong enough that a bull could not ram through it, and tight enough so a pig could not press through it.

At age sixteen, as Abraham Lincoln was approaching his full physical maturity, his skill with an ax opened up limitless possibilities for work. Rail splitters were in steady demand. The best woods for rails came from ash, hickory, oak, poplar, and walnut trees. Typically the rails would be ten feet long and four inches wide.

J. L. G. Ferris painted Lincoln the Rail Splitter *in 1909, the year of
the Lincoln Centennial. The artist, depicting the young Lincoln with an ax,
wished to portray both his strength and his humanity.*

Abraham often would work from sunup to sundown. A skilled
woodsman could regularly make as many as four hundred rails in a day.
The flat rate was twenty-five cents a day, although sometimes the pay
was calibrated to piecework. The rail splitter often erected the fence as
well.

In August 1826, while splitting rails for various farms, Abraham,
Dennis Hanks, and Lincoln's stepbrother-in-law Squire Hall hatched
the idea that they might make more money splitting cordwood for the
steamboats not far from where the Anderson River joined the Ohio.

They received some of their pay in goods. Abraham accepted nine yards of white domestic cloth, which allowed him to have sewn the first white shirt he had ever possessed.

Around this time, Abraham, so handy with his hands, built a scow, a small flat-bottomed boat. One day two men approached him and asked if he would row them and their luggage out to a passenger steamer on the Ohio. Lincoln sculled them out to the boat and loaded their heavy trunks on board. Just as he was about to leave, the two men thanked Lincoln, each tossing a silver half-dollar into his scow. He could scarcely believe his eyes.

Many years later, Lincoln related this story to his secretary of state, William H. Seward, and some other government officials. "Gentlemen, you may think it was a very little thing . . . but it was a most important incident in my life. I could scarcely credit that I, a poor boy, had earned a dollar in less than a day." He declared, "The world seemed wider and fairer before me."

Lincoln's good fortune did not last long. After helping a few more passengers, Lincoln found himself in big legal trouble. John and Lin Dill, Kentucky ferrymen, believed they had the exclusive ferry rights across the Ohio. They charged Lincoln with encroachment. Lincoln was hauled before Squire Samuel Pate, justice of the peace, in Lewisport, Kentucky, and charged with operating a ferryboat without a license. In Lincoln's first law case he was the defendant: *The Commonwealth of Kentucky v. Abraham Lincoln*.

Lincoln pleaded innocence and said that he had not violated any law—he was only responding to requests from passengers on the Indiana side. Squire Pate got down the Kentucky statute book and consulted the relevant law, discovering that it prohibited unlicensed persons transiting persons over or across the river but not to passing steamers in the river. Squire Pate immediately dismissed the charges. As Lincoln sculled back across the Ohio River to Indiana he arrived impressed with the majesty of the law in the hands of a skilled justice of the peace.

LINCOLN REMAINED CLOSE to his sister, Sarah, throughout their childhood. When he was seventeen, Sarah married Aaron Grigsby on August 2, 1826. The new couple moved into a cabin two miles south of the Lincoln cabin. A year and a half after her wedding, Sarah prepared to give birth to the couple's first child. As she struggled through the pains of delivery, she called for her father. Thomas Lincoln set off to fetch a doctor. But it was too late. The child was stillborn. Shortly after, Sarah, age twenty-one, died on January 20, 1828.

By the age of eighteen, Abraham Lincoln had lost both his mother and his sister.

IN THE FALL OF 1828, when Abraham was nineteen, an invitation opened a new horizon. James Gentry, owner of Gentry's store, and one of the wealthiest men in the area, wanted a trustworthy young man to accompany his son, Allen, in taking a cargo flatboat to New Orleans to trade goods. He asked Lincoln.

Lincoln and Gentry left Rockport, Indiana, in late December for the 1,222-mile journey. Lincoln served as the bow hand. When the slow-moving Ohio joined the swifter Mississippi, each boy had to be constantly engaged with navigation. Farther south, the boys began exchanging their cargo for sugar, tobacco, and cotton as they passed by Natchez and entered the lower Mississippi with its moss-festooned oak trees.

Just below Baton Rouge the boys tied their boat up for the night near a plantation where they had been trading. Lincoln would never forget their next experience. As he told reporter John Locke Scripps many years later, "One night they were attacked by seven negroes with intent to kill and rob them." The seven had not counted on the strength and courage of the two young men. Lincoln and Gentry fought off their attackers. "They were hurt some in the melee, but succeeded in driving the negroes from the boat."

A few days later, arriving in New Orleans, they were amazed to see hundreds of ships of all kinds—brigs, schooners, sloops, flatboats, and steamboats—sailing to or from New York and Philadelphia, as well as to Havana and Veracruz. They tied up their boat and walked over the tops of scores of other boats on their way into the city. The bustling waterfront became Lincoln's first glimpse of a city at work. As he walked the cobblestone streets, he saw bales of cotton and large casks of sugar. He observed dried tobacco leaves stripped from their stalks and tied in a bunch called a "hand," and then tightly packed in four-hundred-pound hogsheads. He saw and tasted many of the products of a new market economy.

Young Lincoln visited a city swaggering and dancing as a cosmopolitan center. The two men probably stayed in an area called "the swamp," the boatmen's rendezvous. From its early days, New Orleans's reputation rested in its medley of cultures—French, Creole, Spanish, African, and English. By 1828, the Southern city was filled with slaves. Men, women, and children were bought and sold daily as products in the slave market. Lincoln left no report about his experiences in the city itself, but in light of his later denunciations of slavery, we are left to wonder how his experiences in New Orleans, at the impressionable age of nineteen, influenced his future views.

Lincoln made eight dollars a month for his labor. He earned far more than that in life experience. After a few dizzying days in New Orleans, he and Gentry returned home to Indiana on a steamboat.

IN THE WINTER OF 1830, Thomas Lincoln decided to move on again. John Hanks, Abraham's mother's cousin, had settled in Illinois in 1829 and sent back a report of good soil and an invitation to pull up stakes and come farther west. Thomas Lincoln had moved four times since his first marriage, and now decided to bet his future on the prairies of Illinois.

Abraham pondered what he wanted to do with his life and where he wanted to live. He resisted the desire to leave his family and strike out on his own. Rather, he decided to help his father move. On March 1, after loading their belongings into big ox-drawn wagons, the Indiana Lincolns sold their hogs and corn and said good-bye to their neighbors at Pigeon Creek. Abraham drove one of the wagons west for the 225-mile journey.

The Lincoln caravan probably traveled north to join the Troy–Vincennes Trace, an old ridge route. They no doubt stopped in Vincennes at the end of the first fifty miles of their trek. After four or five days, they crossed the Wabash River, which was swollen by spring rains. As the Lincolns continued west, they left behind the immense forests and tangled underbrush of Indiana to find vast prairies of tall grasses and flowers. When Lincoln crossed the Wabash River from Indiana into Illinois he was twenty-one years old and now legally a man. He differed from the norms of the masculine culture in which he was raised by turning away from alcohol, tobacco, and guns, yet he was exceedingly well liked by the young men in Indiana. Both in ideas and actions, he was learning to listen to his own internal voice.

But many questions remained for Lincoln. Where would he live? What would he do? How could he continue his self-education?

On the evening of March 14, 1830, the Lincoln family camped in the village square in Decatur, Illinois. Decatur, awarded a post office a week before their arrival, was a new town with only a dozen log houses situated in an oak grove.

The next day, the families moved to the north bank of the Sangamon River, where forest and prairie land came together, about seven miles west and two miles south of Decatur. On this site, Abraham and his father built a log cabin and then a smokehouse and a barn. Abraham split rails to fence in their land. No longer obligated to work for his father, he continued to do so during the summer and fall of 1830, but also hired out as a farmhand and rail splitter to his new neighbors.

In the summer of 1830, Lincoln made his first political speech in front of Renshaw's store on Decatur's town square. William Ewing and John F. Posey, candidates for the legislature in Macon County, had gathered a crowd by denouncing "Old Line Whigs" as out of touch with modern issues. When the speakers finished, Lincoln stepped forward to offer a reply. Wearing tow-linen pants, a hickory shirt, and a straw hat, Lincoln surprised and delighted the crowd by refuting the charges, all the time punctuating his remarks with humor. He did not aim his words at the previous speakers, but rather at the crowd. As Lincoln spoke of contemporary issues facing the small community, especially the prospects of navigation on the Sangamon River, he was speaking of his own future in Illinois, with a new life stretching out before him.

CHAPTER 4

Rendering Myself Worthy of Their Esteem
1831–34

EVERY MAN IS SAID TO HAVE HIS PECULIAR AMBITION. WHETHER IT
BE TRUE OR NOT, I CAN SAY FOR ONE THAT I HAVE NO OTHER SO
GREAT AS THAT OF BEING TRULY ESTEEMED OF MY FELLOW MEN, BY
RENDERING MYSELF WORTHY OF THEIR ESTEEM.

ABRAHAM LINCOLN
Springfield's Sangamo Journal, *March 15, 1832*

N A BLUSTERY SPRING DAY IN APRIL 1831, THE RESIDENTS OF THE
recently established village of New Salem, Illinois, clustered on a bluff
to watch three young men struggle furiously with a long flatboat that
had become stranded on the mill dam on the Sangamon River just
below. The crew was attempting to steer the boat, loaded with barrels of
pork, corn, and snorting live hogs, over the dam. With its square end,
the boat had become jammed, with the stern in the water and the bow in
the air. More and more of the cargo was slowly but surely shifting
toward that stern.

The boat's pilot, a gangling fellow in blue-jean trousers, with black
hair tucked under a buckeye-chip hat, was eye catching because of his
tall, angular stature. As he directed his crew's efforts, they borrowed a
smaller boat in order to transfer some of the goods to lighten the load.
Shortly the stranger strode ashore and walked to the cooper shop,
owned by Henry Onstot, to borrow an auger. Returning to the water,
the boatman bored a hole in the end of the flatboat in order to let some
of the water run out. He quickly plugged the hole, and with the boat
thus lightened, they were able to pass over the mill dam.

Before departing, the crew poled the flatboat over to the bank and
came ashore amid the appreciative comments of the admiring crowd.

Thus Abraham Lincoln and the community of New Salem first met each other.

LINCOLN DEPARTED NEW SALEM to pilot the flatboat to New Orleans. He had been engaged by Denton Offutt, an enterprising if sometimes impractical businessman, to head up the voyage down the Mississippi River. Lincoln recruited John D. Johnston, his stepbrother, and John Hanks, his cousin, to join him on the trip.

Lincoln's journey to New Orleans in 1831, unlike his voyage from Indiana three years before, took place without major incident. Once in New Orleans, Lincoln sold the cargo as well as the boat. He then sailed up the Mississippi by steamboat to St. Louis. From St. Louis, he walked to Coles County in southern Illinois to visit his father and stepmother, who had moved there from their first home near Decatur. From there Lincoln walked nearly 180 miles to New Salem, arriving in July, about to break with the past and enter a decisive new chapter in his life. Offutt, taken with the resourceful spirit of the young Lincoln, had offered him a job in a grocery store he intended to start up.

"A STOPPED INDEFINITELY, and, for the first time, as it were, by himself at New Salem." Lincoln would spend only six of his fifty-six years in New Salem, from 1831 to 1837, but he decided to devote nearly one-fourth of his campaign autobiographical statement of 1860 to this time period. He understood he was entering into critical years of development and change.

Lincoln, at age twenty-two, hoped he might find in New Salem a place to begin a new life. Even as he piloted his boat on the Sangamon, in coming to New Salem he intended to cast off some cargo of his former life and separate himself from his father. As he walked to New Salem, he also walked away from his forebears' vocation of farming.

THE TWO WORDS—"New Salem"—rang with impressive promise. Two Southerners, James Rutledge and John Cameron, had founded the village in 1829 on a cliff on the bank of the Sangamon River twenty miles northwest of Springfield. Rutledge and Cameron wanted to build a mill and were looking for a river site with a powerful and steady flow of water.

Settlement in Illinois developed from south to north. When New

Salem was founded, few villages of any size had been settled farther north. Peoria, Dixon's Ferry on the Rock River, and Galena were tiny dots in the midst of the endless prairie. Villages in Illinois were established alongside rivers and lakes with easy access to water and timber. In 1831, the new settlement of Chicago, at the mouth of the Chicago River on Lake Michigan, had a population of sixty.

Like other settlers, Lincoln found the prairies a beautiful but beguiling experience. In the early years of the nineteenth century, no one dreamed one could cultivate them. Beneath what the first farmers called the "sea of grass" lay rich, naturally fertile soil, but the prairie grasses were tethered together for several feet below the surface. More than one pioneer, when first using a simple hoe, felt as if he had hit solid rock in trying to break through the surface.

The residents of New Salem hoped their settlement would become a flourishing river town. By the middle of the decade, New Salem would boast some twenty-five families and perhaps one hundred people.

Road travel in central Illinois was undependable. Travelers had to make their way through mud and mire, and routes were often changed. River travel was much more reliable. In the 1830s, the Sangamon River boasted a larger quantity of water than it does today. The Sangamon flowed into the Illinois at Beardstown, which joined the Mississippi River at Grafton. Rutledge and Cameron, soon to be joined by Lincoln, exuded optimism that light-draft steamboats could navigate the Sangamon.

New Salem had no church, but that did not mean there was an absence of religion. Baptists met in the schoolhouse. Presbyterians and Methodists met in homes. Charles James Fox Clarke, a young man from New England writing home to his mother, took note of the comings of camp meetings in the summers. "Camp meetings are all the rage here now, there is one every week for two months." Methodist evangelist Peter Cartwright conducted several revival meetings in New Salem. While the emotional intensity of the revivals warmed the hearts of many, Lincoln was not among them. The anti-intellectualism and emotionalism of the revivals turned some residents away, while inspiring a search in others for a more rational faith.

ON AUGUST 1, 1831, LINCOLN participated in his first election. He voted at the polling station at John Cameron's house by announcing out loud—no secret ballot here—his choices for Congress, magistrate, and constable to the clerks who sat behind a table. They recorded Lincoln's votes on tally sheets.

At the end of August, Offutt's goods and merchandise arrived from Beardstown. Lincoln helped Offutt unbox them, and the store opened around September 1 in a small log building near the edge of the bluff above the mill. Lincoln and Offutt stocked the shelves with dry goods, seeds, tools, saddles, and guns, as well as sugar, salt, coffee, eggs, and vegetables. Barrels of liquor lined one wall.

Lincoln worked as a clerk in Offutt's store for a salary of fifteen dollars a month. Offutt hired Bill Greene to assist Lincoln, and the two men slept among the crates and barrels in the back storeroom. Greene recalled that the two "slept on the same cott & when one turned over the other had to do likewise."

Bill Greene worked with Lincoln in Denton Offutt's store in New Salem and served in the volunteer militia that elected Lincoln captain during the Black Hawk War.

OFFUTT GAINED A reputation as a braggart, usually about himself and what he could do, but soon he began to brag about his new clerk, Lincoln. He boasted that Lincoln could run faster and jump farther than anyone in the county, and could beat anyone at wrestling. Young frontiersmen liked to participate in a variety of folk games. Offutt's bragging got the twenty-two-year-old Lincoln into a contest he didn't choose.

Jack Armstrong, a strong, muscular man, led a local gang called the Clary's Grove Boys, who took their name from a small village of that name less than three miles from New Salem. In a time when men settled their arguments with their fists, the Clary's Grove Boys were the bullies of the neighborhood. They gained their supremacy by fighting, especially wrestling.

Armstrong was known as the champion wrestler in the area. Not many men were willing to challenge him. Offutt offered up Lincoln as a newcomer who would be more than up to the task. Armstrong and his friends had nothing against Lincoln, but they kept hearing the claims about this new fellow in town.

Wrestling ran in the Lincoln family. His uncle Mord reputedly had a talent for it, and Lincoln had done a fair amount of wrestling growing up in Indiana. His long legs and arms had always given him a great advantage over his opponents.

In the fall of 1831, Armstrong and Lincoln met for a match. Five years older than Lincoln, but ten inches shorter, Armstrong had a reputation for using trickery to win his matches. The accounts of the match vary, offered long after it took place. The two men did not, as the legend has suggested, circle each other with arms free, looking for an opening to dart in and throw the opponent. Rather, they began with prescribed holds, agreed upon in advance, in which strength, leverage, and agility were the primary assets. This custom, passed down from Northern England, favored Lincoln, with his greater height and therefore leverage. Lincoln and Armstrong pushed and pulled until—and here many witnesses are in agreement—Armstrong, in frustration, broke his hold or lost his contact with Lincoln. Under the loose rules of wrestling on the frontier, Lincoln at this point might have been declared the winner, but instead he and Armstrong shook hands and agreed to call the wrestling match a draw.

Lincoln won something more important than a wrestling match that day. He proved his strength and his courage to himself and his new community by fighting the acknowledged champion of the area. After this, the newcomer became accepted in the young male culture of the region.

EARLY ON LINCOLN slept where he worked—in Denton Offutt's store. Later, he followed the practice of nearly all single men of his day: He boarded with various families, staying weeks or even months at a time, earning his keep by doing chores around the house. Farmer James Short recalled, "Frequently when Mr. L was at my house he would help me gather corn." When Lincoln lived with the Bennett and Elizabeth Abell family, she did his washing and he did odd jobs in exchange for a bed.

Lincoln wore characteristic clothing of the day. Jack's wife, Hannah Armstrong, remembered, "I foxed his pants," or made them with a leather lining, and "made his shirts." Lincoln wore a "blue round about coat," a snug jacket preferred by young men, and blue cassinette pantaloons as trousers, which were a combination of cotton and wool. He wore Conestoga shoes, a rough boot. What singled the tall Lincoln out, commented on by many in New Salem, was the persistent gap between the bottom of his pantaloons and the top of his shoes.

IN THE WINTER OF 1832, navigability of the Sangamon River was tested. Excitement grew when Lincoln and the other citizens of New Salem learned that the *Talisman,* a small steamer, had left Cincinnati on a journey to demonstrate that the Sangamon could be used for commercial boat traffic.

Vincent A. Bogue, a businessman, wanted to build a sawmill on the Sangamon River at a place called Portland's Landing. His goal was to service the Sangamon River valley, connecting the people and their produce with the outside world. "I am well aware that the undertaking is *dangerous, difficult,* and *expensive;* still I am willing to risk my all upon it," Bogue wrote. He stipulated that the boat should be "under the direction of some experienced man," one who had "descended the river with flatboats." Lincoln met this qualification and volunteered for the task.

Bogue brought the *Talisman* safely to the confluence of the Illinois and Sangamon rivers at Beardstown on March 9, but the mouth of the Sangamon was jammed with winter ice. Lincoln joined the boat crew in working for four days to make a channel through the ice. The "experienced man," Lincoln helped pilot the *Talisman* as it set off on its triumphant voyage. Men and boys, on foot or horseback, cheered as the boat made its way up the river. The boat passed New Salem and docked at Bogue's mill. Lincoln attended a grand ball in Springfield's new courthouse to celebrate the great event. The *Sangamo Journal* exclaimed, "Springfield can no longer be considered an inland town." Lincoln received forty dollars for his services.

IN 1832, LINCOLN, twenty-three, made his first move into politics. Lincoln's friends, including Bowling Green, the jovial justice of the peace, and James Rutledge, the founder of a debating society, encouraged him to become a candidate for the state legislature. They admired Lincoln, but they also needed a representative in the legislature who could advance their interests, especially their desire to encourage commercial boat traffic on the Sangamon River. After less than one year in New Salem, Lincoln announced his first candidacy in the *Sangamo Journal* on March 15.

> FELLOW-CITIZENS: Having become a candidate for the honorable office of one of your representatives in the next General Assembly of this state, in accordance with an established custom, and the principles of true republicanism, it becomes my duty to make known to you—the people whom I propose to represent—my sentiments with regard to local affairs.

Lincoln directed the bulk of his 1,800-word announcement to a discussion of internal improvements—measures to improve roads, rivers, and canals. He positioned himself as the person most trustworthy on the subject: "It is probable that for the last twelve months I have given as particular attention to the stage of the water in this river, as any other person in the country." On many a day, people from the village had seen Lincoln out in the river measuring the depth of the water in different places and making notes about the river's features. His recent association with the successful voyage of the *Talisman* boosted his reputation.

After briefly discussing the subject of education, Lincoln turned to his conclusion.

> Every man is said to have his peculiar ambition. Whether it be true or not, I can say for one that I have no other so great as that of being truly esteemed of my fellow men, by rendering myself worthy of their esteem. How far I shall succeed in gratifying this ambition, is yet to be developed. I am young and unknown to many of you. I was born and have ever remained in the most humble walks of life. I have no wealthy or popular relations to recommend. My case is thrown exclusively upon the independent voters of this county, and if elected they will have conferred a favor upon me, for which I shall be unremitting in my labors to compensate. But if the good people in their wisdom shall see fit to keep me in the background, I have been too familiar with disappointments to be very much chagrined.

The final paragraph is remarkable for what it discloses about the young Lincoln. In appealing for the sympathy of the community, he underscores his own "ambition"—using the word twice—but modifies this aspiration by suggesting that every man has ambition. Lincoln did not see himself as alone in his desire; he evoked a motivation growing among the young men of his generation, who sought to shape their own lives as over against the well-worn paths of their fathers' lives in the first decades of a new nation. Lincoln shifted the balance and tone of his final words by turning that ambition into a desire "of being truly esteemed of my fellow men." Behind these words is Lincoln's awareness that ambition can lead to selfish egotism in politics. His unvoiced question was: How can I be esteemed? His answer: "by rendering myself worthy."

ON APRIL 19, 1832, a lone rider galloped into New Salem with startling news. Lincoln and other villagers gathered around to hear that Sauk and Fox Indians had left their settlements in Iowa, crossed the Mississippi River, and advanced up the east bank. They were now moving up the Rock River across the northwest corner of Illinois. No one knew their intentions, but some said they wanted to return to their former lands in northern Illinois. Lincoln's initial foray into politics was about to be suspended by a military emergency.

The movements of the Indians caused a panic among the white residents in Illinois. Illinois governor John Reynolds heightened the alarm by calling their actions an "invasion," even though the nearly four hundred warriors were accompanied by three times that many women and children.

Black Hawk, their leader, was an old man, born in 1767. He and his followers were bitter about giving up their homes in a disputed treaty negotiated in 1804. The recent surge of white settlers into Illinois precipitated sporadic hostilities between the settlers and Indians defending their lands.

Reynolds called for recruits to repulse the "invasion." Lincoln promptly volunteered and was sworn into service on April 21. In the military, units elect their own officers. Some of the Clary's Grove Boys put forward Lincoln's name. Bill Kirkpatrick, who owned a sawmill, declared his candidacy. Each of the men was asked to step forward on the village green. The volunteers then formed a line behind the candidate they wanted for captain. Two-thirds of the men fell in behind Lincoln. The rest quickly abandoned Kirkpatrick, making Lincoln the unanimous

The Black Hawk War, precipitated by the movement of Chief Black Hawk and his warriors across the Mississippi back into Illinois in 1832, was the first affirmation of Lincoln's leadership.

choice. Lincoln later described his experience: "to his own surprise, was elected captain of it."

On April 28, Captain Lincoln oversaw the enrollment of his company in the state militia. Jack Armstrong, Lincoln's former wrestling opponent, served as his first sergeant. The next day Lincoln and his men began their march north from Beardstown along an old Indian track near the Mississippi River. Lincoln did not have an easy task instilling discipline in the group of volunteers.

On one occasion, an old Indian named Jack appeared in Lincoln's camp. He showed a paper signed by General Lewis Cass stating he was "a good and true man," but some of the men wanted to kill him. One said, "We have come out to fight the Indians and by God we intend to do so." As tempers flared and rifles rose, Lincoln stepped between Jack and his men. Another man spoke sternly to Lincoln. "This is cowardly on your part, Lincoln." Lincoln replied that if "any man thinks I am a coward let him test it." His words silenced the men in his company and saved Jack's life.

On May 15, just before sunset, Lincoln and his men encountered the deadly results of a battle from the previous day: eleven soldiers' bodies scalped and mutilated. His company helped bury the dead soldiers.

When Lincoln's enlistment expired, he signed up for another twenty days, this time as a private. On June 16, 1832, Lincoln's company was discharged by Lieutenant Robert Anderson, but he enlisted once again. Finally, on July 10, he received his discharge.

Lincoln earned the title of "captain," but he never used it, even though most of the men who served in the Black Hawk War hung on to their titles with pride for the remainder of their lives. Lincoln never participated in combat but expressed his feelings about his military experiences in his 1860 autobiographical statement. "He says he has not since had any success in life which gave him so much satisfaction."

Lincoln had lived in New Salem only nine months when the Black Hawk War intruded into his life. His election as captain represented how quickly he had won the loyalty and affection of his neighbors. He received $125 for his military service. As he walked back to New Salem, he pondered what he should do with this substantial sum.

LINCOLN RETURNED TO New Salem in late July, just two weeks before the election. He began campaigning in earnest. As he began to speak on the campaign trail in Pappsville, a fight erupted in the crowd. Seeing that several men were attacking his friend Rowan Herndon, Lincoln left the platform, pushed through the crowd, picked up the main assailant by the seat of his pants, and threw him six feet. The fighting over, Lincoln resumed his place, and gave one of his shortest political speeches.

> Fellow Citizens, I presume you all know who I am. I am humble
> Abraham Lincoln. I have been solicited by my friends to become
> a candidate for the Legislature. My politics are short and sweet,
> like the old woman's dance. I am in favor of a national bank. I am
> in favor of the internal improvement system and a high protec-
> tion tariff. These are my sentiments and political principles. If
> elected I shall be thankful; if not it will be all the same.

Lincoln won the day in deeds as much as words.

The election for state offices took place on August 6, 1832. Sangamon County was allotted four representatives in the lower house of the state legislature. Lincoln came in eighth in a field of thirteen candidates with 657 votes. He was not too disheartened, however, for in the precinct that included New Salem, he received 277 of the 300 votes.

He had discovered his appetite for politics. Lincoln knew his defeat was largely because he was unknown in the rest of the county, and he was determined to broaden the base of his political support.

LINCOLN LEFT FAMILY and farming behind when he migrated from Indiana, but he did not leave behind his love of learning. The distance that had developed between Abraham and his father was in part over Lincoln's intellectual curiosity and love of reading and learning. Now, "by himself," Lincoln became freer to read. Learning would take on fresh dimensions in the open space of New Salem.

Lincoln quickly became a regular at the debating society that met twice a month. Such societies were springing up across American frontier settlements. Before a tavern fireplace or in a church parlor, men met to debate whether society should care for the poor, whether women should be educated, whether to use public monies to build canals and roads, and whether slavery was right or wrong.

The New Salem debating society became a place for Lincoln to continue his education. In Indiana, he had mimicked preachers and offered impromptu speeches to his boyhood friends, but the debating society provided him his first sustained opportunity to learn the art of speaking.

Robert Rutledge, cousin of James Rutledge, the society's founder, described Lincoln's first attempt to address a meeting. "As he rose to speak his tall form towered over the little assembly." At first nervous, Lincoln wedged his hands deep into the pockets of his pantaloons. "As he warmed to his subject, his hands would forsake his pockets, and would enforce his ideas by awkward gestures." Lincoln's enthusiasm and integrity won him the right to be heard at the debating society, even if his nervousness was all too evident as he struggled with the right words to express his ideas.

"After he was twenty-three and had separated from his father he studied English grammar—imperfectly of course, but so as to speak and write as well as he now does," Lincoln later wrote. A schoolteacher, Mentor Graham, who lived about a mile from New Salem, told Lincoln that John C. Vance, a local farmer, owned a copy of Samuel Kirkham's *English Grammar.* Lincoln walked six miles to ask to borrow the book.

Kirkham's *Grammar* was one of dozens of grammars circulating in the first half of the nineteenth century. In his preface, Samuel Kirkham states that the *Grammar* "professes not to instruct the literary connoisseur" but rather "attempts to accelerate the march of the juvenile mind." Lincoln was not a juvenile, but he was indeed on an intellectual march.

Kirkham divided his subject matter into four sections:

1. Orthography
2. Etymology
3. Syntax
4. Prosody

Lincoln devoured the Kirkham text. Sometimes he stretched out on the counter of Denton Offutt's store as he committed whole sections of the book to memory. Rowan Herndon remembered that Lincoln liked to "read by fire light" at night at Henry Onstot's cooper shop. Kirkham asked the student to learn by rote. "Adverbs qualify verbs, adjectives, and other adverbs." Often Lincoln would wheedle Bill Greene or other friends to help him practice the review tasks at the end of each chapter. Kirkham's orderly progression of teaching helped Lincoln improve his ability to write and to speak the English language.

"HIS MIND WAS FULL of terrible Enquiry—and was skeptical in a good sense," was the way his friend Isaac Cogdal, a farmer and stonemason, described Lincoln's intellectual curiosity. In New Salem, Lincoln felt the freedom to question. Having watched the sectarian rivalries among Baptists, and between Baptists, Methodists, and Presbyterians, Lincoln's inclusive spirit was turned away by denominational divisions.

In Lincoln's early twenties, at the public debating society and in his private reading, he began to ask numerous questions and raise doubts about supposedly established truths. Several books contributed to his growing skepticism. Constantin Volney, French historian and philosopher, wrote *The Ruins* in 1791 at the height of the French Revolution. Volney advocated the overthrow of the twin medieval tyrannies of state and church. Translated into English by Thomas Jefferson, the book offered an Enlightenment critique of revealed religion, arguing that morality was the true measure of faith.

Storekeeper Abner Y. Ellis reported that Lincoln "read some of Tom Pains Works." Paine, a revolutionary propagandist, helped light the fire of the American Revolution when he published *Common Sense* in 1776. Later, while in prison in France during the French Revolution, Paine wrote *The Age of Reason,* which attacked the church and revealed religion. Lincoln read Paine's dismissal of the Bible: "It is a book of lies, wickedness, and blasphemy for what can be more blasphemous than to ascribe the wickedness of man to the orders of the Almighty?"

James Matheny, whom Lincoln met in 1834 when serving as deputy postmaster in Springfield, believed Lincoln's growing affinity for the poetry of Robert Burns also encouraged his skepticism. Burns, a refugee from Scottish Calvinism, cried out against the Presbyterian teachings on predestination. Matheny observed, "Burns helped Lincoln to be an infidel I think—at least he found in Burns a like thinker & feeler."

Whatever Lincoln read often ended up in something he wrote. In the winter of 1834, Lincoln may have written a paper with his views on traditional Christian beliefs. Many New Salem residents remembered hearing of a paper read one evening in James Hill's store that questioned, if not attacked, the divinity of the scriptures in the spirit of Volney and Paine. To voice such questions in a frontier culture steeped in Protestant orthodoxy was to court censure if not ostracism. Lincoln did not finish reading his paper before Samuel Hill snatched it from him and tossed it in the open fire. Hill was either outraged by Lincoln's impiety, or saving his friend from embarrassment.

In New Salem, Lincoln was free to sever ties with his family's Baptist tradition, even though that tradition was present in the village. In his widening circle of reading, he encountered eminent authors who challenged traditional Christian teachings. Lincoln could not go back to the Baptist tradition of his parents.

BY THE END OF the summer of 1832, Lincoln found himself defeated for political office and out of work, Offutt's store having failed in the spring. He could try again for political office in the future, but he needed a job in the present. "He studied what he should do—thought of learning the black-smith trade—thought of studying law—rather thought he could not succeed at that without a better education." He worked all kinds of jobs, including part-time work with storekeeper Ellis, while seeking something more permanent.

Rowan Herndon offered to sell Lincoln his half of a partnership in a New Salem store. Lincoln and William F. Berry, the other partner and one of the corporals in Lincoln's militia company, now attempted to do what a number of other aspirants had failed to do—compete with Samuel Hill, a merchant who had cornered the market in New Salem.

They put up their military pay, personal notes, animals, and land to pursue their dream, but the partners quickly found themselves in trouble.

From the start, they were hobbled by their own habits. Berry enjoyed whiskey, and plenty of it. Lincoln spent as much time talking politics with customers as he did managing the store's ledger. In March, things only got worse when Berry signed his name and Lincoln's to a tavern license enabling them to sell liquor. Barrels of whiskey and bottles of wine, rum, and brandy soon lined the walls and shelves.

"Of course they did nothing but get deeper in debt," Lincoln remembered in 1860. Nine months after opening the store, Lincoln and Berry were in deep financial trouble. Many locals remembered that the decision to sell alcohol—Lincoln did not drink—put a severe strain on the partnership. Lincoln decided to sell his interest in the store to Berry. Years later, an older and wiser Lincoln summarized tersely the end of their joint venture: "The store winked out."

ON MAY 7, 1833, Lincoln was appointed the postmaster of New Salem. President Andrew Jackson, a Democrat, was the first president to bring the post office into the spoils system, where jobs were given to the president's supporters. How then could Lincoln, who had not supported Jackson, earn such an office? He chalked up his government appointment to the fact that the office was "too insignificant, to make his politics an objection."

In 1833, the mail came to New Salem by post rider. Before envelopes and stamps, letters were folded and sealed by wax. Postage was calculated by the number of pages in the letter and the distance it was to travel. Lincoln marked the postage due in the upper right-hand corner of the sealed letter, and the person receiving the letter paid the postage.

As postmaster, Lincoln earned twenty-five to thirty dollars a year. His compensation depended upon receipts that he kept in an old blue sock in a wooden chest under the counter. But the job had other benefits. Lincoln was now a federal official, elevating his position in the community. Most important, the job was not full-time, allowing him to supplement his income. He went back to helping Ellis with his store and lending farmers a hand with harvesting.

His new position also afforded Lincoln the opportunity to get to know people beyond New Salem. Home delivery did not begin in the United States until 1825. When this service began, a surcharge of up to two cents was added to each letter. Lincoln, in delivering letters to far-flung customers, adopted the habit of placing the letters in his hat.

In a letter to his brother, George, Matthew S. Marsh provided a window into how Lincoln carried out his duties: "The Post Master is very careless about leaving his office open and unlocked during the day. Half the time I go in and get my papers, etc., without any one being there as was the case yesterday." But things were not all bad. "The letter was only marked twenty-five [cents] and even if he had been there and known it was double, he would not have charged me any more—luckily he is a clever fellow and a particular friend of mine."

Another benefit for this particular postmaster was the time it allowed to read the many newspapers coming into New Salem, in part because people were slow in calling for their mail. Often, when the newspapers arrived, people gathered around while Lincoln read stories from them. A merchant in New Salem reported that Lincoln "generally Read for the By standers when the male Come which was weekly."

Lincoln began reading regularly the *National Intelligencer* from Washington, which carried fine coverage of Congress. Schoolmaster Graham, commenting on Lincoln's continual learning, said, "His text book was the *Louisville Journal*." The *Journal* offered excellent reporting on both national and regional events and supported Henry Clay, Lincoln's favorite politician. As postmaster, Lincoln had access to other newspapers as well, including the *Cincinnati Gazette* and the *Missouri Republican,* a Democratic newspaper published in St. Louis. Through the newspapers, Lincoln taught himself about politics. He discovered, for the first time, the power of newspapers to influence public opinion, a lesson he would use again and again later on.

LATER IN 1833, while still postmaster, Lincoln found further employment as a surveyor. "[I] accepted, procured a compass and a chain, studied Flint, and Gibson a little, and went at it," he remembered. Hired by Sangamon County surveyor John Calhoun as his deputy, Lincoln served in the northern part of the county. Calhoun was a staunch supporter of President Andrew Jackson. In accepting the job, Lincoln made it known that he would not compromise his political principles.

Lincoln knew nothing about surveying. He acquired a surveyor's vernier compass made by Rittenhouse and Company of Philadelphia, a sixty-six-foot Gunter's chain, some plumb bobs, a set of marking pins, and a set of range or flag poles—all on credit. He already had an ax. He also obtained a horse and set about laying out roads and town sites. In the next years, Lincoln would survey a number of farms as well as the towns of Albany, Bath, Huron, New Boston, and Petersburg. He also surveyed land set aside for public schools. The rapid arrival of settlers made surveying a popular trade.

In January 1834, Russell Godbey employed Lincoln to survey an eighty-acre tract of land six miles north of New Salem and one mile east of the Sangamon River. Godbey said that Lincoln "staid with me all night and Sold him two buckskins—well dressed to fox his Surveyors pants." Surveying had become much more economically viable and politically opportunistic than his job as postmaster. "This procured bread, and kept soul and body together."

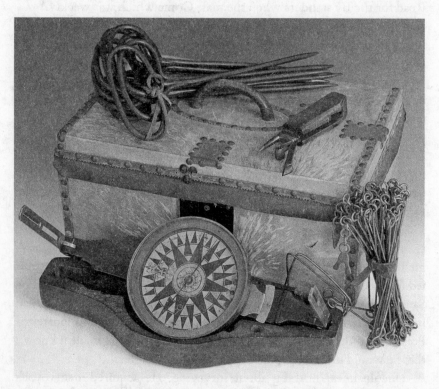

In 1833, Lincoln found employment as a surveyor. His tools included a vernier compass, Gunter's chain, plumb bobs, and a set of marking pins. Lincoln's surveying of both farms and new towns widened his circle of friends.

———

IN THE SPRING OF 1834, Lincoln decided to run for the Illinois legislature a second time. He announced his candidacy in the *Sangamo Journal* on April 19. Thirteen men were running for the four places allotted to Sangamon County for the Ninth General Assembly. What would make this second run any different from the first?

Because the voting was held during a non–presidential election year, the contest turned more on local personalities. Lincoln's circle of friends and acquaintances had increased greatly. Since the last election, Lincoln had held jobs as storekeeper, postmaster, and surveyor. Each job gave him an opportunity to meet a wider sphere of people in Sangamon County. Robert L. Wilson, a Whig politician, recalled, "Every one knew him; and he knew everyone." His reputation for both political skill and speaking ability had also grown. Even as the Whigs and Democrats were rushing to build national party machinery, local issues would continue to be decisive in the summer of 1834.

Over the next four months, Lincoln divided his time between campaigning and surveying, often using the latter to campaign across the countryside. Lincoln campaigned by mounting a stump or sometimes a box. Even as party lines were becoming more defined, and Lincoln was stamped by others as a Whig, he determined to run a bipartisan campaign. In his speeches, he made no mention of either his criticism of Democratic president Andrew Jackson or his support for Whig leader Henry Clay.

Rowan Herndon spoke of Lincoln's campaign style. On a hot summer day in 1834, in the course of his duties as deputy surveyor, Lincoln came to Herndon's new home in Island Grove. Men were working in the field. Herndon introduced Lincoln to them, but some of the men retorted that "they could not vote for a man unless he could make a hand." Lincoln responded, "If that is all I am sure of your votes," and with that he took hold of the cradle used for harvesting grain and led the men one full round of the field. "The boys was satisfied," Herndon remembered, "and I don't think he lost a vote in the crowd."

Lincoln's former client Russell Godbey, a Democrat and a farmer, was a typical Lincoln voter. "I voted for Lincoln in opposition to my own creed & faith in Politics."

When the votes were counted on August 4, 1834, Lincoln was elected. He finished second among the thirteen candidates, trailing the front-runner John Dawson, a Whig eighteen years his senior, by only fourteen votes.

IN HIS CAMPAIGN announcement of 1832, Lincoln had told the people of Sangamon County that his chief desire was to be "esteemed of my fellow men, by rendering myself worthy of their esteem." In a brief two years, Lincoln's abilities and experiences began to coalesce into his gifts of leadership. His intellectual curiosity had pushed beyond the romantic and religious classics he read in his Indiana years to Enlightenment authors who offered critiques of religion. Now feeling at home after living three years in New Salem, he was beginning to find his own voice, not just around the fireside at the country store, but in campaigning in the countryside beyond the little town, where he was known for his clearheaded thinking, whimsical storytelling, and self-deprecating humor. Lincoln's ambitions for public service were about to be tested and shaped in the larger arena of the Illinois Ninth General Assembly.

CHAPTER 5

The Whole People of Sangamon
1834–37

WHILE ACTING AS THEIR REPRESENTATIVE, I SHALL BE GOVERNED BY
THEIR WILL, ON ALL SUBJECTS. . . . I HAVE THE MEANS OF KNOWING
WHAT THEIR WILL IS; AND UPON OTHERS I SHALL DO WHAT MY OWN
JUDGMENT TEACHES ME WILL BEST ADVANCE THEIR INTERESTS.

ABRAHAM LINCOLN
Letter to the editor of the Sangamo Journal, *June 13, 1836*

At 6 A.M. ON FRIDAY, NOVEMBER 28, 1834, ABRAHAM LINCOLN
boarded the weekly stage in Springfield for the ninety-five-mile journey to Vandalia, the Illinois state capital. The coach, crowded with
other Sangamon County representatives, bumped along but Lincoln
didn't mind because of his eagerness to take his seat in the Ninth General
Assembly of Illinois. At some point in the journey, he must have
thought about how far he had traveled in the little more than three years
since he first arrived in New Salem.

Before leaving for Vandalia, Lincoln had asked his friend Coleman
Smoot, a prosperous farmer, "Did you vote for me?" Smoot told him, "I
did."

Lincoln replied, then "you must loan me money to buy Suitable
Clothing for I want to take a decent appearance in the Legislature."

Smoot loaned him two hundred dollars. Lincoln promptly paid sixty
dollars for the first suit he ever owned.

The stage traveled a meandering route by way of Macoupin Point
and Hillsboro. After thirty-four hours, the driver finally blew his horn
to signal they had arrived in Vandalia. Lincoln claimed his bag and followed John Todd Stuart, a prominent Whig leader from Springfield, to
one of the inns on the town square where they would share a room and

a bed. Few people arriving for that session of the Illinois legislature knew anything about Lincoln, but he had traveled a long way in his twenty-five years and came to Vandalia determined to make his mark.

LINCOLN ARRIVED IN a capital invented by politicians. Vandalia had been founded in 1819 as the second capital of the new state of Illinois because the first capital, Kaskaskia, had become untenable due to routine flooding from the Mississippi River. The planners built Vandalia on a heavily timbered bluff in the wilderness above the Kaskaskia River. The Illinois legislature first met there in December 1820.

By December 1834, the second capital had grown to a town of eight hundred to nine hundred people. During the biennial sixty- to seventy-day sessions of the legislature, the town crowded to overflowing with fifty-five representatives and twenty-six senators, as well as lobbyists, office seekers, and hangers on. The state supreme court also met during these sessions, which brought in lawyers, plaintiffs, and witnesses. The small hotels on the town square—the Vandalia Inn, Charter's Tavern, National Hotel, New White House, and the Sign of the Green Tree—each housed thirty to forty people. They were called "boarding taverns" because legislators and lawyers packed their taprooms in the evenings to enjoy strong drink, cigars, and political discussion. Although a statute prohibited it, gambling flourished in all the hotels during legislative sessions.

The capitol building where Lincoln would work was actually the second state capitol erected in Vandalia, the first having burned in December 1823. The plain two-story brick structure on the west side of the public square was ten years old. In addition to meeting rooms for the House and Senate, the capitol contained a courtroom for the Illinois Supreme Court. When Lincoln walked up the stairs to the second floor, he saw that, because the building had been constructed so quickly, the floors sagged and the walls bulged. Falling plaster would often interrupt debates.

ON MONDAY, DECEMBER 1, 1834, Lincoln arrived for his first session in the Illinois legislature. At twenty-five, Lincoln was the second youngest of the fifty-five representatives. Thirty-six representatives were also starting their first term, yet all brought more experience than Lincoln to the task.

On the first day of the new session, most members wore long black coats, white shirts with collars held high by stocks, and a wide band of scarf around their necks. Farmers constituted the largest group in the general assembly; about one-fourth of the members were lawyers. Lincoln participated in drawing lots for seats at a series of long tables, each built to accommodate three members. Each member had an inkstand made of cork. Sandboxes placed around the floor accommodated the many legislators who chewed tobacco. Candles lit the room. A single water pail was present with three tin cups.

On December 3, 1834, the third day of the session, the state of Illinois celebrated its sixteenth birthday. Illinois had grown rapidly from forty-five thousand inhabitants in 1818 to more than two hundred thousand people in 1834. The vast majority of the immigrants were frontier farmers.

Two days later, Lincoln rose for the first time and, in a high tenor voice with a Kentucky accent, intoned, "Mr. Speaker." He introduced his first bill, "an act to limit the jurisdiction of Justices of the Peace." Lincoln's bill ran into difficulties; it was assigned to a committee, and then to a second special committee. Over the next few weeks, he watched his bill bog down in the arcane processes of state legislatures, never to resurface.

In his first weeks in Vandalia, Lincoln answered "present" for each day's session. The roll call did not mark the times he slipped away in the midst of legislative sessions to observe the proceedings of the state supreme court. He had attended local courts in Indiana and Illinois, and he did not want to miss the opportunity to witness the proceedings of a state supreme court.

In the evenings, Lincoln joined the lively conversations around the fireplace in the various inns. Here he heard not simply political gossip and debate, but also legal shoptalk by lawyers who had come to Vandalia to present their cases before the supreme court. These ambitious lawyers, encouraged by alcoholic spirits, spoke freely of the fees they were receiving for their labors.

Along with his public duties in the legislature, Lincoln began to develop another skill while in Vandalia. Long an avid reader of newspapers, Lincoln started writing for them. Simeon Francis, editor of the *Sangamo Journal,* the Whig newspaper in Springfield, was eager to have firsthand reports on the legislative session. On December 13, 1834, the

Sangamo Journal printed a brief letter "From Our Correspondent" summarizing five significant measures that would come before the legislature in the session. Two more letters "From Our Correspondent" would appear in January and February. The letters were from an anonymous hand, but the style and substance sounded like Lincoln, replete with humor.

WITHIN A MONTH, Lincoln had earned the right to be heard in the legislature. In the midst of a long report on internal improvements, William Dawson reminded the House that sometime before, they had moved to fill the post of surveyor for Schuyler County because a report had been received that the incumbent had died. The House nominated and the Senate confirmed Samuel McHatton to be the new surveyor. Representative Dawson had just learned, however, that the incumbent was in fact alive, and now that there was no vacancy, he moved that the nomination of McHatton "be vacated."

Lincoln stood up to protest. He called Dawson's motion an irregularity of parliamentary procedure. Lincoln pointed out the illogicality of having no vacancy, and yet two surveyors. What could the general assembly do? Lincoln offered a solution. "There was no danger of the new surveyor's ousting the old one so long as he persisted not to die." Lincoln then suggested "the propriety of letting matters remain as they were, so that if the old surveyor should hereafter conclude to die, there would be a new one ready made without troubling the legislature."

Lincoln found his legislative voice with irony. He discovered in his first session that humor went a long way in breaking down walls in partisan legislative bodies. Lincoln made an impression on the Speaker, James Semple, a Jacksonian Democrat from Madison. The Speaker appointed Lincoln to ten special committees, and he called upon him regularly to speak to key motions.

The house doorkeeper blew out the candles on February 13, 1835, and the first legislative session of the Ninth General Assembly concluded on the day after Lincoln's twenty-sixth birthday. In his first service as a legislator, Lincoln mostly listened. He was regular in his attendance and learned the political ropes from his roommate Stuart, the Whig leader. After receiving the second part of his salary, $258, Lincoln boarded the stage back to Springfield.

When Lincoln came home, his old boss, Abner Ellis, believed he saw a more self-confident and able Lincoln. "I always thought that Mr. Lincoln improved rapidly in Mind & Manners after his return from Vandalia his first session in the Legislature."

DESPITE HIS NEW SALARY, Lincoln returned home to financial hardship. His former store partner, William F. Berry, had continued his drinking and died on January 10, 1835, leaving considerable debt. Lincoln himself owed more than five hundred dollars on their failed store, and because he and Berry were partners, Lincoln became responsible for Berry's debts as well. Taken together, Lincoln's liability was something over $1,100, a large sum of money in 1835, and equivalent to $25,000 in today's dollars.

In the following months, creditors pressed various judgments against Lincoln. He had to put forward his horse, saddle, bridle, surveying instruments—and his house—to pay off his debts to just one creditor. When Lincoln's goods were put up for sale, James Short, a close friend in New Salem, unbeknownst to Lincoln, bid successfully on all of them and then returned them to Lincoln.

Lincoln's debt was not unusual in a pioneer life based on subsistence farming and a barter economy. It was common for debtors to skip out on their debts, escaping their creditors in the middle of the night. Lincoln's first employer in New Salem, Denton Offutt, did so. Captain Vincent Bogue, owner of the *Talisman,* fled from Springfield.

But Lincoln stayed. He promised all his creditors that he would make good on his debt. He began calling it his "National Debt," suggesting not only that his debt was huge, but that his debtors were from as far away as Cincinnati. Because of this, Lincoln could not pay off his debt in work or in barter; he had to pay it off over time in cash.

From this debacle Lincoln earned a nickname that would stick with him his whole life: "Honest Abe." Yes, Lincoln wanted to become a self-made man, but he was learning that his reputation depended on the opinion of others. His venture with the Lincoln-Berry store may have failed, but his decision to stay and repay his neighbors raised his esteem among a growing circle of friends.

DURING THE CAMPAIGN for the legislature in 1834, Lincoln's friend John Todd Stuart, a successful attorney, had urged Lincoln to study law. Stuart had taken a liking to Lincoln when they served together as volunteers in the Black Hawk War. In Vandalia, Stuart saw potential in Lincoln and went out of his way to encourage him to consider the vocation.

Lincoln had begun reading law books shortly after his arrival in New Salem. He drafted legal documents for his neighbors from an old form book, drawing up a document for James Eastep for a tract of land in 1831, for John Ferguson for the "right and title" for the New Salem ferry in 1832, and several deeds recorded in 1833 and 1834. Jason Duncan, a New Salem doctor, recounted that "as there [were] no Attorneys nearer than Springfield his services were sometimes sought in suits, at law."

Lincoln began arguing cases before the local justice of the peace, Bowling Green. Lincoln formed a friendship with Green, a round man with a large laugh who frequently entertained Lincoln in his home. Lincoln read books in Green's small law library, and he encouraged Lincoln to write out simple legal forms. In Vandalia, Lincoln observed how many of his fellow legislators were both politicians and lawyers, and how Stuart used that prestige to help him become the leader of the Whig minority.

In 1860, Lincoln recalled that in 1834 "he thought of trying to study law," but "thought he could not succeed at that without a better education." Stuart offered to become his mentor.

Like Lincoln, Stuart was from Kentucky, but in everything else the pair could not have been more different. A strikingly handsome man with a captivating manner, he had graduated from Centre College in Danville, Kentucky. Arriving in Springfield in 1828 at barely twenty-one, he had rapidly established a successful law practice. He was elected to the state legislature in 1832 at age twenty-five and quickly became a leader in county and state politics.

After his first session in the state legislature, Lincoln returned to New Salem in the winter of 1835 determined to become a lawyer. At that time, there were only seven law schools in the United States—none in Illinois. In 1832, Massachusetts lawyer Josiah Quincy had described the rudimentary state of the study of law: "Regular instruction there was none; examination as to progress in acquaintance with the law,—none; occasional lectures,—none; oversight as to general attention and conduct,—none." Aspiring lawyers generally learned the profession by studying and clerking in the law office of an experienced attorney.

Stuart, as Lincoln's guide, gave his protégé the run of his law library in the offices of Stuart and Dummer in Springfield, located twenty miles from New Salem. He did not ask Lincoln to be his law clerk but rather gave him every resource at his disposal, believing that Lincoln had both the ability and self-discipline to prepare on his own.

Stuart's law partner Henry Dummer, a New Englander who migrated to Springfield in 1833, recalled how Lincoln appeared in these initial visits. "He was the most uncouth looking young man I ever saw." But Lincoln grew on him. Lincoln "seemed to have but little to say; seemed to feel timid, with a tinge of sadness visible in the countenance, but when he did talk all this disappeared for the time and he demonstrated that he was both strong and acute." Dummer concluded, "He surprised us more and more at every visit."

Lincoln approached the study of law with the same single-minded discipline he had previously applied to the study of grammar, elocution, and surveying. He bought Sir William Blackstone's *Commentaries on the Laws of England,* the standard legal treatise of the day, at an auction. Blackstone, who had been professor of common law at Oxford, wrote his *Commentaries* between 1765 and 1769. Lincoln, in his own words, "went at it in good earnest." He discovered in Blackstone an ordered and comprehensive system that appealed to his rational sensibilities.

Henry McHenry, who married the sister of Jack Armstrong, the wrestler, recalled that in good weather Lincoln could be seen reading his law books sitting "on a goods box under a large white oak tree in Salem, barefooted as he came into the world." In the campaign biography he wrote in 1860, William Dean Howells elaborated on that description.

> His favorite place of study was a wooded knoll near New Salem, where he threw himself under a wide-spreading oak, and expansively made a reading desk of the hillside. Here he would pore over Blackstone day after day shifting his position as the sun rose and sank, so as to keep in the shade, and utterly unconscious of everything but the principles of common law.

LINCOLN DECLARED HIS CANDIDACY for a second term in the Illinois General Assembly on March 19, 1836. Only a few days later, Lincoln took his first formal step toward becoming a lawyer when he entered his name on the record of the Sangamon Circuit Court as a person of good moral character. In these two actions, Lincoln put himself on the dual track of politics and law that he would pursue for almost the next twenty-five years.

Lincoln stated his case for reelection in the *Sangamo Journal*. "In your paper of last Saturday, I see a communication over the signature of 'Many Voters,' in which the candidates who are announced in the Journal, are called upon to 'show their hands.' Agreed. Here's mine!"

A persistent question in American politics is this: Who does a representative represent? Does the legislator vote the will of the constituents or his or her own will? Lincoln, having served one term, made the answer to this question the heart of his announcement. "If elected, I shall consider the whole people of Sangamon my constituents, as well those oppose, as those that support me." At the beginning of his political career, Lincoln laid down a value that would become a lodestar to guide him in his future political profession. "While acting as their representative, I shall be governed by their will, on all subjects upon which I have the means of knowing what their will is; and upon others, I shall do what my own judgment teaches me will best advance their interests."

Lincoln believed that an elected politician held an office for only a brief time at best; the people were the permanent representatives in a republic. In his first session in Vandalia, he had already encountered too many politicians who did not feel the need to be guided by the wishes of the people they represented.

In 1836, as Lincoln embarked on his reelection campaign, President Andrew Jackson, whom Whigs derisively called "King Andrew I," declined to run for a third term. The Democrats, wanting to avoid a divisive contest, decided to rally around a single candidate. Their convention chose Jackson's vice president, Martin Van Buren. The Whigs, not yet organized at a national level and with no national nominating convention, ended up with three sectional candidates, Daniel Webster from New England, William Henry Harrison from the Midwest, and Hugh L. White from the South.

Lincoln concluded the announcement of his candidacy in 1836 by declaring, "If alive on the first Monday in November, I shall vote for Hugh L. White for President." Lincoln had said nothing about presidential politics in his first announcement for the legislature in 1832.

BORN TO COMMAND.

OF VETO MEMORY.

HAD I BEEN CONSULTED.

KING ANDREW THE FIRST.

The power of President Andrew Jackson's presidency hovered over Lincoln's first years in politics. He became a Whig partly in response to "King Andrew I," caricatured here as a despotic monarch. Whigs accused Jackson of usurping the power of Congress.

With his personal popularity rising in 1834, an off year for presidential elections, he had won with the support of both parties. His decision to proclaim his choice for president in his 1836 campaign announcement—White was an anti-Jackson Southern Whig senator from Tennessee—indicated the growing prominence of national politics in local elections.

Lincoln began actively campaigning in the middle of June 1836. Seventeen citizen politicians had declared their candidacies for the Illinois legislature in Sangamon County, and they all traveled on horseback from one grove to the next. The speeches began in the morning and continued into the afternoon, until each candidate had had his opportunity to speak. Robert L. Wilson, a Whig candidate from Athens, described Lincoln's speaking style and content. "Mr. Lincoln took a leading part, espouseing the Whig side of all those questions, manifesting Skill and tact in offensive and defensive debates, presenting his arguments with force and ability."

On Election Day, August 1, 1836, Lincoln received the highest number of votes of the seventeen candidates for the legislature, coming in first in New Salem and third in Springfield. That year, with a growth in population, Sangamon County sent to Vandalia a larger delegation of seven House members and two senators. Most of them still had more experience than Lincoln. All of the newly elected legislators were over six feet tall and were promptly dubbed "the Long Nine," echoing an expression used by sailors to describe a long-barreled cannon that fired nine-pound balls. Just as the longer barrel gave the gun greater range, "the Long Nine" were about to expand the range of the influence of Sangamon County.

ALTHOUGH HE WAS only twenty-seven and beginning his second term, when Lincoln returned to Vandalia in December 1836, the Whigs elected him their floor leader, a sign of his growing standing among his colleagues on the Whig side of the floor.

The tenth session would be long remembered for the remarkable number of future national leaders it included. "The present legislature embraces, perhaps, more talent than any legislative body ever before assembled in Illinois," wrote the *Sangamo Journal*. But the editor could not have predicted that three future governors, six future U.S. senators, eight congressmen, a cabinet member, a number of generals, two presidential candidates, and one future president would eventually emerge from the session.

Lincoln soon met a man whose life and career would forever become linked with his own. Stephen A. Douglas would become better known than many presidents, but that winter at Vandalia he was a twenty-three-year-old attorney from Morgan County elected to his first term. He stood barely five feet tall, had thick brown hair and a face that communicated strength, with a strong jaw and an aggressive chin. Because of his height, some thought he looked like a boy among men, until he spoke. His deep baritone voice commanded attention.

Douglas was born in Brandon, Vermont, on April 23, 1813. Growing up in green mountains and valleys, he studied at the Brandon Academy. In 1830, his family moved to a farm near Canandaigua, by the shimmering lake of the same name, in the Finger Lakes region of western New

York. Here he continued his education at the Canandaigua Academy and began to study law.

On January 1, 1833, Douglas left school to study law full-time on his own. Six months later, twenty years old and confident in his own abilities, he decided to leave his family to seek his fame and fortune in the "great west." After brief stops in Cleveland, Cincinnati, and Louisville, he arrived in St. Louis and called on Edward G. Bates, a former Missouri congressman, but Bates had no opportunities in his law office. On the boat Douglas had heard many fellow immigrants speak glowingly of Illinois, so he set his sights on the prairie state on the other side of the Mississippi.

In November 1833, as Lincoln worked in New Salem as postmaster and surveyor, Douglas stepped off the stage in Jacksonville, Illinois,

Stephen Douglas and Abraham Lincoln met in Vandalia during Lincoln's second term in the Illinois state legislature. Small of stature, Douglas was a powerful Democratic politician who would cross paths with Lincoln again and again in the coming decades.

with five dollars in his pocket. To support himself, he opened a school in nearby Winchester while he continued his law studies. In March 1834, Douglas was examined by the Illinois Supreme Court and granted a certificate to practice law. He set up office in the Jacksonville courthouse.

Politics became his passion. He had read the writings of John Adams, Thomas Jefferson, and Alexander Hamilton and knew well the Federalist Papers. In his first year in Illinois, he established a reputation as an able political debater. At a courthouse meeting in the spring of 1834, after several of Jacksonville's foremost lawyers railed against President Andrew Jackson, Douglas spoke for one hour in a vigorous defense of Old Hickory and his war on the Second Bank of the United States. The crowd cheered Douglas's effort, lifted him to their shoulders, and hailed him the "Little Giant."

Lincoln and Douglas were both in Vandalia for the beginning of the ninth legislative session in December 1834, Lincoln as a first-time legislator, Douglas as an applicant to become the state's attorney for the First Judicial District. If Lincoln and Douglas met, neither recorded their meeting; they were destined to meet two years later.

IN DECEMBER 1836, an expansionist fever sweeping across Illinois generated an internal improvements convention in Vandalia prior to the opening of the legislature. Lincoln had campaigned on the issue in 1832, 1834, and 1836. He now led the push for a whole new system of canals, railroads, and roads that would foster growth and development.

Public meetings up and down the state attracted farmers and businessmen demanding the improvements to better their ability to bring products to market, and newspapers added their voices of support. "It is now time TO ACT," editorialized the *Sangamo Journal*. Supporters pointed out that other states were moving rapidly ahead with internal improvements and that Illinois must do the same if they were not to lose potential new citizens as they moved west. Each legislator brought to Vandalia ideas for projects that should be built in or through their district. Land speculators, hoping to make huge profits from the many proposals, traveled to Vandalia to lobby the legislature.

A few voices tried to slow the process. No studies had been done, they said. No surveys taken. What would be the cost of this bold new plan? From the beginning of his political career, Lincoln was a fervent believer in internal improvements to boost economic nationalism.

Attuned to the rapid developments of the transportation revolution in neighboring states, he had a hard time acknowledging the questions and objections of colleagues concerned about the particular problems and possibilities in Illinois. He argued in the legislature that the improvements would pay for themselves. The pre-assembly convention recommended that the legislature appropriate $10 million to be financed by state bonds.

Governor Joseph Duncan, in his annual message to the legislature, cautioned that the state should provide only one-third of the requested public monies, but the legislators, afraid of private monopolies, raced forward with their plans to fund the entire cost. Lincoln feared the state would be penalized economically if it did not move ahead rapidly. The success of projects in such developed states as New York and Pennsylvania provided a precedent. Some legislators tried to point out that Illinois, a state just emerging from the frontier, did not have the money, manpower, or raw materials of the older, long-settled states. But in a time of expansive plans and hyperbolic rhetoric, not many legislators could focus on the problems when the possibilities seemed so bright.

The House Internal Improvements Committee proposed a $10 million bill for internal improvements on January 9, 1837. The biggest allocation, $3.5 million, was for an Illinois Central Railroad track from Cairo in the south to Galena and the lead mines in the north. Lincoln supported the argument that sister states were "adopting and prosecuting gigantic schemes of improvement" and it was time for "the patriot and enlightened statesmen of Illinois" to act. Governor Duncan threatened to veto the bill. John J. Hardin, a first-term Whig representative from Jacksonville, voiced his concern that the appropriation was precariously large, to no avail.

With Lincoln helping to lead the effort, the House passed the bill on January 31; the Senate followed a few weeks later. The final passage set off wild celebrations. Bonfires were built in the streets of Vandalia. Lincoln and the bill's supporters hailed its passage as the great step forward that would enable Illinois to take its rightful place as a leading state in the West. By the next morning, people eager to acquire property crowded land offices even as the prices doubled, fueled by the prospects of so many improvements across the state.

The enthusiasm would be short-lived. The national financial panic of 1837, caused in part by unbounded speculation—especially in land—brought economic destruction to Illinois. Confidence waned. Banks suspended transactions. The value of land plunged. Some towns disappeared. Governor Duncan suggested stopping the internal improvements already approved, but Lincoln was adamant that the legislature would not curtail the various construction plans. The legislative boom and the economic bust resulted in a $10 million millstone around the necks of Illinois residents for years to come. Four years after the internal improvements package passed, the state of Illinois had a debt of $15 million, and state bonds sold at fifteen cents on the dollar.

BY THE EARLY 1830s, it had become apparent that growth in Illinois was accelerating in the central and northern parts of the state. Vandalia, although situated north of the first capital, Kaskaskia, was still located in the south. On top of this, the legislators discovered that the newly built third capitol building was already too small. They decided to find a new location for the capital. A number of cities—Alton, Peoria, Jacksonville, Decatur—jumped into the contest. Springfield also advanced its case.

As the Whig floor leader, Lincoln, along with the Long Nine, represented the largest delegation of any county in the state. They lobbied hard for Springfield as the most central location in Illinois. This effort required all of Lincoln's legislative skills. He added an amendment obliging the selected city to contribute $50,000 and two acres of land for the new site of state buildings. Lincoln believed the amendment would ensure Springfield's selection as it was the only city that could afford this new stipulation. One of the Long Nine, Robert T. Wilson, said Lincoln "never for one moment despaired" when on more than one occasion "to all appearances" the bill seemed "beyond resuscitation." The voting was contentious, with much horse trading, or railroad trading, taking place. One member, disgusted, cast his vote for Purgatory, a place that could not be found on any Illinois map. Finally, on February 28, 1837, on the fourth ballot, the House and Senate voted to establish the new capital in Springfield. Lincoln and the other members of the Long Nine invited one and all to a lavish celebration party at Ebenezer Capps's tavern, where they consumed eighty-one bottles of champagne and plenty of cigars, oysters, almonds, and raisins.

—

ALARMED ABOUT THE RISE OF ABOLITIONISM and its call for interference with the institution of slavery in the Southern states, Governor Duncan brought to the legislature memorials from Virginia, Alabama, Mississippi, New York, and Connecticut. On January 12, 1837, a resolution deplored "the unfortunate condition of our fellow men, whose lots are cast in thralldom in a land of liberty and peace," but stated that "the arm of the General Government has no power to strike the fetters from them." The purpose of the resolution was both to denounce the abolitionist societies and affirm "that the right of property in slaves, is sacred to the slave-holding States by the Constitution." The resolution stated that the federal government did not have the right to abolish slavery in the District of Columbia without the "consent" of the citizens of the district. Without much debate, the legislature adopted the resolution by a vote of 77 to 6. Lincoln was one of the six who voted no, his first public stand on the issue of slavery.

Illinois, though counting itself a "free" state, was not so free in the 1830s. In the two decades after Illinois became a state in 1818, the largest number of new settlers came from the South. Slavery persisted in the popular folkways of the state despite the provisions against it in the 1818 constitution. And slavery was growing in Missouri, the state's neighbor to the west, which shares a long border with Illinois.

As Illinois grew in population, the debate about slavery became more divisive. Immigrants from New England and New York generally settled in northern Illinois. Although they were a small minority of the total population, they had loud antislavery voices. Immigrants from Virginia, the Carolinas, Tennessee, and Kentucky tended to settle in central and southern Illinois, and most were pro-slavery. But not all. Some, like Thomas Lincoln, had immigrated to Illinois precisely because they did not like slavery in their home states.

In the last days of the legislative session, with Lincoln certainly thinking of the congratulations he would be receiving in Springfield for helping to relocate the capital, he decided to enter a protest. He had already served his most successful term, but he believed he needed to restore some balance to the resolution condemning abolitionism. He wanted to voice his dissent and found a cosponsor in Dan Stone, a Whig lawyer from Springfield. Stone, a Vermonter, opposed slavery.

Lincoln and Stone's "protest against the passage" of the already adopted resolution began, "They believe that the institution of slavery is founded on both injustice and bad policy; but that the promulgation of abolition doctrines tends rather to increase than to abate its evils."

Central to Lincoln's protest was shifting the emphasis on the initiative to end slavery in the District of Columbia. The original resolution stated the matter in the negative: "*Resolved,* that the General Government cannot abolish slavery in the District of Columbia, against the consent of the citizens of said District without a manifest breach of good faith."

Lincoln and Stone turned that part of the resolution upside down by stating, "They believe that the Congress of the United States has the power under the constitution, to abolish slavery in the District of Columbia; but that the power ought not to be exercised unless at the request of the people of said District."

Lincoln and Stone's protest has often been called "cautious," but their amendment should not be underestimated. In 1837, Lincoln publicly defined slavery as both unjust and bad policy. He reversed the resolution's intent on slavery in the District of Columbia by affirming that Congress did have the power to abolish it under the Constitution. Lincoln knew he would gain no political points in central Illinois for the elements in his protest. He made his stand, not with the majority and their willingness to admit only a negative or passive role for government, but rather on government's positive, active role in abolishing slavery.

Twenty-three years later in his autobiographical statement of 1860, Lincoln said little about his terms in the Illinois legislature, but he paused to recall his protest, even taking pains to cite the exact pages of the Illinois *House Journal* in which the protest is still printed. He asked Scripps to insert the entire protest in the campaign biography, which the *Chicago Tribune* writer failed to do.

THE TENTH LEGISLATIVE SESSION adjourned on March 6, 1837, and Lincoln returned to New Salem. The small town was dying as other Illinois towns were rising. The Sangamon River proved to be unnavigable. In 1836, New Salem had lost its post office. It was the beginning of the end. Many residents simply picked up their houses and stores and moved them two miles downstream to the newer town of Petersburg.

While living in New Salem, Lincoln had tested the waters of both politics and law and found that he could navigate both with strength and dexterity. At age twenty-eight, he left New Salem a profoundly different young man from the one who had arrived just six years earlier.

He was ready to move to Springfield, which he had been instrumental in designating as the new capital of Illinois. With his political service moving ahead, and about to become a full-fledged lawyer, he looked forward to the next chapter in his life.

Lincoln moved to Springfield in 1837 and would spend much of his life in the law offices, courts, and stores on this square. The city grew in stature and population when the capital of Illinois moved there from Vandalia in 1839.

CHAPTER 6

Without Contemplating Consequences
1837—42

IF YOU WOULD WIN A MAN TO YOUR CAUSE, *FIRST* CONVINCE HIM
THAT YOU ARE HIS SINCERE FRIEND.

ABRAHAM LINCOLN
Temperance address, Springfield, Illinois, February 22, 1842

ON THE MORNING OF APRIL 15, 1837, ABRAHAM LINCOLN SADDLED
a borrowed horse, packed all his possessions into two saddlebags, and
rode twenty miles into Springfield. He dismounted in front of Abner
Ellis's general store at 103 South Fifth Street, one of the buildings that
crowded the west side of Springfield's town square. Lincoln had worked
for Ellis for a short time in his New Salem store. He entered the Springfield store, put his saddlebags on the counter, and inquired of a young
clerk about a mattress, blankets, sheets, and pillow for a single bed.
Joshua F. Speed, a blue-eyed, slender man who was actually one of the
proprietors, walked about the store with Lincoln as he looked at bedding supplies and noted the costs.

They had never met, but Speed knew a good deal about Lincoln,
who had already made a name for himself as an Illinois politician. Speed
had been present the previous July when Lincoln, running for a second
term in the state legislature, had participated in a candidates' debate.
Speed may have also read the April 15, 1837, *Sangamo Journal,* which
announced that "J. T. Stuart and A. Lincoln, Attorneys and Counselors
at Law, will practice, conjointly, in the Courts of this Judicial Circuit.
Office No. 4, Hoffman's Row, upstairs."

As Lincoln and Speed returned to the front counter with the goods,
Speed took his pencil and slate and calculated the costs of the bedding to
be seventeen dollars.

Lincoln responded, "It is probably cheap enough; but I want to say that cheap as it is I have not the money to pay. But if you will credit me until Christmas, and my experiment here as a lawyer is a success, I will pay you then." After a long pause, he continued, "If I fail in that I will probably never be able to pay you at all."

Speed was struck by the sadness of the man before him. "I never saw so gloomy and melancholy a face in my life." He liked the broad-shouldered young lawyer and offered a solution. "The contraction of so small a debt, seems to affect you so deeply, I think I can suggest a plan by which you will be able to attain your end, without incurring any debt." Speed suggested, "I have a very large room, and a very large double-bed in it; which you are perfectly welcome to share with me if you choose."

"Where is your room?" Lincoln inquired.

"Upstairs." Speed directed Lincoln to the stairs that led to the second floor above the store. Silently, Lincoln picked up his saddlebags and proceeded up the stairs.

In a few minutes Lincoln came back down with a different countenance. He declared, "Well Speed I'm moved."

THE SPRINGFIELD TO WHICH Lincoln arrived in the spring of 1837 was an unprepossessing town of twelve or thirteen hundred inhabitants. Less than twenty years old, it was first settled by trappers and traders in 1818 and had become the seat of Sangamon County in 1821. Local boosters called the county, which was half the size of Rhode Island, "the Empire County" because of its great expanse and natural wealth.

Most of the citizens of Springfield lived in small frame houses. A few impressive two-story brick residences stood out, even as a number of log cabins remained from pioneer times. In the center of town stood a two-story brick courthouse, with small buildings—mostly stores—lining the square around it. On July 4, 1837, two and a half months after his arrival, Lincoln witnessed the laying of the cornerstone at the new Greek Revival state capitol building. He heard an eloquent dedication address by lawyer and politician Edward Dickinson Baker.

An 1836 census revealed that there were nineteen dry goods stores in Springfield, six retail grocery stores, two clothing stores, two shoe stores, and four hotels. Among the craftsmen were tinsmiths, tailors, hatters, shoemakers, carpenters, blacksmiths, and one barber. The young town boasted eighteen doctors and eleven lawyers who served a wide territory embracing a number of counties.

The town's wide streets were not paved. In the wintertime men and women might sink into mud, while in the summer passing carriages and wagons raised billows of dust. Cows, hogs, and chickens meandered through the streets contesting for the right of way. "Hog nuisance" was one of Springfield's greatest irritants. Hog holes greeted residents on nearly every street. The porkers roamed everywhere and citizens debated whether the hogs' filth or constant grunting was the greater annoyance.

When the Illinois legislature voted to make Springfield the new state capital in February 1837, the city began to hum with energy and excitement. Simeon Francis, editor of the *Sangamo Journal,* wrote of the town's new prospects. "The owner of real estate sees his property rapidly enhancing in value; the merchant anticipates a large accession to our population and a corresponding additional sale for his goods; the mechanic already has more contracts offered him for building and improvement than he can execute; the farmer anticipates, in the growth of a large and important town, a market for the varied products of his farm." Springfield's citizens, including Abraham Lincoln, believed the new capital's best days lay ahead.

IN THE SPRING OF 1837 Lincoln received his license as a lawyer. Although a fine achievement for a young man with no family connections and little formal education, this accomplishment brought with it its own kind of terror. True, he had won his way in politics, but central Illinois was filled with outstanding lawyers. It was one thing to receive a license to practice; it was quite another to be able to make a living. How could a young lawyer like Lincoln, with no capital, open an office and obtain clients?

Lincoln's first turn of good fortune occurred when John Todd Stuart told him he needed a new law partner. Any young lawyer would have jumped at the opportunity to become the junior partner of one of Springfield's most successful lawyers. Stuart had had plenty of opportunity to observe Lincoln in the Illinois legislature. In the spring of 1837, he invited Lincoln to join his practice.

Lincoln felt privileged to settle in to Stuart's law office on the second floor in Hoffman's Row at 109 North Fifth Street. The office was not ostentatious; it was furnished only with a couch, table, chair, bench, and what passed for a bookcase.

Lincoln became a junior partner with Stuart just as the national financial crash of 1837, brought on by unbounded speculation and cheap credit, wreaked havoc across Illinois. Thousands of people lost their jobs and homes. As a legislator, Lincoln had been a leading advocate of internal improvements; as a new lawyer, he sought to collect what was due on uncompleted contracts for projects suddenly halted.

The firm of Stuart and Lincoln pleaded cases of libel, trespass, and assault. Lincoln's early cases included collecting for damages to a cooking stove; reclaiming a debt of three dollars for a hog; arguing for the quality of superfine flour; representing the owner of a boat loaded with corn that had been obstructed by fishermen in the Sangamon River; and pleading the authenticity of numerous land titles.

After little more than a year as a lawyer, Lincoln participated in his first criminal case. On the evening of March 7, 1838, Jacob Early, a physician and Methodist preacher, sat before the fireplace in the Spottswood's Hotel in Springfield reading the *Sangamo Journal*. The register of the U.S. Land Office in Galena, Henry B. Truett, entered the room and promptly accused Early of writing a set of resolutions at a recent Democratic convention in Peoria that criticized him and called for his removal from office. Surprised, Early wanted to know who had made this charge. Truett, enraged, began calling Early a "damned coward." Early, feeling threatened, tried to protect himself with a chair. Truett drew a pistol from his coat and, as the two men moved about the room, was able to get off a clear shot and hit Early. Truett ran from the hotel. Early died three days later.

Truett was indicted for murder on March 14, 1838. He retained one of Springfield's most senior lawyers, Stephen Logan, as lead counsel— along with Lincoln, Stuart, Edward D. Baker, and Cyrus Walker—to defend him. Stephen Douglas was appointed to represent the people as prosecuting attorney. The case involved two prominent Democratic politicians, and passions were running high. Lincoln, who would become the master of delaying tactics, helped get the trial adjourned from July to October to help dissipate both passion and prejudice.

The trial began on Monday, October 8, 1838, in the Sangamon Circuit Court located directly below Stuart and Lincoln's office. The lawyers for both sides examined 215 prospective jurors before settling on a final twelve. All of the evidence seemed to point to the guilt of the defendant. Early had even given a dying declaration in which he accused Truett. Prosecutors pointed out that Truett had entered the hotel armed and had fled after the incident.

The novice lawyer Lincoln was entrusted with the closing argument. The defense maintained that Truett had a right to demand whether Early was the author of the Peoria resolution that had so wounded his character. Furthermore, Early had a deadly weapon—a chair—with which he intended to strike Truett. Stephen Logan characterized Lincoln's appeal to the jury as "a short but strong and sensible speech." At the close of Friday, October 12, 1838, Judge Jesse B. Thomas, Jr., gave instructions to the jury, who retired to Stuart and Lincoln's office above the courtroom to deliberate.

On Saturday morning, before a packed court, the jury announced their verdict: not guilty. People rushed to congratulate Lincoln for his closing argument. The Springfield community understood the verdict within the context of frontier society; juries were willing to convict an assassin but not a person caught up in a passionate conflict with another. Lincoln received the large fee of $250 for the case. More important, Lincoln's fame grew as people lauded him as a capable lawyer adept at persuading juries.

AS THE JUNIOR PARTNER AT THE OFFICE on Hoffman's Row in Springfield, Lincoln prepared the legal pleadings and briefs. From the first he was a fine draftsman, writing in a neat hand. When comparing Lincoln's legal writing to that of his peers, one is struck by his absence of corrections. Whether writing a declaration or plea, by the time Lincoln put pen to paper he knew what to say and how to say it. Despite what must have been his anxiety at his new challenge, a calm confidence was evident in his fine writing.

Lincoln could be flexible with his spelling in an era when the art of orthography was not as exact as it would become in later years. He wrote "colateral" and "colatteral" for collateral, and varied his spelling between "prossecution" and "prosecutor." Compared to his contemporaries, however, his spelling was mostly free of peculiarities.

Stuart gave Lincoln the task of keeping the financial records for the firm. One has only to look at the fee book to see that Lincoln was not always adept at this assignment. There are long intervals between entries, and the entries themselves are sometimes quite casual; for example, "I have received five dollars from Deed of Macon, five from Lewis Keeling, five from Andrew Finley, one-half of which belongs to Stuart and has not been entered on the books."

John Todd Stuart decided to make a second run for a seat in Congress within a year of inviting Lincoln to become a partner. He had run in 1836 and lost to Democrat William L. May. His Democratic opponent in 1838 would be Stephen Douglas. The contest between Stuart and Douglas epitomized a campaign on the frontier. The candidates often traveled together, ate meals together, and now and again "slept in the same bed." Stuart and Douglas "debated the issues of the election from the same platform" across the expansive Third Congressional District, which made up one-half of the state's territory. The election took place in August, but it was not until September 1, 1838, that Stuart was declared the winner over Douglas by 36 votes out of 36,495 total.

After Stuart left for Washington in November 1839, Lincoln wrote in their fee book, "Commencement of Lincoln's administration 1839 Nov 2." Lincoln would now miss Stuart's mentoring, yet with his absence, he gained the opportunity to plead a wider variety of cases. In doing so, he was forced to fill in the gaps of his theoretical knowledge. Even more important, he had to stand alone, in small village courtrooms, and before the district court and the Illinois Supreme Court, both of which met in Springfield. During this time, Lincoln seldom sought the advice of other lawyers. He learned early on in law, as in politics, to trust his own counsel.

Lincoln and Stuart's caseload had increased when they decided to expand the territory they would serve. When Lincoln first joined the firm in 1837, both he and Stuart traveled what was then the First Judicial Circuit. In 1839, the legislature divided the state into nine judicial circuits, each circuit presided over by one of nine supreme court judges. Samuel H. Treat served as judge of the new Eighth Judicial Circuit, which included fifteen counties. With Stuart away in Congress, it fell to Lincoln to travel the new circuit, which he did twice a year.

Lincoln journeyed by horseback in the early spring on mud-covered roads and across swollen streams. Bridges were in short supply. The roads usually ran right through the middle of the prairies. There would be stretches where the lawyers could travel nearly all day without meeting anyone. Nearly everyone on the circuit had a latch-string hung on their homes for hospitality for traveling lawyers.

James C. Conkling, Lincoln's Springfield neighbor and a fellow lawyer, described those early days of traveling the circuit. The hotel accommodations were meager. "The rooms were generally crowded with jurors, witnesses, parties litigant" and lawyers. The fortunate slept in beds, sometimes two or three together, but frequently the occupants

Anna Hyatt Huntington's sculpture Life on the Circuit *depicts Lincoln as a young lawyer on horseback, studying as he traveled across the Eighth Judicial Circuit in central Illinois.*

slept on the floor. The coming of the circuit court to these small towns became the center of a community celebration. Farmers and people from adjoining villages flocked to town "not merely to attend court, but to witness a horse-race, or a circus, or some theatrical performance, which were generally the side-shows of a Circuit Court in those primitive places."

Lincoln shone not only by day in court, but also in the evening around the fireplace in a local hotel or tavern. While on the circuit, the lawyers had plenty of time for conversation, cards, music, and playing practical jokes on one another. Lincoln "seemed to possess an inexhaustible fund" of stories and anecdotes. "No one could relate a story without reminding him of one of a similar character." In these sessions, Lincoln also became known for his laughter, taking pleasure in his own humor as well as that of others. There was something about "the heartiness of his own enjoyment" that drew others to him.

Life on the circuit combined politics and law. In traveling the huge Eighth Judicial Circuit, Lincoln was building a name for himself that would translate into votes. The fall term often took place in the midst of political campaigns. Lawyer politicians moved directly from the courthouse to the town square for political debate. As Lincoln learned to practice law inside numerous small-town courtrooms, he came to know and be known by farmers and merchants by staying in their homes and trading in their stores. He also sowed friendships and alliances with other lawyer politicians that he would harvest in future years.

IN SPRINGFIELD, his friendship with Joshua Fry Speed, the store clerk, continued to grow. At twenty-two, Speed was five years younger than Lincoln. He was a fellow Kentuckian, but their backgrounds were very different. Named after his mother's father, Speed was born into a wealthy family on a large estate called "Farmington," five miles southeast of Louisville. His father, John Speed, was a plantation proprietor who owned more than seventy slaves. Young Joshua had attended private schools to prepare him for a professional career. After working for several years in a store in Louisville, he moved to Springfield in 1835. Both young men sought their own identity by leaving their fathers and their fathers' vocations and making fresh starts in a new city.

Speed realized quickly that Lincoln, despite his position in the Illinois legislature, was "almost without friends" in Springfield. Lincoln considered attending a church in Springfield, but remarked, "I've never been to church yet, nor probably shall not be soon. I stay away because I am conscious I should not know how to behave myself." Lincoln, shy in ordinary social relationships, was grateful to Speed for becoming a conduit to new acquaintances. That first winter, Lincoln began to break through some of his social inhibitions. Eight or ten men—"choice spirits"—would gather "by a big wood fire" in Speed's general store to talk, laugh, debate, and carry on a running conversation about many topics. They came night after night "because they were sure to find Lincoln" and his stories and wit. Speed observed the paradox of seeing this reserved man at the center of attention. "Mr. Lincoln was a social man, though he did not seek company; it sought him." After talking politics and sharing stories around the fire, when the others left, Lincoln and Speed would talk for hours into the night.

A SOCIETY ORIENTED AROUND the spoken word rewarded those who learned its ways. In his constant drive for self-improvement, Lincoln sought out opportunities to enhance his speaking ability. In January 1838, he accepted an invitation to speak to the Young Men's Lyceum in Springfield. The Lyceum began in 1835, and by Lincoln's arrival in 1837 occupied a leading cultural place in the community.

On a wintry Saturday evening, the twenty-eight-year-old Lincoln stood to address the Lyceum meeting at the Second Presbyterian Church on "The Perpetuation of Our Political Institutions." He began by offering praise to the founders of the republic. He evoked the inheritance passed down to his generation. The young Lincoln, still learning the art of rhetoric, often used more words than necessary, thus, "We find ourselves under the government of a system of political institutions, conducing more essentially to the ends of civil and religious liberty, than any of which the history of former times tells us." If the major melody in his address was honor to the founders, a contrapuntal theme was the role of Lincoln's generation, just now coming into their maturity, in shaping the nation's future. Their task was much more limited, Lincoln concluded; "'tis ours only, to transmit these" values "to the latest generation."

Underneath Lincoln's towering language we hear a lament. A half century after the election of George Washington as the nation's first president, Lincoln had become convinced that the epic labor of putting together the country had already been consummated. Instead of builders, Lincoln and his generation were conferred the lesser role of transmitters, or custodians.

He did acknowledge his generation's commission to protect the nation's hard-won freedom. Lincoln, always attentive to his social context, spoke of the threat of a "mobocratic spirit" seen in an outbreak of mob violence that had "pervaded the country, from New England to Louisiana." The immediate occasion of the address may have been the murder two and a half months earlier of Elijah Lovejoy, a Presbyterian minister and editor killed defending his abolitionist newspaper in Alton, Illinois, across the river from St. Louis. Lincoln, in embracing the Whig Party in the 1830s, believed that a departure from tradition and order had taken place on the watch of the Democratic Jacksonian administrations.

Lincoln predicted that the danger to "The Perpetuation of Our Political Institutions" would not come from "some transatlantic military giant," but rather from foes and forces that "must spring up amongst us." In words that would be remembered, Lincoln declared, "If destruction be our lot, we must ourselves be its author and finisher. As a nation of freemen, we must live through all time, or die by suicide."

ONE MONTH LATER, on February 24, 1838, Lincoln announced his intention to run for a third term in the Illinois legislature. His championing of internal improvements, followed by the disastrous economic recession of 1837, did not seem to dampen his reelection prospects. By now he had won the trust of an ever-widening part of the public. On August 6, Lincoln received the highest vote total of sixteen candidates.

On a cold Friday morning, November 30, 1838, Lincoln boarded the stage to take his seat in the Eleventh General Assembly, the last to be held in Vandalia. As an indication of how far and fast he had traveled, the Whigs nominated Lincoln for Speaker of the lower house of the legislature. As the candidate of the minority party, Lincoln was defeated on the fourth ballot in a close vote: 43 to 38.

At the beginning of the session, legislators talked incessantly about the status of the internal improvements legislation and program. John J. Hardin of Morgan County brought a resolution calling for an investigation of internal improvements, which he and others called disdainfully the "grand system." In the course of the ensuing debate, Lincoln reaffirmed that "his own course was identified with the system." He was not about to back away now. "We have gone too far to recede, even if we were disposed to do so." Reporting for the Finance Committee on January 17, 1839, he acknowledged the problems in a seriously weakened economy, but remained adamant. "We are now so far advanced in a general system of internal improvements that, if we would, we cannot retreat from it, without disgrace and great loss." After discussing the purchase of still more public lands as part of the program of internal improvements, Lincoln declared, "The conclusion then is, that we *must advance*."

Behind Lincoln's specific proposals for building roads and canals lay his ardent belief in the promise of Illinois. "Illinois surpasses every other spot of equal extent upon the face of the globe, in *fertility* of soil, and in the proportionable amount of the same which is sufficiently level for actual cultivation." At twenty-nine, Lincoln was living proof that in Illinois a young man could begin with nothing and through hard work rise to statewide influence.

The session adjourned on March 4, 1839. As Lincoln prepared to leave Vandalia, he could look back on a record of solid accomplishment, especially in championing transportation as the best means to promote growth throughout the state. From December 1834 through March 1839, he had spent nearly an entire year, forty-four weeks total, in Vandalia. He had arrived largely unknown; he left with a growing reputation for political intelligence, judgment, and honesty.

DURING THE BREAK between legislative sessions, Lincoln joined his fellow Whigs in a series of debates with Democrats in a prelude to the 1840 political campaigns. Stephen Douglas, still regarded as a leader of the Democratic Party despite his congressional defeat, began the debates by defending President Van Buren's plan for a subtreasury system, a new way to solve the old problem of a national bank.

The national bank had been a contentious issue throughout President Jackson's two terms. First proposed by Alexander Hamilton, the Bank of the United States had been chartered in 1791 during the presidency of George Washington as a vehicle to bring order and accountability to banking and currency in the new nation. Charged by its foes with being unconstitutional, the bank was dissolved just twenty years later, in 1811. Faced with financial hardship from the War of 1812, the United States chartered a Second Bank of the United States in 1816. The second bank acted to control notes issued by state banks and private speculative banks.

In 1832, Henry Clay and Daniel Webster passed a bill in Congress to recharter the second bank, even though the charter was not due until 1836. The Whigs wanted to force Jackson's hand in the upcoming presidential election. Sure enough, Jackson vetoed the bill, criticizing the bank for being an enclave of the rich and powerful and in violation of the Constitution, against states' rights, and subversive of the rights of the people. Jackson's successor, Martin Van Buren, pressed ahead to set up an independent treasury, which was called a "subtreasury."

The Whigs were robust proponents of a national bank. Lincoln closed the debate with an intelligent attack on the subtreasury, the centerpiece of a Democratic plan for an independent treasury system. He supported the Whig political belief in the role of government to promote economic growth and development, and the national bank fit well within this philosophy.

The next evening, Lincoln spoke again, but this time his remarks did not hit the target. "Mr. L. of Wednesday night was not the L. of Tuesday." Reporting on the debates, the *Illinois State Register,* a Democratic newspaper in Springfield, accused Lincoln of "clownishness" in his manner and speaking style, which the newspaper advised him to correct. Lincoln, upset with himself, knew he had not done his best. His fellow legislator Joseph Gillespie commented, "He was conscious of his failure and I never saw any man so much distressed." After this, Lincoln was looking for an opportunity to redeem himself.

The Illinois legislature convened in Springfield for the first time on December 9, 1839. With the construction of the new capitol only in the beginning stages, the House met at the Second Presbyterian Church. Springfield, now swelling to nearly three thousand residents, proudly offered hospitality to the arriving legislators.

On the evening of December 26, 1839, after careful preparation, Lincoln offered a speech on the subtreasury. Though he usually spoke with few or no notes, he came prepared with full documentation for an extended address. Clearly disappointed by the small post-Christmas audience, he began by telling the few in attendance that he found it "peculiarly embarrassing" to be put in this situation. He let his pique show as he complained that the reason for the low turnout must be "the greater *interest* the community feel in the *Speakers* who addressed them *then* [referring to Stephen Douglas] than they do in *him* who is to do so *now*." Lincoln declared, "This circumstance casts a damp upon my spirits, which I am sure I shall be unable to overcome during the evening."

In a highly partisan speech, Lincoln criticized the Democratic plan to establish a subtreasury that would collect, hold, and disburse revenues. He complained that the new banking system would decrease the quantity of money in circulation. He spent much of the speech arguing that the subtreasury would be a less secure depository of public money.

But it was his conclusion that attracted widespread attention. Shifting away from the careful, technical descriptions of monetary matters, Lincoln articulated the underlying issues at stake. "Many free countries have lost their liberty; and *ours may* lose hers." Lincoln then launched into an attack against his opponents.

I know that the great volcano at Washington, aroused and directed by the evil spirit that reigns there, is belching forth the lava of political corruption, in a current broad and deep, which is sweeping with frightful velocity over the whole length and breadth of the land, bidding fair to leave unscathed no green spot or living thing, while on its bosom are riding like demons on waves of Hell, the imps of that evil spirit, and fiendishly taunting all those who dare resist its destroying course.

After portraying his opponents' evil intentions in romantic—even apocalyptic—language, Lincoln responded to their challenge in a growing crescendo of strongly evocative words. He started out simply and directly. "Broken to it, I, too may be; bow to it I never will." If his opponents rode the "waves of Hell," Lincoln staked out his own position under the "Almighty Architect" and "before High Heaven." Lincoln, who was always careful of both his words and actions as a politician, declared he was determined to act "without contemplating consequences."

Having made his political stand with a use of the personal pronoun "I" twelve times in the last sentence, he suddenly switched to "we," as if to rally those in his hearing to the cause: "We still shall have the proud consolation of saying to our consciences, and to the departed shade of our country's freedom, that the cause approved of our judgment, and adored of our hearts, in disaster, in chains, torture, in death, WE NEVER faultered in defending."

In his conclusion, the thirty-year-old Lincoln exposed the moral core of his national economic vision. Rejecting the charge that Whigs were the party of privilege, he laid at the feet of his Democratic opponents his indictment of their economic and political corruption. Lincoln's continual use of "I," his long complex sentences, and his use of dramatic contrasts between hell and heaven reflected the spirit of a self-confident if sometimes verbose young legislator. His speech, reprinted widely in the 1840 political campaigns, became a rallying cry. Lincoln portrayed in dramatic moral imagery how the Whigs, contenders but never victors, viewed the stakes in the upcoming presidential election.

The House adjourned on February 3, 1840. On February 10, two days before his thirty-first birthday, Lincoln was praised at an all-day Whig "Festival" in Peoria for "fearlessly and eloquently exposing the iniquities of the subtreasury scheme" in his address six weeks earlier. Lincoln was riding a crest of political popularity.

—

WITH THE LEGISLATURE ADJOURNED, Lincoln entered into a presidential campaign for the first time. Andrew Jackson, elected in 1828, had served two terms and then handpicked his successor, Vice President Van Buren. The combination of the economic panic of 1837 and Van Buren's effete manner compared to his predecessor eroded the electorate's confidence in Van Buren after his first term. At their first national convention in Harrisburg, Pennsylvania, in December 1839, the Whigs turned away from party stalwarts Henry Clay and Daniel Webster and nominated William Henry Harrison, a graying hero of the battle of Tippecanoe in the War of 1812.

Lincoln did not attend the convention but threw himself into the presidential campaign, taking a lead in organizing the Whigs in Illinois. Setting aside his earlier fears that an enlarged party machinery could be ripe for manipulation by party elders, in January 1840, he became a coauthor of a circular that would "appoint one person in each county as county captain," with the precinct captain and section captain "to perform promptly all the duties assigned him." The Whigs, put on the defensive by the organizational structures of their Democratic opponents, were determined to tighten their own organization. "Our intention is to organize the whole State, so that every Whig can be brought to the polls in the coming presidential election."

Lincoln set out on a whirlwind speaking campaign on behalf of Harrison and other Whig candidates in the spring. He spoke at Whig rallies in Carlinville, Alton, and Belleville. He debated Stephen Douglas and other Democrats in Tremont. Many Whig campaigners, sensing that the campaign of 1840 could bring them their first presidential victory, spoke about war-hero Harrison and avoided speaking about the issues. Lincoln, on the other hand, spoke astutely about economic problems. He extolled the Second Bank of the United States, both its "constitutionality" and "utility," and attacked "the hideous deformity and injurious effects" of the subtreasury. The *Quincy Whig* wrote of his speech at Decatur that the opposition forces "have not been able to start a man that can hold a candle to him in political debate."

On August 3, 1840, the day of the state elections, Sangamon County elected five Whigs to the lower house of the Illinois General Assembly. Lincoln voted for four Whigs but, not willing to vote for himself, cast his final vote for a Democrat. He won election to a fourth term, receiv-

PAXTON
STRAIGHT-OUTS.

Buff and Blue,
Tough and True,
For Tippecanoe.

Abraham Lincoln threw himself into the 1840 presidential campaign to elect Whig candidate William Henry Harrison, hero of the battle of Tippecanoe in the War of 1812, as depicted on this campaign ribbon.

ing the lowest number of Whig votes, although 578 more than the leading Democrat.

On August 18, 1840, Lincoln started from Springfield on a campaign trip to the southern part of the state. Traveling through steamy weather punctuated by thunderstorms, Lincoln met with Whig leaders in county-seat towns. Along the route he spoke in Waterloo, debated John A. McClernand about the state bank, and continued on to Carmi, Mount Carmel, Shawneetown, Marshall, and Casey. At Equality, Lincoln was "listened to with so much patience that the Whigs were in extacies."

Lincoln did not simply speak for Harrison, but against Van Buren. The *Sangamo Journal* reported that Lincoln, speaking at Tremont, "reviewed the political course of Mr. Van Buren, and especially his votes in the New York Convention in allowing Free Negroes the right of suffrage."

Lincoln, new to national politics, more than once became antagonistic—if not angry—with adversaries in the campaign. On a summer afternoon, Jesse Thomas, a young Democratic lawyer and politician, criticized Lincoln while speaking in a political debate in the Sangamon County Court. Not present when Thomas began his speech but alerted by friends, Lincoln came quickly. He came angry. He asked for the platform to reply, and then proceeded to assail Thomas. His attack quickly moved beyond the content of Thomas's remarks. "He imitated Thomas in gesture and voice, at times caricaturing his walk and the very motion of his body." The crowd began to yell and cheer. Lincoln, emboldened by the crowd's response, continued his ridicule until Thomas, humiliated and reduced to tears, fled the platform.

The story quickly became known in Springfield as "the skinning of Thomas." The incident would stay in the public memory for years. Lincoln was mortified. Sometime later he found Thomas and offered an apology. The young Lincoln, the man who prized reasonableness, struggled to control his emotions when he felt he was wronged.

In November, the 1840 presidential election drew an astounding 80.2 percent of eligible voters to the polls, up from 57.8 percent in 1836. American political democracy was surging.

For Lincoln, who had worked so hard in the election campaign, the results were bittersweet. Harrison became the first Whig to win the presidency, but he failed to carry Illinois, losing to Van Buren 47,433 to 45,576. The 1840 presidential election represented a coming-of-age in national politics for the thirty-one-year-old Lincoln. His leadership as a party organizer as well as his thoughtful campaign speeches brought him to the forefront of the Whig Party in Illinois.

THE ELECTION OF JOHN TODD STUART to a second term in Congress prompted the senior and junior partner to dissolve their law practice. In four years, the firm had taken on at least seven hundred cases. Stuart had served as Lincoln's first mentor, but when he moved to Washington in 1839, Lincoln lost the benefit of his tutelage.

Lincoln entered immediately into partnership with Stephen T. Logan, the most esteemed jurist in Springfield. Logan, of Scotch-Irish lineage, was small and stern in appearance, with a wrinkled face and an enormous head of red hair. Logan's plain, bedraggled dress and shrill, unappealing voice masked an impressive legal mind. On the bench,

Logan was known both for the impartiality of his courtroom demeanor and his penchant for whittling; he always kept a stack of white pine shingles near at hand.

Before they became partners, Lincoln and Logan had gone head-to-head three times in the Illinois Supreme Court, and the younger Lincoln had won all three court verdicts. Lincoln was idealistic but raw, ready to be seasoned by Judge Logan. The senior partner instructed Lincoln in the discipline of preparation. Stuart, who was more or less absent in their four-year partnership, had pretty much left Lincoln to his own patterns of preparedness. Logan did not allow any spontaneous or slap-dash approaches to serious legal matters.

Logan reread Blackstone every year. He believed that success was a by-product of hard and consistent work. He taught Lincoln that he should know his adversary's case as well as his own so that he was never surprised by the argument of an opponent. He impressed upon Lincoln that it was crucial to understand both the logic and the passion of those who stood on the other side of the courtroom.

EVEN AFTER LIVING for five years in Springfield, Lincoln did not join societies, organizations, or churches. He enjoyed his time alone, when he could read without interruption. Although comfortable in political meetings, he remained uncomfortable in ordinary social gatherings.

He did, however, speak at the meetings of various voluntary societies, especially temperance societies. The American Temperance Society established a Springfield branch in 1832. It was one of thousands of societies springing up in which members took a pledge of total abstinence. On George Washington's birthday, February 22, 1842, Lincoln gave the oration at the first large gathering of the Springfield branch of a new national temperance movement. The Washingtonians, named for the first president, had been founded in Baltimore in 1840. Whereas the American Temperance Union worked through religious organizations, the Washingtonians was a secular organization that appealed directly to the drunkard, seeking to portray him not as a sinner, but as a man to respect.

Lincoln began his address by recognizing that the temperance "cause," although at work for several decades, was "*just now,* being crowned with a degree of success, hitherto unparalleled." He then offered an astute and withering critique of the temperance movement's founding ideas before offering his analysis of the way forward. The problem lay with both leaders and tactics. The earliest champions had been "Preachers, Lawyers, and hired agents," but he faulted all three for their "want of *approachability*." Lincoln asserted that these first leaders lacked sympathy with the very persons they tried to help. He believed there was "too much denunciation against the dram sellers and dram drinkers." Rather than "the thundering tones of anathema and denunciation," Lincoln counseled "the accents of entreaty and persuasion." He spoke out of his own social morality when he told his audience, "If you would win a man to your cause, *first* convince him that you are his sincere friend."

Although ostensibly about temperance, this speech revealed Lincoln's larger understanding of human nature. He argued that if you approach a man and "mark him as one to be shunned and despised . . . he will retreat within himself, close all the avenues to his head and heart." Lincoln set up a contrast between old and new reformers. To the old reformers, "all habitual drunkards were utterly incorrigible, and therefore, must be turned adrift, and damned without remedy." Lincoln found this approach "repugnant to humanity, so uncharitable, so cold-blooded and feelingless."

A problem arising within the new Washingtonian movement was the place and attitude of those who had never been drunkards. "But," say some, "we are no drunkards; and we shall not acknowledge ourselves such by joining a reformed drunkard's society, whatever our influence might be." Lincoln's answer to a secular temperance group critical of the earlier religious reform efforts was, paradoxically, to invoke the central analogy of the Christian narrative. "Omnipotence condescended to take on himself the form of sinful man, and, as such, to die an ignominious death for their sakes, surely they will not refuse submission to the infinitely lesser condescension . . . of a large, erring, and unfortunate class of their own fellow creatures." Despite Lincoln's use of the analogy of Christ's death on the cross, his criticism of earlier religious temperance reformers ended up antagonizing some religious leaders in Springfield.

THE INVITATION TO SPEAK to the Washingtonians in 1842 was one more sign of how far Lincoln had come in his professional and public life in his five years in Springfield. He had now been elected to the Illinois legislature four times. He enjoyed a partnership with one of the most eminent lawyers in Illinois. His distinctive speaking abilities brought him numerous invitations to speak on behalf of Whig candidates and to a variety of reform organizations.

If Lincoln was finding his professional footing in Springfield during these years, privately he often felt awkward and unsure of himself. He was proving himself in his public life with men, but could he find a woman with whom to share his private life?

This first photograph of twenty-eight-year-old Mary Lincoln reveals her style and taste. She wears a silk dress with a large pin and ruffles visible at her wrists. In contrast to the photographs of most other women of the time, she exhibits a feminine sensuality.

CHAPTER 7

A Matter of Profound Wonder
1831–42

I AM NOW THE MOST MISERABLE MAN LIVING. IF WHAT I FEEL WERE
EQUALLY DISTRIBUTED TO THE WHOLE HUMAN FAMILY, THERE WOULD
NOT BE ONE CHEERFUL FACE ON THE EARTH.

ABRAHAM LINCOLN TO JOHN TODD STUART
January 23, 1842

WHEN LINCOLN GREW UP IN INDIANA, HIS STEPMOTHER, SALLY BUSH
Lincoln, remembered, "He was not very fond of girls as he seemed to
me." Anna Caroline Gentry, a schoolmate, reported that Lincoln "did
not go much with the girls—don't like crowds—didn't like girls much."
In New Salem, Lincoln was even shy about waiting on young women in
his store.

But if young women did not know what to make of Lincoln, older
women adored him. In New Salem, several older women mothered this
awkward young man, cooking and cleaning for him and repairing his
clothes. Lincoln reciprocated their affection, finding a safe harbor in
their matronly company. One young woman from New Salem recalled,
"Lincoln loved my Mother and would frequently ask her for advice on
different questions—Such as love—prudence of movements." Jack
Armstrong's wife, Hannah, took a liking to Lincoln. Fun-loving Jack
enjoyed telling people that one of the boys in his family might actually
be "Abe's son," an allusion that Lincoln, although a pretty good practical joker himself, did not find funny. Some of these women, in mother-
ing Lincoln, also wanted to assist him in finding a suitable bride.

IN NEW SALEM, Lincoln broke through his shyness to court the young
Ann Rutledge. He did not need to go far to find her; he had boarded

with the James and Mary Rutledge family in his first months in New Salem.

Ann was eighteen years old when Lincoln arrived in 1831. She was five feet three inches tall and pretty, with blue eyes and light, auburn hair. Bill Greene called her "a young lady . . . of Exquisite beauty." Neighbors remembered her as "intelligent" and "smart." Her brother, Robert Rutledge, said, "My sister was esteemed the brightest mind of the family."

Lincoln was attracted to this gentle young woman but knew that Ann's hand was being sought by several men. She became engaged to John McNeil in 1832. McNeil told Ann he had changed his name from McNamar to McNeil because his father had failed in business, and the son was determined to make enough money to return to New York, pay off his father's debts, and restore the family name. He promised that upon his return from New York they would be married. Ann shared his story with members of her family, some of whom were dubious about its truth.

Her engagement did not discourage Lincoln, and a door opened for him to visit with Ann when McNeil left. How their friendship blossomed into romance is not known. No letters have survived from Ann Rutledge, and nothing in Abraham Lincoln's correspondence tells us about her. How did Abraham overcome his inhibitions?

At some point in 1835, Lincoln and Ann entered into what couples at that time called an "understanding" about their relationship. Ann's cousin, James McCrady Rutledge, about her same age, remembered that while Lincoln was boarding with his uncle, he "became deeply in love with Ann." Lincoln, as postmaster, would be privy to the early letters and then lack of letters from McNeil. It became apparent to everyone that McNeil was not going to return, but vows were honored for a long time in that era. Lincoln and Ann may also have paused because he as yet had no profession except as a part-time legislator, and she wished to pursue more education. Rutledge said his cousin Ann "concented to wait a year for their Marriage after their Engagement until Abraham Lincoln was admitted to the bar." Rutledge firmly believed, "Had she lived till spring they were to be married."

In the long, hot, rainy summer of 1835, Ann fell ill with what people called "brain fever," probably typhoid fever, perhaps caused by the flooding of the Rutledge well. She died on August 25, 1835. Her uncle,

John M. Cameron, a Cumberland Presbyterian minister, preached her funeral sermon.

Lincoln was devastated by Ann's death. He had lost his mother and his sister to early deaths, and now he had lost the first woman he had loved. He had perhaps surprised himself in reaching out to young Ann Rutledge, and now she had been taken from him prematurely.

Lincoln was staying with Elizabeth and Bennett Abell at the time. Elizabeth Abell said later, "It was a great shock to him and I never seen a man mourn for a companion more than he did for her[.] He made a remark one day when it was raining that he could not bare the idea of its raining on her Grave." Robert Rutledge remarked, "The effect upon Mr. Lincoln's mind was terrible; he became plunged in despair, and many of his friends feared that reason would desert her throne." The residents of New Salem, in remembering Abraham and Ann, did not claim they knew the details of their love for each other, but, as Robert Rutledge summarized, Lincoln's "extraordinary emotions were regarded as strong evidence of the existence of the tenderest relations between himself and the deceased."

A LITTLE MORE THAN A YEAR after Ann's death, Lincoln entered into a relationship with a more mature, imposing woman. Mary Owens, born in Green County, Kentucky, in 1808, grew up in a wealthy family, the recipient of a fine education. Lincoln met her while she was visiting her sister, Elizabeth Abell, in New Salem in 1833. Mary, a good-looking woman with dark eyes, black hair, and a generous figure, exhibited a spirited and witty personality.

Three years later, in 1836, Elizabeth Abell prepared to travel to Kentucky to visit her sister. Elizabeth told Lincoln lightheartedly that she would bring Mary back if he would marry her. Mary, twenty-eight, was reaching the age when society would label her an old maid. Lincoln, probably in the same blithe spirit, boasted that he would marry Mary if she returned. After the death of Ann Rutledge, Abell and other women in the village had been encouraging Abraham to look for a wife.

Mary Owens returned to New Salem in November 1836, aware of Lincoln's boast. Their relationship flowered, but from the beginning it also prickled. On one occasion, a party of men and women on horseback on their way to a gathering had to cross a stream. Mary said, "The other gentlemen were officious in seeing that their partners got over safely," but Lincoln never looked back "to see how I got along." When Mary rode up beside him, she remarked, "You are a nice fellow; I suppose you did not care whether my neck was broken or not." Lincoln laughed and replied that he "knew I was plenty smart to take care of myself."

Abraham and Mary had barely begun their courtship when Lincoln left New Salem for the opening of the new legislative session in Vandalia. They may have reached some kind of understanding, but each was already experiencing some apprehension in their relationship. Lincoln was circumspect about the exact nature of his uneasiness. Did he compare this strong, mature woman, a year older than himself, with pretty young Ann? He does not say. Mary, a woman born to privilege, may well have wondered about a man who had not yet established himself in a profession and lacked the social graces of a gentleman.

After two weeks in Vandalia, Lincoln wrote Mary expressing all kinds of discomfort. He began by telling her about his "mortification" in looking for a letter from her and not finding one. In the rest of his letter he talked mostly about himself and said almost nothing about her. Toward the end he confessed that his spirits were not well: "With other

Lincoln began to court Mary Owens, daughter of a well-to-do Kentucky family, about a year after Ann Rutledge's death. They differed in educational background and temperament, and their relationship struggled and then ended.

things I can not account for, have conspired and have gotten my spirits so low, that I feel I would rather be any place in the world than here." As he was about to conclude, perhaps having reread the letter, Lincoln blurted out, "This letter is so dry and [stupid] that I am ashamed to send it, but with my pres [ent] feelings I can not do any better." The letter revealed Lincoln's deep insecurities within himself in relation to women.

Within a month after moving to Springfield in 1837, Lincoln wrote to Mary, who had returned to Kentucky. By now Lincoln seemed to be looking for a way out of their relationship. He told Mary that she would not enjoy living in Springfield. "This thing of living in Springfield is rather a dull business after all, at least it is so to me." He confided, "I am quite as lonesome here as [I] ever was anywhere in my life. I have been spoken to by but one woman since I've been here, and should not have been by her, if she could have avoided it"—an unusual comment to tell another woman. In Lincoln's courtship of Mary Owens, he atypically went out of his way to emphasize the negative. This may have been his obverse way of speaking of his own lack of self-assurance. He wrote, "I am afraid you would not be satisfied" living in Springfield. Women ride about "flourishing" in carriages, but "it would be your doom to see without shareing in it." Owens "would have to be poor without the means of hiding your poverty." Lincoln finally got around to speaking of his own commitments. "Whatever woman may cast her lot with mine, should any ever do so, it is my intention to do all in my power to make her happy and contented."

In August 1837, Lincoln traveled to New Salem to see Mary, who had returned from Kentucky. On the day they parted he wrote her an earnest but painful letter. "I want in all cases to do right, and most particularly so, in all cases with women." He pleaded "ignorance" about her true feelings for him. "What I do wish is, that our further acquaintance shall depend upon yourself." Lincoln then poured out his heart, but in a sentence filled with qualifications. "If you feel yourself in any degree bound to me, I am now willing to release you, provided you wish it; while, on the other hand, I am willing and even anxious to bind you faster, if I can be convinced that it will in any considerable degree, add to your happiness." Finally, he told her, "If it suits you best to not answer this—farewell—a long life and a merry one attend you." He hoped she would write back and "speak as plainly as I do."

She never replied.

Lincoln's letter to Mary Owens on August 16, 1837, reflects his conflicted
feelings about their relationship. He writes mostly about himself
and his feelings, and little about her.

Lincoln found himself deeply hurt—again. Was he blindsided by her silence? Lincoln's letters to Owens revealed him, again and again, conflicted about what to do. It seemed as if his mind told him he should ask her to marry him, but his heart wasn't in it.

That the wound did not heal quickly became apparent by a letter Lincoln wrote nearly eight months later—to another woman. This time he wrote to Eliza Caldwell Browning, the wife of his lawyer friend Orville Browning, and poured out the story of his relationship with

Mary Owens in astonishing detail. By now he was not so complimentary of Mary, writing, a bit cruelly, "for her skin was too full of fat, to permit its contracting in to wrinkles; but from her want to teeth, weather-beaten appearance in general." But the burden of his letter was his own deeply wounded self. He confessed, "I was mortified, it seemed to me, in a hundred different ways. My vanity was deeply wounded by the reflection that I had so long been too stupid to discover her intentions, and at the same time never doubting that I understood them perfectly." It is telling that Lincoln did not write to a male friend. Somehow he felt the freedom to admit to Eliza Browning his lack of social intelligence about women. He admitted something more. Mary Owens "had actually rejected me with all my fancied greatness."

Years later, Mary Owens said that she found Lincoln "deficient in those little links which make up the chain of a woman's happiness, at least it was so in my case." She quickly added, "Not that it proceeded from a lack of goodness of heart." Why did their relationship not work? Mary Owens surmised, "His training had been different from mine, hence there was not that congeniality which would have otherwise existed."

Lincoln, who had lost his first love to death, had now reached a murky parting of the ways with a woman he never really loved.

WHEN THE CAPITAL MOVED to Springfield in 1839, Lincoln began to socialize more than ever before. With the legislature scheduled to meet in Springfield for the first time in December, Lincoln's sense of self-assurance became more secure. He now felt freer to meet young women in the new capital city. He was about to meet the woman who would change his life.

Mary Elizabeth Todd was born on December 13, 1818, in Lexington, Kentucky. Her grandfathers, Levi Todd and Robert Parker, had helped settle Lexington. Her father, Robert Smith Todd, grew up in the family home, Ellerslie, a twenty-room mansion. The Todd family counted as a neighbor Henry Clay, rising Kentucky politician. Six feet tall with brown hair and large brown eyes, Robert Todd became a prominent second-generation leader of Lexington, which fancied itself a civilized town that had moved beyond the frontier.

At twenty-one, Todd married the teenage Eliza Parker, a distant cousin, in 1812. Mary, their fourth child, grew up in a two-story, nine-room, Georgian brick home on Short Street in the center of Lexington. A child of privilege, she knew herself to be part of one of Kentucky's leading political families.

Mary's mother, Eliza, died in the summer of 1825 after the birth of her seventh child, probably from a post-birth bacterial infection, at the age of thirty-one. Mary was six years old. When Mary was eight, her father married Elizabeth Humphreys, a wealthy young woman whose family had strong political connections with the Todds. "Betsy" Humphreys, from Frankfort, nine years younger than her husband, would bear nine children in the following fifteen years. Mary would now grow up in the vortex of an absentee father, often away on business or politics, and a stepmother who many said favored her own children.

Robert Todd was an uncommon father who encouraged the education of his daughters as well as his sons. In the fall of 1827, Mary entered the Shelby Female Academy, housed in a two-story brick house at the corner of Second and Market. Dr. John Ward, an eccentric Episcopal minister, led the school, which was later known as Dr. Ward's Academy.

One of Mary's cousins, Elizabeth Humphreys, remembered her as an aspiring scholar. "Mary was far in advance over girls of her age in education." Dr. Ward believed in beginning class at 5 a.m. on summer mornings and in leading early morning recitations throughout the year. Mary flowered in this disciplined academic atmosphere. Her cousin said, "She had a retentive memory and a mind that enabled her to grasp and thoroughly understand the lessons she was required to learn."

Much of Sunday was spent at the McChord Presbyterian Church. Her father had been one of the founding members of the church. In 1823, when Mary turned five, the church organized the first Sunday school in Lexington. Here Mary participated in the standard Presbyterian education of children and youth by catechizing, a method used by Presbyterians, as well as Congregationalists and many Baptists, in America. Young people were expected to memorize the 107 questions and answers of the *Westminster Shorter Catechism,* beginning with the well-known first question.

Q. What is the chief end of man?
A. The chief end of man is to glorify God and enjoy Him forever.

In 1832, at age fourteen, Mary entered Madame Mentelle's Boarding School. As a rule, Mary would have ended her education after her five years at Dr. Ward's, as only a few thousand girls in America received more than four years of education. Augustus and Charlotte Mentelle, the aristocratic directors of the school, had fled France in 1792 during the French Revolution. Mary received a fine classical education, including French, which set her apart from many of the women she would come to know as an adult.

That year Mary's family moved into a new and even more impressive home on Main Street, with fourteen rooms, both a single and a double parlor, six bedrooms, and formal gardens. The Todds valued both education and fine living.

When Henry Clay visited Lexington in the summer of 1832 while campaigning for the presidency, Mary had already developed a remarkable knowledge of politics. Four years before, at age ten, she had refused on principle to attend a Lexington event honoring presidential candidate Andrew Jackson and had argued with a pro-Jackson neighbor. Now a passionate Whig, she spoke up at a dinner honoring Clay to promise him her support. She quickly added, in everyone's hearing, that she, too, expected to live in Washington some day.

While growing up in Lexington, Mary encountered slavery everywhere. The production of hemp on the bluegrass plantations in the surrounding countryside depended on slave labor. White families used slaves for work inside and outside their homes. By the time Mary was twelve, her father had one slave for every member of his family. The female slaves cooked the meals, washed and sewed the clothes, and looked after the children. The male slaves did everything outside the house, including taking care of the horses.

Lexington was a major slave market. Traders drove groups of slaves—men, women, and children—right past Mary's home on their way to the Deep South. She saw the slaves, young and old, shackled together two by two. As Mary walked to and from school, she frequently observed the slave auctions held at Cheapside, Lexington's public meeting place adjacent to the Fayette County Courthouse on the town square. On another corner of the square stood the black locust whipping post, erected in 1826. As a slave master whipped a slave, a cry would pierce the air of this self-proclaimed civilized town.

BY THE TIME MARY was eighteen, she was considered by her friends, female and male, a pretty young woman. Five feet two inches tall, with soft brown hair, she had a broad forehead, a small upturned nose, blue eyes, and a rosy complexion. Mary exhibited a strong-minded determination to get her way, and the inner circle of her family knew "her temper and tongue." A prominent chin gave the impression of a resolute personality. Her hands darted impulsively in gestures as she spoke.

In the spring of 1837, Mary decided to follow a Todd family pattern and visit Springfield, Illinois. Mary's older sister Elizabeth had married Ninian Edwards, son of the governor of Illinois, and moved with him to Springfield. After the death of their mother, Elizabeth had been as much a mother as a sister to Mary. Their sister Frances also lived in Springfield, as did an uncle, Dr. John Todd, and three cousins, John Todd Stuart, Lincoln's law partner; Stephen T. Logan, his future law partner; and John J. Hardin. The Todds and the Stuarts—Kentuckians, Scottish, and Presbyterian—were forming a veritable clan in Springfield.

In early May, Mary boarded the train for Frankfort, Kentucky, to begin a journey by train, boat, and stagecoach to Springfield. If all connections were made, it would take her two weeks to arrive at Elizabeth and Ninian Edwards's impressive new home on Second Street in the southern part of the city. She may have learned from John Todd Stuart that he had invited a young lawyer named Abraham Lincoln to join him as a partner, but it is doubtful she met Lincoln on this visit. She returned to Lexington in the fall of 1837; they would not meet for another two years.

In the summer of 1839, Mary returned to Springfield, intent on staying this time for more than a visit. She quickly became part of a clique of young women and men calling themselves "the Coterie" who often gathered at the Edwardses' two-story brick home at the top of "Aristocracy Hill." James C. Conkling, a lawyer who had moved to Springfield in 1838 and a member of the Coterie, described Mary as "the very creature of excitement," and said she "never enjoys herself more than when in society and surrounded by a company of merry friends." When one day Mary mimicked the mannerisms of some of her suitors, Ninian Edwards exclaimed, "Mary could make a bishop forget his prayers."

Some of the most marriageable young men in Springfield attended Coterie gatherings, including Stephen A. Douglas; Edward D. Baker; Lyman Trumbull, a slender, good-looking lawyer from Belleville; and James Shields, a native of Ireland, who became auditor of the state of Illinois in 1839. A new invitee was Abraham Lincoln.

Next door to Mary's sister lived attorney Lawrason Levering. His

Ninian and Elizabeth Edwards hosted the Coterie at their home on Aristocracy Hill. Elizabeth never liked Lincoln, believing him to be beneath Mary's social station.

sister, Mercy Levering, a visitor from Baltimore, quickly became Mary's dearest friend in Springfield. For many years Mary and Mercy exchanged long letters. Letter writing was an opportunity for women to share intimate feelings they could not express in public, even in conversation between friends. Mary's correspondence reveals a young woman of intellectual depth and emotional intensity capable of communicating her thoughts and feelings in lucid prose. She wrote in small, slanted script, filling up every sheet right to the borders of the page, her writing style a metaphor for the way she wanted to extend her life right up to and sometimes beyond the prescribed female sphere of her day.

Mary attracted many suitors—old and young, short and tall. A lawyer and legislator named Edwin Webb became very interested, but Mary told Mercy he was "a widower of modest merit," besides "there being a slight difference of some eighteen or twenty summers in our years." Stephen Douglas had moved from Jacksonville to Springfield in 1837 after his appointment as register of the Land Office. He and Mary were seen frequently about town together, and rumors circulated about their relationship. Was it friendship or romance?

ABRAHAM LINCOLN AND Mary Todd probably first became aware of each other in the summer of 1839. They pushed the old axiom "opposites attract" to its limits. Mary described herself a "ruddy *pineknot,*" but in truth she was pretty and perky. Mary's sister Frances described Lincoln as "the plainest man" in Springfield. Mary was well educated, whereas Abraham had received the barest of formal schooling.

The differences between Abraham and Mary's social standing were exhibited for all to see on the dance floor. James Conkling, Mercy's beau, wrote her that when Lincoln danced he gave the impression of being "old Father Jupiter bending down from the clouds to see what's going on." Lincoln disliked dancing, but perhaps he could not resist asking this good-looking, witty young woman. "Miss Todd, I want to dance with you in the worst way," he said.

Later, Mary, with a mischievous smile, recounted the dance to her cousin Elizabeth, saying, "And he certainly did."

There were other, deeper differences, yet to be discovered in this oddly matched couple. But in many ways, they were alike. Both prized education and had worked hard to achieve it. In Mary, Lincoln recognized a soul mate in intellectual curiosity and learning.

Lincoln's courtship of Mary was a romance of the mind as well as the heart. Their mutual enjoyment of ideas and politics put Abraham at ease. They both loved poetry, especially that of Robert Burns, and enjoyed reading aloud to each other. Lincoln, who often led in conversations with men, found himself listening to Mary. Elizabeth Edwards happened upon them once when they were together and observed, "Mary led the conversation—Lincoln would listen and gaze on her as if drawn by some superior power."

Abraham and Mary also shared a passion for politics. The daughter of a leading Whig in Kentucky, she attended speeches for Whig presidential candidate Harrison in 1840 and often discussed politics with her friends. She wrote to Mercy, "This fall I became quite a *politician,* rather an unladylike profession."

But in the midst of delight there arose doubt. Unlike his political self-confidence, Lincoln's confidence that he could succeed in marriage was always on shaky ground. He doubted himself as much or more than Mary. His experience with Mary Owens was still fresh in his mind. At age thirty-one, a part-time politician at the beginning of a career in law, he joined many young men of his time who wondered whether they could support a wife. Remembering the embarrassing attachment of his horse and surveying instruments in New Salem, not to mention his

"National Debt" from his failed store he was still paying off, Lincoln had many questions on his mind as his courtship of Mary advanced.

There was also the matter of the opposition of members of Mary's family. Older sister Elizabeth expressed her resistance to the relationship. She thought that Lincoln, who came to her elegant home in his Conestoga boots, was beneath Mary in every way. "I warned Mary that she and Mr. Lincoln were not suitable. Mr. Edwards and myself believed they were different in nature, and education and raising." She concluded, "They were so different that they could not live happily as man and wife."

Abraham and Mary courted in a sexually segregated Victorian society. Various marriage manuals counseled lovers to "test" each other. Women were encouraged to throw "large and small obstacles in the path of the courting male to measure the depth and intensity of his romantic love." Mary, whether or not she was following the advice of a manual, was very adept at this kind of testing.

A nineteenth-century *Dictionary of Love* stated that doubt was "a great sharpener and intensifier of the tender passions." Lincoln could have been a case study for the *Dictionary of Love,* first with his doubts about his love for Mary Owens, and now his doubts about himself in his developing relationship with Mary Todd.

At some point in 1840, Abraham and Mary's relationship advanced from friendship to courting to an agreement that they might marry. This was not an engagement in the modern sense. He gave her no ring. They told no one of their decision. Rather, they had entered into an "understanding." Mary described this change as having "lovers' eyes."

By the end of that year, however, their relationship suddenly fell apart. It is not clear when or why the break occurred. It may have come on New Year's Day, 1841, but it might also have occurred earlier, during the month of December 1840.

There may have been another woman. Matilda Edwards, daughter of Whig politician Cyrus Edwards and cousin of Mary's brother-in-law Ninian Edwards, arrived at the Edwards home that fall. No one, male or female, could fail to notice the beautiful sixteen-year-old. Mary described her to Mercy Levering as "a most interesting young lady," who has "drawn a concourse of beaux & company around us."

Some contemporaries suggested that Lincoln may have been drawn by the "fascinations" of young Matilda. He certainly may have looked, and Mary may have seen him look, but he also knew he was nearly twice Matilda's age.

Friends differed on who ended the relationship. Conkling thought that Mary broke their understanding; Joshua Speed believed that Lincoln did. Speed said his best friend "went to see 'Mary'—told her that he did not love her." He further believed that "Lincoln did Love Miss Edwards" and "Mary Saw it." Lincoln, acting honorably, told Mary of "the reason of his Change of mind" and she, in turn, "released him." The conversation over, according to Speed, Lincoln "drew her down on his Knee—Kissed her—& parted."

JAMES CONKLING WROTE TO MERCY LEVERING, "Poor L! how are the mighty fallen!" Lincoln had not simply fallen; he was overwhelmed. On January 2, 1841, the clerk of the state legislature called the roll four times, but Lincoln did not answer "Present." On Monday, January 4, Lincoln missed eight votes. On Tuesday, January 5, he did not answer to three afternoon roll calls. Lincoln was always regular in attendance, but his breakup with Mary had plunged him into such despair that he failed to show up to work.

Lincoln's melancholy became the talk of Springfield. Conkling told Mercy that when Lincoln finally returned to the legislature he was "emaciated in appearance and seems scarcely to possess strength enough to speak above a whisper." Joshua Speed removed Lincoln's razor for fear of what his friend might do.

Speed sold his interest in the Springfield store and moved back to his family home in Louisville early in 1841, but, concerned about Lincoln's mental state, invited his friend to visit him. One imagines Lincoln's wonder as, when the circuit court adjourned in August, the young Illinois lawyer traveled to Louisville, turned in from the Bardstown Turnpike, and after crossing a limestone bridge beheld the fourteen-room Federal-style house built for John and Lucy Speed in 1815–1816. Speed described Lincoln's state as "moody and hypochondriac" upon his arrival at Farmington.

Over the next weeks, Lincoln, given a horse and also a slave as a personal attendant, wandered the 550-acre plantation where nearly sixty slaves staffed the home and the eighty acres dedicated to hemp farming. One morning, finding Lincoln alone, Lucy Speed, "pained at his deep depression," presented Lincoln an Oxford edition of the King James Bible. She "advised him to read it—to adopt its precepts and pray for its promises."

Lincoln sent a letter to Mary's cousin, his former law partner John Todd Stuart, on January 23, 1842. "I am now the most miserable man living. If what I feel were equally distributed to the whole human family, there would not be one cheerful face on the earth." Lincoln was pessimistic about his future. "Whether I shall ever be better I can not tell; I awfully forebode I shall not. To remain as I am is impossible; I must die or be better, it appears to me."

Nearly fifteen months later, Lincoln wrote to Speed and referred to "the fatal first of Jany.'41." What did he mean? It has long been assumed that Lincoln was referring to the breaking of his understanding with Mary. Read in the context of a series of letters with Speed, however, in which Speed was struggling with his own engagement and prospective marriage, the reference could also refer to the pain in Speed's life.

Mary also suffered, and her feelings for Lincoln had not diminished with absence and time. Nearly six months after the breakup, she wrote to Mercy, "[Lincoln] deems me unworthy of notice, as I have not met him in the gay world for months, with the usual comfort of misery, imagine that others were as seldom gladdened by his presence as my humble self, yet I would the case were different, that 'Richard' should be himself again, much happiness would it afford me."

When Mary placed quotation marks around "Richard" she was referring to Shakespeare's Richard II. Mary would have been an unusual young woman to be familiar with Shakespeare. At first it seems an odd allusion. Richard II had ascended the English throne as a young man in 1377, but quickly proved to be unwise in his choice of counselors and reckless in his spending of money. Mary may have been expressing her concern about Abraham's mental well-being, and yet her confidence that, despite his humble beginnings, there was royalty in Lincoln's future.

SOMETIME IN 1842, more than a year after the split, Eliza Francis, wife of newspaper editor Simeon Francis, took matters into her own hands. She invited Abraham and Mary to her home, each not knowing the other was coming. Sitting in her parlor, Mrs. Francis urged Abraham and Mary to be friends again. It took a third person to get them to deal with the hurt and pain, and move toward forgiveness and reconciliation. Abraham and Mary began meeting clandestinely at the Francises' home and at the home of Lincoln's physician and Whig friend, Dr. Anson Henry.

That fall, when Lincoln and Mary were participating in the biennial campaigning for state offices, Lincoln gave her an unusual gift. He tied up with a pink ribbon a list of the returns from the last three legislative elections in which he had been one of the winning candidates. Whether Mary found this romantic, we do not know.

One of the most bizarre episodes in Lincoln's life, which brought him face-to-face with the possibility of death, took place just as he and Mary were resuming their relationship. Early in 1842, the State Bank of Illinois had been forced to close. In August, the governor, treasurer, and auditor ordered county tax collectors not to accept the state's own paper notes for payment of taxes and school debts. Only gold and silver would be accepted. Citizens, however, had almost no gold or silver.

The problem escalated when state auditor James Shields issued an order advising state officers how to restore a sound currency. By this time, opposition to the state plan had begun to escalate. Shields, a young Irish immigrant and a rising Democratic politician, became the focus for a vigorous response by Illinois Whigs.

Lincoln, a staunch defender of the state bank, saw an opportunity to harvest some political hay in the upcoming 1842 election for state legislature and governor. Where best to attack the Democrats but in Lincoln's favorite vehicle—the newspaper?

The *Sangamo Journal* had recently printed a satirical letter to the editor from "Rebecca," a country woman who lived in "Lost Townships." This letter, in its homely dialogue, enunciated important Whig ideas. Lincoln contacted editor Simeon Francis suggesting he write a follow-up letter. Lincoln assumed the persona of "Rebecca" and sharpened his writing sword to attack Shields and the Democratic Party's policies. Lincoln showed his letter to Mary, and she and her friend Julia Jayne helped revise its humor and satire.

Published on September 2, 1842, "Rebecca's" letter singled out Shields for ridicule because of his role in the currency dilemma. She minced no words: "Shields is a fool as well as a liar."

Lincoln described Shields at a party in Springfield. "If I was deaf and blind I could tell him by the smell." Placing Shields in the middle of a group of women, the usually gallant Lincoln authored a particularly coarse description: "All the galls about town were there, and all the handsome widows, and married women, finickin about, trying to look like galls, tied as tight in the middle, and puffed out at both ends like bundles of fodder that hadn't been stacked yet, wanted stackin pretty bad."

Silver, the reason for Lincoln's political invective, was now used against Shields with irony. "He was paying his money to this one and that one, and tother one, and sufferin great loss because it wasn' silver instead of State paper." Finally, Lincoln put words in Shields' mouth: "Dear girls, *it is distressing,* but I cannot marry you all. Too well I know how much you suffer, but do, do *remember,* it is not my fault that I am *so* handsome and *so* interesting."

Mary and Julia, caught up in Lincoln's escapade, decided to expand the fun by writing a third Rebecca letter, published in the *Sangamo Journal* on September 16, 1842.

Shields, known for his violent temper, became enraged. He demanded the name of the person who had heaped such scorn upon him. Francis told him it was Lincoln. Lincoln may have allowed Francis to reveal his name, perhaps to protect the names of the two young women. Shields's pride was hurt, but more important, Lincoln had threatened his aspiring political career.

Shields fought back. He confronted Lincoln in Tremont at the Tazewell County Courthouse. He intended to get a retraction from Lincoln. Or else. Shields challenged Lincoln to a duel. The state auditor, who had fought in the Black Hawk War, enjoyed a reputation as an outstanding marksman with pistols.

Dueling had become a recurring feature of American life in the early nineteenth century. The nation had been stunned when Alexander Hamilton died in a duel with Aaron Burr in 1804, but the shock arose from the death of one of America's most talented leaders, not because of a duel. The first American duel took place in 1621 in the Massachusetts Bay Colony. People of all walks of life participated in duels, even as many states passed anti-dueling laws. Dueling, according to the Illinois criminal statute of 1839, was a penitentiary offense, punishable by five years in prison.

As the person challenged, Lincoln had the prerogative to select the weapons. Aware of Shields's skills with firearms, Lincoln chose long cavalry broadswords instead of guns. Six feet four inches tall, Lincoln knew what a tremendous advantage his height and reach gave him over Shields, who was five feet nine inches.

Dueling was not outlawed in Missouri. Just as Hamilton and Burr, nearly forty years earlier, had crossed the Hudson River from New York to New Jersey in 1804, early on Thursday morning, September 22, 1842, two boats embarked from Alton, Illinois, and crossed the Mississippi in the morning mist to a muddy shore on the Missouri side. The party walked a few steps to a clearing that would serve as the dueling ground.

Accounts conflict over what happened next. Some said Lincoln, stretching out his long arm and longer broadsword, cut off the limb of a willow tree high above the combatants and frightened Shields with the demonstration of his extensive reach. Another report said Shields laughed at this gesture. But in his laughter, or his fear, he realized the absurdity of the situation and agreed to make peace. The duel ended before it began.

What are we to make of the near duel between Lincoln and Shields? Did Lincoln, almost unable to stop his participation in the duel, act more like the young wrestler than a mature man? Did he agree to participate to defend the honor of Mary and Julia Jayne, who had written the third letter? It seems certain that Lincoln did not want to harm Shields. He understood he could disarm with a sword, but not with a pistol. Some have suggested that Lincoln and Shields thought they might get political publicity from the duel.

When it was all over, Lincoln felt deeply embarrassed by the whole affair. Years later, when people would bring up the duel, Lincoln quickly let it be known that he did not want to discuss it.

WITH THE DUEL BEHIND HIM, and now reunited with Mary, Lincoln still struggled over whether he should marry Mary. He wrote to his friend Speed for advice. Lincoln had received letters from Speed as his friend struggled over his own engagement to Fanny Henning. Now Lincoln wanted to know how it had turned out. "Are you now, in *feeling* as well as *judgment,* glad you are married as you are?" Lincoln recognized that "from any body but me, this would be an impudent question not to be tolerated," but he was confident that Speed would accept the question from him, his closest friend. "Please answer it quickly as I feel impatient to know."

Speed must have responded, but no letter exists. Years later Speed wrote, "One thing is plainly discernable—If I had not been married & happy—far more happy than I ever expected to be—He would not have married."

On Friday morning, November 4, 1842, Abraham and Mary announced that they intended to marry—that very evening. The couple did not tell anyone in advance. There was much to do and little time to do it.

They decided on a private marriage service. Lincoln called at the brown frame house at Eighth and Jackson to ask the Reverend Charles Dresser, rector at St. Paul's Episcopal Church, if he would marry them in his home. When Mary broke the news of her wedding to her sister and brother-in-law, Elizabeth and Ninian Edwards erupted over the suddenness of the decision. Elizabeth had long objected to Lincoln, but now that the deed was going to be done, Ninian insisted, as Mary's legal guardian, that the wedding take place in their home.

Lincoln purchased a wedding ring at Chatterton's Jewelry Store on the west side of the town square. He had the ring inscribed "Love is Eternal." Around noon, Lincoln asked fellow Springfield lawyer James H. Matheny to be his best man. Mary hurried to ask her cousin "Lizzie" Todd and her good friend Julia Jayne to stand up with her. Elizabeth Edwards, fretting about what food to provide, sent out to Dickey's, Springfield's only bakery, for gingerbread and beer, and later decided to bake a cake, which did not turn out well.

At seven o'clock on a rainy, tempestuous evening, the thirty-three-year-old Lincoln and the twenty-four-year-old Mary took their places in front of the fireplace of the Edwardses' parlor. On the mantel two lamps were lit. The great difference between their heights, he an angular six feet four inches, and she barely five feet two inches, was striking. Mary wore a white muslin dress skirt. The Reverend Dresser, dressed in the vestments of the Episcopal Church, led the wedding service from the Book of Common Prayer. Abraham and Mary exchanged their vows, pledging themselves to each other. Saying "With this ring I thee wed," Lincoln slid the band on Mary's finger.

ONE WEEK AFTER Lincoln's wedding, he wrote to his friend Sam Marshall, an attorney in Shawneetown, Illinois, concluding his letter, "Nothing new here, except my marrying, which to me, is a matter of profound wonder."

From now on, Lincoln's life would be like the three-legged stool that he had made as a boy in Indiana. The three legs gave the stool stability; if one leg were ever shortened or lengthened, the balance could become precarious. In the first leg of his adult life, Lincoln found success in politics; in the second leg, he established himself as a lawyer; in the third leg, he entered into marriage. The challenge that lay ahead would be how Lincoln could balance on all three legs as he reached for higher political office.

This first known photograph of Abraham Lincoln was made by
Nicholas H. Shepherd in his daguerreotype store on the Springfield town square.
Lincoln's muscular hands reveal his past, but his dress points to his future as a congressman.

CHAPTER 8

The Truth Is, I Would Like to Go Very Much
1843–46

LET THE PITH OF THE WHOLE ARGUMENT BE
"TURN ABOUT IS FAIR PLAY."

ABRAHAM LINCOLN
Letter to Benjamin F. James, editor,
Tazewell Whig, December 6, 1845

A DOOR TO LARGER POLITICAL SERVICE UNEXPECTEDLY OPENED
for Abraham Lincoln at the beginning of 1843. John Todd Stuart, his
former law partner who had represented the Third Congressional District as the first Whig congressman from Illinois, announced that he
would not seek a third term in the House of Representatives. Lincoln,
having declined in the previous year to run for a fifth term in the state
legislature, eagerly stepped forward to present his credentials for Congress.

When Lincoln arrived in Illinois in 1830, the state was still entitled to
only one representative, the same as when it achieved statehood in 1818.
By 1833, with rising immigration, the number increased to two, and
then three in 1835. For the elections of 1843, Illinois would have seven
seats. The new Seventh Congressional District would be made up of
eleven counties, the majority of the population coming from Sangamon
County.

The Whigs believed they could win the new Seventh District. Three
men—John J. Hardin, Edward D. Baker, and Abraham Lincoln—all
young lawyers, veterans of the Black Hawk War, and friends in the Illinois legislature, now became rivals for the Whig nomination to Congress. Everyone knew that winning the Whig nomination would be
tantamount to winning the general election. The political race was on.

—

JOHN J. HARDIN, one year younger than Lincoln, was born in 1810 into a prominent political family in Frankfort, Kentucky. He graduated from Transylvania University in Lexington, studied law with Chief Justice John Boyle of the Kentucky Supreme Court, and entered the legal profession in 1831. That same year, Hardin moved to Illinois, setting up a law practice in Jacksonville, the county seat of Morgan County. Tall, with dark hair and dark eyes, Hardin had a bold face that reflected his determined personality. He was an excellent speaker, even though he had a slight speech impediment. He served in the Black Hawk War in 1832. First elected to the state legislature in 1836, he gave up his seat in 1842, the same year that Lincoln stepped down. As a fellow Whig, Hardin had actively opposed Lincoln on the internal improvements legislation. As a personal friend, Hardin had attempted to stop the duel between Lincoln and James Shields.

Edward D. Baker, two years younger than Lincoln, was born in London, England, and immigrated to the United States with his family in 1816. Baker lived in Philadelphia until 1825, when his family moved to British socialist Robert Owens's utopian community in New Harmony, Indiana. Later that same year, they settled in Illinois, first in Belleville and then in Carrollton. In 1835, Baker opened a law office in Spring-

John J. Hardin, a talented lawyer and politician from Jacksonville, counted himself as one of Lincoln's friends but became his opponent for the Whig nomination to Congress in 1843.

Lincoln thought so much of Whig politician Edward D. Baker that he named his second son Edward after his good friend. Baker and Lincoln vied for the support of the Sangamon County Whigs in the run-up to the congressional election of 1843.

field. Stunningly handsome and tall, with blue eyes, Baker was an inspiring if impetuous person. He was a lay minister in the Disciples of Christ Church, a denomination formed in 1832 from two revival streams, "Christian" and "Disciples," which aimed to restore New Testament Christianity. Baker's preaching experience prepared him to be a persuasive orator at Whig political rallies. He was elected to the state legislature in 1837 and to the state senate in 1840. Whig politics brought Baker and Lincoln together as kindred spirits.

IN HIS CAMPAIGN for Congress, Lincoln employed an aggressive multi-pronged strategy. Months before the election, he began writing Whig friends about his congressional aspirations. On February 14, 1843, he wrote Richard S. Thomas, fellow lawyer and active Whig from Virginia, Illinois. "Now if you should hear any one say that Lincoln don't want to go to Congress, I wish you as a personal friend of mine, would tell him you have reason to believe he is mistaken. The truth is, I would like to go very much." Lincoln's political ambition, muted in his first races for the state legislature, became more direct and visible when he decided to run for Congress.

On March 4, 1843, the Whigs published an "Address to the People of Illinois," signed collectively by five politicians, including Lincoln, who likely penned it. Who else but Lincoln would have pled for political action by appealing to Aesop, "that great fabulist and philosopher," and to Jesus, "he whose wisdom surpasses that of all philosophers," who "declared that 'a house divided against itself cannot stand' "? The campaign circular concluded, "At every election, let every whig act as though he knew the result to depend upon his action."

In advocating a convention system for nominating candidates, Lincoln moved to the front rank of Whigs. He knew the Democrats had advanced their party's interests in recent years in part because of their adoption of a convention system, which ensured that the party would unite behind one candidate rather than divide its votes among several candidates. Many Whigs had resisted a convention system because they feared party bosses would easily manipulate it, putting forward candidates who were not the choice of the people. But Lincoln could see that a convention system could help Whigs at both the state and national level. The first nominating convention for the new Seventh District was scheduled to be held on May 1, 1843.

As the convention approached, two difficulties clouded Lincoln's candidacy. First, his opponents charged that as a result of his recent marriage to Mary Todd, he was now a candidate of the wealthy and influential. These detractors accused Lincoln of being a member of "the Junto," a group of prominent business and political leaders in Springfield. Lincoln's new brother-in-law Ninian Edwards was also a member of the Junto. Edwards's aristocratic airs did not go over well with the Whigs, and Lincoln became guilty by association. Lincoln commented on the irony of this in a letter to Martin S. Morris, a delegate from Menard County. "It would astonish if not amuse the older citizens to learn that I (a strange, friendless, uneducated, penniless boy, working at ten dollars per month) have been put down as the candidate of pride, wealth, and aristocratic family distinction."

A second problem was the issue of religion. It was well known that Lincoln was not a member of any church. Mary attended the Episcopal Church, viewed by many as the church of the wealthy. Baker, on the other hand, was an active member of the Disciples of Christ Church and had become known for his spellbinding lay sermons. The Whigs had always taken pride in their affirmation of Protestant Christian values. They criticized Democrats for either having no religious faith or having the wrong faith, by which they meant the Catholic faith.

In his letter to Morris, Lincoln wrote, "There was the strangest combination of church influence against me." He said that Mary had relatives in both the Presbyterian and Episcopal churches, and that often "I had been set down as either the one or the other." But lately, he complained, "it was everywhere contended that no ch[r]istian ought to go for me, because I belonged to no church, was suspected of being a deist, and had talked about fighting a duel." He went on to tell Morris that Baker was not the cause of his problems. "I only mean that those influences levied a tax of a considerable per cent, upon my strength throughout the religious community." Lincoln's letter points to the role of religion in American politics in Lincoln's day.

Whigs from across Sangamon County met for the first step in the nominating process on March 20, 1843. The Baker followers arrived early at the statehouse in Springfield and managed to outmaneuver the Lincoln supporters. After the first ballots, Baker led. In the afternoon, the Baker supporters asked Lincoln, in the name of party unity, to withdraw his name, for it had become obvious that he would not win.

But then an odd thing happened. The group wanted Lincoln to become the chairman of the Sangamon County delegation. He tried to decline, but they persisted, and Lincoln, an early advocate of the convention system, found it difficult to say no. And so it was that Lincoln arrived in the morning a candidate for Congress and left in the evening chairman of a delegation pledged to Baker. Lincoln, able to see the humor in any situation, wrote to Speed, "In getting Baker the nomination, I shall be fixed a good deal like a fellow who is made a groomsman to a man who has cut him out and is marrying his own dear gal."

LINCOLN JOINED WHIGS from across the district who assembled for the convention at the Tazewell County Courthouse in Pekin on May 1. Lincoln arrived at the head of the Baker delegation. He knew he had lost his bid to be elected in 1843, but he had not lost his ambition to serve in Congress.

John J. Hardin won the Whig nomination for Congress. At this point Lincoln stood and urged the convention to adopt a resolution endorsing Baker as "a suitable person to be voted for by the Whigs of the district" in the succeeding election. The district convention adopted his motion by a vote of 18 to 14. In effect, the delegates were agreeing that Hardin should serve only a single term. Lincoln argued for a principle of rotation, a practice already in place in many states. The agreement, in spirit if not in letter, would hopefully assure Lincoln the nomination after Baker.

The Whig convention to select their candidate for Congress in 1843 was held at the Tazewell County Courthouse in Pekin. Lincoln lost the nomination to Hardin, but suggested a rotation system whereby first Edward Baker and then he would be assured nomination as the candidates for future terms.

Lincoln left Pekin on good terms with Baker, but in disagreement with Hardin about the principle of rotation. Ten days later, Lincoln, having heard that Hardin had some doubts "whether the whigs of Sangamon will support [him] cordially," wrote to Hardin. "You must at once, dismiss all fears on that subject. We have already resolved to make a particular effort to give you the largest majority possible in our county." He sought to reassure Hardin. "We have many objects for doing it. We make it a matter of honor and pride to do it; we do it, because we love the whig cause; we do it, because we like you personally."

On Election Day, Lincoln voted for the offices of justice of the peace and constable, but for no other candidates. Since voting was still done by voice, Lincoln's vote became known. He did not vote for Hardin or any of the Whig candidates for county and state offices. An explanation was never offered. Hardin won the seat for Congress in the new Seventh District, receiving a majority of 504 votes in Sangamon County.

THE CONGRESSIONAL CAMPAIGN of 1843 began just as Abraham and Mary Lincoln started their married life together. They rented one room at the Globe Tavern, a two-story plain wooden hotel on the north side of Adams Street, for four dollars a month, including board. The Lincolns lived in a cramped eight-by-fourteen-foot room on the second floor and took their meals in a common room with both long-term boarders and hotel guests. A gathering place for Whig politicians, the Globe was noisy day and night, in part because the hotel doubled as the main office for the stage lines serving Springfield. A bell rang at odd hours announcing the arrival of a stage.

The Lincolns' first child, Robert Todd Lincoln, named after Mary's father, was born on August 1, 1843, nine months after their wedding. They called him Bob. The joy of his birth took some of the sting out of losing the nomination. After the baby's birth, Lincoln began addressing his wife as "Mother." She called him, in Victorian fashion, "Mr. Lincoln."

Shortly after Robert's birth, Abraham and Mary rented a frame cottage at 214 South Fourth Street for $100 per year. This three-room residence was but a way station on the road to purchasing a house. Lincoln, now making about $1,500 a year as an up-and-coming lawyer and working hard to retire the last of his "National Debt" from his New Salem days, began looking for a permanent home.

Early in 1844, Abraham and Mary purchased their first home, the very same one-and-a-half-story frame house at Eighth and Jackson where Lincoln had called on the Reverend Henry Dresser on the day of their wedding sixteen months earlier. Lincoln agreed to pay Dresser $1,200 in cash plus the transfer of a lot immediately west of the public square that Lincoln and his law partner Stephen T. Logan had acquired together two years earlier.

Abraham, Mary, and nine-month-old Bob moved into their new home on Friday, May 3, 1844. What mixed emotions this event must have brought. Abraham's mind may have wandered back to the many places he had lived over the past thirteen years, none of which he could call home. Mary might have remembered the grand brick homes she had lived in while growing up in Lexington, Kentucky, or the magnificent Springfield home of her sister and brother-in-law, Elizabeth and Ninian Edwards, where she had lived for three years. This new home was far less than anything she had known before, while for Lincoln it was far more.

The house, situated on a slight elevation, appeared a bit higher than some of the neighboring homes. Built in a Greek Revival style, it was typical of many of the newer Springfield homes and located a mere seven blocks from Springfield's center and Lincoln's law office.

Since houses were not numbered in Springfield until 1873, they were usually identified with nameplates on the front door. The front door of the Lincoln home bore a simple black doorplate inscribed with silvered Roman characters: "A. Lincoln."

THE NEW HOUSE would remain the Lincoln family's center for the next seventeen years. A second child, Edward Baker Lincoln, named after Edward Baker, Lincoln's friend and political colleague, was born on March 10, 1846.

Harriet Chapman, the daughter of Lincoln's stepsister Sarah Elizabeth Johntson Hanks, came to the Lincoln home shortly after they moved in, working as a hired girl for a year and a half. She reported how much Lincoln enjoyed reading, especially aloud. His typical posture was to "turn a Chair down on the floor and put a pillow on it and lie there for hours and read." She added her voice to the general observation that Lincoln was "remarkably fond of Children."

Mary was also an avid reader. She, too, typically read aloud, and Abraham sometimes asked her to read to him. After their wedding, the Lincolns subscribed to the semiweekly *Lexington Observer and Reporter*. Mary took pleasure in reading aloud from her home paper to her husband.

She enjoyed reading the novels and poems of Sir Walter Scott to her eldest son, Bob. One day she heard noises outside the front window. She looked to see Bob and a little playmate engaged in "a battle royal." Bob was brandishing a fence paling instead of a lance, and declaring in a shrill voice, " 'This rock shall fly from its firm base as soon as I.' " Mary, sparkling with laughter, exclaimed from Scott's *Lady of the Lake*, " 'Gramercy, brave knights. Pray be more merciful than you are brawny.' "

IN THE SPRING OF 1841, Lincoln began working with his new partner, Stephen T. Logan. Though the two men were quite different in temperament, Lincoln enjoyed a much closer working relationship with Logan, nine years older, than with Stuart. The senior partner was conscientious, industrious, and exact in his approach to the law. Logan was no orator, but he argued his cases with persuasive, rational power. In the aftermath of the financial panic of 1837, Congress passed the Bankruptcy Act on February 1, 1842, the first such act in forty years. Logan and Lincoln pled more than seventy cases, representing both creditors and debtors but primarily arguing for relief for debtors, before the act was repealed thirteen months later.

Lincoln and Logan moved into offices on the third floor of the new Tinsley building on Springfield's downtown square in August 1843. A trapdoor connected the offices to the federal courtroom, from which the lawyers could listen in on the proceedings below. Lincoln was presenting more and more cases before the Supreme Court of Illinois, and his professional reputation was growing. Lawyers who lived far from Springfield began to refer their cases to him, confident that he would argue them with skill before the state's highest court.

A fresh opportunity opened up for Lincoln when Logan decided to give up traveling and asked his junior partner to represent the firm on the Eighth Judicial Circuit. By 1843, the Eighth Judicial Circuit included fourteen counties in central Illinois. Lincoln, on occasion, traveled beyond the circuit, all the way to Clark County, near the Indiana line, and into Madison County, on the Missouri border, to participate in cases. The firm was becoming one of the most prominent in the state.

Logan grew to appreciate his young partner's distinctive skills. "I have seen him get a case and seem to be bewildered at first, but he would go at it and after a while he would master it. He was very tenacious in his grasp of a thing that he once got hold of."

After three successful years, Lincoln's partnership with Logan came to an end in 1844. Logan informed Lincoln that he wished to take his son David as a partner. This was understandable, and the partners parted and remained friends.

Logan and Lincoln handled approximately 850 cases together. Lincoln learned self-discipline and the art of case preparation from Logan, who had served previously as a circuit judge and had taught Lincoln to see cases from every possible point of view. Having learned much about the law and the courts, Lincoln was eager to start his own firm and began to search for a partner.

IN DECEMBER 1844, Lincoln selected an unlikely candidate, one that got Springfield's tongues wagging. William Herndon, an intellectually curious but opinionated and garrulous young man, was born in Greensburg, Kentucky, on December 25, 1818; his father, Archer Herndon, had moved his family to Illinois in 1820. After struggling with farming, they relocated in Springfield in 1825. Archer started the Indian Queen Tavern and Hotel, the first hotel of any prominence in Springfield, located at Second and Jefferson. Seven-year-old Billy had helped his father serve drinks and stable horses. Archer served in the Illinois Senate for eight years and had been one of the "Long Nine" who joined Lincoln's effort to move the state capital from Vandalia to Springfield.

Archer Herndon possessed no formal education, but he was determined his children should receive what he was denied. After paying for his son to attend the Springfield schools, he sent Billy to the preparatory department of Illinois College in Jacksonville in the fall of 1836.

During his year there, Billy enhanced his budding interest in philosophy, borrowing from the library the school's allotment of one large book or two small books for each student each week. He also got into more than his allotment of trouble with school officials for his clowning around and practical jokes.

Illinois College had grown from the dream of John M. Ellis, a Presbyterian missionary, who embraced the need for education in the West in 1829. Edward Beecher left his pulpit at the renowned Park Street Church in Boston to become the first president of the college in 1830. President Beecher and faculty members Jonathan B. Turner and Julian M. Sturtevant all brought their antislavery convictions with them from New England. They believed that immediate conversion should put people on the road to immediate abolition, the urgent goal of American moral reform. Beecher played a major role in the founding of the first antislavery society in Illinois in 1837.

Archer Herndon, a Jackson Democrat and pro-slavery man, had sent his son off to college, not expecting he would return as a convinced Whig and an antislavery man. When Billy came home to Springfield he argued with his father over his new antislavery convictions and moved out of his father's house. He ended up working in Speed's general store and was invited to stay in the room above the store with Speed and Lincoln.

Lincoln had encouraged Herndon to read law in the office of Logan and Lincoln in 1841. Herndon was admitted to the bar on December 9, 1844. When Lincoln invited Billy to join his practice, he was twenty-six, nine years younger than Lincoln.

Lincoln and Herndon rented an office in the new Tinsley Building on the public square in Springfield. A shingle with the names "Lincoln & Herndon" hung from hinges at the foot of the stairway.

From the beginning, Lincoln called Herndon "Billy," while the junior partner addressed him as "Mr. Lincoln." In their partnership, Lincoln decided he would travel the circuit while young Herndon would manage the firm and look after the books, a task Lincoln never liked. But Herndon proved no more adept at fiscal accountability than Lincoln; much of the time the books went neglected. As Logan's junior partner, Lincoln had received only one-third of the firm's proceeds. Although he was now the senior partner, Lincoln split all fees evenly with his new younger colleague.

EVEN AS LINCOLN was changing law partners, he became deeply involved in the political campaigns of 1844. The presidential contest pitted Henry Clay of Kentucky, leader of the Whigs, against James K. Polk of Tennessee, who as Speaker of the House had been President Andrew Jackson's chief lieutenant in the bank war. James G. Birney of Michigan, a former Whig, was the standard-bearer of the antislavery Liberty Party. Throughout the campaign, Lincoln received many invitations to speak on behalf of Clay and various Whig candidates, which reflected his growing stature as a rising Whig politician.

He was invited to speak in southern Indiana and looked forward to returning to his boyhood home for the first time in fifteen years. On Thursday morning, October 24, 1844, Lincoln left Springfield by horseback. Journeying from the prairies of Illinois east to Indiana he met the changing colors of fall in the maple, oak, beech, hickory, and walnut forests of southern Indiana.

While speaking about a protective tariff at Rockport on October 30, 1844, a man about Lincoln's age entered the courthouse. In the middle of his speech, Lincoln exclaimed, "There is Nat." Lincoln had recognized his old schoolmate Nathaniel Grigsby. He stopped, "walked over the benches," and joyfully greeted his boyhood friend.

The next day, Lincoln traveled to Gentryville where he visited more old friends. His visit to his boyhood haunts in the Pigeon Creek area stirred mixed memories. "I went into the neighborhood in that State in which I was raised, where my mother and only sister were buried," he told an acquaintance later.

A year and a half later, in letters to Andrew Johnston, a lawyer in Quincy, Lincoln wrote of the "poetizing mood" triggered by the emotional experience of returning to his boyhood home. Lincoln included a poem about his feelings of visiting Indiana again.

> *My childhood's home I see again,*
> *And sadden with the view;*
> *And still, as memory crowds my brain,*
> *There's pleasure in it too.*

Lincoln confessed he was not sure "whether my expression of those feelings is poetry." Even so, he needed to articulate such deep emotions.

> *Near twenty years have passed away*
> *Since here I bid farewell*
> *To woods and fields, and scenes of play,*
> *And playmates loved so well.*

He concluded with a sense of death and loss.

> *I range the field with pensive tread,*
> *And pace the hollow rooms,*
> *And feel (companion of the dead)*
> *I'm living in the tombs.*

Lincoln told Johnston that he could publish these words, anonymously, if he wished, in the *Quincy Whig,* which Johnston did two and a half years later.

THE PRESIDENTIAL ELECTION OF November 1844 disappointed Lincoln and the Whigs. James K. Polk, a rather colorless Democrat, outpolled Clay, with Birney, the antislavery candidate of the Liberty Party, a distant third. The contest turned on just a few counties in several states. Clay, a slaveholder, was nonetheless the infinitely better candidate than Polk, who had promised the annexation of Texas, which meant the possibility of the extension of slavery into a new state. Lincoln, deeply disappointed, believed if Birney had not been in the race, Clay would have won.

The defeat taught Lincoln that abolitionists and other extreme antislavery men would rather be right—what he called "righteous"—than win. That the election result continued to gnaw at him was evident in correspondence eleven months later with Williamson Durley of Hennepin, who called himself an abolitionist and a "Liberty man." Lincoln told Durley, "If the whig abolitionists of New York had voted with us last fall, Mr. Clay would now be president, whig principles in the ascendant, and Texas not annexed."

Lincoln recounted to Durley that he had met another Liberty man who said his religious principles forbade him to vote for Clay, a slaveholder. "We are not to do *evil* that *good* may come," the man had said. Lincoln, quite exercised, offered both his own religion and logic in response. "This general, proposition is doubtless correct; but did it apply? If by your votes you could have prevented the *extention, &c.* of slavery, would it not have been *good* and not *evil* to have used your votes even though it involved the casting of them for a slaveholder?" Using biblical imagery, Lincoln stated, "By the *fruit* the tree is to be known. An *evil* tree can not bring forth *good* fruit. If the fruit of electing Mr. Clay would have been to prevent the extension of slavery, could the act of electing have been *evil*?" Sensitive to the misuse of religion, Lincoln would never forget this political lesson.

IN THE FALL OF 1845, Lincoln began his campaign to win the Whig nomination for Congress, even though the Whig district convention was eight months away. He had met with Baker, who had succeeded Hardin, and received assurances that he would not run for a second term. In September, Lincoln traveled to Jacksonville to meet with Hardin. Two months later, he wrote Henry E. Dummer, Stuart's former law partner, "I strongly suspect, that Genl. Hardin wishes to run again." Lincoln knew he needed to make sure that Hardin would not be in a favorable position to seek another nomination.

He decided to put in place a comprehensive strategy. He wrote letters to prospective delegates, appealing to their sense of fairness. In his letter to Dummer, Lincoln reminded him of the agreement in 1843 between Hardin, Baker, and himself. "I know of no argument to give me a preference over him, unless it be 'Turn about is fair play.' " Lincoln was careful not to disparage Hardin. To Dr. Robert Boal of Lacon, he wrote, "That Hardin is talented, energetic, usually generous and magnanimous, I have, before this, affirmed to you, and do not now deny. You know that my only argument is that 'turn about is fair play.' This he, practically at least, denies." On January 8, 1846, Congressman Baker published in the *Sangamo Journal* his declaration of withdrawal, the timing of his announcement coordinated between him and Lincoln. Three days later Boal wrote to Hardin, "I do not well see how we can avoid adopting the maxim that 'turn about is fair play,' whether right or wrong, this is my only reason for favoring the pretensions of Mr. Lincoln."

Lincoln began courting newspaper editors. His new law partner, William Herndon, observed, "He never overlooked a newspaper man who had it in his power to say a good or bad thing of him." Lincoln understood the power of the press to influence public opinion. He wrote four letters to Benjamin F. James, editor of the *Tazewell Whig,* in December 1845 and January 1846, discussing the campaign and asking him about the likely positions of other editors and newspapers. Lincoln told James he needed seventeen votes to win the nomination over Hardin at the Whig convention and then listed where they were likely to come from in each county. He concluded by counseling the editor, "In doing this, let nothing be said against Hardin . . . nothing deserves to be said against him. Let the pith of the whole argument be 'Turn about is fair play.' "

Lincoln had become practiced in the politics of personal persuasion. He decided to visit as many delegates, or persons influential with delegates, as he could. "It is my intention to take a quiet trip through the towns and neighbourhoods of Logan county, Delevan, Tremont, and on to & through the upper counties." At the same time, Lincoln did not want to take anything for granted. He told editor James, "Don't speak of this, or let it relax any of your vigilance."

Lincoln believed that he was poised to win the nomination at the district convention. Hardin received this same message, even from his friends. One of Hardin's ardent supporters wrote him that Lincoln "spins a good yarn, is what we call a clever fellow, has mixed much with our citizens, and has done much in sustaining Whig principles in Illinois. . . . Our people think that it is Abraham's turn now."

Still, Hardin pursued his goal of returning to Congress. He and his supporters proposed Lincoln for governor, but he was not interested. Next, Hardin put forward a plan to cancel the district convention and instead have a district primary in each county, stipulating that each candidate and his friends could not campaign outside their own county.

Behind these public maneuvers, a private correspondence was taking place between the two political opponents. Hardin wrote Lincoln on January 16, 1846, about his new rules for electing candidates. He argued that the convention system, which Lincoln had labored to put in place, was undemocratic because it limited those who could run for office. Lincoln replied on January 19, "I am entirely satisfied with the old system under which you and Baker were successively nominated and elected to congress." Hardin replied to Lincoln in a second letter. The contents of that letter, not preserved, can be inferred, for Lincoln returned a lengthy letter, answering Hardin point by point. Lincoln, who had every reason to be irritated by Hardin, wrote with conciliation. "I believe you do not mean to be unjust or ungenerous; and I, therefore am slow to believe that you will not yet think *better* and think *differently* of this matter." Hardin was not yet ready to accept Lincoln's reasoning, for he sent his complete twelve-step proposal to the *Sangamo Journal* on February 16.

Within days of receiving Hardin's proposals, however, the *Sangamo Journal* and other Whig newspapers printed an announcement that Hardin was withdrawing from the contest.

The Whigs of the Seventh Congressional District convened in the Menard County Courthouse in Petersburg on Friday, May 1, 1846. The Committee on Nominations put forward Abraham Lincoln's name, which was unanimously adopted. Starting with the May 7, 1846, issue, the *Sangamo Journal* carried as its masthead:

AUGUST ELECTIONS
For Congress
ABRAHAM LINCOLN
of Sangamon County

WITHIN TWO WEEKS of Lincoln's nomination, distant dramatic events began that would have unforeseen implications for Lincoln's political career. Military skirmishes between U.S. and Mexican forces in a disputed borderland prompted President Polk to declare war against Mexico on May 11, 1846. Though there were questions about who had initiated the hostilities, when Congress concurred with the president on May 13, war fever swept the country. Large cities and small hamlets alike rallied around the flag in patriotic meetings.

Springfield held a mass rally on May 30, 1846. John Hardin, a brigadier general in the Illinois militia, volunteered to organize the First Illinois Regiment of Volunteers, and seventy men signed up. Edward Baker, in Washington, announced he would soon lead the Fourth Illinois Regiment. Addresses offered by a number of leaders, including Lincoln and Governor Thomas Ford, called for "prompt and united action to support the Mexican War."

Some influential Whigs saw Polk's war declaration as a thinly disguised attempt to gain more territory for slavery. But these Whigs were immediately caught in the dilemma of how they could simultaneously resist the president, support the troops, and not appear to be unpatriotic.

TWO DAYS BEFORE the Springfield rally, the Democrats announced Lincoln's opponent in the election for Congress: Peter Cartwright, one of the most colorful figures on the frontier. Cartwright, famous as a revivalist, had traveled by horseback through Methodist circuits in Kentucky, Tennessee, Ohio, Indiana, and Illinois. A preacher and a reformer, he became an avowed enemy of both slavery and whiskey.

Twenty-four years older than Lincoln, Cartwright was born on September 1, 1785, in Amherst County, Virginia. As a young child, he moved with his family to Logan County, Kentucky, near the Tennessee border. At the turn of the century, a series of camp meetings in the region ignited what was called "the Great Revival." In 1801, in Cane Ridge, Kentucky, upward of twenty thousand people camped for days in a festival atmosphere in order to hear protracted preaching. The fifteen-year-old Cartwright was converted at one of those camp meetings. He joined the Methodist Church and quickly began his vocation as a revival preacher.

Cartwright settled in Sangamon County in 1824 because, as he would state in his autobiography, "I would get entirely clear of the evil of slavery." Cartwright hated slavery, but he also despised abolitionism because he believed the rhetoric and tactics of abolitionists made it more difficult to speak with slave owners about changing their ways.

After four years in Illinois, Cartwright turned his religious convictions into political action by running for state office; he was elected to the Illinois General Assembly in 1828. Defeated in 1830, he ran again in 1832, this time coming in ahead of a young Abraham Lincoln from New Salem, defeated in his first run for political office.

Now, fourteen years later, Lincoln and Cartwright squared off to become the representative of the Illinois Seventh Congressional District. A rugged man, about five feet ten inches tall, Cartwright bore his nearly two hundred pounds on a medium frame. His resolute personality exuded from a face with high cheekbones, a firm jaw, and piercing black eyes. Cartwright's Methodist district overlay some of the same territory as the Seventh District, but the Democrats knew they faced an uphill battle in the one supposedly safe Whig district in the state.

The trail of the campaign for Congress in 1846 has left few tracks. Lincoln and Cartwright never appeared together at any point in the contest. No debates took place.

In the latter days of the campaign, Whig friends informed Lincoln that "Mr. Cartwright was whispering the charge of [religious] infidelity against me" in some northern counties in the Seventh District. Lincoln was unsure of what to do. In a letter to Allen Ford, editor of the *Illinois Gazette* in Lacon, he stated that "Cartwright, never heard me utter a word in any way indicating my opinion on religious matters, in his life." Lincoln thought that "nine out of ten have not heard the charge at all," and to answer it might only lift up questions about his religious beliefs his opponent intended to raise. Lincoln finally decided to publish a handbill answering the charges, sent it to selected counties, and left it to the discretion of his friends as to whether it would help or harm.

In the handbill, Lincoln acknowledged that Cartwright had charged him to be "an open scoffer at Christianity." In response he declared, "That I am not a member of any Christian Church, is true; but I have never denied the truth of the Scriptures; and I have never spoken with intentional disrespect of religion in general, or of any denomination of Christians in particular." He admitted that "in early life," he had believed in the "Doctrine of Necessity," which he defined as "the human mind is impelled to action, or held in rest by some power, over which he has no control." He quickly added, "The habit of arguing thus however, I have, entirely left off for more than five years." Finally, Lincoln declared, "I do not think I could myself, be brought to support a man for office, whom I knew to be an open enemy of, and scoffer at, religion." Though distributed as a handbill, the statement was not published in newspapers until after the election.

Cartwright might have been a popular preacher and revivalist, but he was a poor campaigner. Some voters, including Democrats, did not believe a preacher should be involved in politics. By the time the voting took place, the result was a foregone conclusion. In the election, held on August 3, 1846, Lincoln received 6,340 votes to Cartwright's 4,829. Lincoln won the most decisive victory so far in the Seventh District, running ahead of the winning margins of both his predecessors, Baker and Hardin.

"BEING ELECTED TO CONGRESS, though I am very grateful to our friends, for having done it, has not pleased me as much as I expected," wrote Lincoln to Speed, two months after his election. Perhaps the lack of elation was in part due to the fact that in the political calendar of those years, it would be sixteen months before Lincoln would take up his seat in Washington in December 1847.

During this long interval, Lincoln decided to attend the great Rivers and Harbors Convention in the summer of 1847. He traveled by stage-coach for four days on his first visit to Chicago, joining more than ten thousand people in the mud-flat town on July 4, 1847. The first national convention ever held in this rising city of sixteen thousand drew businessmen and farmers, politicians and the press, eager to encourage navigation and business on rivers and lakes.

President Polk's veto of the Rivers and Harbors Appropriation Bill in August 1846 was the impetus for the convention. Polk called the effort at internal improvements unconstitutional, arguing that many of its appropriations were not federal in scope but limited to a single state. The Whigs, who had long championed internal improvements, seized a strategic opportunity to present their case. The decision to hold the convention "at the terminus of lake navigation," recognized not simply the large number of rivers and lakes affected, but the huge migration of people to the West.

On the morning of July 6, 1847, David Dudley Field, a prominent New York lawyer, spoke in defense of the position of the Polk administration. He rejected the obligation of the federal government to help develop the navigation of the Illinois River, which traversed a solitary state.

Lincoln stood to offer a reply, speaking for the first time before a national audience. His full remarks were not recorded, but Field's remarks brought out the best of Lincoln's satire. Lincoln, who as usual had done his homework, learned that Field favored a federal appropriation for the Hudson River in New York. Lincoln asked "how many States the lordly Hudson ran through."

Lincoln's remarks made an indelible impression on a leading New York newspaper editor. Horace Greeley, a reformer and politician at heart, and founding editor of the New York Tribune, always had a nose for the up-and-coming. He thought he spied it in the tall congressman-elect. The next day, Greeley wrote in appreciation, "Hon. Abraham Lincoln, a tall specimen of an Illinoian, just elected to Congress from the only Whig District in the state, spoke briefly and happily in reply to Mr. Field."

CONGRESSMAN-ELECT ABRAHAM LINCOLN posed for his first photograph, a daguerreotype, sometime in the last half of 1846, perhaps shortly after his election to Congress. The daguerreotype was a process that created an extremely detailed image on a sheet of copper plate without the use of a negative.

Lincoln was the perfect candidate for early daguerreotypists, who sought out political figures to photograph so they could place their finished products in the front of their studios to attract other customers. By 1850, there were more than seventy daguerreotype studios in New York City. Even in the small city of Springfield there were as many as four photographers by the late 1840s.

Nicholas H. Shepherd opened his Daguerreotype Miniature Gallery above the drugstore of J. Brookie at the northwest corner of the square in Springfield. He first advertised his photographic services in the *Sangamo Journal* on October 30, 1845, and probably approached Lincoln as a rising political figure to pose for a photograph. He offered to take a separate daguerreotype of Mary. Robert Lincoln remembered that these photographs of his parents hung on the wall in a prominent place in their Springfield home.

Photography in 1846 was subject to the limitations of a craft and technology still in its infancy. Abraham and Mary had to sit still for up to fifteen minutes, which meant that their facial expressions appear direct and unsmiling. In his first photograph, Abraham Lincoln, at thirty-seven, wears the clothes of a successful lawyer and politician. His slicked-down hair is not the tousled mop familiar to Lincoln's friends; it was surely arranged by the photographer or his assistant in an effort to reflect Lincoln's station. His large, muscular hands are a striking feature that could not be rearranged. His eyes reflect a man determined to make his mark in Congress.

Lincoln admired three legislators for their oratory. Henry Clay of Kentucky, John C. Calhoun of South Carolina, and Daniel Webster of Massachusetts became known as "the Great Triumvirate."

CHAPTER 9

My Best Impression of the Truth
1847–49

AS YOU ARE ALL SO ANXIOUS FOR ME TO DISTINGUISH MYSELF,
I HAVE CONCLUDED TO DO SO, BEFORE LONG.

Abraham Lincoln to William H. Herndon, December 13, 1847

ABRAHAM AND MARY LINCOLN PREPARED TO LEAVE SPRINGFIELD
for Washington on October 25, 1847, cheered on by Springfield's *Illinois
State Journal*. "Success to our talented member of Congress! He will find
many men in Congress who possess twice the good looks, and not half
the good sense, of our own representative."

Two days before departing, Lincoln leased their family home at
Eighth and Jackson to Cornelius Ludlum, a brick contractor from Jacksonville, for ninety dollars a year. As the Lincolns embarked on their
six-week journey, they looked forward to visiting Mary's family in Lexington. It was her first visit home since 1839. Her father, Robert S.
Todd, had visited Springfield, but her stepmother, Elizabeth, and step-
brothers and -sisters, had never met her husband.

The Lincolns traveled from Springfield by stage to Alton, where
they boarded a packet steamboat to take them down the muddy waters
of the Mississippi past St. Louis. At Cairo, the southernmost tip of Illinois, they transferred to a river steamer to journey up the clearer waters
of the Ohio River. As the steamboat plowed north, with autumn colors
in view on both the Indiana and Kentucky shores, Lincoln may have
remembered his first trip on the Ohio thirty-one years before. He passed
Thompson's Landing where, as a nine-year-old boy, he and his family
disembarked in 1816 and began the trek to their new home at Pigeon
Creek. The four Lincolns continued by boat on the Kentucky River to
Frankfort, Kentucky, where they boarded the Lexington and Ohio

train, which consisted of a small steam locomotive and a solitary coach car, for the bumpy thirty-mile ride to Lexington. On November 2, 1847, a raw, windy day, the whole Todd family stood near the front of the brick mansion on West Main Street to greet them. Mary walked in first with little Eddie in her arms, followed by Abraham carrying four-year-old Bob.

The three-week sojourn in Lexington gave Lincoln plenty of opportunity to observe slavery once again. Every day he encountered it in the Todd household. Slave auctions were held at Cheapside in the center of Lexington most weeks. Lincoln also confronted the issue every time he picked up a Lexington newspaper. On November 3, 1847, the *Lexington Observer and Reporter* printed a notice:

NEGROES FOR SALE.

35 NEGROES IN LOTS TO SUIT PURCHASERS OR THE WHOLE, CONSISTING OF FIELD HANDS, HOUSE SERVANTS, A GOOD CARRIAGE-DRIVER, HOSTLERS, A BLACKSMITH, AND WOMEN & CHILDREN OF ALL DESCRIPTIONS.

James H. Farish

Lincoln would also have seen plenty of advertisements about runaway slaves. A reward of five hundred dollars was offered for the arrest of a forty-year-old slave named Joshua, "who is slow of speech, with a slight choking when agitated and who professes to be a preacher."

While in Lexington, Lincoln was afforded the singular opportunity to attend a political meeting organized by Mary's father featuring an address by Henry Clay. Lincoln had admired Clay for many years, but they had never met. His political vision was indebted to Clay's "American System" of economic advancement through internal improvements and fiscal accountability. How fortuitous to hear Clay, his political hero, discuss the vexing subjects of the war with Mexico and American slavery just weeks before Lincoln would take his seat in the Thirtieth Congress.

At age seventy, Clay evoked strongly mixed emotions among his political friends and foes. Some labeled him the "Star of the West," a courageous, brilliant, eloquent politician who had devoted his life to the noble cause of the Union. Others found Clay ambitious, ruthless, and a demagogue, whose silver voice was not to be believed, and who was tak-

Lincoln, stopping in Lexington, Kentucky, on his way to Washington, heard Clay deliver a fiery speech declaring his opposition to war with Mexico.

MR. CLAY TAKING A NEW VIEW OF THE TEXAS QUESTION.

ing power away from the states and giving it to the federal government. Despite his age and the counsel of friends, Clay was testing the waters for a fourth run for the presidency.

Clay began his speech by telling his Lexington audience that the day was "dark and gloomy, unsettled and uncertain," because of the "unnatural" war with Mexico. Clay's son, Henry, Jr., had been killed at the battle of Buena Vista the previous February. By the summer of 1847, the Mexican War had become a partisan issue, with most Whigs opposing it, and Democrats, appealing to a sense of Manifest Destiny and seeing it as an opportunity to extend slavery, supporting it. In vivid detail, Clay recounted the blunders and lies that had led to the "perils and dangers" the United States now faced.

He contrasted the war with Mexico with what he called "the British War" of 1812, arguing that the earlier war was defensive and "just," while the present engagement with Mexico was "no war of defense, but one unnecessary and of offensive aggression." Clay laid the blame at the feet of President Polk. The Kentucky senator rose to the height of his oratory in declaring that although Congress may have initially acquiesced in supporting the president's request to raise fifty thousand troops, "no earthly consideration would have ever tempted or provoked me to vote for a bill, with a palpable falsehood stamped on its face." He invoked the Constitution in urging the Congress to stand up and now resolve the proper purposes of the war.

In concluding, Clay asked his audience to join with him "to disavow, in the most positive manner, any desire, on our part, to acquire any foreign territory whatever, for the purpose of introducing slavery into it." He reiterated his "well known" beliefs about slavery. "I have ever regarded slavery as a great evil," but the slaves were here, and their future should be finally resolved "with a due consideration of all the circumstances affecting the security, safety, and happiness of both races."

THE LINCOLNS PREPARED TO LEAVE Lexington on Thanksgiving Day, November 25, 1847. In the morning they attended services in the new sanctuary of the Second Presbyterian Church. The guest preacher was Robert J. Breckenridge, a well-known Presbyterian minister and politician, "noted for his hostility to slavery." Breckenridge's opinions were printed regularly in the *Lexington Observer and Reporter,* but the words of the sermon that Lincoln heard on his final day in Lexington were not preserved.

In the afternoon, the Lincolns began their trip by stage, boat, and finally by train to Washington. They arrived in the nation's capital six days later on the evening of December 2, 1847. They went directly to Brown's Indian Queen Hotel, a marble-fronted moderately priced hotel on Pennsylvania Avenue. Lincoln registered his family as "A. Lincoln & Lady 2 children, Illinois."

They did not stay long at Brown's, soon moving into rooms at a boardinghouse operated by Ann Sprigg, a widow from Virginia. The boardinghouse was the fourth in a row of houses known as Carroll Row on East First Street between A and East Capitol streets, located where the Library of Congress stands today.

LINCOLN ARRIVED EAGER TO EXPLORE Washington, which had a population of more than thirty-five thousand, including nearly eight thousand slaves and two thousand free Negroes. It was only the thirteenth largest city in the nation. Many members of Congress lived in one of the new hotels in the downtown area, such as the United States and the

National. In 1847, shortly before the Lincolns arrived, the City Hotel, at the northwest corner of Pennsylvania Avenue and Fourteenth Street, had been remodeled by the brothers Edwin D. and Henry A. Willard. The new Willard Hotel quickly achieved the reputation as the finest hotel in Washington.

The national capital, not quite five decades old, remained an almost-city. Carriages rattled over the rough cobblestones of Pennsylvania Avenue, the main thoroughfare. Charles Dickens, visiting the United States five years earlier, had described Washington as "the City of Magnificent Intentions," with "spacious avenues, that begin in nothing, and lead nowhere; streets, mile-long, that only want houses, roads, and inhabitants; public buildings that need but a public to be complete." Pennsylvania Avenue was the lone street lit by oil lamps, and only when Congress was in session.

"Washington may be called the headquarters of tobacco tinctured saliva," wrote Dickens, appalled by the manners, especially the pervasiveness of chewing tobacco, of his American cousins. He described a scene where "several gentlemen called upon me who, in the course of the conversation, frequently missed the spittoon at five paces." More seriously, Dickens expressed his disgust at the slave pens and slave auctions in the nation's capital.

THE THIRTIETH CONGRESS of the United States convened on December 6, 1847, the customary first Monday of December. The Capitol was located directly across the street from Ann Sprigg's boardinghouse. Each day, Lincoln passed the colossal statue of George Washington by American sculptor Horatio Greenough in the eastern Capitol gardens. The controversial neoclassical statue, commissioned for the Capitol in 1832, had proved to be too heavy for its floor.

The House of Representatives met in a space south of the Rotunda that would become today's National Statuary Hall. The original chamber, burned by the British in 1814, had been rebuilt and reopened in 1819. A statue of Clio, the muse of history, stood above the entrance. The Hall appeared like an ancient Greek theater, with a richly draped Speaker's chair at the front. For all of its architectural beauty, the Hall, like the older chamber, was an acoustical nightmare. Not only was it hard to hear, but the lofty arched ceiling redirected speeches and conversations.

The Thirtieth Congress comprised 232 members, or only a little

*Abraham Lincoln arrived in Washington in December 1847, to be greeted
by this view of the Capitol, located directly across from Ann Sprigg's
boardinghouse, where he and Mary lived.*

more than half of the 435 members of today's House of Representatives. The national legislature represented a cross-section of a rapidly changing nation. Over half the members were, like Lincoln, serving their first term. Only two members in the whole House were over sixty-two.

On their second day in session, the representatives drew their seat locations by lot. The seats were arranged in six semicircular rows. Lincoln drew seat 191, placing him in the back row on the left, or Whig, side. Lincoln received appointments to two committees: Post Offices and Post Roads and the Expenditures of the War Department.

The House membership of the Thirtieth Congress included a few men who would play significant roles in the country's future political struggles. Joshua R. Giddings, a strapping six-foot-two-inch Whig from the Western Reserve of Ohio, led the radical antislavery forces in the House and would become a prominent abolitionist in the years before the Civil War. Democrat Andrew Johnson, six weeks older than Lincoln and his future vice president, represented Tennessee. Johnson voted against almost every government appropriation, including the painting of portraits of presidents, paving Washington's streets, and establishing the Smithsonian Institution, as well as all antislavery activity.

From the day he arrived, Horace Greeley, editor of the *New York Tribune,* began trying to reform the House, especially its penchant for waste and greed. The mileage paid to members for their travel to and from Congress was supposed to be computed according to the most direct route. Determined to take on the "mileage-elongators," Greeley published in the *Tribune* the monies received by each member. For just one session of Congress, Greeley calculated an excess of $47,223.80. Greeley's list revealed that Lincoln was one of the chief culprits. Congressman-elect Lincoln understood that he would be reimbursed for this trip to Washington at the amount of forty cents per mile. The shortest route from Springfield to Washington was 840 miles. Lincoln sent in a bill for 1,626 miles, almost twice the shortest route, and thereby collected $1,300.80 in reimbursement. Greeley published, for all to see, $676.80 as the excess amount received by Lincoln.

One Southerner especially caught Lincoln's eye and ear. Alexander H. Stephens, a Whig congressman from Georgia, introduced a resolution arguing against seizing Mexican territory. The war was "a wanton outrage upon the Constitution." In a blistering one-hour speech, Stephens attacked President Polk's policies as "dishonorable," "reckless," and

Lincoln was impressed with Alexander Stephens, a small Whig congressman from Georgia, after hearing him deliver a speech criticizing the war with Mexico.

"disgraceful." Young Charles Lanman, the future historian of Congress, was present in the House gallery for the first time and was captivated by the "wonderful earnestness" of Stephens's speech. But Lanman also said to a friend seated with him that he did not think the gaunt speaker "would live to finish his speech."

Lincoln, too, found himself deeply impressed with Stephens's speech. He wrote to "Billie Herndon," "Mr. Stephens of Georgia, a little slim, pale-faced, consumptive man, with a voice like Logan's, has just concluded the very best speech, of an hour's length, I ever heard." Lincoln, who always appreciated splendid oratory, concluded, "My old, withered, dry eyes, are full of tears yet."

Lincoln was eager to see the oldest and most distinguished member of Congress. John Quincy Adams was eighty when the Thirtieth Congress convened. Adams, son of the nation's second president, John Adams, was the only person to be elected to the House of Representatives after serving as president. He had defended the slave mutineers of the *Amistad* in 1839. In 1844, he finally achieved the removal of the "gag rule" that had long prevented the introduction of antislavery petitions. Adams had been feeble since a stroke in 1846, and Lincoln immediately sensed an aura of greatness about the ancient New England patriarch who would die shortly after Lincoln's arrival.

Although diligent in his attendance in the House, Lincoln sometimes

Lincoln was eager to see John Quincy Adams, former president and a member of the Thirtieth Congress.

crossed over to sit in the Senate gallery and listen to the speeches. He had heard Henry Clay, not presently in the Senate, in Lexington. Now he wanted to hear the other two giants of "the Great Triumvirate."

The first, Daniel Webster, born in 1782, had risen to fame in New England as a lawyer and a politician. Friends said he looked like a lion, a large man with a great head—"Godlike Daniel" some called him—with black hair and black eyes. He spoke with an eloquent voice that often prompted tears in his audience, as when he spoke in 1820 at the two hundredth anniversary of the landing of the Pilgrims at Plymouth Rock. Steeped in the Bible, Shakespeare, and Milton, Webster became a spokesman for the collective aspirations of first New England and then the Union. Lincoln was thoroughly familiar with Webster's 1830 Senate debate with South Carolina's Robert Hayne over states' rights and slavery: Webster had defended the Union with these famous words, "Liberty and Union, now and forever, one and inseparable."

The third member of the triumvirate, John C. Calhoun, was born two months after Webster, on March 18, 1782, on a flourishing farm in the red hills of South Carolina's up-country. He traveled eight hundred miles north to study at Yale College, graduating in 1804. Calhoun was an angular figure, whose age accentuated his pale face and submerged eyes; his graying hair stood straight up on his head. For the past four decades Calhoun had served in both the House and Senate, as secretary of war and secretary of state, and as vice president of the United States under Presidents John Quincy Adams and Andrew Jackson. Calhoun had earned a reputation as a "metaphysical" politician who approached issues theoretically. In the final session of the Twenty-ninth Congress, he presented a series of resolutions on slavery, and Lincoln may well have heard Calhoun speak of them during the Thirtieth Congress. Calhoun argued that Congress did not have the power to legislate on the presence of slavery in the new territories. To prevent citizens of Southern states to enter any of the territories with their property—slaves—would discriminate against the equality of the citizens of those states.

On December 12, 1847, Lincoln wrote Herndon telling him, "As soon as the Congressional Globe and Appendix [the official record of the proceedings of Congress], begins to issue, I shall send you a copy of it regularly." He asked his law partner "to preserve all the numbers so that we can have a complete file of it." The new congressman may have only been on the job one week, but he was already thinking of building his political files for the future.

Lincoln also took advantage of the free mailing privileges for members of Congress by sending to his constituents copies of many speeches. He sent out 7,080 copies of his own speeches, as well as 5,560 copies of speeches by other members, including Daniel Webster.

JOSHUA GIDDINGS, THE CONGRESSMAN FROM OHIO, used Ann Sprigg's boardinghouse as a place to bring antislavery congressmen together. In addition to Lincoln, eight other Whigs boarded there, including several leading abolitionists. Their presence guaranteed that slavery was a regular topic of conversation at meals. Lincoln had never before been around so many able politicians with such deep and earnest moral convictions about slavery.

Samuel C. Busey, a young medical doctor who took his meals at the boardinghouse, found himself intrigued with Lincoln's manner in conversations. Busey said that Lincoln would often interrupt tense conversations with an anecdote that had a healing effect on everyone, including the disputants. "When about to tell an anecdote during a meal he would lay down his knife and fork, place his elbows upon the table, rest his face between his hands, and begin with the words, 'that reminds me.' " As Lincoln began, "everybody prepared for the explosions sure to follow." Lincoln had the ability to influence "the tenor of the discussion" so that the parties engaged would either separate in good humor or continue the conversation free of discord. Dr. Busey recalled that Lincoln's "amicable disposition made him very popular with the household."

SPEECHES REMAINED AT the heart of the daily working of the House of Representatives in this sixth decade after the nation's founding. Both the House and Senate still retained a parliamentary ethos that would entirely disappear in the next century. Modern-day tourists, on their first visit to Congress, might be shocked to learn that a speaker often speaks to an empty chamber. In Lincoln's time, visitors lined up to hear such celebrated speakers as the Great Triumvirate orate grandly on the leading issues of the day. The best legislators were by common agreement the best speakers, persons who could persuade their colleagues in long, well-attended speeches.

Most congressmen and senators prepared their speeches carefully, spending hours and sometimes days writing and rewriting. But they never read their speeches. A contemporary observer reported, "They would have been laughed out of the House had they come into the hall with, and attempted to *read* a written speech." This was not a possibility. "These men met each other face to face," speaking with eloquence and passion.

Good speaking and good listening, however, did not always go together. Maria Horsford, the wife of New York Whig congressman Jerediah Horsford, in writing home to her children, described the high intensity and noise of the House chamber. "The confusion and noise of the House of Representatives is wearying. . . . I never saw a district school dismissed at noon so rude and noisy . . . more like a hundred swarms of bees." The noise was continually punctuated by cries of "Speaker"—"Speaker"—"Speaker" in voices rising "higher and higher."

On the second day of the session, President Polk delivered his third annual message to Congress, the vast majority of it dealing with the war with Mexico. Calling the United States "the aggrieved nation," Polk claimed, "History presents no parallel of so many glorious victories achieved by any nation within so short a period." Indeed, by the time Lincoln heard Polk's message, the fighting was all but over. General Zachary Taylor had won victories at Palo Alto, Resaca de la Palma, and Monterrey, and fought off a Mexican attack at Buena Vista in February 1847. General Winfield Scott had led an expedition of ten thousand U.S. soldiers to capture Veracruz and then led an assault on the capital, Mexico City, securing the surrender of the Mexican defenders on September 14, 1847.

Polk came to Congress seeking ratification of his plan to demand that Mexico pay the United States an indemnity in a cession "of a portion of her territory." The president appealed to the Louisiana Purchase of 1803 and the cession of Florida of 1819 as precedents. He rejected the attacks of critics who said that the United States should take the high moral ground of accepting no territory. Polk replied, "The doctrine of no territory is the doctrine of no indemnity . . . and if sanctioned would be a public acknowledgment that our country was wrong and that the war declared by Congress with extraordinary unanimity was unjust and should be abandoned—an admission unfounded in fact and degrading to the national character."

Freshmen congressmen sometimes struggled to find their speaking voices in the new terrain of the nation's capital. But Lincoln, only one week after he took his seat in the Thirtieth Congress, wrote a third time to Herndon, declaring, "As you are all so anxious for me to distinguish myself, I have concluded to do so, before long."

Two weeks after Polk's annual message, on December 22, 1847, Lincoln rose to introduce a series of eight resolutions asking the president to inform the House about specific actions of the United States. Lincoln's speech began by using direct quotes from President Polk's message to Congress of May 11, 1846, and his annual message to Congress in December 1846 and 1847. Lincoln's purpose was to challenge the president's veracity. The burden of the first-term congressman's remarks was contained in his preface to the resolutions: "This House desires to obtain a full knowledge of all the facts which to establish whether the particular spot of soil on which the blood of our *citizens* was so shed, was, or was not, *our own soil,* at that time." Lincoln was directly challenging the president's assertion that the Mexicans fired the first shot in the war. He used the word "spot" again in the first resolution, as well as in the second and in the third, driving home his point that the spot was not on our soil but actually on the soil of Mexico, thus making the United States the initial aggressor. Lincoln's resolutions were not remarkable, offering a summary of objections that had been heard by other Whigs in the hallways of Washington and in newspapers throughout the country. But because of Lincoln's use of the innocuous word "spot," the challenges would become known as the "spotty" resolutions. He was only getting started.

THE WHIGS' ATTACKS on "Mr. Polk's War" resumed in the new year. On January 3, 1848, in the course of a debate on a resolution offering thanks to General Taylor, Congressman George Ashmun of Massachusetts proposed an amendment stating that the war with Mexico had been "unnecessarily and unconstitutionally begun by the President of the United States." The amendment received the votes of eighty-five Whigs, including Lincoln.

Nine days later, Lincoln rose again, this time to speak to the broader implications of the war. In a thoroughly prepared speech, Lincoln articulated the difference between supporting the troops and supporting the president and his policies. He stated that back in May 1846, he believed that whatever concerns there might be about the constitutionality or necessity of the war, "as citizens and patriots," persons should "remain

Lincoln challenged President Polk's assertion that Mexican troops fired the first shot in the war with Mexico. Lincoln demanded to know whether the particular "spot of soil" where the blood was shed was in the United States.

silent on that point, at least until the war had ended." He said he continued to hold this view until he took his seat in Congress and heard President Polk "argue every silent vote given for supplies, into an endorsement of the justice and wisdom of his conduct."

Lincoln told the House that he had examined all of the president's messages to see if Polk's assertions about precedents measured up to the truth. "Now I propose to show, that the whole of this,—issue and evidence—is, from the beginning to end, the sheerest deception." After analyzing six propositions of the president's evidence, Lincoln offered his own precedent. "Let him answer with *facts,* and not with arguments. Let him remember he sits where Washington sat, and so remembering, let him answer as Washington would answer." In the heat of a present-day controversy, Lincoln found it useful to appeal to the founding fathers.

In escalating rhetoric, Lincoln went on to question both Polk's motives and conscience. "I more than suspect already, that he is deeply conscious of being in the wrong—that he feels the blood of this war, like the blood of Abel, is crying to Heaven against him." Lincoln concluded with a final pummel. President Polk "is a bewildered, confounded, and miserably perplexed man," he said. Lincoln's strong words against the sitting president spread quickly beyond the nation's capital.

BACK IN ILLINOIS, Lincoln's forceful assault on President Polk took Lincoln's friends and foes by surprise. Yes, many Whigs were against the war, but after Lincoln's speech many people in his district came to believe his words bordered on treason. Illinoisans, proud of the effort of the American troops, resented what they said was Lincoln's failure to support them.

From so long a distance, Lincoln's votes were misrepresented by his local opponents and misunderstood by many of his friends. Lincoln went on to vote yes on all bills to fund the troops and their supplies. On January 12, 1848, he gave a speech meant to show that one could support the troops and not the president, a distinction difficult to communicate in a time of patriotic fever.

The Democratic *Illinois State Register* in Springfield tore into Lincoln. "Thank heaven, Illinois has eight representatives who will stand by the honor of the nation." Recalling the military heroism of Illinois soldiers, the *Register* said of Lincoln, "He will have a fearful account to settle with them, should he lend his aid in an effort to neutralize their efforts and blast their fame." The *Register* printed what they hoped would be Lincoln's political epitaph: "Died of Spotted Fever."

Even Billy Herndon expressed concern about his law partner's vote for the Ashmun Amendment, firing off a letter on January 19, 1848. Lincoln replied immediately, "If you misunderstand, I fear other friends will also." Lincoln told Herndon, "I will stake my life, that if you had been in my place, you would have voted just as I did." He asked Herndon, "Would you have voted what you felt you knew to be a lie?"

What really upset Lincoln was the way Polk and the Democrats shrewdly tried to conflate support for the war and voting to send supplies for the troops. "I have always intended, and still intend, to vote supplies," Lincoln told Herndon. The Democrats, he said, "are untiring in their effort to make the impression that all who vote supplies . . . of necessity, approve the President's conduct in the beginning of it." The Whig position, as Lincoln explained, "from the beginning, made and kept the distinction between the two."

Herndon wrote a second letter and Lincoln replied again. It was obvious now that the partners did not agree on whether any president becomes the "*sole* judge" in initiating war. Lincoln defended the "provision of the Constitution giving war-making power to Congress." He told Herndon, "Allow the President to invade a neighboring nation, whenever *he* shall deem it necessary to repel an invasion, and you allow him to do so, *whenever he may choose to say* he deems it necessary for such purpose—and you allow him to make war at pleasure."

IN MARCH 1848, Lincoln's curiosity about his ancestors in America became jogged by correspondence from a long-lost relative named Solomon Lincoln. In replying to a letter of inquiry from Solomon Lincoln, Lincoln wrote, "We have a vague tradition, that my great-grandfather, John Lincoln, went from Pennsylvania to Virginia; and that he was a quaker. Further back than that, I have never heard anything." His curiosity aroused, Lincoln decided to ask James McDowell, the former governor of Virginia and now a colleague in the House, "whether he knew persons of our name there." McDowell replied he did know of a David Lincoln. Lincoln wrote a second letter to Solomon Lincoln three weeks later telling him of this new discovery.

Lincoln, "much gratified," received a letter from David Lincoln on March 30, 1848. He quickly replied, "There is no longer any doubt that your uncle Abraham, and my grandfather was the same man." Lincoln peppered David Lincoln with questions. "Was he or not, a Quaker? About what *time* did he emigrate from Berks count, Pa. to Virginia? Do you know any thing of your family (or rather I may now say, *our* family) farther back than your grandfather?" Far from being uninterested in his family background, Lincoln wanted to find out more. Ironically,

Solomon Lincoln wrote to Abraham Lincoln from Hingham, Massachusetts, where Lincoln's ancestors first settled in America—a fact that Abraham Lincoln would never know.

IN THE SPRING OF 1848, Mary Lincoln and their boys left Washington and returned to Lexington. She had grown weary of her confinement in Ann Sprigg's boardinghouse, where much of the time she found herself alone with her two small children. Lincoln attended sessions of Congress during the day and often spent his evenings in Whig caucuses.

The correspondence between Abraham and Mary from the spring of 1848—some of the few letters between them that have survived—reveals how their affection grew stronger in absence. Lincoln wrote on April 16, 1848, "In this troublesome world, we are never quite satisfied. When you were here, I thought you hindered me in attending to business but now, having nothing but business—no vanity—it has grown exceedingly tasteless to me." Lincoln admitted, "I hate to stay in the old room by myself." He wanted to include a greeting from others, but remembered that not everyone at Ann Sprigg's thought kindly of her, so he wrote, "All the house—or rather all with whom you were on decided good terms—send their love to you. The others say nothing." He also asked Mary, in the future, "Suppose you do not prefix the "Hon" to the address on your letters to me any more."

Mary wrote in May telling Abraham that she wanted to return to Washington to be with him. He replied, playfully, "Will you be a *good girl* in all things, if I consent?" This was undoubtedly another reference to her behavior with other guests at the boardinghouse. "Then come along, and that as *soon* as possible. Having got the idea in my head, I shall be impatient till I see you."

The correspondence between Abraham and Mary, in the sixth year of their marriage, brings to light both the depth of their love and the difficulties in their relationship. Lincoln, as was often his way, gently teased Mary about her strained relations with some of the boarders, but his comments also hint at tensions between them. Mary, pretty and perky, could also be difficult and demanding.

WITH MARY AND the two boys gone, Lincoln had more time to continue his self-education. He attended sessions of the U.S. Supreme Court, hearing Daniel Webster argue a case before the highest court in the land. He certainly got a glimpse of Roger B. Taney of Maryland, who in 1836 had been appointed by President Andrew Jackson to replace the legendary John Marshall as chief justice of the United States.

Lincoln frequently walked across the street from the boardinghouse to the Library of Congress. The Library began in 1800 when the capital moved from Philadelphia to Washington. During the War of 1812, when the British burned the Capitol, they used books from the Library of Congress to kindle the inferno. The Library began to rebuild itself when former president Thomas Jefferson offered his private library to Congress. After partisan wrangling, Jefferson's offer was accepted and Congress purchased his library of 6,487 volumes for $23,950. The books were transported by wagons from Monticello to Washington. The fledgling Library continued in its temporary quarters until August 1824, the last year of James Monroe's presidency, when it moved into its new home in the center of the west front of the Capitol.

Twenty-three years later, Abraham Lincoln became one of the Library of Congress's most active borrowers. Where the new congressman spent his free time became "a puzzle, and a subject of amusement" to his fellow representatives. They observed, "He did not drink, or use tobacco, or bet, or swear." What Lincoln was doing was "mousing among the books" at the Library. Lincoln often selected books to take to his room at the boardinghouse, wrapping them in a bandana, placing a stick in the knot, and transporting them over his shoulder. To his fellow congressmen, whatever else they thought of Lincoln, many were convinced: "He is a bookworm!"

THERE WAS A presidential election in 1848, and in June Lincoln attended the Whig convention in the Chinese Museum Hall in Philadelphia. The contest pitted Henry Clay against General Zachary Taylor. Intellectually, Lincoln leaned toward Clay and his ideas, but he supported Taylor for a strictly pragmatic reason: The Whigs needed to win. The Whigs took a page from the Democrats, who had nominated General Andrew Jackson in 1828 and 1832, and nominated their own military hero, General Zachary Taylor, as their presidential candidate in 1848.

Taylor, a down-home fellow known as "Old Rough and Ready," had served in the military for forty years. He was best known for leading his troops to an unlikely victory at the desperate battle of Buena Vista in the Mexican War. He did not write or speak well and was woefully ignorant of foreign affairs. The Whigs hoped that Taylor, a strong

Lincoln made the pragmatic decision to back General Zachary Taylor, a hero of the Mexican War, over Henry Clay in the 1848 presidential election.

nationalist, could appeal to their Northern constituents because of his experience in the military. At the same time, they hoped he would also draw in Southerners because he was from Louisiana and owned a plantation with one hundred slaves in Mississippi.

Taylor's nomination allowed Lincoln and other young Whigs in the House to continue to attack the Democrats for beginning an unjust war, but at the same time extol one of the generals responsible for winning it. Taylor's political record was nonexistent, but he offered the hope of electability. "I am in favor of Gen: Taylor as the whig candidate for the Presidency because I am satisfied we can elect him, that he would give us a whig administration, and that we can not elect any other whig." The other Whig, unnamed, was Henry Clay. Lincoln said as much in a letter to a friend in Illinois: "Our only chance is with Taylor. I go for him, not because I think he would make a better president than Clay, but because I think he would make a better one than Polk, or Cass, or Buchanan." In 1848, Lincoln's political pragmatism triumphed over his idealism.

The Democrats nominated Lewis Cass of Michigan. Cass had fought in the War of 1812, had been secretary of war in the Jackson administration, and was serving as U.S. senator from Michigan. On the slavery issue, Cass favored what he called "popular sovereignty," letting the residents of each of the new territories decide whether they wanted slavery or not.

A third antislavery party, the Free Soil Party, emerged in 1847–48 as a protest to both Cass, who they feared would allow "squatter sovereignty" in the territories, and to Taylor, a slave owner. The Free Soil Party nominated former president Martin Van Buren as their candidate in 1848. This loose coalition of former Liberty Party men, plus antislavery Whigs and Democrats, campaigned on the slogan "Free soil, free speech, free labor, free men."

As the long, hot summer term of Congress wound down, presidential politicking warmed up. Presidential campaigning in the early nineteenth century was largely the work of surrogates. Most Americans thought it unseemly for candidates to speak on their own behalf. Before the Thirtieth Congress adjourned, the candidates' supporters took to the floor to give their best political orations. On July 27, 1848, Lincoln found himself speaking eighth behind three Democrats and four Whigs in the House before a packed gallery. After hours and hours of speeches, how could Lincoln stand out?

He decided to turn the Cass criticism of Taylor against their man. The Democratic speakers that day had complained that they did not know either the principles or policies of General Taylor. Lincoln answered by giving an exposition of Whig principles—tariff, currency, and internal improvements. But Democrats contended that the Whigs had deserted all of their principles and taken refuge under General Taylor's military armor. Lincoln could smell an opening.

What about the military coattail of General Jackson? "Like a horde of hungry ticks you have stuck to the tail of the Hermitage lion to the end of his life." Part of Cass's reputation was his military exploits in the War of 1812. As Lincoln zeroed in on Cass, he exclaimed, "You democrats are now engaged in dovetailing onto the great Michigander . . . tying him to a military tail."

Lincoln now raised suspicions about Cass's war record by presenting a self-deprecating recital of his own military record. "By the way, Mr. Speaker, did you know that I am a military hero?" Lincoln captivated his listeners by declaring, "Yes, sir; in the days of the Black Hawk war, I fought, bled, and came away." By now it was clear that he was mocking Cass's military career. "Speaking of Gen: Cass' career, reminds me of my own." Lincoln spoke satirically with a set of derisive comparisons about battles, weapons, and enemies, all meant to say that Cass saw no more action than Lincoln did. Finally, in sardonic humor, Lincoln told his colleagues, now convulsed in laughter, "If he saw any live, fighting

Indians, it was more than I did; but I had a good many bloody struggles with musquetoes."

Reporting on Lincoln's speech, the *Baltimore American* described his power to mesmerize an audience. Lincoln "was so good natured, and his style so peculiar, that he kept the House in a continuous roar of merriment." Lincoln's mannerisms caught the eye of the reporter as it did that of his fellow congressmen. "He would commence a point in his speech far up one of the aisles, and keep on talking, gesticulating, and walking until he would find himself, at the end of a paragraph, down in the center of the area in front of the speaker's desk. He would then go back and take another *bead,* and work down again." Lincoln, perhaps feeling more at home, offered an old-fashioned Illinois stump speech in the well of the House of Representatives.

MARY, BOB, AND EDDIE returned to Washington at the end of July, finding husband and father busily engaged in the last two weeks of the first session of Congress. After an all-night meeting on August 13, 1848, Congress adjourned for the summer. Lincoln decided to spend the recess working for Taylor's election.

In early September, with a basic stump speech in hand, Lincoln left Washington with his family for a campaign tour in Massachusetts. The Bay State had been a Whig stronghold, led by such giants as Daniel Webster and Rufus Choate, but lately Whig unity and dominance was fracturing. Many members, outraged about the lack of progress on the issue of slavery, were joining the emerging Free Soil Party just as the 1848 presidential campaign got into full swing. By the middle of the 1840s, two groups of New England Whigs had fallen into dispute. "Conscience Whigs" saw the battle over slavery as a moral struggle; "Cotton Whigs," while admitting the evils of slavery, nevertheless did not want to completely alienate the South, whose cotton was needed in New England's textile mills. As Lincoln prepared to speak in Massachusetts, he knew many Massachusetts Whigs were deeply upset that the Whig presidential candidate, General Taylor, owned slaves in Louisiana.

Lincoln arrived in Worcester on Tuesday, September 12, 1848, the eve of the Whig state convention. Andrew Bullock, a local Whig politician, was planning a public rally for the evening but all of the speakers had declined his invitation to speak. Hearing that the Illinois congressman was in Worcester, he found Lincoln at the Worcester House and asked him to address the rally. That evening at 7 p.m., Lincoln, dressed in a long linen duster, arrived at the city hall to find more than one thousand people crammed inside. The chairman of the meeting introduced Lincoln as a "Free Soil Whig," which he did not deny.

Dusting off the speech he gave in the Congress in July, Lincoln spoke for two hours. He had two main goals in mind. First, he wanted to assure the audience that Taylor did embody Whig values. Second, Lincoln drove home the point that Van Buren, the Free Soil candidate, could not win the election; a vote for Van Buren would end up being a vote for the Democratic candidate Cass. Lincoln had vowed never to forget the lesson of the presidential campaign of 1844, that moral purity can be self-defeating if it opens the door to political defeat. The *Springfield* (Massachusetts) *Republican* reported that the audience "frequently interrupted" Lincoln "by loud cheering." The *Boston Daily Advertiser* was impressed with his initial speech. "Mr. Lincoln has a very tall and thin figure, with an intellectual face, showing a searching mind, and a cool judgment." The Whig newspaper called Lincoln's oration a "truly masterly and convincing speech."

Three days later, Lincoln arrived by train in Boston. The different districts in this city of 130,000 were connected not by horsecars but by a number of stagecoach lines. Used to rude hostelries in central Illinois, Lincoln and his family enjoyed their stay at the stylish Tremont House.

In succeeding days, Lincoln traveled by train to speak in Lowell, Dorchester, Chelsea, Dedham, Cambridge, and Taunton. On Thursday evening, September 21, 1848, Lincoln addressed the Union Hall in Taunton, a city humming with industrialization. A Taunton Whig newspaper, the *Old Colony Republican,* captured the dynamism of Lincoln as a public speaker and described the way Lincoln "advanced upon his hearers."

> It was an altogether new show for us—a western stump speaker. . . . Leaning himself up against the wall, as he commenced, and talking in the plainest manner, and in the most indifferent tone, yet gradually fixing his footing, and getting command of his limbs, loosening his tongue, and firing up his thoughts, until he had got possession of himself and of his audience.

The content of Lincoln's speech struck the reporter as even more distinctive. "Argument and anecdote, wit and wisdom, hymns and prophecies, platforms and syllogisms, came flying before the audience like wild game before the fierce hunter of the prairie." The reporter concluded, "There has been no gathering of any party in a region where the responses of the audience were so frequent and so vigorous."

The climax of his speaking tour was a giant Whig open-air rally in the evening in Boston. The main speaker for the evening was not Lincoln, but William H. Seward. A former governor of New York, the slender Seward had been elected to the Senate in 1848 and spoke in Boston as an established leader in the antislavery movement. Seward gave a formal address, arguing that a third Free Soil Party, however well intentioned in their ideas, could only draw away votes from the Whigs and help elect Democrats who would do nothing to stop the spread of slavery.

Seward gave such a lengthy speech that by the time Lincoln was introduced, it was already 9:30. But Lincoln was not about to cut short his remarks. He spoke for a full hour, the *Boston Courier* reporting that Lincoln spoke "in a most forcible and convincing speech, which drew down thunders of applause." The next evening Lincoln and Seward, who would go on to become Lincoln's secretary of state, shared a room in Worcester. Seward recalled, "We spent the greater part of the night talking about anti-slavery positions and principles." Lincoln told Seward, "I have been thinking about what you said in your speech. I reckon you are right. We have got to deal with this slavery question, and got to give much more attention to it hereafter than we have been doing."

WITH HIS SPEAKING obligations in New England completed, Lincoln and his family finally started for home. He stopped in Albany, New York, to meet Millard Fillmore, the Whig vice presidential candidate, and Thurlow Weed, founder of the *Albany Evening Journal* and a close friend of Seward's. In Buffalo, the Lincolns took a boat trip to see Niagara Falls. Lincoln was "overwhelmed in the contemplation of the vast power the sun is constantly exerting in quiet, noiseless operation of lifting water *up* to be rained *down* again." He wrote some notes about this experience, thinking of turning it into an essay. "It calls up the indefinite past. When Columbus first sought this continent—when Christ suffered on the cross—when Moses led Israel through the Red Sea—nay, even when Adam first came from the hand of his Maker—then as now, Niagara was roaring here."

The Lincolns traveled on the steamer *Globe* from Buffalo to Chicago, covering the 1,047 miles in the astounding time of sixty hours. During the voyage, the ship became stranded on a sandbar. The captain called for the hands to collect loose planks and empty casks and barrels and try to force them under the boat to help lift it off the sandbar. Lincoln observed this operation closely, perhaps remembering similar problems in navigating the Sangamon and the Mississippi.

On October 10, 1848, the Lincolns finally arrived home in Springfield. Lincoln quickly learned that many of his constituents held him in disfavor. While campaigning for Taylor in the Seventh District, Lincoln found himself criticized for opposing President Polk on the war with Mexico. The *Illinois State Register* wrote, "Lincoln has made nothing by coming to this part of the country to make speeches. He had better have stayed away." Nevertheless, on Election Day, November 7, Lincoln joined the cheering in his hometown when Taylor won the presidency, carrying the Seventh District by nearly fifteen hundred votes.

IN LATE NOVEMBER Lincoln left Springfield to return to Washington for the final, short, session of the Thirtieth Congress, reporting "present" on Saturday, December 7, 1848.

The rump session would be dominated by rancorous debates on slavery, both about the territories and in the nation's capital. Lincoln had been largely silent during the debates over slavery in the first session, but he returned to Washington determined to offer a compromise measure. Twelve years earlier, in the Illinois legislature, Lincoln had advocated the abolition of slavery in the nation's capital, but only with the approval of Washington's citizens. He now wrote a proposal in the same spirit. Lincoln showed it to Joshua Giddings on January 8, 1849, who encouraged him to go forward even though the abolitionist Ohio congressman disapproved of the feature of compensation for the owners of slaves.

Lincoln stood on January 10 to announce his intention to present a bill in his final session in the House. Lincoln aimed for conciliation in a bitterly divided Congress. On the one hand his bill would allow officers of slaveholding states to bring their slaves to the nation's capital while on government business. Lincoln's bill also allowed for the arrest of fugitive slaves who might escape into the District. But Lincoln was clear in his first and main point: "No person within the District shall ever be held in slavery within it."

The next evening, at Mrs. Spriggs's boarding house, the Whig boarders remained after dinner to discuss Lincoln's bill. Giddings wrote

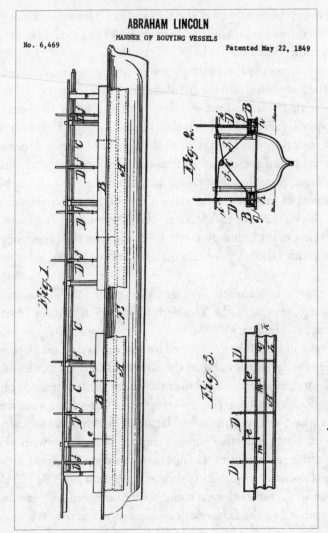

ABRAHAM LINCOLN
MANNER OF BOUYING VESSELS
No. 6,469   Patented May 22, 1849

In March 1849, Lincoln applied for a patent in Washington for his invention to help lift boats over sandbars or shoals.

in his diary of Lincoln's proposal: "I believed it as good a bill as we could get at this time."

On January 12, Lincoln intended to introduce his bill but ultimately did not. In a matter of days he discovered that support for his compromise measure had dried up and his bill never made it into the hopper, the wooden box near the Speaker's desk in which all new bills were deposited before being printed for consideration by committees. In speaking of what Lincoln hoped would be the results of compensated emancipation, he crafted language ("such slaves shall be forever free") that he would revisit at a future time.

ON FEBRUARY 12, 1849, Congressman Abraham Lincoln turned forty. Three weeks later, the Thirtieth Congress worked all night to conclude its business, finally adjourning at 7 a.m. on Sunday, March 4. On Monday, March 5, a gray cloudy day, Lincoln attended the inauguration of President Zachary Taylor.

Two days later, Lincoln argued his first and only case before the U.S. Supreme Court. While in Congress he had watched cases argued, but now he had the delight of standing before the nine black-robed justices. On March 7, 1849, Lincoln argued *Lewis for use of Longworth v. Lewis,* referred to the high court from the U.S. Circuit Court in Illinois, which involved a disputed meaning of a statute of limitations. On March 13, 1849, Chief Justice Roger Taney ruled against Lincoln's plea.

Three days later, Lincoln applied for a patent, the only president ever to do so. Lincoln had long had an engineer's curiosity about mechanical appliances. When staying with a farmer while traveling on the circuit, he delighted in getting down on the ground and inspecting from every angle a new farm implement. The impetus for this patent grew from his experience on his trip home the previous October, when his boat became stuck on a sandbar. Once back in Springfield, Lincoln built a scale model of his invention with help from Walter Davis, a mechanic with an office near Lincoln's law office. In his application for a patent, Lincoln stated he had "invented a new and improved manner of combining adjustable buoyant air chambers with a steam boat or other vessel for the purpose of enabling their draught of water to be readily lessened to enable them to pass over bars, or through shallow water, without discharging their cargoes."

Lincoln was pleased with his new patent, but ship owners did not flock to use it. Herndon, always a bit skeptical about his partner's idealistic schemes, reported that "the threatened revolution in steamboat architecture and navigation never came to pass."

Lincoln remained in Washington working tirelessly on political patronage and taking part in speaking engagements in cities near Washington. He advocated a number of claims for fellow Illinois citizens with the new administration. As the only Whig congressman from Illinois, he viewed these patronage opportunities as ways to strengthen the

Whig Party. Lincoln wrote many letters recommending everyone from Edward Baker for a place in the cabinet to many friends in Illinois for local offices. Despite his efforts, Lincoln bemoaned, "Not one man recommended by me has yet been appointed to any thing, little or big, except a few who had no opposition."

The leading patronage office in Illinois was the commissioner of the General Land Office, land being the key commodity in the West. The position offered a salary of three thousand dollars per year. Initially, Lincoln lobbied for Cyrus Edwards, brother of Ninian Edwards. But Lincoln's friend Edward Baker, now a member of Congress from Galena, had his own candidate, Don Morrison. Neither the candidates nor the sponsors could agree to compromise. Some of Lincoln's friends suggested that he himself become the compromise candidate, but he declined. "I must not only be chaste but above suspicion."

Finally, on March 20, 1849, Lincoln started the arduous trip home to Illinois. A chastened Lincoln arrived in Springfield on Saturday evening, March 31. His return was not greeted with the well wishes of the press and public with which he had left for Washington only sixteen months earlier. The Whigs, adhering to the rotation system, had run Lincoln's former law partner Stephen Logan for Congress, but he had suffered a narrow defeat in his effort to become the fourth consecutive Whig to represent the Seventh Congressional District. Lincoln received plenty of blame for the defeat. Democrats murmured that Lincoln had provided "aid and comfort to the enemy." Wiser pundits recognized that Logan's crusty manner and lack of speaking ability did not measure up to that of Lincoln and the previous Whig candidates.

The deadlock for the Land Office position threatened to be broken when another candidate suddenly entered the contest. Justin Butterfield, a prominent Chicago attorney and ardent supporter of Clay, had contested the presidential campaign of Zachary Taylor to the end, and had not worked to build up the Whig Party in Illinois. Lincoln wondered aloud why he should now receive this patronage plum. "He is my personal friend, and is qualified to do the duties of the office but of the one hundred Illinoisians, equally well qualified, I do not know of one with less claims to it."

Learning that Butterfield was Secretary of the Interior Thomas Ewing's probable choice, and upset by the cumulative evidence that Taylor supporters were not receiving their deserved patronage positions, Lincoln decided to pursue the position for himself. He quickly orchestrated a letter-writing campaign by his friends to Secretary Ewing, even asking Mary to write letters to supporters on his behalf. He also tried to go around Ewing and appeal directly to President Taylor. But unknown to Lincoln, several Whigs in Springfield had written to Secretary Ewing criticizing Lincoln for his speech in Congress against the Mexican War, "which inflicted a deep and mischievous wound upon the Whole Whig party of the state."

On June 10, 1849, Lincoln rushed back to Washington to lobby for the job, believing that letters sent to Ewing had somehow been withheld from President Taylor. He arrived on June 19 only to learn two days later that Taylor had followed Secretary Ewing's recommendation and appointed Butterfield. Lincoln was devastated.

When Lincoln returned to Springfield he wrote Ewing, "I opposed the appointment of Mr. B because I believed it would be a matter of discouragement to our active, working friends here, and I opposed it for no other reason." He told the secretary of the interior, "I never did, in any true sense, want the job for myself."

In August 1849, Lincoln was offered a second-place prize: secretary of the Oregon Territory. He quickly wrote to Secretary of State John M. Clayton to decline the office. In September, Secretary Ewing offered him the governorship of Oregon. He took some time to consider this offer, which Mary argued against. Lincoln recognized the future power of the states forming in the Far West, but he also knew that Oregon was at that moment in the hands of Democrats, and thus he saw little future there for a Whig politician. He believed the office would mean political exile. He declined the position.

LINCOLN HAD CAMPAIGNED for the Illinois legislature by vowing to be a legislator who would faithfully advocate the beliefs and opinions of the people he represented; he was now criticized for taking a position on the Mexican War that was unrepresentative of the beliefs of the people of his district. Secretary of State Clayton and Secretary of the Interior Ewing had offered him positions he did not want and refused to give him the one position he would have accepted. Herndon would say later that when Lincoln returned to Springfield, he "determined to eschew politics from that time forward and devote himself entirely to the law."

CHAPTER 10

As a Peacemaker the Lawyer
Has a Superior Opportunity
1849–52

PERSUADE YOUR NEIGHBORS TO COMPROMISE WHENEVER YOU CAN.

ABRAHAM LINCOLN
Notes for a Law Lecture ca. July 1, 1850

BRAHAM LINCOLN RETURNED TO ILLINOIS IN THE SPRING OF 1849, his single term in Congress ended by his principled but unpopular stand against the Mexican War. His only career option was to resume practicing law. Ever since 1832, when he made his first unsuccessful run for the state legislature, Lincoln had been campaigning for political office. With time now to devote to his law firm, Lincoln hoped to increase its reputation and boost his income to better support Mary and their two boys. Grant Goodrich invited him to Chicago for what might have become a lucrative law partnership, but Lincoln replied, "If [I] went to Chicago then [I] would have to sit down and Study hard—That would kill [me]." Lincoln preferred the kind of law he could practice in the federal and superior courts in Springfield, as well as the small rural communities of central Illinois's Eighth Judicial Circuit. Years later, Lincoln would recall, "From 1849 to 1854, both inclusive, [I] practiced law more assiduously than ever before."

William Herndon had kept the firm busy during Lincoln's time in Washington. From 1847 to 1849, Herndon used a fee book in which there was a heading: "These cases attended to since Lincoln went to Congress." Herndon offered to share with his senior partner the fees collected for these cases, but Lincoln refused, saying that he had no right to any of these monies.

After his failed political career, Lincoln often pondered the question of the purpose and meaning of his life. In 1850, Lincoln told Herndon, "How hard, oh how hard it is to die and leave one's country no better than if one had never lived." Herndon noticed the marked effect the downturn in his political fortunes had upon Lincoln in these years. "It went below the skin and made a changed man of him."

As Lincoln returned to the practice of law, he determined to continue his self-education. He looked forward to traveling alone for hours, or even a whole day, on the open prairies, well-worn editions of Shakespeare and the Bible as his traveling companions. He found mental refreshment in the poetry of Lord Byron and Robert Burns, whose rhyming stanzas he always read aloud. At the end of each carnival-like day in court, Lincoln always found time for solitude and reflection.

As Lincoln traveled the vast physical territory of the circuit, he ventured into new intellectual territory. He bought a copy of Euclid's *Elements* and set himself the task of memorizing the Greek mathematician's six geometrical theorems. He would often study by candlelight late at night while his fellow lawyers slept.

Lincoln's reading offered him the opportunity to go deeper into his own spirit and broader into the land of imagination. From 1849 to 1854, Lincoln would cultivate a profound interior life.

FOR MUCH OF 1849, Lincoln walked the nearly seven blocks from his home to his office in Springfield every day, sometimes arriving as early as 7 a.m. For a Whig committed to order, Lincoln kept his law office mostly in disorder. The floor was never clean. John H. Littlefield, who studied law with Lincoln during this time, discovered while attempting to clean the office that a variety of discarded fruit seeds had sprouted in the dirt and dust. Attorney Henry C. Whitney described the windows in Lincoln's office as "innocent of water and the scrubman since creation's dawn or the settlement of Springfield."

When Lincoln arrived at his office, he immediately stretched out on the worn leather couch, the central piece of furniture in the room. It was too small for his large frame, so he would put one foot on a chair and the other on a table nearby. Once positioned, Lincoln began to read the newspapers—always out loud, no matter who was present. Lincoln's reading aloud annoyed Herndon. Once, when Herndon asked his senior partner why he read aloud, Lincoln answered, "When I read aloud two senses catch the idea: first, I see what I read; second, I hear it, and therefore I can remember it better."

Both Lincoln and Herndon read newspapers insatiably. After returning from Washington, Lincoln subscribed to the *New York Tribune,* Horace Greeley's influential national newspaper; Washington's *National Intelligencer,* the great Whig newspaper; and the *Chicago Tribune,* founded in 1847, which advocated a Whig and Free Soil opinion on slavery. Herndon encouraged Lincoln to subscribe to several leading antislavery papers as well, including the *Anti-Slavery Standard,* the official weekly newspaper of the American Anti-Slavery Society; and the *National Era,* a weekly abolitionist paper published out of Washington.

Sometimes, when Herndon pressed his antislavery views upon Lincoln, the senior partner would counter that it was important to hear the Southern side as well. As Lincoln struggled with the issue of slavery, he wanted to consider all points of view. Out of these exchanges, Lincoln decided to subscribe to several Southern newspapers. The *Richmond Enquirer* set the standard in Southern journalism and had become a leading voice in the surge toward secession. The *Charleston Mercury* espoused a fierce pro-slavery position and regularly let loose journalistic attacks on the North, especially abolitionists. These divergent newspapers became instruments for Lincoln's thinking and brooding about slavery. "Let us have both sides at the table," Lincoln told Herndon. "Each is entitled to its day in court."

Lincoln delegated some of his legal research to Herndon, but the senior partner always wrote out his own pleadings. He had written many when he worked as a junior partner with John Todd Stuart, but nearly all of the pleadings for the Logan and Lincoln firm had come from Stephen Logan's hand. Now Lincoln returned to the laborious practice of writing these long legal documents in his elegant penmanship.

The law had changed a great deal in the twelve years since Lincoln began practicing with Stuart in the spring of 1837. Formality in the courtroom began to replace the informality that had reigned during the 1830s and '40s. Legal precedent had become ascendant over argument. Spontaneous oratory, for the most part, had been replaced by careful preparation and presentation. Instead of the clear meaning of the law applying to all cases, now the complex meaning of the law applied to specific cases.

A POPULAR SAYING in Lincoln's day was that the Bible, Shakespeare, and Blackstone's *Commentaries* made up the foundation of any well-stocked legal library. The best lawyers in the first half of the nineteenth century were typically well versed in both literature and law. After the Civil War, the trajectory of law would point to professional training and specialization. From this perspective, some observers describe pre–Civil War lawyers as wanting in their preparation, but from another point of view we can see that they approached law from the established tradi-

COMMENTARIES

ON THE

LAWS OF ENGLAND:

IN FOUR BOOKS;

WITH

AN ANALYSIS OF THE WORK.

BY

SIR WILLIAM BLACKSTONE, KNT.
ONE OF THE JUSTICES OF THE COURT OF COMMON PLEAS.

IN TWO VOLUMES,
FROM THE EIGHTEENTH LONDON EDITION.

WITH A

LIFE OF THE AUTHOR, AND NOTES:
BY

CHRISTIAN, CHITTY, LEE, HOVENDEN, AND RYLAND:
AND ALSO

REFERENCES TO AMERICAN CASES,

BY A MEMBER OF THE NEW-YORK BAR.

VOL. I.—BOOK I. & II.

NEW-YORK:
W. E. DEAN, PRINTER & PUBLISHER, 2 ANN STREET.
COLLINS, KEESE & CO., 254 PEARL STREET.
1838.

Lincoln used Blackstone's Commentaries *as a foundation
of self-education in the law.*

tions of Western literature and religion. One can find frequent descriptions of lawyers' eloquence in the pre–Civil War courtroom, where literary and rhetorical expression had a high value. As for Lincoln, his growing eloquence sprang not from a knowledge of legal precedent, but from his familiarity with the classic resources of the Bible, works of history and biography, and literature, especially Shakespeare.

Some lawyers who practiced with Lincoln reported his knowledge of the law was lacking. But one needs to qualify this observation by understanding both the observer and the context. Stephen Logan, Lincoln's second partner, remembered, "Lincoln's knowledge of law was very small when I took him in," but, of course, this recollection came from a man who wanted to be remembered for helping tutor the young Lincoln. Judge David Davis, who would become one of Lincoln's best friends out on the circuit in the 1850s, offered a more balanced assessment. Lincoln may not have been a meticulous student of the law but, when pressed by necessity, he used the available sources of legal information. Davis said, "Sometimes Lincoln studied things, if he could not get the rubbish of a case removed." In many ways Lincoln approached the practice of law in a way typical of the busy lawyers who traveled the large judicial circuits in frontier states.

When Lincoln did need to brush up on the law, he would walk across the street to use the resources of the Illinois Supreme Court Library housed in the statehouse. He also relied on published digests containing summaries of important cases. The *United States Digest* covered cases from both state and federal courts; the *Illinois Digest* was also a fast and reliable tool for researching cases.

TWICE A YEAR, in the spring and fall, Lincoln traveled more than five hundred miles for a cycle of the Eighth Judicial Circuit. The circuit, which expanded and contracted during this time, stretched across an area of nearly fifteen thousand square miles, larger than the state of Connecticut. Lincoln's schedule was the exception to that of other lawyers of his day: Most practiced law in only a few counties surrounding their hometown and office.

Lincoln enjoyed the itinerant lifestyle of a circuit lawyer. When he rejoined the circuit in the fall of 1849 for the first time after leaving Congress, he switched from traveling by horseback to a buggy pulled by his horse "Old Buck," who had seen better days. Instead of saddlebags, he now carried his legal papers, a few books, and an extra shirt in a carpetbag. On September 17, 1849, he bought a large cotton umbrella for seventy-five cents as protection from the Illinois weather. He had his name sewed inside with white thread and tied the umbrella together with twine to keep it from flying open.

Lincoln had grown up in the forests of Indiana, but he became enthralled by the endless prairies of Illinois. The prairies were a striking mixture of blue stem, Indian, and Canadian white rye grasses. By summer's end, they were a foot higher than Lincoln's head. As the Indian summer of late September gave way to October's cooler nights, the prairies turned from green to tawny and vermilion. Black-eyed Susans, goldenrod, and sawtooth sunflowers came into final bloom, thriving not simply from the fall rains, but also from the rich subsoil beneath the prairies. In the woodlands, the foliage of red and white oaks blazed orange and dark purple in the last days of October and early November. The prairies were wondrously silent, with only the voice of an owl or a fox to break Lincoln's solitude.

For all of their beauty, however, the prairies could be treacherous. The weather was always changing. By October, Lincoln had to be prepared for thunderstorms, winds, and sleeting snow, which could turn the roads into rivers of mud. Fire, generated by just a spark in the autumn's tall grass, could roar across the prairies with tremendous speed, overtaking travelers and destroying farms. Blizzards could suddenly blow out of the north and produce drifts that could kill man and beast.

Nonetheless, after spending sixteen months in the nation's capital, Lincoln seemed to relish traveling the byways of the Eighth Judicial Circuit. The circuit was growing in population and offered new legal opportunities as well as friendships. He set to work reestablishing old relationships and making new ones that would become key to regaining his prominence as a lawyer, as well as to his future reentry into politics.

Lincoln was especially eager to see Judge David Davis again. Lincoln had first met lawyer Davis in 1835. While Lincoln served in Congress, the legislature had elected Davis judge of the Eighth Circuit. Born on his grandfather's plantation in Sassafras Neck on the eastern shore of Maryland in 1815, Davis had graduated from Kenyon College, in the interior of Ohio, in 1832. One of his classmates was Edwin M. Stanton, a young man from Steubenville, Ohio, who suffered from asthma.

After graduation, Davis worked in the law office of Henry W. Bishop in Lenox, in western Massachusetts. In 1835 he decided to travel west to

Judge David Davis would become one of Lincoln's closest legal and political friends.

practice law. After first settling in Pekin, Illinois, he moved twenty-five miles east to Bloomington, a town of 450 residents built north of a large grove of trees known as Blooming Grove.

Lincoln differed from Davis in many ways. Judge Davis, a congenial aristocrat, dressed immaculately. By the time Lincoln began traveling with Davis on the Eighth Circuit, the judge, five feet eleven inches tall, weighed nearly three hundred pounds; Lincoln's six-foot-four-inch frame carried less than two hundred pounds. Davis's huge size made it impossible for him to share a bed with Lincoln in hotels. He was so large he had to ride about the circuit in a buggy drawn by not one but two gray mares.

Despite these superficial differences, Davis formed a highly favorable opinion of Lincoln. In a letter Davis said, "Lincoln is the best Stump Speaker in the State." During the 1850s the lives and careers of Abraham Lincoln and Judge David Davis would intertwine repeatedly as they traveled from court to court in the small towns of central Illinois.

IN THE FALL OF 1849, Lincoln met Leonard Swett, a new lawyer on the circuit. Originally from Maine and a veteran of the Mexican War, Swett began practicing law in 1849 in Clinton, Illinois, a small town not far from Bloomington. A tall, erect man with a bright, intelligent face, he started traveling the Eighth Judicial Circuit just as Lincoln returned to it.

In October 1849, they met for the first time in front of the Greek Revival courthouse in Mount Pulaski. Immediately Swett, sixteen years younger, and Lincoln formed a friendship that would last sixteen years.

That fall, Lincoln, Davis, and Swett formed what the lawyers on the circuit would call "the great triumvirate," an homage to Calhoun, Clay, and Webster. Enjoying one another's company, they traveled everywhere together and often stayed in the same hotel rooms. Other lawyers admired their abilities and chuckled at their invariable high jinks and humor. This triumvirate would not only become significant in the legal courts of central Illinois, but one day in political circles in Illinois and beyond.

WHILE THERE HAVE always been many lawyers who became politicians, Lincoln was one of the few politicians who later became a lawyer. Lincoln was a Whig in the statehouse before he became a Whig in the courthouse. He brought to the practice of the law a constellation of Whig ideas.

As a first principle, Whigs believed in order. Lincoln thought that the nation could not modernize and expand so long as lawlessness and violence remained prevalent in society. As a Whig, Lincoln was convinced that laws could be used to build a political and social framework. Lincoln also embraced the Whig idea of government serving as a protector of community ideals and moral values.

Lincoln's politics were not of the cut-flower variety, which bloomed only for the moment; rather, they grew from the deep soil of tradition. In the 1850s, he referred more and more in his speeches and writings to the ideas of the nation's founders—especially George Washington, John Adams, Benjamin Franklin, Thomas Jefferson, and James Madison—citing them as precedents for the problems and possibilities of his own day.

Lincoln was also coming to believe that every generation needed to redefine America for its own time. Back in 1838, in his speech to the Young Men's Lyceum in Springfield, he had declared that the role of his generation was quite limited—they were to "transmit" the ideas and institutions of the founders to their own and future generations. But by the 1850s, Lincoln was beginning to arrive at a creative balance—often a creative tension—between past traditions and the new and different possibilities of the present and future.

AS LINCOLN TRAVELED THE EIGHTH CIRCUIT, he kept abreast of the political events in Washington. He applauded the efforts of Senator Henry Clay, who in January 1850 was busy cobbling together a series of measures to ease the growing tensions between the North and the South. The seventy-year-old Clay had introduced eight resolutions proposing "an amicable arrangement of all questions in controversy between the free and slave states, growing out of slavery." Clay hoped his resolutions, which would become known as the Compromise of 1850, would promote "a great national scheme of compromise and harmony."

Clay's initiatives produced high drama. His two celebrated senior colleagues, John C. Calhoun and Daniel Webster, also at the end of their years of service, determined to respond.

On March 4, 1850, Calhoun, sixty-seven, sat at his Senate desk, too weak to speak, coughing incessantly, as the last major speech of his life was read by Virginia senator James M. Mason. In the speech, Calhoun asked, "How can the Union be preserved?" and then followed with a second question, "How has the Union been endangered?" He answered both questions by rehearsing how first the Northwest Ordinance and then the Missouri Compromise had kept Southern interests out of Western territories and states. Calhoun declared that the spiritual cords that bound the nation together had already been broken in the recent divisions of three leading Protestant denominations—Baptist, Methodist, and Presbyterian. He saw this separation as a dire trend and wondered whether the political cords would be severed also. He warned against further compromise.

Three days later, Calhoun returned to the Senate to hear Daniel Webster speak in favor of Clay's resolutions. Expectations reverberated throughout Washington, and all the seats in the Senate chamber were filled, with people sitting in the aisles. Webster began, "I wish to speak to-day, not as a Massachusetts man, nor as a northern man, but as an American." He declared, "I speak to-day for the preservation of the Union." He then surprised his audience by chastising abolitionists and declaring that he could never support the Wilmot Proviso, which would keep slavery out of any territory acquired from Mexico. In the end, he supported each of Clay's proposals, including the strengthening of the fugitive slave law.

Even from afar, Lincoln understood that the Compromise of 1850 was only a temporary truce. Each of the Compromise's planks had been acrimoniously debated. California would enter the Union as a free state. The territories of New Mexico, Nevada, Arizona, and Utah would be organized without a declaration about slavery, leaving it to the citizens to decide. The slave trade, but not slavery, would be abolished in Washington and the District of Columbia. The Compromise settled a boundary dispute between Texas and New Mexico. In the deepest bow to the South, which had not received another slave state in the deal, the Compromise amended the old Fugitive Slave Act of 1793 to require citizens to assist in recapturing runaway slaves and denying those slaves a jury trial.

Although it held the nation together, the Compromise of 1850 satisfied no one. Abolitionists only increased their efforts to end slavery once and for all. Conductors on the Underground Railroad stepped up their activities so that between 1850 and 1860 more than twenty thousand slaves traveled from farms to safe houses along the track from the United States to Canada. The new fugitive slave law instituted a reign of terror with free blacks being detained and sent to the South without trial. Many Southerners were extremely dissatisfied as well, arguing that Clay, the Great Compromiser, had sold out his native South.

For three old actors—Clay, Calhoun, and Webster—the debate on the Compromise of 1850 would be their last curtain call in the Senate. Calhoun died on March 31, 1850, before the debate ended. Clay and Webster would both die in the next two years. The vexing issue of slavery, if temporarily defused, would be left to the will and wiles of America's next generation to resolve. Far away from the Washington stage, Lincoln read reports of the Compromise of 1850 in the *Congressional Globe* and in his regular diet of newspapers, but made no public comment.

IN THE SUMMER of 1850, Lincoln started taking notes for a lecture on the law and lawyers. Although there is no record of Lincoln ever delivering this lecture, the ideas expressed in the notes reveal his self-understanding of his profession.

"I am not an accomplished lawyer," Lincoln began with self-deprecation. He confessed, "I find quite as much material for a lecture in those points where I have failed, as in those wherein I have been moderately successful." Lincoln here gave voice to a principle—the willingness to both admit mistakes and learn from them—that was becoming a part of his moral character.

He believed "the leading rule" for any lawyer was "diligence." Lincoln counseled, "Leave nothing for to-morrow which can be done today. . . . Whatever piece of business you have in hand, before stopping, do all the labor pertaining to it which can then be done." He advised lawyers preparing a common-law suit to "write the declaration at once."

Lincoln also offered a brief on the utility of public speaking. "It is the lawyer's avenue to the public. Extemporaneous speaking should be practiced and cultivated." Though he recognized that there were many qualities of a successful lawyer, he believed this one virtue trumped all others. "However able and faithful he may be in other respects, people are slow to bring him business if he cannot make a speech."

At the heart of his lecture was a definition of his understanding of the calling of a lawyer. "As a peacemaker the lawyer has a superior opportunity of being a good man." Here Lincoln offered his most practical advice: "Discourage litigation." Life in the frontier states was marked by disputes. Rural and townsfolk were ready to "go to law" over the least aggravation. Lincoln's counsel: "Persuade your neighbors to compromise whenever you can. Point out to them how the nominal winner is often the real loser—in fees, expenses, and waste of time." At this point, Lincoln seems to anticipate a question from his imagined audience: Is not litigation the very source of a lawyer's business and fees? He answers, "There will still be business enough."

LINCOLN UNDERSTOOD HIS ROLE as a lawyer to be a mediator in the various small communities in which he practiced law. Abram Bale, who moved to the New Salem area from Kentucky in 1839, hired Lincoln in February 1850 to represent him in a dispute with the Hickox brothers over $1,000 of "good, merchantable, superfine flour." Lincoln, drawing upon both his farming and storekeeping experience, argued that the twenty barrels of flour were not fairly characterized; they were instead inferior in quality. He knew he had a good case, but in the midst of the proceedings he counseled his client to settle. "I sincerely hope you will settle it. I think you *can* if you *will,* for I have always found Mr. Hickox a fair man in his dealings." Lincoln then told Bale, "I will charge nothing for what I have done, and thank you to boot." He further encouraged his client, "By settling, you will most likely get your money sooner; and with much less trouble and expense."

Lincoln was a mediator more than a prosecutor. Just as in his speeches he was sensitive to the attitudes and questions of his audiences, in the courtrooms of the Eighth Judicial Circuit he worked hard to understand the motives and attitudes of clients, witnesses, and judges. He was responsive to the differing local contexts in which he practiced. He was often the only lawyer who stayed out on the circuit over the course of an entire fall and spring cycle. Lodging in homes, he shared folks' leisure time on the weekends and learned their concerns, struggles, and questions. In his understanding of the lawyer as mediator, Lincoln recognized that cases that at first glance seemed to be between two persons almost always involved the whole community in these small towns. His active presence in these communities gave Lincoln both a standing and sensitivity to local institutions and sentiments. Even though justice was universal, Lincoln appreciated that in crucial ways law was local.

In the spring of 1850 the *Illinois Citizen* in Danville captured both Lincoln's abilities and his growing reputation as a lawyer.

In his examination of witnesses, he displays a masterly ingenuity . . . that baffles concealment and defies deceit. And in addressing a jury, there is no false glitter, no sickly sentimentalism to be discovered. In vain we look for rhetorical display. . . . Seizing upon the minutest points, he weaves them into his argument with an ingenuity really astonishing. . . . Bold, forcible and energetic, he forces conviction upon the mind, and, by his clearness and conciseness, stamps it there, not to be erased. . . . Such are some of the qualities that place Mr. L. at the head of the profession in this State.

Lincoln practiced law as a peacemaker. His early cases concerned individuals, not companies or corporations. Whether about hogs, cooking stoves, land, or slander, they almost always involved persons who knew each other face-to-face and had got crossways.

The reason Lincoln urged so many of his clients to settle was that he knew these people needed to go on living next to one another in their small villages and towns after they had their day in court. The skills he was developing as a lawyer—especially the subtle art of mediation— would one day soon be put to use on a much larger circuit.

WITH LINCOLN SPENDING more and more time traveling, his life as a lawyer, a politician, and a family man teetered out of balance. Politics, for the moment, had diminished while his legal practice had become all consuming. Any hopes that Mary may have had that Abraham would be home more often now that he was back from Washington were soon dashed. In 1850, his first full year home, Lincoln was away from Springfield 175 days.

Mary bore these absences as one who felt abandoned. At age six, she had lost her mother. One year later, her father had married a woman to whom Mary never grew close. For much of Mary's childhood her father was absent, often away on business or politics.

She dealt with her sense of desertion and loss by focusing intently on her children. Whereas family manuals from this period advised nursing children for up to ten months, Mary nursed each of her boys for nearly two years. One of the boys always slept with her, whether or not Lincoln was home. With no nurse and no grandparents nearby, Mary raised her children almost as a single mother.

And then death tumbled in. In July 1849, just as the family was returning from Washington, Mary's father, Robert Todd, died suddenly of cholera while campaigning for the Kentucky Senate. Five months later, little Eddie Lincoln, age three and a half, fell ill. Mary nursed the boy through December and January, but the medical practice of the day could do little to combat what was probably pulmonary tuberculosis. After fifty-two days of suffering, Eddie Lincoln died at 6 a.m. on February 1, 1850.

The death of Eddie brought tremendous sadness to both Abraham and Mary. The Lincoln home was filled with the sound of Mary weeping. She probably did not go to the cemetery, where she might break down, for the convention of the time dictated that women grieve in private. Everything we know about Mary suggests that Eddie's death struck a tremendous blow to her sense of self and her stability.

How Lincoln responded to the death of his young son is more difficult to determine. Herndon reported that Lincoln sank deep into melancholy. A friend recalled Lincoln trying to comfort Mary by entreating her, "Eat, Mary, for we must live." Three weeks after Eddie's death, Lincoln wrote, "We miss him very much."

IMMEDIATELY AFTER EDDIE'S DEATH, Abraham and Mary attempted to contact the man who had married them, Reverend Charles Dresser of St. Paul's Episcopal Church, where Mary worshipped, to ask him to conduct the funeral service. Unfortunately, Dresser was out of town.

And so the Lincolns turned to the Reverend James Smith, the new minister at Springfield's First Presbyterian Church. The funeral service was held at the Lincolns' home at 11 a.m. on February 2. Both before and after the funeral, Smith brought pastoral care and comfort to the grieving parents.

Less than two years later, Mary joined First Presbyterian, a congregation founded in 1828 that had first met in the home of her uncle John Todd. In joining First Presbyterian, Mary reconnected with the Presbyterian church she had attended as a girl in Lexington. She became a member on October 13, 1852, "by examination." The ruling elders of the congregation heard her narrative of faith, what they called in the session minutes "experimental religion." The Lincolns rented pew number twenty in the seventh row for an annual fee of fifty dollars.

Originally from Scotland, the Reverend James Smith immigrated to the United States as a young man who was a confirmed deist, having read Constantin Volney and Thomas Paine. He took pleasure in challenging the religious ideas of camp-meeting preachers near his home in southern Indiana. But upon listening to the preaching of a Cumberland Presbyterian Church minister, Smith was converted. He was licensed to preach in 1825.

Smith wrote *The Christian's Defence* in 1843. The book grew out of his debates with a popular freethinker, Charles G. Olmstead, over eighteen successive evenings in Columbus, Mississippi, in 1841. Smith defended the authority and truthfulness of the Old and New Testaments. In critiquing contemporary deviations from true faith, he was concerned that "the exercises of the understanding must be separated from the tendencies of the fancy, or of the heart," a reference to the emotional, revivalist faith from which he was just then emerging.

Smith's increasing intention to embrace a more rational faith gradually led him to the Presbyterian Church in 1844. He was called to First Presbyterian Church in Springfield in the spring of 1849, less than one year before the death of Eddie Lincoln. In October 1849, after the death of Mary's father, the Lincolns traveled to Lexington, Kentucky, to help settle her father's estate. While browsing in the library at the Todd home, Lincoln came across Smith's 650-page treatise.

When Lincoln met Smith in Springfield, around the time of Eddie's death, he either asked for or was offered a copy of *The Christian's Defence*. Robert Lincoln remembered that a copy of Smith's book sat on the bookshelf in the Lincoln home at Eighth and Jackson. Smith's logical presentation of the Christian faith must have appealed to Lincoln's penchant for order and reason. Put off by the emotionalism of the revivalist religion of his youth, Lincoln would have likely agreed with Smith's proposal that when pondering religion "the mind must be trained to the hardihood of abstract and unfeeling intelligence." Smith contended that in matters of faith "everything must be given up to the supremacy of argument."

In the early 1850s, Lincoln attended First Presbyterian Church infrequently. He was away traveling on the Eighth Circuit each fall and spring, in addition to other travels as a lawyer and politician. Nevertheless, in the spring of 1853, Lincoln accepted an invitation to be one of three lawyers to represent the church in a suit in the Sangamon Presbytery.

John Todd Stuart, Lincoln's former law partner and a member of First Presbyterian, remembered that Lincoln began to attend church on a more regular basis in the late 1850s. Both Abraham and Mary appreciated Smith, "an intellectual, powerful man," who, in the words of Mary's close cousin Lizzie Grimsley, "could thunder out the terrors of the law as well as proclaim the love of the Gospel." Lincoln, who had pushed away his father's emotional expressions of faith when he moved to New Salem in the 1830s, began to take another look at religion.

LESS THAN A YEAR after Eddie's death, Mary's grief was relieved in part when she gave birth to William Wallace Lincoln on December 21, 1850. He was named after Mary's brother-in-law Dr. William Wallace. The Lincolns' third son would grow to become the boy most like his father.

A fourth son, Thomas Lincoln, was born on April 4, 1853, named after Abraham's father. He quickly acquired the nickname "Tad," short for "Tadpole," the way he looked at birth. Tad grew to be a prankster in a family of boys who were mischief makers—with their father's consent and often encouragement.

Tad Lincoln was baptized at First Presbyterian Church on April 4,

1855. Thomas was the only son born after Mary joined First Presbyterian Church and seems to have been the only one of the Lincoln boys who was baptized. All the boys regularly attended Sunday school at the church. The Lincolns were becoming fond of Pastor James Smith and frequently invited him to their home. Lincoln discovered in Smith someone who had also doubted as a young man, had also read Volney and Paine, but had come to affirm both reason and faith.

LINCOLN, THOUGH NOT SEEKING PUBLIC OFFICE himself, continued to lobby for public offices for his friends. He wrote to President Taylor in January 1850, to recommend Stephen T. Logan for U.S. judge of the District Court of Illinois. In the spring of 1850, Lincoln's name was put forward by a Whig newspaper for another term in Congress, but he quickly quashed the idea.

In July 1850, while in Chicago to participate in a case before the U.S. District Court, Lincoln learned that President Taylor, after participating in patriotic ceremonies on a hot July 4, had contracted a stomach ailment and died five days later. In Chicago, two committees immediately planned an event to memorialize the dead president. Receiving word that Lincoln was in town, they invited him on July 22 to give a eulogy. Honored by the request but concerned that he had less than two days to prepare, Lincoln replied, "The want of time for preparation will make the task, for me, a very difficult one to perform, in any degree satisfactory to others or to myself."

Nevertheless, on July 24, 1850, Lincoln offered a eulogy at city hall. The address had all the marks of words prepared in a hurry. Lincoln took much of his eulogy from Taylor's 1848 campaign biographies, some of which contained inaccurate information.

Lincoln did, however, use the occasion to offer his perspective on contemporary politics. "I fear the one *great* question of the day, is not now so likely to be partially acquiesced in by the different sections of the Union, as it would have been, could Gen. Taylor have been spared to us." Lincoln, never as enamored of Taylor as he was of Henry Clay, nonetheless had hoped that the president, a slave owner, would be a mediating figure in the growing crisis over slavery.

In Lincoln's unusual conclusion, he reminded his audience "that *we, too, must die.*" He concluded with six entire stanzas from the poem "Mortality" by Scottish poet William Knox, which he had discovered in a newspaper in 1846 and committed to memory.

The eulogy said as much about Lincoln as it did about Taylor. Lincoln, through the poem, evoked his own struggles with the meaning of life and death.

> *Yea! Hope and despondency, pleasure and pain,*
> *Are mingled together in sun-shine and rain;*
> *And the smile and the tear, and the song and the dirge,*
> *Still follow each other, like surge upon surge.*

Lincoln had known melancholy and despondency.

> *'Tis the wink of an eye, 'tis the draught of a breath,*
> *From the blossoms of health, to the paleness of death.*
> *From the gilded saloon, to the bier and the shroud.*
> *Oh, why should the spirit of mortal be proud!*

The poem, with its summoning of eternal and unchanging rhythms of life, appealed to Lincoln in his quest for meaning and fulfillment.

SOON AFTER THE BIRTH of Willie, Lincoln received a letter from his stepbrother, John D. Johnston, telling him that his father was quite ill and might not recover. Thomas Lincoln and his second wife, Sara Bush Lincoln, had lived on a farm on Goosenest Prairie in Coles County in southeastern Illinois since 1840. Johnston reminded Lincoln that he had written two previous letters and wondered why he had received no reply. Lincoln, acknowledging the receipt of both letters, wrote, "it is no[t because] I have forgotten them, or been uninterested about them— but because it appeared to me I could write nothing which could do any good." Lincoln added, "You already know I desire that neither Father or Mother shall be in want of any comfort either in health or sickness while they live," and added that his stepbrother should use his name "to procure a doctor, or anything else for Father in his present sickness." Lincoln then asked his stepbrother to convey to his father a consolation of faith: "Tell him to remember to call upon, and confide in, our great and good, and merciful Maker, who will not turn away from him in any extremity. He notes the fall of a sparrow, and numbers the hairs of our heads; and He will not forget the dying man, who puts his trust in Him."

It has been suggested by some that Lincoln's religious words were an unconvincing appeal to the language of the primitive Baptist faith adhered to by Lincoln's parents. But it is more plausible that Lincoln offered heartfelt language that he himself had heard from the Reverend Smith eleven months earlier at the funeral of his son Eddie and now conveyed as a consolation to his own father.

In his conclusion, Lincoln wrote of the distance that had grown between son and father. "Say to him that if we could meet now, it is doubtful whether it would not be more painful than pleasant."

Thomas Lincoln died five days later on January 17, 1851. Lincoln did not attend the funeral. The distance could not be bridged.

AS SOLE HEIR, Lincoln inherited the eighty-acre farm on the Goosenest Prairie. He had no wish to benefit from the farm and sold it to his stepbrother for one dollar on August 12, 1851.

When, near the end of that year, he learned that Johnston was considering selling the land and moving to Missouri, Lincoln could not restrain his outrage. "I have been thinking of this ever since; and can not but think such a notion is utterly foolish." He peppered Johnston with questions. "What can you do in Missouri, better than here? Is the land richer? Can you there, any more than here, raise corn, & wheat & oats, without work? Will any body there, any more than here, do your work for you?" Lincoln did not mince words. "I feel it is my duty to have no hand in such a piece of foolery." He was particularly upset on "*Mother's* account," that the lack of Johnston's labor and income would leave his stepmother destitute.

Lincoln, in reading over this strong letter, began his final paragraph, "Now do not misunderstand this letter, I do not write it in any unkindness." He told his stepbrother he wrote "to get you to *face* the truth . . . your thousand pretences for not getting along better are all non-sense—they deceive no body but yourself." Lincoln's final sentence articulated not simply his hopes for his brother, but his own creed. "*Go to work* is the only cure for your case."

SENATOR HENRY CLAY died in Washington, D.C., on June 29, 1852. On July 6, Springfield suspended all city business in recognition of a day of national mourning. The citizens of Springfield held two memorial meetings, one at the Episcopal church led by the Reverend Charles Dresser, who read the "Service for the Dead" from the Book of Common Prayer, and the second at the state capitol with a eulogy delivered by Lincoln. What Jefferson had meant to Madison, Clay had meant to Lincoln.

Lincoln began his speech by relating the birth of the nation to the birth of Clay. "The infant nation, and the infant child began the race of life together." Lincoln built his eulogy around the lessons that Clay's life could still offer the country. Commenting on Clay's "comparatively limited" education, Lincoln said that it "teaches at least one profitable lesson," that "one can scarcely be so poor, but that, if he *will,* he can acquire sufficient education to get through the world respectably." Lincoln may have exaggerated Clay's lack of education, but in introducing this theme he offered his identification with the politician he idealized.

Unlike hundreds of other eulogies to Clay, Lincoln's highlighted the Kentuckian's vigorous engagement with slavery throughout his political life. He emphasized that Clay, from the beginning of his public career, "ever was, on principle and in feeling, opposed to slavery." Acknowledging the paradox that Clay was a slave owner, Lincoln declared that he had nonetheless been "in favor of gradual emancipation of the slaves in Kentucky." Lincoln admired Clay for opposing "both extremes" on slavery: those who would "shiver into fragments the Union" and those who would "tear to tatters the Constitution" in their desire to overthrow slavery immediately. Lincoln was intent to "array his name, opinions, and influence," against "an increasing number of men" who, Lincoln feared, were beginning to assail "the declaration that 'all men are created free and equal.' "

Lincoln offered this tribute to Clay three years after he had last held public office. He had no future political office in sight. His eulogy memorialized his ideal politician, but it also enunciated the ideals that would bring Lincoln once again into public life, much sooner than he anticipated.

This photograph from October 17, 1854, by Polycarp Von Schneidau in Chicago, captures an intellectual, if not crafty, Lincoln in the year he reentered politics.

CHAPTER 11

Let No One Be Deceived
1852–56

OUR REPUBLICAN ROBE IS SOILED, AND TRAILED IN THE DUST. LET US
REPURIFY IT. LET US TURN AND WASH IT WHITE, IN THE SPIRIT, IF
NOT THE BLOOD, OF THE REVOLUTION.

ABRAHAM LINCOLN
Speech at Peoria, Illinois, October 16, 1854

"WE WERE THUNDERSTRUCK AND STUNNED; AND WE REELED AND FELL IN
utter confusion." Abraham Lincoln spoke these words in one of his first
responses to the passage of the Kansas-Nebraska Act of 1854. He found
himself quickly caught up in the midst of a tempest, and his words
revealed his keen awareness that he was not prepared for the political
task before him. Yet, he would discover in the months ahead how to
speak with new definition and clarity about the meaning of the promise
of America in the national debate about slavery. The ways in which Lincoln responded to this storm would mark a significant turning point in
his life.

ON JANUARY 4, 1854, Senator Stephen A. Douglas, chairman of the
powerful Committee on Territories, brought to the Senate a bill to set
up a government in the vast Nebraska Territory. The urgency grew
from mounting pressure to organize this territory in the center of the
old Louisiana Purchase. President Jefferson's acquisition from France in
1803 of more than one million square miles had expanded the area of
the United States all the way from the Mississippi River to the Rocky
Mountains and from the Gulf of Mexico to the Canadian border. At the
time of the Louisiana Purchase, the United States consisted of seventeen
states—nine free and eight slave—of almost equal population.

Political infighting over the organization of the sizable Nebraska Territory had broken out in earlier Congresses, and four previous bills had foundered over disagreements about the extension of slavery. Douglas now offered what he called a "compromise" measure, arguing that local control, what he called a long-held American "sacred" value, would finally mitigate the issue of slavery. In its final form the act provided for not one but two new territories, Nebraska and Kansas. The bill stated that "all questions pertaining to slavery in the territories were to be left to the decision of the people residing therein." The intent of Douglas's bill was to transfer the power to decide whether or not slavery would be permitted from Congress to the people in the territory.

The storm began the moment the Kansas-Nebraska Act was introduced. Salmon P. Chase, elected to the Senate from Ohio in 1849 by a coalition of Free Soilers and Democrats, was chosen point man for the counterattack. Chase would be ably assisted by Charles Sumner, the new senator from Massachusetts, also elected by Free Soilers and Democrats. The tall, handsome Chase questioned Douglas's interpretation of American history and declared that the leaders of the revolutionary generation had abhorred slavery, had tolerated it as the price of gaining approval for the Constitution, and, by restricting its future growth, had expected it to die out by the second or third generation of the new nation. In the course of his remarks, Chase charged that the Illinois senator had "outSouthernized the South."

Douglas was surprised and angered by the intensity of the criticisms. A dramatic moment occurred when Senator Edward Everett of Massachusetts brought to the Senate a 250-foot-long memorial against the bill signed by 3,050 New England ministers of various denominations. Douglas was furious at what he described as religious leaders inappropriately meddling in politics.

On March 2, 1854, the Senate began a final debate on the bill. Everyone wanted to speak, bickering ensued, and insults were exchanged. On March 3, exhaustion set in and liquor broke out. At dusk, the candles in the great chamber were lit so that the debate could continue. Douglas finally began his summation at eleven-thirty in the evening with the galleries still packed. He rested his case in his belief that popular sovereignty would in the long run "destroy all sectional parties and sectional agitations." After a nonstop session of more than seventeen hours, at five o'clock in the morning on March 4, the Senate passed the Kansas-

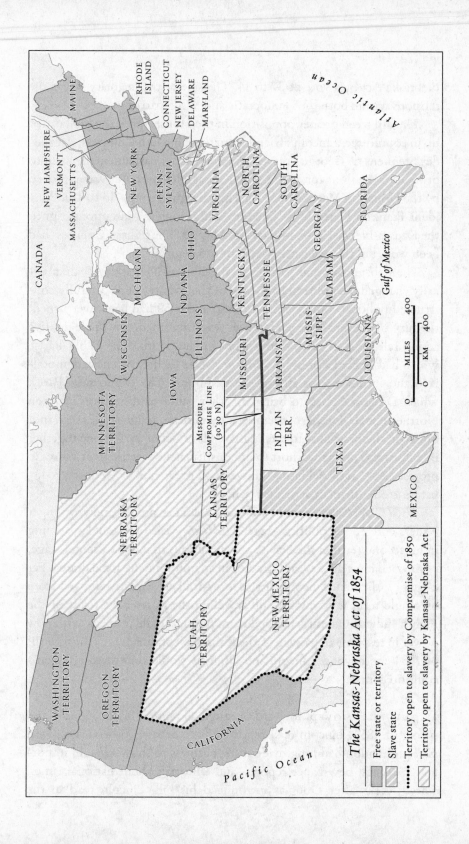

The Kansas-Nebraska Act of 1854

Free state or territory

Slave state

Territory open to slavery by Compromise of 1850

Territory open to slavery by Kansas-Nebraska Act

Missouri Compromise Line (30°30′ N)

CANADA

WASHINGTON TERRITORY

OREGON TERRITORY

MINNESOTA TERRITORY

NEBRASKA TERRITORY

KANSAS TERRITORY

UTAH TERRITORY

NEW MEXICO TERRITORY

CALIFORNIA

MEXICO

TEXAS

INDIAN TERR.

IOWA

WISCONSIN

MICHIGAN

ILLINOIS

INDIANA

OHIO

MISSOURI

ARKANSAS

LOUISIANA

MISSISSIPPI

ALABAMA

GEORGIA

FLORIDA

TENNESSEE

KENTUCKY

VIRGINIA

NORTH CAROLINA

SOUTH CAROLINA

MAINE

NEW HAMPSHIRE

VERMONT

MASSACHUSETTS

RHODE ISLAND

CONNECTICUT

NEW YORK

PENN-SYLVANIA

NEW JERSEY

DELAWARE

MARYLAND

Atlantic Ocean

Gulf of Mexico

Pacific Ocean

MILES 0 400
KM 0 400

Nebraska Act by a vote of 37 to 14. The size of the majority belied the tensions within both the Democratic and Whig parties.

The bill faced greater opposition in the House. With the bill bottled up in committee, Lincoln's friend from the Thirtieth Congress, Alexander Stephens of Georgia, played an experienced parliamentary hand to bring it to the floor for a vote. The Kansas-Nebraska Act was approved by the House on May 22, 1854, in a much tighter vote, 113 to 110. President Franklin Pierce, who lined up with Douglas's intentions, signed the Kansas-Nebraska Act into law on May 30. The fight in Congress had been won, but the real battle was about to begin.

The debate over and passage of the Kansas-Nebraska Act dramatically changed the political landscape of the country. The carefully constructed political compromises of 1820 and 1850 had been overturned; the fury of the antislavery advocates was intensified; but the legislative action fell short of mollifying many in the South. The Whig Party, which had elected a president only six years earlier, was now demoralized and in disarray; it struggled to respond. The Democratic Party, which Douglas hoped to bring together, suffered dissension between Northern and Southern members. American religious leaders, not united in their response to the Fugitive Slave Act of 1850, came together in pulpits and press to exhort their constituencies to raise their voices in protest. An "anti-Nebraska" movement grew quickly, enlisting disparate groups that cut across party lines.

With Clay, Calhoun, and Webster no longer present, new, younger leaders entered the political stage. The forty-year-old Douglas, serving in his second term in the Senate and ambitious to move to center stage, positioned himself as a leading actor in an unfolding national drama. Far offstage, Abraham Lincoln, at age forty-four, five years removed from his single term in Congress and traveling the dusty back roads of the Eighth Judicial Circuit, emerged from political exile to speak with new power in response to passage of the Kansas-Nebraska Act. In the months of 1854 and beyond, Lincoln and Douglas would find themselves on a collision course.

AS THE BILL MOVED forward through Congress in the winter and spring of 1854, Lincoln read reports of the debate in the *Congressional Globe*. Herndon had long made it his business to show Lincoln important speeches, newspaper reports, and editorials about national issues. Three weeks after Douglas introduced his bill, Lincoln read in the

National Era "An Appeal of Independent Democrats" over the names of six congressional leaders, including Senators Chase and Sumner, plus his friend from the Thirtieth Congress Joshua Giddings of Ohio. The "Appeal" was filled with inflammatory language. "We arraign this bill as a gross violation of a sacred pledge; as a criminal betrayal of precious rights; as part and parcel of an atrocious plot to exclude from a vast unoccupied region immigrants from the Old World and free laborers from our own States, and convert it into a dreary region of despotism, inhabited by masters and slaves."

The fact that Lincoln failed to speak out was not surprising. He did not hold political office, nor was he a candidate for office. He was, however, extremely busy with his general law practice. In January and February, he began work on an appeal before the Illinois Supreme Court of his first large case for the Illinois Central Railroad, *Illinois Central v. McLean County.* He was continuously involved in court cases until the Sangamon Circuit Court adjourned in Springfield on June 15, 1854. And he continued to practice his regular intellectual discipline. His notes from the 1850s include reflections on law, government, slavery, sectionalism, Stephen A. Douglas, and the formation of the Republican Party.

In the early months of 1854, the anti-Nebraska movement acceler-

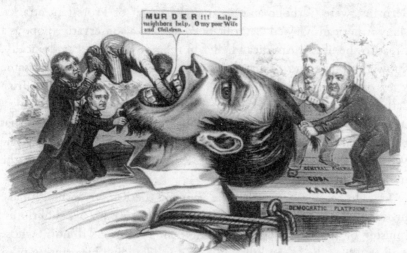

FORCING SLAVERY DOWN THE THROAT OF A FREESOILER

*The artist places the blame on the Democrats for the violence against
Free Staters in Kansas in the wake of the Kansas-Nebraska Act.*

ated the disintegration of the Whigs, but Lincoln was, if anything, loyal. He remained faithful to the party of Clay and was not ready to abandon the Whig heritage or its future.

And he did not know for sure which way the political winds were blowing. In the 1850s, the nation experienced its largest reordering of political parties in its history. The Liberty Party, abolitionists energized by an evangelical perfectionist theology, had experienced some success in the early 1840s, especially in New York, but its base was too radical and its ideology too focused to allow it to become a national party. The Free Soil Party showed promise of broader appeal in 1848, enticing both Whigs and Democrats in New England, New York, and across the northern tiers of the Midwestern states to join its ranks, but it had yet to achieve a wider appeal. Both parties developed from a groundswell of Northern antislavery and sectional sentiment.

In these same years, Lincoln was discouraged by the nativism sweeping the country. Immigration had surged in the 1840s, bringing newcomers fleeing revolutions in continental Europe and famine in Ireland. In response, an anti-immigration movement had sprung up. Various secret societies coalesced in the early 1850s into the American Party, popularly known as Know-Nothings, because members, when asked about their organization, steadfastly declared their ignorance of the party. The largest group of immigrants—the Irish—as well as many Germans, were Catholic and became the target of Protestant attacks. Many Americans viewed Catholic obedience to a conservative pope as a threat to the liberal American belief in religious liberty. Paradoxically, Know-Nothings and other nativist groups often attracted the same voters who were for temperance, hostile to the hard-drinking Irish Catholics, and against slavery. This appeal to nationalism united Whigs, Democrats, and Free Soilers into a Know-Nothing movement that experienced some spectacular election victories in 1854 and 1855. The New York Herald even predicted the Know-Nothings would win the presidency in 1856.

Lincoln became heartsick as he watched the Know-Nothings make inroads into the Whig Party. He wrote to Owen Lovejoy, abolitionist minister of the Congregational church in Princeton, Illinois, whose brother, Elijah, had been killed in 1837 for defending his printing press in Alton, "I do not perceive how any one professing to be sensitive to the wrongs of the negroes, can join in a league to degrade a class of white men." He was more adamant in a letter to his old friend Joshua

Lincoln became dismayed by the nativist movement's inroads into the Whig Party in the 1850s. "The Know Nothing Citizen" depicts a fair-haired young man meant to be the embodiment of the native-born citizen.

Speed. "I am not a Know-Nothing. That is certain. How could I be?" Lincoln then addressed the dizzying events unfolding across the nation.

> Our progress in degeneracy appears to me to be pretty rapid. As a nation, we began by declaring that "*all men are created equal.*" We now practically read it, "all men are created equal, *except negroes.*" When the Know-Nothings get control, it will read "all men are created equal, except negroes, *and foreigners, and catholics.*" When it comes to this, I should prefer emigrating to some country where they make no pretence of loving liberty—Russia, for instance, where despotism can be taken pure, without the base alloy of hypocrisy.

LINCOLN WATCHED FROM A DISTANCE as another new party struggled to be born. Starting in 1852, a moderate antislavery movement began to attract disgruntled Whigs, Democrats, and Free Soilers. If the problem of slavery became a primary catalyst for this new movement, its first leaders also expressed long-held economic beliefs about protective tariffs, internal improvements, and the use of public lands in the West. The urgency to act now grew from their sense that their ideas were being blocked by a Southern oligarchy that for too long had exercised too much power in Washington. Opposition to the Kansas-Nebraska Act led to local meetings in Wisconsin and Michigan, as well as in Vermont, Maine, Ohio, Indiana, and Iowa. This new movement was called by different names, but the name "Republican"—probably first used in Ripon, Wisconsin, in February 1854—quickly became its calling card. Concerned about the future, these early Republican leaders saw themselves as heirs to the old Jeffersonian Democratic-Republicans of the past.

IN 1854 OR 1855, Lincoln wrote two notes on slavery.

The first, perhaps referring to George Fitzhugh's *Sociology of Slavery,* stated, "Although volume upon volume is written to prove slavery a good thing, we never hear of the man who wishes to take the good of it, *by being a slave himself.*" Fitzhugh, a Virginia lawyer and social theorist, had argued in his 1854 book that the slave was "but a grown up child" who needed the protections provided by Southern society, whereas free labor in the North could be easily exploited.

Lincoln began his second note with a philosophical question. "If A. can prove, however conclusively, that he may, of right, enslave B.— why not B. snatch the same argument, and prove equally, that he may enslave A? . . . You say A. is white, and B. is black. It is *color,* then; the lighter, having the right to enslave the darker?" He tried out the same argument with the characteristics of "*intellectual* superiority" and "*interest.*" In each case, his response is, be careful, "you are to be slave to the first man you meet," with a color, intellect, or interest superior to yours. This fragment is a rare glimpse of a private Lincoln puzzling out the most public problem of the day.

Lincoln's reading, contemplation, and writing was his means not simply to acquire more knowledge or to prepare for a future speech, but to forge his moral character. Always an astute observer of the character of others, he was keenly aware of his own moral development. Lincoln attempted to clarify his ethical identity even as he prepared to speak with new clarity about the moral issues facing the nation.

Many of the ideas in these notes, and sometimes the exact language, would later find their way into his speeches. Although remembered as a grand spontaneous speaker, Lincoln increasingly preferred careful preparation before making a speech.

He also listened. On a warm July day in 1854, Cassius M. Clay, an antislavery editor from Kentucky, lectured in Springfield as part of his tour of Illinois. Denied the use of the rotunda of the statehouse because of his abolitionist views, Clay spoke in a grove of trees at the edge of town. Lincoln was present, "whittling sticks as he lay on the turf."

Clay aimed his rhetorical guns at Douglas and his Springfield mouthpiece, the *Illinois State Register,* edited by Douglas defender Charles H. Lamphier. Clay, born the son of a large Kentucky slaveholder, was a cousin of Henry Clay, Lincoln's political hero. As a student at Yale, young Cassius became impressed with the dynamism of New England's free white labor economy. On his return to Kentucky, he saw with fresh eyes the impoverishment of his own region, which he attributed to its reliance on black slave labor. The way that Clay connected free men with free labor struck a responsive chord in Lincoln.

Clay centered his remarks in Springfield on fidelity to the Declaration of Independence as the key to the present debate on slavery. "The Declaration of Independence asserted an immortal truth. It declared political equality as to personal, civil, and religious rights." When he turned his firepower on the Kansas-Nebraska Act, Clay took aim at the economic impact on the new states. "As men of commerce, mere men of the world, conscious that slavery leads back to barbarism, we cannot look with indifference upon the conversion of this vast region to slavery." Lincoln, imbued with a belief in everyone's right to rise, was critical of slavery for denying that right.

LINCOLN FINALLY SPOKE out in late August 1854, three months after the passage of the Kansas-Nebraska Act. He spoke in response to a request from Richard Yates to assist in his campaign for reelection to Congress in Lincoln's home district. Yates was an early opponent of the Kansas-Nebraska Act, condemning it in March on the floor of the House of Representatives. On Friday, August 25, Lincoln traveled to Yates's home in Jacksonville and stayed overnight; the two traveled together to the Scott County Whig Convention in Winchester. Lincoln's speech focused on "the great wrong and injustice of the Missouri Compromise, and the extension of slavery into free territory." The local newspaper believed Lincoln offered "a masterful effort . . . equal to any upon the same subject in Congress."

On September 12, 1854, Lincoln addressed a German anti-Nebraska gathering in Bloomington, Illinois. The German immigrants in Illinois, numbering more than thirty thousand by 1850, had been moving away from their initial support for the Democratic Party over the issue of slavery. In a season of increasingly incendiary rhetoric, Lincoln addressed the German audience in a decidedly different tone. He was inclusive rather than abusive. "He first declared that the Southern slaveholders were neither better, nor worse than we of the North," reported the *Bloomington Pantagraph*. He further stated, "If we were situated as they are, we should act and feel as they do; and if they were situated as we are, they should act and feel as we do. We never ought to lose sight of this fact in discussing the subject." Lincoln, who in his early political career had attacked opponents without mercy, began his remarks with a plea for understanding for the people of the South, who others just now joining the anti-Nebraska coalition delighted in vilifying.

Lincoln's speech was more a history lesson than a harangue. He recounted the story of the development of the Mississippi River valley after it was acquired from the French. He invoked the name and precedent of Thomas Jefferson, whom Lincoln identified as a Southerner—a Virginian—who had declared that "slavery should never be introduced into" the territories. Lincoln appealed to the precedent of the Missouri

Compromise of 1820, which declared that for all time the territories north of the 36°30′ latitude line, the southern boundary of Missouri, "should be free."

IN THE 1850S, STEPHEN A. DOUGLAS was becoming one of the most visible national politicians. The Little Giant, small in stature, wielded a mighty hammer with his potent words. Douglas's friends and critics puzzled over how such an astute politician could so misread the signs on the Nebraska horizon. Did he not understand that his actions would raise a storm of protest? Personal motives are exceedingly complex, and Douglas acted from an assortment of them. He started with a belief in local self-government. Douglas also had a desire to help the West grow. He wanted to damp down the extremists, both in the North and South, on the slavery issue. He hoped his actions could bring the Democratic Party together. Last—some would say first—Douglas was a man with an enormous political ambition.

Whoever dared challenge Douglas would inevitably create a large space for himself. Beginning in late 1854, Lincoln stepped into that space; he would challenge Douglas again and again in the coming months and years.

When Congress adjourned on August 7, 1854, Douglas hurried home to Illinois to defend both his bill and his reputation. Some friends urged him to stay away. He joked that he could have journeyed to Illinois by the light of the burning effigies of himself.

On September 1, 1854, Douglas prepared to speak in Chicago. In the early evening, the bells of local churches began a steady funeral dirge to sound their disapproval. More than eight thousand people crammed into Market Square on a sultry summer evening, with hundreds more sitting in the windows and on the rooftops of adjoining buildings. As the Little Giant began to speak, the audience greeted him with an eerie silence. Before long, his words were met by catcalls and hisses. Shaking his fists, his face flushed with anger, he accused the crowd of being a mob. After suffering two hours of alternating taunts and silence, he gave up and stomped off the platform.

Determined to make his case, Douglas set out on a statewide speaking tour trailed by newspaper reporters, and always met by a variety of anti-Nebraska speakers eager to rebut his remarks. Douglas's announced purpose was to educate the public about the true meaning of the Kansas-Nebraska Act. Learning from the Chicago experience, he attempted to restrain his temper, but he could not restrain himself from shouting epithets—"Abolitionists," "Black Republicans," and "Nigger-lovers"—as the crowds grew hostile.

When Douglas arrived in Bloomington on September 26, 1854, Lincoln was waiting. He was eager to bring his months of solitary reading and preparation, and his weeks of honing his speeches, into an engagement with the author of the Kansas-Nebraska Act. The *Illinois State Register* groused that Lincoln "had been nosing for weeks in the State Library pumping his brain and his imagination for points and arguments." Bloomington resident Jesse W. Fell, a friend of Lincoln's, proposed that Douglas join Lincoln in a debate, but Douglas refused, replying that this was his meeting. Douglas spoke in the afternoon at the courthouse. As he concluded, the crowd called out, "Lincoln, Lincoln, Lincoln." Although present, Lincoln declined to respond at that moment, instead inviting the crowd to return to hear him speak in the evening.

A few hours later, Lincoln responded to Douglas's characterization of the new party as "Black Republicans," dismissing this remark as a "pander to prejudice." Lincoln asked the audience to compare the old Douglas of 1849 with the new Douglas of 1854. The old Douglas had spoken "in language much finer and more eloquent than" Lincoln had about the Missouri Compromise. "This Compromise had become canonized in the hearts of the American people as a sacred thing, which no ruthless hand should attempt to disturb." Lincoln then asked, "Who was it that uttered this sentiment? What 'Black Republican'?" As the crowd roared in laughter, a voice cried out: "Douglas." Lincoln laid out in elaborate detail the "sophistry" by which the Missouri Compromise had been abandoned in order to pass the Kansas-Nebraska Act. Lincoln had done his historical detective work. He carried with him clippings of Douglas's speeches. His speech at Bloomington sparkled with wisdom and wit.

ONE WEEK LATER, both Lincoln and Douglas attended the opening of the Illinois State Fair in Springfield. Douglas spoke outdoors on October 3, 1854, and for a second time he turned down an invitation to appear on the same platform with Lincoln. When heavy rains swamped the fairgrounds, Douglas spoke in the hall of the House of Representatives. While Douglas made his address, Lincoln listened in the lobby, pacing back and forth. With the speech over and the crowd leaving the hall, Lincoln stood on the stairway announcing that he would answer Douglas the next day.

The next afternoon, Lincoln appeared at two o'clock in the Hall of Representatives, which was crowded to overflowing on a muggy afternoon. Lincoln, dressed only in shirt sleeves and ill-fitting pants, invited Douglas, in his usual formal attire, to sit directly in front of him in the first row.

Horace White, a twenty-year-old correspondent for the *Chicago Tribune,* later wrote that Lincoln spoke that day with "a thin, high-pitched falsetto voice of much carrying power, that could be heard a long distance in spite of the hustle and bustle of the crowd . . . [with] the accent and pronunciation peculiar to his native state, Kentucky."

Lincoln's speech at Springfield bore the marks of an orator who had revised and refined a basic speech that he had given for more than a month. In the highly charged atmosphere he began with conciliation. "I do not propose to question the patriotism, or to assail the motives of any man, or class of men; but rather to strictly confine myself to the naked merits of the question." As for slavery, he made it clear that throughout his speech he intended to "MAKE and KEEP the distinction between the EXISTING institution, and the EXTENSION of it." Lincoln offered "a clear understanding" of the logic and meaning of the Missouri Compromise by again focusing on Jefferson, whom he called "the most distinguished politician of our history." He took pains to point out that Jefferson, who opposed the extension of slavery in the legislation of the Northwest Ordinance, was himself a slaveholder.

At the heart of the speech Lincoln took up Douglas's "sacred right of self-government." Douglas had argued that the Kansas-Nebraska Act was not about slavery, going so far as to say that he was "indifferent" about slavery. At this point in his speech, Lincoln's historical narrative suddenly became an ethical indictment.

> This *declared* indifference, but as I must think, covert *real* zeal for the spread of slavery, I can not but hate. I hate it because of the monstrous injustice of slavery itself. I hate it because it deprives our republican example of its just influence in the world— enables the enemies of free institutions, with plausibility, to taunt us as hypocrites.

Lincoln asked his audience to consider what "popular sovereignty" would become at the end of the day. This line of thinking, Lincoln said, "forces so many really good men amongst ourselves into an open war with the very fundamental principles of civil liberty—criticising the Declaration of Independence, and insisting that there is no right principle of action but *self-interest*."

In this speech, and his others in 1854, Lincoln developed an alternating rhythm of conciliation and challenge. Having exercised his moral indignation over the slavery he hated, he quickly returned to empathy for the people of the South. He began with a bow to the past. "When southern people tell us they are no more responsible for the origin of slavery, than we; I acknowledge the fact." He then moved from past to present. "When it is said that the institution exists, and that it is very difficult to get rid of it, in any satisfactory way, I can understand and appreciate the saying." Finally, he personalized the problem by putting the onus on himself, and by implication, his audience, when he declared, "I surely will not blame them for not doing what I should not know how to do myself." With these generous words, he identified with not only the South, but many in the central Illinois audience he was attempting to persuade.

Lincoln, who delighted in rhetorical contrasts, then quoted Alexander Pope's *Essay on Criticism,* " 'Fools rush in where angels fear to tread,' " and told his audience, "At the hazard of being thought one of the fools . . . I rush in, I take the bull by the horns." He was at his best in winsomely combining high and low culture, often through self-deprecation.

Lincoln focused his attention on the "great argument" for the repeal of the Missouri Compromise, the right of self-government. He set about to unmask the doctrine, but first gave it its due. "The doctrine of self government is right—absolutely and eternally right—but it has no just application, as here attempted." Why not? For Lincoln, it was a prior belief that needed to be settled: "It all depends upon whether a negro is *not* or *is* a man." His voice rising in intensity and volume, he declared: "When the white man governs himself, that is self-government; but when he governs *another* man, that is *more* than self-government—that is despotism."

What was the answer? Lincoln, appealing to what he called his "ancient faith," declared, "Let no one be deceived. The spirit of seventy-six and the spirit of Nebraska, are utter antagonisms; and the former is being rapidly displaced by the latter." He believed America was witnessing a march backward from the moral values of the Declaration of Independence.

Then he employed biblical imagery to ressurect the truth of the Declaration of Independence. He issued a call for repentance in the highly evocative, apocalyptic imagery of the book of Revelation where, in the context of the persecution of Christians in the Roman Empire, John the Elder described how the robes of the Christian martyrs had been washed and made white, the symbol for purity. "Our republican robe is soiled, and trailed in the dust," Lincoln said. "Let us repurify it. Let us turn slavery from its claims of 'moral right,' back upon its existing legal rights, and its arguments of 'necessity.' " Just as the writer of the book of Revelation called people to return to their first faith, Lincoln called for a return to the first faith of the founders. "Let us return it to the position our fathers gave it; and there let it rest in peace. Let us re-adopt the Declaration of Independence, and with it, the practices and policy, which harmonize with it."

For Lincoln's audiences, the meaning of his argument would not necessarily have been understood. Before 1854, Lincoln had appealed to the Declaration of Independence only twice in his public remarks, first in the speech to the Young Men's Lyceum in 1838, and then in his eulogy for Henry Clay. Starting in 1854, Lincoln would reach back behind the Constitution to invoke the Declaration again and again.

For the revolutionary generation, the Declaration of Independence was primarily about the present act of separation from Great Britain. Their emphasis was not so much on the introduction,

> We hold these truths to be self-evident, that all men are created equal, that they are endowed by their Creator with certain unalienable Rights, that among these are Life, Liberty and the pursuit of Happiness.

as the conclusion,

> That these United Colonies are, and of Right ought to be Free and Independent States, that they are Absolved from all Allegiance to the British Crown, and that all political connection between them and the State of Great Britain, is and ought to be totally dissolved.

For the first fifteen years after 1776, the Declaration languished in neglect. The framers of the Constitution barely mentioned it, either in substance or language, in their deliberations.

It reentered the national dialogue when the new Democratic-Republican Party of Thomas Jefferson challenged the Federalists for office in the first years of the nineteenth century. The Federalists, with no love for Jefferson, focused their patriotic national celebrations not on July 4 but on February 22, the birthday of George Washington.

Lincoln grew up attending Fourth of July celebrations where the entire Declaration would be read. Yet, by the 1840s, many of Lincoln's fellow Whigs interpreted the Declaration and the Revolution as not "the creation of something new," but rather a recognition of a reality that had already been realized in the earlier colonial experience. Thus, Rufus Choate, Massachusetts conservative Whig politician, declared in 1834, "The Declaration of Independence, the succeeding conduct of the war, the establishment of our local and general governments" were not new developments but simply "effects, fruits, outward manifestations!" For many Whigs, the Declaration became noteworthy chiefly as a historical signpost. This view, as Lincoln well understood, defused the Declaration as an impetus for reform in mid-nineteenth-century American life.

As the debate over slavery escalated, Southerners also weighed in on the meaning of the Declaration. In a June 27, 1848, Senate debate over how Oregon should be organized, Senator John C. Calhoun of South Carolina argued that government meddling with slavery was embedded in the "false and dangerous assumption" that "all men are created equal." Calhoun stated that this idea had been "inserted in the Declaration of Independence without any necessity" to the main purpose of separation from Great Britain. Furthermore, he argued that the Declaration's contention was "a hypothetical truism" about human equality in the state of nature, drawn from the writings of John Locke and Algernon Sidney, but in the present political state the idea that "all men are created equal" was "the most false and dangerous of all political error."

In his speech at Springfield, Lincoln cut through the political, social, and economic arguments about slavery to expose the moral issue at stake. His intellectual imagination shone in his use of the Declaration of Independence as the centerpiece of his argument.

The next day, Lincoln wrote out a summary of the speech for the *Illinois State Journal*. Herndon wrote a *Journal* editorial on the speech, stating, "The anti-Nebraska speech of Mr. Lincoln was the profoundest in our opinion that he has made in his whole life." Twelve days later, Lincoln offered essentially the same speech in Peoria. This time he wrote out the entire speech for publication, and thus it became known as the Peoria speech, which, distributed as an 1854 campaign document, began to spread the word about Lincoln beyond Illinois.

ON OCTOBER 4, 1854, the same day that Lincoln spoke at the state fair, two Congregational ministers, Owen Lovejoy and Ichabod Codding, attempted to gather a group in Springfield with the intention of starting a Republican state party. Melding their evangelical theology to abolitionist practice, they wished to draw all free-soil groups together. Wanting to hear Lincoln speak, they postponed their meeting. When they met the next day, Lincoln, although invited, did not attend. According to Herndon, who was empathetic with the radical Republican ideals but knew his partner was not, he counseled Lincoln to get out of town, "under the pretense of having business in Tazewell County."

With or without Lincoln's presence, Lovejoy and Codding were so impressed with his speech two days before that they hoped to recruit him for the new party's leadership. In their enthusiasm, they placed Lincoln's name on a new state committee without his approval.

This action was one of what would become a growing number of attempts in the 1850s to define Lincoln even as he was struggling to define himself. One reason that Lincoln got on so well with Herndon was that he knew that his junior partner, who held more radical views on slavery than did Lincoln, would not attempt to impose his views or misrepresent Lincoln's opinions. This could not be said for other friends, colleagues, and even acquaintances, who not only sought to define Lincoln but also co-opt him for their cause.

When Lincoln discovered a few weeks later what Lovejoy and Codding had done, he wrote a strongly worded letter to Codding. "I have been perplexed to understand why my name was placed on that committee. I was not consulted on the subject; nor was I apprized of the appointment." He quickly added, "My opposition to the principle of slavery is as strong as any member of the Republican party."

Why was he not willing to join? First, Lincoln continued to hope for the rejuvenation of the Whig Party. Second, he was concerned that the Republicans seemed to be a narrow party of extreme abolitionists rather than a broad party of antislavery men. Indeed, Lovejoy and Codding's meeting in Springfield had advocated the immediate abolition of slavery across the nation and the repeal of the 1850 Fugitive Slave Act. Because of the convention's radical stance, the *Illinois Journal,* which allied itself with Lincoln, discouraged the forming of a Republican Party in Illinois. Finally, as Lincoln began to consider running for political office again, he wondered if the emergent Republican Party would have staying power. Lovejoy and Codding had met with only a few dozen people in Springfield and had failed to persuade other prominent Whigs to join, and thus a Republican Party in Illinois never got off the ground in 1854.

WHEN LINCOLN REEMERGED in politics in the congressional elections of 1854, he said that "he took the stump with no broader practical aim or object than to secure, if possible, the reelection of Hon Richard Yates to congress." But things were moving quickly. As anti-Nebraska men sought to pack the state legislature, they approached Lincoln about running. A group of Know-Nothings also informed him that their party had nominated him—secretly—for the legislature. On September 3, Dr. William Jayne, Lincoln's family physician, placed an announcement of the candidacy of Lincoln and Logan for the state legislature in the *Illinois State Journal*. The surprise announcement angered Mary Lincoln, who marched down to the offices of the newspaper and demanded that the editor take the announcement out. The next day, Dr. Jayne called on Lincoln to make his case in person. Years later, Jayne remembered Lincoln's response. Deeply upset, Lincoln exclaimed, "No—I can't. You don't know all. I say you don't begin to know one-half and that's enough."

What didn't Jayne know? The state legislature may have seemed to Lincoln a step backward after having served in the House of Representatives. Lincoln never explained his reservations, but he quickly changed his mind. He announced his candidacy as a Whig for the state legislature, believing it could help Yates in his tight race for Congress and, at the same time, strengthen the Whigs in the legislature. The 1854 elections confirmed the power of the anti-Nebraska movement in Illinois. On election day Lincoln received the highest number of votes of any candidate in Sangamon County.

At some point during this period, Lincoln set his sights on a higher goal. In the closing weeks of the campaign for the state legislature, he started speaking beyond his district, traveling as far as Chicago, an indication that he was considering a run for the U.S. Senate. In one speech in Chicago, in addition to his usual blasts at Douglas, he took aim at a recent detractor of the Declaration of Independence, Senator John Pettit, a Democrat from Indiana, who had spoken in favor of expanding slavery into Kansas. In 1853, on the Senate floor, Pettit said that the Declaration's decree that "all men are created equal" was not a "self-evident truth" but instead "is nothing more to me than a self-evident lie." Lincoln now asked, "What would have happened if he had said it in old Independence Hall? The door-keeper would have taken him by the throat and stopped his rascally breath awhile, and then have hurled him into the street."

James Shields, Lincoln's old dueling foe, had been elected to the Senate in 1849. At the time, all U.S. senators were elected by state legislatures. Everyone agreed that Shields could be defeated by an anti-Nebraska candidate in the election of 1855. Lincoln's appetite for public office, stimulated by the responses to his anti-Nebraska speeches, became whetted once again.

But immediately after his election to the legislature, Lincoln made an unsettling discovery. He learned that the state constitution mandated that the legislature could not elect one of its own members as senator. By winning one election, he made himself ineligible for a second election. On November 25, 1854, after more than two weeks of deliberations, Lincoln declined his recently won seat in the legislature.

Lincoln's withdrawal did not sit well. Some among the Whigs, the anti-Nebraska coalition, and the Know-Nothings felt betrayed. A number believed that Lincoln was an opportunist putting personal ambition ahead of both cause and party.

As Lincoln began his campaign for the U.S. Senate, he displayed his resourcefulness as a politician. In the space of five days in November, he wrote numerous letters to friends all over the state asking them for their support. It was time to call in the chits he had earned in both his legal and political careers. With Charles Hoyt, prominent merchant in Aurora, the bond was legal. Lincoln had represented Hoyt in a lengthy lawsuit in Chicago over the patent for a water wheel in 1850. Four years later, Lincoln wrote to ask for his political support. For others, it was primarily political. Lincoln asked Joseph Gillespie, a political colleague from southern Illinois, whether he intended to make a run and told him, "I do not ask you to yield to me." Lincoln also wrote to editors, such as Hugh Lemaster, editor of the *Fulton Republican* at Lewistown. In each letter, Lincoln thanked his correspondents for their support, and concluded by requesting "the names, post-offices, and '*political* position' of members round about you." He included a copy of his Peoria speech in each letter.

As Lincoln surveyed his prospects, he understood he had much work to do. In order to win election he would need to gain the votes of some anti-Nebraska Democrats. The majority of Democrats, in revolt against Douglas, were cozying up to the well-liked governor Joel A. Matteson. An alternative was Lyman Trumbull, a former Illinois secretary of state and Supreme Court justice, who had just been elected to Congress from the Eighth District. Trumbull's wife, the former Julia Jayne, was Mary Lincoln's close friend. The regular Democrats despised Trumbull because of his anti-Nebraska stance, but he was attracting the interest of independent Democrats who had broken ranks with Douglas, and yet would never vote for an old-line Whig.

Lincoln stepped up his efforts in December, bringing in old friends and colleagues to help. Judge David Davis wrote letters and Leonard Swett traveled the state to line up elected officials for Lincoln. Responses to Lincoln's November letters were encouraging. Charles Hoyt promised his support: "It will give me pleasure to do what I can for your appointment to the Sennet." Hugh Lemaster responded, "We want some one that can stand right up to the little Giant (*excuse me*) it takes a great Blackguard (you know) to do that—*and thou art* (excuse again) *the man.*"

Abraham Lincoln ran against Lyman Trumbull, an anti-Nebraska Democrat, for a U.S. Senate seat in 1854–55.

Lincoln made a special effort to reach out to Elihu B. Washburne. A Galena attorney and former Whig, Washburne was one of the first Republicans elected to Congress. On December 11, 1854, Lincoln wrote that he was "a total stranger" to members of Washburne's northern district and asked, "Could you not drop some of them a line?" On December 14, Lincoln wrote again, complaining that "my most intimate friends" in Chicago "do not answer my letters," and asking Washburne to contact both Republicans and Democrats. On December 19, after hearing concerns about whether he would represent the rapidly growing northern part of the state, Lincoln assured Washburne he would represent the whole state.

When the legislature assembled in Springfield on January 1, 1855, Lincoln wrote the names of all one hundred members of the Senate and House on seven pages of lined paper. After each name he placed a "W" for Whig, "D" for Democrat, or "A.N.D." for Anti-Nebraska Democrat. He wrote a number of copies of his list and sent them to some of his key contacts across the state. Davis, Swett, and several others came to Springfield to help. On January 6, Lincoln sent a detailed analysis to Washburne of his assessment of where things stood. He was cautiously optimistic. "I cannot doubt but I have more committals than any other one man."

After delays caused by the fiercest Illinois snowstorm in twenty-four years, the House and Senate convened in joint session at 3 p.m. on February 8, 1855, to begin the balloting. Mary Lincoln watched the proceedings from the packed gallery.

At the end of the first ballot, Lincoln had 45 votes; followed by Shields, the incumbent, with 41; Trumbull with 5; and Governor Matteson and eight other candidates with 1 vote each. Lincoln was seven votes short of a majority. Lincoln had told Washburne two months earlier, "I do not know that it is much advantage to have the largest number of votes at the start." Nothing changed much through five more ballots; although Lincoln slowly declined to 34 on the fifth ballot, his vote total was back to 36 on the sixth ballot. On the seventh ballot, the regular Democrats made their flanking move. They abandoned Shields, who fell from 41 to 1, and shifted their votes to Matteson, who rose from 0 to 44. On the eighth ballot, Lincoln dropped to 27 and on the ninth to 15. Meanwhile, Matteson had risen to 47, the most that any candidate had yet received and only four votes short of election.

What could Lincoln do? On the one hand, Lincoln hoped that if he could prevent Matteson from winning on one or two more ballots, his original backers might return to him. His old legal colleagues Stephen Logan and Judge Davis encouraged him to hang on. On the other hand, Lincoln was worried that Matteson might be able to win away some of Trumbull's backers. At this critical moment, Gillespie asked Lincoln what he should do. "You ought to drop me and go for Trumbull," Lincoln advised. Lincoln had decided he could not take the chance that the Democrats could elect the pro-Nebraska Matteson. He released his backers and instructed his friends to go for Trumbull, a Democrat but an avowed anti-Nebraska man. Lincoln decided that the long-term cause of stopping slavery trumped his short-term ambition. Trumbull was elected on the tenth ballot with the necessary 51 votes.

BALLOTS FOR UNITED STATES SENATE
1855

	1ST	2ND	3RD	4TH	5TH	6TH	7TH	8TH	9TH	10TH
Lincoln	45	43	41	38	34	36	38	27	15	0
Shields	41	41	41	41	42	41	1	0	0	0
Trumbull	5	6	6	11	10	8	9	18	35	51
Matteson	1	1	0	2	1	0	44	46	47	47

Lincoln was both philosophical and gracious in defeat. The next day he told Congressman Washburne, "I regret my defeat moderately, but I am not nervous about it." He added, "On the whole, it is perhaps as well for our general cause that Trumbull is elected."

Lincoln's family and friends did not take the defeat as well. Mary Lincoln broke off her long friendship with Julia Trumbull, who had stood up with Mary at her wedding. Thinking of her role within her own marriage, Mary believed Julia could have influenced her husband's political decision making.

Logan and Davis were furious. Lincoln, they pointed out, who began with 45 votes, actually had 47 different people vote for him, whereas Trumbull had begun with only 5 votes.

Immediately after his defeat, Lincoln told Gillespie "he would never strive for office again." Yet with more time to consider all that had taken place, Lincoln began to see things in a different light. He realized that the person who had been defeated was not Matteson, nor Shields, nor even himself, but Douglas. Douglas had become the personification of the Kansas-Nebraska Act, which, its critics said, opened the door to slavery, not just in the territories, but everywhere. Lincoln told Washburne, "his defeat now gives me more pleasure than my own gives me pain."

Lincoln respected Trumbull and his sharp, logical mind, and knew he would provide a balance to Douglas in the Senate. On the evening after the election, Ninian and Elizabeth Edwards hosted a reception that had originally been intended as a victory party. The defeated Lincoln surprised many by attending. Elizabeth tried to console him by saying she knew he must be very disappointed. He replied, "Not *too* disappointed to congratulate my friend Trumbull," and with those words walked over to shake the hand of the new senator. Trumbull, admiring Lincoln's behavior, later wrote him: "I shall continue to labor for the success of the Republican cause and the advancement at the next election to the place now occupied by Douglas of that *Friend,* who was instrumental in promoting my own."

"I WAS DABBLING IN POLITICS; and, of course, neglecting business. Having since been beaten out, I have gone to work again." So Abraham Lincoln wrote a long-overdue letter to a New York law firm on March 10, 1855.

Lincoln had foreseen the future of railroads a full twenty years before they brought a revolution in transportation to Illinois. In his first announcement of candidacy for the Illinois legislature in 1832, Lincoln declared, "No other improvement that reason will justify us in hoping for, can equal in utility the rail road." As he returned from his stint in the U.S. House of Representatives in 1849, the first railroad was winding its way south from Chicago. Innumerable problems and roadblocks resulted in only 110 miles of track being laid by 1850.

Lincoln started representing the Illinois Central Railroad in 1852. First greeted as a boon to transportation, the Illinois Central quickly established a reputation as a large and unpopular bully. It was infamous for striking cows on the rails, setting barns on fire with stray sparks, and losing the freight of its customers.

The railroads needed friends in high places to succeed. Lincoln, like other political leaders, "chalked his hat," or traveled on railroad passes, regularly. Politicians were lobbied heavily in the state legislature by every small town that wanted to be on the new railroad line. Many politicians and lawyers would become wealthy through land speculation close to the routes of railroad lines. Satisfied to earn his livelihood from his law practice, Lincoln turned away from such speculation, though it was practiced with lucrative results by his close friend David Davis. Railroads needed lawyers to represent them in the contracts and contentions in the 1850s. Lincoln, with his growing stature, found the railroads coming to his door seeking his legal services.

From 1852 through the end of the decade, Lincoln would represent the railroads in about fifty cases, although seldom alone, in five counties in the Eighth Circuit and in appellate cases before the Supreme Court. He was never an employee of the Illinois Central, the most powerful railroad in the state, although he did serve at various times on a retainer. He also brought suit against it on a number of occasions.

Lincoln's work for the railroad was a departure from his previous legal practice. When he advocated the "economic right to rise" in America, he had in mind the upward path of the farmer or small proprietor that he had come to know in the 1830s and 1840s. He had grown up as a lawyer in a face-to-face society in which he urged his clients to settle because they had to live with one another in small communities. Most of the clients stood on more or less equal footing with one another. As a Whig, he upheld the ideal of the independence of each person, but as a lawyer in the 1850s he represented a powerful corporation determined to use its corporate muscle for profit.

Even when dealing with corporations, Lincoln looked for opportunities to be a mediator. In 1854, he wrote to Milton Brayman, solicitor of the Illinois Central, about an old man from DeWitt County who wanted Lincoln to sue the railroad because it did not keep its word regarding the erection and repair of fences. Lincoln offered advice to Brayman that the railroad should be careful to mend its fences, both physical and political. "A stitch in time may save nine in this matter."

As the Illinois Central proceeded with construction, it completed a section in 1853 between La Salle and Bloomington in McLean County. Thereupon county officials presented a bill for a tax assessment. The railroad protested, arguing that under the provisions of its charter the legislature had exempted it from all county taxes with the proviso that it pay a charter tax of 5 percent of its annual gross revenues for the first six years after its incorporation in 1851, and 7 percent thereafter. McLean officials argued the state did not have the power to exempt the railroad from county taxation. The railroad was in trouble if every county attempted to levy a tax.

Both sides contacted Lincoln as each prepared to go to court. He believed at issue "is the largest law question that can now be got up in the State." Approached by the county, he replied that he needed an official letter promising payment if they wanted him to represent them. "I can not afford, if I can help it, to miss a fee altogether." After waiting eighteen days, Lincoln wrote the Illinois Central that he would accept their offer. Four days later, Brayman sent Lincoln a personal check for $250 as a retainer for the case.

McLean County engaged the services of a prominent team of lawyers—Stephen Logan, John Todd Stuart, and Benjamin S. Edwards. This was Lincoln's first big case for the Illinois Central and he well understood that success could lead to many more. He prepared carefully. In his appeal on February 28, 1854, Lincoln, for precedent, cited twenty-six cases: four decisions from the U.S. Supreme Court and twenty-two decisions from thirteen state courts. Because of the significance and complexity of the case, the circuit court ordered the case reargued before the Illinois Supreme Court.

The Supreme Court heard the case a final time in January 1856. Lincoln argued that because the railroad was held in trust by the state it was exempt from taxation for its first six years while being built. He defended the authority of the legislature to take such action. Judge Walter G. Scates upheld Lincoln's argument, ruling that the legislature had the authority to exempt the railroad's payment of county taxes. In his long opinion, Judge Scates cited thirteen of the precedents from Lincoln's appeal.

Lincoln, overjoyed with the result, believed he had salvaged for the railroad at least $500,000. He presented a bill in person in Chicago of $2,000 for his fee.

The bill was rejected. The railroad replied that Lincoln's request was as much as Daniel Webster might have charged. Rebuffed, Lincoln started back for Springfield. Stopping in Bloomington, he consulted with a few fellow attorneys. His peers, surprised at Lincoln's submission of such a modest fee, encouraged him to resubmit a bill for $5,000. When the railroad again refused to pay, Lincoln brought suit in January 1857, in the McLean Circuit Court. Six months later, a jury returned a verdict to pay the plaintiff the full amount of five thousand dollars.

Lincoln would work for the Illinois Central again. This episode tells us how far he had come as a lawyer in twenty years. The man with the reputation as a peaceful mediator for his clients took a stand for himself against the largest corporation in Illinois.

DURING THE FALL CIRCUIT in 1855, Lincoln interrupted his usual routine for a patent case that was attracting national attention. The "Reaper Case," as it would become known, would be a crucial test case with huge implications for the growing farm community. It also offered a splendid opportunity for a rising Illinois lawyer.

Cyrus McCormick, born three days after Lincoln in 1809, had invented a mechanical reaper in Virginia that could mow, gather, tie, and stack wheat, thereby combining the functions of earlier harvesting machines. McCormick patented his machine in 1834 and started a factory in Chicago in 1847. John H. Manny developed a similar machine in Wisconsin and subsequently moved his factory to Rockford, Illinois. McCormick sued Manny for infringement, demanding damages of $400,000.

Both sides were prepared to hire the best lawyers and spend whatever it took to win the case. McCormick retained nationally known lawyers Edward M. Dickerson of New York and Reverdy Johnson of Washington. The Manny Company hired the country's leading patent lawyers, George Harding of Philadelphia and Peter H. Watson of New York, as well as Edwin M. Stanton, a rising young lawyer from Pittsburgh. Because the case was to be tried in the federal court in Chicago, Harding sent Watson to Illinois in June to find a prominent local lawyer who would have the trust of the federal judge. Watson, a short, stout man, with red hair and beard, upon meeting the tall, dark Lincoln at his home, was unenthusiastic. Nevertheless, he invited Lincoln to join the defense team and gave him a $500 retainer, telling him there would be a substantial fee upon completion of a successful case. Watson also told Lincoln that he would deliver the closing argument as the Illinois lawyer on the case.

Lincoln determined to give this case his most careful preparation. On July 7, 1855, while in Chicago for the summer session of the U.S. Federal Court, he went out to Rockford and spent time at the Manny factory becoming familiar with their reaper. On July 23, he wrote to Watson, concerned that he had not yet received depositions for the case.

"During August, and the remainder of this month, I can devote some time to this case, and, of course, I want all the materials that can be had." Lincoln's letter received no answer. Frustrated, Lincoln finally wrote to the Manny headquarters in Rockford on September 1, seeking materials and asking for clarification about the place of the trial. In the weeks before the trial, the case was transferred from Chicago to Cincinnati.

On the morning of September 19, 1855, as Harding and Stanton were walking to the courthouse from the Burnett House in Cincinnati, they came across, in Harding's words, "a tall rawly boned, ungainly back woodsman, with coarse, ill-fitting clothing" standing on the stone steps. Remembering Watson's uncomplimentary description of Lincoln, they knew it had to be the Springfield lawyer. Lincoln suggested that they go up to the courthouse "in a gang," but Stanton prevailed upon Harding to walk without Lincoln.

In Cincinnati, the Manny Company lawyers informed Lincoln he would not give the final argument. In fact, he would have no role in the case. Harding never opened the lengthy brief that Lincoln had prepared. When informed of this, Lincoln asked that the brief be returned so he might destroy it.

The case lasted a week. In all this time, the defense team never included Lincoln in their deliberations, nor even invited him to join them for their meals at the hotel. Judge John McLean entertained all the lawyers at a dinner at his home, but Lincoln was not invited.

Lincoln felt humiliated. He remained in Cincinnati, attending all the court sessions—now reduced to the role of a spectator. He admired the lawyers' expertise in the technical matters of patents. After the case was decided in favor of the Manny Company, Watson sent Lincoln a check as payment for his participation. Lincoln returned the check, replying that he had no right to any fee beyond the original retainer. Watson sent him the check again, saying he had earned it by his preparation. Lincoln finally cashed it.

Stanton, who was known for his brusque manners and often acidic tongue, was especially rude to Lincoln. He is reputed to have described Lincoln as "a long, lank creature, from Illinois, wearing a dirty linen duster for a coat." Lincoln told Herndon after he returned to Springfield that he had been "roughly handled by that man Stanton." Stanton, a careful letter writer, wrote in great detail about what he called "the most important Patent case that has ever been tried," but said nothing about Lincoln in his letters. The two men would meet again seven years later in very different circumstances.

AS LINCOLN RETURNED to his successful law practice, he continued to be deeply concerned about politics, staying abreast of developments, agonizing over party realignments, and biding his time. Though he did not make public speeches, he did reveal his thoughts and struggles in private letters.

On July 18, 1855, he opened a package containing a gift: *Scrap Book on Law and Politics, Men and Times,* by George Robertson, an old friend who was presently professor of law at Transylvania University in Lexington, Kentucky. The volume contained Robertson's speeches and letters from a distinguished legal and political career spanning more than forty years. On August 15, Lincoln wrote to Robertson to thank him and to offer his thoughts on issues triggered by Robertson's lectures.

Robertson, as a young Kentucky congressman in 1819, had spoken of the prospect of "the peaceful extinction of slavery." Lincoln replied, "Since then we have had thirty six years of experience; and this experience has demonstrated, I think, that there is no peaceful extinction of slavery in prospect for us." Lincoln was saying privately in 1855 what he would not yet say publicly. "The signal failure of Henry Clay, and other good and great men, in 1849, to effect anything in favor of gradual emancipation in Kentucky, together with a thousand other signs, extinguishes that hope utterly."

Lincoln also responded to Robertson's discussion of liberty. "On the question of liberty, as a principle, we are not what we have been." He continued, "When we were the political slaves of King George, and we wanted to be free, we called the maxim 'all men are created equal' a self-evident truth; but now when we have grown fat, and have lost all dread of being slaves ourselves, we have become so greedy to be *masters* that we call the same maxim 'a self-evident lie.' " What did all this mean? "The fourth of July has not quite dwindled away; it is still a great day—*for burning fire-crackers!!!*"

Lincoln voiced both despair and hope. "The Autocrat of all of Russia will resign his crown, and proclaim his subjects free republicans sooner than our American masters will voluntarily give up their slaves." He then posed what he believed to be "Our political problem. Can we, as a nation, continue together *permanently—forever*—half slave, and half free?" Lincoln concluded with a confession and a hope. "The problem is

too mighty for me. May God, in his mercy, superintend the solution."
This poignant letter to Robertson, at a time when Lincoln was making
no speeches, tracked his thinking as he brooded over ideas that would
become central to his future attack upon slavery.

On August 24, 1855, Lincoln wrote an even more revealing letter to
Joshua Speed. He had received an earlier letter from Speed in which his
good friend wrote that it had become clear that he and Lincoln now had
quite different positions on the nature and prospect of slavery. Speed
stated that he may well be against slavery in principle, but in practice, in
Lincoln's paraphrase, "You say that sooner than yield your legal right to
the slave—especially at the bidding of those who are not themselves
interested, you would see the Union dissolved." Lincoln was here confronted, not with an anonymous opponent or an avowed enemy, but
with the ideas of his oldest and dearest friend.

At the outset of his letter, Lincoln recalled their common experience
in 1841 when they encountered ten or twelve slaves "shackled together
with irons" on a steamboat traveling from Louisville to St. Louis. Fourteen years later, Lincoln told Speed, "That sight was a continual tor-
ment to me; and I see something like it every time I touch the Ohio, or
any other slave-border." He then challenged his old friend. "You ought
rather to appreciate how much the great body of the Northern people
do crucify their feelings, in order to maintain their loyalty to the constitution and the Union." Lincoln was pained to see that he and Speed
"differ about the Nebraska-law." In private, Lincoln said to Speed, "I
look upon that enactment not as a *law,* but as *violence* from the beginning. It was conceived in violence, passed in violence, is maintained in
violence, and is being enacted in violence."

Speed, in his letter, had asked Lincoln where he stood. Lincoln
answered, "That is a disputed point. I think I am a whig; but others say
there are no whigs, and that I am an abolitionist. When I was in Washington I voted for the Wilmot Proviso, a measure enacted by the opponents of slavery to prevent its introduction into territories acquired in
the Mexican War, as good as forty times, and I never heard any one
attempting to unwhig me for that. I now do more than oppose the
extension of slavery." Lincoln exaggerated how many times he had voted
for the Wilmot Proviso, but once more he disclosed his continuing
struggle with identity—including party identity—even as he told his
friend that others were seeking to identify him in ways he was not willing to accept.

IN THE WINTER OF 1856, Lincoln was rethinking his affiliation with the Whigs as the party continued to splinter, but whether from loyalty or obstinacy, he did not rush to join any of the new movements. On Washington's birthday, a Republican national organizing convention was to meet in Pittsburgh. The Republican train was gaining speed. Would Lincoln climb aboard?

In early February, two men came to Springfield to raise money and secure arms for the "free-state" forces in Kansas. William Herndon helped organize a meeting to hear their appeal, and in the midst of much excitement, belligerence, and exaggeration, Lincoln was asked to speak. He counseled moderation and spoke against coercion that would lead to bloodshed. "Revolutionize through the ballot box, and restore the Government once more to the affections and hearts of men by making it express, as it was intended to do, the highest spirit of justice and liberty." At the end of the meeting Lincoln made a donation to be forwarded to free-state supporters in Kansas. As usual, Lincoln remained more moderate in public than in his more candid conversations with trusted friends.

On February 22, 1856, Lincoln boarded the train for Decatur. Paul Selby, editor of the *Morgan Journal* in Jacksonville, and William Usrey, editor of the *Illinois State Chronicle* in Decatur, had issued a call for an anti-Nebraska meeting, which was endorsed by editors of twenty-five Illinois newspapers. The purpose of the meeting was to plan for the coming state and national elections. The planners had invited one well-known political figure to attend. Lincoln, who had cultivated a relationship with newspaper editors, accepted their invitation. The editors agreed to oppose the introduction of slavery into the territories and work for the restoration of the Missouri Compromise. They called for an anti-Nebraska convention to meet in Bloomington in May.

At a banquet that evening at the Cassell House, one of the editors proposed that Lincoln run for governor. Lincoln quickly replied that it would not do to have an old-line Whig head the ticket; it would be better to try to elect an anti-Nebraska Democrat. Richard J. Oglesby of Decatur, a hero of the Mexican War, was called upon to make a toast. He toasted Lincoln "as the warm and consistent friend of Illinois, and our next candidate for the U.S. Senate."

Lincoln rose and said, "The latter part of that sentiment I am in favor of." He then addressed the dinner guests. He told them that "not being an editor" reminded him of "the ugly man riding through a wood who met a woman, also on horseback. She stopped and exclaimed, 'Well, for land sake, you are the homeliest man I ever saw.'

" 'Yes, madam, but I can't help it,' said he.

" 'No, I suppose not,' she observed, 'but you might stay at home.' "

Lincoln gave the editors his word that he would "buckle on his armor for the approaching contest."

In the spring, Herndon took the lead in calling for a county convention to select delegates for the anti-Nebraska convention in Bloomington. Lincoln was out of town and Herndon, confident that he knew Lincoln's sentiments, signed his name. The list of delegates was then published in the *Illinois State Journal*.

The list had barely been printed when John Todd Stuart stormed into Herndon and Lincoln's law office asking, "Did Lincoln authorize you to sign the list?"

Herndon replied with an emphatic "No."

Stuart quickly responded, "Then you have ruined him." Stuart, who had been Lincoln's first mentor in the study of law, was yet another person wishing to define him. By 1856, Stuart had become deeply concerned that Lincoln was being recruited by the Republicans, whom he equated with radical abolitionism.

Herndon thought he knew Lincoln's mind, but immediately wrote him in Tazewell County where he was attending court. He told Lincoln how much of a stir this was causing among his conservative friends. Herndon needed a response right away.

Lincoln responded: "All right; go ahead. Will meet you—radicals and all."

ON MAY 28, 1856, Lincoln traveled by train from Danville to Decatur on his way to Bloomington. Upon learning there was no train north until the following morning, he strolled about town with other delegates to the upcoming anti-Nebraska convention. While sitting on the trunk of a fallen tree, Lincoln reminisced about coming to Decatur twenty-five years earlier as a young man from Indiana. He pointed to the exact place on the public square where he had stopped the wagon and team of oxen he was driving. Lincoln confessed he was worried about what might transpire in Bloomington. He feared the radicals in the northern counties would be well represented in Bloomington, but voiced his concern that there might not be many representatives from the conservative southern Illinois counties.

Arriving in Bloomington the next day, Lincoln made his way to Judge Davis's mansion where he was invited to stay. Later he stopped in a small jewelry store where he bought his first pair of spectacles for thirty-seven and a half cents. He told his walking companion, lawyer Henry C. Whitney, that "he had got to be forty-seven years old, and 'kinder' needed them."

In the evening, a crowd gathered in front of the Pike House hotel and called for speeches. Lincoln stepped forward, claimed he wasn't prepared to speak that evening, but then proceeded to do so. He talked about the "outrages" in Kansas and said, "A man couldn't think, dream, or breathe of a free state there, but what he was kicked, cuffed, shot down and hung."

On the morning of May 29, 1856, everyone was eager for the arrival of the Chicago dailies. Isaac N. Arnold, a former Democrat and now Free Soil politician from Chicago, stood on the main stairway and read from two stories that the delegates had been following. Eight days earlier a huge Kansas posse, including Missouri "border ruffians," had swept into Lawrence, Kansas, with the intent of striking terror among the rising free-state population. Finding that the free-state leaders had fled, they proceeded to throw two printing presses into the streets and turned five cannon on the Free State Hotel, finally setting the building on fire. Although no one was killed, homes and businesses were pillaged, and the story of the "Sack of Lawrence" ignited antislavery men across the North.

Arnold then read aloud about events in Washington. Senator Charles Sumner of Massachusetts had delivered an eloquent but bitterly antagonistic "Crime against Kansas" speech on May 19 and 20, 1856, including fierce personal criticisms of Senator James Mason of Virginia and Senator Andrew P. Butler of South Carolina. On May 22, as the Senate was adjourning, Sumner was attacked by young South Carolina representative Preston S. Brooks, a nephew of Butler, and beaten into bloody unconsciousness with a walking cane.

With everyone talking about Kansas and Sumner, the convention was called to order. About 270 delegates, mostly from northern and central Illinois, joined together in Major's Hall, located on the third floor over Humphrey's Cheap Store. The call that had gone out was for

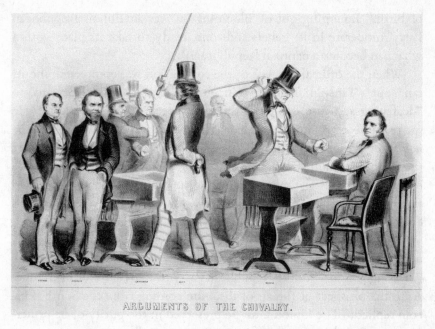

ARGUMENTS OF THE CHIVALRY.

*The artist pictures the caning of Senator Charles Sumner on May 22, 1856.
Above the scene were words from Henry Ward Beecher: "The symbol of
the North is the pen; the symbol of the South is the bludgeon."*

a "State Convention of the Anti-Nebraska Party of Illinois." There were at least two stumbling blocks for using the name "Republican." First, the name had become associated with the abolitionists, and many delegates detested the abolitionists as much as they did Douglas. Second, Douglas had been using the characterization "Black Republicans" as a way to play the race card.

Orville Browning, conservative lawyer from Quincy, led the effort to put together a platform. In its final form, it did not embrace the demands of the abolitionists, but rather reiterated the older logic that Congress had the right to keep slavery out of the territories. It condemned the repeal of the Missouri Compromise and called for the immediate admission of Kansas as a free state. With a nod to the Germans—a potential new force for the Republicans—it remained silent on temperance. As for the vexing issue of nativism, it included the statement that the new party would "proscribe no one, by legislation or otherwise, on account of religious opinions, or in consequence of place of birth." Emerging out of Bloomington was an Illinois Republican Party, moderate in its beliefs and tone, ready to take its place within what had become a national Republican Party.

When the official business of the convention was completed, shouts rang out, "Lincoln! Lincoln! Lincoln!" Lincoln stepped forward, to "deafening applause," to make the final speech of the convention. He spoke for nearly an hour and a half. The speech was so powerful that the newspaper reporters in the hall, spellbound, put down their pencils after the opening minutes and failed to record what Lincoln said. It was reportedly one of the most compelling speeches of his life. Some said that he spoke extemporaneously, but by now Lincoln never approached even the possibility of such a speech without careful preparation.

The *Alton Weekly Courier* was the only newspaper that carried a summary of the speech, and it was exceedingly brief. Lincoln spoke of the "pressing reasons" for the Republican Party to step forward at this time. As to the prospect of threats of disunion coming from the South, Lincoln replied, "The Union must be preserved in the purity of its principles as well as the integrity of its territorial parts."

Because no stenographic reporter recorded the address, it has acquired the title of Lincoln's "Lost Speech." It's surprising that Lincoln, even though he spoke without notes, did not later write the speech out, at least in summary form, for publication by local newspapers. Yet, his passion and eloquence were not lost on his audience. Herndon wrote ten years later, "I have heard or read all of Mr. Lincoln's great speeches, and I give it as my opinion that the Bloomington speech was the grand effort of his life. . . . He had the fervor of a new convert; the smothered flame broke out; enthusiasm unusual to him blazed up, his eyes were aglow with an inspiration, he felt justice."

IT WILL FOREVER BE DEBATED whether Lincoln's political career was essentially continuous or whether there was a new beginning in 1854. The friends who knew him best—even with their great respect for what he had already accomplished—would say there was something new in the anti-Nebraska Lincoln. In 1854, with the speech he delivered at Springfield and again at Peoria, he laid the foundation of ideas he would build upon in the next six years. Like anything new, Lincoln's ideas went through a refining process. He began with opposition to the extension of slavery in the West in the political disguise of "popular sovereignty." But he had long ago learned that simple opposition to expansion could never carry the day. Where he began to distinguish himself from his peers was his ability to offer affirmation—of the old Declaration of Independence and of a new vision for America.

Beneath the public figure dwelt a private man forging a deeper moral character as he clarified his personal and political identity. As Lincoln's political star began to rise, his friends and colleagues often tried to define and sometimes even restrict who he was becoming. But the dynamism of the developing Lincoln could not be confined. Emphasizing his "ancient faith" in the Declaration of Independence, he was not to be bound even to the American Revolution and the founding generation. Though he grieved for the Whig Party, its passing opened up new prospects for political achievement and service that he had not known before. With the birth of the Republican Party, Lincoln left Bloomington with no political office but with something much more important—a political vision for the promise of America that would lead him into the future.

*While Lincoln was in Chicago working on a lawsuit, some attorney friends asked him
for a photograph. He replied, "I don't know why you boys want such a homely face."
Alexander Hesler tried to brush Lincoln's hair away from his forehead. This
"tousled hair" photograph made Lincoln smile and pleased his friends.*

CHAPTER 12

A House Divided
1856–58

I BELIEVE THIS GOVERNMENT CANNOT ENDURE, PERMANENTLY HALF *SLAVE* AND HALF *FREE*.

I DO NOT EXPECT THE UNION TO BE *DISSOLVED*—I DO NOT EXPECT THE HOUSE TO *FALL*—BUT I *DO* EXPECT IT WILL CEASE TO BE DIVIDED.

ABRAHAM LINCOLN
Speech at the Republican convention, Springfield, Illinois, June 16, 1858

IN JUNE 1856, ON THE EVE OF THE FIRST NATIONAL REPUBLICAN convention in Philadelphia, Abraham Lincoln was far away in Urbana, Illinois. He had arrived on Tuesday, June 17, to attend a special session of the Champaign County Court. He checked into a room at the American House hotel where he was joined by his close friends Judge David Davis and lawyer Henry C. Whitney.

The proprietor, John Dunaway, called his guests to meals by beating vigorously on a gong situated directly under the room where the three jurists slept. On Thursday morning, after their sleep was disturbed for a second morning, Davis and Whitney, by a majority vote, elected Lincoln to deal with the noisy annoyance. The next day, after the morning session of court, Lincoln went back to the hotel, took the gong down, and "secreted" it between two layers of a dining room table. When the proprietor attempted to call his boarders to the noon meal, he looked high and low but could not find the missing gong. When Whitney and Davis reached their room, there sat Lincoln, "looking amused, sheepish, and guilty, as if he had done something ridiculous as well as reprehensible." The prank deserved a great laugh, and no one laughed harder than Lincoln.

The following day, June 20, 1856, the Chicago papers, arriving about the time of the noon court break, announced that Lincoln had received 110 votes for vice president at the Republican national convention, the second highest of any candidate. Davis and Whitney were "jubilant" at the news. Davis, recalling the prank of the day before, playfully admonished Lincoln: "Great business for a man who aspires to be Vice President of the United States." To their surprise, the news "made slight impression on Lincoln." Finally, he responded, "I reckon it's not me. There's another Lincoln down in Massachusetts. I've an idea he's the one."

The Republicans in Philadelphia offered a validation that Lincoln had become a national Republican leader. Yet, the forty-seven-year-old Lincoln, for a long time reluctant to join the Republican Party, had not held an elected office for seven years and was only one and a half years removed from his defeat for the U.S. Senate seat from Illinois. Given the whirlwind of events since he reemerged into politics two years before, who could dare predict what the next two years might bring for A. Lincoln, the man with the self-deprecating sense of humor.

THE REPUBLICAN CONVENTION convened on June 17 at the Musical Fund Hall in Philadelphia. The party nominated John C. Frémont as its first presidential candidate. A forty-three-year-old military man and explorer, Frémont had become a hero after his expeditions through the American West. Born in the South, he had served briefly as one of the first two senators from California. He was strongly opposed to slavery. As a celebrity with great name recognition, Frémont won on the first ballot, with 530 votes to 37 for Judge John McLean of Pennsylvania, whom Lincoln had favored.

Delegates nominated fifteen names for vice president. Illinois delegate William B. Archer persuaded John Allison, a congressman from Pennsylvania, to nominate Lincoln. Archer, who had known Lincoln for thirty years, made a seconding speech on behalf of Illinois, calling Lincoln "as pure a patriot as ever lived."

Lincoln garnered 110 votes on the first ballot, trailing only William L. Dayton, a former senator from New Jersey, who polled 221 votes. Most impressive was that Lincoln received votes from eleven states, stretching from Maine to California. Dayton was elected on the second ballot. Two days later, Archer wrote to Lincoln, "had we moved earlier," he might have stood a stronger chance at the nomination.

Lincoln learned that a number of people outside of Illinois had stood up to commend his nomination. Lincoln wrote to one of them, John Van Dyke of New Brunswick, New Jersey, who had served with Lincoln in the Thirtieth Congress. He told Van Dyke, "When you meet Judge Dayton present my respects, and tell him I think him a far better man than I for the position he is in."

LINCOLN THREW HIMSELF into the 1856 presidential campaign. Unlike 1852, when he had done little campaigning for the Whig presidential nominee, General Winfield Scott, Lincoln spoke everywhere on Frémont's behalf. On June 23, 1856, in Urbana, he praised "the gallant Fre-

Lincoln stumped for the first Republican presidential ticket, John C. Frémont and William Dayton, in 1856.

mont," and promised he would "devote considerable of his time to the work" of seeking his election.

The Democratic Party, deeply split over the issue of slavery, "bleeding Kansas," and the ongoing debate over the role of the states versus the federal government, nominated James Buchanan of Pennsylvania over Stephen Douglas as their presidential candidate. Buchanan's political advantage was his absence. He had been out of the country the past four years serving as ambassador to England, and thus he was the only candidate not tarnished by the bruising battles over the Kansas-Nebraska Act. Douglas, who had worked hard to become his party's star, was now seen by some as too controversial to be elected. Buchanan won the nomination on the seventeenth ballot. The party platform supported "popular sovereignty" as the means of settling the issue of slavery in the territories.

The presidential election of 1856 became a story of contrasts. Buchanan was born into a well-to-do family in Pennsylvania. He had never married. A tall, handsome man, he wore stiff, high stocks about his jowls that accentuated both his height and his formal personality. He had served five terms in the House of Representatives and ten years in the Senate. He also had served as minister to Russia under President Jackson and secretary of state under President Polk, and came to the campaign fresh from his service as minister to the Court of St. James's in England under President Pierce. Never had a candidate brought more political experience to a presidential campaign.

Frémont was born in Georgia, an illegitimate child of a father who came to the United States as a penniless French-Canadian refugee. He married Jessie Benton, the beautiful daughter of Senator Thomas Hart Benton of Missouri. Benton, a champion of Western expansion, helped Frémont get assignments in the 1840s to explore the entire American West. Frémont capitalized on five successful expeditions, traveling across the Rocky Mountains to California, to position himself as a young hero of a new party. Ironically, it was Buchanan, as secretary of state, who convinced the Senate to publish Frémont's *Exploring Expedition to the Rocky Mountains* in 1842, which had enhanced Frémont's fame. Seldom had a candidate brought less political experience to a campaign.

The Republicans set out to campaign on the theme "Free Soil, Free Speech, and Frémont." Stories of "bleeding Kansas" were kept alive by on-the-scene reports in Horace Greeley's *New York Tribune*. Democrats countered that Frémont was a "black abolitionist," the front man for a party of radicals.

In this frenzied environment, Lincoln spoke out on the campaign trail in support of Frémont, but the scope of his speeches was broader than support for the candidate, whom he did not know. Long sections of his speeches consisted of historical and philosophical analysis and made almost no reference to Frémont.

In the summer of 1856, Lincoln privately wrestled with a number of ideas. He wrote a long note to himself—undated, but probably from July—in which he sought to define the issues at stake in the campaign. He began, as he almost always did in his private notes, with a problem. "It is constantly objected to Fremont & Dayton, [Frémont's vice-presidential candidate] that they are supported by a *sectional* party, who, by their *sectionalism,* endanger the National Union." The Democrats continually charged that the Republicans, because of their strong anti-slavery beliefs, represented only the North and parts of the West, and thus could never be a national party. Lincoln believed that the issue of sectionalism, "more than all others," was causing persons "really opposed to slavery extension, to hesitate." This was the "reason, I now propose to examine it, a little more carefully than I have heretofore done, or seen it done by others."

In his private reflection, Lincoln engaged in a systematic examination of all the issues involved in sectionalism. He began by exploring the ways Democrats tried to make the Republican question—"Shall slavery be allowed to extend into U.S. territories, now legally free?"—into a sectional issue. In his answer, Lincoln engaged in a long backward gaze at previous candidates for president, noting which ones were from free and slave states. He pointed out that in 1844, the Democratic Party had nominated a Southern candidate, James Polk of Tennessee, but since 1848, as the debate over the extension of slavery escalated, the Democrats nominated only Northern candidates, "each vieing to outbid the other for the Southern vote."

Questions punctuate every paragraph in Lincoln's note. Toward the end, he asked, "Then, which side shall yield?" His answer:

Do they really think the *right* ought to yield to the *wrong?* Are they afraid to stand by the *right?* Do they fear that the constitution is too weak to sustain them in the right? Do they really think that by right surrendering to wrong, the hopes of our constitutions, our Union, and our liberties, can possibly be bettered?

This note demonstrates a major reason Lincoln was becoming such a persuasive public speaker. He was willing to engage in the hard task of examining an opponent's arguments fully and fairly.

WHILE IN CHICAGO to try cases before the federal court, Lincoln accepted an invitation to address a Saturday evening open-air meeting in Dearborn Park on July 19, 1856. Referring to the Democrats' nomination of Buchanan, Lincoln said it "showed how the South does not put up her own men for the Presidency, but holds up the prize that the ambition of Northern men may make bids for it." The *Chicago Democratic Press* reported that Lincoln "demonstrated in the strongest manner, that the only issue before us, is freedom or slavery."

In Galena on July 23, 1856, Lincoln spoke of the challenge of Millard Fillmore, candidate of the Know-Nothings, who in 1856 officially adopted the name the "American Party." Fillmore, elected as the Whig vice president in 1848, had succeeded to the presidency in 1850 upon the death of Zachary Taylor. As president, Fillmore's signing of the Fugitive Slave Act in September 1850 quickly alienated many Whigs. When the Whig Party collapsed in the early 1850s, Fillmore refused to join the new Republicans. The Know-Nothing American Party nominated Fillmore at their convention in February.

Fillmore's appeal came from his nativist platform commitment: "Americans must rule America." He accused both the Democrats and the Republicans of being "Disunionists." Lincoln was deeply concerned that Fillmore's American Party could deny the Republicans an election victory by playing the role of the spoiler, as he had seen the Liberty Party do before. In the conclusion of his Galena speech, Lincoln exclaimed, "All this talk about the dissolution of the Union is humbug—nothing but folly. *We* won't dissolve the Union, and *you* SHAN'T."

During the 1856 campaign, Lincoln received invitations to speak in Indiana, Michigan, Wisconsin, and Iowa—recognition of his growing national stature within the Republican Party. The only out-of-state invitation he accepted was to a huge Republican state "concourse" in Kalamazoo, Michigan. On August 27, Lincoln followed the logic of his July private note by declaring that the crux of the campaign was "to learn what people differ about." He stated, "The question of slavery, at the present day, should be not only the greatest question, but very nearly the sole question." He presented the arguments of his opponents, repeating the questionable charge of the *Richmond Enquirer* "that their slaves are far better off than Northern freemen." He also responded to the complaint that Frémont and his supporters were abolitionists and that the Republicans were disunionists. Lincoln's rhetorical strategy was to ask his audience the questions that he wanted to answer. After praising the United States as "the wonder and admiration of the whole world," he responded to the question, "What is it that has given us so much prosperity?" by responding, "That every man can make himself."

LINCOLN RETURNED HOME on October 28, 1856, after four months of vigorous campaigning. By his own count he had spoken more than fifty times during the presidential campaign. Although his speeches appeared to reporters and audiences to be extemporaneous, little did they realize how much prior effort, including writing his private notes, went into them. The *Amboy Times* captured the distinctiveness of Lincoln's maturing political speaking, observing, "His language is pure and respectful, he attacks no man's character or motives, but fights with arguments."

Lincoln came home to a house divided. Mary did not support Frémont. She wrote her younger half sister Emilie Todd Helm in Lexington, contrasting her political views with those of her husband. Knowing Emilie's strong Southern viewpoint, Mary first defended her husband. "Altho' Mr L is, or was a *Fremont* man, you must not include him with so many of those, who belong to *that* party, an *Abolitionist*." She further explained, "All he desires is, that slavery, shall not be extended, let it remain where it is." Mary then explained her own political position. "My weak woman's heart was too Southern in feeling, to sympathize with any but Fillmore."

On Tuesday, November 4, 1856, a cold and muddy election day in Springfield, Lincoln was the 226th voter at polling place number two. Across the nation there was intense interest and an immense turnout. People stood in queues for more than two hours in New York City to vote. Nearly 83 percent of the nation's eligible voters went to the polls, up nearly 7 percent from the election of 1852.

Lincoln had to wait for several days before the results became known in Illinois. In the end, Frémont lost, but William Bissell won for governor by a majority of five thousand, the first statewide victory for the new Republican Party. As Lincoln had feared, the Fillmore vote hurt Frémont, but the American Party vote ran below expectations.

Although Buchanan triumphed in the electoral college with 174 votes to 114 for Frémont and 8 for Fillmore, he did not win a majority of the popular vote. He received 1,832,955 votes (45.3 percent) compared to 1,340,537 (33.1 percent) for Frémont, and 871,955 (21.6 percent) for Fillmore. Buchanan won five Northern states—New Jersey, Pennsylvania, Indiana, Illinois, and California—and every Southern state except Maryland, which went for Fillmore. Frémont won Maine, New Hampshire, and Michigan, which had been Democratic mainstays. But he received only 1,196 votes in the South.

President-elect Buchanan, greeting supporters at Wheatland, his estate on the outskirts of Lancaster, Pennsylvania, offered his interpretation of his victory. "The storm of abolition against the South has been gathering for almost a quarter of a century," he said, a reference to the growth of antislavery sentiment in the North. More recently, "Republicanism was sweeping across the North like a tornado." Then he offered a prediction for the future, one that would prove entirely wrong. "The night is departing, and the roseate and propitious morn now breaking upon us promises a long day of peace and prosperity for our country."

Upon reflection, Republicans called the 1856 presidential election a "victorious defeat." Privately, many Republican leaders complained that Frémont had proved to be long on bravado and short on both political experience and wisdom. There were, however, many encouraging signs for the future. Frémont had defeated Buchanan by more than 80,000 votes in New York. Buchanan's margin of victory in Indiana was less than 2,000 votes, and less than 1,000 votes in Pennsylvania. If the Frémont and Fillmore votes were combined, Frémont would have won both Illinois and New Jersey. If Frémont had won Pennsylvania, and either Indiana or Illinois, the Republicans would have been victorious. In less than twelve months, the Republican Party had become the strongest party in the North. The Republican candidate in 1860 would stand a real chance of winning the presidential election.

LINCOLN HAD PLAYED A VITAL ROLE in the 1856 election. With his help, Republicans had won the complete state ticket in Illinois. Although without office, he had nevertheless become the leading Republican in Illinois by the end of 1856. One month after the election,

Lincoln was introduced to the "deafening cheers" of three hundred people at a Republican banquet at the Tremont House in Chicago. Recalling that throughout the campaign the Republicans had been "assailed as the enemies of the Union," Lincoln declared that the new party was, above all, "the friend of the Union." Responding to the recent final annual message of outgoing president Franklin Pierce, in which he had trumpeted the "triumph of good principles and good men," Lincoln declared that Buchanan did not triumph in the recent election, but that "all of us who did not vote for Mr. Buchanan, taken together, are a majority of four hundred thousand." He noted that during the campaign, the *Richmond Enquirer*, "an avowed advocate of slavery," had invented the phrase "State equality." In his closing charge to these Republican stalwarts, Lincoln declared, "Let us reinaugurate the good old 'central ideas' of the Republic." What did these ideas mean in the present crisis? "We shall again be able not to declare, that 'all States as States, are equal,' nor yet that 'all citizens as citizens are equal,' but to renew the broader, better declaration, including both these but much more, that 'all *men* are created equal.' " Lincoln asked his audience, "Can we not come together" around this basic belief?

Even in the midst of his growing public esteem, Lincoln struggled privately with insecurity when he compared his political career to that of his longtime rival, Stephen Douglas, the senior senator from Illinois. In December 1856, Lincoln spelled out his struggle on a scrap of paper. "Twenty-two years ago Judge Douglas and I first became acquainted." Lincoln, for his eyes only, admitted, "Even then, we were both ambitious; I perhaps, quite as much so as he." What about today? "With *me,* the race of ambition has been a failure—a flat failure; with *him* it has been one of splendid success." He quickly added, "I affect no contempt for the high eminence he has reached." Having confessed his envy, though, Lincoln offered a soulful affirmation about his hope that others could share in his own search for eminence, "so reached, that the oppressed of my species, might have shared with me in the elevation." Lincoln, knowing of Douglas's disdain for African-Americans, declared that whatever ascent he may yet experience might be accompanied by the rise of the "oppressed"—those who had been the subject of every one of his addresses since 1854. He concluded, "I would rather stand on that eminence, than wear the richest crown that ever pressed a monarch's brow."

THE STORY IS TOLD of Lincoln returning to Springfield after three months away on the circuit. When he encountered his neighbor, James Gourley, Lincoln asked in jest, "Do you know where Lincoln lives?" After a moment, Lincoln, with a wry smile, pointed to his house and exclaimed, "He used to live here!" Lincoln's feigned disorientation was a sharp comment on what Mary Lincoln had wrought.

Thirteen years after the purchase of their home at Eighth and Jackson, Mary began the effort to raise their modest cottage into a full two-story house. Having grown increasingly independent through her husband's long absences, Mary had become the manager of the Lincoln household. She wanted more space for a family of three rambunctious boys, Robert, Tad, and Willie, plus a live-in maid. Her husband was now making about three thousand dollars a year from his law practice. She believed the Lincolns deserved a home more in keeping with her husband's position as a prominent lawyer and politician, and where she could entertain more. In September 1854, she sold eighty acres of farmland in Sangamon County her father had given her for $1,200, further enhancing her independence.

Contractors Daniel Hannon and Thomas A. Ragsdale began constructing a new east wing of the house. Mary's cousin's wife said in a letter that the Lincolns had "commenced raising" the back part of their house. "I think they will have room enough before they are done, particularly as Mary seldom uses what she has." The new construction meant that Mary and Abraham would have separate but connecting bedrooms. This arrangement was common in middle-class families and not a commentary on their marriage or sexual relations. Visitors reported that Lincoln often entertained business guests in his bedroom.

As the project approached completion, Mary bought wallpaper and new furniture from John Williams and Company. She shifted some of her massive Empire pieces upstairs and placed the new, early Victorian pieces in the downstairs formal front parlor and the family sitting room. The final cost of the expansion was $1,300. Lincoln returned to find a fine-looking home newly adorned with light brown paint and dark green shutters. The renovations were in the Greek Revival tradition of the times, which Lincoln approved, with its associations with classical tradition and democracy.

Mary Lincoln was very ambitious for her husband's political career.

Her many dinners and receptions in their newly renovated house provided space for him to network with political friends visiting the Illinois state capital. In the winter of 1857, conversations at these gatherings often turned to politics and the U.S. Supreme Court.

ALEXIS DE TOCQUEVILLE, in his travels in America in the 1830s, had examined the place of the Supreme Court in comparison to the high courts of England and other nations in Europe. He concluded, "A more

Chief Justice Roger Taney delivered the majority
opinion in the Dred Scott case in 1857.

immense judicial power has never been constituted in any people." Yet in the growing political crisis of the 1850s, the Court had been largely silent. It was the only one of the three branches of government not deeply involved in the conflict over the extension of slavery into the federal territories. But the Court was about to exercise its power. Beginning in December 1856, news spread that the Supreme Court would consider a case that had been making its way through the lower courts for more than ten years.

In 1830, Dr. John Emerson, an army surgeon working at the Jefferson Barracks near St. Louis, bought a slave named Dred Scott. Scott accompanied Emerson to Fort Armstrong at Rock Island, Illinois, in 1833, and then to Fort Snelling, in the northern part of the Louisiana Territory, near present-day St. Paul, Minnesota, in 1836. Scott returned with Emerson to Missouri in 1838. When Emerson died in 1843, Scott sought to buy his freedom from Emerson's widow. When she refused, he petitioned the Missouri Circuit Court at St. Louis on April 6, 1846, seeking his freedom, arguing that he had lived for three years in a free state.

Scott lost his first trial on a technicality but won a second trial in 1850 when the Missouri court ruled that once a slave left Missouri he should be considered free. Mrs. Emerson proved to be as determined as Scott, appealing the court's decision.

Scott's final hope was an appeal to the U.S. Supreme Court. Montgomery Blair, a former resident of St. Louis, agreed to represent Scott without fee. Blair, at age forty-one, whose father, Francis Preston Blair, Sr., had been a member of Andrew Jackson's "kitchen cabinet," had established his own reputation as a lawyer in Washington. The Supreme Court announced it would hear the case during its term in December 1856.

Chief Justice Roger B. Taney presided at the December hearing. Taney, born into a wealthy slaveholding family in southern Maryland in 1777, had served as both attorney general and secretary of the treasury in the Jackson administration, before being appointed the fifth chief justice of the United States in 1836. Standing before Taney and eight associate justices, Blair contended that Emerson had emancipated Scott when he took him both to the free state of Illinois and to the Louisiana Territory, where slavery was prohibited. He also presented examples from five states that had treated African-Americans as citizens, as had Missouri in earlier years.

Montgomery Blair represented Scott, contending that he became emancipated when his owner brought him into free territory.

Politicians and the press buzzed with rumors of what the Court would or would not do. Congressman Alexander Stephens of Georgia wrote to a friend, "The decision will be a marked epoch in our history." The *New York Courier* wrote, prophetically, "The Court, in trying this case, is itself on trial."

Reading reports of the trial, Lincoln wrote a private note on the Dred Scott case, probably in January 1857. He began with a question: "What would be the effect of this, if it should ever be the creed of a dominant party in the nation?" He pondered the "full scope" and the "narrow scope" of the result if the Supreme Court ruled that Dred Scott was still a slave. Lincoln did not argue his own position, but was preparing himself if the position of Douglas and his followers in the Democratic Party prevailed. He wrote that whatever the Court's decision on this constitutional question, it must be obeyed.

The Supreme Court heard oral arguments on February 11, 1857. Senator Henry Geyer of Missouri argued that "blacks are not citizens" even if taken into free territories. Reverdy Johnson, the former attorney general of the United States, presented an impassioned defense of slavery, contending, "Slavery promises to exist through all time, so far as human vision can discover."

Interest in the case heightened when President Buchanan referred to it in his inaugural address on March 4, 1857. Buchanan, coming into office convinced the problems in the country were the fault of the

Northern abolitionists, was determined to reach out to the Southern pro-slavery members of his own party. He believed the long-awaited decision in the Dred Scott case could be a major step in that direction. In his address he stated that "it is understood" that the case will "be speedily and finally settled." How did he come to this understanding? He had spoken with Chief Justice Taney in late February and learned the basic outline of the verdict. Trying to head off opposition, Buchanan declared, "To their decision, in common with all good citizens, I shall cheerfully submit."

Only two days after Buchanan's inauguration, at eleven o'clock on March 6, 1857, Taney and the eight black-robed justices entered the Supreme Court on the ground floor of the Capitol. Customarily, when the Supreme Court announced its opinions, it did so in splendid isolation, but on this Friday morning newspaper reporters and spectators filled the chamber. Taney, only eleven days before his eightieth birthday, began reading in a low, at times almost muted, voice from a manuscript held in his unsteady hands. For the next two hours he read the Court's 7–2 decision.

The Court ruled, first, that Scott was not a citizen and therefore not entitled to sue in federal court. Rehearsing the long arc of history, Taney declared that blacks had "been regarded as beings of an inferior order, and altogether unfit to associate with the white race, either in social or political relations." Second, the Court ruled that the U.S. Congress's presumption of authority to exclude slavery from the federal territories was unconstitutional. To make this move, the chief justice engaged in a judicial juggling act with fact and interpretation. He had to admit that the first Congress did enact the Northwest Ordinance of 1787 forbidding slavery in those territories it covered, but that subsequent Congresses had no right to forbid slavery in future territories acquired by the United States. Third, reiterating the decisions of the lower courts, Taney found that Dred Scott was and would always be a slave according to Missouri law.

Taney may have hoped to bring peace to the beginning of Buchanan's administration, but instead the decision unleashed a storm of protest. Republicans charged partisanship. William Lloyd Garrison, Wendell Phillips, and other leading abolitionists went further and called for immediate disunion. Their focus was on the fact that five of the nine justices came from the South. Taney and the other justices, who hereto-

Holy Bible

Thou shalt not deliver unto the master his servant which has escaped from his master unto thee. He shall dwell with thee. Even among you in that place which he shall choose in one of thy gates where it liketh him best Thou shalt not oppress him.
Deut XXIII.15.

Effects of the Fugitive-Slave-Law.

Declaration of independence.

We hold that all men are created equal, that they are endowed by their Creator with certain unalienable rights, that among these are life, liberty and the pursuit of happiness.

The fugitive slave law, passed in 1850, became a source of continuing controversy. This print shows a group of four black men—possibly freedmen—ambushed by a posse of six armed whites in a cornfield.

fore had toiled in near obscurity, were negatively profiled in Northern newspapers. In the South, the decision was hailed as a victory.

LINCOLN MADE NO IMMEDIATE public comment after the Court's decision. Instead, he worked tirelessly in private to understand every facet of the opinion, just as he had done after the Kansas-Nebraska Act was announced. Understanding that the Dred Scott decision was an attack upon the principles of the new Republican Party, he bided his time, preparing to speak at the right moment.

Stephen Douglas also remained silent about the decision throughout the spring. On June 7, 1857, at the invitation of the U.S. District Court in Springfield, Douglas broke his silence. Lincoln was in the audience.

Douglas declared that the "main proposition" of the Dred Scott decision was that "a negro descended from slave parents . . . is not and can not be a citizen of the United States." He attacked those who would say that the Declaration of Independence pledged equality for African-Americans. "No one can vindicate the character, motive, and conduct of the signers of the Declaration of Independence, except upon the hypothesis that they referred to the white race alone, and not to the African, when they declared men to have been created free and equal." Douglas insisted that the signers were referring solely to white British subjects.

Douglas's speech attracted national attention. James Gordon Bennett's Democratic *New York Herald* offered an enthusiastic endorsement for more than the speech. "The curtain of 1860 is partially lifted, and we have a peep behind the scenes." The *Herald* believed, "As a democratic Presidential aspirant, Mr. Douglas is now without a rival in the great Northwest."

Lincoln, roused by Douglas's address, decided to answer him directly. For two weeks in June, he studied in the Illinois Supreme Court's law library on the first floor of the state capitol. He read the written opinions of the justices, drawing especially on the dissent of Associate Justice Benjamin Curtis, and perused commentaries on the decision in a variety of newspapers.

On the evening of June 26, 1857, Lincoln offered his response in the statehouse. It was not the kind of answer many expected. Walking in with law books under his arms, Lincoln's speech was not that of a Republican firebrand, but rather a thoughtful, calm address.

He began by assuring his audience that he did not agree with those who advocated resisting the Court's ruling. Instead, he said he believed as much as Douglas—"perhaps more"—in obedience to the rulings of the judiciary, especially when they involved matters of the Constitution. He quickly added, "But we think the Dred Scott decision is erroneous. We know the court that made it, has often over-ruled its own decisions, and we shall do what we can to have it to over-rule this."

Lincoln, relying on his legal sleuthing, instructed his audience on the true way a Supreme Court decision could be accepted by everyone. The decision would need to be unanimous, without "partisan bias," based in precedent, and making use of agreed-upon "historical facts." Lincoln then proceeded to demonstrate how this decision did not inspire public confidence because it failed on every one of these points.

In Lincoln's earlier speeches, he assailed the immorality of slavery but seldom spoke of the condition of slaves. This time, in the midst of historical argument contrasting the days of the founders with the present day, Lincoln's language became emotional when he described the bondage of African-Americans. "All the powers of earth seem rapidly combining against him. Mammon is after him; ambition follows, and philosophy follows, and the Theology of the day is fast joining the cry." What has been the result? "They have him in his prison house; they have searched his person, and left no prying instrument with him. One after another they have closed the heavy iron doors upon him, and now they have him, as it were, bolted in with a lock of a hundred keys." Lincoln, in his evocative word portrait, declared it was "grossly incorrect" to say, as Douglas and many in the South claimed, that African-American slaves were better off today than at the birth of the nation in 1776.

One by one, Lincoln took up Douglas's points, often quoting him at length. A main target was Douglas's charge that those who opposed the Dred Scott decision supported racial equality. Lincoln, in the strategy of a debater, first conceded there was "a natural disgust in the minds of nearly all white people, to the idea of an indiscriminate amalgamation of the white and black races." He repeated Douglas's infamous charge that when Republicans evoked the Declaration of Independence, they "do so only because they want to vote, and eat, and sleep, and marry with negroes!"

Now, having conceded, Lincoln objected. "Now I protest against that counterfeit logic which concludes that, because I do not want a black woman for a *slave* I must necessarily want her for a *wife*. I need not have her for either, I can just leave her alone." Both then and now, people quoting Lincoln often stop here. But Lincoln continued with his main point, words that many have failed to cite. "In some respects she certainly is not my equal; but in her natural right to eat the bread she earns with her own hands without asking leave of any one else, she is my equal, and the equal of all others." Lincoln, in step with his audience, was unwilling to call an African-American his social equal. But the power of his logic was not what he denied but what he affirmed.

Having taken on Douglas, Lincoln quickly turned to Chief Justice Taney, for both, in Lincoln's eyes, were guilty of using and abusing the Declaration of Independence. The chief justice had stated that Jefferson's self-evident truths that "all men are created equal" would "seem to embrace the whole human family," but argued that the language did not mean what it said. It was "too clear for dispute that the enslaved African race were not intended to be included."

Lincoln, momentarily backed into a corner by the argument that if the framers of the Declaration of Independence intended to include African-Americans within the phrase, "all men are created equal," why did they not, "at once," actually place them on an equality with the whites? Lincoln offered a striking but subtle answer: "I think the authors of that notable instrument intended to include *all* men, but they did not intend to declare all men equal *in all respects*. They did not mean to say all were equal in all respects. They did not mean to say all were equal in color, size, intellect, moral developments, or social capacity." Lincoln said the founders did define, "with tolerable distinctiveness, in what respect they did consider all men created equal—equal in 'certain inalienable rights, among which are life, liberty, and the pursuit of happiness.' This they said, and this meant."

Lincoln built into his affirmation a creative tension between intent and action. He admitted that at the time of the Declaration of Independence, all men were not "then" enjoying such equality, or even that the framers had the power to "confer" such equality. Lincoln believed the framers were thinking in the future tense so that the "*enforcement*" of this right "might follow as fast as circumstances should permit." Speaking in his own future tense, Lincoln looked forward to imagine how the equality of all persons might be transformed from intent to reality. He fervently hoped that the "maxim" that "all men are created equal" should be "constantly looked to, constantly labored for, and even though never perfectly attained, constantly approximated, and thereby constantly spreading and deepening its influence, and augmenting a happiness and value of life to all people of all colors everywhere."

Although Lincoln delivered a forceful reply to Douglas, it failed to satisfy all Republicans. For some, his words seemed like a scholarly lecture that lacked the white heat of indignation. One responded that it was "too much on the old conservative order." Not a few wondered if the genial Lincoln was a match for the firebrand Douglas.

LINCOLN'S RESPONSE to the Dred Scott decision was his only political speech in 1857. Lincoln spent the bulk of the political off-year busy in his law practice. His cases ranged from repaying a personal friendship from his New Salem days to the corporate contest between river and rail.

By the middle of the 1850s, picturesque and romantic travel on the Mississippi, which would soon inspire Mark Twain's *Huckleberry Finn* and *Life on the Mississippi,* was in its final chapters, although not many suspected so at the time. Railroads had snaked across the land and now forded rivers by bridge. In 1854, the Rock Island Bridge Company announced plans to build the first bridge to span the Mississippi River. The proposed bridge, between Rock Island, Illinois, and Davenport, Iowa, sparked public protests stoked by river interests, such as ferry operators. In a case brought in July 1855, Associate Justice John McLean of the U.S. Supreme Court sustained the company's rights to build the bridge. Constructed with more than 620,000 pounds of cast and wrought iron, the bridge finally opened on April 21, 1856, when a single locomotive, the *Des Moines,* crossed to the cheers of people and the sound of church bells on both banks of the river.

Just two weeks later, on May 6, 1856, the steamer *Effie Afton,* a fast and sleek side-wheeler with a deck 230 feet long and side wheels 30 feet in diameter, sailed up the Mississippi from its home port in Cincinnati. In the evening, as the pilot maneuvered his way through the snags and reefs of the mighty river swollen by spring rains, he came for the first time to the new bridge. The boat slowed as it attempted to navigate into the draw of the bridge. Suddenly, one of its side wheels struck one of the piers, and the huge boat bounced over against the pier on the other side. The impact jarred a small coal stove on board, and within minutes the boat was burning. Passengers and crew managed to escape, but the *Effie Afton* sank with all its cargo. The wooden trusses of the bridge caught fire, and a section fell into the river. By the next day, the entire bridge had collapsed into the Mississippi.

The destruction of the boat and bridge stirred up deep feelings on the river and in towns along the Mississippi. For the next few weeks, steamboat captains blew their whistles in that part of the Mississippi to mark the obliteration. The *St. Louis Republican* denounced the bridge as "an intolerable nuisance," and editorialized, "We have rarely seen such illustration of supercilious insolence, as have been presented by advocates of the bridge." The *Chicago Tribune,* taking the exact opposite opinion, responded that the facts of the case "do not warrant the incessant clamor" of those who insisted that river bridges should be torn down. "We trust that the outcries of the St. Louis and river press may be silenced."

John S. Hurd, owner of the *Effie Afton,* sued to recover the value of the boat and cargo, $65,000 in total, from the Rock Island Railway, the bridge's parent company. The ostensible parties in the suit were *Hurd v. Rock Island Bridge Co.,* but the real opponents embraced much larger entities: Chicago, the railroads, and east-west traffic versus St. Louis, the riverboats, and north-south travel.

Norman B. Judd, general counsel for the Rock Island Railway, wanted the best lawyer possible to join him in defending the railroad. One of the five anti-Nebraska Democrats who had opposed Lincoln's bid for the Senate in 1855, Judd had become a Republican and now served as chairman of the Republican state committee. He turned to Lincoln to lead the defense in this high-profile case that attracted national attention.

In preparation for the trial, Lincoln, with his omnivorous craving for information, traveled to the scene of the disaster. He interviewed Benjamin Brayton, Sr., the engineer who designed the bridge, about bridge construction. He sat down at the head of the new bridge with Ben Brayton, Jr., and with his long legs hanging over the edge, questioned the fifteen-year-old boy about the currents of the river. He hired several men to pilot the steamer *Keokuk* through the draw of the bridge to check the boat's responses to the winds and the currents in relation to the piers. He conducted experiments by placing different kinds of objects in the water and observing them drifting toward the draw. Lincoln, at the height of his legal practice, understood well that complicated court cases are often won or lost well before the judge brings down his gavel to begin the formal court proceedings.

The case began in Chicago sixteen months later on September 8, 1857, with Supreme Court justice McLean presiding. The structure of the federal court system called for each Supreme Court justice to serve as the presiding judge of one of the nine circuit courts. The *Chicago Democratic Press* devoted extra space to the trial because the case involved "a fundamental national struggle" between "the great natural channel of trade of the Mississippi Valley" and the railroads, "the great artificial lines of travel and communication." The lawyers for the plaintiff called fifty men who made their living on rivers, including captains and pilots; each argued that the bridge was an obstacle to river traffic. Judd and Lincoln called six engineers, as well as many ordinary citizens, who testified that the bridge was perfectly safe. Judd charged that the misfortune of the *Effie Afton* was due simply to "the carelessness of her officers."

On the afternoon of September 22, 1857, Lincoln began the defense's closing argument. The absence of an official court record was fortunately remedied by a newspaper reporter who, using the new skill of shorthand, wrote out in detail Lincoln's extensive address. In a highly contentious case, being tried each day in the press, Lincoln began by say-ing "he did not propose to assail anybody." He had "no prejudice" against steamboats or against St. Louis. Rather, he asked the jury to stand with him as they witnessed the "astonishing growth" of the West, of Illinois, and of Iowa, and other young communities west of the Mis-sissippi. Why were they growing so rapidly? Because of the free flow of east-west travel now enhanced by the railroad. Did the jury want to compare north-south to east-west travel? Lincoln, the master of facts, told them that from September 6, 1856, to August 8, 1857, 12,586 freight cars and 74,179 passengers had passed over the rebuilt Rock Island Bridge. He also pointed out that during this same time period river traffic was closed "four days short of four months" due to ice in the river. He presented statistics showing that of the 959 subsequent boat passings under the bridge, only 7 had suffered any kind of damage. His real point was that the accidents were "tapering off." Lincoln declared, "As the boatmen get cool, the accidents get less."

When Lincoln resumed his closing argument the next morning he appeared with a wooden model of the *Effie Afton*. Employing all of his former skills as boatman and surveyor, he spoke to the jury of the angu-lar position of the piers, the course of the river, the speed of the cur-rents, the depth of the channel, and the speed of the boat, all to demonstrate that the boat crashed into the pier of the bridge because of the pilot's carelessness and because her starboard wheel had not been working.

Lincoln understood that this case was about the collision, not simply of boat and bridge, but of past and future. No one enjoyed rivers and boats more than Lincoln. As a teenager, he had traveled down the Mis-sissippi to New Orleans in one of the great and harrowing adventures of his life, almost getting killed in an assault. He first came to New Salem by boat, and almost immediately upon settling there became a leading proponent of developing boat traffic on the Sangamon as a way of enhancing the future of his new home. He had patented a device to help boats surmount sandbars and shoals in rivers and lakes. But, by the 1850s, Lincoln understood that to hug too tightly to the boat's tiller was to cling to the past. Lincoln's political grammar always gravitated to the future tense.

On September 24, 1857, Judge McLean announced that the jury, which voted 9 for the bridge and 3 against, was deadlocked and thus dis-missed. Litigation against the bridge would continue all the way until

December 1862, when the U.S. Supreme Court decided the bridge could remain. Five years after the original trial, a war, not a bridge, would suspend all commercial business on the Mississippi River.

IF THE *EFFIE AFTON* CASE was about the future, in the fall of 1857 Lincoln was drawn back to his past in a case growing out of the behavior of some rowdies at a religious revival. In August, a two-week evangelistic camp meeting was held at Virgin's Grove near the site of New Salem, which had been abandoned by 1840. On August 29, at a makeshift bar on the outskirts of the meetings, William "Duff" Armstrong, twenty-four-year-old son of Jack Armstrong, Lincoln's wrestling friend from New Salem, and another young man named James Norris got into a fracas with James Metzker. Norris struck Metzker with a three-foot block of wood while Armstrong hit him with a slungshot, a lead weight wrapped in a leather pouch and fastened to thongs. Metzker died while attempting to escape on his horse. Duff Armstrong and James Norris were charged with murder. Duff's mother, Hannah, appealed to Lincoln, asking if he would help. He said he would.

Duff Armstrong's case came to trial on May 7, 1858. Norris had already been convicted in an earlier, separate trial. In the courtroom, on the second floor of the Cass County courthouse in Beardstown, Lincoln

Lincoln defended Duff Armstrong, son of his old wrestling partner, Jack Armstrong, in a murder trial in 1858.

took great care in selecting the jury, preferring young men in their twenties who might sympathize with another, admittedly wild young man. Charles Allen, the key witness, swore that from a distance of thirty yards, at eleven o'clock in the evening, he saw clearly how the fight developed. When asked how he could be so certain, he answered that the moon was shining directly above. At that moment the outlook seemed dim for the defendant.

Lincoln's cross-examination of Allen began in an understated way. He enticed from the witness, through different questions, the repeated assertion that he had seen clearly what had happened. Lincoln, who had been speaking in a conversational tone, suddenly changed his demeanor and approach. In a dramatic moment, he called for an almanac, which a court officer brought him. Lincoln read from *Jayne's Almanac* the decisive sentence that the moon had already set before the fight ensued on the evening of August 29, 1857. The witness could not have seen what he asserted he saw. As several members of the jury stated later, "The almanac floored the witness."

There were tears in Lincoln's eyes when in his closing argument he told the jury "of his once being a poor, friendless boy; that Armstrong's father took him into his house, fed and clothed him & gave him a home." William Walker, Lincoln's cocounsel in the trial, remembered that Lincoln spoke "of his kind feelings toward the mother of the prisoner, a widow." J. Henry Shaw, who prosecuted the case for the state, believed, "It was generally admitted that Lincoln's speech and personal appeal to the jury saved Armstrong."

When the trial was over Lincoln went down to Beardstown to visit Duff's mother. She asked him what she owed him for his legal services. He replied, "Why—Hannah, I shant charge you a cent—never."

WHILE LINCOLN, IN 1857, was enjoying the most productive year in his legal career, he kept one eye on the latest news about Stephen Douglas. The calm that seemed to have settled in over Kansas was deceptive. In Lecompton, the territorial capital, located on the south bank of the Kansas River between Topeka and Lawrence, a constitutional convention convened on September 7 on the second floor of a new black-walnut clapboard building. The delegates had been selected in an election on June 15, but nearly all the antislavery men, who distrusted the territorial legislature, had boycotted it. The results of the sham election were trickling in just as Lincoln was answering Douglas at Springfield on June 26. Lincoln, in his speech, called the voting in Kansas "altogether the most exquisite farce ever enacted."

The meeting at Lecompton proposed two options. Voters could choose to endorse a constitution with "no slavery" but that legalized slavery for those already there—about two hundred slaves—and their progeny. Or voters could choose a constitution "with slavery" that legalized new slaves brought into the territory as well as those who were already there. The convention proposed that there be an election, not on the whole constitution, but only on the plank on slavery. When the election was held in December the vote for slavery—again with most antislavery men boycotting—was 6,143 to 569.

President Buchanan, who had wished the vote had been on the entire constitution, nevertheless offered his endorsement and encouraged Congress to move forward quickly to admit Kansas as a new slave state. When the new Congress assembled in December, Buchanan, who was lobbied by Southern leaders, offered his first annual message to an expectant Congress. In it he praised "the great principle of popular sovereignty" as he embraced the provisions in the Lecompton Constitution.

The next day, December 9, 1857, Stephen Douglas answered the president. He condemned the Lecompton arrangement as a sham. Furthermore, he announced he would fight Buchanan and his allies over it. Why? Lecompton, an effort by a small minority, went completely against the principles of popular sovereignty. He accused Buchanan of misinterpreting the meaning of the Kansas-Nebraska Act. To be sure, Douglas was unhappy with the Buchanan administration; he had learned early on that he would not be the trusted adviser and dealmaker he expected to be. But the real issue for Douglas was popular sovereignty. "I have spent too much strength and breadth and health, too, to establish this great principle in the popular heart, now to see it frittered away."

When the Senate reconvened in January 1858, an unlikely spectacle began taking place. Douglas, who in 1854 had served as floor manager of the Kansas-Nebraska Act, now allied himself with Republican senators Salmon Chase, Henry Wilson, and Benjamin Wade. Wilson, an antislavery senator from Massachusetts, opined that if Douglas would cross the aisle and become a Republican, it would "bring more weight to our cause than any ten men in the country."

Douglas's sudden change prompted the question in all quarters:

What was he up to? Horace Greeley, ever the kingmaker, editorialized in the *Tribune,* "His course has not been merely right, it has been conspicuously, courageously, eminently so." Greeley counseled Republicans that they throw in with Douglas or face certain defeat in the upcoming senatorial election. Following Greeley's lead, a Republicans for Douglas movement began to gather momentum in the East.

Lincoln, with his ear ever attuned to the latest political news, was deeply alarmed. At the end of 1857, he wrote three letters to Senator Lyman Trumbull. He asked, what is "your general view of the then present aspect of affairs?" On December 28, Lincoln wrote, "What does the New-York *Tribune* mean by its constant eulogising, and admiring, and magnifying Douglas?" Did Greeley speak for "the sentiments of the republicans in Washington"? Had leaders in Washington "concluded that the republican cause, generally, can be best promoted by sacrificing us here in Illinois"? Lincoln acknowledged to Trumbull that he had heard of "no republican here going over to Douglas," but he was concerned that "if the Tribune continues to din his praises into the ears of its five or ten thousand republican readers in Illinois, it is more than can be hoped that all will stand firm." Lincoln's plans for a Senate race against Douglas in 1858 were suddenly being challenged. The usually patient Lincoln was plainly fretful.

Trumbull replied on January 3, 1858, attempting to calm Lincoln's anxieties. He began by admitting to Lincoln that "the unexpected course of Douglas has taken us all somewhat by surprise." He told Lincoln of the responses of some Republicans. "Some of our friends here act like fools in running & flattering Douglas." Trumbull wrote that Douglas "encourages it & invites such men as Wilson, Seward," and others "to confer with him & they seem wonderfully pleased to go." Trumbull did not want Lincoln to take these reports at face value, but to understand that William Seward's motivation in offering public praise for Douglas was to further fuel the division growing in the Democratic Party. Trumbull assured Lincoln, "I have no sort of idea of making Douglas our leader either here or in Ills. He has done nothing as yet to commend him to any honest Republican."

This letter revealed Trumbull's admiration for Lincoln, the man he had defeated for the Senate three years earlier in January 1855. Trumbull concluded by assuring Lincoln that he would work for the election to the Senate "of that *Friend* who was instrumental in promoting my own." After he signed his letter, Trumbull added a final sentence. His wife, Julia Jayne Trumbull, who was once one of Mary Lincoln's dearest friends before the rupture caused by the 1855 Senate race, was sitting by her husband as he completed the letter. She admired Lincoln and told her husband that Lincoln was "too modest to understand whom I mean by 'that friend.' " Heeding his wife's advice, Trumbull added that Lincoln was the friend "who magnanimously requested his friends just at the right moment to cast their votes for me."

AS THE WINTER OF 1858 slowly turned into spring, the air began to go out of Douglas's balloon. Republicans in Illinois increasingly resented the intrusion of Greeley and other eastern Republicans in their affairs. Joseph Medill's *Chicago Press &Tribune* fumed, "There seems to be a considerable notion pervading the brains of political wet-nurses at the East, that the barbarians of Illinois cannot take care of themselves."

To the observant eye, Lincoln's bid for the Senate, despite the winter panic over Douglas, was coming into focus in the spring for important reasons. First, while being an old-line Whig had hurt Lincoln in his Senate bid in 1855, it was helping him in 1858. Both Governor Bissell and Senator Trumbull were former old-line Democrats. There was a general consensus that it was time to honor an old-line Whig with the other Illinois Senate seat. Second, Lincoln rose to the top of the available former Whigs because of the "sacrifice" of his candidacy three years earlier that had led to the election of Trumbull. Trumbull had personally recognized the debt, but it was also being spoken of by other politicians as well as the editors of Republican newspapers.

In the midst of pressure from eastern Republicans to embrace Douglas, Illinois Republicans came up with a novel idea. Up until this time, the legislature would select the nominee from a variety of candidates. Why not short-circuit that process by holding a convention and agreeing upon only one candidate, whom everyone could then rally around? As German-American leader Gustave Koerner put it, "We must make them understand that *Lincoln* is our man." Lincoln endorsed the idea of a convention in an April 24, 1858, letter to Illinois secretary of state Ozias Hatch. "Let us have a state convention in which we can have a full consultation: and till which, let us stand firm, making no committals as to strange and new combinations." Lincoln, although confident, remembered that he had lost out in 1855 to a new combination, even as some Republicans were still talking about combining with Douglas.

In April, the pace of events quickened. Republican leaders, including William Herndon, who represented Lincoln, met in Chicago and endorsed the idea of holding a convention in Springfield on June 16, 1858.

AS LINCOLN WAS GEARING UP to run for the Senate, he was also exploring an additional career as a public lecturer. He was inspired by the traveling lecturers who began coming to Springfield in the 1850s. Lincoln heard two of Ralph Waldo Emerson's three lectures at the statehouse in January 1853. Bayard Taylor, a renowned world traveler, had lectured on "the Arabs" in 1854, and, by popular demand, returned in 1855 to lecture on Japan, India, and "the Philosophy of Travel." Other lecturers included Horace Greeley, Henry Ward Beecher, and New England Unitarian minister Theodore Parker. The biggest crowds turned out to hear (and see) Lola Montez, an actress and dancer, lecture on "Fashion."

Lincoln decided to try his hand as a homegrown lecturer. On April 6, 1858, Lincoln delivered a lecture on "Discovery and Inventions" in Bloomington. Lincoln's thesis was that of all the creatures on Earth, man "is the only one who *improves* his workmanship." He then traced innumerable inventions and discoveries that were of "peculiar value" because of their "efficiency in facilitating other inventions and discoveries." As an example, he trumpeted the printing press, which "gave ten thousand copies of any written matter, quite as cheaply as ten were given before. Consequently a thousand minds were brought into the field where there was but one before."

Lincoln delivered this same lecture again nearly one year later in February 1859, in Jacksonville, Decatur, and Springfield. It demonstrated Lincoln's commitment to progress, especially his appreciation of the changing arts of communication, although much of his material was cobbled together from Old Testament references and *Encyclopedia Americana* articles. Despite Lincoln's personal and political popularity, his general public lectures never caught fire with the small audiences in attendance.

IN THE MONTHS LEADING UP to the Republicans' June nominating convention, Lincoln turned down all speaking invitations and started the most extensive preparation for any speech he had ever made. Yes, he would be building on all of his speeches since 1854, but this time he decided to write out the speech in its entirety. He wrestled with ideas on scraps of paper and the backs of envelopes. The Lincoln who returned from Congress in 1849 not knowing if he could ever be elected again, who had been defeated for the Senate in 1855 when he and his friends thought surely he would win, well understood that this was his last opportunity to win election to the Senate, his highest aspiration to public office. Behind closed doors, Lincoln wrote, revised, and edited what he intended to say at the historic state convention.

The evening before the convention, Lincoln shared his speech with a dozen friends. After asking them to sit down at a round table, Lincoln read his entire address slowly. He asked each man for his response "to its wisdom or polity." One by one each responded. One, unnamed, burst out, a "damned fool utterance." John Armstrong, a Sangamon County builder, declared that the speech "was too far in advance of the times." Still another voiced his concern that the speech would "drive away a good many voters fresh from the Democratic ranks." Only William Herndon, who had heard an earlier version of the speech, offered his affirmation. Armstrong remembered that Herndon, while admitting that perhaps the speech was ahead of its time, urged Lincoln to "lift the people to the level of this Speech." Lincoln sat silently. He then rose, walked back and forth, and responded, "The time has come when these sentiments should be uttered." His friends feared the speech would be heard as too radical, but by now Lincoln had learned to trust his own judgment.

JUNE 16, 1858, dawned a "lovely" day in Springfield. Euphoric Republicans, sensing victory in the air, strolled around the state capital in grand spirits. For only the second time in the history of the nation a state convention was gathering to nominate a candidate for the U.S. Senate. Because there were no hard-and-fast rules on credentials, about one thousand delegates poured into Springfield.

The nomination of Lincoln began with the Chicago delegation bringing their banner into the hall as the crowd cheered: "Cook County Is for Abraham Lincoln." A delegate from Peoria moved that the convention adopt the motto "Illinois Is for Abraham Lincoln."

"Hurrahs" shook the statehouse. By the close of the afternoon, the editor of the *Chicago Journal* submitted an endorsement: "Resolved that Abraham Lincoln is the first and only choice of the Republicans of Illinois for the United States Senate, as the successor of Stephen A. Douglas." The cheers and hurrahs went on and on. Finally, the convention, still in a celebratory mood, adjourned for dinner.

The convention reconvened at eight o'clock. On a terribly warm and humid evening, with not nearly enough chairs to accommodate everyone, the Hall of Representatives became "crowded almost to suffocation." The angular Lincoln, at age forty-nine, rose and walked the few steps to the table at the front of the hall. He turned to face an audience that suddenly became silent. Although thoroughly prepared, Lincoln had decided to speak without his manuscript. He was, as always in delivering a speech, nervous. He began:

> If we could first know *where* we are, and *whither* we are tending, we could then better judge *what* to do, and *how* to do it.
>
> We are now far into the *fifth* year, since a policy was initiated, with the *avowed* object, and *confident* promise, of putting an end to slavery agitation.
>
> Under the operation of that policy, agitation has not only, not *ceased,* but has *constantly augmented.*
>
> In *my* opinion, it *will* not cease, until a *crisis* shall have been reached, and passed.
>
> "A house divided against itself cannot stand."
>
> I believe this government cannot endure, permanently half *slave* and half *free.*
>
> I do not expect the Union to be *dissolved*—I do not expect the house to *fall*—but I *do* expect it will cease to be divided.
>
> It will become all one thing, or all the other.
>
> Either the *opponents* of slavery, will arrest the further spread of it, and place it where the public mind shall rest in the belief that it is in course of ultimate extinction; or its *advocates* will push it forward, till it shall become alike lawful in all the States, *old* as well as *new*—*North* as well as *South.*
>
> Have we no tendency to the latter condition?

Lincoln began the most important address of his political career with short brushstrokes, painting the state of affairs of the nation in the middle of 1858. It was "the *fifth* year" since a "policy was initiated"—the policy was unnamed but everyone present knew it was the Kansas-Nebraska Act. A "*confident* promise" had been put forth that there would be an "end to slavery agitation." The promise had been offered by President Buchanan in his inaugural address fifteen months earlier. The repetition of the word "agitation" conjured up in the imaginations of Lincoln's listeners the cacophony of events symbolized in "bleeding Kansas."

As Lincoln painted the problem, the audience grew eager to hear his answer. He offered his solution by switching from an opening "we" to an "In *my* opinion." Lincoln told them: "A house divided against itself cannot stand." He had quickly reached his thesis sentence. Lincoln declared, by the use of a biblical metaphor drawn from Jesus admonishing the Pharisees (Matthew 12:25), that there was no longer any middle position between slavery and freedom.

As with all of Lincoln's best ideas, he had worked with this "house divided" metaphor on several occasions stretching back fifteen years. He employed it in a Whig campaign circular in 1843. He put it as a question in his philosophical letter to George Robertson of Transylvania University in 1855. Judge T. Lyle Dickey, who had shared the platform with Lincoln at a speech in Bloomington on September 12, 1856, remembered that he used it on that evening. Whatever its past use, this scriptural image would become the signature theme of this address and the senatorial campaign to follow.

The Bible, for Lincoln, always possessed a present dimension. The invocation of this biblical metaphor pointed beyond itself and allowed him to make several points. First, he declared that the status quo on slavery was no longer acceptable. He qualified this assertion with the historical modifier "permanently." Lincoln was offering a forecast, but not a timetable, for the future of slavery in America. Second, the logical Lincoln told his audience:

1. He did "not expect the Union to be *dissolved*."
2. He did "not expect the house to *fall*."
3. But he did "expect it will cease to be divided."

In his developing speaking style, Lincoln relished repetition. He twice told the audience what he did not expect. But it was actually the same thought, stated first literally (Union) and then figuratively (house). Telling the audience what he *did not* expect increased their anticipation for what he *did* expect. He predicted, boldly, that the nation would cease to be divided.

How would this come to be? Lincoln offered more than one possibility. At first, it might sound as if Lincoln was repeating what he had been saying since 1854, namely that his only goal was to "arrest" the spread of slavery into the territories. Furthermore, Lincoln stated that extinction would follow from restriction. He believed he was saying nothing more than Jefferson had said, but this provocative part of his introduction quickly became open to misunderstanding.

Although Herndon suggested Lincoln wrote the "House Divided" speech in the weeks immediately prior to its delivery, Lincoln had actually laid the foundation of the address seven months before in one of his most extensive private notes. The impetus for the note, about three-quarters as long as the speech itself, may have been the suggestion that Republicans support Douglas for reelection to the Senate in 1858. About three-quarters of the way through his private reflection, Lincoln noted that this "angry agitation" over the extension of slavery was not confined to the political arena. He chose one example to illustrate the growing problem. "Presbyterian assemblies, Methodist conferences, Unitarian gatherings, and single churches to an indefinite extent, are wrangling, and cracking, and going to pieces on the same question."

He then crafted the idea in a way that would link this private rumination to his future public speech.

I believe the government cannot endure permanently half slave and half free. I expressed this belief a year ago; and subsequent developments have but confirmed me. I do not expect the Union to be dissolved. I do not expect the house to fall; but I do expect it will cease to be divided. It will become all one thing or all the other. Either the opponents of slavery will arrest the further spread of it, and put it in course of ultimate extinction; or advocates will push it forward till it shall become alike lawful in all the States, old as well as new. Do you doubt it? Study the Dred Scott decision, and then see how little even now remains to be done.

In Lincoln's speech seven months later, some whole sentences are drawn word for word from his extended private note. The major difference between the note and the speech is its rhetorical structure. Whereas Lincoln employed the "house divided" metaphor toward the end of the note, as the culmination of the logic of his thinking, in the speech he moved it up to the beginning, as the thesis that undergirded the specifics that would follow from it.

After Lincoln's tightly written thesis, he muses about a conspiracy that would make slavery a national institution. He goes into great detail to describe the "*working* points of that machinery" by employing a house-building analogy that would have been familiar to nearly everyone in his audience: "When we see a lot of framed timbers, different portions of which we know have been gotten out at different times and places and by different workmen—Stephen, Franklin, Roger, and James . . ." Suddenly, dramatically, Lincoln moves from metaphor to naming names. Everyone in the audience knew he was speaking of Senator Stephen Douglas, ex-president Franklin Pierce, Chief Justice Roger Taney, and President James Buchanan. As the audience took in these names, Lincoln completed the scaffolding by hammering in the last nail. "We find it impossible to not *believe* that Stephen and Franklin and Roger and James all understood one another from the beginning, and all worked upon a common *plan* or *draft* before the first lick was struck."

He concluded this section by suggesting that this unholy conspiracy was working toward a second Dred Scott decision "declaring that the Constitution of the United States does not permit a *state* to exclude slavery from its limits." He told his audience that such a result grew from chief carpenter Douglas's "doctrine of 'care not whether slavery be voted down or voted up.' " Lincoln is arguing that no one should be misled that this controversy is only about the territories. One day people in the North will wake up to discover that the proponents of the Dred Scott decision wish to open the doors to slavery in the supposed free states.

In the third section, still concerned that Douglas might draw off some Republicans in the upcoming election, Lincoln sought to portray Douglas, despite his opposition to the Lecompton Constitution, as no friend of the Republican cause. He told his audience he had heard people whisper "*softly,* that Douglas is the *aptest* instrument" to oppose that "dynasty" that is the Buchanan administration because "he has regularly voted with us" against the charade of the Lecompton Constitution. These nameless friends "remind us that *he* is a very *great man,* and that the largest of *us* are very small ones." At this point, in high drama, with his right arm outstretched, Lincoln thundered, "But 'a *living dog* is better than a *dead lion.*' " Here Lincoln was turning again to the Bible, this time quoting from Ecclesiastes 9:4, "For to him that is joined to all the living there is hope: for a living dog is better than a dead lion." This ancient

Jewish declaration received its meaning from the contrast between the lowest and highest of animals. Lincoln knew he could never claim Douglas's exalted status, but pointed beyond himself to the exalted cause he served.

He declared that Douglas, despite his popularity, was "a *caged* and *toothless*" leader, because he was on the wrong side of the moral issue of slavery. "How can he oppose the advances of slavery? He don't *care* anything about it." Popular sovereignty was an empty promise if in the end it had nothing to say about one man owning another man. Resorting to irony, Lincoln identified himself in the phrase "the largest of *us* are very small ones"—Lincoln may be tall in height but knew he was small in public stature compared to Douglas—but the cause he represented would bring him the victory.

Lincoln's 3,173-word speech, which took less than thirty minutes to deliver, was actually brief in comparison to the average political addresses of the time. Twenty-four of the twenty-seven words in the opening sentence were one syllable long. He underlined twenty words in the introduction, which he made sure were italicized in the printed text.

With his speech completed, Lincoln gave his text to the young reporter Horace White of the *Chicago Tribune,* requesting that he take it to the office of the *Illinois State Journal*. Before White could finish proofreading the speech, Lincoln "came into the composing room . . . and looked over the revised proof." He told White he wanted the speech printed exactly as he had delivered it. He was beginning his run for the Senate and intended these ideas to serve as the platform that would lead him to victory.

This photograph at Macomb, Illinois, was taken five days after Lincoln's first debate with Stephen Douglas in Ottawa. Photographer T. Painter Pearson asked Lincoln on the morning of August 26, 1858, if he wanted a mirror to "fix up." He said no. "It would not be much of a likeness if I fixed up any."

CHAPTER 13

The Eternal Struggle Between These Two Principles
1858

I SHALL HAVE MY HANDS FULL. HE IS THE STRONG MAN OF THE
PARTY—FULL OF WIT, FACTS, DATES, AND THE BEST STUMP-SPEAKER,
WITH HIS DROLL WAYS AND DRY JOKES, IN THE WEST. HE IS AS HON-
EST AS HE IS SHREWD.

STEPHEN A. DOUGLAS ON ABRAHAM LINCOLN
June 1858

THERE IS NO REASON IN THE WORLD WHY THE NEGRO IS NOT ENTI-
TLED TO ALL THE NATURAL RIGHTS ENUMERATED IN THE DECLARA-
TION OF INDEPENDENCE, THE RIGHT TO LIFE, LIBERTY, AND THE
PURSUIT OF HAPPINESS. I HOLD THAT HE IS AS MUCH ENTITLED TO
THESE AS THE WHITE MAN.

ABRAHAM LINCOLN
The first debate with Stephen A. Douglas at Ottawa, Illinois, August 21, 1858

THE CHEERS FOR LINCOLN'S "HOUSE DIVIDED" SPEECH HAD BARELY
died down when the criticism started up. To many, whether friend or
foe, Lincoln's words had sounded like the language of abolitionism. His
biblical metaphor seemed to be a prophecy of civil war. Lincoln found
himself on the defensive before the campaign had even begun.

His friends were concerned. Leonard Swett, his close friend from the
Eighth Judicial Circuit, believed Lincoln had defeated himself with the
first ten lines of the speech. John Locke Scripps, the editor of the *Chicago
Democratic Press,* while joining in the widespread praise of the speech,
wrote Lincoln to warn that "some of my Kentucky friends who want to
be Republicans" objected to the "House Divided" metaphor. "This

they hold is an implied pledge on behalf of the Republican party to make war upon the institution in the States where it now exists."

Lincoln thanked Scripps for his support, "and yet I am mortified that any part of it should be construed so differently from any thing intended by me." Lincoln explained that his language did not assert the power of the federal government "to interfere with slavery in the States where it exists." He told Scripps that whenever the effort to spread slavery into the territories "shall be fairly headed off," by whatever means, then it will be on its way to "ultimate extinction"—what the founders had presumed would happen when they formed the nation.

STEPHEN DOUGLAS LEARNED of Lincoln's speech just as the Thirty-fifth Congress was adjourning in Washington. Douglas confided to John W. Forney, the editor of the *Philadelphia Press,* "I shall have my hands full. He is the strong man of the party—full of wit, facts, dates, and the best stump-speaker, with his droll ways and dry jokes, in the West. He is as honest as he is shrewd, and if I beat him, my victory will be hardly won."

When Douglas returned to Chicago in early July 1858, cheering crowds greeted his arrival at the Great Central Depot aboard a special four-car train. Douglas heard artillery boom a 150-gun salute and saw welcome banners hanging from windows as he rode in an open carriage to the Tremont House. To many, he remained the leader of Illinois politics.

On the evening of July 9, 1858, Douglas opened his Senate campaign with a speech from the Tremont House's balcony. Lincoln, at Douglas's invitation, sat in a chair behind the senior senator. Douglas's speech revealed the themes he would emphasize in the coming campaign. At the outset, he underlined "that great principle of self-government to which my life for many years past has been, and in the future will be devoted." Douglas took credit for the victory over the Lecompton Constitution, but immediately pointed out that his opposition had nothing to do with the issue of slavery. Douglas's speeches always combined defense and offense. He defended the Dred Scott decision, arguing that Republican criticism of the ruling failed to understand that "this government of ours is founded on the white basis. It was made by the white man, for the benefit of the white man, to be administered by white men."

With his challenger present, Douglas complimented Lincoln, saying he was a "kind, amiable, and intelligent gentleman, a good citizen and

Stephen Douglas, "the Little Giant," all of five feet four inches, would travel more than five thousand miles in his campaign and debates against Lincoln.

an honorable opponent." But then he returned to offense. Focusing on the "House Divided" speech, Douglas declared, "It is no answer . . . to say that slavery is an evil and hence should not be tolerated. You must allow the people to decide for themselves whether it is a good or an evil." He warned that Lincoln was calling for "a war of sections, a war of the North against the South, of the free states against the slave states." Douglas hoped that his strong offense would put Lincoln on the defense.

The next evening, Lincoln answered Douglas from the same balcony. He began in the self-deprecating manner that endeared him to audiences. He told the crowd that he would read from Douglas's speech, "provided I can find it," as he struggled to bring out a rumpled copy of the *Chicago Press and Tribune* from his coat pocket. He quoted Douglas's story about how the Russians at the battle of Sebastopol (1854–55) had not stopped to inquire who their fusillade of bullets would hit, and Douglas said neither would he. Lincoln responded, "Well now, gentlemen, is not that very alarming?" which drew loud laughter from the crowd. "Just to think of it! Right at the outset of his canvass, I, a poor, kind, amiable, intelligent [laughter] gentleman [laughter and renewed cheers] I am to be slain in this way. Why, my friend, the Judge, is not only, as it turns out, not a dead lion, nor even a living one—he is the rugged Russian Bear!" The crowd responded with "roars of laughter and loud applause."

Lincoln devoted the first part of his speech to defending his position, talking about popular sovereignty and the Lecompton Constitution. He addressed Douglas's criticism that Lincoln was in favor of war between North and South. "I did not say that I was in favor of anything. . . . I only said what I expected would take place. I made a prediction only—it may have been a foolish one perhaps." Lincoln became quite personal in explaining his lifelong opposition to slavery. "I have always hated slavery, I think as much as any Abolitionist. I have been an Old Line Whig. I always hated it, but I have always been quiet about it until this new era of the Nebraska Bill began."

In concluding, Lincoln lifted up the Declaration of Independence as the standard we might never reach perfectly, but to which we should nevertheless strive. He made his point by offering another biblical analogy. "My friend has said to me that I am a poor hand to quote Scripture." Lincoln was sensitive to the criticism that because he was not a member of any church he was not entitled to use the Bible. "I will try it again, however." Lincoln appealed to "one of the admonitions of the Lord, 'As your Father in Heaven is perfect, be ye also perfect.' " Lincoln declared, "The Savior" had set up a standard of perfection but did not expect any human beings to reach it. Just so, the Declaration of Independence set a standard, "all men are created equal. . . . I say . . . let it be as nearly reached as we can."

THE CAMPAIGN FOR the U.S. Senate was off and running. Lincoln stayed in Chicago to consult with his advisers before heading home to Springfield. Within days, Douglas traveled south from Chicago like a conquering hero. He rode in a special car complete with flags and a banner that read "Stephen A. Douglas, the Champion of Popular Sovereignty." At a stop in Joliet, a twelve-pound cannon on a special flatcar was attached to the train. As the train approached each small town, two young men in semi-military dress fired the cannon to announce Douglas's arrival. He arrived with his vivacious second wife, Adele. At only twenty-three, she was twenty-two years younger than her husband and offered a lively contrast to the often dour Douglas. She was a hit on the campaign trail, with both the ladies and the men.

On July 16, 1858, Lincoln traveled from Springfield to Bloomington to hear Douglas speak. When Douglas finished, loud calls went up for Lincoln to reply. He came to the front and received "three rousing cheers" from the crowd. Lincoln declined to speak, saying, "This meeting was called by the friends of Judge Douglas, and it would be improper for me to address it."

All interest now focused on Springfield. As the Douglas train neared the state capital, the cannon began firing every minute. This time, Douglas spoke in the afternoon and Lincoln in the evening. Douglas covered much of the same ground as in his Chicago and Bloomington speeches. He sought to distance himself from Lincoln's assertion that he was an instrument in the extension of slavery. He first complimented and then condemned Lincoln. He is "a kind-hearted, amiable, good-natured gentleman . . . and there is no objection to him, except the monstrous revolutionary doctrines with which he is identified and which he conscientiously entertains."

When Lincoln addressed a large crowd that evening, he spoke at length about how popular sovereignty had been nullified by the Dred Scott decision. He charged Douglas with "having been a party to that conspiracy and to that deception for the sole purpose of nationalizing slavery." In affirming the Declaration of Independence, he challenged Douglas that if he did not believe that all men are created equal, to come forward with an amendment: "Let them make it read that all men are created equal except negroes."

Up to this point Lincoln had decided, with the encouragement of his advisers, that as the challenger it would be a good idea to follow Douglas from place to place and attempt to speak after him. But the shadowing annoyed Douglas and his followers. The *Chicago Times* charged that Lincoln could not draw crowds on his own. Before long, some of Lincoln's advisers began to question this strategy. They believed it put Lincoln on the defensive, and usually ended up attracting only a portion of the crowd that first heard Douglas. By the end of July, Lincoln had stopped trailing after Douglas and wrote a series of letters to friends in different communities explaining his change of tactics. "I should be at your town to-day with Judge Douglas, had he not strongly intimated in his letter, which you have seen in the newspapers, that my presence, on the days or evenings of his meetings would be considered an intrusion." Lincoln did not want to back away from challenging Douglas directly, but he needed to find a way to do so on a more equal footing.

Six weeks into the campaign, Lincoln and his advisers came up with the idea that would change the whole shape and tenor of the contest. They offered Douglas the opportunity for an extended series of debates, envisioning upward of fifty.

Lincoln was taking a risk. Douglas, with much more experience as a legislator than Lincoln, had built a reputation in the Senate as an outstanding debater. Some of Lincoln's friends feared the Little Giant would run roughshod over their man.

These fears notwithstanding, Lincoln wrote a formal challenge to Douglas on July 24, 1858. "Will it be agreeable to you to make an arrangement for you and myself to divide time, and address the same audiences during the present canvass?" As the incumbent, Douglas feared he had little to gain. He was also concerned that a third candidate, a Buchanan Democrat, might yet enter the field. But in the American West, a man could be labeled a coward if he refused a challenge.

Cornered, Douglas countered. He agreed to debate Lincoln, but not all over the state. Douglas proposed to limit the debates to seven, which would take place in seven of the nine congressional districts. There was no need for debates in Chicago and Springfield, where the candidates had spoken already. Douglas insisted on deciding the details of the debates. On July 29, 1858, on the way to speaking engagements, Lincoln and Douglas met outside the little town of Bement to hammer out final particulars. Douglas named the places and dates to fit his schedule. Two days later, after a week of negotiations, Lincoln wrote from Springfield, "I accede, and thus close the arrangement." Just as the corn was growing tall under the warm summer sun on the Illinois prairies, the campaign

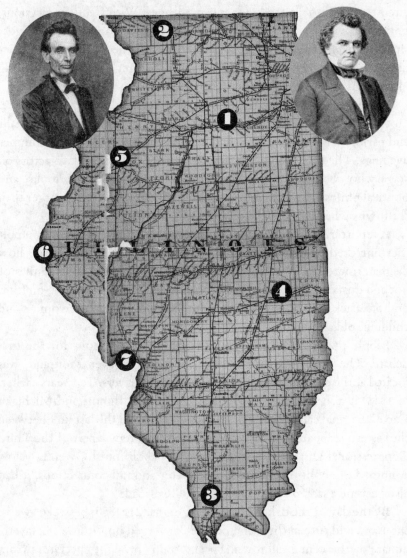

This map of Illinois shows the places of the seven debates between Lincoln and Douglas in the late summer and fall of 1858.

between Lincoln and Douglas was suddenly about to grow into the kind of historic event neither man could have imagined.

IN THE 1850S, in rural and small towns across Illinois, politics and religion were often the main shows in town. The preachers held forth on Sunday. The visiting lecturers spoke on cold winter evenings. Towns vied with one another to host the annual summer county fairs. Visiting circuses were anticipated by people of all ages. With frequent elections, politics provided year-round drama, entertainment, and sources for gossip. The seven Lincoln-Douglas debates became the Fourth of July picnic, summer revival meeting, county fair, visiting circus, and visiting lecturer all rolled into one grand pageant.

People came from miles around, arriving early and staying late. Hotels overflowed with guests, with visitors sleeping on cots in halls and parlors, or on pews in churches, or on the streets on warm summer evenings. The debates became dramatic theater featuring two actors on stage who could not have been more different in height, looks, and political philosophies. The enthusiastic audiences were often larger than the towns where the debates were held.

A reporter for the *New York Post* captured the intense interest in politics mirrored in the Lincoln-Douglas debates. "It is astonishing how deep an interest in politics this people take. Over long weary miles of hot and dusty prairie the processions of eager partisans come—on foot, on horseback, in wagons drawn by horses or mules; men, women, and children, old and young."

People poured into Ottawa, in north central Illinois, for the first debate. The green town of Ottawa, population seven thousand, was located at the confluence of the Fox and Illinois rivers. Ten years earlier, in 1848, it also became a canal town astride the Illinois and Michigan Canal, the final canal built in the United States and the last link between the eastern seaboard and the Gulf of Mexico. Ottawa, part of the Third Congressional District, was represented by abolitionist Owen Lovejoy. A hotbed of abolitionism, with both water and rail connections, it had also become a stop on the Underground Railroad.

By the day of the debate, Saturday, August 21, 1858, between twelve thousand and fifteen thousand people converged on Ottawa's Lafayette Square at the center of town. Special trains brought spectators from Chicago. With no chairs provided, people prepared to stand for hours under the scorching sun. To make matters worse, the *New York Evening*

Post reported that from sunrise to high noon "Ottawa was deluged in dust." Patriotism was unfurled everywhere in the bright colors of flags, banners, and bunting. A cannon was fired at irregular intervals, punctuating the already noisy atmosphere.

Lincoln arrived at noon aboard a special Chicago and Rock Island seventeen-car train packed with his supporters. A vast crowd greeted him at the depot, from which he was taken by a carriage decorated with evergreens to the home of Mayor Joseph O. Glover to rest until the debate. Douglas made his grand entrance into Ottawa in a carriage drawn by four white horses.

Shortly after two o'clock, already behind schedule because of the crush of people, the dignitaries made their way to the speakers' stand, where representatives of the press and timekeepers jostled for space to witness and monitor the event. Lincoln and Douglas took the center seats, flanked by Congressman Lovejoy, Mayor Glover, and Chief Shabbona, elderly leader of the Ottawa Tribe. By the rules of the debates, the first participant would speak for one hour, followed by a response of one and a half hours, with the first speaker given a final half hour for a rebuttal. Douglas would have the advantage of beginning and concluding four of the seven debates, including the first one. The crowds felt free to cheer, jeer, and offer questions and comments.

After an opening recapitulation of his leadership in passing the Kansas-Nebraska Act, Douglas spent the majority of his first hour attacking Lincoln's speeches and actions since 1854. Douglas, recognizing that he needed to climb a steep hill in a strongly Republican district, determined not to defend his record, but rather to force Lincoln to defend his.

He accused Lincoln and Illinois senator Lyman Trumbull of entering into an arrangement to dissolve the Whig and Democratic parties and "to connect the members of both into an Abolition party under the name and disguise of a Republican party." Douglas focused his attack on the early Republican meeting convened by Lovejoy in Springfield in October 1854. The week before the Ottawa debate, Douglas had written to his friend Charles H. Lamphier, editor of the *Illinois State Register* in Springfield, seeking details about the platform enacted at that meeting. Douglas, in a dramatic gesture, held up the resolutions of the meeting of the "Black Republicans." He declared that his purpose in reading the resolutions was to ask Lincoln seven questions to see "whether he will stand by each article in that creed and carry it out." At that point a voice in the crowd called out, "Hit him again." Douglas resumed, "I ask Abraham Lincoln to answer these questions, in order that when I trot him down to lower Egypt [the extreme southern part of Illinois] I may put the same questions to him again. . . . My purposes are the same everywhere."

Douglas assured the audience that, knowing Lincoln for twenty-five years, "I mean nothing personally disrespectful or unkind to that gentleman." He proceeded to offer flattering remarks about Lincoln's life and career, but salted each remark with satire. He described Lincoln as a "flourishing grocery-keeper" in New Salem—translation: Lincoln sold liquor. He offered mock praise for Lincoln as a congressman who "distinguished himself by his opposition to the Mexican war, taking the side of the common enemy against his own country." Finally, Douglas read the introduction of the "House Divided" speech. Even as the audience responded with "good," Douglas declared Lincoln's words were "revolutionary and destructive of the existence of this government."

Douglas was also adept at turning national issues into local problems. Thus, he attacked Lincoln on his criticism of the Dred Scott decision by asking the audience "Are you in favor of conferring upon the negro the rights and privileges of citizenship?" ("No, no!") "Do you desire to strike out of our State Constitution that clause which keeps slaves and free negroes out of the State, and allow the free negroes to flow in and cover your prairies with black settlements?" ("Never!") Douglas assailed Lincoln by playing up to the prejudices and fears of his audience. "I do not question Mr. Lincoln's conscientious belief that the negro was made his equal, and hence is his brother, [laughter], but for my own part, I do not regard the negro as my equal, and positively deny that he is my brother or any kin to me whatever."

After an hour, Lincoln rose to offer his response. The crowd cheered so loudly and long that it was several minutes before he could begin. As he began to speak, he held in his hand a book containing Douglas speeches, editorials from newspapers, and several quotations he intended to use, including some from the founding fathers.

Henry Villard, a twenty-three-year-old German immigrant hired to cover the debates for the *Illinois Staats-Zeitung,* captured the unusual characteristics of Lincoln as a speaker. "He had a lean, lank, indescribably gawky figure, an odd-featured, wrinkled, inexpressive, and altogether uncomely face." As for his mannerisms, "He used singularly awkward, almost absurd, up-and-down and side-wise movements of his

Lincoln kept a scrapbook filled with Douglas speeches, newspaper editorials, and quotations from the founding fathers as a ready resource to use during the debates.

body to give emphasis to his arguments." And yet, observed Villard, in Lincoln one saw "a thoroughly earnest and truthful man, inspired by sound convictions." A reporter for the *New York Evening Post* wrote, "I must confess that long Abe's appearance is not comely. But stir him up and the fire of his genius plays on every feature. . . . You have before you a man of rare power and magnetic influence." Whereas Douglas had been pretentious, often demeaning, and sometimes angry, Lincoln appeared comfortable, self-deprecating, and often humorous in his remarks.

Lincoln, in response to Douglas's attacks, replied, "When a man hears himself misrepresented, it provokes him—at least, I find it so with myself; but when the misrepresentation becomes very gross and palpable, it is more apt to amuse him." As the crowd laughed, Lincoln began his defense. One by one, he refuted Douglas's accusations in a style that delighted the crowd. After rebutting each charge—for example, that he agreed to "sell out the old Whig party"—Lincoln would end by saying, "Yet I have no doubt he is *conscientious* about it," satirizing the very word that Douglas had used to characterize him. Finally, Lincoln dismissed Douglas's attacks about the supposed first Republican platform in 1854 by turning to "my friend Mr. Lovejoy," who was seated on the platform. "He will be able to recollect that he tried to get me into it, but I would not go in."

Douglas used his final half hour to resume his offensive. He charged that Lincoln had not answered his questions. After he finished, supporters swarmed the stage and lifted a startled and embarrassed Lincoln to their shoulders.

The highly political press reported two different debates at Ottawa. The *Chicago Press & Tribune*'s headline crowed: "Twelve Thousand Persons Present: The *Dred Scott* Champion Pulverized." The *Chicago Times,* by contrast, emblazoned: "Lincoln's Heart Fails Him! Lincoln's Legs Fail Him! Lincoln's Tongue Fails Him." The reader, searching for the truth between such politically biased reporting, might wish to turn to the text of the debate. Reporter Horace White and stenographer Robert R. Hitt covered the debates for the pro-Lincoln *Chicago Press & Tribune,* while Henry Binmore and James B. Sheridan, two shorthand reporters, wrote on the debates for the pro-Douglas *Chicago Times*. The difficulty was that the texts in the two newspapers sometimes varied on crucial words or phrases.

The rival campaign staffs attempted to use the debate postmortem to influence public opinion. Lincoln's closest friends sent their congratulations. Judge David Davis wrote, "Everybody here is delighted with the rencontre at Ottawa." Richard Yates, on whose behalf Lincoln delivered his first speech when he reentered politics in 1854, applauded, "We were *well satisfied* with you at Ottawa." As for Lincoln, the day after the Ottawa debate, he wrote Joseph O. Cunningham, editor of the *Urbana Union,* "Douglas and I, for the first time this canvass, crossed swords here yesterday; the fire flew some, and I am glad to know I am yet alive."

Behind closed doors, however, Lincoln and his advisers were not so pleased with his performance. Henry C. Whitney, his friend from the Eighth Judicial Circuit, dispirited, wrote that even Lincoln's friends said "Dug had now got you where he wanted you—that you had *dodged* on the platform." Lincoln went to Chicago to meet with his advisers. Norman Judd, chairman of the Republican state central committee, and Joseph Medill and Charles Ray of the *Chicago Press & Tribune* gave him strong medicine. "Don't act on the *defensive* at all." Lincoln and his strategists worked on questions he could ask Douglas. Ray implored Congressman Elihu Washburne, in whose congressional district the next debate would be held, "When you see Abe at Freeport, for God's sake tell him to 'Charge Chester! Charge!' " Medill, speaking of Douglas, added, "You are dealing with a bold, brazen, lying rascal and you must '*fight the devil with fire*.' " Finally, Lincoln was urged by his friends, "For once leave modesty aside."

THE SECOND DEBATE took place six days later in Freeport, on the banks of the Pecatonica River, a few miles south of the Wisconsin line. In spite of overcast skies and the threat of rain, upward of fifteen thousand people converged on this town of seven thousand. More than a thousand traveled the six-hour train ride from Chicago. Although not as antislavery as Ottawa, Freeport sat at the hub of a strongly Republican area.

Lincoln arrived by special train the morning of the debate and was escorted to the new, stylish Brewster House. In the early afternoon, he traveled the short distance from the hotel to the debate site in a broad-wheeled Conestoga wagon accompanied by a group of farmers. There he met Douglas. The attire of the debaters was a study in contrasts. Douglas was dressed in a ruffled shirt, a dark blue coat with shining buttons, light trousers, well-shined shoes, and a white brim hat. Lincoln wore a stovepipe hat, a coat with too-short sleeves, and baggy trousers so short they showed off his rough Conestoga boots. Lincoln and Douglas partisans held aloft a variety of competing banners, including "All Men Are Created Equal" and "No Nigger Equality."

Lincoln, speaking for the first hour, immediately struck a more confident tone in this second debate. At the end of the Ottawa debate, Douglas had accused Lincoln of answering only one of his seven "interrogatories." At Freeport, Lincoln wasted no time in answering all seven, doing so in crisp one-sentence answers, which he later expanded upon. He did not support the repeal of the Fugitive Slave Act. "I shall be exceedingly glad to see slavery abolished in the District of Columbia." Although direct, his answers contained no new revelations.

At Freeport, Lincoln became the hunter and Douglas the hunted. Lincoln took the offensive by asking Douglas four questions, the second being the most critical. "Q. 2. Can the people of a United States Territory, in any lawful way, against the wish of any citizen of the United States, exclude slavery from its limits prior to the formation of a State Constitution?"

Lincoln's advisers, especially Joseph Medill, had encouraged him to ask this question. It was meant to push Douglas to speak about the meaning of popular sovereignty within the new legal landscape of the Dred Scott decision. Certainly this was not a new question for Douglas. "Mr. Lincoln has heard me answer [it] a hundred times from every stump in Illinois." Yet Lincoln, who would return to popular sovereignty again and again in the debates, decided to make him answer it at Freeport. Douglas came into the debates trying to straddle the fence between popular sovereignty and Dred Scott. Lincoln believed the Supreme Court's decision had effectively put a roadblock in front of popular sovereignty. He held that if Douglas endorsed the Supreme Court decision, he could not at the same time support self-government. Lincoln hoped his question would force Douglas off the fence.

Lincoln then turned his focus to the Republican meeting of October 1854, which Douglas had pounced on in the first debate. Lincoln admitted that six days earlier he had not known whether the resolutions Douglas read from had actually been passed at the Springfield meeting. His own recent research, done by Herndon, had revealed several important facts.

1. The meeting did not call itself the Republican State Convention.
2. No resolutions were passed in Springfield.
3. The resolutions Douglas read from had been passed later at a meeting in Kane County.
4. Lincoln was at neither meeting.

Lincoln spelled out his case as if he were a lawyer in a courtroom, turning to the jury of the Freeport audience and exclaiming, "It is *most extraordinary* that he should so far forget all the suggestions of justice to an adversary, or of prudence to himself, as to venture upon the assertion of that which the slightest investigation would have shown him to be wholly false." Prosecutor Lincoln rested his case to a response of tumultuous cheers.

Douglas was forced to begin his one-and-a-half-hour reply responding to Lincoln's four questions. His answer to question two was direct. "It matters not what way the Supreme Court may hereafter decide as to the abstract question whether slavery may or may not go into a territory under the Constitution, the people have the lawful means to introduce it or exclude it as they please." Why? "Slavery cannot exist a day or an hour anywhere, unless it is supported by local police regulations."

Douglas's answer to Lincoln, while not new, received widespread attention in the press, who quickly dubbed it the "Freeport Doctrine." Douglas may have been seeking to separate himself from the Buchanan Democrats in Illinois, but his answer further alienated him from the pro-slavery Democrats in the South.

Whenever cornered, Douglas resorted not to ideas, but to aggression. A good defense, he believed, was a good offense. His favorite tactic was to characterize Lincoln as part of the "Black Republicans." He used the term "Black Republicans" thirteen times at Ottawa and eighteen times at Freeport. He also referred to Lincoln's ideas by using the terms "abolition" and "abolitionizing."

After answering Lincoln's four questions, Douglas suggested Lincoln needed more help from his advisers if he was to craft more questions. He named among Lincoln's advisers Frederick Douglass, the well-known African-American writer and editor, abolitionist, and Republican. He began his race-baiting by acknowledging that some people in Freeport "think that Fred. Douglas is a good man." He then told a story that he said took place the last time he was in Freeport. "I saw a carriage and a magnificent one it was, drive up and take a position on the outside of the crowd; a beautiful young lady was sitting on the box seat, whilst Fred. Douglas and her mother reclined inside." The story provoked a flurry of responses—"Right," "What have you to say against it?" "What of it?"— to which he replied, "All I have to say of it is this, that if you, Black Republicans, think that the negro ought to be on social equality with your wives and daughters, and ride in a carriage with your wife, while you drive the team, you have a perfect right to do so." He concluded, "Those of you who believe that the negro is your equal and ought to be on an equality with you socially, politically, and legally; have a right to entertain those opinions, and of course will vote for Mr. Lincoln."

Douglas was a master of negation. If momentarily caught off guard by Lincoln's charges about the supposed Springfield resolutions of October 1854, he quickly recovered and tried to change the subject by going on the attack. He said that the real import of the resolutions was their radical abolitionist content, not whether they had been approved "on the right 'spot.' " Douglas then launched into a diatribe about Lincoln's unpatriotic behavior for criticizing the Mexican War during his term in Congress.

Lincoln had the opportunity for a rebuttal for the first time at Freeport. He failed to follow up on his questions to Douglas and spent most of the time defending his own record.

Most of Lincoln's supporters believed he did a much better job at Freeport. He had seized the initiative with his four questions. He was less repetitive than Douglas. Yet, there was still concern in the Lincoln camp. Medill, who had encouraged Lincoln to ask the hard-hitting second question, was more discouraged than encouraged. The day after the debate, Medill wrote that Douglas was better on the stump than Lincoln and "the popular sympathy is more on his side than Lincolns."

FREDERICK DOUGLASS WAS NOT one of Lincoln's advisers, but he cautiously admired Lincoln from a distance. Born in 1818, nine years after Lincoln, Douglass grew up as a slave near the Tuckahoe River and Baltimore, Maryland. He never knew his father, a white man, and was separated from his mother when he was very young. After what he described as "a religious awakening" at thirteen, his passion for reading found its focus in the Bible. In 1838, Douglass escaped from slavery by traveling in disguise on a train from Baltimore to Philadelphia. Settling as a laborer in New Bedford, Massachusetts, Douglass joined the abolitionist movement led by William Lloyd Garrison. In 1847, Douglass broke with Garrison, embracing the tactics of political action and rejecting Garrison's reliance on moral suasion. Moving to Rochester, New York, Douglass began publishing his own abolitionist journal, the *North Star.* By the 1850s, Douglass had become the leading African-American spokesman in America, attacking slavery and advocating a greater role in society for free blacks in the North.

Speaking in Poughkeepsie, New York, Douglass told an audience commemorating the twenty-fourth anniversary of emancipation in the British West Indies that "the contest going on just now in the State of Illinois is worthy of attention." He observed that "Slavery and Anti-

Slavery are at the bottom of the contest" and characterized Stephen Douglas as "one of the most restless, ambitious, boldest and unscrupulous enemies with whom the cause of the colored man has had to contend." He then turned, briefly, to "the great speech of Mr. Lincoln," quoting the introduction to the "House Divided" speech, commending it as "well and wisely said."

THE DEBATES WERE ONLY a small part of the campaign in the summer and fall of 1858. Lincoln, by his own count, delivered sixty-three speeches; Stephen Douglas said he delivered more than one hundred. In the nearly three weeks between Freeport and the next debate at Jonesboro, Lincoln gave eight speeches, plus responses at several conventions and rallies. Although he focused his campaign on the middle of the state, he traveled the length of Illinois.

The Lincoln-Douglas debates would have been physically impossible before the late 1850s. During his Senate campaign, Lincoln traveled 3,400 miles by train, 600 miles by carriage, and 350 miles by boat, for a total of 4,350 miles. Douglas traveled 5,277 miles, mostly by special train, with his own car, which allowed him to rest between towns and spend time with his wife, Adele. Lincoln traveled as a passenger on regular trains, without Mary, who stayed home with the boys. Exuberant supporters often accompanied him, giving Lincoln little time for rest.

For the third debate, Lincoln went down into "Little Egypt," a narrow neck of land at the convergence of the Ohio and Mississippi rivers, wedged between Kentucky and Missouri, with its best-known town named Cairo. The region was rural, poor, and strongly Democratic. It was also known for its hatred of blacks. Jonesboro, with its eight hundred residents, lay three hundred miles south of Chicago, and farther south than Richmond, Virginia.

This was not Lincoln land. In his twenty-five years in politics, Lincoln had not spent much time in the state's southernmost counties. John C. Frémont had received only forty-six votes in Union County, in which Jonesboro was located, in the 1856 presidential election.

For Lincoln, a man who reveled in discoveries and inventions, a thrilling part of his stay in Jonesboro occurred in the sky the night before the debate. On September 14, 1858, he sat on the Union House's porch to watch Donati's Comet and its fiery tail race past the earth. Italian Giovanni Battista Donati, who discovered the comet on June 2, 1858, calculated that the comet, one of the brightest to be observed in the nineteenth century, would not be visible again for two thousand years.

The next morning, on a hot and humid day, 1,200 to 1,500 people came to Jonesboro. Some spectators made the trek from Kentucky and Missouri. Douglas arrived with his private cannon.

The setting for the debate was simple, the platform constructed of rough planks placed across logs. A table in the center of the platform gave newspaper reporters a place to write. The seats for Lincoln and Douglas and the various dignitaries were ordinary chairs brought from nearby homes.

Douglas knew his challenge in this southern region of Illinois was not from the Republicans, but from that faction of the Democratic Party loyal to President Buchanan. He needed to reassure these conservative Democrats, given his rejection of the Lecompton Constitution, of his party orthodoxy. He did so by attacking Lincoln on his "House Divided" speech, trying to show that Lincoln was not a moderate but actually a collaborator with radical abolitionists.

Lincoln, speaking second, added an additional question to the four he had asked at Freeport: "If the slaveholding citizens of a United States Territory should need and demand Congressional legislation for the protection of their slave property in such territory, would you, as a member of Congress, vote for or against such legislation?"

Douglas responded with a general answer that "it is a fundamental article of the Democratic party creed that there should be non-interference by Congress in the States and territories."

Toward the end of his presentation at Jonesboro, knowing he could not win over a hostile audience by argument, Lincoln reached out to them with identification. "Did the Judge talk of trotting me down to Egypt to scare me to death? Why, I know this people better than he does. I was raised just a little east of here. I am a part of this people. But the Judge was raised further north, and perhaps has some horrid idea of what this people might be induced to do."

At Jonesboro, Lincoln tried not to become defensive. For the most part, he succeeded in parrying the thrusts of his Democratic antagonist.

THREE DAYS LATER, Charleston welcomed Lincoln as a favorite son with an eighty-foot pictorial banner hung across the main street with the caption: "Abe's Entrance Into Charleston Thirty Years Ago." The painting depicted Lincoln, the pioneer boy, driving three yoke of oxen as his family entered Illinois from Indiana. The Douglas contingent answered with their own banner with the caption, "Negro Equality," showing a white man, a Negro woman, and a mulatto boy.

The fourth debate would take place in Coles County in east central Illinois, an old-line Whig district that Lincoln knew well. Some in the crowd had known his father and stepmother, who had settled in Coles County in 1831. Thomas Lincoln had died in 1851, but his beloved stepmother, Sally Bush Johnston Lincoln, still lived in an old log cabin south of Charleston. She did not attend the debate.

Both Lincoln and Douglas entered Charleston on the morning of September 18, 1858, like heroes at the head of elaborate processions with bands and banners. In the Lincoln procession was Bowling Green College's marching band, which had traveled fifty miles from Terre Haute, Indiana, to march for their Indiana son. Prominent in the procession was a large wagon filled with thirty-two young women wearing white dresses with long red and blue sashes, each holding a banner for one of the thirty-two states in the Union. A banner above the wagon read:

Westward thy Star of Empire takes it way,
    Thy Girls *Link-on* to Lincoln,—
Their Mothers were for Clay.

Following the wagon was a young woman on horseback with a sign bearing the motto "Kansas will be free!"

In this rural district of cornfields, when the time for early morning farm chores was over, between twelve thousand and fifteen thousand spectators thronged the dusty roads of Charleston. Men, women, and children from Bloody Hutton, Dogtown, Paradise, Muddy, and Goosenest Prairie converged on the agricultural society fairgrounds west of the town. A special eleven-car train brought in spectators from Indiana. By ten o'clock, the streets leading to the public square were nearly impassable.

At 2:45, Lincoln opened the debate with an introduction that would become the subject of much interpretation and misinterpretation. At his hotel that morning, he said, an elderly gentleman had wanted to know whether "I was really in favor of producing a perfect equality between the negroes and white people." After the laughter died down, Lincoln said he had not intended to say much on this subject in Charleston, but thought he would devote five minutes to the question.

He then issued a series of statements defining where he stood on racial equality. "I will say that I am not, nor ever have been in favor of bringing about in any way the social and political equality of the white and black races, [applause],—that I am not nor ever have been in favor of making voters or jurors of negroes, nor of qualifying them to hold office, nor to intermarry with white people." After stating his own opinion, Lincoln went on to say that he had never met a person "in favor of producing a perfect equality, social, and political, between negroes and white men."

Lincoln, by the fourth debate, had grown tired of Douglas's continual race-baiting. He decided to take on Douglas's constant criticisms by clarifying his own position and appealing to the generally held norms of the community where he was speaking. Furthermore, Lincoln appealed to the laws of the state of Illinois, which expressly forbade marriage between whites and blacks.

"Race prejudice seems stronger in those states that have abolished slavery than in those where it still exists, and nowhere is it more intolerant than in those states where slavery was never known." So wrote Alexis de Tocqueville in *Democracy in America* in 1833. Few white Americans were without aversion to black Americans in the 1840s and 1850s. White attitudes were based on an assumption of the inferiority of African-Americans. This prejudiced mind-set permeated both the South and the North.

Although the first Illinois constitution in 1818 outlawed slavery, by the time of a revised constitution, anti-black feeling was on the rise. A proposal at the 1847 Illinois constitutional convention to extend the right of suffrage to blacks was defeated by a vote of 137 to 7. Article 14 of the revised constitution of 1848 directed the general assembly to enact laws prohibiting black migration to Illinois. More than three-fourths of Illinois voters approved the new constitution.

Ironically, antislavery and racist attitudes walked hand in hand. Only a few aggressive abolitionists contemplated social equality with African-Americans as a possibility. Republicans who campaigned in the 1850s understood that it was prudent to deny any interest in social equality as part of achieving some measure of political rights for African-Americans.

Lincoln had one more method to try to silence Douglas's "great apprehension." It was his favorite tactic. Whereas Douglas resorted to anger, Lincoln employed humor. Lincoln said he understood that laws against social equality rightly belonged to the states and that Douglas seemed to be "in constant horror" about measures that might be brought forward in the state legislature to promote equality of the races. What was Lincoln's solution? "I propose as the best means to prevent it that the Judge be kept at home and placed in the State Legislature to fight the measure."

Norman Judd had written to Lincoln before the debate at Charleston, "Allow me to suggest that in your next joint debate where you have the opening you make your entire opening a series of charges against Douglas leaving all statement of your own views for your reply." Lincoln followed Judd's advice. Taking leave of the remarks about popular sovereignty and Dred Scott that had been so prominent in the first three debates, Lincoln instead focused on the accusation that Douglas, despite his protest of the Lecompton Constitution, was part of a conspiracy to impress slavery on Kansas. Senator Lyman Trumbull, who had returned to Illinois in August to campaign against Douglas, had first made this charge, based on his knowledge of Douglas's insider trading in the Senate. Douglas had denounced the charges before, but Lincoln renewed them at Charleston in an at-times wearying recitation of Trumbull's version of the story.

When Douglas stepped forward to speak, he expressed astonishment. "I am amazed that Mr. Lincoln should now come forward and endorse that charge, occupying his whole hour in reading Mr. Trumbull's speech in support of it." In Douglas's conclusion, he referred to Lincoln's opening remarks about Negro equality and left his audience questioning whether Lincoln was in favor of Negro citizenship.

The fourth debate did little to boost Lincoln. His opening remarks about equality were read and heard in quite different ways among different audiences. Some thought he was simply acknowledging the attitudes of the overwhelming majority of those in south central Illinois. Others, reading about the debate in Chicago and northern Illinois, wondered if this was the same Lincoln of the "House Divided" speech. Many observers, then and now, reading only two sentences and not the full two paragraphs, failed to understand that Lincoln's purpose in raising the issue of social equality was to get Douglas off his back. It was a short-term political tactic.

—

LINCOLN SPENT THE NEXT DAY with relatives in Coles County. He visited with his stepmother, giving her fifty dollars before he left the next morning at four o'clock to resume his campaigning. In the nineteen days before the next debate in Galesburg, Lincoln would crisscross the state in a hurly-burly schedule of speech making, sometimes two or three times in a day.

Lincoln continued to refine his thinking on slavery by writing on his steady supply of small slips of paper. The catalyst for one of his notes was reading *Slavery Ordained by God,* an 1857 book by Frederick A. Ross, a Presbyterian minister from Huntsville, Alabama. The book, based on lectures and sermons, became an instant bestseller among pro-slavery advocates. Ross argued that slavery was a beneficent and ordering institution.

Lincoln began his musing with a question: "Suppose it is true, that the negro is inferior to the white, in the gifts of nature?" He understood that most white Americans accepted the assumption of inferiority, but he did not stop there. Pondering that supposition, Lincoln wrote, "Is it not the exact reverse justice that the white should, for that reason, take from the negro, any part of the little which has been given him?" Lincoln offered his answer. "Give to him that is needy" is the Christian rule of charity; but "Take from him that is needy" is the rule of slavery.

Ross had argued that slavery was the will of God, to which Lincoln wrote, "Certainly there is no contending against the Will of God; but still there is some difficulty in ascertaining, and applying it, to particular cases." He then proposed a case. Dr. Ross has a slave named Sambo. Lincoln asked, "Is it the Will of God that Sambo shall remain a slave, or be set free?" Lincoln pondered the options. "The Almighty gives no audible answer to the question, and his revelation—the Bible—gives none—or, at most, *none* but such as admits of a squabble, as to its meaning." Lincoln quickly added, "No one thinks of asking Sambo's opinion of it." Lincoln wrote that the last option was for Dr. Ross to decide. If he decided that Sambo was to remain a slave, "he thereby retains his own comfortable position." If "he decides that God wills Sambo to be free," it will mean that he "has to walk out of the shade, throw off his gloves, and delve for his own bread." Lincoln asked whether Ross will be guided by "that perfect impartiality" which was the best means of making decisions. Lincoln anticipated Ross's answer: "But, slavery is good for some people!!!" and rebutted that slavery is "peculiar" in "that it is the only good thing which no man ever seeks the good of, *for himself.*"

This complex reflection on slavery was something Lincoln was not yet prepared to say in public. After carefully considering all the options, Lincoln's anger boiled over in the conclusion of his note. "Nonsense! Wolves devouring lambs, not because it is good for their own greedy maws, but because it [is] good for the lambs!!!" The triple exclamation points revealed Lincoln's deep feeling as he struggled with the immorality of slavery, especially as it was defended by religious leaders. Lincoln was ever alert to the mishandling of religion.

In a second note, written in this same period, Lincoln began, "But there is a larger issue than the mere question of whether the spread of negro slavery shall or shall not be prohibited by Congress." Lincoln asserted that even the Buchanan papers, such as the *Richmond Enquirer* and the *New York Day-Book,* understood the issue. Both newspapers pointed to the assertion by Senator John Pettit of Indiana that the doctrine of equality in the Declaration of Independence was "a self-evident lie." As for Senator Douglas, Lincoln said he "regularly argues against the doctrine of the equality of men." Lincoln concluded that the "common object" of Douglas and his allies was to subvert the clear avowal in the Declaration of Independence and "to assert the natural, moral, and religious right of one class to enslave another."

THE LARGEST CROWD of the seven debates converged on Knox College in Galesburg in northern Illinois on Thursday, October 7, 1858. Galesburg, a town of 5,500, was Republican, antislavery, and a stop on the Underground Railroad. Heavy rains had fallen the day before, and on debate day icy winds tore down signs and ripped up banners. But not even the elements could keep 15,000 to 20,000 spectators away. An eleven-car train came from Chicago. A twenty-two-car train from Peoria, crammed full with 2,200 passengers, was slowed by mechanical problems and did not arrive until near the end of the debate. Despite the winds, numerous banners vied with one another for creativity. A representation of a two-donkey act showed Douglas attempting to ride Popular Sovereignty and Dred Scott. Try as he might, he was unable to keep his balance and was sent sprawling. Another banner was inscribed "Small-fisted Farmers, Mud Sills of Society, Greasy

Mechanics, for A. Lincoln," a refutation of the recent Southern charge that laborers in the North were at least as exploited as slaves in the South.

At 2:30, Lincoln and Douglas were driven to the college in identical carriages. Because of the bitter conditions, the platform had been moved from an open space on the college campus to abut the east side of Old Main, the central building on campus. According to a later reminiscence, both Lincoln and Douglas had to climb through a window in Old Main to get to the platform. Lincoln, never at a loss for words, was heard to say, "Well, at last I have gone through college."

Douglas began and quickly settled into his regular speech. By this fifth debate Douglas appeared exhausted, with a hoarse voice that did not carry his words beyond the first few rows of the audience. He defended popular sovereignty and attacked both Republicans and Buchanan Democrats. He accused Lincoln of shifting his message according to the geography of the debate. "In the extreme northern part of the state he can proclaim as bold and radical abolitionism as ever Giddings, Lovejoy, or Garrison enunciated." In the southern part of the state, Douglas claimed Lincoln identified himself as "an old line Whig, a disciple of Henry Clay." Douglas summed up his criticism by telling the crowd, "Mr. Lincoln's creed cannot travel."

Lincoln, by contrast, seemed restored at Galesburg. His nineteen days of travel, spent speaking with thousands of people in Urbana, Jacksonville, Winchester, Pittsfield, Metamora, and Pekin, had not tired but rather renewed his spirits. Lincoln, who could be introspective and took pleasure from time alone to read and to write, was energized by contact with all sorts of people on the campaign trail.

Taking heart from this strongly Republican community, Lincoln began with the Declaration of Independence. Douglas had insisted that the Declaration's opening words were never intended to include Negroes. Lincoln countered with his strongest statement in the debates about the Declaration's intent. "I believe that the entire records of the world, from the date of the Declaration of Independence up to within three years ago may be searched in vain for one single affirmation, from one single man, that the negro was not included in the Declaration of Independence." As for Douglas's contention that Jefferson did not intend to include Negroes because he was the owner of slaves, Lincoln replied by recalling Jefferson's words, offered late in his life, that "he trembled for his country when he remembered that God was just." Lincoln elicited "great applause" when he thundered, "I will offer the highest premium in my power to Judge Douglas if he will show that he, in all his life, ever uttered a sentiment at all akin to that of Jefferson."

Lincoln also charged head-on into Douglas's criticism that Lincoln changed his message on Negro equality depending on where he was speaking. Lincoln pointed out that all his speeches were in print so everyone could read them. He denied that there was any conflict between what he said at the various debates. Lincoln then turned Douglas's criticism to his advantage by addressing the moral dimension of the debate about slavery. In summarizing Douglas's position, Lincoln reminded the audience that "every sentiment he utters discards the idea that there is any wrong in Slavery."

Lincoln's supporters were exuberant about his performance at Galesburg. The *Quincy Whig* reported, "When Douglas concluded, 'Old Abe' mounted to the stand, and was received with three such tremendous cheers." The Republican paper believed "he met, and successfully refuted, every argument made by Judge Douglas." Lincoln did so by seizing the moral high ground. He charged Douglas with "blowing out the moral lights around us." Lincoln declared, "Judge Douglas, and whoever like him teaches that the negro has no share, humble though it may be, in the Declaration of Independence, and so far as in him lies, [muzzles] the cannon that thunders its annual joyous return" every Fourth of July.

THE SIXTH DEBATE took place on October 13, 1858, at Quincy. Nestled on the banks of the Mississippi River, just across from Missouri, Quincy was settled by New Englanders who named the town in 1825 for then president John Quincy Adams. Quincy was like many cities in central Illinois—contested territory between Republicans and Democrats. Boats from Hannibal, Missouri, and Keokuk, Iowa, swelled the crowd to between ten thousand and fifteen thousand who gathered at Washington Park on a sunny but cool day.

Lincoln arrived by train in the morning and was invited to ride in a decorated carriage, although he said he preferred to "foot it to Browning's," his friend Orville Browning's home, where he would rest until the debate. Nevertheless, a large procession guided Lincoln. Central in the procession was a model ship on wheels drawn by four horses and labeled "Constitution."

Carl Schurz, an immigrant who had fled the failed revolution in Germany of 1848–49, traveled from Watertown, Wisconsin, to witness the debate. Later, Schurz recalled that Lincoln's

charm did not, in the ordinary way, appeal to the ear or to the eye. His voice was not melodious; rather shrill and piercing, especially when it rose to its high treble in moments of great animation. His figure was unhandsome, and the action of his unwieldy limbs awkward. He commanded none of the outwardly graces or oratory as they are commonly understood. His charm was of a different kind. It flowed from the rare depth and genuineness of his convictions and his sympathetic feelings.

He said that Lincoln's "voice was not musical, being rather high-keyed and apt to turn into a shrill treble in moments of excitement." But it did possess "an exceedingly penetrating, far-reaching quality." Lincoln's movements especially struck Schurz. "His gestures were awkward. He swung his long arms sometimes in a very ungraceful manner. Now and then, to give particular emphasis to a point, he would bend his knees and body with a sudden downward jerk and then shoot up again with a vehemence that raised him to his tiptoes and made him look taller than he was."

Carl Schurz, a German immigrant from Wisconsin, traveled to Quincy to hear Lincoln in the sixth debate. Schurz would become instrumental in mobilizing the large German population in the Midwest behind Lincoln.

Lincoln began the debate by denying that his remarks about Negro civil rights at Charleston were any different from what he had said at Ottawa or would affirm at Quincy. Whenever Lincoln bowed to the norms of his day as to the impossibility of social equality between the races, he always concluded with the greater possibility, not yet fully realized, inherent in the Declaration of Independence: "In the right to eat the bread without leave of anybody else which his own hand earns, he is my equal and the equal of Judge Douglas, and the equal of every other man." To this the crowd cheered loudly.

Lincoln concluded his opening hour with a compelling repetition of his charge that slavery is morally wrong. "When Judge Douglas says that whoever, or whatever community, wants slaves, they have a right to have them, he is perfectly logical if there is nothing wrong in the institution; but if you admit that it is wrong, he cannot logically say that anybody has a right to do wrong." Lincoln stated that the issue was not whether he or Douglas was right or wrong, but whether slavery was right or wrong. If, Lincoln declared in his final sentence, "we can get all these men who believe that slavery is in some of these respects wrong, to stand and act with us in treating it as a wrong—then, and not till then, I think we will in some way come to an end of this slavery agitation."

Douglas, on the defensive, was forced to respond to Lincoln's charge that he would not say whether slavery was right or wrong. "I tell you why I will not do it. I hold that under the Constitution of the United States, each state of this Union has a right to do as it please on the subject of slavery." He then spent much of his time disputing that he was conspiring with Pierce, Buchanan, and Taney to open the territories to slavery. Near the conclusion of his remarks Douglas stated, "This republic can exist forever divided into free and slave States."

Lincoln, in his rebuttal, immediately seized upon Douglas's remark. "We are getting a little nearer the true issue of this controversy, and I am profoundly grateful for this one sentence." Lincoln said that he had no desire to argue with slavery in Kentucky or Virginia, but that Douglas would be happy to see slavery extend not just into the Western territories but into the Northern states.

AFTER THE QUINCY DEBATE, both Lincoln and Douglas boarded the *City of Louisiana* for the 115-mile passage down the Mississippi River to Alton, site of the final debate. Alton was snuggled among bluffs at the confluence of the Mississippi and Illinois rivers. When the ship arrived the next morning, Mary and fifteen-year-old Robert were waiting to greet Lincoln. They had traveled from Springfield on the Sangamon-Alton Railroad, which ran a half-price excursion fare to the debate. Robert, a member of the Springfield Cadets, was smartly dressed in a blue coat with white pants. Gustave Koerner, who had served as president of the Republican convention that nominated Lincoln for the Senate, had also traveled to Alton. Koerner found Lincoln in the sitting room at the Franklin House. Lincoln encouraged Koerner to go upstairs and speak with Mary because "she is rather dispirited" about her husband's political chances. Koerner expressed his confidence to her "of carrying the State and tolerably certain of our carrying the Legislature."

In 1837, Alton had been the scene of the murder of Presbyterian abolitionist Elijah Lovejoy, who was defending his press from a pro-slavery mob. In 1858, this town in southwestern Illinois remained sympathetic to slavery, Douglas, and Democrats. The *White Cloud* and *Baltimore* steamboats offered one-dollar round-trip fares from neighboring St. Louis, bringing in from Missouri more Douglas supporters. Some visitors even made the trip from Kentucky. On a beautiful fall day, organizers of the final debate were disappointed that the crowd would number only between five thousand and six thousand, some spectators saying that by now everyone knew what both Lincoln and Douglas would say.

Douglas began the debate looking like a man the worse for wear from the debates and the campaign. His voice could barely be heard as he summarized his arguments of the previous six debates. On the offense in debate one, by debate seven he made the odd decision to focus his defense on his decisions relating to Lecompton. Obviously distressed by Lincoln's renewed emphasis on the Declaration of Independence at Galesburg and Quincy, Douglas, in a barely audible voice, declared, "I hold that the signers of the Declaration of Independence had no reference to negroes at all when they declared all men to be created equal. They did not mean negro, nor the savage Indians, nor the Fejee Islanders, nor any other barbarous race."

Lincoln, in contrast, appeared tanned and eager for the final debate. Always conscious of his audience, Lincoln acknowledged that the citizens of Alton were linked with "strong sympathies by birth, education, and otherwise, with the South." Not content to concede any audience, however, Lincoln recalled his father's decision to move from a slave state to a free state, and then asked: "How many Democrats are there about here who have left slave states and come into the free state of Illinois to get rid of the institution of slavery?" One voice interrupted and said, "A thousand." Another added, "One thousand and one," to which Lincoln responded, "I reckon there are a thousand and one."

Douglas, at Quincy and again now at Alton in Madison County, had tried to put on the mantle of Henry Clay, arguing that the architect of the Compromise of 1850 would never have acceded to Lincoln's radical views. But no one loved Clay and his speeches more than Lincoln. Perturbed that Douglas tried to pass himself off as a follower of Clay, Lincoln reached into his coat and pulled out his notebook filled with extracts from important speeches. He read a long section from one of Clay's speeches to show that the Great Compromiser believed in the great "fundamental principle" from the Declaration of Independence that all men are created equal, even as Clay understood that principle had not yet become fully realized in American society.

Toward the end of this final debate, when Lincoln must have been tired, he rose to the height of his eloquence. Focusing his final comments on Douglas's constant refrain that he did not care whether slavery was voted up or down, Lincoln responded that the real issue was the morality of slavery. "That is the issue that will continue in this country when these poor tongues of Judge Douglas and myself shall be silent." Lincoln declared the issue to be "the eternal struggle between these two principles—right and wrong—throughout the world." He continued,

> They are the two principles that have stood face to face from the beginning of time; and will ever continue to struggle. The one is the common right of humanity and the other the divine right of kings. It is the same principle in whatever shape it develops itself. It is the same spirit that says: "You work and toil and earn bread, and I'll eat it."

THE TWENTY-ONE HOURS of debate were over. The story of the Lincoln-Douglas debates of 1858 needs to be understood on its own terms and not from a backward glance from future events, when Douglas became at best a foil and at worst caricatured or marginalized. At the time of the debates, Douglas was a leading national actor while Lincoln was regarded solely as an Illinois politician.

How was the voter to decide? Most attended only one debate. At the outset, Lincoln had to discredit the idea that he was a radical abolitionist, whereas Douglas had to deny that he was a pro-Southern defender of slavery. There were many other issues that Lincoln and Douglas might have included in their debates—currency policy, tariffs, immigration, railroads—but the focus was almost exclusively on slavery. The debaters and the audiences agreed that this was the most important issue facing the nation.

There was a great deal of repetition in the debates, often with each debater reading long quotations from previous speeches. Douglas stuck to his theme of self-government. Lincoln invoked the Declaration of Independence again and again. Douglas began strong and put Lincoln on the defensive with his attacks and questions. Lincoln gathered momentum in the final three debates, beginning at Galesburg, both in his physical presence and his decision to focus on the moral dimension of slavery. Douglas, when under stress, resorted to anger and sarcasm. Lincoln, when pushed, reflexively responded with humor, a lighter touch that created a bond of trust with audiences. Lincoln, whether in his private notes to himself or in his public debates with Douglas, grew in his ability to communicate his ideas both clearly and forcefully.

The debates were over, but the campaign continued. Lincoln, after spending several days in Springfield, was off again. In the final two and a half weeks he was alternately discouraged and encouraged, as were his closest advisers. Stepping off the train in Naples on October 18, 1858, Lincoln saw fifteen "Celtic gentlemen" and wondered if these Irishmen were being brought into Illinois to vote. The next day, he heard that four hundred Irish laborers were arriving in Schuyler County to work on the railroad, arriving just before Election Day. On October 20, Lincoln wrote to Norman Judd, "I now have a high degree of confidence that we shall succeed, if we are not over-run with fraudulent votes to a greater extent than usual."

A few days later, Judge David Davis expressed his apprehension. "Outside Republicans from the East, Mr. Greeley—Truman Smith &c have thrown cold water on the election of Lincoln." A difficult blow to Lincoln's chances for election came at the end of the campaign. A letter written by Senator John J. Crittenden of Kentucky on August 1, 1858, announcing his support for Douglas, was held until the last week of the campaign when it could do the most damage. Lincoln and Crittenden had served together in the Thirtieth Congress. Crittenden viewed himself as Clay's political heir. Astonished and hurt that a Kentucky Whig would enter the Senate campaign against an Illinois Whig, Lincoln had written Crittenden in July telling him that a story was being whispered "that you are anxious for the reelection of Mr. Douglas." Lincoln told Crittenden, "I do not believe the story, but still it gives me some uneasiness. I do not believe you would so express yourself. It is not in character with you as I have always estimated you." Unfortunately for Lincoln, the story proved to be true. Crittenden admired Douglas's stand against the Lecompton Constitution and believed that a vote for Douglas was a vote against the Buchanan administration. Crittenden's support for Douglas, trumpeted by the *Illinois State Register* in Springfield, certainly served to undercut Lincoln with some old-line Whigs, especially in the critical counties of central Illinois.

Lincoln chose to give his last speech of the campaign in Springfield on Saturday, October 30, 1858. An enthusiastic crowd of five thousand made it almost impossible for Lincoln to be heard. He became quite personal and emotional in his final words before friends and admirers. "Ambition has been ascribed to me," Lincoln acknowledged.

> I claim no insensibility to political honors; but today could the Missouri restriction be restored, and the whole slavery question replaced on the old ground of "toleration" by *necessity* where it exists, with unyielding hostility to the spread of it, on principle, I would, in consideration, gladly agree, that Judge Douglas should never be *out,* and I never *in,* an office, so long as we both or either, live.

He had ended on the high road of principle.

LINCOLN VOTED EARLY in Springfield on Election Day, Tuesday, November 2, 1858. A cold rain covered the Illinois prairies and fell "incessantly" throughout the day in the state capital, turning the streets into a "horrid condition." The *Illinois State Journal* reported that "Street fights are not as numerous as expected," but by sundown, the "city prison is nearly full."

Republican candidates for the state legislature won the popular vote, 125,430 to 121,609. But Democrats won the contest for seats in the legislature by a vote of 54 to 46. Lincoln lost a split decision. It would be the legislators who would vote on January 5, 1859, and thus decide who would be the next U.S. senator. This Senate election, with its appeal to the people rather than to state legislators, was a first step on the long road toward the Seventeenth Amendment, ratified in 1913, which would call for the direct election of senators.

After monitoring the results far into the night at the telegraph office, Lincoln headed wearily for home. Some years later he recalled that on that dark and rainy evening he slipped, "but I recovered . . . and I said to myself, '*It's a slip and not a fall.*' "

IN A POSTELECTION INQUEST on their defeat, Republicans complained about the inequities of an antiquated apportionment of various Illinois legislative districts. William Herndon wrote a long letter to Theodore Parker, a New England transcendentalist minister, detailing what he deemed were "the causes of our defeat." He blamed Horace Greeley: "His silence was his opposition"; he chastised Crittenden: "Thousands of Whigs dropped us just on the eve of the election, through the influence of Crittenden"; and he blamed the pro-slavery men who "went to a man for Douglas." Finally, Herndon blamed "thousands of roving, robbing, bloated, pock-marked Catholic Irish" imported from St. Louis and other cities.

Lincoln did not blame anyone. If there was one person he might have blamed, it was Crittenden. The Kentucky senator wrote Lincoln on October 27, 1858, stating that the publication in several Democratic newspapers of a private letter stating why he was supporting Douglas was "unauthorized." Crittenden's letter, in the confusion of the election, had been picked up at the post office but, Lincoln said, "was handed me only this moment." Everyone around him was blaming Crittenden but, Lincoln wrote, "It never occurred to me to cast any blame upon you." In a final sentence, Lincoln expressed magnanimity in defeat. "The emotions of defeat, at the close of a struggle in which I felt more than a merely selfish interest, and to which defeat the use of your name contributed largely, are fresh upon me, but even in this mood, I can not for a moment suspect you of anything dishonorable." Lincoln's magnanimity grew in part from his ability to attribute the best motives to those who were his opponents.

The *Chicago Press & Tribune,* under the editorship of Joseph Medill and Charles Ray, said it best on November 10, 1858, five days after Election Day.

Mr. Lincoln is beaten. We know of no better time than the pres- ent to congratulate him on the memorable and brilliant canvass he has made. He has created for himself a national reputation that is both envied and deserved; and though he should hereafter fill no official station, he has done the cause of Truth and Justice what will always entitle him to the gratitude of his party and the keen admiration of all who respect the high moral qualities, and the keen, comprehensive and sound intellectual gifts he has dis- played.

On November, 19, 1858, Lincoln wrote Dr. Anson Henry, his for- mer doctor and Whig associate, now living in Oregon. He told his old friend, "I am glad I made the late race. It gave me a hearing on the great and durable question of the age, which I could have had in no other way, and though I sink out of view, and shall be forgotten, I believe I have made some marks which will tell for the cause of civil liberty long after I am gone."

Mathew Brady took this photograph of a beardless Lincoln,
in New York to deliver his Cooper Union address. It was later
called "the photograph that made Lincoln president."

CHAPTER 14

The Taste Is in My Mouth, a Little
1858–60

LET US HAVE FAITH THAT RIGHT MAKES MIGHT, AND IN THAT FAITH,
LET US, TO THE END, DARE TO DO OUR DUTY AS WE UNDERSTAND IT.

ABRAHAM LINCOLN
Cooper Union address, February 27, 1860

ON NOVEMBER 3, 1858, THE DAY AFTER LINCOLN'S DEFEAT IN THE SENATE
election, Jeriah Bonham, editor of the *Illinois Gazette* in Lacon, asked,
"What man now fills the full measure of public expectation as the
statesman of to-day and of the near future, as does Abraham Lincoln? . . . We believe we but express the wish of a large majority of the
people that he should be the standard-bearer of the Republican Party
for the presidency in 1860."

Three days later, the *Commercial Register* of Sandusky, Ohio, carried a
brief notice: "An enthusiastic meeting is in progress here to-night in
favor of Lincoln for the next Republican candidate for President."

These first calls for Lincoln to run for president came from small-
town, little-known newspapers. But on November 10, 1858, only a
week after Lincoln's defeat, the *Chicago Tribune* printed the *Commercial
Register*'s announcement without comment in the "Personal and Political" column of its popular weekly edition. The following day, the
Chicago Democrat stated that Illinois should "present his [Lincoln's] name
to the National Republican Convention, first for President, and next for
Vice President." The *Illinois State Journal* of Springfield printed the
"Lincoln for President" story from Sandusky on November 13, 1858,
but it was buried in the "City Items and Other Matters" column without editorial comment.

Other newspapers would add their approbation at the end of 1858, but the speculation about Lincoln's future in higher office often was as much about praising him for what he had accomplished in the debates in 1858 as about what he might achieve in 1860. Some of this commendation mentioned Lincoln at the end of a list of potential candidates, which usually started with Senator William H. Seward of New York and Senator Salmon P. Chase of Ohio, and often included Edward G. Bates of Missouri and Senator Simon Cameron of Pennsylvania.

AT DUSK ON A COLD DECEMBER DAY, as Lincoln was leaving the McLean County courthouse in Bloomington, Jesse Fell, lawyer, land speculator, and the founder of the *Bloomington Pantagraph,* met him on the south side of the public square. Fell asked whether he could have a word in his brother Kersey's law office. Fell and Lincoln had roomed together as members of the state legislature at Vandalia in the early 1830s. He had been one of the organizers of the Republican convention in Bloomington in 1856. He nominated Lincoln for the Senate in June 1858, and was secretary of the Republican State Committee. As the two sat amid calf-bound legal books, Fell told Lincoln he had recently returned from an extensive trip to Pennsylvania, New York, and New England. Everywhere he traveled he found people asking the question: "Who is this man Lincoln?" Fell responded that there were two giants in Illinois, a little one they knew, "but that you were the big one they didn't all know."

Fell told Lincoln he could become a viable candidate for president in 1860, but it was critical that his name become better known in the East, especially in Pennsylvania. He knew from his wide-ranging contacts that Seward, thought by many to be the leading candidate for the Republican nomination for president, was not popular in Pennsylvania. If Pennsylvania, and several other states in the East, were to rally behind Lincoln, they would first need to know more about him. Fell proposed that Lincoln write an autobiographical statement to be published in several Eastern newspapers.

"Oh, Fell, what's the use talking of me for the Presidency," Lincoln replied, "whilst we have such men as Seward, Chase, and others, who are so much better known to the people?" Lincoln told Fell, "Everybody knows them. Nobody, scarcely, outside of Illinois, knows me." Fell was particularly struck by what Lincoln said next. "Beside, is it not, as a matter of justice, due to such men, who have carried this movement forward to its present status, in spite of fearful opposition, personal abuse, and hard names?"

Lincoln concluded, "I admit the force of much that you say, and admit that I am ambitious, and would like to be President; I am not insensible to the compliment you pay me, and the interest you manifest in the matter, but there is no such good luck in store for me, as the Presidency of these United States." Besides, "there is nothing in my early history that would interest you or anybody else." With these words, Lincoln put on his "dilapidated" shawl and walked out into the darkness.

At the very moment that Lincoln was saying no to Fell's initiative, he was taking his own initiative to publish his personal scrapbook of the debates. Throughout the summer and fall of 1858, Lincoln, by scissors and paste, had placed in a two-hundred-page scrapbook the texts of speeches and debates, primarily from the *Chicago Press and Tribune* and the *Chicago Times*. On virtually every page, he wrote in his distinctive handwriting titles, captions, a variety of notes, and corrections to the texts. Four days after he met with Fell, he told Henry C. Whitney, "There is some probability that my Scrap-book will be reprinted."

Lincoln was actually ambivalent about the presidency in December 1858. Fell's request may have collided with Lincoln's innate caution or with his Victorian sense of modesty in speaking about oneself, whereas the texts of the debates were a public record. Lincoln's ambition was not simply to preserve the historical record of the debates, but to advance his reputation. In the winter of 1858–59, consumed by his law practice and averse to letting the scrapbook out of his hands, Lincoln made no headway in securing a publisher.

FOUR DAYS AFTER the November election, Lincoln and Herndon were back in court in Springfield. For nearly six months, Lincoln had neglected his law practice. He went without income and paid nearly all of his own expenses during the Senate campaign. When state Republican chairman Norman Judd wrote after the election requesting his help in paying off Republican campaign debts, Lincoln replied, "I have been on expenses so long without earning any thing that I am absolutely without money now for even household purposes."

Lincoln returned to his law office to answer clients complaining of lack of action on their lawsuits. Samuel C. Davis and Company, wholesale merchants in St. Louis, had written Lincoln on October 1, 1858, annoyed that their "interests have been so long neglected." Lincoln replied on November 17, explaining that he had just seen their letter because he had been "personally engaged the last three or four months." Usually even tempered, Lincoln betrayed his annoyance. "I will have no more to do with this class of business. I can do business in Court, but I can not, and will not follow executions all over the world." Lincoln concluded by offering to "surrender" these matters to other lawyers.

Lincoln's attempt to balance law and politics had become more difficult than ever before. His impatience came through in a number of letters to clients. In November, he wrote former governor Joel Matteson that "we have performed no service" in a case for the Chicago and Alton Railroad, "but we lost a cash fee offered us on the other side." In December, he told lawyer William M. Fishback, "I wish you would return and take charge of this business" with Samuel C. Davis and Company. After receiving two letters from a cousin in Lexington, Kentucky, Lincoln replied, "It annoys me to say that I can not collect money now."

Lincoln's only speeches during the four months after the election took place in courtrooms. In the early spring of 1859, he resumed traveling the Eighth Judicial Circuit, which had been reduced from fourteen to five counties in 1857. Completing the circuit in Danville in early May, he returned to Springfield, where he handled a heavy caseload before the U.S. Circuit Court until the end of June.

THE YEAR 1859 would be full of political surprises for Lincoln, but it did not start out that way. On January 5, the Illinois legislature gathered in Springfield to cast their votes for the U.S. Senate. Rumors persisted that there would be some defections from the Democratic ranks, with some pro-Buchanan legislators expressing their anger at Douglas by voting for Lincoln. In the end, however, all fifty-four Democrats voted for Stephen Douglas and all forty-six Republicans voted for Lincoln.

Bitterly disappointed, Lincoln pondered his options for 1860. He wrote to Judd, "In that day I shall fight in the ranks, but I shall be in no ones way for any of the places." Lincoln's comment meant that he had decided not to seek the other U.S. Senate seat from Illinois in 1860 because Lyman Trumbull would surely run for a second term. Lincoln was sounded out by friends to run for governor, but he was not interested in a state office, even the highest one. Now beaten twice for the

Senate, this meant Lincoln's only course seemed to be to wait six more years until 1864 to challenge Douglas—again.

His main political task at the beginning of 1859, now that he had become the recognized leader of the Republicans in Illinois, was marshaling a party many predicted would soon splinter and divide. Lincoln's leadership was based on loyalty forged through lengthy years in Illinois politics and in the camaraderie of the Eighth Judicial Circuit. These Lincoln men were joined by a few former Democrats, whom Lincoln had known for much less time, but who had come to appreciate both his integrity and political abilities.

Lincoln would demonstrate his political wisdom not only in bringing these men together, but in occasionally keeping them apart. They trusted Lincoln, but many distrusted one another. The advisers were rivals both for Lincoln's attention and for Illinois political offices. Norman Judd, a former Democrat, was resented by former Whigs for the power he wielded as chairman of the Illinois Republican State Central Committee. He was a resident of northern Illinois, and many believed he slighted the crucial counties in central Illinois in the 1858 Senate campaign. Richard Yates and Leonard Swett, who both disliked Judd, became his rivals for the Republican nomination for governor in 1860. "Long John" Wentworth and Judd carried on a feud through the pages of two Republican papers vying for dominance, Wentworth's *Chicago Democrat,* and the *Chicago Tribune,* which took Judd's side. Wentworth, in commenting on the Republican organization in the state, summed up the problem in a letter to Judge David Davis. "I look upon the whole management as making Lincoln incidental to the project of certain men for the future."

ON APRIL 13, 1859, Thomas J. Pickett, editor of the *Rock Island Register,* wrote Lincoln that he was eager to write to "the Republican editors of the State on the subject of a simultaneous announcement of your name for the Presidency." Lincoln replied immediately, "I must in candor say I do not think myself fit for the Presidency," adding, "I certainly am flattered, and gratified, that some partial friends think of me in that connection; but I really think it best for our cause that no concerted effort, such as you suggest, should be made." Lincoln was not being unduly modest. He was fully aware of the shortcomings of his candidacy, which he believed would be brought into the open if he decided to throw his hat in the ring. He was painfully aware of his lack of education. He had served only a single term in Congress, and was certain that "spotty" Lincoln, the congressman who critics said had failed to support the troops, would be dredged up from his past. He had never held an executive post as had the two front-runners, Seward and Chase, each having served as governor of their states.

Though he refused Pickett's offer, Lincoln was aware that his influence was expanding beyond Illinois in the spring of 1859, when political leaders in other states began to ask for his help.

Lincoln received an invitation to attend a festival in Boston in April 1859, in honor of the birthday of Thomas Jefferson. He could not attend but sent a letter. "All honor to Jefferson," Lincoln declared across the miles and years. Alert to the ironies in American history, Lincoln recalled that two great parties had been formed at the birth of the Republic, but seventy years later they had completely changed places. Modern Republicans, descendants of the old New England Federalists, paradoxically, had ended up preserving the principles of Jefferson. Lincoln illustrated his point by the story of two drunken men who engaged in a fight with the result that "each having fought himself *out* of his own coat, and *into* the other." The contemporary application: "The democracy [Democrats] of to-day hold the *liberty* of one man to be absolutely nothing, when in conflict with another man's right of *property*. Republicans, on the contrary, are for both the *man* and *dollar;* but in cases of conflict, the man *before* the dollar." Lincoln's compelling words would receive wide circulation in the Republican press.

In May, Lincoln turned down an invitation to speak at the founding convention of the Republican Party in Kansas but presented his counsel about identity and membership: "The only danger will be the temptation to lower the Republican Standard in order to gather recruits. . . . In my judgment such a step would be a serious mistake—would open a gap through which more would pass *out* than pass *in*." To Kansas Republicans, Lincoln offered his definition of "the o[b]ject of the Republican organization—the preventing the spread and nationalization of Slavery."

He began to offer his advice on passionately debated issues in other states he believed would impact the prospects for Republican victories in 1859 and 1860. In Ohio, a contentious issue was the Fugitive Slave Act of 1850. The controversy was raised to a fever pitch in the fall of 1858 when a federal marshal arrested John Price, a slave who had lived in

Oberlin for some time. Residents of Oberlin stormed the hotel in nearby Wellington where Price was being held, freed him, and took him back to Oberlin, where the president of Oberlin College hid him in his home before friends spirited him away to Canada.

Lincoln was paying attention when Ohio Republicans, with emotions running high, met in a convention in Columbus on June 2, 1859. The convention enacted a plank in their party platform calling for "a repeal of the atrocious Fugitive Slave Law." Lincoln, in response to these actions, wrote Ohio governor Salmon P. Chase. In an earlier letter Lincoln had expressed his gratitude to Chase for traveling to Illinois to campaign for him the previous summer. He called Chase "one of the very few distinguished men, whose sympathy we in Illinois did receive last year." But they had never met. Lincoln now told Chase that the action of the convention "is already damaging us here." He concluded by imploring, "I hope you can, and will, contribute something to relieve us from it."

Chase replied by declaring that this advice was inconsistent with the "avowal of our great principles" so evident in "your own example in that noble speech of yours at Springfield which opened the campaign last year." Chase did not give an inch, replying that he believed the fugitive slave law to be unconstitutional, unduly harsh, and not possible to be carried out.

Lincoln responded a week later by stating that, in theory, he believed Congress did have the authority "to enact a Fugitive Slave Law." In practice, Lincoln was not so interested in discussing "constitutional questions" as he was concerned that "the introduction of a proposition for repeal of the Fugitive Slave Law, into the next Republican National Convention, will explode the convention and the party."

In May, Lincoln received a letter from Dr. Theodore Canisius, publisher of the *Illinois Staats-Anzeiger,* who was concerned about Republican involvement in a recent law passed in Massachusetts that obliged two years' residence by immigrants after naturalization before they would be allowed to vote. Germans, the largest immigrant group in Illinois, worried that the Massachusetts law could spread to Illinois. Lincoln, who had worked hard to reach out to the German population, replied, "As I understand the Massachusetts provision, I am against its adoption in Illinois, or in any other place where I have a right to oppose it."

Lincoln's priorities were voiced in a letter to Schuyler Colfax, a young Indiana congressman. Lincoln told Colfax his concern was to

Salmon P. Chase, antislavery governor and senator from Ohio, would begin to cross paths with Lincoln often, starting in 1858, before becoming a rival for the Republican nomination for president in 1860.

"hedge against divisions in the Republican ranks generally, and particularly for the contest of 1860." Lincoln believed, "The point of danger is the temptation in different localities to '*platform*' for something which will be popular just there, but which, nevertheless, will be a firebrand elsewhere." He then named these "platform" issues: agitation against foreigners in Massachusetts; resistance to the fugitive slave law in New Hampshire; the repeal of the fugitive slave law in Ohio; and "squatter sovereignty" in Kansas. Lincoln told Colfax, "In these things there is explosive matter enough to blow up half a dozen national conventions." Thinking ahead to 1860, he concluded, "In a word, in every locality we should look beyond our noses; and at least say *nothing* on points where it is probable we should disagree." Lincoln wrote to Chase, Canisius, and Colfax on individual matters, but the letters demonstrate the beginnings of his national party leadership.

LINCOLN EXPANDED HIS NATIONAL influence by wielding his most developed political weapon: public speaking. Since 1854, Lincoln had spoken outside his home state only one time, in Michigan, but in 1859 he would speak in five states—Ohio, Indiana, Wisconsin, Iowa, and Kansas—and turn down invitations to speak in five more.

The initial spark for his expanded speaking engagements was fanned by Lincoln's old rival, Stephen Douglas. When the *Ohio Statesman* in Columbus announced on September 1, 1859, that Douglas would campaign in Ohio to support Democratic candidates in the upcoming state elections, the Republican leadership was startled. On the same day, William T. Bascom, secretary of the Ohio Republican State Central Committee, wrote Lincoln inviting him to speak in several cities in Ohio because "We desire to head off the little gentleman."

Lincoln was ever alert to the staying power of what he called "Douglasism." He discerned that Douglas, blamed by Buchanan supporters for defeats in the recent elections for Congress and stripped of his chairmanship of the powerful Committee on Territories in an effort led by senators Jefferson Davis, John Slidell, and Jesse Bright, remained a resilient politician.

Despite his setback, Douglas did not retreat from popular sovereignty. Instead, he decided to write a "manifesto" to promote his views. He had promoted popular sovereignty as a self-evident practical remedy for the imploding sectionalism of the day, but now he decided to explain the doctrine in broader theoretical and historical terms. In April 1859, Douglas contacted historian George Bancroft for assistance in understanding the principles involved in the conflict between the colonies and Great Britain. Douglas believed his essay was an opportunity both to give him the last word in the debates with Lincoln and also to answer Senator Albert G. Brown of Mississippi, who had attacked his ideas in the Senate in the winter of 1859. He published his long essay in

September in Fletcher Harper's *Harper's Magazine*, the foremost literary periodical in the nation.

Douglas's manifesto, "The Dividing Line Between Federal and Local Authority: Popular Sovereignty in the Territories," produced an instant impact. At the outset, Douglas took as one of his foils Lincoln's "House Divided" speech to argue that for these Republican leaders, "there can be no peace on the slavery question—no truce in the sectional strife—no fraternity between the North and South, so long as this Union remains as our fathers made it—divided into free and slave states, with the right on the part of each to retain slavery so long as it chooses, and to abolish it whenever it pleases." Douglas argued that popular sovereignty was the "great principle" of American history. The image of a dividing line was taken from the "immortal struggle between the American Colonies and the British Government." He appealed to the "fathers of the Revolution" to anchor his ideas on self-government. He argued that for the revolutionary generation, slavery was always regarded as a domestic question to be decided locally. Lincoln read Douglas's essay carefully, biding his time to the day when he would have the opportunity to respond.

The opportunity came in Ohio. On September 15, 1859, Abraham and Mary boarded a train for Columbus. Mary, increasingly ambitious for her husband's political future, relished this political trip. On the long train ride, she talked about their son Robert, whom they had recently sent off for Phillips Exeter Academy in New Hampshire. Earlier in the year, Robert had failed fifteen of his sixteen entrance exams for Harvard, and thus the decision by his parents to enroll him for one more year of preparation in one of the nation's leading preparatory schools. Whereas Douglas had been met at the train station in Columbus by a large crowd and a thirteen-gun salute, the Lincolns were not even greeted by a welcoming committee, and they walked alone to the Neil House.

Lincoln spoke twice in Columbus, including on the east terrace of the state capitol where Douglas had spoken six days earlier, but neither speech was well attended. Lincoln asked, "Now, what is Judge Douglas' Popular Sovereignty?" Lincoln answered, "It is, as a principle, no other than that, if one man chooses to make a slave of another man, neither that other man nor anybody else has a right to object." Making sport of the recent *Harper's* essay, Lincoln stirred the crowd to laughter when he declared, "His explanations explanatory of explanations explained are interminable."

A larger crowd greeted Lincoln in Cincinnati. In the audience he recognized people from Kentucky who had crossed the Ohio River to hear him. He aimed many of his forceful remarks at them. "I am what they call, as I understand it, a 'Black Republican.' I think Slavery is wrong, morally, and politically. I desire that it should be no further spread in these United States, and I should not object if it should gradually terminate in the whole Union." He told these people from his native state, "I say to you, Kentuckians, that I understand you differ radically with me upon this proposition, that you believe Slavery is a good thing; that Slavery is right; that it ought to be extended and perpetuated in this Union." Lincoln surely surprised his audience when he said, if you feel this way, "I only propose to try to show you that you ought to nominate for the next Presidency, at Charleston, my distinguished friend Judge Douglas."

In Ohio, Lincoln offered speeches that challenged Douglas's assumption that the founding fathers, because some were slave owners, could not possibly have contemplated outlawing slavery in the future. Lincoln wanted to test this assumption by following the actions of these early leaders in subsequent votes, for example, the vote on the Northwest Ordinance of 1787. Lincoln declared it was the Northwest Ordinance that forbade slavery, not the exercise of popular sovereignty by states of the old Northwest.

On his way home, Lincoln stopped in Indianapolis, where he spoke for two hours at the Masonic Hall. With Douglas still on his mind, Lincoln quoted the leitmotif of Douglas's essay: "Our fathers, when they framed the Government under which we lived, understood this question just as well, and even better, than we do now." Lincoln responded, "Our fathers who made the government, made the Ordinance of 1787." He reminded his audience that Indiana "more than once petitioned Congress to abrogate the ordinance entirely" so they could "exercise the 'popular sovereignty' of having slaves if they wanted them." Congress refused. If it were not for Congress, Lincoln declared, "Indiana would have been a slave state."

Lincoln's political tour in Ohio bore fruit in a surprising turn of events. At some moment during the train trip from Columbus to Cincinnati, Lincoln remembered that he had left his debates scrapbook behind in his room at the Neil House. Frantic, he requested the assistance of Republican leaders in procuring its safe return, his plea bringing its existence to light. Before long, the Republican State Central

Committee, working with Columbus publisher Follett, Foster and Company, contacted Lincoln about publishing an edition of the scrapbook that would include Lincoln's Ohio speeches. Lincoln was delighted, since conversations in the spring with Illinois publishers had resulted in no offers.

When Lincoln returned home from his Ohio speaking tour, he renewed his correspondence with Ohio politician Thomas Corwin. A former governor of Ohio who had recently been elected to the House of Representatives, Corwin wrote to Lincoln on September 25, 1859, expressing concern that the Republican party's unremitting talk about slavery "will make the contest in 1860 a hopeless one for us."

Lincoln replied in a remarkable letter, long lost but recently found, expressing his belief about the role slavery should play in the presidential election of 1860. "What brought these Democrats with us! The Slavery issue. Drop that issue, and they have no motive to remain, and will not remain, with us. It is idiotic to think otherwise." Lincoln clarified exactly what kind of candidate the Republicans should nominate.

> Do not misunderstand me as saying Illinois must have an extreme antislavery candidate! I do not so mean. We must have, though, a man who recognizes that Slavery issue as being the living issue of the day; who does not hesitate to declare slavery a wrong, nor to deal with it as such; who believes in the power, and duty of Congress to prevent the spread of it.

"Idiotic." Lincoln had never used that word before. In this letter, Lincoln, without betraying any sense that he might be that candidate in 1860, speaks in 1859 about his strong conviction that the Republican nominee ought to be someone who has demonstrated his opposition to the extension of slavery.

Corwin replied to Lincoln's letter on October 17. "Six months hence we shall see more clearly what at this time must remain only in conjecture." The Ohio Congressman, who would become a strong supporter of Abraham Lincoln, proved to be prophetic.

WHILE BUSY IN COURT EACH DAY, Lincoln closely followed the 1859 elections held in a number of states. On October 14, the long-awaited results revealed that Republicans had triumphed in Indiana, Ohio,

Pennsylvania, Minnesota, and Iowa. Returning on Saturday evening to Springfield, he had scarcely arrived at his residence when several hundred townspeople marched to Eighth and Jackson to persuade "Mr. Lincoln, the 'giant killer,' " to speak at the capitol.

Sometime that Saturday evening, or perhaps the next day, Lincoln opened the mail that lay waiting for him. In the stack was a telegram that read,

> Hon. A. Lincoln.
>   Will you speak in Mr. Beechers church Broolyn on or about the twenty ninth (29) november on any subject you please pay two hundred (200) dollars.
> James A. Briggs

Lincoln had long admired the Reverend Henry Ward Beecher, one of America's most prominent ministers. But who would the audience be? What would he say in this prominent setting? Lincoln had never been offered so large a fee to speak.

On Monday morning, Lincoln bounced into his office eager to share his telegram with Herndon. His younger partner remembered how Lincoln "looked much pleased" at the invitation. Lincoln, eager to accept but knowing the demands of his law practice and his own need to prepare thoroughly, wrote requesting a date three months later, toward the end of February 1860. Lincoln's "compromise" was accepted.

Lincoln understood that he had been invited to deliver a lecture, not a campaign speech. Herndon pointed out that the invitation might be part of an effort by the New York committee to chip away at the candidacy of Seward, whose outspoken criticism of nativism and "Irrepressible Conflict" speech of 1858, in which he spoke of the inevitable collision of the North and South's two social systems, made some leading Republicans nervous about his prospects in a presidential election. Further sleuthing revealed that Briggs, who tendered the invitation, was a Salmon Chase supporter. Lincoln's excitement was tempered by awareness that the response to his recent lectures on "Discoveries and Inventions" had been underwhelming. Despite his confidence in his political stump speaking, he understood the address to an audience of Eastern sophisticates in Brooklyn would try his abilities.

As Lincoln was enjoying the invitation, startling news broke that threatened to upset the entire antislavery movement. On the evening of Monday, October 16, 1859, John Brown, a fifty-nine-year-old abolitionist, led a band of twenty-one men, sixteen white and five black, in a raid against the U.S. arsenal at Harpers Ferry in Virginia. Brown's plan was to use the raid as an opening attack to provide slaves with arms. But Brown had failed to notify any slaves of his intentions. After thirty-six hours, with no rebellion incited, Brown and his men surrendered inside the arsenal on October 18 to a detachment of U.S. Marines commanded by Lieutenant Colonel Robert E. Lee.

Leaders in the South, frightened, became furious when Brown aroused sympathy in the North. They quickly accused Northern abolitionists and Republicans of offering aid and comfort to such slave rebellions. Lincoln, the "Black Republican," began preparations for his Brooklyn address as the nation's politicians and newspapers continued to blame and praise Brown during his imprisonment and trial.

Lincoln took advantage of the long lead time to be "painstaking and thorough" in his research for his lecture. It was not as though he started fresh, for he had been building a foundation in his speeches in Ohio. But there was much work to do. Herndon observed Lincoln as "he searched through the dusty volumes of congressional proceedings in the State Library, and dug deeply into political history."

On the last day of November 1859, Lincoln started for Kansas to fulfill a demanding speaking tour leading up to its crucial state election on December 6. On December 1, in the frontier town of Ellwood, on the evening before the hanging of John Brown, Lincoln offered his first public comment on the former Kansan. He stated that the attack by Brown was wrong for two reasons: It was "a violation of law" and "futile" in terms of its effect "on the extinction of a great evil."

Traveling down the Missouri River to Leavenworth, Lincoln told his audience in crowded Stockton's Hall that the election in Kansas was not about a popular sovereignty that did not care whether slavery was right or wrong, but solely about the morality of "the slavery question." In his conclusion, Lincoln offered a dire warning. "Old John Brown has been executed for a crime against a state." If Kansas decided to join with those who would "undertake to destroy the Union," then "it will be our duty to deal with you as old John Brown has been dealt with."

Lincoln returned home to discover that rumors were continuing to rock the Republican boat. In response to whispers that Lincoln might run for Trumbull's Senate seat in 1860, and that Judd was secretly back-ing Trumbull, Lincoln said he would never run against Trumbull because "I would rather have a full term in the Senate than in the Presidency."

In the middle of December, Judd traveled to New York for a meet-ing of the Republican National Committee to select the site for the 1860 Republican convention. The loyalists for each leading candidate came to lobby for a city favorable to their man. Judd listened patiently as Seward partisans argued for Buffalo, New York; Chase supporters made a case for Cleveland or Columbus, Ohio; Cameron's people wanted Harris-burg, Pennsylvania; and Bates's men lobbied for St. Louis, Missouri. Lincoln revealed the state of his thinking in a letter to Judd a week ear-lier. "I find some of our friends here, attach more consequence to get-ting the National convention into our State than I did, or do." Fortunately for Lincoln, the astute Judd understood the importance of the choice better than the man he was representing. Judd argued that since Illinois did not have a leading candidate, Chicago would be an ideal neutral site. In the final vote, Chicago defeated St. Louis by one vote.

ON DECEMBER 20, 1859, a full year after Jesse Fell had asked for an autobiography, Lincoln wrote, "Herewith is a little sketch, as you requested. There is not much of it, for the reason, I supposed, that there is not much of me." Lincoln included an instruction, "If anything is to be made out of it, I wish it be modest, and not to go beyond the mate-rial," and a restriction, "Of course it must not appear to have been writ-ten by myself."

Lincoln surprised Fell by sending him only 606 words. In a political era of outsized campaign biographies, it was not what Fell was expect-ing.

> I was born Feb. 12, 1809, in Hardin County, Kentucky. My par-ents were both born in Virginia, of undistinguished families— second families, perhaps I should say. My mother, who died in my tenth year, was of a family of the name of Hanks, some of whom now reside in Adams, and others in Macon counties, Illi-nois. My paternal grandfather, Abraham Lincoln, emigrated from Rockingham County, Virginia, to Kentucky, about 1781 or 2, where, a year or two later, he was killed by indians, not in battle,

but by stealth, when [where?] he was laboring to open a farm in the forest. His ancestors, who were quakers, went to Virginia from Berks County, Pennsylvania. An effort to identify them with the New-England family of the same name ended in nothing more definite, than a similarity of Christian names in both families, such as Enoch, Levi, Mordecai, Solomon, Abraham, and the like.

My father, at the death of his father, was but six years of age; and he grew up, litterally without education. He removed from Kentucky to what is now Spencer county, Indiana, in my eighth year. We reached our new home about the time the State came into the Union. It was a wild region, with many bears and other wild animals still in the woods. There I grew up. There were some schools, so called; but no qualification was ever required of a teacher, beyond *"readin, writin, and cipherin,"* to the Rule of Three. If a straggler supposed to understand latin, happened to so-journ in the neighborhood, he was looked upon as a wizzard. There was absolutely nothing to excite ambition for education. Of course when I came of age I did not know much. Still somehow, I could read, write, and cipher to the Rule of Three; but that was all. I have not been to school since. The little advance I now have upon this store of education, I have picked up from time to time under the pressure of necessity.

I was raised to farm work, which I continued till I was twenty two. At twenty one I came to Illinois, and passed the first year in Macon county. Then I got to New-Salem (at that time in Sangamon, now in Menard county, where I remained a year as a sort of Clerk in a store. Then came the Black-Hawk war; and I was elected a Captain of Volunteers—a success which gave me more pleasure than any I have had since. I went the campaign, was elated, ran for the Legislature the same year (1832) and was beaten—the only time I ever have been beaten by the people. The next, and three succeeding biennial elections, I was elected to the Legislature. I was not a candidate afterwards. During this Legislative period I had studied law, and removed to Springfield to practice it. In 1846 I was once elected to the lower House of Congress. Was not a candidate for re-election. From 1849 to 1854, both inclusive, practiced law more assiduously than ever before. Always a whig in politics, and generally on the whig electoral tickets, making active canvasses. I was losing interest in politics, when the repeal of the Missouri Compromise aroused me again. What I have done since then is pretty well known.

If any personal description of me is thought desirable, it may be said, I am, in height, six feet, four inches, nearly; lean in flesh, weighing, on an average, one hundred and eighty pounds; dark complexion, with coarse black hair, and grey eyes—no other marks or brands recollected. Yours very truly A. LINCOLN

It was a spare autobiography at best. Lincoln offered no substantive comments on the past five years of his political career nor mention of the debates with Douglas.

Lincoln still struggled with uncertainty about his national political prospects, but his self-understanding was being shaped by the affirmation of others. In the last five months of 1859, he had tested the political waters by traveling more than four thousand miles to deliver twenty-three speeches. He looked forward to speaking in Brooklyn. Even if he was unsure whether he could stand equal to Seward, Chase, Cameron, and Bates, he had come to believe it was time to send forth a trial balloon by complying with Fell's request.

Fell sent Lincoln's autobiography to his friend Joseph J. Lewis, a prominent Republican lawyer in West Chester, Pennsylvania. Lewis was perplexed because he expected much more than the minuscule autobiography he received. He immediately wrote Fell asking for more information. Finally, Lewis wrote his own biography of Lincoln of nearly three thousand words and arranged for both biographies to be printed on February 11, 1860, in the *Chester County Times*. Copies were sent to other newspapers in Pennsylvania. The *Chicago Press & Tribune* printed the autobiography, with an editorial affirmation, on February 23.

WHEN THE CALENDAR TURNED the page to January 1, 1860, the presidential guessing game became more earnest. Lincoln understood that an early announcement of his candidacy would prompt criticism from rivals who, at this point, were pleased to consider him as a candidate for vice president. In the nineteenth century, the most successful candidate at party conventions was often the one who did not seem to be seeking the office.

On a cold January evening, when many lawyer-politicians were in Springfield arguing cases before the federal and Supreme Court, a small group of Republicans invited Lincoln to meet in the inner office of Illinois secretary of state Ozias Hatch. Some were thinking of nominating Lincoln as the favorite son of Illinois with no conviction that he could win. After considerable discussion, Lincoln was asked "if his name might be used at once in connection with the coming nomination and election." Lincoln "with his characteristic modesty doubted whether he could get the nomination even if he wished it." Someone then asked Lincoln, if he failed to get the nomination for president, would he accept the nomination for vice president. This time he did not hesitate. "No." Lincoln requested that he could have until the next morning to consider their invitation to be a candidate for president.

How did Lincoln ponder this request? What did he say to Mary? He left no recollection about his deliberation or their discussion. The next morning he gave his friends permission, if they were "pleased" to do so, to work for him.

On a sunny February 8, 1860, the Republican State Central Committee met and selected Decatur and May 23 as the place and time of the Republican state convention. A person notably absent from the decision was Lincoln's longtime friend Orville Browning. That evening Lincoln called upon Browning at Room 30½ at the American House. Browning, who was supporting Bates, recorded what Lincoln said in his daily diary. "It is not improbable that by the time the National convention meets in Chicago [Lincoln] may be of the opinion that the very best thing that can be done will be to nominate Mr. Bates."

In January and February 1860, the newspapers proposing Lincoln's name for the national ticket, both for vice president and president, grew in number. William O. Stoddard's Central Illinois Gazette, in the thriving town of West Urbana (modern-day Champaign), was one of the first newspapers to place Lincoln's name at the top of its columns in bold Gothic type. But these mastheads and editorial endorsements were mostly still in small-town papers.

On February 16, 1860, the Chicago Press & Tribune endorsed "the nomination of Lincoln for the first place on the National Republican ticket." The Tribune, under the leadership of Joseph Medill and Charles Ray, was becoming a major paper in the West. Medill, previously an editor in Cleveland, had been courted in the fall by supporters of Senator Chase of Ohio. Medill traveled to Washington in December to speak with members of Congress. He stayed into January, buttonholing whomever he could to talk about Lincoln. Day by day, the *Tribune* printed Medill's reports under the column "Presidential." The forceful February 16 editorial, probably written by Ray but with input from state chairman Judd, declared that the *Tribune*'s endorsement of Lincoln was not simply as a favorite son, but as the one candidate who could carry Pennsylvania, New Jersey, Indiana, and Illinois. Medill followed up the editorial with a letter, signed "Chicago," reporting that in Washington he now heard Lincoln's name talked about for president "ten times as often as it was a month ago."

ONE WEEK AFTER the *Tribune*'s endorsement, Lincoln prepared to leave for Brooklyn to seek an even larger endorsement. He was confident about his preparation because, as Herndon observed, "No former effort in the line of speech-making had cost Lincoln so much time and thought as this one." On the morning of George Washington's birthday, Lincoln boarded a train at 11:15. Mary prevailed upon him to take her trunk instead of his old worn luggage.

On his departure, the Democratic *Illinois State Register* offered its biting assessment of Lincoln's mission: "SIGNIFICANT.—The Hon. Abraham Lincoln departs to day for Brooklyn, under the engagement to deliver a lecture before the Young Men's Assn. of that city, in Beecher's church. Subject, not known. Considerations, $200 and expenses. Object, presidential capital. Effect, disappointment."

After two and a half days' onerous travel aboard five trains, Lincoln's long train trip ended on Saturday in Jersey City where he boarded the Paulus Street ferry for the trip across the Hudson River. Upon arriving at the splendid six-story Astor House, Lincoln learned for the first time that he would not deliver his lecture at Plymouth Congregational Church in Brooklyn, but at the Cooper Union in New York.

On Sunday, Lincoln worshipped at the church in Brooklyn Heights where he had expected to deliver his lecture. He came to hear Henry Ward Beecher, who had assumed the pulpit shortly after the church was formed in 1847. Lincoln had followed Beecher's opposition to the Kansas-Nebraska Act and his aid to "bleeding Kansas." Visitors from across the United States came to see and be seen as Beecher regularly preached to congregations of 2,500 on Sunday mornings. Worshippers would have noticed the tall Lincoln, as his custom was to stand, out of respect to a God whom he always called "The Almighty," during morning prayers.

Lincoln attended Plymouth Congregational Church in Brooklyn Heights in order to hear Henry Ward Beecher, one of America's most popular Protestant ministers.

On Monday, on a walking tour of New York, Lincoln entered the new studio of photographer Mathew Brady, located at the corner of Broadway and Bleecker Streets. Brady had opened his first Daguerreian Miniature Gallery in New York in 1844, and his first studio in Washington in 1849, where he photographed President Zachary Taylor and his cabinet. As Lincoln waited in the reception room, he met George Bancroft, the eminent historian whose work was popularly known as "Bancroft's History" of the United States. Lincoln plied his humor on Bancroft. "I am on my way to Massachusetts where I have a son at school, if, report be true, already knows much more than his father."

Brady invited Lincoln into his "operating room" and sized up his subject. The photographer asked if he might adjust Lincoln's collar. "Ah," responded Lincoln, "I see you want to shorten my neck."

"That's just it," Brady answered, and both of them laughed. For the first time in his life, Lincoln was posed standing rather than sitting down. Brady's use of a pillar behind Lincoln's right shoulder, and a table with books at his left hand, suggested not a Western frontier man, but the kind of erudite Eastern man Brady usually photographed. The photographer found himself challenged by Lincoln's new but crumpled black suit. Finally, one of Brady's assistants opened the lens to capture Lincoln's likeness on a wet-plate glass negative.

The photograph portrayed a Lincoln about to be auditioned at Cooper Union. It reflected Lincoln's strength, but without the rough skin and tousled hair of earlier photographs. His firm expression, with his jaw set, may be attributed either to the ordeal of mid-nineteenth-century photography or to his self-confidence about that evening's lecture.

Lincoln arrived at the redbrick Cooper Union on Seventh Street between Third and Fourth avenues as snow was falling. Peter Cooper's experimental school was a beehive of free classes ranging from art to engineering. Shortly before eight o'clock, guests began arriving in the basement auditorium, ultimately filling about three-quarters of the 1,800 seats. William Cullen Bryant, editor of the *New York Evening Post,* who had met Lincoln briefly in Illinois during the Black Hawk War, introduced Lincoln as "a gallant soldier of the political campaign of 1858."

Lincoln rose to speak. Charles C. Nott, a young lawyer and one of the event's planners, described the speaker.

The first impression of the man from the West did nothing to contradict the expectation of something weird, rough, and uncultivated. The long, ungainly figure, upon which hung clothes that, while new for the trip, were evidently the work of an unskillful tailor; the large feet; the clumsy hands, of which, at the outset at least, the orator seemed to be unduly conscious; the long, gaunt head capped by a shock of hair that seemed not to have been thoroughly brushed out made a picture which did not fit in with New York's conception of a finished statesman.

Lincoln began in his Indiana twang, "Mr. Cheerman . . ." After losing his place in his first few sentences, his nervousness dissipated and he settled in confidently to his long introduction, which achieved its power from his meticulous grasp of historical data. He had constructed his speech around a declaration Senator Douglas had made: "Our fathers, when they framed the Government under which we live, understood this question just as well, and even better, than we do now." Lincoln stated, "I fully indorse this, and I adopt it as a text for this discourse." In a remarkable rhetorical strategy, Lincoln would repeat Douglas's declaration fifteen times in his speech.

As Lincoln began to question the meaning of Douglas's words, one imagines that each time Lincoln repeated the question, the audience, becoming aware of Lincoln's strategy, leaned forward in their seats, eager to hear how this resourceful Westerner would question, probe, rebut, and reframe Douglas's affirmation. At the same time, Lincoln asked the question that had steered his meticulous research: "Does the proper division of local from federal authority, or anything in the Constitution, forbid our Federal Government to control as to slavery in our Federal Territories?"

Lincoln enthralled his audience. He started by identifying the thirty-nine "fathers" as those who signed the Constitution at the Constitutional Convention in 1787. He inquired how those thirty-nine expressed their understanding about the expansion of slavery into the territories in both preceding and following years through legislative votes. He specified the persons voting: four in 1784, two in 1787, seventeen in 1789, three in 1798, two in 1804, and two in 1819–20. Some voted on the issue more than once. Lincoln found twenty-three had made choices concerning this question, with no proof of the other sixteen acting in any way. Twenty-one of the twenty-three who understood the question "better than we," acted consistently under the belief that the federal government did have the right to exercise power over slavery in the territories.

Lincoln's Cooper Union speech was really three speeches in one. With a transitional, "But enough!" Lincoln proceeded from speaking to the North to speaking to the South. He knew there was probably no one from the South in the audience, but, nevertheless, "if they would listen—as I suppose they will not—I address a few words to the Southern people." What followed was a brief but powerful rhetorical section in which Lincoln convened a colloquy of accusations and answers.

You say we are sectional.	We deny it.
You say we have made the slavery question more prominent than it formerly was.	We deny it.
You charge that we stir up insurrections among your slaves.	We deny it.

Lincoln said that Southerners loved to quote George Washington's warning against sectionalism in his Farewell Address but conveniently forgot that Washington had earlier signed the act "enforcing the prohibition of slavery in the Northwestern Territory." Lincoln's aim, by this and other examples, was to show that the responsibility for the divisional discord lay not with the North but with the South.

"But you will not abide the election of a Republican President!" Lincoln sealed this second section by a declaration and a story. "You say, you will destroy the Union; and then, you say, the great crime of having destroyed it will be upon us!" Lincoln asked his audience to imagine a highwayman holding a pistol to his ear and then muttering: " 'Stand and deliver, or I shall kill you, and then you will be a murderer!' "

In the final section, Lincoln spoke "a few words now to Republicans." After summarizing his historical arguments, he offered a ringing ethical avowal. This speech, as indeed Lincoln's political posture in 1860, has often been depicted as conservative, but his conclusion is directed toward those conservative Republicans who would concede too much to the South in search of an ephemeral peace. He made his point with a compelling cadence of question and answer.

Will they be satisfied if the Territories be unconditionally surrendered to them?	We know they will not.
Will it satisfy them if . . . we have nothing to do with invasions and insurrections?	We know it will not.

Lincoln finally asked: "What will convince them?" His answer: "This, and this only: cease to call slavery wrong, and join them in calling it right."

Lincoln's Cooper Union address concluded with an ethical imperative, first what we cannot do, and second, in a sentence that Lincoln capitalized, what we must do.

Neither let us be slandered from our duty by false accusations against us, nor frightened from it by menaces of destruction to the Government nor of dungeons to ourselves. LET US HAVE FAITH THAT RIGHT MAKES MIGHT, AND IN THAT FAITH, LET US, TO THE END, DARE TO DO OUR DUTY AS WE UNDERSTAND IT.

When Lincoln concluded, the audience leapt to its feet in volley after volley of applause. The next day, four New York newspapers published the entire text of the address. Horace Greeley, in the *Tribune*, offered his wholehearted praise. "Mr. Lincoln is one of Nature's orators, using his rare powers solely and effectively to elucidate and to convince, though their inevitable effect is to delight and electrify as well."

At Cooper Union, Lincoln exhibited not only oratorical eloquence but political sagacity. Speaking in Seward's home state, invited by a person partial to Chase, with the shadow of the Little Giant following him, Lincoln understood he needed to deflate, if not defeat, both Seward and Douglas, and place himself in the moderate center of the Republican Party. Eschewing Western stump-style speaking, with its heavy use of humor and satire, Lincoln demonstrated that his increasingly broad range of oratory could connect with an elite audience of the leaders of New York society.

The most telling appraisal may have come from Mayson Brayman, a Springfield lawyer who had lived in Lincoln's home when he was in Washington during his term in Congress. Brayman, a Democrat, had been asked by Lincoln to stand in the back of the hall and raise his hat on a cane if Lincoln's voice was not being heard. The next day, Brayman wrote to William Bailhache, an owner of the *Illinois State Journal,* of the transformation he had witnessed at Cooper Union. Brayman found it "somewhat funny, to see a man who *at home,* talks along in so familiar a way, walking up and down, swaying about, swinging his arms, bobbing forward, telling droll stories and laughing at them himself, *here in New-York,* standing up stiff and straight, with his hands quiet, pronouncing sentence after sentence, in good telling English."

THE FOLLOWING DAY, Lincoln left for New England. He had long planned to visit his son Bob at Exeter, in New Hampshire, but after Cooper Union he accepted requests to speak in three New England states. Over the next eleven days, Lincoln delivered eleven speeches, with a day for rest on the Sabbath. After speaking in Providence, Rhode Island, he delivered speeches in New Hampshire at Concord; Manchester, where he was introduced as the next president of the United States; Dover; and finally at the town hall at Exeter. All of his speeches were variations on the themes of his Cooper Union address.

Lincoln spent Saturday and Sunday with Bob at Phillips Exeter Academy. He was proud of his oldest son, but there never seemed to be the same bond between them as there was with Tad and Willie, whom Lincoln often spoiled. Now, with the two younger boys not present, a distinctive opportunity presented itself for the father and his eldest son to become companions. After Bob's painful humiliation of being denied entrance to Harvard, father Abraham was pleased and proud of his son's commitment to education at Exeter. On Sunday, "according to Bob's orders," Lincoln worshipped at Second Congregational Church. In the

Lincoln visited his oldest son, Robert, a student at Phillips Exeter in Exeter, New Hampshire, immediately after speaking at Cooper Union.

evening, Bob invited some of his friends to meet his suddenly famous father.

A letter from James Briggs was waiting for Lincoln in Exeter. Briggs, the man who had invited Lincoln to speak at Cooper Union, was ecstatic. "Enclosed please find 'check' for $200. I would that it were $200,000. for you are worthy of it."

Lincoln wrote Mary from Exeter, "I have been unable to escape this toil. If I had foreseen it, I think I would not have come east at all." He offered his understated assessment of the Cooper Union address. "The speech at New York, being within my calculation before I started, went off passably well and gave me no trouble whatever." He told Mary of the problem of speaking "before reading audiences who had already seen all my ideas in print."

Leaving Bob on Monday morning, March 5, 1860, Lincoln proceeded to Hartford, Connecticut. During the day Lincoln talked with Gideon Welles at Brown and Gross's bookstore. Welles, an ex-Democrat, was a member of the Republican National Committee. It was common knowledge that Welles despised Seward, who he believed was a spokesman for special interests in neighboring New York. Lincoln and Welles met again in the afternoon at the offices of the *Hartford Evening Press,* which Welles founded in 1856 to foster the Republican cause.

As Lincoln traveled through New England, he became aware of what was being called "the great shoemakers' strike." The strike began in Lynn, Massachusetts, but quickly spread to other New England states. Controversy raged over the rights of shoemakers to strike for better wages and conditions. Lincoln, responding to the strikes, declared at Hartford, "I am glad to know that there is a system of labor where the laborer can strike if he wants to! I would to God that such a system prevailed all over the world."

After completing his speech, Lincoln was escorted to his hotel by the "Wide-Awakes," a newly formed group of young Republican men who marched in solemn military procession with torches held aloft. They adopted their name from a recent *Hartford Courant* description of them as "wide awake." The men, who wore glazed hats and capes to shield them from the oil of the torches, injected color into political campaigns and sheltered Republican marchers from the brickbats of Democratic spectators.

The next evening, Lincoln took the night express train from Bridgeport, Connecticut, to New York. After hearing Dr. Beecher one more time on Sunday morning, he asked to visit the Five Points House of Industry, an industrial mission reaching out to abandoned children established in 1852 by Lewis M. Pease, an inventive Methodist minister.

On Monday, March 12, 1860, after more than two weeks in the East, Lincoln departed on the Erie Railroad across New York. He was in demand for more speeches but had decided it was time to return west with bracing Eastern political winds at his back. New York and New England had proved to be decisive in his journey of self-discovery.

LINCOLN FELT TIRED but renewed upon his return to Springfield. His trip to New York, and his often overlooked circuit of New England, had turned out to be a listening as well as a speaking tour. In places that he had only read about, he heard from new friends about possibilities for higher political office that he had barely allowed himself to think about not many months before. Back home, his old friends rushed to offer "earnest congratulations" for his success in the East. Newspaper conjecture about Lincoln and the Republicans' convention in Chicago rushed ahead. The *Chicago Press & Tribune* and the *Illinois State Journal* had kept their readers abreast of Lincoln's speaking tour by printing the accolades from the New York and New England newspapers. The Cooper Union address, published in pamphlet form by the *New York Tribune*, was about to be published by the *Illinois State Journal*. Herndon observed that Lincoln's "recent success had stimulated his self-confidence." It was as if the affirmation he had received in New York and New England finally convinced a cautious Lincoln that he had the support to seek the highest office in the land. Herndon observed, "It was apparent now to Lincoln that the Presidential nomination was within his reach."

In the last week of March, Lincoln traveled to Chicago to participate in the "Sandbar Case" before Judge Thomas Drummond in the federal court. While in Chicago, sculptor Leonard Volk asked him to sit for a bust. Volk had studied sculpture in Italy, a trip sponsored by his brother-in-law, Stephen Douglas. Honoring Lincoln's busy schedule, Volk decided to keep the sessions to a minimum by beginning with a life mask. Lincoln endured with good humor the process of letting wet plaster dry on his face and then Volk's removing it by stretching his skin.

Lincoln's success in the East evidenced itself in expanded support in Illinois. At the end of February 1860, the Republican National Committee had announced they were moving the starting date of the Chicago convention up from June 13 to May 16. In March and April, Lincoln and his advisers set out to translate this surge of goodwill into hard votes at the rapidly approaching convention.

An unexpected benefit of speaking in Ohio, Kansas, New York, and New England was a new group of friends and self-appointed advisers. From Columbus, Samuel Galloway, a lawyer and politician, wrote to offer an astute evaluation of the other candidates in the field. He wanted Lincoln to know that "there will be but little fervent attachment to Mr Chase in the Ohio delegation." Galloway predicted that "after one or two ballotings he will not receive more than 1/4th of the vote." As for Seward, he "will doubtless enter the Convention with the largest plural-ity vote—He cannot however be nominated unless Pennsylvania & New Jersey give him their votes." Lincoln must have been heartened when Galloway concluded, "The *concurrent* opinion of our most intelligent politicians is that either you or Bates will be nominated."

Lincoln, in his reply, revealed his thinking on his chances. "My name is new in the field; and I suppose I am not the *first* choice of a very great many." Starting from this assumption, Lincoln laid out his campaign strategy. "Our policy, then, is to give no offence to others—leave them in a mood to come to us, if they shall be compelled to give up their first love."

From Connecticut, James F. Babcock, editor of the *New Haven Palladium* and host for Lincoln's lecture in March, wrote, "I have heard your name mentioned more freely than ever in Connection with the Chicago nomination, and by some who have had other views, or whose feelings were previously committed in favor of another." Connecticut and Rhode Island, unlike Massachusetts, were conservative states that would not back Seward.

Lincoln replied to Babcock in a tone both curious and cautious. "As to the Presidential nomination, claiming no greater exemption from selfishness than is common, I still feel that my whole aspiration should be, and therefore must be, to be placed anywhere, or nowhere, as may appear most likely to advance our cause." While not making known his intentions to Babcock, he did include the names of eleven "confidential friends" in Ohio, Iowa, and Illinois "with whom you might correspond."

On April 29, 1860, two and a half weeks before the Republican convention in Chicago, Lincoln offered his most direct comment yet on his candidacy. Senator Trumbull had written Lincoln with a detailed evaluation of the various candidates, and asked "to be put fully in possession of your views." Lincoln replied, "As you request, I will be entirely frank. The taste *is* in my mouth, a little." The "a little" has often been left off Lincoln's declaration when quoted. Lincoln's letter was significant because it showed him willing to discuss with Trumbull the strengths and weaknesses of Seward, Bates, and Judge John McLean, the latter being the candidate Trumbull favored.

When Lincoln wrote Trumbull, he was still awaiting the results of the Democratic convention in Charleston, South Carolina, "to know who is to lead our adversaries." He understood that the choice of the

Democratic candidate in Charleston could well influence the choice of the Republican candidate in Chicago. He would have a long wait.

The Democratic convention had begun on April 23, 1860, with a clash between Douglas supporters' promotion of popular sovereignty and Southern delegates' insistence on a federal slave code for the territories. The discordant convention culminated in fifty delegates from Southern states walking out. After ten days and fifty-seven ballots, unable to nominate their presidential candidate, the convention disbanded on May 3 with the decision to meet again six weeks later in the friendlier environs of Baltimore.

IT HAS OFTEN been suggested that Lincoln was his own political manager, but this judgment does not explain the effectiveness of his campaign. Offered as a way to extol Lincoln's political genius, it actually undervalues the astute ways he worked with colleagues. Lincoln's genius was his ability to draw upon the talents of others, meld together diverse personalities who often did not trust one another, and then listen to their advice, recognizing that it was sometimes wiser than his own.

David Davis laid aside his judicial robes to become Lincoln's campaign manager in 1860. Lincoln said of his corpulent friend, "I keep no secrets from him." Leonard Swett, inseparable from Lincoln and Davis on the Eighth Judicial Circuit, told Lincoln in December 1854 to use him in any way that could help him and continued, unceasingly, to offer his services in all of Lincoln's election campaigns. Norman Judd, the former anti-Nebraska Democrat whom Trumbull described as "the shrewdest politician . . . in the State," was Lincoln's key adviser in 1858 and would play a crucial role in 1860.

Lincoln's advisers, many self-appointed, never functioned as a single, organized group, instead relating to Lincoln singly or in groups of three or four. They served as his agents in the quite different northern, central, and southern sections of Illinois. Up until the spring of 1860, advisory meetings were mostly held on an on-call basis, related to Lincoln's being in the vicinity or to deal with a specific problem or issue.

In early May 1860, delegates converged on Decatur for the state Republican convention. Lincoln's advisers realized it was crucial that he arrive in Chicago with the unanimous support of the Illinois delegation with its twenty-two votes, but this would not be easy, as Seward enjoyed support in northern Illinois and Bates in southern Illinois. Lincoln arrived on May 8 but did not plan to participate in the meeting. On May 9, Decatur resident Richard J. Oglesby, chairman of the convention, announced, "I am informed that a distinguished citizen of Illinois, and one whom Illinois will ever delight to honor, is present, and I wish to move that this body invite him to a seat on the stand." With a flair for the dramatic, he paused and finally shouted: "Abraham Lincoln!" Cheers shook the fragile tent. Lincoln was found, apprehended, and to his surprise began to be passed "kicking, scrambling—crawling—upon the sea of heads" to the stage at the front of the tent. When Lincoln was finally upright, he "rose bowing and blushing," and thanked the convention for their "Manifestations of Esteem."

The dramatics had only begun. Oglesby was about to become yet another friend who wished to define Lincoln. He announced that an "Old Democrat had something he wished to present to this meeting." The cry went up: "Receive it!—Receive it!" Nineteenth-century politics was replete with political nicknames: "Old Hickory" in 1828, "Tippecanoe and Tyler Too" in 1840, and "The Pathfinder" in 1856. By 1860, Lincoln was most often referred to as "Old Abe." Oglesby was certain that sobriquet was not sufficient.

Oglesby knew that old John Hanks, the first cousin of Lincoln's mother, who as a young man had lived on and off with the Lincolns for four years in Indiana, was a resident of Decatur. Hanks was a Democrat, but no matter. Oglesby got in touch with Hanks and went with him to get some black walnut and honey locust rails that Lincoln and Hanks had split together thirty years earlier during Lincoln's first year in Illinois.

From the back of the tent, John Hanks and a friend marched triumphantly in carrying two rails and a banner that read:

ABRAHAM LINCOLN
The Rail Candidate
FOR PRESIDENT IN 1860
TWO RAILS FROM A LOT OF 3,000 MADE IN 1830
BY THOS. HANKS AND ABE LINCOLN—WHOSE
FATHER WAS THE FIRST PIONEER IN MACON COUNTY

The banner was not completely correct, for it was John, the bearer of the sign, who had split the rails, and Thomas Lincoln was not the first pioneer in Macon County. But no one in the assembly cared about accuracy at that moment as they burst into applause that went on for more than ten minutes. When Lincoln finally stood to acknowledge their acclaim, he recalled that when he immigrated to Illinois he spent a season in Macon County and helped cultivate a farm on the Sangamon River, where he built a cabin and "split rails."

"Honest Abe" could not vouch that he had split the rails brought to the tent, but "he had mauled many and many better ones since he had grown to manhood." The cheers started up again. The symbol of "the Rail Splitter," pointing to the rights of free labor as opposed to slave labor, added a new emotion to the Lincoln boom.

ON MAY 12, 1860, *Harper's Weekly* published a double-page illustrations displaying the faces of eleven "prominent candidates" for the Republican nomination to be decided at Chicago. Front and center in the lithograph was the craggy face of Seward. In the bottom row, to the

Harper's Weekly *published on May 12, 1860, images of all the candidates for the Republican presidential nomination. Lincoln's image is far away from the center, which is occupied by William Seward, an indication of the magazine's estimation of their chances for the nomination.*

left, was the Brady photograph of Lincoln. The biographies of the contenders were on another page. Lincoln's biography was the last and the least.

Special trains crammed full of delegates began arriving in Chicago on May 12 and 13, 1860. Most Republicans came to Chicago expecting that a man of great reputation and long public service would be the nominee. Seward and Chase, both of whom had served as senator and governor, fit that bill. Both had strong antislavery credentials, with Chase to the left of Seward. However, after attacks on Republicans about the John Brown affair, many delegates were eager to embrace a more moderate voice as their standard-bearer in 1860. Simon Cameron, a tall Scot, newspaper editor, businessman, and senator, could fit that profile, but a reputation for unsavory business practices stuck with him, and he was having trouble picking up support beyond his native Pennsylvania. Onetime slaveholder Edward Bates, living tranquilly in St. Louis, was not presently holding elective office but had advanced his candidacy by writing public and private letters. Lincoln thought highly of Bates's chances as a safe, conservative alternative to Seward and Chase. Bates's major stumbling block was his nativist record, which frightened the large German populations in Illinois and Wisconsin. Editor Horace Greeley, once a strong supporter of Seward but now a major player in the stop-Seward movement, was putting his chips on Bates. Associate Supreme Court Justice John McLean was seventy-five years old in 1860 but appealed to some who embraced the safe values of the past. Lincoln had supported his candidacy for the Republican nomination in 1856.

Chicago was a jaunty city of more than one hundred thousand people whose jerry-built buildings hollered that it was a city in a hurry. Rapidly becoming the manufacturing and trade center of the Midwest, the city boasted fifteen railroads. The spires of fifty-six churches dominated the skyline. Most of the streets were paved only with long oak planks, beneath which lived an army of rats that came out each night to ravage the city's uncollected garbage. The arriving delegates encountered buildings decorated with festive banners and bunting. The fastest growing city in America wanted to put on its best face—a largely Republican one—which could lend a hand to "Old Abe." The center of activity was "the Wigwam," a structure 100 by 180 feet, built to accommodate ten thousand people. Inside the Wigwam were patriotic displays of state coats of arms, flags, and busts of distinguished Americans.

THE REPUBLICANS IN NOMINATING CONVENTION, IN THEIR WIGWAM AT CHICAGO, MAY, 1860.

*The Republican convention met in the Wigwam, a tentlike structure
built to hold upward of ten thousand people.*

On May 12, 1860, David Davis arrived in Chicago to find that all the major candidates had established headquarters except Lincoln. He promptly rented two rooms at the Tremont House, paid the bill from his own pocket, and went to work around the clock. He drew together an inner circle of managers: lawyers from the old Eighth Circuit such as Leonard Swett, Stephen Logan, and Henry C. Whitney; several of Lincoln's political colleagues, including Norman Judd, Jesse Fell, Jesse Dubois, and Ozias Hatch; and newspapermen Joseph Medill and Charles Ray. Davis gave each man specific assignments. Almost everyone in Illinois was from somewhere else, so Davis dispatched his associates to visit the delegations of their home states: Richard Yates and Stephen Logan to work on delegates from Kentucky; Swett to speak with delegates from Maine; and Ward Hill Lamon, an old lawyer friend, to lobby the Virginia delegation. Orville Browning had told Lincoln in February he was supporting Bates, but he had a change of heart and proved invaluable in speaking with delegates leaning toward the St. Louisian.

The massive Davis sat behind a large table receiving reports from his lieutenants. From time to time, he would speak with an arriving state delegation. A critical delegation was Indiana, with twenty-six votes, which arrived with a majority for Bates. Davis understood that Lincoln, aside from being simply a favorite son, needed to garner votes from some other states on the first ballot if he was to make a move on the second and third ballots. It was Davis's policy not to put other candidates down, but to lift Lincoln up. His purpose was to secure pledges that Lincoln would be a delegation's second choice to which they would turn if their first choice faltered.

In Springfield, Lincoln was biding his time between his law office and the telegraph office on the north side of the public square. The accepted protocol was that candidates not appear at conventions. Lincoln told Swett, "He was almost too much of a candidate to go, and not quite enough to stay home." Lincoln's team in Chicago was a good deal more confident than the candidate himself. On May 13, 1860, Dubois wired Lincoln, "We are here in great confusion things this evening look as favorable as we had any right to expect."

On Tuesday, May 14, 1860, one day before the convention opened, the *Chicago Press & Tribune* ran a huge headline: "The Winning Man—Abraham Lincoln." Lincoln received numerous telegrams from friends and advisers in Chicago. Nathan M. Knapp, chairman of the Scott County Republican Committee, who had long believed that Lincoln did not fully appreciate "his own power," sent a telegram after conversations with the Indiana delegation. "Things are working; keep a good nerve—be not surprised at any result." He told Lincoln, "We are laboring to make you the second choice of all the Delegations we can where we cannot make you first choice."

On this tumultuous Tuesday, some of Lincoln's friends were signaling him that it might help if he were present in Chicago to make his case and answer questions, but Davis and Dubois were adamant: "Dont come unless we send for you." Editor Ray of the *Chicago Tribune* sent what Lincoln must have received as a mixed message. "Don't be too sanguine. Matters now look well and as things stand to-day I had rather have your chances than those of any other man. But don't get excited."

The convention opened at noon on Wednesday, May 16, 1860. As the proceedings began in the Wigwam, twice as many watched outside as could fit inside. The first afternoon was devoted to organization and the appointment of committees.

Thursday, May 17, 1860, a warm, balmy day, was devoted to the adoption of the platform, which tempered the tone but not the basic conviction of the 1856 convention's condemnation of the extension of slavery. The platform also contained planks that Lincoln had long supported: a protective tariff, dear to the hearts of Pennsylvania and New Jersey delegates; federal support for rivers and harbors, important for Chicago and Detroit; a homestead act for free land, which was imperative for farmers in the West and for German-Americans; and building a railroad to the Pacific Ocean, supported by delegates from Iowa, Missouri, Oregon, and California.

The Illinois delegation took little part in the public platform debates because they were trolling for votes in private meetings with key delegations. The Lincoln camp knew that Seward was strongest in the northern tier of states where Republicans could expect to win in 1860—Maine, Massachusetts, New York, Michigan, Wisconsin, and Minnesota. The most intense attention was focused on the four crucial states that Buchanan had won in 1856—Illinois, Indiana, Pennsylvania, and New Jersey.

On the same day, Edward L. Baker, editor of the *Illinois State Journal,* arrived in Chicago. He brought with him a copy of the *Missouri Democrat,* which he handed to Davis. Lincoln had written in pencil on the edge of the paper: "Make no contracts that will bind me." It has long been debated how Davis did or did not act upon this message. At the time, he was negotiating with Pennsylvania and its rich harvest of fifty-four votes. If Senator Simon Cameron of Pennsylvania could be offered a cabinet post, it might make the difference, but Lincoln was signaling that he would have none of it. Davis may have offered a position to Cameron, but it is more likely he said that certainly Pennsylvania would deserve a place in a Lincoln cabinet. Lincoln's terse instruction revealed his earliest thought on the way he intended to govern.

IN CHICAGO, balloting commenced on Friday, May 18, 1860, at 10 a.m. Davis may have been the campaign manager, but no one had prepared for this day longer than Judd. As the one who had secured the convention for Chicago, he took charge of seating arrangements, placing the New York and Pennsylvania delegations at opposite ends of the Wigwam where they would have great difficulty conversing. As a railroad lawyer, he arranged for special excursion fares to bring Lincoln supporters from all over the state. Finally, Judd had extra tickets printed, so that on Friday morning additional Lincoln supporters arrived at the Wig-wam early, thereby denying places to Seward supporters. Once inside, the Lincoln "shouters" drowned out the outnumbered Seward backers.

In Springfield, Lincoln braced himself for rebuff once again. At eight-thirty he walked over to James Conkling's law office located over Chatterton's jewelry store. Lincoln had learned that Conkling, who had been at the Republican convention, had unexpectedly returned from Chicago. Conkling was out, but later in the morning Lincoln found his friend in. Stretching his long frame on an old settee by the front win-dow, Lincoln asked Conkling what he expected to happen that day at the convention. Conkling answered that he believed Lincoln would be nominated because there was so much opposition to Seward. Lincoln replied that "he hardly thought this possible," and that if Seward was blocked, the nomination would go to Bates or Chase. Lincoln presently declared, "Well, Conkling, I believe I will go back to my office and practice law."

In Chicago, Seward's name was the first to be placed in nomination by the renowned lawyer William M. Evarts. Judd stood second to nom-inate Lincoln. Caleb B. Smith of Indiana, who had served in Congress with Lincoln, seconded the nomination.

The clerk began the balloting, not by alphabetical order, as is the cus-tom today, but by geographical order. The clerk shouted, "Maine." Maine gave ten votes to Seward and six votes to Lincoln: surprise. But Maine's split vote was no surprise to Davis and his lieutenants. New York cast its seventy votes for Seward. No surprise.

In Springfield, just before noon, editor Baker burst into Lincoln's office with the results of the first ballot: Seward 173½; Lincoln 102; Cameron 50½; Chase 49; Bates 48; and McLean 12. Lincoln and his advisers believed that Seward had arrived in Chicago with at least 150 votes. Lincoln knew that Seward's vote total had to include all 70 votes from New York, the largest state. This meant Seward had barely more than 100 votes from the other delegations. The most heartening news was that Indiana cast all of its 26 votes for Lincoln. Lincoln had told Browning that Bates could well be the benefactor of the stop-Seward movement, but no state gave the majority of its votes to Bates. Two hundred thirty-three votes were needed for the nomination.

In Chicago, delegates cried out, "Call the Roll," eager for the sec-ond ballot to begin. Vermont. The Green Mountain state, which had

William H. Seward, senator from New York, arrived in Chicago as the leading candidate.

given its ten votes on the first ballot to favorite son Senator Jacob Col-
lamer, called out, "Ten votes for Lincoln." Lincoln garnered five new
votes from Rhode Island and Connecticut, where he had spoken so
effectively not more than two months earlier. The Keystone state,
Pennsylvania, which every delegate knew was critical to a Republican

victory in 1860, after some delay, called out "Forty-eight votes for Lincoln." A gain of forty-four votes. The vast army of Lincoln supporters inside and outside the Wigwam shouted and cheered. Delaware changed all six of its votes from Bates to Lincoln. The clerk continued, with Lincoln picking up a few votes here and there as the roll call moved west.

The results of the second balloting were announced: Seward 184½; Lincoln 181; Chase 42½; Bates 35; Dayton 10; McLean 8; Cameron 2; and Clay 2. Lincoln had picked up seventy-nine votes while Seward gained only eleven. Instantly, everyone knew Lincoln was gaining.

In Springfield, Lincoln was fidgety. He decided to walk over to the Illinois and Mississippi telegraph office to see if there were any new telegrams. Finding none, he proceeded to the offices of the *Illinois State Journal*. On the way over he stopped to talk with some young men with whom he had played the game of "fives," an early form of handball, on the previous day. After a few minutes, a telegram arrived with the surprising results of the second ballot.

In Chicago, the third ballot began immediately amid tremendous excitement inside and outside the Wigwam. Maine, New Hampshire, Vermont: no changes. Massachusetts took four votes from Seward and gave them to Lincoln. Lincoln also gained in Rhode Island, Connecticut, Pennsylvania, Maryland, and Kentucky. The clerk called Ohio. Lincoln had spoken in Ohio and earned friends there. Medill, who had lived in Ohio for more than twenty years before moving to Chicago, had been sitting in and working on the Ohio delegation. The Wigwam gasped when Ohio awarded Lincoln twenty-nine votes, a pickup of fifteen.

As the roll call moved west, hundreds of pencils scratched everywhere, keeping a running tally. Lincoln had now reached 231½. He needed only one and a half more votes to be nominated. David Cartter, chairman of the Ohio delegation, a Cleveland lawyer, rose to speak in a Wigwam suddenly silent. "I-I a-a-rise, Mr. Chairman, to a-a-nounce"—Cartter stuttered, as he always did—"the c-c-change of f-four votes, from Mr. Chase to Abraham Lincoln."

In Springfield, where Lincoln sat in a large armchair in the offices of the *Journal,* a telegram was run in telling him he was nominated on the third ballot. Another telegram, moments later, told him that the New York delegation moved to make the nomination unanimous. More and more telegrams poured in, including one from Nathan Knapp: "We did it—glory to God." Lincoln accepted congratulations all around. Presently he told the growing throng of friends, "Well gentlemen there is a little woman at our house who is probably more interested in this dispatch than I am."

*Shortly after Lincoln's nomination as the Republican candidate,
he sat for this photograph in Springfield at the suggestion of
campaign biographer Joseph H. Barrett.*

CHAPTER 15

Justice and Fairness to All
May 1860–November 1860

LINCOLN BEARS HIS HONORS MEEKLY.

ORVILLE BROWNING
Diary entry, June 12, 1860

ON THE EVENING OF MAY 18, 1860, A LARGE RALLY ASSEMBLED AT THE statehouse in Springfield. Picking up the symbol of the Rail Splitter, several hundred men arrived with rails, which they stacked at the statehouse doors like muskets. Afterward, a large parade wound its way to the Lincoln home. After a serenade, Lincoln told the cheering crowd he "did not suppose the honor of such a visit was intended particularly for himself, as a private citizen, but rather the representative of a great party." That evening, across the Midwest and the East, Republicans gathered in small and large communities for "ratification rallies." In the stacks of telegrams Lincoln received on May 18, David Davis, his campaign manager, counseled, "Write no letters & make no promises till You see me write me at Bloomington when to see you I must see you soon."

Lincoln had learned in the early evening the convention had nominated Hannibal Hamlin of Maine for vice president. Hamlin, born the same year as Lincoln, 1809, taught school and published a Democratic newspaper before being admitted to the bar in 1833. A strong-willed Mainer, he sought to abolish the death penalty and was hostile to the extension of slavery. He was elected to Congress in 1843 and entered the Senate in 1848. His nomination balanced Lincoln, a former Whig from the West, with a former Democrat from the East. In the practice of mid-nineteenth-century politics it was not unusual that Lincoln would not be consulted about the choice of a vice presidential running mate.

The next day, George Ashmun of Massachusetts, president of the convention, and various chairmen of state delegations—almost all of whom had originally supported other candidates—traveled to Springfield to bring the official notification of Lincoln's nomination. Carl Schurz, German-American leader from Wisconsin who was a strong supporter of Seward, recalled that Lincoln received the delegation in the north parlor of "his modest frame house." Most had never even seen Lincoln and looked at him "with surprised curiosity." Lincoln stood "tall and ungainly in his black suit of apparently new but ill-fitting clothes." Abraham and Mary had disagreed over whether to serve liquor or not. Lincoln, with great respect for the temperance movement, prevailed, and ice water was served. He also broke the demeanor of the stuffy notification ceremony when he asked a surprised Governor Edwin D. Morgan of New York what his height was. Walking out of the house, Judge William D. Kelley told Schurz, "Well, we might have done a more brilliant thing, but we could hardly have done a better thing."

AN IRONY OF THE 1860 CAMPAIGN was that Lincoln stayed home in Springfield more than he ever had before, as was the custom of nineteenth-century politics. Lincoln believed his record to be in plain sight in his speeches, many of which were now being bundled together in campaign pamphlets. He told everyone he would be home for the summer.

Lincoln did pledge that, if elected president, he would govern by the motto "Justice and fairness to all." By "all," he meant a widening set of concentric circles of his constituencies. He would not distinguish among Republicans who did or did not support him. He had always worked with Democrats and intended to do so again. Most important, he would make no distinction between North and South.

In this spirit, Lincoln's first initiative in his campaign was to reach out to his Republican opponents. On Monday, May 21, 1860, David Davis expressed his concern about New York and how the disaffection of Seward supporters could play into the hands of Douglas. On May 24, Thurlow Weed, Seward's shrewd campaign manager, arrived in Springfield for what Lincoln and Davis hoped would be the beginning of a rapprochement with his chief rival. Weed wrote later of that initial visit that he sensed from the first that Lincoln revealed "such intuitive knowledge of human nature, and such familiarity with the virtues and infirmities of politicians, that I became impressed very favorably with his fitness for the duties which he was not unlikely to be called upon to discharge." On the same day, Orville Browning, dispatched by Lincoln and Davis to St. Louis, met with Edward Bates, his second rival, to try to bring him on board. Bates told Browning that he would write a public letter endorsing Lincoln.

Lincoln himself wrote to Salmon P. Chase, his third rival. "Holding myself the humblest of all whose names were before the convention, I feel in especial need of the assistance of all." To Schuyler Colfax, who had supported Bates, Lincoln wrote, "You distinguish between yourself and my *original friends*—a distinction which, by your leave, I propose to forget."

WHILE THE REPUBLICANS were uniting, Lincoln watched from Springfield as the Democrats and others were dividing. From late April through June, five nominating conventions produced three more presidential candidates. A week before the Republican convention, former Whigs and Know-Nothings who could back neither the Republicans nor the Democrats, and were hoping to avoid disunion, met in Baltimore to found the Constitutional Union Party with the promise to save "the Union as it is." They nominated John Bell, a former Whig who had opposed the Kansas-Nebraska Act, and Edward Everett, former president of Harvard and secretary of state under President Fillmore.

The Democrats, after the disaster at Charleston, reconvened on June 18, 1860, in Baltimore. One hundred and ten "fire-eaters" walked out when once again the convention would not agree to a resolution recognizing slavery in the territories. Following marathon balloting, the convention nominated Stephen Douglas for president and Herschel V. Johnson of Georgia for vice president.

The Southern Democrats, convening in another location in Baltimore after their walkout, reconvened in Richmond on June 28, 1860, and nominated Buchanan's incumbent vice president, John C. Breckinridge of Kentucky, for president, and Joseph Lane of Oregon for vice president, on a pro-slavery platform.

At the end of this unprecedented cycle of conventions, all signs favored Lincoln and the Republicans. Douglas would be his main contestant in the North. Breckinridge and Douglas would do battle in the South, with Bell hoping to do well in the border states. Lincoln assessed his chances in a letter to Anson G. Henry in Oregon, "We know not what a day may bring forth; but, today, it looks as if the Chicago ticket will be elected." He added, "I think the chances were more than equal that we could have beaten the Democracy *united*. Divided, as it is, its chance appears indeed very slim."

CAMPAIGN BIOGRAPHIES CONSTITUTED a major feature of nine-teenth-century political campaigning. William Dean Howells, a twenty-three-year-old editorial writer for the *Ohio State Journal* in

John Bell, a former Whig senator from Tennessee, led the Constitutional Union Party ticket.

Columbus, was engaged by Follett, Foster and Company, the same firm that had recently published Lincoln's scrapbook of the Lincoln-Douglas debates, to write a biography of Lincoln. The publisher suggested that Howells go to Springfield to interview Lincoln himself. Howells, at the beginning of a brilliant literary career during which he would write more than one hundred books from 1860 to 1920, declined, saying later, "I missed the greatest chance of my life." Instead, he commissioned a young law student, James Quay Howard, to interview Lincoln. When Lincoln received his copy in the early summer, he sat down with his Farber pencil to insert corrections and additions, most of them small, in the Howells text.

The most popular biography came from the pen of John Locke Scripps, senior editor of the *Chicago Press & Tribune*. Scripps interviewed

Stephen Douglas, Lincoln's longtime opponent, led the Northern Democratic ticket.

Lincoln in Springfield in June. When his thirty-two-page pamphlet biography, published by the *New York Tribune,* appeared in mid-July, the Republican organization inundated the public with what they called "Campaign Document No. 1." They based their claim in part on the extensive interview Scripps did with Lincoln, thereby lending a semi-official authority to it.

On July 17, 1860, Lincoln received a letter from Scripps that may have given him a chuckle. Scripps wrote, "I believe the biography contains nothing that I was not fully authorized to put into it." But then he quickly added, "In speaking of the books you read in early life, I took the liberty of adding Plutarch's Lives. I take it for granted that you had read that book. If you have not, then you must read it at once to make my statement good." Lincoln made no reply to Scripps, but the *Chicago*

John C. Breckinridge, Kentucky senator, led the Southern Democratic ticket.

Tribune author learned that Lincoln, never missing a beat, made "frequent humorous allusions to it."

THE LINCOLN-HAMLIN CAMPAIGN started quickly. With so many people coming to see him, and quickly realizing he could not work out of his law office, he accepted the offer of Governor John Wood to use the governor's room on the second floor of the statehouse. John G. Nicolay, the serious, hardworking assistant to Secretary of State Hatch, who had been on loan to Lincoln, now became his one-man staff. Nicolay, born in Essingen, Germany, immigrated to the United States with his family when he was six. First living and attending school in Cincinnati, a city of German immigrants, he kept moving west with his family, finally arriving in Illinois. Young Nicolay went to work for the *Pike County Free Press* in Pittsfield, a New England town set down on the prairies, and by twenty-three was its editor. Now twenty-eight, Nicolay was five feet ten inches tall, and a rail-thin 125 pounds. He had blue eyes and brown hair, his "slow smile" partially hidden behind a mustache and small beard. Nicolay was a young man who loved words, whether it was the Bible, especially the Old Testament, printed in German letters, the plays of Shakespeare, or his editorials in a Whig newspaper. All of these qualities helped build a relationship of mutual trust and appreciation with Lincoln.

John G. Nicolay, quiet and efficient, became Lincoln's one-man staff in his campaign for the presidency.

Nicolay had been the custodian of Illinois state election records in Hatch's office, and Lincoln, an assiduous student of these records, was regularly in conversation with him. Now the two shared Lincoln's campaign office, which, while large, had no anteroom, no security, so visitors came and went all day long.

To his chagrin, Lincoln discovered that he had become a celebrity. Every day an army of politicians, reporters, photographers, portrait painters, and others arrived in Springfield. Yet, for all of the crush of people to see him, his new elevated status brought little change to his personal habits and his relationships with people, be they old friends or new acquaintances. Three weeks after his nomination, his old friend Orville Browning, after visiting Springfield's campaign office, wrote in his diary, "Lincoln bears his honors meekly."

Photographer Alexander Hesler of Chicago traveled to Springfield to take four photographs of Lincoln on June 3, 1860. Lincoln particularly liked one photograph that captured his facial expression at the crowning moment of his maturity. Lincoln commented, "That looks better and expresses me better than any I have ever seen." Mary and some others, however, did not like it. Lincoln believed "their objection arises from the disordered condition of the hair." Lincoln concluded, "My judgment is worth nothing in these matters."

Through the weeks of the hot Illinois summer, Lincoln said nothing about his policies. He did not discuss what he would do about the disgruntled South. His standard reply to questions was that his ideas could be found in his published speeches. When pressed, he added that he did not want to say anything that could be misinterpreted. Lincoln's posture did not mean he was passive or inactive. He kept abreast of events in the states and flagged his concerns to friends and allies.

He also continued to act as a peacemaker, using the skills he had learned in the small towns of the Eighth Judicial Circuit and in the rough-and-tumble state politics of Illinois. He had successfully steered the Republican boat through troubled waters in Illinois in 1859 and now he sought to do the same on a national stage in 1860. Because he did not campaign publicly, it is easy to miss how much he did behind the scenes.

Looking east to the state of New York, Lincoln became aware of the long-running Republican division between the William Seward–Thurlow Weed constituency and the Free Soil Democratic wing of the party led by William Cullen Bryant, editor of the *New York Post,* with support from Horace Greeley. Lincoln kept hearing that Douglas would mount a tremendous campaign in New York and feared that unhappy

*Abraham Lincoln and Hannibal Hamlin
led the Republican ticket in 1860.*

Seward supporters might sit out the presidential election. In August, Lincoln wrote to Weed, "I think there will be the most extraordinary effort ever made, to carry New-York for Douglas." Even though the New York Republicans were confident of victory, Lincoln admonished, "Still it will require close watching, and great effort" to keep Douglas contained. Continuing to hear of divisions within the New York Republican Party, Lincoln sent word that he "neither is nor will be . . . committed to any man, clique, or faction." Lincoln's policy, in New York and elsewhere, was "to deal fairly with all."

In Pennsylvania, a feud between Senator Simon Cameron and Andrew Curtin, Republican candidate for governor, threatened Republican solidarity in the second largest state in the Union. David Davis and Leonard Swett visited Pennsylvania in August on a fact-finding mission and reported back to Lincoln. Lincoln then wrote to members of the

Pennsylvania Republican State Committee. "I am slow to listen to criminations among friends, and never expose their quarrels on either side. My sincere wish is that both sides will allow by-gones to be by-gones, and look to the present and future only."

MARY LINCOLN WAS EAGER to join her husband's campaign in ways that most previous candidates' wives were not. In past presidential campaigns, the wives of candidates were seldom seen and never heard. But Mary had inherited from her father a passion for politics, and for years she had put that enthusiasm to work encouraging her husband and, in an "unwomanly" way for her time, offering her counsel on all manner of politics and people. From early in their marriage, when Lincoln was running for state office, again while he served in Congress, and even when he was seemingly exiled to the Eighth Judicial Circuit, Mary had her eyes on faraway horizons. Even if Mr. Lincoln was not always an ideal husband, traveling away from her too often and not present to her when he was at home, she recognized long before others his abilities, which she believed would carry him one day all the way to the presidency.

If Lincoln did not go to the people, the people came to him. He met supporters in his home as much as at his temporary election office. As daily visitors to Springfield came to take the measure of Lincoln's leadership abilities, many were also eager to take the measure of Mary's abilities as hostess and conversationalist. As the candidate welcomed visitors to his office in the statehouse, she welcomed many of these same people to their home at Eighth and Jackson. Newspapers of the day seldom talked about the wives of politicians, but the *New York Tribune* departed from this tradition to offer a first assessment of Mary Lincoln on May 25, 1860. Greeley's newspaper wrote that Mary Lincoln was "amiable and accomplished . . . vivacious and graceful," and reported that she was "a sparkling talker."

Through her love of letter writing to correspondents, known and unknown, across the country, Mary campaigned for her husband from Springfield. Most of her letters have vanished, but a sample of her writing is found in a reply to the Reverend Dyer Burgess, a Presbyterian minister in Constitution, Ohio, who was both antislavery and anti-Mason (some people feared that the Masons were a secret movement attempting to rule the nation). Burgess wrote that, as a Republican, he wanted to support Lincoln but needed assurances that he had never been a member of a secret society. Mary replied, "Mr. Lincoln has never been a Mason or belonged to any secret order."

Mary received a note shortly after Lincoln's nomination from Annie Parker Dickson, a cousin living in Cincinnati. She and her husband, William Martin Dickson, an attorney and active Republican, had entertained Lincoln when he was in Cincinnati for the "Reaper Case" in 1855. The note read, "You are an ambitious little woman and for many reasons I am delighted with your success." Dickson was only voicing what others, especially women, had observed for a long time.

One of Mary's regular correspondents was Hannah Shearer, sister of Noyes W. Miner, a Baptist minister and the Lincolns' neighbor. After the death of her first husband, Edward Rathbun, Hannah had married John Henry Shearer, a physician, and moved to Brooklyn, New York. Shortly before the election, Mary wrote, "You used to be worried, that I took politics so coolly you would not do so, were you to see me now. Whenever I *have time,* to think, my mind is sufficiently exercised for my comfort."

With her husband home, Mary acted as a consultant—not about issues, but about people. Mary had long believed her husband was too trusting of others. She had strong opinions about his political colleagues. She did not like or trust Norman Judd. She relied on David Davis. Unlike her husband, she held grudges. She still harbored resentment toward Lyman Trumbull, who had defeated Lincoln for the Senate in 1855, and had not repaired her relationship with his wife, Julia Jayne Trumbull. From May through November 1860, Mary was with Abraham nearly every day, expressing her opinions and counting herself as his chief adviser. It was one of their longest periods together.

AN INSIGHT INTO Mary and Abraham Lincoln's home life was provided by young Frank Fuller, a friend of Robert's from Phillips Exeter who visited in the summer of 1860. After Frank called on Lincoln at the statehouse, Lincoln invited him home to dinner. Lincoln did not invite anyone to dinner without Mary's prior consent, but Fuller found himself "warmly welcomed by Mrs. Lincoln." He brought Mary a gift of a slim book of poems by Albert Laighton, a young poet from Portsmouth, New Hampshire. She told him of her delight in poetry and quizzed young Fuller about the poet and the poems.

As the family seated itself in the dining room, Lincoln asked Fuller if he offered grace at meals. He replied that it was his practice to read a couple of lines of poetry. As Lincoln bowed his head, Fuller asked the blessing of "the Supreme Power"

> That made our frames, sustains our lives,
> And through all earthly change survives.

In the conversation at dinner the young Phillips Exeter student discovered that Lincoln had committed to memory a good deal of the Bible, especially, he told him, the Sermon on the Mount and the Twenty-third Psalm.

AFRICAN-AMERICAN LEADER Frederick Douglass, returning to Rochester in 1860 from a speaking tour in England and Scotland, tried to take stock of the multiplying political candidates poised to run for the presidency. He had been a supporter of Seward, who was a subscriber to Douglass's antislavery newspaper, the *North Star,* and whose career he had followed as a fellow New Yorker.

In June, Douglass offered a perceptive analysis of Lincoln in the *Douglass' Monthly.* He praised Lincoln as "a man of unblemished private character; a lawyer, standing near the front rank of the bar of his own State, has a cool, well balanced head; great firmness of will; is perseveringly industrious; and one of the most frank, honest men in political life." Noting that nineteenth-century political parties had habitually turned away from their best statesmen for president—Daniel Webster and Henry Clay—and nominated men of lesser stature—William Henry Harrison, James Polk, Zachary Taylor, and Franklin Pierce—Douglass observed, "Mr. Lincoln possesses great capacities, and is yet to be proved to be a great statesman, it is lucky for him that a political exigency moved his party to take him on trust and before his greatness was ripe, or he would have lost his chance." And what of Douglass's hopes for Lincoln as president?

> When once elected it will be no longer dangerous for him to develop great qualities, and we hope than in taking him on a "profession of faith," rather than on the recommendations of his political life, his party will witness his continual "growth in grace," and his administration will redound to the glory of his country, and his own fame.

Douglass, utilizing two metaphors for the Christian journey of faith, offered one of the most prescient predictions of Lincoln's journey of political leadership.

"ON MONDAY NIGHT some miserable, infamous, low-flung, narrow-minded, ungodly, dirt-eating, cutthroat, hemp-deserving, deeply dyed, double-distilled, concentrated miscreant of miscreants, sinned against all honor and decency, by cutting down and sawing down two or three Republican poles in this city." This editorial in Springfield's *Illinois State Journal* was referring to huge poles, some as high as one hundred feet, to which were fastened the banners of parties and candidates. What the editorial really highlighted was the enthusiasm, intensity, and contentiousness of political campaigning in Illinois at midcentury.

Political campaigns were the chief source of entertainment of the day. Events ran the gamut from rallies, parades, and pole raisings, to picnics, fireworks, excursions, and illuminations, and sometimes riots. The enthusiasm for political campaigns rivaled earlier nineteenth-century religious revivals and could be compared to the twentieth-century embrace of spectator sports. People all over the nation were paying attention as four candidates sprinted toward the finish line.

On a thousand platforms across the North, Republican leaders stumped for Lincoln. Seward and Chase barnstormed across the Midwest. In their speeches they depicted Lincoln, emphasizing his humble origins, as a man of the people. They extolled him as a lawyer and a decisive debater. Women, who could not vote, were nevertheless quite present at political rallies, carrying banners that declared,

Westward the star of Empire takes it way,
We link-on to Lincoln, as our mothers did to Clay.

A highlight of the summer campaign took place on August 8, 1860, when Springfield hosted an "immense" rally at the fairgrounds to honor its townsman candidate. The *Illinois State Journal*'s headline blared: "The Prairies on Fire for Lincoln." The *Journal* used a full three columns to describe the rally, beginning the first column with an image of an elephant bearing its trunk, the first known use of the elephant as a symbol for the Republican Party. The words "We Are Coming" stood beneath the elephant, followed by "Clear the Track."

A parade, led by Wide-Awakes, came to Lincoln's home to convey him to the fairgrounds. When he arrived, the crowd, aroused at the sight of their candidate, stampeded his carriage, lifted him bodily above the mob, and carried him to one of the five speakers' stands.

Lincoln, overcome with emotion, nevertheless kept his cool. Adjusting his stovepipe hat, he told the huge crowd, "It has been my purpose, since I have been placed in my present position, to make no speeches." He did admit, "I confess with gratitude . . . that I did not suppose my appearance among you would create the tumult which I now witness."

Lincoln's problem became how to extricate himself from that tumult. When the crowd surrounded and stopped his carriage, George Brinkerhoff, a clerk in the state auditor's office, joined with several other men in pulling Lincoln out of the carriage and "slipped him over the horses tail on to the saddle [and] led the horse to town."

In August, Lincoln was particularly delighted to receive a letter of congratulations from his old friend Edward Baker. Writing from San Francisco, Baker, having known Lincoln for a quarter century, pinpointed the two characteristics that best described the president-elect. Baker wrote, "The reward that fidelity and courage, find in your person will infuse hope in many sinking bosoms, and new energy in many bold hearts." Lincoln would need both fidelity and courage for the challenges ahead.

WITH HIS OPPONENTS DIVIDED, Lincoln was confident he would win, but he was taking nothing for granted. In the nineteenth century, state elections took place throughout the calendar year; the victories of Republicans in Maine and Vermont in August seemed to many a harbinger of good things to come. Lincoln looked forward eagerly to the results of elections in early October in the crucial states of Pennsylvania, Ohio, and Indiana.

Lincoln believed that early state elections could have a domino effect, influencing voters in other states. When he heard that expected September victories in two congressional districts in Maine might not materialize, and that Governor Israel Washburn's margin of victory in his race for reelection might be much smaller than originally predicted, he wrote an urgent letter to Senator Hamlin, his vice presidential running mate, who was from Maine. "Such a result . . . would, I fear, put us on the down-hill track, lose us the State elections in Pennsylvania and Indiana, and probably ruin us on the main turn in November."

Even with direction from Lincoln and a national committee, much of the campaign was under the control of state Republican organizations. This meant that in Massachusetts voters heard a strong antislavery message, whereas in Pennsylvania that message was muted in favor of one about protective tariffs. In the West, Republicans emphasized commitments to homestead opportunities and the building of the transcontinental railroad. Nonetheless, Republicans everywhere extolled the virtues of Lincoln and of sustaining the Union.

Douglas, whom Lincoln knew to be his chief rival, threw aside the nineteenth-century tradition of campaign abstention, and launched a strenuous crusade, believing he still could carry the populous free states with their large electoral votes. He put far more weight on the threats from the South than did Lincoln, and therefore tried to circulate the message that only his election could bring about peace between North and South.

The Little Giant and his supporters held nothing back in their attacks on Lincoln. Douglas partisans accused Lincoln of being a Deist—someone who believed only in natural religion—and circulated stories of Lincoln's near duel with James Shields. They charged that Lincoln had once joined a secret Know-Nothing lodge in Quincy and dredged up the story of Lincoln's supposed lack of support for the troops in the Mexican War. Both Douglas and John Bell, presidential candidate of the Constitutional Union Party, sought to portray Lincoln and the Republicans as the party of disunion.

In response to these attacks, Lincoln said nothing about secession. His policy was not to credit such fears, even in the fall of 1860. He believed talk of secession in the South was mostly bluster. He remained confident that, as a son of the South, he understood the mind of the Southern people. He continually referred people to his written speeches, because he believed Southerners would find in them his repeated promise not to touch slavery where it already existed in the South. In response to a letter in early August, Lincoln replied, "The people of the South have too much good sense, and good temper, to attempt the ruin of the government."

In Springfield, Lincoln was isolated from the secessionist talk, but throughout the summer and fall of 1860, there was much foreboding across the South. Around the cracker barrels at country stores and on porches of sprawling mansions, people turned Lincoln into a caricature. Southerners depicted him as a Black Republican who was secretly aligned with abolitionists ready to unleash slave rebellions throughout the South. Southerners did not read Lincoln's speeches, but they heard that Douglas had accused him in 1858 of favoring Negro equality. The spirit of 1776 was being rekindled in the South; this time the enemy was not the despotic British, but the tyrannical North about to elect an unknown man from the West.

Lincoln rejoiced, and also expressed a sense of relief, when victories in Pennsylvania, Ohio, and Indiana were announced at the beginning of the second week of October. On October 12, 1860, Lincoln wrote to Seward, "It now looks as if the Government is about to fall into our hands."

All through October, Lincoln maintained his policy of silence. Although some supporters suggested that he write a public letter in the last days of the campaign setting forth his key ideas and allaying fears in the South, he continued with his strategy and said nothing.

ON A SUNNY ELECTION DAY MORNING, Tuesday, November 6, 1860, Lincoln received visitors at his office in the statehouse. He had never voted for himself in an election and was not planning to do so today. William Herndon persuaded him that he could clip off the presidential electors at the top of the ballot and still cast his vote for the state offices.

In the afternoon, Lincoln walked over to the courthouse to vote. Everywhere Lincoln went on this Election Day, people cheered and followed him. He went home for an early supper with Mary and the boys. He returned to the statehouse by seven, where he intermittently received scattered and inconclusive reports of election results from across the country.

At nine, Lincoln and David Davis and a few others went to the telegraph office. With increasing rapidity, the tapping of the telegraph keys began to spell out Republican victories across the North. Lincoln had one remaining fear. If he did not win New York, with its thirty-five electoral votes, he might not win a majority, and the election would be decided in the House of Representatives. Shortly after midnight, the results from New York signaled that Lincoln would be the sixteenth president of the United States.

With victory assured, Lincoln walked over to Watson's Confectionery, where Mary and other Republican women had prepared a victory supper. As he entered, the women greeted him, "How do you do,

Mr. President!" After eating, he went back to the telegraph office and stayed until nearly two o'clock to monitor the results.

By everyone's remembrance, Lincoln remained remarkably calm through the long evening. He did exclaim that he was "a very happy man . . . who could help being so under such circumstances?" As church bells rang, and cheering exploded, Lincoln finally headed for home. "Mary, Mary, we are elected."

This Lincoln photograph by Samuel G. Alschuler in Chicago on November 25, 1860, shows the president-elect's new whiskers.

CHAPTER 16

An Humble Instrument in the Hands of the Almighty
November 1860 – February 1861

I NOW LEAVE, NOT KNOWING WHEN, OR WHETHER EVER, I MAY
RETURN, WITH A TASK BEFORE ME GREATER THAN THAT WHICH
RESTED UPON WASHINGTON.

ABRAHAM LINCOLN
Farewell address at Springfield, Illinois, February 11, 1861

IN THE FIRST DAYS AFTER HIS ELECTION, ABRAHAM LINCOLN TOOK THE
initial steps to build his administration and determine his policies. He
faced a problem never encountered by any of his predecessors—how to
preserve the nation. For all his gifts and abilities, Lincoln still did not
fully understand the very real possibilities for secession and war while
he remained isolated in Springfield. Thinking of himself as a son of the
South, he failed to appreciate that Kentucky, as a border state, was not
representative of Southern opinion. With his upbeat mind-set, removed
from the information and intrigue of Washington, as well as Southern
state capitals, he remained optimistic that all would yet be well.

Lincoln and his Republican colleagues had become used to persistent
enmity between North and South, which, for nearly thirty years, had
always stopped short of war. Lincoln, as the first president ever elected
by a minority, sectional electorate, faced twin challenges: how to defend
the Union but not resort to war, and how to save the Union but not give
in to compromise. These challenges would grow, not diminish, in the
long months ahead.

"WELL, BOYS, YOUR TROUBLES are over now," Lincoln greeted some
newspapermen on the morning after the election; "mine have just
begun." Lincoln had gone home at 2 a.m., but not to sleep. Both exhil-

arated and exhausted, "I then felt, as I never had before, the responsibility that was upon me. I began at once to feel that I needed support, others to share with me the burden."

Lincoln stayed up pondering whom he should name to his cabinet. He had been thinking about this question for some time, but on this night he wrote down eight names on a slip of paper:

Lincoln	Judd
Seward	Chase
Bates	M. Blair
Dayton	Welles

Lincoln listed himself at the top, but within the list. The other seven names all had some kind of leadership experience, in business or politics, whereas Lincoln was keenly aware that he had no executive experience. All were on record as against the extension of slavery into the territories. Lincoln included his three major Republican rivals, William Seward, Salmon Chase, and Edward Bates. The four other men listed had come into the Republican ranks from previous Free Soil and Democratic affiliations. Lincoln seemed to be aiming for geographical balance. Gideon Welles came from New England (Connecticut); William Seward and William Dayton from Northeastern states (New York and New Jersey); Norman Judd and Salmon Chase from the Northwest (Illinois and Ohio); and Edward Bates and Montgomery Blair from border states (Missouri and Maryland). Lincoln would hold this list close to his chest.

IT TOOK SEVERAL DAYS for the returns to reveal the final shape of the election. Lincoln won with 180 electoral votes, followed by 72 for John Breckinridge, 39 for John Bell, and 12 for Stephen Douglas. Lincoln won the popular contest with 1,866,452 votes to 1,376,957 for Douglas, 849,781 for Breckinridge, and 588,879 for Bell. This highly spirited election drew 82.2 percent of the eligible voters to the polls, making it the second highest turnout in the nation's history. Lincoln won all of the free, Northern states, dividing the electoral votes of New Jersey with Douglas. Despite finishing second in the popular vote, Douglas won only Missouri. Bell won three states in the upper South: Virginia, Kentucky, and Tennessee. Breckinridge won the rest of the South.

In the midst of celebration, there was some sobering news. Lincoln was the first Republican elected as president, but he won with only 39.9 percent of the popular vote, and with almost a million votes less than the combined total of his three opponents. The Republicans had failed to win either chamber of Congress. The most portentous warning for a party that had steadfastly denied it was a sectional party was that Lincoln and Hannibal Hamlin won not one vote in ten Southern states.

Immediately after the election, Lincoln committed one of his greatest errors of political judgment by failing to grasp the growing agitation over secession spreading across the South. Senator Truman Smith of Connecticut tried to alert him when he wrote Lincoln a long letter on November 7, 1860. Smith had become aware of a group, "among the most respectable citizens of New York," who were speaking out against Lincoln's election and plans for the nation. The senator told Lincoln,

> Public exigencies may be such as to make it incumbent on a successful candidate to speak out, not to repel slander, for that is of little consequence, but to disarm mischief makers, to allay causeless anxiety, to compose the public mind, and to induce all good citizens to . . . "judge the tree by its fruit."

Lincoln replied on November 10, 1860, "It is with the most profound appreciation of your motive, and highest respect for your judgment too, that I feel constrained, for the present, at least, to make no declaration for the public." Lincoln's decision to be silent muted his greatest strength—speaking persuasively to any audience.

President-elect Lincoln now sought to organize for a long transition. It would be four months before he would be inaugurated in Washington on March 4, 1861. This extended time would remain the pattern in American politics until the second term of Franklin Delano Roosevelt in 1937, when the date for the presidential inauguration was shifted from March 4 to January 20.

Lincoln continued to use the governor's room on the second floor of the statehouse, a room about fifteen by twenty-five feet in size, with long windows looking out on the south and east sides of the square. He arrived each morning looking much the same, except for a fringe of beard he had begun to grow. Eleven-year-old Grace Bedell of Westfield, New York, had written him on October 15, 1860, urging him to grow a beard. She told Lincoln, "You would look a great deal better for your face is so thin. All the ladies like whiskers and they would tease their husbands to vote for you and then you would be President."

John G. Nicolay, Lincoln's one-man campaign staff, now became his one-man transition team. Lincoln worked at a corner table with his secretary. "Heaps and hills" of newspapers were piled everywhere. Letters cascaded in from Republican leaders recommending themselves or others for offices. Lincoln dictated responses or wrote them in his own hand. Hate mail from the South also arrived regularly, constantly comparing Lincoln to the devil. The writers threatened him with death by hanging, gibbet, and stiletto. Most were not signed with real names, but rather by the "Southern Brotherhood" or other such organizations.

Lincoln greeted friends, politicians, reporters, and visitors in his corner office from ten until twelve. At noon, he walked home for lunch with Mary and the boys. He returned to work with Nicolay in the early afternoon and held another open house from three until five-thirty. The young newspaperman Henry Villard, posted to Springfield to cover Lincoln for the *New York Herald,* recorded the scene in the first days after Lincoln's election. "He sits or stands among his guests, throwing out hearty Western welcomes, asking and answering questions, joking, endeavoring to make matters every way comfortable to all present."

People even followed Lincoln home at night and "he was once more crowded upon in his parlor, and had to undergo another agony of presentations . . . by the constant influx of an ill-mannered populace." Mary enjoyed the visibility and attention, but she had "to endure," night after night, the complete first floor of her home filled with visitors, as many "callers ask each other, 'Is that the old woman?' " Villard, who had covered Lincoln in the debates in 1858, was impressed that Lincoln's personality had not changed with his election. "He is precisely the same man as before—open and generous in his personal communications with all who approach him."

UNDER RELENTLESS PRESSURE to speak about his policies as the future president, Lincoln partially broke his silence on November 20, 1860. Senator Trumbull was slated to speak at a Republican victory celebration in Springfield, and Lincoln gave him two paragraphs to insert into his speech. Lincoln sat beside Trumbull as he announced that under the new Republican administration "each and all of the States will be left in as complete control of their own affairs respectively, and at as perfect liberty to choose, and employ, their own means of protecting property, and preserving peace and order within their respective limits, as they have ever been under any administration."

These words were meant to reassure the South, but the speech continued with words that took away that assurance. "Disunionists *per se,* are now in hot haste to get out of the Union, precisely because they perceive they can not, much longer, maintain apprehension among the Southern people that their homes, and firesides, and lives, are to be endangered by the action of the Federal Government." Lincoln's insertion revealed that he wrongly believed the secessionists represented only a tiny minority of Southern sentiment. His concluding words were the most surprising of all. "I am rather glad of this military preparation in the South. It will enable the people the more easily to suppress any uprisings there, which their misrepresentations of purposes may have encouraged." Fortunately, Trumbull decided not to include these two sentences, and the public never heard them.

Trumbull's address satisfied no one. The Democratic-leaning *New York Herald* charged that the president-elect seemed to be either cut off from "all knowledge of the Southern revolutionary movements of the day; or that he is so completely under the control of his party advisors that he dare not speak; or that he feels himself unequal to the crisis, and is afraid to speak."

Though following the nineteenth-century tradition of refusing to speak publicly before inauguration, in private Lincoln worked tirelessly to influence events in the coming months, by both affirmation and rejection of ideas brewing in Congress. On November 21, 1860, Lincoln left Springfield, for the first time in more than six months, for a three-day meeting with Vice President–elect Hamlin and several others in Chicago.

Calling himself a private citizen, Lincoln purchased tickets on the Chicago, Alton, and St. Louis Railroad. He and Mary traveled with Lyman and Julia Trumbull—Mary was now speaking to Julia—in a regular crowded train car. Lincoln also invited Joshua Speed and his wife, Fanny, to come from Kentucky, as he wished to surround himself with friends, even as he sought to build a government mostly with men he had never met. Lincoln spoke with Speed, a Southerner who disagreed with Lincoln about slavery, about a cabinet position, but his longtime friend was not interested.

In Chicago, Lincoln explained to Hamlin and Trumbull that he

Lincoln looked forward to meeting with Vice President—elect Hannibal Hamlin at a conference in Chicago in November 1860.

wanted to reach out to his rivals, especially Seward, Bates, and Chase; he wanted to tap the best talent available for the difficult road ahead. He was most concerned about getting Seward on board as secretary of state. He wondered if Seward, rejected by the convention, might in turn reject Lincoln's invitation. He entrusted Senator Hamlin, wise to the ways of Washington politics, to handle the negotiations with Seward. As Trumbull listened to Lincoln's rationale to secure the most able leaders for the cabinet, he began to assume that Lincoln "would lean heavily on members of his Cabinet and leave many crucial decisions to them."

ON DECEMBER 3, 1860, Lincoln waited anxiously for news from Washington: On this day the Thirty-sixth Congress would assemble and receive President Buchanan's fourth and final annual message. Buchanan was popularly known as a "doughface," a derogatory term for the Northerners who, pliable like dough, adapted their views to appease Southern leaders on slavery. In his farewell, the seventy-year-old president placed responsibility for the national crisis on the North. "The long continued and intemperate interference of the northern people with the question of slavery in the southern States has at length produced its natural effects." How could the present crisis be settled? "All that is necessary" is for the South "to be let alone and permitted to manage their domestic institutions in their own way."

President Buchanan told the states of the South there was no legal right under the Constitution to proceed to acts of secession, because the United States was an organic Union and not merely a voluntary association of states. Having denied that the federal government, under his leadership, was guilty of any abuse of Southern rights, Buchanan put Lincoln on notice. "Reason, justice, a regard for the Constitution, all require we shall wait for some overt and dangerous act on the part of the President elect, before resorting to such a remedy." Finally, Buchanan declared that he did not have the power to mediate the conflict between the federal government and the states, something only Congress had the power to do.

Lincoln, upon reading the address, felt dismay at Buchanan's assessment of the crisis. He realized that the lame-duck president would continue to be part of the problem.

IN HIS INCOMING CORRESPONDENCE, Lincoln found a number of letters advocating the inclusion of Senator Simon Cameron of Pennsylvania in the cabinet. He had not included Cameron in his original list, in part because he had heard a steady refrain of charges that Cameron was a wire-puller whose politics always ended up being economically profitable for himself. Now, as Lincoln sought to resolve the final shape of the cabinet, a tug-of-war developed between pro- and anti-Cameron forces.

Lincoln also reread a letter from Henry J. Raymond. From his post as editor of the *New York Times,* Raymond had become aware of the public misunderstanding about the intentions of Lincoln and the new Republican administration. He had written to urge Lincoln to make some reassuring statement and, rather audaciously, sent Lincoln some sentences of what the president-elect ought to say. Lincoln, having sat on Raymond's letter, now replied that he believed his policy of silence had "a demonstration in favor of my view." Lincoln had been talked into inserting words into Trumbull's speech, but now he asked Raymond, "Has a single newspaper, heretofore against us, urged that speech [upon its readers] with a purpose to quiet public anxiety?" Lincoln, irritated and reaching for a way to express his discontent to the *New York Times* editor, concluded with Jesus's words " 'They seek a sign, and no sign shall be given them.' " Jesus's words were delivered to "an evil and adulterous generation"; Lincoln characterized his own generation as possessed by " 'Party malice' and not 'public good.' "

Lincoln's first choice for his cabinet was Seward, but he did not consider the effect that New York politics, as well as the rumor mill, would have on his wish. While Lincoln proceeded in his own mind with all deliberate speed, others wondered aloud why he was taking so long to decide on the key appointment of secretary of state. This interval of silence allowed for the anti-Seward factions in New York to recycle their criticisms. Then political gossip began to circulate that Lincoln did not really want Seward but intended to offer him the position with the expectation that Seward would decline it. As these rumors drifted back to Springfield, Lincoln took up his pen on December 8, 1860, to write Seward directly. He admitted he had "delayed so long to communicate" because of what he thought was "a proper caution in this case." As for the gossip, "I beg you to be assured that I have said nothing to justify these rumors. . . . It has been my purpose, from the day of the nomination at Chicago, to assign you, by your leave, this place in the administration." Several days later, Seward thanked Lincoln for the honor of the invitation, but asked for more time to consider it.

Lincoln now contacted Bates, next in priority for the cabinet. Lincoln offered to travel the ninety miles to meet the august, bearded Bates in St. Louis, but the old-line Whig believed that would be demeaning for the president-elect, and offered to come to Springfield instead. They met in Bates's room at the Chenery House on December 15, 1860. Lincoln offered him the position of attorney general, which he accepted. Immediately after their conference, Bates confided to his diary that he found Lincoln "free in his communications and candid in his manner."

LINCOLN BELIEVED THAT ONE WAY to reassure the South that his was not a sectional government was to include at least one Southerner in his cabinet. Hamlin had supported this idea in their face-to-face meeting in Chicago, as did Seward and Judge Davis. Lincoln considered James Guthrie, a Kentuckian who had served both as president of the Louisville and Nashville Railroad and as secretary of the treasury in the Pierce administration. Lincoln sent Speed to feel out Guthrie who, about to turn seventy-two, said he supported the Union but did not want the position.

As he deliberated over his cabinet, Lincoln learned of a striking speech delivered by one of the most reasonable Southern leaders, Alexander Stephens, his old Whig colleague from the Thirtieth Congress, who had recently retired from Congress. On November 14, 1860,

Stephens, even more shrunken in form than when Lincoln had known him, had pleaded in a speech to the Georgia legislature, "Don't give up the ship. Don't abandon her yet."

Someone called out, "The ship has leaks in her."

"Let us stop them if we can," replied Stephens.

Lincoln wrote to Stephens requesting a copy of his speech. Stephens sent the speech on December 14, along with the injunction, "The country is certainly in great peril, and no man ever had heavier or greater responsibility resting upon him than you have in the present momentous crisis."

After studying Stephens's speech, Lincoln replied on December 22, 1860, asking, "Do the people of the South really entertain fears that a Republican administration would, *directly,* or *indirectly,* interfere with their slaves, or with them, about their slaves? If they do, I wish to assure you, as once a friend, and still, I hope, not an enemy, that there is no cause for such fears." Lincoln might have stopped there, but did not. "You think slavery is *right* and ought to be extended; while we think it is *wrong* and ought to be restricted. That I suppose is the rub."

Stephens replied on December 30, 1860. "In addressing you thus, I would have you understand me as being not a personal enemy, but as one who would have you do what you can to save our common country." Yet, Stephens did believe slavery was right, and resented any party that continued to make slavery the primary issue in the country. Lincoln had undoubtedly misinterpreted Stephens's understanding of the Union. He felt a Union upheld by force was "nothing short of a consolidated despotism." In concluding, Stephens appealed to wisdom from Proverbs 25:11 to encourage Lincoln to speak publicly before it was too late. "A word fitly spoken by you now would be like 'apples of gold in pictures of silver.' " Lincoln never replied.

Although Lincoln was a reconciler by nature, and his first instinct was to reach out to his former rivals, after Stephens's reply he became more hesitant about including Southerners in his cabinet. In an editorial he placed in the *Illinois State Journal* on December 12, 1860, affirming the "frequent allusion to a supposed purpose on the part of Mr. Lincoln to call into his cabinet two or three Southern gentlemen, from the parties opposed to him politically," he asked two questions.

1. Would such a person "accept a place in the cabinet?"
2. "Does he surrender to Mr. Lincoln, or Mr. Lincoln to him, on the political differences between them?"

Seward, Thurlow Weed, and Judge Davis nevertheless continued to press Lincoln to consider a Southerner. He hosted Weed for a two-day meeting in Springfield on December 20 and 21, 1860. They were joined by Davis and Swett. Weed, a tall man whose elongated nose was compared by cartoonists to Cyrano de Bergerac's, had earned a reputation as a tough political operator in New York. He found himself surprised by his attraction to Lincoln. "While Mr. Lincoln never underestimated the difficulties which surrounded him, his nature was so elastic, and his temperament so cheerful, that he always seemed at ease and undisturbed." Lincoln told Weed that "the making of a cabinet" was not nearly as easy as he had supposed.

Weed encouraged Lincoln to have at least two members of the cabinet from slaveholding states, but Lincoln wondered if these "white crows" could be trusted over the long haul. Vice President–elect Hamlin proposed North Carolina congressman John A. Gilmer, a slaveholder and former Whig. Gilmer had written a long letter to Lincoln on December 10, 1860. "For one politically opposed to you" Gilmer had encouraged Lincoln to write a "clear and definite exposition of your views," which "may go far to quiet, if not satisfy all reasonable minds, that on most of them it will become plain that there is more misunderstanding than difference." To probe what differences there were, Gilmer asked Lincoln six detailed questions. Lincoln replied on December 15 with a question of his own: "May I be pardoned if I ask whether even you have ever attempted to procure the reading of the Republican platform, or my speeches, by the Southern people?" Lincoln wanted to know why a new statement would "meet a better fate? . . . It would make me appear as if I repented for the crime of having been elected, and was anxious to apologize and beg forgiveness." Lincoln referred Gilmer to chapter and verse in the published *Joint Debates* but also answered his questions in some detail. In the end, he said to Gilmer what he said to Alexander Stephens: "You think slavery is right and ought to be extended; we think it is wrong and ought to be restricted." Lincoln did, however, authorize Weed to explore a cabinet position with Gilmer. The matter lingered on through January, Lincoln telling Seward on January 12, 1861, that he still hoped Gilmer would "consent to take a place in the cabinet." Gilmer wrote on January 29 declining the invitation.

A struggle ensued over whether to appoint Henry Winter Davis, a former Whig, or Montgomery Blair, a former Democrat, both from

Maryland, where they were locked in a bitter rivalry for leadership of the Republican Party. In the end, Blair prevailed. At some point Weed asked Lincoln if it was wise to give former Democrats a majority of one in the new cabinet. Lincoln, with his wrinkled smile, replied, "But why do you assume that we are giving that section of our party a majority of the cabinet? You seem to forget that *I* expect to be there; and counting me as one, you see how nicely the cabinet would be balanced and ballasted."

With Bates and now Blair joining the cabinet, Lincoln was content that his choices would appease Southerners. He overestimated the effect the appointment of two border-state politicians—one of whom had been a candidate for the Republican nomination for president—would have on the South's perception of him and failed to understand the violent feelings represented by leaders such as Senators Jefferson Davis of Mississippi, Robert Toombs of Georgia, and John Slidell of Louisiana.

IN LINCOLN'S TRANSITION WINTER, he would spend much more time than he expected in dealing with a Republican house divided. The Republicans of 1856 found cohesion in their role as an opposition party. The Republicans in the winter of 1860–61 had become an institution in power torn between radicals and conservatives who represented different regions and had different viewpoints on slavery and the South.

Lincoln won his leadership spurs in Illinois by building a coalition brought together by initial opposition to the Kansas-Nebraska Act and Stephen Douglas and staying together because of its hatred of Pierce, Buchanan, and Democratic corruption. Many ex-Whigs and ex-Democrats became Republicans more for what they were against than what they were for. Now, Lincoln faced Republican acrimony not only in states such as Pennsylvania, New York, and Maryland, but also on the national stage of the House and Senate in Washington.

The question on everyone's lips was where Lincoln stood in the midst of this spectrum of beliefs. His nomination gave all sides hope that he was on their side. Conservatives voted for him both because he was a former Whig, and because they could not vote for Seward. Radicals knew of his persistent stand against the extension of slavery. As rumors swirled about his cabinet selections, some Republicans became fearful he would surround himself with old-line Whigs; others worried that he would be open to too many ex-Democrats. All factions within the party believed they could persuade him to move in their direction.

In Congress, Republicans and many Democrats—having lost confidence in President Buchanan—scurried to forge some kind of consensus on secession. With Lincoln publicly silent in Springfield, others stepped in to fill the void. Seward became viewed by many as the unofficial head of the party. Once he accepted his new role as secretary of state—a position that in the first seventy-two years of the Republic exhibited far more power over administrative policy than in modern times—he began to exercise leadership, sometimes on his own accord.

Old John J. Crittenden, the unobtrusive seventy-three-year-old senator from Kentucky, offered compromise legislation that he hoped could stop the secessionist impulse. Born during the Constitutional Convention and first entering the Senate at the inauguration of President James Monroe in 1817, Crittenden, an old-line Henry Clay Whig, had seen it all. With his still-erect angular frame, sparkling dark eyes, iron-gray hair, and a tobacco quid in his jaw, he was calm and thoughtful in demeanor. He shone not in speeches on the Senate floor but in the art of private negotiation.

If Lincoln believed he knew Kentucky, Crittenden was convinced he understood it much better. His legislation grew from his experiences in a border state he thought of as three states. Unbridled secessionists nestled together on the southern border with Tennessee, Unionists tended to live along the Ohio River in northern Kentucky, and the central part of the state was inhabited by people who simply wanted to get along. Crittenden believed that in this sense Kentucky represented a microcosm of the nation at large.

Crittenden rose in the Senate on December 18, 1860, to offer a comprehensive package of six constitutional amendments that would remove slavery from federal jurisdiction for all time. The Kentucky senator believed that all agreements since 1787 had been legislative compromises that were always subject to overturning by later Congresses. The first amendment would reinstate the Missouri Compromise all the way to the Pacific Ocean with the effect of protecting slavery south of the line. The second amendment would prohibit Congress from abolishing slavery in slave states. He also called for a congressional resolution on the fugitive slave law that would recognize the law as constitutional but amend it to take out some clauses "obnoxious" to citizens in the North.

Lincoln watched from Springfield as what became known as the Crittenden Plan gathered momentum. Petitions poured into Congress supporting it. Business interests in the North and some Republican leaders believed it could provide a way out of the mounting crisis.

Lincoln opposed the Crittenden Plan because it would permit slavery to expand into the West. Congressman Elihu B. Washburne and Senator Lyman Trumbull were Lincoln's eyes and ears in Congress during these critical months. Washburne wrote from Washington, "The secession feeling has assumed proportions of which I had but a faint conception when I saw you at Springfield, and I think our friends generally in the west are not fully apprised of the imminent peril which now environs us." Lincoln, aware that anxiety would push some in his own party toward compromise, wrote to Trumbull, "Let there be no compromise on the question of *extending* slavery. Stand firm. The tug has to come, & better now, than any time hereafter." Three days later, Lincoln wrote to Washburne, "Prevent, as far as possible, any of our friends . . . entertaining propositions for compromise of any sort. . . . hold firm, as with a chain of steel."

Despite popular support for the Crittenden Plan, including the backing of some Republicans, Lincoln won high marks for steeling Republicans in the Senate to back away from the illusory compromise.

THE SOUTHERN PRESS was filled with indignation at Lincoln's election. "The election of Lincoln . . . means all the insult . . . that such an act can do," spewed the *Wilmington* (North Carolina) *Herald*. The *New Orleans Crescent* summed up the editorial comment of countless Southern papers: "The Northern people, in electing Mr. Lincoln, have perpetrated a deliberate, cold-blooded insult and outrage on the people of the slaveholding states." In the border states of Delaware, Maryland, Kentucky, and Missouri, editors spoke out against talk of secession and disunion. St. Louis's *Missouri Democrat,* a Republican newspaper, wrote, "Throughout the campaign . . . [Lincoln] has been portrayed by most newspapers as an Abolitionist; a fanatic of the John Brown type. Never was a public man so outrageously misrepresented." Nevertheless, the *Richmond Enquirer,* which Lincoln had long read to keep up with the sentiment of the South, charged that "the Northern people, by a sectional vote, have elected a President for the avowed purpose of aggression on Southern rights." The *Enquirer* concluded, "This is a *declaration of war.*"

Lincoln continued to believe that the strong Southern talk was mostly bluff. The North had encountered this bluster before, in 1820 and 1850, and also at the time of the formation of the Republican Party in 1856. The plantation owners were angry, but Lincoln was convinced that the ordinary yeoman farmers, whom he believed he understood, would not, in the end, go along with disunion. He continued to think that sensible leaders would stop any final moves toward separation.

The "tug" Lincoln spoke of in his letter to Trumbull became a jolt on December 20, 1860, when a South Carolina convention, meeting in Charleston, voted unanimously to secede from the Union. The die was cast. Or was it? As politicians and editors raged, everyone wondered about Lincoln's attitude. Even as he refrained from public speaking, people looked to the *Illinois State Journal* for clues to Lincoln's thinking. The *Journal* editorialized that South Carolina could not pull out of the Union without a fight. "If she violates the laws, then comes the tug of war." Editor Baker, in regular conversation with Lincoln, had taken Lincoln's tug analogy from the Trumbull letter. "The President of the United States has a plain duty to perform." The *Journal* worried, "Disunion by armed force, is treason, and treason must and will be put down at all hazards."

Over the next forty days, one by one, the states of Mississippi, Florida, Alabama, Georgia, Louisiana, and Texas voted themselves out of the Union, quickly taking over federal institutions, including forts and arsenals. The whole North waited to see if Virginia, North Carolina, Tennessee, and Arkansas would follow.

IN THE MIDST OF the Union's disintegration, Lincoln made a major priority the preparation of his inaugural address to be delivered in Washington on March 4, 1861. He had begun his research shortly after his election, borrowing from the Illinois State Library *The Statesman's Manual,* a volume published in 1854 that contained the addresses and messages of presidents from 1789 to 1849. Lincoln examined President Andrew Jackson's proclamation in the nullification controversy of 1832. As he had done before his Cooper Union address, Lincoln was looking for historic precedents.

In late December, with the coming of a new governor and the convening of the state legislature scheduled on January 7, 1861, Lincoln had to give up his office in the statehouse. Joel Johnson, who owned an office building on the Springfield square, offered Lincoln the use of two offices on the second floor.

Lincoln discovered that these new offices, even busier than the old,

The *Charleston Mercury's headline trumpeted South Carolina's
secession from the Union on December 20, 1860.*

were not an ideal place to work on an inaugural address. He accepted an invitation from Clark Moulton Smith, his brother-in-law, to use a room on the third floor of his store as his writing space. Lincoln wrote and revised at an old merchant's desk, which contained plenty of pigeon-holes for his many notes.

In January, Lincoln asked Herndon to acquire copies of two speeches he had long appreciated. As a young man living in New Salem, Lincoln had read Daniel Webster's reply to Robert Hayne. In 1830, after Senator Robert Hayne of South Carolina had defended the right of nullifica-tion—arguing that ultimate power rested in the states, which could withdraw from the Union—on the floor of the Senate, Senator Webster of Massachusetts replied to him, closing with the memorable words, "Liberty and Union, now and forever, one and inseparable." Lincoln also asked for a copy of Senator Henry Clay's memorable speech in support of the Compromise of 1850.

By late January, Lincoln asked William H. Bailhache, one of the owners of the *Illinois State Journal,* to secretly print copies of his inaugural address. For an address of this magnitude, he decided to seek the suggestions of a few friends. He asked Judge Davis to read the entire address, but he made no suggestions. Lincoln put copies of his address, plus notes for speeches for the trip to Washington, in a black oilcloth handbag, which he gave to his son Robert for safekeeping on the train and in the cities they would be visiting in February.

TOWARD THE END OF JANUARY, Lincoln began his farewells to family and friends. On January 30, 1861, Lincoln slipped away from reporters and office seekers and traveled by train and horse and buggy to Farmington, a small remote community in Coles County. He wished to see his aging stepmother, Sarah Bush Lincoln. The summer before, when she heard of her stepson's nomination, she feared that if elected something terrible would happen to him. Lincoln also wanted to visit his father's grave, which had stood unmarked since 1851. On this trip, Lincoln ordered a stone marker for it.

Returning to Springfield, Lincoln concluded many personal and family matters. He rented the beloved family home to Lucian Tilton, the retired proprietor of the Wabash Railroad, for $350 a year. The Lincolns sold much of their furniture. They gave away their floppy-eared dog Fido to neighbor boys John and Frank Roll, whose father, John Roll, was the carpenter who had helped remodel the Lincoln home. Fearing a violation of privacy, Mary burned heaps of old letters and papers in the rear alley. Lincoln left a batch of his letters and papers for safekeeping with Elizabeth Grimsley, Mary's cousin. Mistaking the speeches and letters for trash, Grimsley's maid would later burn most of the contents, which included Lincoln's "Discoveries and Inventions" speech as well as the partial drafts from his "House Divided" speech. On February 7, 1861, the Lincolns moved out of their home to the Chenery House, a hotel across from Lincoln's office.

On his final day in Springfield, Sunday, February 10, 1861, Lincoln walked to his law office at 105 South Fifth Street to meet his law partner, Herndon. Lincoln rested his large frame on the comfortable sofa one last time. After the two men reminisced about old times and conferred about unfinished legal business, Lincoln requested that the sign board on its rusty hinges at the foot of the stairway should remain. "Let it hang there undisturbed. . . . If I live I'm coming back some time, and then we'll go right on practicing law as if nothing had ever happened."

On that final evening, Lincoln took some Chenery House cards, turned them over, and wrote, "A. Lincoln, Executive Mansion, Washington." The nearly one hundred days as president-elect in Springfield had come to a close.

ON MONDAY MORNING, February 11, 1861, Lincoln arrived at the small, brick Great Western railway station to begin the journey to Washington. The day dawned cold with rain dripping from low-hanging clouds.

Lincoln had notified the press that he would offer no speech. After the many farewells of recent days, Lincoln believed there was no need for more words. Newspaperman Villard captured a compelling scene. "The President elect took his station in the waiting-room, and allowed his friends to pass by him and take his hand for the last time." Lincoln's "face was pale, and quivered with emotion so deep as to render him almost unable to utter a single word."

The ringing of the engine bell alerted Lincoln that it was time to depart. As Lincoln stepped out onto the platform, friends and neighbors who had come to say their good-byes crowded each side of the special train. Despite his publicly announced intention not to speak, the crowd thronging around the rear platform encouraged their neighbor to offer some remarks.

In response to these requests, Lincoln hesitated, gathering himself to offer a speech he had not intended to give. Caught off guard, in the poignancy of this moment, Lincoln bared his spirit in deeply emotive language: "My friends—No one, not in my situation, can appreciate my feeling of sadness at this parting. To this place, and the kindness of these people, I owe everything." Though his personality usually prompted him to conceal rather than to reveal his emotions, he now spoke openly. The sadness etched in his face was voiced in his words. In twelve succinct words, Lincoln offered heartfelt appreciation to a city where he had lived for nearly twenty-four years, and to his neighbors, and friends.

Then Lincoln quickly moved from past to present: "I now leave, not knowing when, or whether ever, I may return, with a task before me greater than that which rested upon Washington."

Until now, Lincoln had steadfastly avoided speaking about the task that lay ahead. Now, in the midst of spontaneous remarks about community and family, he inserted what might sound like an audacious comment about himself.

Lincoln, as a young boy, had developed a reverence for George Washington through his reading of Mason Locke Weems's *Life of George Washington*. In his address in 1838 to the Young Men's Lyceum, Lincoln had spoken of the less important role of his own generation compared to that of the giants who came before. As a young man, he had said he was standing at the end of the revolutionary generation now being carried away by "the silent artillery of time." Now an "old man" by his own reckoning, he was being summoned by some unsearchable fate or providence "to a task greater than Washington." These words were not boastful. They were offered with a sense of an appointment with destiny.

Lincoln concluded,

Without the assistance of that Divine Being, who ever attended him, I cannot succeed. With that assistance I cannot fail. Trusting in Him, who can go with me, and remain with you and be every where for good, let us confidently hope that all will yet be well. To His care commending you, as I hope in your prayers you will commend me.

He devoted 63 of his 152 words to sketching the omnipresence of God.

The God that Lincoln invoked was more than the creative first force cited by Jefferson. Lincoln appealed to a God who acted in history— who attended George Washington in the past, was able to *go* with Abraham Lincoln to Washington in the present, and would *remain* with Lincoln's friends in Springfield in the future.

In saying "To His care commending you, as I hope in your prayers you will commend me," Lincoln reached for prayer as the invisible connective tissue that would bind him to those he was about to leave.

Lincoln's capacity to connect with his audience was demonstrated in their response. His encouragement to pray elicited shouts of "We will do it, we will do it." As Lincoln turned to enter the train, three cheers split the air, and in a few moments the train chugged slowly forward into the dark morning.

As Lincoln took his seat in the passenger car, the powerful Rogers locomotive began to pull the train slowly east. Newspaper correspondents Henry Villard, Edward L. Baker of the *Illinois State Journal,* and Henry M. Smith of the *Chicago Tribune* crowded around Lincoln and asked about the speech. In response, Lincoln started to write out what he had said. The effects of a moving train made the task difficult, and at the beginning of the fifth sentence, Lincoln handed the paper to John Nicolay, who took up the task of writing while Lincoln dictated.

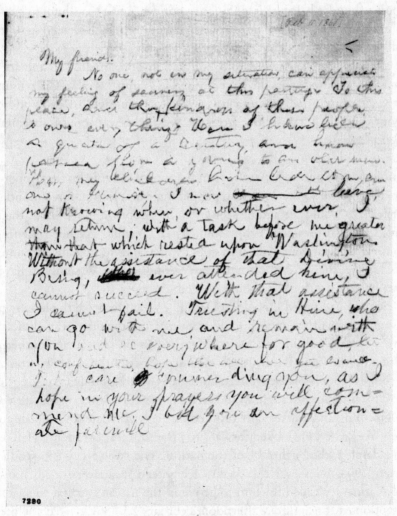

Lincoln, after delivering his farewell address in Springfield, tried to write it down on a bumpy train. He finally dictated it to John Nicolay, who completed writing the brief speech.

Back in Springfield, Lincoln's friend James Conkling described the audience's response to Lincoln's farewell remarks when he wrote his son, Clinton, a good friend of Bob Lincoln's, the next day. As for the crowd, "Many eyes were filled to overflowing." Of "Mr. Lincoln," his "breast heaved with emotion and he could scarcely command his feelings sufficiently to commence."

In the next day's paper, Edward L. Baker editorialized in the *Journal,* "We have known Mr. Lincoln for many years; we have heard him speak upon a hundred different occasions; but we never saw him so profoundly affected, nor did he ever utter an address which seemed to us so full of simple and touching eloquence."

Lincoln's farewell words did not stay in Springfield. His remarks appeared in newspapers the next day and in *Harper's Weekly*. Citizens in large cities and small towns across America were eager to know more about this gangly rail splitter from the West who was about to become their president.

LINCOLN'S JOURNEY TO WASHINGTON would provide his first opportunity to speak to the American people since his election three months earlier. He would see and be seen by more people in more places than any American president before him. After Lincoln's extended silence, politicians, press, and ordinary people were eager to take his measure. Yet his speeches on his journey from Springfield to Washington have usually been overlooked or undervalued.

Seward had urged Lincoln in December 1860 to make the long trip through some of the most populous states, from the prairies of Illinois, across central Indiana and Ohio, down to Cincinnati to the Southern border on the Ohio River. In Cleveland and Pittsburgh, Lincoln would encounter people on the western border of the urban-industrial edge of an expanding America. He would arrive in New York in a region settled by New England Yankees and proceed through the center of the state to New York City. He looked forward to his visit to Independence Hall in Philadelphia, the birthplace of the nation. The twelve-day trip would cover 1,904 miles over the tracks of eighteen separate railroads. Lincoln's itinerary called for him to arrive in the nation's capital to a gala reception late on Saturday afternoon, February 23, 1861, ten days before his inauguration.

The events of the twelve days took on the festive moods of a carnival, a political rally, and a religious revival. Between the major cities, the train would make numerous stops at small towns decorated with American flags. Lincoln would say again and again that the celebrations were not about a person, but about an office and a nation. He insisted that the guest lists should not be partisan. In that spirit, he invited supporters of Stephen Douglas, John Breckinridge, and John Bell to ride with him.

Whatever the original reasons for the journey, by the time of Lincoln's departure from Springfield it had become controversial. Seward had long ago changed his mind about the wisdom of the trip. He wrote on December 29, 1860, informing Lincoln of a Southern plot to seize the capital on or before March 4. Seward stated, "I therefore renew my suggestion of your coming earlier than you otherwise would—and coming in by surprise—without announcement." Lincoln did not take Seward's counsel and continued planning his extended preinaugural trip. Nicolay wrote that Lincoln "had no fondness for public display," but well understood "the importance of personal confidence and live sympathy" between a leader and his constituents.

AS IF LINCOLN'S TRAIN TRIP to Washington were not drama enough, a second train with another president-elect departed on the same day, February 11, 1861, bound for his own inauguration. Only one week before Lincoln's departure, on February 4, delegates from six Southern states gathered in Montgomery, Alabama, to begin the task of hammering out a new nation. Four days later, this Confederate convention adopted a provisional constitution. The next day, they unanimously elected a provisional president, Jefferson Davis, and a provisional vice president, Lincoln's friend Alexander Stephens of Georgia.

Starting on February 11, 1861, all eyes across the nation were fixed on not one but two trains. After departing from Springfield, Lincoln's moved slowly east through Indianapolis, Columbus, and Pittsburgh toward Washington. Davis, after leaving his plantation, Brierfield, in Mississippi, was carried by boat to Vicksburg, and then traveled by train in a roundabout route to Jackson, Chattanooga, and Atlanta, and then west toward Montgomery, the Confederate capital. The public's fascination with these two journeys to two capitals was chronicled in the *New York Times* on February 11, 1861, in two columns placed side by side:

The New Administration   The New Confederacy

LINCOLN'S TRAIN ARRIVED at its first overnight stop at Indianapolis right on schedule at 5 p.m. on February 11, 1861. Governor Oliver P. Morton, Indiana's first native-born governor, welcomed Lincoln who, on the first of many occasions, had to reply extemporaneously to welcoming words by a local politician. In his remarks Lincoln offered what would become an oft-repeated demur: "I do not expect, upon this occasion, or on any occasion, till after I get to Washington, to attempt any lengthy speech."

Lincoln referred to himself as an "accidental instrument." He would work with this metaphor in several ways in the days ahead. In Indianapolis, he restricted his responsibility as president by saying his role was "temporary" and "for a limited time." His real purpose, he said, was to encourage the responsibilities ordinary citizens must ask of one another.

During an evening reception for members of the Indiana legislature, Lincoln grew impatient as he asked for the speeches that he had entrusted to his son. The boy and the bag were missing. When Robert, who was being called "the Prince of rails" by his young friends, finally arrived, he explained that he had left the oilcloth bag with the hotel clerk. Lincoln bid a hasty departure to the reception, and his long legs carried him quickly down the stairs to the hotel lobby. Burrowing through the pile of luggage, Lincoln attacked the first bag that looked like his, but it surrendered only a dirty shirt, playing cards, and a half-empty whiskey bottle. He quickly discovered his bag and recovered the copies of the inaugural address and other speeches, the whole episode good for a laugh at the end of an exhausting day.

While in Indianapolis, Lincoln gave Orville H. Browning, who had accompanied Lincoln on the train, one of the copies of his inaugural address. Upon his return to Springfield, Browning wrote his response to Lincoln. He made a single proposal, which he wrote at the bottom of the page of Lincoln's text. He suggested that Lincoln "modify" the passage: "All the power at my disposal will be used to reclaim the public property and places which have fallen; to hold, occupy and possess these, and all other property and places belonging to the government, and to collect the duties on imports; but beyond what may be necessary for these, there will be no invasion of any State."

Browning told Lincoln, "On principle the passage is right as it now stands. The fallen places ought to be reclaimed. But cannot that be accomplished as well, or even better without announcing the purpose in your inaugural?" He suggested revising the sentence to delete the clause, "to reclaim the public property and places which have fallen."

JEFFERSON DAVIS'S PRESIDENTIAL TRAIN pulled into Jackson, Mississippi, on the evening of February 11, 1861. Encircled by well-wishers, he spoke at the capitol to an audience that "occupied every available inch of space." Davis declared that he deplored war but would face it "with stern serenity of one who knows his duty and intends to perform it." He asserted that England and France will "not allow our great staple to be dammed up within our limits." Finally, if war came, Davis promised to "go forward . . . with a firm resolve to do his duty as God might grant him power."

THE PRESIDENTIAL SPECIAL arrived in Columbus on February 13, 1861, punctually at 2 p.m. Lincoln went directly to the capitol, where he addressed the Ohio legislature. In his prepared remarks he said, "I have not maintained silence from any want to real anxiety. It is a good thing that there is no more than anxiety, for there is nothing going wrong. . . . We entertain different views upon political questions, but nobody is suffering anything."

Lincoln's remark "there is nothing going wrong" added to the controversy that was building toward his inauguration. Supporters contended that his remarks were part of a strategy to diminish public alarm. Critics argued that Lincoln's remarks exposed a president-elect out of touch with the forces gearing up for civil war.

Meanwhile, Jefferson Davis traveled through Mississippi and Alabama on February 14, 1861, the firing of cannons welcoming him at many stops. In Stevenson, in northeastern Alabama, he told the crowd he expected the border states to become part of the Confederate States of America within sixty days. He also declared that "England will recognize us, and . . . grass will grow in the northern cities where the pavements have been worn off by the tread of commerce." Davis concluded by saying he "hopes for peace but is prepared for war."

ON THE MORNING OF FEBRUARY 15, 1861, Lincoln spoke from the balcony of the Monongahela House in Pittsburgh to a crowd of five thousand standing under umbrellas. After Columbus, he was determined to sidestep questions about an impending civil war and instead spoke about the tariff, a topic of great importance in Pennsylvania. He declared that because there was no direct taxation, a tariff was necessary. "The tariff is to the government what a meal is to the family." In speaking about protections for home industries, Lincoln stated, "I must confess I do not understand the subject in all its multiform bearings."

Villard characterized the Pittsburgh speech as "the least creditable performance" of the entire trip. "What he said was really nothing but crude, ignorant twaddle." He believed that this speech proved Lincoln to be "the veriest novice in economic matters."

Next, Lincoln backtracked to Cleveland. Here he was entering greater New England, for the northern tier of Ohio was settled by westward-moving Yankees from the New England states. New England, and by extension northern New York and northern Ohio, were the regions that supported abolitionism most strongly. Cheering spectators stood in deep mud along Euclid Street. Lincoln told the assembled crowd, "Frequent allusion is made to the excitement at present existing in our national politics, and it is as well that I should also allude to it here. I think that there is no occasion for any excitement. The crisis, as it is called, is altogether an artificial crisis."

These remarks only fueled the controversy begun in Columbus. Did the president-elect not understand the escalating crisis?

The nation's greatest orator read the daily newspaper reports of Lincoln's speeches. Edward Everett, a native of Massachusetts, had served with distinction in a multiplicity of offices for over four decades. He began as a young professor at Harvard in 1819 and later returned as president of the nation's oldest college. Everett served Massachusetts as congressman, senator, and governor and represented the United States as secretary of state and minister to England. On February 15, 1861, he wrote in his diary, "These speeches thus far have been of the most ordinary kind, destitute of everything, not merely of felicity and grace, but of common pertinence." Everett, who believed that speeches were a mirror revealing the character of the person, had formed an opinion about Lincoln. "He is evidently a person of very inferior cast of character, wholly unequal to the crisis."

LINCOLN LEFT CLEVELAND on the morning of February 16, 1861. The train traveled east again, through Ohio and across the northwest corner of Pennsylvania. Entering New York, the Presidential Special chugged along the shore of Lake Erie. The first stop was Westfield, where a banner was stretched across the tracks emblazoned, "Welcome Abraham Lincoln to the Empire State."

He told the crowd that several months earlier he had received a letter from a "young lady" from Westfield. His correspondent recommended that he "let his whiskers grow, as it would improve my personal appearance." Lincoln had accepted her counsel, and now he wished to know if she was present in the crowd. A small boy cried out, "There she is Mr. Lincoln." Grace Bedell, a blushing eleven-year-old girl with dark eyes, stepped from the crowd, and President-elect Lincoln gave her several hearty kisses "amid the yells of delight from the excited crowd."

Lincoln arrived in Buffalo in the afternoon. Exhausted, at the half-

Lincoln, upon his arrival in Westfield, New York, asked to see Grace Bedell, the young girl who had written to tell him he would look better in whiskers.

way point of his long train trip, he rested on the Sabbath, attending church the next day with former president Millard Fillmore. Across the street from Lincoln's hotel, a banner on the Young Men's Christian Association building was inscribed with words of reply to Lincoln's farewell remarks at Springfield: "We Will Pray For You."

JEFFERSON DAVIS ENDURED his longest day of traveling and speaking on February 16, 1861. Arriving in Atlanta at about four o'clock in the morning, he spoke at midmorning, taking aim at Northern abolition-ism, especially "its systematic aggression upon the constitutional rights of the South for the last forty years."

After the speech, Davis boarded his special car on the Atlanta and West Point Railroad and headed west across Georgia. During the day he stopped to speak in Fairburn, Palmetto, Newman, Grantville, LaGrange, and West Point. At each stop he was greeted by women wav-ing their handkerchiefs. Entering Alabama, the Davis train stopped for speeches at Opelika and Auburn. A correspondent for the *New York Tri-bune* reported that Davis would give elements of the same speech several times during his many stops. Davis arrived in Montgomery, Alabama, at 10 p.m. at the completion of his eight-hundred-mile train trip.

On Monday, February 18, 1861, while Lincoln's train traveled through the Mohawk Valley toward Albany, Lincoln learned that Jeffer-son Davis had taken the oath of office as provisional president of the Confederate States of America, and Alexander Stephens the oath of office as vice president. In Montgomery, Davis gave his inaugural address from the portico of the Alabama capitol building, which was now the capitol of the Confederacy. Without a national anthem, the band played "La Marseillaise," the national anthem of France.

Davis spoke to his fellow Southerners, to the citizens of the United States, and to foreign nations who had a vital interest in the availability of cotton. He never mentioned Lincoln. The speech was remarkably mild; some in the audience had expected to hear a trumpet call to war. As for oratory, the second sentence of the address was typical.

> Looking forward to the speedy establishment of a permanent government to take the place of this, and which by its greater moral and physical power will be better able to combat with the many difficulties which arise from the conflicting interests of separate nations, I enter upon the duties of the office to which I have been chosen with the hope that the beginning of our career as a Confederacy may not be obstructed by hostile opposition to our enjoyment of the separate existence and independence which we have asserted, and, with the blessing of Providence, intend to maintain.

This sentence of one hundred words reveals the limitations of Davis's leadership. The sentences would only get longer as the speech unfolded.

The contrast to Lincoln's economy of language and rhetorical artistry would become even more apparent in the four years to come.

LINCOLN ARRIVED IN NEW YORK CITY on Tuesday, February 19, 1861, at 3 p.m. with what had to be mixed emotions. He was returning to the scene of his triumph at Cooper Union the previous winter, but though he had carried the state in the election, he received less than 35 percent of the vote in the city.

An apprehensive crowd estimated at more than two hundred thousand greeted Lincoln. One astute observer was Walt Whitman, the young poet who was in the midst of negotiations with a Boston publisher to bring out an expanded third edition of his *Leaves of Grass*. Whitman found himself on the top of a Broadway omnibus stalled in traffic. He took the measure of Lincoln for the first time.

> I had, I say, a capital view of it all, and especially of Mr. Lincoln, his look and gait—his perfect composure and coolness—his unusual and uncouth height, his dress of complete black, stovepipe hat pushed back on the head, dark-brown complexion, seam'd and wrinkled yet canny-looking face, black, bushy head of hair, disproportionately long neck, and his hands held behind him as he stood observing the people.

Whitman wrote of Lincoln, "He look'd with curiosity upon that immense sea of faces, and the sea of faces return'd the look with similar curiosity."

The poet spied hostility as well as curiosity and admiration in the crowd. "Many an assassin's knife and pistol lurk'd in hip or breast-pocket there, ready, as soon as break and riot came."

Another interested eyewitness was George Templeton Strong. Strong, a lawyer, Episcopal vestryman, and trustee of Columbia College, was a careful observer of political events. In 1835, at age fifteen, he began to write in uniform blank books every evening before he went to bed. He wrote for the next forty years. The diary, ultimately comprising nearly four and a half million words, would remain unknown to the public for more than fifty years after Strong's death in 1875. A supporter of Seward, Strong had been following Lincoln's trip as it wound its way toward New York. He wrote an appraisal in his diary. "Lincoln is making little speeches as he wends his way towards Washington, and has said some things that are sound and credible and raise him in my esteem." However, Strong confided, "But I should have been better pleased with him had he held his tongue altogether."

Strong walked uptown on Broadway the next afternoon to join the crowd welcoming Lincoln. Later that evening Strong recorded in his diary, "The great rail-splitter's face was visible to me for an instant, and seemed a keen, clear, honest face, not so ugly as his portraits."

AFTER LINCOLN HAD SPENT more than a week on the Presidential Special, newspapers across the North and South began to weigh in with their assessments of his preinaugural speeches. The *Baltimore Sun,* with ardent Southern sympathies, offered the opinion, "He approaches the capital of the country more in the character of a harlequin," or a character in a comedy. "There is that about his speechification which, if it were not for the gravity of the occasion, would be ludicrous." The pro-Lincoln *Chicago Tribune* countered, "The wiseacres who indulge in criticism of the verbal structure of Mr. Lincoln's recent speeches" were off the mark. The *Tribune*'s defense pointed out that former presidents George Washington and Andrew Jackson did not have the "gift of gab" when asked to speak extemporaneously.

Yet some pro-Lincoln editors were worried. Samuel Bowles, editor of the *Springfield* (Massachusetts) *Republican,* had been enthusiastic about Lincoln when he heard him speak in Boston in 1848, and the paper had supported Lincoln in the 1860 election. But Bowles was concerned as he read reports of Lincoln's speeches. On February 26, 1861, he wrote to Henry L. Dawes, a member of Congress from Massachusetts, of his discouragement both with Lincoln and the disagreements rankling the Republican Party. Bowles told Dawes, "Lincoln is a 'simple Susan.' "

Among Republicans in Congress trepidation abounded. In several speeches, when Lincoln seemed to be supporting coercion of the South, his words were taken to be a refutation of Seward's efforts at conciliation. In other speeches, Lincoln seemed to point toward a policy of moderation. Questioners wondered whether Lincoln was wavering in his position or even certain of his own opinion.

Charles Francis Adams, the son and grandson of presidents, whom Seward would soon propose to Lincoln to become minister to England, was deeply concerned. He confided to his diary on February 20, 1861, "[Lincoln's speeches] betray a person unconscious of his position as well as the nature of the contest around him." Adams thought that Lincoln was "good-natured, kindly," but he considered the president-elect "frivolous and uncertain." In Adams's evaluation, Lincoln's speeches "put to flight all notions of greatness."

THE PRESIDENTIAL SPECIAL departed New York at 9:05 a.m. on February 21, 1861, reaching Trenton, the state capital of New Jersey, at 11:50 a.m. Speaking in the Senate chamber, Lincoln told the legislators that of all the accounts of the "struggles for liberties," none remained so fixed in his mind as Washington crossing the Delaware and winning the battle at Trenton on December 26, 1776.

At Indianapolis, Lincoln had spoken of himself as an "accidental instrument." At Trenton, he changed his meaning and his metaphor: "I shall be most happy indeed if I shall be an humble instrument in the hands of the Almighty, and of this, his almost chosen people." Lincoln often pointed to his humble beginnings, but his depiction of the American people as an "almost chosen people" is one of his most enigmatic phrases. The concept that Americans were God's chosen people arrived with the Puritans. This identity flourished in the eighteenth century and, whether in secular or religious versions, undergirded the revolutionary generation that founded a new nation in 1776. In the middle of the nineteenth century, Americans added the sense of "manifest destiny," the right and duty to inhabit and civilize the whole of the continent to promote the great experiment in democracy.

Lincoln never clarified "almost." Is his qualification an allusion to slavery? In an era of absolutes, whether sponsored by abolitionists or secessionists, Lincoln could live comfortably with the uncertainties facing an "almost chosen people."

Lincoln reached Philadelphia at 4 p.m. on Thursday, February 21, 1861. In response to greetings from Mayor Alexander Henry, Lincoln declared his fidelity to the Declaration of Independence and the Constitution. "All my political warfare has been in favor of the teachings coming forth from that sacred hall." Lincoln used fiery imagery from the Psalms to swear his allegiance: "May my right hand forget its cunning and my tongue cleave to the roof of my mouth, if ever I prove false to those teachings."

The next day, the booming of cannon and the ringing of church bells announced the celebration of the birthday of George Washington. Early in the morning, Lincoln traveled by carriage to Independence Hall where he participated in the raising of the new American flag with

Lincoln, bareheaded, raised the flag at Independence Hall in Philadelphia. F. DeBourg took this photograph just after sunrise on George Washington's birthday, February 22, 1861.

thirty-four stars, the final star for Kansas, which had been admitted as a state on January 29, 1861. Lincoln told the huge crowd, "I have never had a feeling, politically, that did not spring from the sentiments embodied in the Declaration of Independence."

He had offered this sentiment a number of times since his reemergence into politics in 1854, but Lincoln must have taken special delight in affirming his loyalty to the Declaration of Independence at the place where the sacred document was signed more than eighty-four years before. To underline his commitment to this principle, he told his audience, "I would rather be assassinated on the spot than to surrender it."

On the previous evening, Lincoln had been startled to learn of a plan to kill him before he could reach Washington. In his room at the Continental Hotel, Lincoln met Allan Pinkerton, a Chicago detective whose company worked for the Philadelphia, Wilmington, and Baltimore Railroad. Pinkerton informed Lincoln that his detectives had uncovered a plot to assassinate him as his train car was pulled by horses through the streets of Baltimore in the middle of the day. Pinkerton insisted that no one in the presidential party be told of the plot and that Lincoln take a train for Washington that night. He refused. He insisted on keeping his date at Independence Hall.

Lincoln left Philadelphia at 9 a.m. for the 106-mile trip to Harrisburg, the state capital of Pennsylvania. Governor Andrew Curtin met Lincoln and took him to the state capitol, where he addressed the legislature in joint session.

At dusk, the plans for Lincoln's secret trip to Washington were put into action. Instead of traveling with his usual stovepipe hat, Lincoln wore a soft Kossuth hat given to him in New York. At Philadelphia, Lincoln boarded a sleeping car, accompanied by only Pinkerton and Ward Hill Lamon, his Illinois lawyer friend and now bodyguard, but no one slept. Lincoln was so tall that he "could not lay straight in his berth." The train arrived in Baltimore at about 3:30 a.m., and Lincoln's car was transferred to the Camden Street Station, where he boarded a Baltimore and Ohio train and waited in the dark for thirty minutes before departing at 4:15 a.m. for Washington. Lincoln arrived at the Baltimore and Ohio depot at New Jersey Avenue and C Street at six in the morning, almost ten hours ahead of his scheduled late-afternoon arrival and reception. He arrived in Washington virtually alone, unannounced and unrecognized.

Allan Pinkerton, a Chicago detective who uncovered a plot to assassinate Lincoln in Baltimore, accompanied the president-elect on a secretive night journey to Washington.

Lincoln, exhausted from his twelve-day train trip, went to Mathew Brady's studio probably the day after his arrival in Washington. Alexander Gardner took five poses of a president-elect deep in thought.

CHAPTER 17

We Must Not Be Enemies
February 1861–April 1861

THE MYSTIC CHORDS OF MEMORY, STRETCHING FROM EVERY BAT-
TLEFIELD, AND PATRIOT GRAVE, TO EVERY LIVING HEART AND
HEARTH-STONE, ALL OVER THIS BROAD LAND, WILL YET SWELL THE
CHORUS OF THE UNION, WHEN AGAIN TOUCHED, AS SURELY THEY
WILL BE, BY THE BETTER ANGELS OF OUR NATURE.

ABRAHAM LINCOLN
First inaugural address, March 4, 1861

AS THE SUN WAS ABOUT TO RISE OVER WASHINGTON ON SATURDAY
morning, February 23, 1861, Abraham Lincoln, arriving incognito at the
Baltimore and Ohio railway depot, was met by a party of one. Congressman Elihu B. Washburne stepped out from behind a pillar, "caught
hold of Lincoln," and exclaimed, "Abe, you can't play that on me." Allan
Pinkerton, on Lincoln's left, "hit the gentleman with a punch," causing
Washburne to stagger back. The detective, worried that the plot to smuggle the president-elect through Baltimore in the middle of the night had
been discovered, stepped toward what he assumed was an assailant, when
Lincoln intervened. "Don't strike him—that is my friend Washburne."

Indeed, Washburne, Lincoln's Republican colleague from Galena,
Illinois, had discovered Lincoln's new schedule from William Seward's
son, Frederick. Seward had intended to meet Lincoln at the station, but
overslept. With calm restored, Washburne arranged for a carriage to
take Lincoln to the Willard Hotel at the corner of Pennsylvania Avenue
and Fourteenth Street. Because of his unexpected early arrival, the
hotel gave Lincoln temporary quarters before lodging him later that day
in Parlor Suite 6, consisting of two bedrooms and two parlors on the
corner of the second floor overlooking the White House.

Lincoln joined Governor Seward, as he liked to be called, who had hurried to the hotel for breakfast. Seward's appearance was both unusual, with his slender build and beaklike nose, and impressive, with his vigorous personality conveyed through his animated eyes. Lincoln had met Seward only twice, once in September 1848, when they both campaigned in New England on behalf of presidential candidate Zachary Taylor, and five months earlier, when Seward traveled through Springfield in the midst of a campaign tour in the West. Now Seward informed Lincoln of up-to-the-minute occurrences in the frenzied capital.

Lincoln's secret arrival created a sensation. George Templeton Strong, reading the "Extras" published by noon in New York, recognized the problems the early morning arrival could create for the president-elect. He wrote in his diary, "This surreptitious nocturnal dodging or sneaking of the President-elect into his capital city, under cloud of night, will be used to damage his moral position and throw ridicule on his Administration."

Frederick Douglass, capturing the poignancy of Lincoln's arrival from the vantage point of black Americans, wrote,

> He reached the Capital as the poor, hunted fugitive slave reaches the North, in disguise, seeking concealment, evading persuers, by the underground railroad, between two days, not during the sunlight, but crawling and dodging under the sable wing of night. He changed his programme, took another route, started at another hour, traveled in other company, and arrived at another time in Washington.

In the end, Douglass declared, "We have no censure for the President at this point. He only did what braver men have done."

ON HIS FIRST MORNING IN WASHINGTON, Lincoln called on President Buchanan and his cabinet at the Executive Mansion. Buchanan's manner suggested that he could not wait for the inauguration of the new president.

Lincoln requested that the Illinois delegation meet with him at the Willard at 4 p.m. He especially wanted to speak with Senator Stephen Douglas. Their relationship in recent years had been as opposing candidates for the Senate and for the presidency. Although attention has often focused on Lincoln reaching out to his Republican rivals, Lincoln's rapprochement with Douglas, his Democratic rival, in whose shadow he had lived his whole political life, was even more remarkable. Lincoln was shocked at Douglas's appearance. He did not look well. Lincoln surmised the strain of constant campaigning had taken its toll. He had heard that Douglas was drinking too much. On this afternoon, Lincoln expressed his delight to see his old Illinois competitor. The two men shared more in common than the casual observer might have thought. They both believed in the indivisibility of the Union. A newspaper correspondent reported a "peculiarly pleasant" meeting between the two leaders. Later in the day, Adele Douglas, "with graceful courtesy," called on Mary Lincoln.

Lincoln went to Seward's home at 7 p.m. for a private dinner with Seward and Vice President–elect Hamlin. Seward, pleased with his initial day with Lincoln, wrote that evening to his wife, Frances, of his first impressions. "He is very cordial and kind toward me . . . simple, natural, and agreeable."

The next day, Sunday, Lincoln joined Seward for worship at St. John's Episcopal Church on Lafayette Square. Upon their return to his hotel, Lincoln asked Seward if he would read his inaugural address and suggest any changes. Lincoln had earlier asked David Davis and Orville Browning, longtime friends, for their suggestions. When Lincoln requested Seward to scrutinize his speech, he approached a new colleague: a former rival who was not yet a friend.

Lincoln must have been surprised when Seward responded with a seven-page letter containing forty-nine suggestions, as well as two options for a new final paragraph. Working with the final version printed in Springfield, Seward had carefully numbered every line on the seven pages as the template for his editorial effort. He told Lincoln, "Your case is quite like that of Jefferson." Thomas Jefferson won a contentious election not finally decided until thirty-six ballots were cast in the House of Representatives in February 1801. At Jefferson's inauguration on March 4, 1801, the resentment of the defeated Federalists could be felt almost everywhere, especially in the visible absence of Federalist John Adams, defeated for a second term as president. Seward reminded Lincoln that Jefferson "sank the partisan in the patriot in his inaugural address, and propitiated his adversaries by declaring: 'We are all Federalists, all Republicans.' " Seward advised, "Be sure that while all your administrative conduct will be in harmony with Republican principles and policy, you cannot lose the Republican Party by practicing in your advent to office the magnanimity of a victor." Lincoln integrated, if sometimes recast, twenty-seven of Seward's forty-nine suggestions.

THE NINE DAYS BETWEEN Lincoln's arrival in Washington and his inauguration were both exhilarating and exhausting. On Monday afternoon, Seward, who had acquired the nickname "the premier" because of the lead role he hoped to play in the new administration, squired Lincoln to the Capitol. Lincoln walked into the Senate chamber and shook hands with senators from both sides of the aisle. In the House of Representatives, where he had served one term more than a decade before, he accepted congratulations from Republicans as well as a few—but not all—of the remaining Southern members. Finally, Lincoln called upon the Supreme Court, conversing with Chief Justice Roger Taney and the other justices responsible for the Dred Scott decision of 1857.

One visitor immediately gained access to the president-elect. Francis Preston Blair, patriarch of a distinguished Kentucky Democratic family, had supported Edward Bates at the Republican convention, but he quickly offered his support and advice to Lincoln. Blair first came to Washington in 1830 when President Andrew Jackson asked him to become the founding editor of the *Congressional Globe*. Approaching his seventieth birthday, Blair, with his sons Montgomery and Francis, Jr., had become prominent in the politics of two critical border states, Maryland and Missouri.

Blair had gained Lincoln's confidence with a long, incisive letter in January wherein he offered useful evaluations of the various personalities in Washington. He warned Lincoln about the political efforts in Washington to compromise with the South. "You are about to assume a position of greater responsibility than Washington ever occupied." Why? Because the states had grown far more powerful than the colonies. However, Blair stated, there existed a crucial difference between then and now. "Washington had to assist him in administration the genius and virtue of Adams, Jefferson, and Hamilton," whereas Lincoln was surrounding himself with cabinet members, such as Seward and Simon Cameron, of "greedy & unscrupulous ambition that really rejoices in the principle that 'every man has his price.' " Blair counseled Lincoln that "neither you, nor they can change their natures." Blair did offer a word of encouragement. "You need not depend on clerks or Cabinets if your own sound & honest sense is known to preside in the administration."

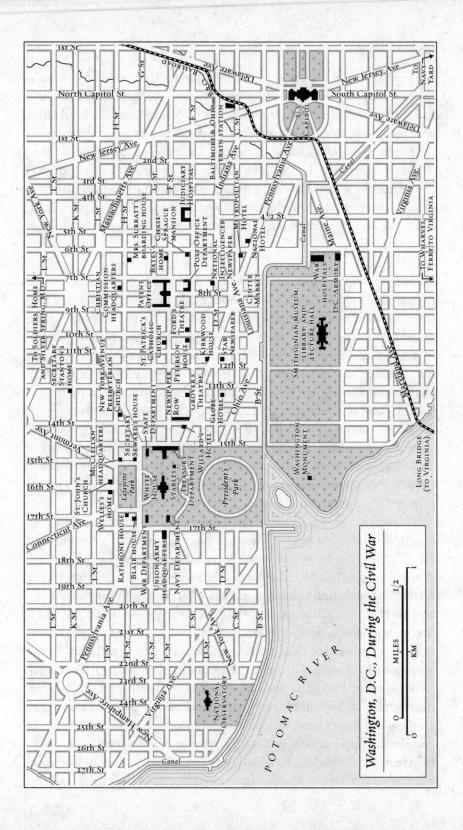

Washington, D.C., During the Civil War

Throughout the week, Lincoln found himself honored and feted at celebrations, dinners, and receptions. Gideon Welles, whom Lincoln had met in Connecticut after his Cooper Union address and would now appoint as secretary of the navy, reported, "A host of ravenous partisans from Maine to California" including "a large proportion of those Whigs long excluded from office," descended upon Washington and "besieged the White House." Lincoln told reporter Henry Villard, "It was bad enough in Springfield, but it was child's play compared with this tussle here. I hardly have a chance to eat or sleep. I am fair game for that hungry lot."

IN THE MIDST OF innumerable requests for meetings, Lincoln worked to complete his cabinet—or so he thought. At each social gathering Lincoln found himself under immense pressure as Republican leaders pressed the credentials of their friends and colleagues. Newspaper editors, especially Horace Greeley of the *New York Tribune* and James Gordon Bennett of the *New York Herald,* were enjoying publishing continually shifting lists of who would or should join the cabinet.

On Tuesday afternoon, February 26, 1861, Lincoln returned to the Senate to carry out a plan he had decided upon in Springfield. He requested to see each Republican senator in alphabetical order. He asked only one question: Who was their choice for secretary of the treasury? Lincoln did not ask what they thought of Cameron or Chase. Lincoln surprised the senators and cabinet watchers by his open posture.

Although seeking counsel from many persons, Lincoln carried with him in his right vest pocket the small piece of paper in which he first listed his choices for the cabinet. The final list would not differ much from the original list jotted down on the evening of his election. He did invite Senator Simon Cameron of Pennsylvania to join the cabinet. He met with Ohio senator Salmon Chase in Springfield, and again in his first days in Washington, but had not yet tendered him a formal invitation for a cabinet position. Lincoln had settled on the tall Marylander Montgomery Blair, son of Francis Preston Blair, for postmaster general, which allowed him to say he had included Southerners in his cabinet. Blair spoke of secessionists with disdain, which helped explain the growing dislike between Blair and Seward. Indiana believed it had been promised an appointment by David Davis. Lincoln had decided on fifty-two-year-old Caleb Smith, whom he knew from his term in Congress, when several from the Hoosier state suggested Schuyler Colfax, thirty-seven-year-old congressman from South Bend. In the end, Lincoln settled on the person he knew, the bland Smith, for the Interior Department. Lincoln, concerned that Colfax believed he was passed over because of his alleged pro-Douglas activity in 1858, wrote to him, "When you were brought forward I said 'Colfax is a young man—is already in position—is running a brilliant career, and is sure of a bright future in any event'—With Smith, it is now or never.' " Lincoln concluded, "I now have to beg that you will not do me the injustice to suppose, for a moment, that I remember any thing against you in malice."

Just when everything seemed settled with the cabinet, Seward resigned on the eve of the inauguration in a terse letter. "Circumstances which have occurred since I expressed to you in December last my willingness to accept the office of Secretary of State seem to me to render it my duty to ask leave to withdraw that consent." What circumstances? Seward did not say, but Lincoln knew he had objected strenuously to the prospect of the appointment of Salmon P. Chase to the cabinet.

What could Lincoln do? On the morning of his inauguration, while the inaugural parade lined up in the street below, Lincoln wrote out a reply and gave it to John Nicolay to copy. He told his secretary, "I can't afford to let Seward take the first trick." Having only a day to consider Seward's request, Lincoln wrote that the reception of the note was extremely "painful" but "I feel constrained to beg that you will countermand the withdrawal." Lincoln had heard and seen that Seward had many opponents in Washington, but Lincoln had come to value his abilities. "The public interest, I think, demands that you should; and my personal feelings are deeply enlisted in the same direction." He asked Seward to answer by 9 a.m. on March 5, 1861, the first working day of the new administration. On the evening of March 4, Seward called on Lincoln at the Executive Mansion and the two "had a long and confidential talk." Seward withdrew his letter and agreed to "remain."

Lincoln's absorption with completing his cabinet left him open to criticism. Charles Francis Adams believed that in Lincoln's first weeks in Washington he seemed "more intent on the distribution of offices than on the gravity of the crisis" in the South. Gideon Welles, the new secretary of the navy, wrote that Lincoln "was accused of wasting his time in a great emergency on mere party appointments."

MARCH 4, 1861, dawned windy, cool, and overcast. A crowd of between twenty-five and thirty thousand, including a large number of

"Western men," began arriving in the early hours to find places close enough to hear Lincoln's address. Riflemen stationed themselves on the rooftops of buildings along Pennsylvania Avenue. Soldiers on horseback patrolled all the major crossroads. Sharpshooters kept the inaugural platform under close watch from windows in the Capitol.

Precisely at twelve o'clock, President-elect Lincoln came out a side door of the Willard. He wore a new black suit, a white shirt, and black boots. He had on a tall black hat and held in his hand an ebony cane with a gold head. While a band played "Hail to the Chief," Lincoln waved away a closed carriage and took his seat in an open four-seated carriage opposite President Buchanan, where he could be seen by the people. Buchanan "appeared pale and wearied." As the carriage bounced along the cobblestones of Pennsylvania Avenue, Buchanan said to Lincoln, "If you are as happy in entering the White House as I shall feel on returning to Wheatland you are a happy man."

In Lincoln's time, the inaugural parade preceded the inaugural address. One hundred marshals, dressed in blue, orange, and pink, guided their horses at the front of the parade. All along the parade route, between the White House and the Capitol, American flags soared in the breeze from open windows. Soldiers were grouped so closely around the open presidential carriage that it was difficult to see Lincoln. Ahead, rising over the nation's capital, Lincoln could see the Capitol. The wooden dome that Lincoln saw when he arrived for his single term in Congress in 1847 had been taken down. A decision had been made in 1855 to build a new iron dome. All Lincoln could see on this inaugural day was the arm of a huge crane extending up from the unfinished dome.

No inaugural address had ever been presented in such turbulent times. Rumors raced through the capital of threats to Lincoln and of attacks on Washington. Hundreds of disgruntled Southerners remained in the capital on Inauguration Day.

Lincoln took his place in the front row on the massive platform that had been constructed on the east front of the Capitol. Stephen Douglas sat nearby. Lincoln had asked silver-haired Senator Edward D. Baker of Oregon, who as a young legislator in Illinois had outshone Lincoln as a speaker, to introduce him. As Lincoln stood, he realized there was no place to put his top hat and cane. Douglas stepped forward and asked if he could hold them. Lincoln took out his steel-rimmed spectacles and stepped forward to the small speaker's table.

Lincoln saw a very different Capitol when he returned to Washington in 1861.
The old dome was removed in 1856, and at the time of his inauguration a crane can be seen
sticking through the opening of what will become the new dome.

"Fellow citizens of the United States," he began. After an opening self-reference, Lincoln began a pattern of directing attention away from himself to the larger persona of American political bodies: "a Republican administration . . . the Union . . . the American people . . . the national authority . . . the Constitution . . . the people." He was determined to use nonpartisan language. At a time when the Northern press, and many politicians, were using inflammatory language, Lincoln stayed away from such volatile words as "enemy," "secessionists," or even "Confederacy." His initial rhetorical move was toward conciliation.

Lincoln's instinct told him to move directly to the real source of tension in his audience: "Apprehension seems to exist among the people of the Southern States that by the accession of a Republican Administration their property and their peace and personal security are endangered." By the time of Lincoln's inauguration, seven states had seceded, but by saying "Southern States," he affirmed that they were still part of the Union. He would not use the name "Confederate States of America."

He sought to allay their anxieties: "There has never been any reasonable cause for such apprehension. Indeed, the most ample evidence to the contrary has all the while existed and been open to their inspection. It is found in nearly all the published speeches of him who now addresses you."

Lincoln's lawyerly reasoning governed the structure and content of most of the address. As a lawyer-politician, he referred the jury-

This distant view by an unknown photographer captures the crowd gathering before the east front of the unfinished Capitol for Abraham Lincoln's inauguration on March 4, 1861.

audience to the precedent of his own speeches. He did not present himself as prepared to do something new, but rather to follow the ideas and practices that he had advocated since the middle of the 1850s.

Lincoln bowed further toward conciliation when he announced he would continue to support the fugitive slave law. Why did he introduce a discussion of this controversial law so early in his address? He believed he had more to gain from those in favor of the law than to lose from those opposed to it. Introducing the fugitive slave law also offered Lincoln the opportunity to underline his larger point. In taking the oath as president, he intended to uphold the Constitution in all matters. He hoped his language would send a signal that the South had nothing to fear in this new president from the West.

Horace Greeley, sitting behind Lincoln, recalled that as the audience listened quietly he almost expected to hear the crack of rifle fire. But the quiet was broken only by the noise of a spectator crashing down from his perch in the top of a tree.

Lincoln's high-pitched voice and his Kentucky accent struck many Easterners in the audience as inelegant, but Lincoln's ideas, to the sympathetic listener, were substantial. "I hold, that in contemplation of universal law, and of the Constitution, the Union of these states is perpetual. Perpetuity is implied, if not expressed, in the fundamental law of all national governments. It is safe to assert that no government proper, ever had a provision in its organic law for its own termination."

Cheers greeted his words about the perpetuity of the Union. He had decided in Springfield to make the central theme of his address the indivisibility of the Union. Lincoln declared that states had the right to uphold their own domestic institutions, not on the basis of state sovereignty, but because of their respective roles within the nation. He reminded his audience that "the Union is much older than the Constitution."

But Lincoln knew he could not discuss the Constitution for too long. He needed to speak about what was on the listeners' minds: the very real possibilities of "bloodshed and violence." He wanted to establish a baseline: Any violence would not come from his administration. He employed the phrase "national authority," contrasting his constitutional legitimacy with all lesser authorities.

As Lincoln pivoted from conciliation to firmness, he began by characterizing the actions of the leaders of the secession movement. "Plainly, the central idea of secession is the essence of anarchy."

Attempting to call to mind memories of 1776, secessionists had clothed themselves in a righteous second war of independence, but Lincoln forcefully disrobed their actions by calling them "anarchy" and "despotism." Sounding like a teacher of constitutional law, Lincoln made the case that "no State, upon its own mere motion, can lawfully get out of the Union." He declared that, "in view of the Constitution and the laws, the Union is unbroken" and he understood it to be his duty as president to ensure "that the laws of the Union be faithfully executed in all the States." Then, as if remembering his conciliatory side, he quickly added, "I trust this will not be regarded as a menace, but only as the declared purpose of the Union that it will constitutionally defend, and maintain itself."

No one was more caught up in Lincoln's address than Stephen Douglas. As Lincoln spoke, Douglas whispered under his breath, "Good," "That's so," "No coercion," and "Good again." Lincoln concluded with two dramatic paragraphs. First, he skillfully combined challenge and affirmation, driving home his point by employing one of his favorite rhetorical devices, opposition:

> In your hands, my dissatisfied fellow countrymen, and not in mine, is the momentous issue of civil war. The government will not assail you. You can have no conflict, without being yourselves the aggressor. You have no oath registered in Heaven to destroy the government, while I have the most solemn one to "preserve, protect and defend" it.

Lincoln, after being widely criticized for months for failing to understand the threat to the Union, now named the crisis. He wanted the historical testimony to be unambiguous about who the antagonist would be. "The government will not assail *you*." Conciliation, the main motif of the speech, yielded in this penultimate paragraph to determination.

After speaking for nearly thirty minutes, Lincoln turned to his concluding paragraph. In his first and second drafts of the address, he had ended with a question: "With you and not with me is the solemn question, 'Shall it be peace or a sword?' " Seward urged Lincoln to employ a different conclusion: "some words of affection—some of calm and cheerful confidence." Seward achieved the reputation of being a fine speaker, but a comparison affords an opportunity to observe how Lincoln transformed Seward's words into his own prose poetry.

Seward	Lincoln
1. I close.	I am loath to close.
2. We are not, we must not be, aliens or enemies, but fellow-countrymen and brethren.	We are not enemies, but friends. We must not be enemies.
3. Although passion has strained our bonds of affection too hardly, they must not, I am sure they will not, be broken.	Though passion may have strained, it must not break our bonds of affection.
4. The mystic chords which, proceeding from so many battlefields and so many patriot graves, pass through all the hearts and all the hearths in this broad continent of ours, will yet again harmonize in their ancient music when breathed upon by the guardian angel of the nation.	The mystic chords of memory, stretching from every battlefield, and patriot grave, to every heart and hearth-stone, all over this broad land, will yet swell the chorus of the Union, when again touched, as surely they will be, by the better angels of our nature.

Lincoln pared away all superfluous words. He made use of assonance, which placed together words or syllables with related sounds. He employed alliteration, which brought close together the same consonant and sound five times in the final two sentences, and encouraged the connection of words within the paragraph for the hearer: break, bonds, battlefield, broad, better.

He used symbolic images to shape a rhetoric of unity. The power of his appeal grew as he called to mind the figure of "the mystic chords of memory." Lincoln, who understood better than anyone the power of words, but who had been silent for the previous ten months, now spoke with the hope that he could bridge the growing divide to appeal to mutual feelings for the Union.

At the conclusion of the address, Chief Justice Taney stepped forward. A bowed, lean figure in his black gown, Taney may have remembered the previous presidents he had sworn in—Van Buren, Harrison, Tyler, Polk, Taylor, Fillmore, Pierce, and Buchanan—as he prepared to swear in a ninth president. Lincoln placed his left hand on the Bible, raised his right hand, and repeated the oath of office. As Lincoln ended the oath, the cheering began. One of the first to congratulate Lincoln was Senator Douglas. Artillery boomed salute after salute to the newly inaugurated sixteenth president.

IMMEDIATELY AFTER LINCOLN'S INAUGURATION, citizens in small hamlets and large cities congregated at newspaper offices eager for telegraphic reports of his address. The next day, the first newspaper responses reflected the nation's divided opinion. In a highly politicized press, critics read Lincoln's words through their own partisan glasses.

Greeley's *New York Tribune* liked the firmness of Lincoln's remarks. "The avowal of purpose . . . is unequivocal, unhesitating, firm, and earnest." The *New York Times,* then a barometer of conservative opinion, editorialized that "conservative people are in raptures over the Inauguration." The two newspapers in Illinois that had long supported Lincoln applauded. The *Chicago Tribune* stated, "No document can be found among American state papers embodying sounder wisdom and higher patriotism." The *Illinois State Journal* in Springfield proclaimed, "The Inaugural Address of our noble Chief Magistrate has electrified the whole country."

The anti-Lincoln papers heard much to criticize. The *Chicago Times* deplored the address as "a loose, disjointed, rambling affair." The *New York Herald* criticized Lincoln's words as "neither candid nor statesmanlike; nor does it possess any essential dignity or patriotism." Comparing Lincoln to his praiseworthy predecessors, the *Herald* declared the address "would have caused a Washington to mourn, and would have inspired a Jefferson, Madison, or Jackson with contempt."

Southern newspapers did not hear the conciliation that Lincoln believed was one of the twin pillars of his address. The *Richmond Enquirer* excoriated the address as "the cool, unimpassioned, deliberate language of the fanatic," believing Lincoln's aim to be "the dismemberment of the Government with the horrors of civil war." The *Charleston Mercury,* an important Southern voice whose editorials were often republished in Northern newspapers, berated Lincoln's "lamentable display of feeble inability to grasp the circumstances of the momentous emergency."

In response, the *New York Times* questioned whether newspapers in the South had even taken time to read the address. "Before the Inaugural has been read in a single Southern State, it is denounced, through the telegraph, from every Southern point, as a declaration of war."

George Templeton Strong conveyed in his diary the sense of anticipation the inaugural caused in New York City. He reported that on Wall Street, "news from Washington" was "awaited impatiently." Newspapers printed special editions at noon and 1:30 p.m. Strong read the first half of Lincoln's inaugural in the second edition of the evening papers. The next day, he had time to read the entire inaugural address and speak with colleagues who liked Lincoln's conciliatory and cautious approach. Strong, whose diary is fascinating in the ways that he brings in opinions other than his own, offered his response: "I think there is a clank of metal in it." Strong believed that Lincoln's address "is unlike any message or state paper of any class that has appeared in my time." What Strong especially liked was that the inaugural "seems to introduce one to *a man* and to dispose one to like him."

Two American leaders with whom Lincoln was destined to cross paths in dramatic encounters during his presidency were each dispirited in reading the address. Edward Everett followed the reactions to Lincoln's oratory from his home on Summer Street in Boston. On March 4, 1861, after receiving the inaugural address by telegraph, he lauded Lincoln's "conciliatory" tone in his journal, but expressed the opinion that Lincoln's intention to hold the forts would "result in Civil War." On April 3, he noted that all of the opinions of the English press had now arrived, and wrote that Lincoln's inaugural address "is almost universally spoken of as feeble, equivocal, and temporizing. It has evidently disappointed public expectation." He went on to express his empathy for the new president. He believed that Lincoln was caught between the abolitionist beliefs of the Republicans he knew well in New England and the president's own instincts for magnanimity. "The truth is the President's situation is impossible."

Frederick Douglass, from his home at the northwest corner of Robinson Drive and South Avenue in Rochester, New York, was not so charitable. Wrought up with "tension and frustration" during the months of the secession crisis, he characterized the address as "little better than our fears." It was a "double-tongued document, capable of two constructions, and conceals rather than declares a definite policy." Douglass contended what cartoonists were illustrating: "No man reading it could say whether Mr. Lincoln was for peace or war." Douglass had followed Lincoln's attacks on Stephen Douglas's race-baiting in their 1858 debates and now found the "denial of all feeling against slavery . . . wholly discreditable to the head and heart of Mr. Lincoln." Worst of all, in Douglass's eyes, was Lincoln's announced intention to abide by the fugitive slave law. As for what black Americans could expect from the new president, Douglass wrote, "Some thought we had in Mr. Lincoln the nerve and decision of an Oliver Cromwell; but the result shows that we merely have a continuation of the Pierces and Buchanans, and that the Republican President bends the knee to slavery as readily as any of his infamous predecessors."

EARLY ON TUESDAY MORNING, March 5, 1861, Lincoln went to his new White House office where the very first paper given to him was a military communication requiring urgent attention: a letter from Major Robert Anderson, commander of the Union garrison at Fort Sumter, the five-sided fort constructed on a shoal in South Carolina's Charleston harbor. Anderson wrote that he had supplies to last only six weeks. Unless resupplied, he would be forced to surrender. Lincoln was fully aware of the pressure put upon President Buchanan to surrender Fort Sumter after South Carolina seceded in December, but never had a newly inaugurated president faced such an immediate challenge. In his inaugural address, Lincoln had attempted to balance conciliation and firmness. How would he execute this balance in responding to the threat to Fort Sumter?

At noon, Lincoln sent to the Senate, meeting in extra session, the list of his cabinet.

Secretary of State, William H. Seward, New York
Secretary of the Treasury, Salmon P. Chase, Ohio
Secretary of War, Simon Cameron, Pennsylvania
Secretary of the Navy, Gideon Welles, Connecticut
Secretary of the Interior, Caleb B. Smith, Indiana
Attorney General, Edward Bates, Missouri
Postmaster General, Montgomery Blair, Maryland

The Senate confirmed each cabinet nominee, and the next day each was inducted into office.

Absent from the floor of the Senate when the votes on cabinet positions were taken, Chase was taken aback when colleagues rushed up to congratulate him after he returned. A man of tremendous pride who believed in the right political protocol, Chase sought Lincoln out to decline the nomination. The president explained that it would be embarrassing to both of them if he did not accept the appointment. Chase resigned his seat in the Senate and wrote to Lincoln later that day, "I accept the post which you have tendered me."

Lincoln's first executive act, the selection of his cabinet, sent a strong signal both of his own sense of security and the direction of his leadership. Rather than choosing lesser yes-men, he surrounded himself with some of the nation's most able men: three ex-Whigs, Seward, Bates, and Smith, and four ex-Democrats, Chase, Cameron, Welles, and Blair. Some Republicans immediately criticized Lincoln for the majority of ex-Democrats in his cabinet, but he countered that he, as a former Whig, made the cabinet perfectly balanced: four to four. Lincoln had learned in Illinois how to bring divergent voices together, and he now set out to do this on the larger stage of Washington.

Lincoln convened his first cabinet meeting on the evening of March 6, 1861. The cabinet gathered, in the order of their seniority, around the table in the center of Lincoln's office. An engraved oil portrait of Andrew Jackson stared down at this gathering of old Whigs, old Democrats, and the new Republican president. Lincoln intended this initial meeting to be only introductory. Attorney General Edward Bates confided to his diary that he found the first cabinet meeting "uninteresting."

LINCOLN CAME TO THE PRESIDENCY lacking executive experience, and his first weeks in office did little to inspire confidence that he could launch and run a new administration.

A large walnut table, piled with books and maps, dominated his sizable office on the second floor of the White House. Here Lincoln conducted cabinet meetings on Tuesdays and Fridays, but cabinet officers soon learned not to depend on their regularity. Lincoln often worked at an old upright mahogany writing desk by the middle windows of the south wall facing the Washington Monument and further to the Potomac River. His secretaries, John Nicolay and John Hay, described his desk as looking like it came from "some old furniture auction." Lincoln used the pigeonholes of the desk, as earlier in Illinois he had used his stovepipe hat and desk drawers, as repositories for his legendary notes to himself. Two horsehair sofas and wooden chairs were scattered about the room in no particular arrangement. More maps hung above the sofas. Oilcloth covered the floor. Lighted by gaslights and heated by a fireplace, the room functioned as a working office, not a ceremonial office, even though Lincoln received many of his guests there. The president could call for Nicolay and Hay with a bell cord close to his desk.

Lincoln was well aware that, in the words of David Davis, "he had no administrative ability until he went to Washington." At first he tried to do everything by himself. He acknowledged to Robert L. Wilson, a member of the "Long Nine" of the Illinois House of Representatives in the 1830s, his initial floundering. "When [I] first commenced doing the duties, [I] was entirely ignorant not only of the duties, but of the manner of doing the business" of the presidency.

Hay remembered, "There was little order or system about it. . . . Those around him strove from beginning to end to erect barriers to defend him against constant interruption, but the President himself was always the first to break them down." Senator Henry Wilson of Massachusetts, who as chairman of the Military Affairs Committee would work closely with Lincoln, once tried to counsel him about his availability to people: "You will wear yourself out." Lincoln replied, "They don't want much; they get but little, and I must see them."

It has been suggested that Lincoln, innately cautious, was a reactor rather than an initiator. Certainly, in his first months in office, Lincoln felt his way, and the press of events called for a steep learning curve. But there is a difference between being cautious and being passive. While Lincoln never offered any philosophy of leadership, it is possible to observe principles that guided his development of policy, his relationships with colleagues, and his command of the war. Once in Washington, to the surprise of many, Lincoln was a quick learner.

LINCOLN WAS NOT PREPARED to deal with the crisis of Fort Sumter at the beginning of his presidency. He had determined in Springfield to preserve the Union without war, and he was aware of his inexperience in military matters. His previous method of dealing with crises, such as the Kansas-Nebraska Act or the Dred Scott decision, was to take months to research, think, and brood in private, before announcing his public response. But Anderson's memorandum informed the War Department that there were only weeks to decide what to do.

Now Lincoln faced a far-reaching choice. He had to deal with the thorny problem of Fort Sumter on Charleston harbor in South Carolina, as well as Fort Pickens, constructed to fortify Pensacola, in the northern part of seceded Florida. The main show was Fort Sumter. Lincoln could surrender Fort Sumter and hope that this might keep the four states of the upper South and four border states from joining the secession, or he could attempt to resupply the forts and take the probable risk of starting a civil war. He asked Buchanan's secretary of war Joseph Holt, a Unionist Kentuckian who had agreed to stay on while Lincoln waited for Simon Cameron to assume his duties, whether the Kentuckian Robert Anderson could be trusted. Holt said he could. Lincoln would find himself asking this question many times about government officials and military officers in the opening weeks of his administration. The new president needed time to think and to plan, but the clock was ticking.

In the following days, Lincoln conferred with cabinet secretaries and army and navy men about how to tackle the problem in the Charleston harbor. He listened respectfully as Secretary of State Seward argued strongly against resupplying Fort Sumter in order to preserve the peace. Welles, after several of these conferences, wrote of the president in his diary, "He was disinclined to hasty action, and wished time for the Administration to get in working order."

On Saturday evening, March 9, 1861, when Lincoln reconvened his new cabinet, he invited General Winfield Scott, the hero of the Mexican War, to join the discussion. Scott, old and obese, had been studying Anderson's dispatches. He urged, in the strongest terms, an evacuation of Fort Sumter. Everyone at the cabinet meeting, with the exception of Postmaster General Montgomery Blair, agreed.

Despite the majority sentiment to withdraw, Lincoln decided to seek more information. Later, he wrote out three questions for General Scott. Lincoln convened another cabinet meeting on March 11, 1861, to share Scott's answers. Scott advised that to undertake a mission to resupply Fort Sumter would take a fleet of war vessels, five thousand regular troops, plus twenty thousand volunteers. Lincoln read the sobering final sentence of Scott's reply. "To raise, organize, & discipline such an army, would require new acts of Congress & from six to eight months."

On the same day, Francis Blair, Sr., Montgomery Blair's father, called upon Lincoln at the White House and told him "the surrender of Fort Sumter . . . was virtually a surrender of the Union unless under irresistible force—that compounding with treason was treason to the Govt." The next day the elder Blair wrote to Montgomery, who passed the letter on to Lincoln. The elder Blair half apologized—"I may have said things that were impertinent"—for his strong words with the president. Hearkening back to the resolve of President Jackson in the nullification crisis with South Carolina in 1832, the Blairs, father and sons, were committed to stiffening the backbone of Lincoln.

Two days later, Montgomery Blair hurried to the White House to introduce Lincoln to his brother-in-law, Gustavus Fox, a short, sturdy former naval officer who was now in private business in Massachusetts. Fox, at the urging of the Blairs, presented an inventive plan to resupply Fort Sumter. He had offered his plan to President Buchanan in February, who had turned him away, but Lincoln heard him out. Having studied the Confederate defenses, Fox proposed sending a large steamer, carrying troops, accompanied by two New York tugboats, carrying supplies. Arriving by daylight, he would test Confederate intentions and probe the vulnerable places in their defenses, and then run in men and supplies by the cover of night.

Impressed, Lincoln presented the plan at the cabinet meeting of March 15, 1861. Fox told the cabinet he was willing to risk his life in leading the relief effort. After the meeting, Lincoln sent a note to each cabinet member with a single question: "Assuming it to be possible to now provision Fort-Sumter, under all the circumstances, is it wise to attempt it?"

On Monday, March 18, 1861, with a spring snow hanging on in Washington, Lincoln sat alone at his desk to review the seven responses from his cabinet.

William Seward, secretary of state, writing in his suite of two rooms on the second floor of the State Department building at the corner of Pennsylvania Avenue and Fifteenth Street, offered an extended answer that was summed up in one conviction, "I would not provoke war in any way *now*." No.

Salmon Chase, secretary of the treasury, after voicing concern that "the attempt will so inflame civil war," concluded "it seems to me high improbable that the attempt . . . will produce such consequences." A qualified yes.

Simon Cameron, secretary of war, influenced by the arguments of the army officers, answered, "It would be unwise now to make such an attempt." No.

Gideon Welles, secretary of the navy, believed the attempt would need to have both a military and a political component, but on both counts, "I do not think it wise." No.

Caleb Smith, secretary of the interior, after weighing the conflicting army and navy recommendations, concluded, "It would not be wise under all circumstances." No.

Edward Bates, attorney general, after sifting the legal arguments, concluded, "I do not think it *wise now* to attempt to provision Fort Sumter." No.

Montgomery Blair, postmaster general, alone, voiced his strong support for provisioning Fort Sumter, on two counts. First, he believed this action would inspire a like-minded courage among loyal Unionists in the South. Second, not to do so "will convince the rebels that the administration lacks firmness." Such an evacuation would signal an unwillingness "to maintain the authority of the United States." Yes.

The count was 5 to 2, a clear majority against a relief mission, but Lincoln was not yet prepared to abandon Fort Sumter. He decided to test some of the conjectures of his advisers. To gather yet more information, he sent Fox to see Anderson and investigate the problems and possibilities in a defense of Fort Sumter. He also dispatched Ward Hill Lamon and Stephen Hurlbut, an old Illinois friend who had grown up in Charleston, for a second reconnoiter mission. Seward had argued that Unionism was strong if temporarily silent in South Carolina. Lincoln wanted to test this thesis. Fox returned on March 25, 1861, more ready than ever to attempt the resupply mission. Hurlbut and Lamon returned on March 27 reporting that the American flag could not be seen flying anywhere. "The Sentiment of National Patriotism always feeble in Carolina, has been Extinguished."

As the crisis at Fort Sumter focused inordinate attention on Lincoln, everyone sought to take the measure of the new president. William Howard Russell, special correspondent of the *Times* of London, had earned an international reputation from twenty years of reporting on events in Ireland, India, and the Crimean War. Russell had arrived in New York in the middle of March and hurried on to Washington. On March 27, 1861, the generously proportioned London correspondent was taken to the White House. Russell recorded in his diary his first impressions of Lincoln.

There entered, with a shambling, loose, irregular, almost unsteady gait, a tall, lank, lean man, considerably over six feet in height, with stooping shoulders, long pendulous arms, terminating in hands of extraordinary dimensions, which, however, were far exceeded in proportion by his feet. He was dressed in an ill-fitting, wrinkled suit of black, which put one in mind of an undertaker's uniform at a funeral; round his neck a rope of black silk was knotted in a large bulb, with flying ends projecting beyond the collar of his coat; his turned-down shirt-collar disclosed a sinewy, muscular yellow neck, and above that, nestling in a great black mass of hair, bristling and compact like a ruff of marching pins, rose the strange quaint face and head, covered with its thatch of wild republican hair, of President Lincoln.

Russell, known to be disdainful of everything not English, left his first encounter with Lincoln "agreeably impressed with his shrewdness, humor, and natural sagacity."

The clock was running down at Fort Sumter. As it did, Americans of all political persuasions were growing impatient with the president.

Senator John C. Breckinridge of Kentucky, Southern Democratic presidential candidate in 1860, was the voice of the remnant of Southerners still in Congress. Breckinridge kept pressing for information on Lincoln's policies and criticized the North for being unwilling to compromise. On March 28, 1861, Lyman Trumbull introduced a Senate resolution to support, but also to prod, Lincoln. "Resolved, the opinion of the Senate, the true way to preserve the Union is to enforce the laws of the Union." As Lincoln's political career ascended, Trumbull's relationship with Lincoln had begun to cool. Trumbull viewed Lincoln as "ambitious but indecisive, a compromiser who could be swayed by knowledgeable advisors" like Seward. The final words of his resolution read: "It is the duty of the President . . . to use all means in his power to hold and protect the public property of the United States." Trumbull, distrusting Seward and unsure of Lincoln, wanted not simply to encourage the president, but to make him accountable to the consensus he hoped the Republicans were building in Congress.

Also on March 28, 1861, General Scott told Lincoln, once again, that Fort Sumter could not be resupplied. Lincoln, who corresponded with General Scott all through the long secession winter, had come to Washington with great admiration for the old military hero. In one of Lincoln's first acts of presidential leadership, he made the painful decision to respectfully disagree with those whom he respected. That night, Lincoln slept not at all.

By March 29, 1861, Good Friday, Lincoln had decided to resupply

Fort Sumter, "but he took care to make it as unprovocative as possible." He informed his cabinet at their noon meeting that, with only two weeks left before supplies would run out, he was ordering Welles and Cameron to draw up plans for the relief of the fort. Gustavus Fox went to New York to take charge of naval preparations to sail for Charleston harbor. Lincoln had made his first real decision as commander in chief.

The weeks of nonstop debate and indecision had taken a toll. Lincoln told a military officer, "If to be the head of Hell is as hard as what I have to undergo here, I could find it in my heart to pity Satan himself." Sam Ward, a Washington insider, noted on March 30, " 'Abe' is getting heartily sick of 'the situation'—It is hard for the Captain of a new Steamer to 'work this passage.' " Ward wrote that the day before, Lincoln had told a mutual friend he was "in the dumps."

WHEN THE LINCOLNS ARRIVED in Washington, a number of churches had invited them to attend Sunday worship. Two days after the inauguration, the First Presbyterian Church invited President and Mrs. Lincoln to accept a pew in their church, free of rent. Many Protestant congregations in the nineteenth century charged pew rents as a means of raising money for church budgets. First Presbyterian, which enjoyed its reputation as "the church of the presidents," boasted that Presidents Jackson, Van Buren, Polk, Pierce, and Buchanan had worshipped there. It was made up largely of Democrats and had until recently included many of the Southern members of Congress.

On the first Sunday after inauguration, the Lincolns worshipped at the New York Avenue Presbyterian Church. The next week a deacon from the church brought a plat, or map, of the pews to the White House for inspection. No free rent.

New York Avenue was an Old School congregation, whereas First Presbyterian Church was New School. The Presbyterian Church had split in 1837 over a number of theological and organizational issues. Both traditions were grounded in the Bible, but the Old School rooted itself in a rational doctrinal tradition, whereas the New School was more open to experience expressed in the revivalism of the Second Great Awakening. The New School committed itself to political reform, especially antislavery reform, whereas the Old School held that the church should not involve itself in political questions.

Phineas Densmore Gurley was the minister at New York Avenue. He had graduated first in his class at Princeton Theological Seminary in

1840. A fine-looking man of large frame and voice, Gurley stood squarely in the American Old School Presbyterian understanding of Reformed theology. American Presbyterians strove to balance a high view of God with a low view of humanity. A denomination that prized learned ministers, they nevertheless understood God not as the first principle in philosophy but as the primary actor in history. Lincoln, ever attuned to paradox, appreciated the Presbyterian belief that the sinfulness of human beings did not lead to passivity, because Christian men and women were called to be instruments of divine purpose in society.

Though Lincoln had attended the First Presbyterian Church in Springfield infrequently, he would become more regular in his attendance at New York Avenue Presbyterian Church, and Gurley would become a regular visitor in the White House. Lincoln sent his first quarterly check for the pew rent of fifty dollars a year.

"WANTED—A POLICY." In an editorial on April 3, 1861, the *New York Times* charged the new Republican administration with "a blindness and a stolidity without parallel in the history of intelligent statesmanship." Editor Henry J. Raymond aimed his criticism at Lincoln. "He must go up to a higher level than he has yet reached, before he can see and realize the high duties to which he has been called."

As painful as it must have been to hear this charge from a leading newspaper that had supported his election, Lincoln found himself blindsided by the person closest to him in his cabinet. Seward, increasingly perturbed by what he came to believe was Lincoln's lack of leadership, finally reacted in exasperation. On Sunday, March 31, 1861, he had drafted a letter, "Some Thoughts for the President's consideration." Seward's son, Frederick, delivered the letter to the president on Monday morning, April 1.

"We are at the end of a month's administration and yet without a policy either domestic or foreign. . . . Further delay to adopt and prosecute our policies for both domestic and foreign affairs would not only bring scandal on the Administration, but danger upon the country." What was the solution? Seward stated, "It must be somebody's business to pursue and direct it incessantly." And who should the leader be? "Either the President must do it himself, and be all the while active in it; or Devolve it on some member of his Cabinet." Certainly Seward did not consider himself out of line. In the first half of the nineteenth century, the secretary of state assumed a major share of leadership in presidential administrations.

Lincoln replied immediately, responding point by point. He acknowledged that he and Seward had disagreed over the question of resupplying Fort Sumter. The president declared he did have a new policy and reiterated the policy outlined in his inaugural address. He reminded Seward, who had been helpful in reviewing the second draft of the address, "This had your distinct approval at the time." Yet Lincoln probably never sent his carefully worded letter, the first of many letters he wrote as president but never sent, deciding it would be better to speak with Seward in person. Lincoln told Seward, "If this must be done, *I* must do it."

Lincoln took another significant step forward on April 1, 1861. He wrote a short note to General Scott asking, "Would it impose too much labor" to "make short, comprehensive daily reports to me of what occurs in his Department, including movements by himself, and under his orders, and the receipt of intelligence?" Framed politely, as a question, it was in fact an order that indicated Lincoln's belief that he needed to become more directly involved in the military's day-by-day operations. That Lincoln read these reports carefully was evident nearly three weeks later when he wrote a memo to himself, "No report from Gen. Scott this 19. April 1861."

On a warm Saturday, April 6, 1861, with the trees beginning to leaf out and the peach trees blossoming in the capital, political tensions were mounting. Lincoln directed Secretary of War Cameron to dispatch a courier, Robert S. Chew, to Charleston with a message for Governor Andrew W. Pickens of South Carolina: "An attempt will be made to supply Fort-Sumter with provisions only; and that, if such attempt be not resisted, no effort to throw in men, arms, or ammunition, will be made." After a series of aggravating delays, on April 9, Fox sailed from New York, with his small fleet planning to rendezvous off Charleston harbor.

Governor Pickens quickly notified Jefferson Davis of Lincoln's message. The leaders of the Confederacy found Lincoln's action to be a direct threat. The Confederate cabinet met and decided to seek the immediate surrender of Fort Sumter. At noon on April 11, 1861, a message was sent to Major Anderson demanding surrender. He refused.

In the meantime, the sailing of the relief mission to Fort Sumter had run afoul of yet another squabble between cabinet members, a feud between Seward and Welles. Seward, who believed that Fort Pickens should be reinforced but Sumter evacuated, intervened at the last moment to persuade Lincoln to divert the warship *Powhatan* to accompany the mission to Fort Pickens instead of to Fort Sumter. Fox was unaware of the change, which would deprive him of his most powerful weapon.

As Lincoln waited to hear news of Fox's relief expedition, Jefferson Davis and his military leaders attacked. At 4:30 a.m. on April 12, 1861, Brigadier General Pierre G. T. Beauregard ordered a Confederate battery to open fire on Fort Sumter, thirty-nine days after Lincoln's inaugural address. A single red ball arced ominously over Fort Sumter and exploded. Quickly, forty-three guns and mortars circling the harbor opened fire. Anderson deliberately held his fire until 7 a.m., when Captain Abner Doubleday fired at a South Carolina shore battery. Fort Sumter had been built to repel a naval, not a land, assault. Anderson's best guns were mounted on the top tier of the fort, but this meant the men manning them would be most vulnerable to incoming fire.

The attack on Fort Sumter on April 12–13, 1861, galvanized Northern opinion to defend the Union. The attack is dramatized in this illustration from Harper's Weekly, *April 27, 1861.*

A powerful Atlantic storm had delayed Fox's depleted fleet, and he discovered off Charleston that he had lost his three tugboats. As the bombardment proceeded, the captains of the *Pawnee* and *Harriet Lane* believed it too treacherous to navigate their ships around the sandbar at the mouth of the harbor; they could only watch helplessly from afar.

At noon on April 13, after thirty-three hours, and four thousand shots and shells, Anderson ordered a white flag raised in surrender. Fox's flotilla finally arrived to ferry Anderson and his small garrison back to the North. Anderson held in his hands a tattered American flag. The Confederates had fired the first shot of the Civil War.

WASHINGTON BECAME ALIVE with the news about the bombardment of Fort Sumter. The mood was a curious mixture of foreboding and expectation: relief that the long stalemate was over, and an adventurous—if reckless—spirit ready to go to war. Horatio Nelson Taft, who came to Washington to work in the Patent Office in 1858, expressed the sentiment of many when he wrote in his diary for April 13, 1861, "Everybody much excited, and all will soon be compelled to 'show their hands,' *for* or *against* the Union."

Abraham and Mary Lincoln worshipped that Sunday morning at the New York Avenue Presbyterian Church. In his sermon, Phineas Gurley pointed to "God, in his merciful providence" offering "another opportunity for counsel, for pause, for appeal to Him for assistance before letting loose upon the land the direct scourge which He permits to visit a people—civil war." Gurley concluded with a prayer that the "counsels of the Administration might be sanctified and blessed."

In the afternoon, Lincoln was working alone when Stephen Douglas arrived unexpectedly. Lincoln took from his desk a draft of the proclamation he planned to issue the next day. The two men studied Lincoln's text. Lincoln intended to ask for 75,000 volunteers to join the army. "I would make it 200,000," declared Douglas. The two men talked together for almost two hours, their meeting marked, in Douglas's words, by a "cordial feeling of a united, friendly, and patriotic purpose."

Douglas later spoke of their meeting. While emphasizing that he was opposed to the administration, and that he had been against the attempt to resupply Fort Sumter, he declared that he was now united with the president in the need for strong action. Douglas reported they "spoke of the present & future, without reference to the past." When Douglas met a friend at the telegraph office who asked about Lincoln, he replied,

"I've known Mr. Lincoln a longer time than you have, or than the country has; he'll come out right, and we will all stand by him." The account of Douglas's conversation with Lincoln was printed widely.

As the war broke out, Lincoln had the freedom to act without the restraint of Congress, which wasn't in session, but he knew he could not act alone. He needed the authorization of Congress in order to prosecute and to pay for the war. But the legislative branch of the government was not scheduled to convene as the new Thirty-seventh Congress until the first Monday in December.

On April 15, 1861, Lincoln issued a proclamation calling for a special session of Congress to convene on July 4, 1861. The coming storm, of which Lincoln had spoken many times, had arrived in the waters off Charleston, South Carolina. Within the next two months, Virginia, Arkansas, North Carolina, and Tennessee would join the Confederacy, bringing the number of states to eleven.

At the time, and ever since, critics have scrutinized Lincoln's words and actions in an attempt to understand his intentions during this crisis. Did Lincoln, given contradictory advice by his political and military advisers, arrive at a result beyond his control? Or, by his decision to resupply Fort Sumter, did he control events, forcing the Confederacy to fire the first shot at Fort Sumter? As Lincoln had said in his inaugural address, "The government will not assail *you*. You can have no conflict, without being yourselves the aggressors." Did he do everything in his power to forestall open hostilities between the North and the South?

In the next months, Lincoln offered an explanation of his actions to two friends. Of the military officers he met in March and April, he had come to especially admire naval officer Gustavus Fox. He wrote to him on May 1, 1861, "You and I both anticipated that the cause of the country would be advanced by making the attempt to provision Fort-Sumpter, even if it should fail; and it is no small consolation now to feel that our anticipation is justified by the result." Ten weeks after the event, Lincoln told his old friend Orville Browning, "The plan succeeded. They attacked Sumter—it fell, and thus did more service than it otherwise could." Lincoln did confess to Browning, "All the troubles and anxieties of his life had not equaled those which intervened between this time and the fall of Fort Sumter."

As Lincoln encountered these troubles, he began to find his footing. Respectfully seeking the advice of his senior general, becoming painfully aware that his secretary of state was charting his own course, listening to the discordant voices of his cabinet, Lincoln proved to be not passive but prudent as he determined his own course on Fort Sumter. The whole constellation of decisions leading to the first shot of the Civil War in South Carolina revealed the initial signs of Lincoln's emerging presidential leadership.

President Abraham Lincoln sat for this photograph in Mathew Brady's studio in Washington in April 1861. Some said at the time that this photograph showed a shrewd if not cunning look—an accusation seized upon by his opponents.

CHAPTER 18

A People's Contest
April 1861–July 1861

THIS ISSUE EMBRACES MORE THAN THE FATE OF THESE UNITED
STATES.

ABRAHAM LINCOLN
Message to Congress in special session, July 4, 1861

ON THE MORNING OF APRIL 15, 1861, THE CITY OF WASHINGTON SHUDDERED
with panic. Everywhere citizens looked, they found streets barricaded
and buildings blocked by police and soldiers. The navy commandeered
boats on the Potomac and set up pickets along the river. Many businesses
were closed.

In the White House, Lincoln paced his second-floor office above the
East Room, visibly concerned about the security and safety of the city.
His secretaries, John Nicolay and John Hay, found Lincoln in a state of
"nervous tension." The president reached for his telescope, climbed out
on the roof of the Executive Mansion, and scanned the Potomac, looking for any boats conveying Union troops. He then turned his lens
toward Alexandria, where, in the midst of church steeples and chim-
neys, he could see Confederate flags flying in the breeze.

In the days after the fall of Fort Sumter, residents of the capital
struggled to comprehend the unfolding political turmoil. On April 17,
1861, came a report from Richmond that Virginia would schedule a
vote in May. The next day, a small company of Union soldiers set fire to
Harpers Ferry, where the states of Maryland and Virginia met, before
the Union installation could be overrun by a larger Confederate force.
On April 19, Baltimore erupted in riot as Southern sympathizers tried
to stop New England troops from passing through their city on their
way to Washington. By April 20, federal authorities at the immense

Norfolk Naval Shipyard in Portsmouth, Virginia, were burning buildings and scuttling eleven ships in anticipation of a takeover by Confederate troops. And on Sunday evening, April 21, rioters seized the telegraph office in Baltimore, cutting off all communications from Washington to the North. The next day, Horatio Nelson Taft wrote in his diary, "We are in a beleaguered City with enimies on every side and at our doors."

Lincoln wondered aloud: Who would defend Washington? The national army, commanded by seventy-four-year-old General Winfield Scott, comprised only sixteen thousand men, the majority spread across seventy-nine outposts on the Western frontier. Almost one-third of its officers were leaving their commissions to join the Confederacy. To make up for the shortage of troops in or near Washington, Scott was forced to organize a few new regiments of old regulars, who called themselves the Silver Grays. Cassius M. Clay, wearing three pistols, organized a group of Kentuckians, while Senator-elect Jim Lane, a veteran of the Kansas border wars, organized his Frontier Guards, who set up headquarters in the East Room of the White House to the delight of Tad and Willie Lincoln. More vigilantes than military men, Clay's battalion was stationed at the Willard Hotel while Lane's Frontier Guards stood guard around the Executive Mansion.

SCOTT WAS TOO OLD and obese to command the Union forces, but Lincoln did seek his counsel for recommendations for the post. Without hesitation, Scott suggested Virginian Colonel Robert E. Lee.

Lee, the son of Revolutionary War hero "Light Horse" Harry Lee, graduated from West Point in 1829, earning the distinction as the first cadet to graduate from the academy without a single demerit. In 1831, Lee married Mary Anna Randolph Custis, the great-granddaughter of Martha Washington, at her parents' home, Arlington House, just across the Long Bridge from Washington. Posted to the Corps of Engineers, Lee served on General Scott's staff in the Mexican War, where he distinguished himself for his leadership of troops. After the war, Lee became superintendent of the military academy at West Point. He achieved further recognition for leading the force of marines that captured Harpers Ferry in the raid against John Brown in 1859.

Lincoln asked Francis Blair, Sr., a fellow Southerner, to approach Lee about commanding the Union forces. Lee, who had been undergoing a deep internal struggle about where his loyalty lay, told Blair that he deprecated secession, but he could not take up arms against his native state of Virginia. After speaking with Blair, Lee went to see Scott, a Virginian who had been a father figure to him, to deliver the same message. Lincoln was disappointed to learn that Lee quickly accepted an invitation from Governor John Letcher of Virginia one week later, April 25, 1861, to become a major general in command of all of Virginia's forces.

WAR FEVER SPREAD quickly across the North. Lincoln issued a proclamation calling up seventy-five thousand troops from state militias to serve as three-month volunteers to suppress what he called an insurrection "by combinations too powerful to be suppressed by the ordinary course of judicial proceedings." For his authority, Lincoln relied upon a provision of a 1795 militia law.

In the North and Northwest, the response to Lincoln's proclamation was overwhelming. Maine governor Israel Washburn, Jr., wired his guarantee: "The people of Maine of all parties will rally with alacrity to the maintenance of the government." Ohio's governor William Dennison assured Lincoln that he "will furnish the largest number you will receive." Governor Oliver P. Morton of Indiana promised ten thousand men "for the defense of the nation and to uphold the authority of the Government."

Lincoln's request for troops from the border states elicited replies that ranged from evasive to defiant. William Burton, governor of Delaware, delayed his answer but finally replied that his state had no militia law. Governor Beriah Magoffin of Kentucky replied brusquely, "Kentucky will furnish no troops for the wicked purpose of subduing her sister Southern States." Claiborne Fox Jackson, the new governor of Missouri, replied, "Your requisition, in my judgment, is illegal, unconstitutional, and revolutionary in its object. . . . Not one man will the state of Missouri furnish to carry on any such unholy crusade."

Massachusetts governor John A. Andrew, one of a coterie of radical Northern leaders, had begun assembling regiments in January, long before Lincoln even took office. As Lincoln's call to arms raced across the telegraph in April, the Massachusetts troops, with new rifles, were marching in a sleet storm on the Boston Common. Andrew responded, "Dispatch received. By what route should I send?"

Governor Andrew asked a troubling question. As the troops from the North proceeded toward Washington, they came upon the same problem that Lincoln had encountered nearly two months earlier: how to pass through the narrow neck of Maryland, which commanded the only railroad links to Washington. Maryland, a border state, was filled with Southern sympathizers. Baltimore, located at the top of the Chesapeake Bay, was the center for three major railroads to the West and the North.

The Sixth Massachusetts Volunteer Infantry was the first military unit to approach Washington. The seven hundred men arrived in Baltimore on the Philadelphia, Wilmington, and Baltimore Railroad at the President Street Station at noon on April 19, 1861. Immediately, horse-drawn cars began to transport the troops through the city so that their cars could be hooked up to a Baltimore and Ohio engine at Camden Station, one mile away, for the trip to Washington. Word spread quickly that troops from the abolitionist stronghold of Massachusetts had arrived in Baltimore. The soldiers had not gone far along Pratt Street before an angry crowd jeered and then began throwing bricks and stones at them. Panicking, some soldiers fired into the crowd. Twelve civilians and four soldiers died in the riot; scores were injured. The unrest in Baltimore inflamed secessionist passions in the South even as the editors of several Northern newspapers called for Baltimore to be burned to the ground. The riot helped galvanize both Union and Confederate commitments. With no casualties at Fort Sumter, the Baltimore riot of April 19 drew the first blood of the Civil War.

Through these fearful days, authorities in Maryland pressured the president. Unionist governor Thomas Hicks and Baltimore mayor George W. Brown wired Lincoln, "Send no more troops here." In Lincoln's reply on April 20, 1861, he thanked the governor and the mayor for their attempts to preserve the peace, but declared, "Now, and ever, I shall do all in my power for peace, consistently with the maintenance of government." That evening, John Hay wrote in his diary, "The streets were full of the talk of Baltimore. . . . The town is full tonight of feverish rumours about a meditated assault upon this town."

On April 22, 1861, a Baltimore committee of fifty called on Lincoln at the White House to acknowledge the independence of the Southern states and to ask that no more troops be sent through Baltimore. Lincoln's patience had run out. He reminded the Baltimore delegation, "Your citizens attack troops sent to the defense of the Government, and yet you would have me break my oath and surrender the Government without a blow." In Lincoln's answer he sought to remind his audience of presidential precedent: "There is no Washington in that—no Jackson in that—no manhood or honor in that." He asked the representatives how the troops were supposed to get to Washington. "Our men are not moles, and can't dig under the earth; they are not birds, and can't fly through the air." This abrasive challenge by Maryland authorities stiffened Lincoln's resolve to defend the capital and the Union.

Lincoln was looking out of the upstairs windows of the Executive Mansion on April 24, 1861, when the troops of the Sixth Massachusetts Volunteers finally reached Pennsylvania Avenue. Clara Barton, a thirty-nine-year-old U.S. Patent Office clerk from Massachusetts, organized a relief program for the soldiers of her home state, beginning on that day a lifetime of nursing and philanthropy. Seeing the troops, Lincoln felt a momentary sense of relief, but he worried that secessionists from Maryland might use the same Baltimore and Ohio tracks to assault the capital. Lincoln hosted some of the wounded officers and men at the Executive Mansion. He commended their courage and wondered aloud about what had happened to the regiments from other states, none of which had arrived in Washington. "I began to believe that there is no North. The Seventh regiment is a myth. Rhode Island is another. You are the only real thing."

But two days later, the Seventh Regiment of the New York State Militia arrived in Washington after bypassing Baltimore, sailing down the Chesapeake Bay to Annapolis, Maryland, and traveling by train the thirty miles to the capital. In the spring sunshine, Lincoln waited outside the White House as the soldiers, with their splendid regimental brass band, marched up the entire length of Pennsylvania Avenue. Their arrival "created much enthusiasm and relief." The gloom of the ten days following Fort Sumter disappeared as windows were opened and people took to the streets to meet the young Union soldiers. Lincoln waved his welcome to the troops.

"WANTED—A LEADER!"

Even as Lincoln enjoyed reviewing the Seventh New York Regiment, the criticism of his leadership grew louder. He had long since learned to discount condemnation from opposition Democratic newspapers, but it became more difficult to ignore criticism from his friends. On April 25, 1861, he read an editorial in the *New York Times,* opining, "In every great crisis, the human heart demands a leader that incarnates its ideas, its emotions and its aims. Till such a leader appears, everything is disorder, disaster, and defeat. The moment he takes the helm, order, promptitude and confidence follow as the necessary result. When we see such results—we know that a hero leads." Something about this particular article compelled Lincoln to clip and save it, including its final charge: "No such hero at present directs affairs."

Lincoln faced another challenge when Southern sympathizers in Maryland started cutting telegraph wires, burning bridges, and doing everything in their power to disrupt communications between the North and the capital. Maryland, a state noted for its crabs, was situated geographically like one, with claws pinching in on the capital from three sides.

On April 27, 1861, Lincoln gave an order to his top commander, General Scott, authorizing him "to suspend the writ of habeas corpus" if "an insurrection against the laws of the United States" erupted anywhere along a line from Philadelphia to Baltimore to Washington. The president instructed Scott to make arrests without specific charges. The right of habeas corpus, which protects citizens from illegal detention, requires that a prisoner be brought before a court to decide the legality of his arrest.

The responses to the suspension of habeas corpus created another predicament for Lincoln. Since the termination of the Revolutionary War seventy-eight years before, Americans had sailed upon a remarkably peaceful sea, with brief interruptions for the War of 1812 and the Mexican War. Unlike Europeans and Latin Americans, Americans had become accustomed to living in an open society. The nation was a society of small towns, where most citizens never saw a national army, never encountered a national police force, and encountered little federal intrusion. Authority was vested in the town mayors or constables. Now, in 1861, the arrest of citizens by a national army created a sensation. It caused people to consider, many for the first time, the vessel—the Constitution—in which they were sailing. Fortunately, the person at the helm was an astute lawyer and adroit politician.

A test case of habeas corpus came one month later when John Merryman was arrested on May 25, 1861, at his home in Cockeysville, Maryland, for allegedly drilling troops to aid the secessionist movement. Merryman was imprisoned at Fort McHenry, the star-shaped brick fort best known for its defense of Baltimore harbor in the War of 1812. Merryman's lawyer petitioned the federal court in Baltimore to look at the charges against him under the writ of habeas corpus.

The federal judge who heard the case just happened to be Chief Justice Roger Taney, who had offered the majority opinion in the Dred Scott case in 1857. Merryman obtained a writ from Taney ordering that he be either tried before a regular court or released. When Taney sent his order to Fort McHenry to be served, the officer in charge refused to receive it, citing Lincoln's order.

The Constitution, article 1, section 9, specifies that the right of habeas corpus "shall not be suspended, unless when in cases of rebellion or invasion the public safety may require it." The Constitution does not say who is authorized to suspend the privilege, but most legal experts, up until 1861, believed the power belonged to Congress, because the suspension clause was found in article 1, which enumerated congressional power. The framers of the Constitution, working against the background of resistance to the powers of a king, George III, placed the habeas corpus clause under congressional power because they were wary of an American president someday assuming monarchical powers.

Habeas corpus became the only principle of English common law that found its way into the Constitution. In the years leading up to the Civil War, habeas corpus, and corollaries to it, was not studied in law schools nor was it a part of the curriculum at West Point. When habeas corpus was discussed, the debate arose over the contentious fugitive slave law. The writ of habeas corpus came to symbolize America's commitment to individual freedom. While Lincoln believed that secession went against the Constitution, many argued that arbitrary arrest did as well. Lincoln understood that he had defied the mainstream of judicial opinion in his actions.

In the end, Lincoln chose a course of no action: He did not respond, appeal, or order the release of Merryman. Chief Justice Taney, on May 28, 1861, ruling in *Ex parte Merryman,* gladly delivered a sermon to Lincoln and the nation about the true meaning of the Constitution. Taking care to strike his title as presiding judge of the U.S. Circuit Court, Baltimore, in favor of chief justice, he argued that Lincoln was usurping the role of both Congress and the judicial branches of government in his employment of the military to carry out his purposes. Taney warned that Lincoln was on the road to becoming a military dictator. Nevertheless, the president's decisive action was applauded by the Republican press.

ON MAY 3, Lincoln issued a proclamation calling for an additional 42,034 three-year volunteers and 18,000 sailors, as well as expanding the regular army by 22,714 men. By the end of May, the war was beginning to achieve a human face, for no one more than Lincoln.

Somehow during the first confusing days of the Civil War, Lincoln found time to correspond with a young soldier named Elmer E. Ellsworth. Born in Saratoga County, New York, in 1837, Ellsworth had moved to Springfield, Illinois, in August 1860, to read law in Lincoln's office. Boyish in appearance, only five feet six, with clean-cut features, Ellsworth quickly became like a son to Lincoln. He accompanied the Lincolns on the Presidential Special to Washington. With Robert away at Harvard, Ellsworth became like an older brother to the two younger Lincoln boys, even catching the measles from them.

Ellsworth, after meeting a French Zouave veteran, Charles A. De-Villier, reorganized the Sixtieth Regiment of the Illinois State Militia into a Zouave unit. Ellsworth led his fifty young American men, dressed in bright red, blue, and gold uniforms with jaunty red caps with orange or gold decoration. In city after city, Ellsworth's Zouaves mesmerized audiences as they went through their military routines: marching, retreating, parrying and thrusting their bayonets, and loading and firing their Sharps rifles in every possible position, even kneeling and on their backs.

After Fort Sumter, Ellsworth hurried to New York City, where he organized the New York Zouaves, an 1,100-man volunteer regiment made up of New York firemen. Returning to Washington on April 29, 1861, he paraded his disciplined troops up the "Ave," the locals' name for Pennsylvania Avenue. Thereafter, almost daily, Ellsworth paraded his men in front of the Executive Mansion, and sometimes on the South Lawn, for Lincoln to review with pride.

When Virginia formally seceded on May 23, 1861, Ellsworth prepared his men to march on Alexandria. Landing at the Alexandria waterfront early on the morning of May 24, Ellsworth led his men to the telegraph office to cut all communication to the South. Spying a Confederate flag flying from the Marshall House, a three-story hotel, Ellsworth crossed the street and went inside. He took down the flag, but as he was coming back down the stairs, James W. Jackson, the hotel owner, shot and killed him with a double-barrel shotgun. Elmer Ellsworth was the first commissioned officer to die in the Civil War.

An officer brought news of Ellsworth's death to the White House. The young captain found Lincoln in the library and told him the sad news. At that moment, Senator Henry Wilson of Massachusetts and a

DEATH OF COL. ELLSWORTH,

after hauling down the rebel flag, at the taking of Alexandria, Va. May 24th 1861.

Elmer Ellsworth, almost like a son to Abraham Lincoln, was the first Union officer to die in the Civil War. This illustration depicts the deed of the first hero killed in battle.

reporter entered the library. Lincoln, stunned and heartbroken, turned to the visitors, extended his hand, and said simply, "Excuse me, but I cannot talk."

Abraham and Mary went down to the Washington Navy Yard to view Ellsworth's body. The president ordered it to lie in state in the East Room. A funeral service took place in the White House on May 26, 1861. Throughout the North, Ellsworth became a symbol of courageous young men willing to give their lives for the Union. His death also helped shake off any remaining complacency in the Northern public.

Overcome with grief, Lincoln wrote a letter to Ellsworth's parents on the day before the funeral. "In the untimely loss of your noble son, our affliction here, is scarcely less than your own." He described Ellsworth's sterling qualities, "a fine intellect, an indomitable energy, and a taste altogether military, constituted in him, as seemed to me, the best natural talent, in that department, I ever knew." Lincoln then turned to his own relationship with the young man—"as intimate as the disparity of our ages, and my engrossing engagements, would permit." He added, "What was conclusive of his good heart, he never forgot his parents. . . . In the hope that it may be no intrusion upon the sacredness of your sorrow, I have ventured to address this tribute to your brave and early fallen child. May God give you that consolation which is beyond all earthly power." Lincoln's letter, the first of hundreds he would write to the parents or spouses of fallen soldiers, is remarkable in both its affection and eloquence—written by a man consumed in grief.

THE MOST PUBLIC MAN in America lived in a White House that served as both home and office. The West Wing, which houses the current White House offices, would not be added until 1902 by President Theodore Roosevelt. This arrangement became the setting of an odd mixture of politics and pomp.

William Howard Russell, correspondent of the *Times* of London, described the White House as "the moderate mansion." He and other visitors from abroad compared it unfavorably to London's Buckingham Palace or Paris's Tuileries. Abraham and Mary Lincoln, on the contrary, were impressed with a home that had thirty-one rooms set amid twenty-two acres of woodlands. To try to add to the dignity of the residence, President James K. Polk had placed a bronze statue of Thomas Jefferson on the North Lawn in 1848. President Buchanan had built a conservatory to replace a greenhouse, but admittedly much of the sur-

Mathew Brady took this photograph of Mary Lincoln sometime in 1861.
She is proud of her role as the hostess of the White House and is seen here
in a beautiful gown with a floral headdress.

rounding woodlands were untidy and contained old, unused buildings and sheds. There was also the marshy Ellipse that slanted down to the Potomac River. The White House had obtained city water just two years before the Lincolns arrived.

Inside, the Executive Mansion—as it was called on official stationery until the presidency of Theodore Roosevelt—boasted the large elegant East Room, the ornate Red Room with a piano, and the lovely Blue Room, on the main floor. On their first evening in their new home,

Mary Lincoln led a tour of inspection and was surprised to find the upstairs family quarters in shabby condition, with cracked wallpaper, worn carpets, dilapidated draperies, and furniture that looked like it had belonged to the first residents, John and Abigail Adams. Rather than an Executive Mansion, most of the private residence had the appearance of a run-down hotel.

Mary Lincoln believed she was prepared, by family background and education, to be "First Lady," a title that had been conferred for the first time in 1857 upon Harriet Lane, the orphaned daughter of bachelor James Buchanan's much-loved sister. At age forty-two, Mary eagerly set out to take responsibility for the public life in the White House.

She welcomed her new position. If her husband was the new commander in chief in the masculine public sphere of the nation, she wanted to be the commander in chief in the feminine sphere of the home. As her husband took the lead in building a ragtag army into a modern, well-equipped military, she became determined to turn the run-down White House into a modern, well-furnished public place for the people.

Mary found herself living a difficult "semiprivate" life, a space in between the customary private lives of women in the nineteenth century, and the public life of the new First Lady of the White House. She had always taken pleasure in the political aspects of public life. In Illinois, she had grown accustomed to being a part of her husband's inner circle, offering him counsel and advice. In Washington, she expected to do the same.

But Mary was not prepared for the cold reception she would receive in Washington. She found herself excluded from Washington society by various cliques of women. Although Mary was a Southerner by birth, the Southern women who remained in Washington rebuffed her because they deemed her husband the "Black Republican." On the other hand, Eastern women snubbed her because they saw her as an uncivilized frontier woman from the West.

Soon after arriving in Washington, Mary decided to restore the Executive Mansion both as a personal home and as a public space. Not since Dolly Madison, a half century earlier, had a First Lady approached her task with such resolve. Ever since 1841, Congress had provided twenty thousand dollars annually for refurbishing the White House. Few of her predecessors had spent the full allowance. Harriet Lane, Buchanan's niece, had focused her attention on social events on the main floor and spent nothing on the living quarters on the second floor. Mary

Lincoln got busy spending the allowance on furniture, wallpaper, rugs, and china.

In early May, Mary set off for New York and Philadelphia. Accompanied by her cousin Lizzie Grimsley and William Wood, who had been in charge of the Lincolns' travel arrangements from Springfield to Washington, she attacked the finest stores in New York and Philadelphia. Alexander T. Stewart, known as "the Merchant Prince" of New York, hosted Mary at a dinner party and she returned the favor by buying two thousand dollars' worth of rugs and curtains at his marble emporium on Broadway. This would be the first of eleven buying trips by the First Lady.

CONGRESS RETURNED ON the first days of July 1861 to prepare for the special session. George Templeton Strong, who traveled to the capital during these same days, observed that Washington in early July was not for the fainthearted. "For all the detestable places, Washington is the first—in July, and with Congress sitting." He described his experiences: "Crowd, heat, bad quarters, bad fare, bad smells, mosquitoes, and a plague of flies transcending everything within my experience." Strong invoked Old Testament imagery to express his impressions of Washington and its best hotel. "Beelzebub surely reigns there, and Willard's Hotel is his temple."

Lincoln had begun to compose his July 4 message to Congress in May. He had never written an executive report to a legislative body before. As the day approached, the president changed his open-door policy and would not see anyone except for members of the cabinet or high officials. He worked in his office alone, often speaking words aloud before he put pencil to paper.

While writing and revising, Lincoln would sometimes look up and, in a brooding mood, gaze through the window, past the South Lawn, at the red sandstone Smithsonian Institution, which had only been completed in 1855, and beyond to the unfinished Washington Monument. Lincoln had been present when the cornerstone for the monument was laid in a grand patriotic ceremony on July 4, 1848. In the intervening years, work on the monument had stalled and then stopped. Improper management and a lack of funds dampened public support. At the outbreak of the Civil War, the monument still stood at 176 feet high, only about one-third of its final 555⅝ feet. The grounds surrounding the monument had been turned into an open grazing pen for cattle, sheep,

Lincoln could look through the south window of his office at the Washington Monument.
As a congressman, he was present on July 4, 1848, for the laying of the cornerstone,
but the monument remained unfinished in 1861.

and pigs, giving it the name "the Washington National Monument Cattle Yard." One of Lincoln's heroes was George Washington, and the stoppage of work on the monument, coupled with the suspension of the completion of the dome of the Capitol, symbolized the fragile condition of the Union in the early summer of 1861.

As Lincoln moved from the first to the second draft of his July 4 address, he invited his cabinet to look over the proof sheets. Secretary of State Seward again became an editor, offering more than twenty revisions. Once more, his editing was aimed at "softening the expression and eliminating potential problems," but his revisions did not have the same impact as they had on Lincoln's inaugural address. In the end, Lincoln's chief editor was Lincoln himself; he revised again and again, making nearly a hundred revisions in the several versions of the text.

After the secession of eleven states, the new Thirty-seventh Congress comprised 105 Republicans and 43 Democrats in the House of Representatives and 31 Republicans and 10 Democrats in the Senate. Democrats had lost almost half their representation in Congress. A new force in Congress were the "War Democrats," those from the South who supported Lincoln's efforts to preserve the Union, such as Senator Andrew Johnson from Tennessee, whose home state was the last Southern state to secede.

There was also a deeply felt absence. Stephen Douglas, Lincoln's longtime opponent, had died on June 3, 1861, in Chicago, probably of cirrhosis of the liver. He was only forty-eight years old. To the end, Douglas had gone far out of his way to express his support for President Lincoln. At Douglas's death, Lincoln ordered the White House and government buildings draped in bereavement bunting. Department offices closed.

In 1861, the president did not deliver an annual message to Congress in person. George Washington and John Adams, the nation's first two presidents, had personally delivered their annual messages, but Thomas Jefferson changed this tradition. Jefferson held a deep aversion to the monarchical configuration from which the colonies freed themselves. He believed the symbol of the president speaking to Congress smacked of the old order, in which the king or queen spoke from on high to Parliament. He declared a clean break from his two Federalist predecessors by saying he would not address Congress in person, but rather send up a written message. Jefferson's practice lasted more than one hundred years, all the way into the early twentieth century. Woodrow Wilson broke with this precedent in his first year as president when he spoke in person to Congress about the State of the Union in 1913.

On July 4, 1861, all the members of Congress gathered for a chief ceremonial occasion in the young republic: the reading of a presidential message. The clerk read Lincoln's words in a dull monotone.

At the outset, Lincoln restated the policy he had announced in his inaugural address: to pursue "all peaceful measures" to avoid war, reminding friend and foe that the policy of his administration was to rely on the peaceful measures of "time, discussion, and the ballot box." He continued, "And this issue embraces more than the fate of these United States. It presents to the whole family of man, the question, whether a constitutional republic, or a democracy—a government of the people, by the same people can, or cannot, maintain its territorial integrity, against its own domestic foes."

In Lincoln's opening paragraphs, he signaled that his audience was to be more than Congress. He directed his remarks to the people of the South and the North, as well as to foreign governments who were making up their minds about their posture toward the Union and the new Confederate government.

Lincoln introduced his discussion of the suspension of habeas corpus by acknowledging that "the attention of the country has been called to the proposition that one who is sworn to 'take care that the laws be faithfully executed,' should not himself violate them." After addressing the ramifications of his actions, he asked a question that anyone in his audience could understand: "To state the question more directly, are all the laws *but one* to go unexecuted, and the government itself go to pieces, lest that one be violated?" In the end, Lincoln went out of his way to offer assurance. "Whether there shall be any legislation upon the subject, he was content to rely on the better judgment of Congress." In his discussion of habeas corpus, he wanted Congress to know he believed he had acted "very sparingly," but would act decisively in the future to preserve the Union.

At the center of the address, Lincoln acted as a political guide eager to lead the way through a thicket of thorny definitions. For Lincoln, definitions mattered. It mattered most that this was not a war between the government of the United States and the government of the Confederate States of America. To use such terms would be to cede to the Southern states the constitutional prerogative of secession.

> This is essentially a People's contest. On the side of the Union, it is a struggle for maintaining in the world, that form, and substance, of government, whose leading object is, to elevate the condition of men—to lift artificial weights from all shoulders—to clear the paths of laudable pursuit for all—to afford all, an unfettered start, and a fair chance, in the race of life.

The Civil War has been interpreted as a war to preserve the Union, but at the beginning of the war Lincoln declared the Union not an end, but a means to an end that was more than a particular system of political organization. For Lincoln, the Union was an ecology of political, social, and economic life that could nourish the common person's opportunity to pursue their dreams, unrestricted by artificial obstacles.

This address demonstrates Lincoln's ability to combine both homely and high language in a new kind of American presidential communication. In his extended discussion of secession, he referred initially to its proponents by saying "they commenced by an insidious debauching of the public mind." He continued his assault by arguing that "they invented an ingenious sophism," an argument ultimately invalid, even if correct in form. After this high level of oratory—albeit in a communication read by a clerk—Lincoln suddenly exclaimed, "With rebellion thus sugar-coated, they have been drugging the public mind of their section for more than thirty years."

The government printer John D. Defrees, when he received Lincoln's draft before July 4, objected to Lincoln's phrase "sugar-coated." Defrees had served as a member of the Indiana state legislature and had led the Indiana delegation at the Republican convention in Chicago. A politician and a printer, he informed Lincoln that sugar-coated "lacked the dignity proper to a state paper." Lincoln replied, "Well, Defrees, if you think the time will come when people will not understand what 'sugar-coated' means, I'll alter it; otherwise, I think I'll let it go."

One of Lincoln's greatest gifts was his ability to give voice to the war aspirations of the Union in compelling prose. On July 4, he did so by combining conservative and liberal goals. Lincoln's ideas were conservative as he spoke of defending a deep-rooted, established order; they were liberal when he spoke of promoting and extending the rights of all people.

In his message to the special session of Congress, Lincoln told his critics that he was, indeed, in charge. As he had answered Seward's challenge in private, he now spoke in public. The speech was as much about establishing Lincoln's political and moral authority to lead as anything else. In answer to the *New York Times* and other newspapers and politicians, Lincoln offered a policy that would be acted upon in the more than seventy provisions Congress would pass in the remaining twenty-eight days of the session.

THE RESPONSE TO LINCOLN'S MESSAGE signified that at the beginning of the war almost all sides were willing to support the president. Politicians from both parties supported Lincoln's proposal that Congress appropriate $400,000 to support an army of 400,000 men. Once in session, Congress boosted the amounts to $500,000 for an army of 500,000 men.

George Curtis, an editorial writer for *Harper's Monthly* and *Harper's*

Weekly, read Lincoln's address with great interest. Living on Staten Island, Curtis had gone to Chicago to support his fellow New Yorker William Seward for the Republican nomination for president. After Lincoln was elected, Curtis expressed doubts about Lincoln's capacity to lead the nation.

The July 4 address changed his appraisal of Lincoln. In a letter to a younger friend, he offered his assessment. Curtis thought Lincoln's "message was the most truly American message ever delivered." As a literary critic, he believed Lincoln's words were "wonderfully acute, simple, sagacious, and of antique honesty!" Curtis concluded, "I can forgive the jokes and the big hands, and the inability to make bows. Some of us who doubted were wrong."

In the midst of all of the accolades for Lincoln's address, African-American abolitionist editor Frederick Douglass offered a lonely but prescient commentary. "In the late Message of our honest President, which purports to give an honest history of our present difficulties, no mention is, at all, made of slavery. . . . Any one reading that document, with no previous knowledge of the United States, would never dream from anything there written that a slaveholding war was waged upon the Government, determined to overthrow it." Douglass gave voice to millions when he declared, "The proclamation goes forth at the head of all our armies, assuring the slaveholding rebels that slavery shall receive no detriment from our arms."

Indeed, Lincoln made no mention of slavery in his address, for in July 1861, the war was solely about preserving the Union. Lincoln understood this to be the sentiment of the Northern people. Elected by a minority of the citizenry, he needed the loyalty of Democrats, who remained distrustful of the intentions of Republicans. Lincoln believed he must continue to reiterate this message of fighting solely to preserve the Union if he was to hold on to the border states.

PARTISAN POLITICS WERE QUIETED briefly after Lincoln's July 4, 1861, message to Congress, but throughout April, May, and June, volunteers had streamed into both the Union and Confederate armies. The presence of troops from almost every Northern state, visible in daily parades in and around Washington, increased the call of politicians and newspaper editors to begin marching south. When the Confederate Congress announced they would convene on July 20 in Richmond, their new capital, only one hundred miles south of Washington, the pressure on

Lincoln and his generals grew. One question dominated the daily conversations of the Northern public: "When would the army march toward Richmond?"

Starting on June 26, 1861, managing editor Charles A. Dana placed this aggressive caption at the top of the editorial columns of the *New York Tribune* in bold italics.

> ***Forward to Richmond! Forward to Richmond!***
> ***The Rebel Congress must not be allowed to meet there***
> ***on the 20th of July.***
> ***By that date the place must be held by the National Army!***

The same headline ran every day for eleven straight days.

While Lincoln sought the right generals to lead the Union troops, he also had to contend with the so-called newspaper generals of New York. Horace Greeley, editor of the *New York Tribune,* Henry J. Raymond, editor of the *New York Times,* James Gordon Bennett, editor of the *New York Herald,* and William Cullen Bryant, editor of the *New York Evening Post,* saw their jobs as not only reporting but shaping public opinion from their offices on newspaper row in New York City. Immediately after Fort Sumter, they began demanding action. Throughout late April, May, and June, the newspaper generals counseled and cajoled the president. They advised that the war should be carried to Baltimore, Richmond, Charleston, Atlanta, and Montgomery. They made the case that if the border states did not respond immediately to a call to arms, their citizens should be treated as traitors.

In the special session of Congress, the question about Richmond dominated deliberations. All around Washington, the capital regiments assembled, drilled, and paraded, but nearly three months had passed since Lincoln's April 15, 1861, proclamation and still there was no major military engagement. Most of the soldiers were ninety-day militia, everyone well aware that their obligations of service would be up in the later part of July.

Behind the scenes, Lincoln was shocked to learn the army was unprepared for war. He watched, in disappointment, as the War Department and the Navy Department struggled to become effective. The military bureaucracy was frustratingly inefficient. Seventy-two years after the inauguration of its first president, the United States boasted no professional military literature and thus an absence of critical military theory in the preparation of army officers at West Point. The Bureau of Topographical Engineers owned few accurate maps of the South.

Rivalries broke out between Cameron and Welles over the preparation for and conduct of the war, with both men complaining that Seward was constantly interfering with their authority and jurisdiction. Lincoln believed the public wanted the military to move soon, or he ran the risk of cooling the ardor of war fever.

Lincoln asked General Scott; Irvin McDowell, commander of the Union forces in Virginia; Quartermaster General Montgomery Meigs; and other senior military leaders to attend a special cabinet meeting to discuss a summer offensive. He directed everyone's attention to a map on the wall of his office and said he wanted McDowell to attack a Confederate force at Manassas, Virginia, a rail junction thirty miles southwest of Washington. Scott dissented, arguing that the army could not possibly be ready to fight until the fall.

Scott then presented to the full cabinet his own plan. He would tighten the blockade on the East Coast and then, with sixty thousand troops, sail down the Mississippi River from Cairo, Illinois, to the Gulf of Mexico, establishing a string of forts along the way: his so-called "boa constrictor" plan. The South thus sealed, the Union would wait for calmer voices to drown out the fire-eaters, as Union sentiment in the South rose. The press, when hearing of this plan, named it for a different snake, the anaconda, the largest and most powerful snake in the Western Hemisphere, who lived in water and killed its prey by constriction or squeezing. Scott's "Anaconda Plan" failed to consider what the Southern troops would be doing while the Northern troops took several months to travel to and sail down the Mississippi. Lincoln knew that the public would never have the patience for Scott's plan. In listening to his daily visitors, he came to understand that his Northern audience needed to see some results if he and the Union would retain their support.

After this, Lincoln focused on finding a leader to produce real results. He believed he found this man in Brigadier General McDowell. Born in Columbus, Ohio, in 1818, McDowell grew up in France before returning to study at West Point. Six feet tall, square and strong, he had put on considerable weight by the summer of 1861. He had a reputation as a gargantuan eater—at one time consuming a whole watermelon for dessert—yet he abstained from alcohol, tobacco, and coffee. McDowell had served on Scott's staff in the campaign from Veracruz to Mexico

*Irvin McDowell became the
first American general to
lead an army of thirty
thousand men into battle.
He also suffered the ignominy
of the Union defeat at Bull Run
at the end of July 1861.*

City. His career had been pushed along in Washington by influential
Ohio senator John Sherman and Secretary of the Treasury Salmon
Chase. Honest and upright, McDowell could also be stern and inflexi-
ble. Now, at age forty-two, he was about to become the first general in
America to lead an army of thirty thousand men into battle.

But it was now McDowell's turn to demur. He told Lincoln and the
cabinet that his men could not possibly be ready to march in July. He
had an undersized staff, his men were untrained volunteers, and he did
not even possess a map of Virginia that showed anything beyond the
main roads. Scott rallied to the defense of McDowell, saying he agreed
that the army was unprepared.

But Lincoln believed it was time to act, and countered McDowell's
objections. "You are green, it is true; but they are green, also; you are all
green alike." As commander in chief, Lincoln ordered McDowell to
prepare for his men to march by July 9.

LINCOLN ROSE EARLY on a warm, muggy Sunday morning, July 21,
1861, as McDowell, twelve days behind schedule and unsure of his inexperienced troops, began his march to the meandering, tree-lined Bull
Run River, several miles north of Manassas Junction. McDowell's plan
was straightforward: He would lead his army of thirty thousand recruits

in three columns against a Confederate force of twenty thousand recruits, commanded by Brigadier General Pierre G. T. Beauregard, who had been in charge of the Confederate forces that shelled Fort Sumter. Although outnumbered, Beauregard, making his headquarters at the farmhouse of Wilmer McLean, believed he could take advantage of the lay of the land and the bends in the river.

McDowell's movements caught no one by surprise. Confederate operatives in Washington conveyed his plans to General Beauregard, but there was no need to do so. McDowell's march became a spectator sport as politicians, ladies with picnic baskets, and a ragtag assembly of onlookers traveled south from Washington to witness the great victory that would prelude the march on Richmond.

McDowell crossed the Bull Run River and started to turn the Confederate left. Men on both sides, who had never before been in battle, fought fiercely. McDowell believed he had the Confederates outnumbered. Union troops quickly forced the Confederates into retreat up Henry House Hill. Telegraphs of the initial successes were sent to the War Department in Washington every fifteen minutes from Fairfax, ten miles from the battle. But the Union attacks were too uncoordinated, and attack and counterattack swelled back and forth. McDowell held on to his two reserve brigades instead of using them strategically in battle.

One Confederate general held his ground. Thomas Jackson, a West Point graduate and a devout Presbyterian layman, had begun the day on his knees in prayer in his tent. When other Confederate forces were falling back before Union artillery and troops, Jackson's West Point friend Barnard Bee pointed his sword toward the crest of Henry Hill and called out, "Look, men, there is Jackson standing like a stone wall." The little-known Jackson, wearing his blue faculty member's uniform from the Virginia Military Institute, pointed his left hand to the sky and rallied his men. When McDowell brought forward more artillery pressure, a New York regiment that had moved toward the pines where Jackson was located suddenly found themselves overrun by James E. B. "Jeb" Stuart and his First Virginia Cavalry.

LINCOLN ASKED SCOTT on the morning of July 21, 1861, for his assessment of the prospects of the battle. The general assured the president that everything was going well. Lincoln, as was becoming his custom, went off to church.

After lunch, he walked over to the War Department's telegraph office to read some of the telegrams coming from the battle. Mounted couriers, coordinated by twenty-five-year-old Andrew Carnegie, sustained telegraph communication with General McDowell's headquarters. At 3 p.m., as Lincoln pored over maps, the telegraph spelled out in Morse code, "Our army is retreating."

Alarmed, Lincoln walked to Scott's office, only to find the general fast asleep. Awakened, the general counseled the president that there was always an ebb and flow in battles and not to worry. Reassured, the president went for a carriage ride to the Naval Yard.

When Lincoln returned, Secretary of State Seward handed him a telegram from McDowell. "The day is lost. . . . Save Washington and the remnants of this army. . . . The routed troops will not reform." Lincoln returned to the telegraph office at intervals until after midnight, when all telegraph messages ceased.

How did this calamitous defeat happen? As Jackson held his ground for nearly three hours, Confederate reinforcements had arrived from the South. Although the Southern army would quickly develop a reputation for lightning-like cavalry, the use of the railroad helped change the Battle of Bull Run. Nine thousand men in the Shenandoah Valley loaded themselves and their horses into freight and cattle cars and traveled on the Manassas Gap Railroad, sometimes as slowly as four miles per hour because of the weight of the horses, toward Manassas and Bull Run. Their arrival and counterattack stunned the Union forces, which began to retreat in panic. McDowell tried to regroup north of Bull Run, but it was no use.

Soldiers retreated all the way back to Washington, sometimes overtaking the surprised spectators. Senators Benjamin Wade of Ohio and Zachariah Chandler of Michigan, who had ridden out to enjoy the fruits of victory with rifles in hand, now were aghast as soldiers, horses, and wagons hurried back to Washington. Wade, enraged, leapt from the wagon, shouting, "Boys, we will stop this damned run-away." Brandishing his rifle, along with Chandler and several others, he blocked the road and "commanded an immediate halt" to the retreating soldiers.

In the middle of the night, Lincoln learned that after ten hours of fighting, almost nine hundred men, including five hundred Union soldiers, lay dead on the fields of Henry House Hill, Matthews Hill, and Chinn Ridge. The hopes of both North and South for a quick war were shattered. A spiral of violence was just beginning. The South had won a great tactical victory, but even more important, the Confederacy stalled any march into Virginia until 1862.

For Lincoln, Bull Run was an alarming defeat. He pulled his cabinet together for an emergency late-night meeting at the War Department. Afterward, Lincoln could not sleep. He lay on a lounge all night, but from time to time talked with soldiers and spectators returning from the battle. Senator Chandler arrived at midnight to give Lincoln his report of the disastrous battle. The President was shaken.

In the South, they were jubilant. An unknown Southern poet wrote:

> Yankee Doodle, near Bull Run
>   Met his adversary,
> First he thought the fight he'd won,
>   Fact proved quite contrary.
> Panic-struck he fled, with speed
>   Of lightning glib with unction,
> Of slippery grease, in full stampede,
> From famed Manassas Junction.

In the wake of the defeat at Bull Run, political leaders put aside their partisanship in order to rally to the Union cause and restate the purpose of the war. On Monday, July 22, 1861, John J. Crittenden from Kentucky and Andrew Johnson from Tennessee introduced identical resolutions in the House and Senate "which gave expression to the common sentiment in the country," that the war was not being waged "for the purpose of interfering with the rights of established institutions of those States, but to defend and maintain the *supremacy* of the Constitution, and to preserve the Union." The resolution passed in the House on July 22 and in the Senate on July 25. After the defeat at Bull Run, even most of those who wanted the war to be about ending slavery voted for this resolution.

"Today will be known as BLACK MONDAY." Diarist George Templeton Strong in New York City captured the mood in the North. "We are utterly and disgracefully routed, beaten, whipped by secessionists." After such a defeat, charges and allegations were leveled at the military. General McDowell, who had not counted on the arrival of Confederate reinforcements, became the initial focus of the criticism. A teetotaler, McDowell was even accused of being drunk in battle. But quickly the censure targeted his boss, General in Chief Winfield Scott. He may have been a hero of the Mexican War, but public opinion said he was far past his prime and ought to retire.

Two days later, Lincoln found himself in conversation with four Illinois congressmen and Scott when the old general exclaimed, "Sir, I am the greatest coward in America! I will prove it. I have fought this battle, sir, against my judgment; I think the President of the United States ought to remove me for doing it."

Lincoln, taken aback, replied, "Your conversation seems to imply that I forced you to fight this battle."

Lincoln's remark seemed to throw Scott off balance. He responded, "I have never served a President who has been kinder to me than you have been."

As accusations swirled in Congress, the press, and the public, Lincoln refused to indulge in any finger pointing. If there would be any responsibility for defeat, he would bear it upon his broad shoulders. He knew it was not a time for looking backward but forward. Lincoln had learned some valuable lessons and he was preparing to act upon them. After the disastrous defeat at Bull Run, Lincoln knew he needed to find military leadership he could rely upon. In the late summer and fall of 1861, this was his most urgent priority.

This photograph, perhaps taken by Mathew Brady toward the end of 1861, may have captured Lincoln in a candid moment. The photographer, sensing he had caught Lincoln deep in reverie, asked him to retain this reflective pose.

CHAPTER 19

The Bottom Is Out of the Tub
July 1861–January 1862

THE STRUGGLE OF TODAY, IS NOT ALTOGETHER FOR TODAY—IT IS
FOR A VAST FUTURE ALSO.

ABRAHAM LINCOLN
Annual message to Congress, December 3, 1861

ARTICLE 2, SECTION 2 OF THE CONSTITUTION STATES, "THE PRESIDENT
shall be Commander in Chief of the Army and Navy of the United
States, and of the militia of the several States, when called into the service of the United States," but it does not identify the range or restric-
tions of the president's military responsibilities. In the months after Bull
Run, Lincoln began to take the role of commander in chief in new,
dynamic, and controversial directions. Although he had held the title
during the first four and a half months of his presidency, he only truly
began to assume the position in the summer and fall of 1861.

Four of Lincoln's fifteen predecessors—George Washington, Andrew
Jackson, William Henry Harrison, and Zachary Taylor—came to the
presidential office with military experience, each having served as a commanding officer. Presidents James Madison and James Polk, neither of
whom had military experience, presided over the nation's two wars since
the War of Independence—the War of 1812 and the Mexican War. Both
Madison and Polk largely delegated to military leaders the military strategy and operations in each conflict. Lincoln, at the beginning of his presidency, followed this pattern, delegating this function to General in
Chief Winfield Scott. After the disaster of Bull Run, he was ready to
take up the yet-to-be-defined duties of commander in chief.

Lincoln came to the presidency keenly aware of his limited military
experience. In the Black Hawk War in 1832, he had served for three

months as a private and a captain. By contrast, Jefferson Davis, the president of the Confederate States of America, had graduated from West Point, commanded a regiment that fought bravely at the battle of Buena Vista in the Mexican War, and served with distinction as secretary of war from 1853 to 1857 in the administration of Franklin Pierce.

Following his inauguration in March, Lincoln's posture toward Scott and other senior military officers had been initially respectful and deferential. After carefully considering their opinions during the crisis leading up to Fort Sumter, Lincoln took his first steps as commander in chief in questioning some of the assumptions of his military leaders. Three months later, in the run-up to the battle at Bull Run, Lincoln challenged Scott's Anaconda Plan, and advocated Irvin McDowell's advance on Bull Run.

After the humiliating defeat, Lincoln turned his full attention to the military strategy that would carry out his national policy. Although he would, at times, vacillate between deference and decision with his new military leaders, as summer turned into fall he began to assume responsibilities that had never been wielded before by an American president. By early 1862, he would become a hands-on commander in chief.

"WARS, COMMOTIONS, AND REVOLUTIONS, we thought were for other and less favored lands, but for us an uninterrupted future of peaceful growth." So spoke Lincoln's Illinois friend Julian M. Sturtevant, president of Illinois College, in an address to the alumni of Yale College immediately after the defeat at Bull Run. Sturtevant offered a sober warning that Lincoln certainly heard. "These were the delusive daydreams of our national childhood . . . to be rudely dissolved by the stern, sad realities of experience."

Immediately after Bull Run, Lincoln decided to change generals. At 2 a.m. on July 22, 1861, General Lorenzo Thomas sent a telegram to young General George B. McClellan, summoning him from western Virginia to Washington. "Circumstances make your presence here necessary." McClellan would take the place of McDowell and serve directly under General Scott.

McClellan was only thirty-four years old when, the next morning at daylight, he rode on horseback sixty miles to Wheeling, Virginia, boarded a train to Pittsburgh, and from there traveled on to Washington. He arrived in the capital late on Friday afternoon, July 26, 1861, as a hero. His only victories up to this point had been in small battles in

This photograph of General George B. McClellan captures the handsome features of the man called "Young Napoleon," who became the first military hero of the Civil War.

western Virginia, pushing out Confederate defenders in the state's northwestern counties. But his conquests helped ignite efforts by Unionists in the area to repeal Virginia's ordinance of secession and to form their own state of West Virginia. The Union was ready for a hero, and McClellan, with an erect, strong build and a handsome face with gray eyes and dark hair, looked and acted the part.

The next morning, Lincoln welcomed McClellan to the White House to inspect his new general. Afterward Congress lionized McClellan and he was introduced all around. Lincoln invited him to attend a cabinet meeting in the afternoon. When McClellan told Winfield Scott, who was not invited, of the invitation, the old general became irritated at what he took to be a snub. He detained McClellan so that he missed the cabinet meeting. When McClellan later apologized to Lincoln, the president "seemed more amused than otherwise." That same evening, McClellan wrote his wife, Ellen Marcy, "I find myself in a new & strange position here—Presdt, Cabinet, Genl Scott & all deferring to me—by some strange operation of magic I seem to have become *the* power of the land." Three days later he wrote Ellen he was "quite overwhelmed by the congratulations I received & the respect with which I was treated." Members of Congress "tell me that I am held responsible for the fate of the Nation." McClellan was confident in his ability. "It is an immense task that I have on my hands, but I believe I can accomplish it."

George Brinton McClellan was born to a family that traveled in the upper circles of Philadelphia society. A precocious student, George was educated in private schools before entering West Point at age fifteen, the youngest in his class. He graduated in 1846 second in a class of fifty-nine, but believed that it was only an injustice by faculty members that denied him finishing first.

On September 26, 1846, Second Lieutenant McClellan sailed from New York for Brazos Santiago, Texas, near the mouth of the Rio Grande. He began his service in the Mexican War in the Corps of Engineers, sometimes under the direction of Captain Robert E. Lee. McClellan advanced to first lieutenant, and his abilities and courage in battle marked him for future leadership.

After the Mexican War, McClellan returned to West Point to administrative and part-time teaching duties for three years. Discouraged by the slow rate of promotions in the peacetime army, he transferred to a position as captain in the newly formed First Cavalry in 1855. Here he undertook a number of assignments, including an entire year in Europe studying the tactics used in the Crimean War. He came back to the United States in April 1856, and set to work writing a report on his findings. Returning with a hundred books and manuals from Europe, fluent in French and German, and teaching himself Russian, McClellan focused in his report on the siege at Sebastopol and concluded with a highly informative manual for American cavalry. He completed his special assignments as a protégé of the activist secretary of war Jefferson Davis.

McClellan resigned his commission in the army on January 15, 1857, which surprised his army friends. He decided there was a bright future in business, and at age thirty he became the chief engineer of the Illinois Central Railroad at a beginning salary of $3,000, more than twice his army pay.

Lincoln first met McClellan through his work for the Illinois Central Railroad. In 1857, the main line of the Illinois Central traversed 704 miles from Chicago to Cairo. By this time McClellan, who had grown up a Whig, had become a conservative Democrat who blamed the "ultras" in both Republican and Democratic parties for the growing sectional conflict. In Lincoln's debates with Stephen Douglas in 1858, McClellan actively supported Douglas and invited the Little Giant to make use of his private Illinois Central car for his campaign against Lincoln. Some believe that the first encounters between these two quite different men, in what McClellan described as "out-of-the-way county-seats" in Illinois, sowed the seeds of future difficulties, but neither Lincoln nor McClellan ever offered such a suggestion.

AFTER MCCLELLAN ARRIVED in Washington in the summer of 1861, the public was keen to learn more about this new military hero. He proved more than willing to oblige. He visited Mathew Brady's studio on Pennsylvania Avenue and struck a military pose with his right hand pressed into his coat in replication of Napoleon. As small *cartes de visite,* the photographs were sold across the North. Newspaper correspondent William Russell and others began calling him the "Young Napoleon."

"Confidence Renewed" was the title of an August 1, 1861, *New York Tribune* editorial praising McClellan's first days on duty. McClellan saw his immediate task as reestablishing order in the capital. He would sometimes spend twelve hours in the saddle, chewing tobacco, rounding up military stragglers, clearing the barrooms, and wanting to see and be seen by both his men and residents. The soldiers started calling him "Little Mac," and offered a cheer when he approached, to which he would respond by raising and twirling his cap. When he stopped to talk to soldiers, he pledged no more retreats, asking them if they were ready to fight.

Lincoln was eager to fight, too, and asked McClellan to present a strategic plan to end the South's insurrection. On August 2, 1861, "Little Mac" submitted his ambitious proposal to the president. He wanted "to move into the heart of the enemy's country, and crush out this rebellion in its very heart." Rather than Scott's slow concentric squeezing of the enemy, McClellan proposed a quick strike by a huge army that would win the war in one climactic battle. "The force I have recommended is large—the expense is great." Lincoln's reaction to this plan is not known. McClellan's plan was long on reach and short on realism, requiring more than double the number of men presently in the ranks.

AS COMMANDER IN CHIEF, Lincoln understood that he faced a steep learning curve. Yet his whole adult life had consisted of self-education, and he welcomed the challenge. Just as he had become a self-taught lawyer in rural Illinois, he now set out to teach himself military theory and strategy.

A day after Bull Run, Lincoln wrote out the lessons to be learned from defeat, following his lifelong habit of putting his thoughts to paper as a way of guiding himself through a difficult problem. He listed nine action steps, encompassing everything from "making the Blockade effective" in the East to instructing General John C. Frémont to "push forward his organization and operations in the West." Four days later, Lincoln continued on the same page with two additional items, one for the eastern theater—the need to seize Manassas and Strasburg in Virginia—and one for the western theater—the proposal to move on both Memphis and eastern Tennessee.

By November John Hay wrote, "The President is himself a man of great aptitude for military studies." By now Lincoln was so present at the War Department that "many of the orders issuing from the War Department are penned by the hand of the President." In December, John Nicolay observed that Lincoln "gave himself, night and day, to the study of the military situation. He read a large number of strategical works. He pored over the reports from the various departments and districts of the field of war. He held long conferences with eminent generals and admirals, and astonished them by the extent of his special knowledge." Increasingly, military books piled up on the long cabinet table in his office. One of the books he read was *Elements of Military Art and Science* by Henry W. Halleck, a general and military theorist.

"The poor President!" William Howard Russell, the world's first war correspondent, became aware of Lincoln's trips to the Library of Congress.

> He is to be pitied . . . trying with all his might to understand strategy, naval warfare, big guns, the movement of troops, military maps, reconnaissances, occupations, interior and exterior lines, and all the technical details of the art of slaying. He runs from one house to another, armed with plans, papers, reports, recommendations, sometimes good humoured, never angry, occasionally dejected.

Russell, who continually undervalued Lincoln's abilities, believed it was unwise for the president to immerse himself in the details of military theory and strategy. Time would tell who was correct.

Lincoln understood from the beginning that his role as commander in chief was in service to both his political vision and military realities. Carl von Clausewitz, the Prussian soldier and educator, wrote in *On War* (*Vom Kriege*), "The political objective is the goal, war is the means of reaching it, and means can never be considered in isolation from their purpose. Therefore, it is clear that war should never be thought of as *something autonomous* but always as an instrument of policy." Although there is no evidence that Lincoln ever read von Clausewitz, he would nonetheless appropriate the German theorist's thesis while pursuing his own political objectives.

Lincoln quickly learned that his own military leaders were often the greatest obstacles to military policy. The professional military leaders, almost all graduates of West Point, were trained for the battlefield. Used to operating within a chain of command that did not include political leaders, and certainly not the president, many did not take kindly to Lincoln's growing involvement in what they saw as their field of expertise. As Lincoln would become more and more a hands-on commander in chief, tensions with some of his military leaders would grow.

Lincoln began to insist that he as president was the first and last authority in setting military policy. Critics railed that he was expanding the power of the presidency, some going so far as labeling him a "dictator." Perhaps the greatest irony, some said, was that thirty years before, a young Lincoln had joined the bitter criticism against "King Andrew" Jackson—calling *him* a dictator. Now Lincoln had selected the old general's portrait to hang in his office. But it needs to be remembered that Lincoln followed three weak and ineffectual presidents. The odor of Buchanan's indecision in the year leading up to the Civil War still stuck in the nostrils of Washington politicians, even in Buchanan's own Democratic Party.

THE PROCESS OF RAISING a large army quickly proved to be much more complicated than Lincoln could ever have imagined. Never before had an American general commanded an army larger than the fourteen thousand men Scott had led in the War with Mexico.

A persistent difficulty in 1861 was not securing the number of recruits—the army was quickly oversubscribed with volunteers—but rather putting in place a workable military organization. A number of problems immediately arose.

The Constitution spoke about the army and navy of the United States as well as the state militias. Military officers who owed their rank and service to a professional military system of recruitment and review led the army and navy. The militias, on the other hand, were state home guards who often owed their recruitment and review either to the political officers of the respective states or to the person who raised the regiment and served as its commanding officer. To complicate matters, a number of units were ethnic regiments, such as German regiments, which often recruited men from more than one state. The problem, as Lincoln came to understand it, was how to coordinate a national military comprising the regular army and navy plus both state militias and ethnic units into a cohesive fighting force.

From the vantage point of the professional military, as well as that of Secretary of War Simon Cameron, the various militias too often operated by their own rules under the jurisdiction of local officials. From the point of view of state political officials and the leaders of the militias, the professional army and the Department of War presented needless bureaucratic obstacles to men who simply wanted their opportunity to fight to preserve the Union. The problem was exacerbated when state officials or leaders of regiments went over the heads of Scott and Cameron and made their cases directly to the president. Lincoln was always ready to cut through the red tape to accommodate regiments of all kinds. His typical response was to write Cameron, as he did seven times between May 13 and 26, 1861, with essentially the same message: "If the Secretary of War can accept the Regiments named within, I shall be greatly gratified."

In his role as commander in chief, the president had to appoint generals subject to Senate confirmation. In an extremely politicized era, Lincoln acquiesced to the long traditional practice of appointing well-known politicians as "political generals." He became amused and sometimes irritated by the process, but believed it was necessary in the beginning months of building up a huge army.

Lincoln allowed the custom to flourish for several reasons. First, governors and senators used their political influence as a form of military patronage. As a reward for political loyalty, or to accede to the wishes of political blocs of voters, influential leaders recommended men whose résumés consisted not of military experience but of political allegiance. Thus, Massachusetts governor John A. Andrew appointed Benjamin Butler, wealthy lawyer and powerful politician, to the overall command of the four Massachusetts regiments at the beginning of the war.

In May, Lincoln wrote to calm an irritated New York governor Edwin Morgan, a Republican governor he could not afford to upset. Morgan was angry that the "Union Defense Committee" of the city of

New York was raising fourteen regiments "quite independent and irrespective of authority from the Executive of New York." The governor complained that this action "cannot fail to result in confusion and serious disaster." Lincoln's answer was a masterpiece of diplomacy. He distinguished between a *substantial* wrong and a *technical* wrong in the question of jurisdiction. In his final sentence to Morgan, Lincoln summed up the attitude he had taken about raising an army. "The enthusiastic uprising of the people in our cause, is our great reliance; and we can not safely give it any check, even though it overflows, and runs in channels not laid down in any chart."

Second, the appointment of a wide range of political generals helped foster the political allegiance of German, Irish, Polish, and other ethnic groups. On May 13, 1861, Lincoln wrote to Simon Cameron to recommend Carl Schurz, who had raised four German regiments in New York, for brigadier general. "I am for it, unless there be some valid reason against it." A number of the ethnic political generals, like Schurz and Franz Sigel, became outstanding recruiters, expanding their ranks to great effect. Sigel was extremely popular with German recruits who proudly shouted, "I fights *mit* Sigel!"

Lincoln also appointed political generals for his own larger national policy. To lead the Union as a president elected by less than half of the electorate, he understood his need to court and include the opposition Democratic Party. An important way to do so was to appoint Democrats as political generals. In the first years of the Civil War, Lincoln accepted the appointments of Butler, John A. Logan, John A. McClernand, and Daniel E. Sickles: all Democrats. These and other Democratic leaders represented constituencies in sections or states, such as southern Ohio, Indiana, and Illinois, where the war was not popular.

As commander in chief, Lincoln quickly understood that a mass mobilization of troops was almost totally dependent on the efforts of state and local politicians. He knew he was riding a teeter-totter between professional and political soldiers and he needed to give equal weight to both sides to keep the army in balance. As the war moved forward, he believed the qualifications of soldiers would be quickly judged and won by their conduct on the battlefield.

LINCOLN SOON BECAME a frequent caller at George McClellan's headquarters, in a capacious home at Jackson Square on Pennsylvania Avenue at Nineteenth Street, two blocks from the War Department. McClellan set up the first floor for staff offices and a telegraph office and used the second floor for his living quarters. He convened staff meetings in the morning and rode to the various troop encampments in the afternoon. On two occasions, he made surveillances from Professor Thaddeus Lowe's hydrogen balloon.

Lincoln came calling to seek military news and talk strategy, while usually finding time to tell a few humorous stories. McClellan came to resent these visits as bothersome and the president as an annoyance. Like so many others, McClellan underestimated the man behind the droll stories: Lincoln, in fact, used these visits to size up his young general.

Less than two weeks into his new command, McClellan became convinced that his army would soon be under siege. On August 8, 1861, McClellan wrote a pessimistic memorandum, officially to General in Chief Scott, but he had aide Thomas M. Key deliver a copy on the same day to the president—without Scott's knowledge. McClellan portrayed a dire military landscape that, without ever saying so directly, cast aspersions on Scott's leadership. Citing "information from spies, letters and telegrams"—never identified—he wrote that the Confederacy was sending massive reinforcements because "the enemy intend attacking our positions on the other side of the river as well as to cross the Potomac North of us." How large was this force? "I am induced to believe that the enemy has at least one hundred thousand men in front of us." (Their actual numbers were closer to forty thousand.) After inflating the enemy's strength, Little Mac deflated the capacity of the army he had inherited: "I feel confident that our present army in this vicinity is entirely insufficient for the emergency; and it is deficient in all the arms of service—Infantry—Artillery and cavalry." A pattern of alarm and exaggeration was being set in motion. McClellan would defend himself by saying he was holding fast to his "one safe rule of war"—always be ready for the worst.

McClellan's memo infuriated Scott. The aged general, feeling the brunt of the tactics of America's Young Napoleon, wrote Secretary of War Cameron on August 9, 1861, and asked him to put him on the list for retirement. However, Scott wanted to hang on long enough to be sure that the young upstart McClellan would not be his successor. He hoped to anoint General Henry Halleck, the writer and editor of books on military theory that Lincoln had begun to read, to take his place.

Lincoln, ever the mediator, immediately sprang into action. First he walked over to McClellan's headquarters to both confront and counsel his young general. After reproving McClellan for the content and tone of the letter to his superior, Lincoln asked him to retract the letter by the end of the day. In McClellan's new letter he wrote, "I yield to your request, and withdraw the letter referred to." Later, Lincoln walked over to Scott's headquarters, showed him McClellan's second letter, and asked the general to withdraw his resignation. Scott thanked Lincoln for his "patriotic purpose of healing differences," but declined to withdraw his resignation. He told the president that he could not overlook or forgive his "ambitious junior" for his disrespect and for going around him directly to the president "without resort to or consultation with me, the nominal General-in-Chief of the Army."

"The Presdt is an idiot," wrote McClellan to his wife, Ellen, on the evening of August 16, 1861. If McClellan had publicly agreed to a truce, in his private letters to his wife he saw demons and adversaries everywhere—"wretched politicians" he called them. "Seward is the meanest of them all." "Welles is weaker than the most garrulous old woman." As for Lincoln, "The Presdt is nothing more than a well meaning baboon."

Over the next months, Lincoln would spend far more time with McClellan than any of his generals. It was as if he saw potential greatness in this young man and hoped he could nurture his abilities. Lincoln encouraged him and tried to reason with him. McClellan, for his part, was never able to take advantage of the leadership and insight that the president was only too willing to offer. After a tea at the White House, he told Ellen, "I found 'the original gorilla,' about as intelligent as ever. What a specimen to be at the head of our affairs now!"

On September 27, 1861, the simmering dispute between McClellan and Scott boiled over when Scott complained he was the last to know of McClellan's plans, and yet civilians in the administration always seemed to know. Finally, Lincoln had had enough. He wanted Scott respected for his long service to the country, but recognized that McClellan represented the future. On October 18, Lincoln accepted the old general's resignation, effective October 31. On the morning of November 1, Lincoln appointed McClellan general in chief of the army, the nation's top military post. That evening, Lincoln walked to McClellan's home to promise his full support. "Draw on me for all the sense I have, and all the information," he told his new general. "In addition to your present command, the supreme command of the army will entail a vast labor upon you."

"I can do it all," McClellan replied.

THROUGHOUT THE SUMMER OF 1861, Lincoln became increasingly concerned that the border states of Maryland, Delaware, Kentucky, and Missouri would join with the eleven states of the Confederacy. With their agricultural, industrial, and military resources, the fifteen states would become a much more potent adversary.

Lincoln was convinced he didn't need to worry about Delaware, with its less than two thousand slaves. Actually, the tiny state was really two Delawares, a northern, Republican, antislavery Delaware, and a southern, Democratic, pro-slavery Delaware. Seventy-five percent of Delaware's slaves lived in the Nanticoke River basin in the far southwestern corner of the state. Despite this division, most residents of this small state believed it would be suicide not to stay within the Union. Besides, Delawareans were proud of their heritage as the first state to enter the Union. When Georgia first approached the state to secede, the Delaware legislature answered back, "As Delaware was the first state to adopt, so will she be the last to abandon the Federal Constitution."

Maryland, which was smaller in population than the states of Kentucky and Missouri, posed large strategic problems because of its location. It not only surrounded the capital on three sides, but on and over its land passed key railroad and telegraph communications to the North and West. Union sentiment abounded among the small farmers of western Maryland while the eastern shore and southern Maryland supported slavery and often secession. Baltimore was a tinderbox where both sides vied for power.

The phrase "an iron hand in a velvet glove" was probably coined by Napoleon, but it became Lincoln's method of dealing with Maryland. He had seen the problems firsthand earlier that spring when the troops of the Sixth Massachusetts Militia were attacked as they traveled through Baltimore. From this episode, Lincoln had learned that he needed to work hard to cultivate and support Unionist sentiment in the border states. He could sometimes do this best by not overreacting to secessionist threats, which only played into the hands of Confederate sympathizers. He had gone to the limits of his iron hand with his suspension of habeas corpus, but he believed this strong action was necessary to keep open communications to and from the capital. Backward glances at Lincoln's controversial suspension of habeas corpus have often overshadowed what many of Lincoln's contemporaries saw as the president's quite limited actions in Maryland. While members of his own Republican Party demanded that Maryland be made to pay for its secessionist sympathizers and Baltimore "plug uglies," Lincoln believed that to err on the side of conciliation was the best path forward in the volatile state. When Postmaster General Montgomery Blair reported to Lincoln that "our office holders have been quietly installed in Baltimore," Hay reported that the president responded "that if quiet was kept in Baltimore a little longer Maryland might be considered the first of the redeemed."

Lincoln's hopes were to be realized in the fall elections. Helped by Union soldiers who traveled home to vote and by the presence of Union troops on guard in the state, Augustus W. Bradford, an earnest Unionist, was elected governor, ensuring that Maryland would remain within the Union ranks.

"I HOPE TO HAVE GOD ON MY SIDE, but I must have Kentucky." Lincoln was reported to have offered this observation early in the Civil War. If Maryland was the capital's contentious neighbor, Kentucky was the keystone in the bridge of four border states that spanned from East to West.

All Kentuckians knew that the state had given birth to two sons who were now presidents. Jefferson Davis was born in 1808 in Christian County a year before Lincoln. As a boy, Lincoln moved with his family to the free state of Indiana; Davis moved to the slave state of Mississippi. In the election of 1860, of the four border states, Lincoln did the worst in his home state, receiving only 1,364 votes in Kentucky. Despite the election result, Lincoln believed that as a native son he knew this border state better than the other three.

Lincoln understood that connections of family, commerce, and slavery moved Kentucky on the currents of the Ohio and the Mississippi rivers toward the South. But Lincoln also believed that the long Whig tradition exemplified by Henry Clay, the political hero of his youth, would continue to hold the state within the Union. On June 14, 1861, as a monument to Clay was dedicated in the Lexington cemetery, spectators placed a flagstaff in the extended right hand of the statue and "the Stars and Stripes were unfurled amid hearty cheers."

Kentucky was strategically valuable as a safeguard between the Old Northwest states of Ohio, Indiana, and Illinois, and the Confederate state of Tennessee. Furthermore, whoever controlled Kentucky's natural boundaries of the Ohio and Mississippi rivers, as well as the Cumberland and Tennessee rivers within the state, would immediately secure huge military advantages. Through the years, Lincoln had stayed in touch with Kentucky by subscribing to Lexington's polar opposite newspapers, the now Unionist *Observer* and the secessionist-leaning *Statesman*. Lincoln also hoped to rely on his old friend Joshua Speed, his influential brother, James Speed, seventy-four-year-old senator John Crittenden, and Presbyterian minister and politician Robert J. Breckinridge for information and counsel.

Kentucky's Democratic governor, Beriah Magoffin, wanted secession. He had replied angrily to Lincoln's call for troops, but was outvoted and outmaneuvered, and was out of office by August. While the state House of Representatives proclaimed a policy of "neutrality," each side, Unionists and pro-Confederates, hoped to tip the balance in their direction.

Lincoln was careful not to awaken any more hostility against the Union. The president spoke with Kentucky senator Garrett Davis, a strong opponent of secession, and told him that "he contemplated no military operations that would make it necessary to move any troops over her territories." Aware of the chorus of Republican senators and newspaper editors calling for forceful action, Lincoln believed that respect for Kentucky's public stance of neutrality in the short term was the best strategy for winning his native state to the Union side in the long term. He did this by his public commands not to recruit volunteers or to move troops against Kentucky unless attacked.

Behind Lincoln's public posture, however, he appointed Major General Robert Anderson, the hero of Fort Sumter and a native Kentuckian, to the command of the new Department of Kentucky, its headquarters located in Cincinnati, just across the Ohio River. Lincoln also agreed to permit William Nelson, a former navy officer, to smuggle five thousand rifles into the state. A delighted Joshua Speed wrote Lincoln on May 27, 1861, "We have beaten them at their own game." What Speed meant was that Governor Magoffin had secretly borrowed money to procure guns from New Orleans, but what arrived were out-of-date flintlocks. By contrast, Speed told Lincoln, "The distribution of the small number received has had a most salutary influence. . . . Giving strength and confidence to our friends."

Lincoln's stealth and patience paid off as Confederate military leaders grew impatient. Alarmed at what they believed were imminent Union military moves into the state, Confederate forces under impulsive general Gideon Pillow violated Kentucky's neutrality by seizing Columbus in the western tip of the state on September 4, 1861. Pillow and his superior, General Leonidas Polk, a former Episcopal bishop, believed that from this base they could control river traffic on the Mississippi. That decision triggered a countermove by Union forces under the command of a little-known brigadier general from Illinois named Ulysses S. Grant. On September 6, Grant occupied Paducah, Kentucky, giving the Union control of the mouth of the Tennessee River, which flowed into the Ohio. From that point forward, though still officially neutral, Kentucky was on the side of the Union.

OF ALL THE BORDER STATES, Lincoln was least familiar with Missouri. It would become his greatest challenge. Missouri's threat to the Union was geographic. If in Confederate control, it could bar river traffic on the middle length of the "Father of Waters," the Mississippi. Missouri had been the staging ground for the Lewis and Clark expedition in 1806 and for the Pony Express in 1860, which would carry Lincoln's inaugural address to California in March 1861. Under the stars and bars, Missouri could become the staging ground for incursions into southern Illinois, Kentucky, and Tennessee, as well as cut off communications with the West.

As in Kentucky, the outbreak of the Civil War found a Southern sympathizer occupying the governor's office. Claiborne Jackson, a conservative Douglas Democrat, called for a special convention to vote on secession, but the delegates voted resolutely to stay within the Union.

The secessionists coveted the St. Louis Arsenal with its sixty thousand stand of arms and other military supplies. When Governor Jackson directed the mobilization of several hundred soldiers in the state militia, Union Captain Nathaniel Lyon, a fiery antislavery Republican from New England, confronted the militia on May 10, 1861. Fighting spilled into the streets of St. Louis, resulting in twenty-eight deaths and seventy-five injuries. The next two months witnessed continued skirmishing, not simply between Union and Confederate troops, but within the Union ranks, between military leaders General William S. Harney, commander of the Department of the West, and Lyon, as well as between political leaders Congressman Frank Blair, Jr., and Attorney General Edward Bates.

Lincoln, still relying on the advice of the Blair family, decided to make a fresh start in Missouri by appointing General John C. Frémont to head the Department of the West. Frémont, now forty-eight, handsome, with graying hair and piercing eyes, was the first Republican candidate for president in 1856. He met with Lincoln at the White House before heading west and reported that Lincoln told him, "I have given you *carte blanche;* you must use your own judgment and do the best you can." Frémont arrived at his headquarters in St. Louis on July 25, 1861, just after the Union was defeated at Bull Run.

General Frémont did not get off to a good start. He rented an opulent mansion on Chouteau Avenue for six thousand dollars a year. He made himself largely inaccessible, surrounding himself with Hungarian and Italian guards in showy uniforms at the gates, while citizens and soldiers sought, often in vain, to see him. While Frémont remained in St. Louis, the impetuous Lyon picked a fight at Wilson's Creek, ten miles south of Springfield, Missouri, and a long 215 miles from his supplies in St. Louis, against a Confederate force that outnumbered him two to one. Lyon was killed in battle, the first Union general to die in the Civil War. Frémont's initial supporters, the Blairs, and Hamilton R. Gamble, a Lincoln loyalist who led the provisional state government as governor, wondered aloud why the aloof Frémont did not reinforce Lyon.

Confederate forces, encouraged by their victory at Wilson's Creek, continued to wreak havoc across the Missouri countryside. Desperate, Frémont declared martial law, pushing aside Governor Gamble. Acting solely on his own authority, he issued a proclamation on August 30, 1861, that freed the slaves belonging to all rebels in the state. Frémont, by his action, was expanding the purpose of the war to include the liberation of slaves. Frémont, in far-off Missouri, suddenly had Lincoln's undivided attention.

Alarmed, the president wrote Frémont at once. "I think there is great danger that the closing paragraph, in relation to the confiscation of property, and the liberating slaves of traitorous owners, will alarm our Southern Union friends, and turn them against us—perhaps ruin our rather fair prospect for Kentucky." Lincoln asked, not ordered, Frémont to "modify" the paragraph. Lincoln saw that the measure about slaves could quickly undo everything that he had been attempting to accomplish in Kentucky and Maryland. He told Frémont that no commander,

GEN. FREMONT'S PROCLAMATION.

MARTIAL LAW IN MISSOURI

ALL REBELS TAKEN IN ARMS TO BE SHOT.

REBELS' PROPERTY CONFISCATED.

Slaves of Rebels Declared Free.

11428—

PROCLAMATION OF GEN. FREMONT.
St. Louis, Saturday, Aug. 31, 1861.

The following Proclamation was issued this morning:

"HEADQUARTERS OF THE WESTERN DEPARTMENT,
"St. Louis, Aug 31, 1861.

"Circumstances, in my judgment of sufficient urgency, render it necessary that the Commanding General of this Department should assume the administrative powers of the State. Its disorganized condition, the helplessness of the civil authority, the total insecurity of life, and the devastation of property by bands of murderers and marauders who infest nearly every county in the State and avail themselves of the public misfortunes and the vicinity of a hostile force to gratify private and neighborhood vengeance, and who find an enemy wherever they find plunder, finally demand the severest measures to repress the daily increasing crimes and outrages which are driving off the inhabitants and ruining the State. In this condition the public safety and the success of our arms require unity of purpose, without let or hindrance, to the prompt administration of affairs.

"In order, therefore, to suppress disorders, to maintain as far as now practicable the public peace, and to give security and protection to the persons and property of loyal citizens, I do hereby extend, and declare established, martial law throughout the State of Missouri. The lines of the army of occupation in this State are for the present declared to extend from Leavenworth by way of the posts of Jefferson City, Rolla, and Ironton, to Cape Girardeau on the Mississippi River.

"All persons who shall be taken with arms in their hands within these lines shall be tried by court-martial, and, if found guilty, will be shot. The property, real and personal, of all persons in the State of Missouri who shall take up arms against the United States, and who shall be directly proven to have taken active part with their enemies in the field, is declared to be confiscated to the public use; and their slaves, if any they have, are hereby declared free.

"All persons who shall be proven to have destroyed, after the publication of this order, railroad tracks, bridges or telegraphs, shall suffer the extreme penalty of the law.

"All persons engaged in treasonable correspondence, in giving or procuring aid to the enemies of the United States, in disturbing the public tranquillity, by creating and circulating false reports or incendiary documents, are in their own interest warned that they are exposing themselves.

"All persons who have been led away from their allegiance are required to return to their homes forthwith; any such absence without sufficient cause will be held to be presumptive evidence against them.

"The object of this declaration is to place in the hands of the military authorities the power to give instantaneous effect to existing laws, and to supply such deficiencies as the conditions of war demand. But it is not intended to suspend the ordinary tribunals of the country where the law will be administered by the civil officers in the usual manner, and with their customary authority while the same can be peaceably exercised.

"The Commanding General will labor vigilantly for the public welfare, and in his efforts for their safety, hopes to obtain not only the acquiescence, but the active support of the people of the country.
"J. C. FREMONT,
"Major-General Commanding"

These newspaper headlines broadcast the news of John C. Frémont's proclamation of August 30, 1861, which freed the slaves of enemies of the Union in Missouri.

no matter how high his rank, could set national policy in the guise of military action. Lincoln reserved to himself this right. Though Lincoln was obviously upset, his conclusion was remarkably evenhanded in dealing with the senior military officer. "This letter is written in a spirit of caution and not of censure."

Frémont decided to send his reply in the person of his wife. On September 8, 1861, Jessie Benton Frémont boarded a train in St. Louis ready to defend her husband's reputation as well as his point of view on slavery. After two days and two nights sitting up in hot, squeaking cars, she arrived at the Willard Hotel in Washington. Immediately upon her arrival, without an opportunity to bathe or rest, she sent a message to the president requesting a meeting. To her surprise, a reply came back immediately: "Now, at once. A. Lincoln." It was after 9 p.m.

She was in a state of high tension as she was ushered into the Red Room. In a short while, Lincoln entered and, leaving the door ajar, remained standing without offering her a seat. Lincoln's every indication was that he was not there for a long conversation. She handed him her husband's letter, explaining that she wanted to be sure it reached him. He took the letter and stood under the chandelier to read it. Finally, looking up, Lincoln told her, "It was a war for a great national idea, the Union," and that "General Frémont should not have dragged the Negro into it—that he never would if he had consulted with Frank Blair. I sent Frank there to advise him." With that, Mrs. Frémont launched into her own defense of her husband's actions, implying that her husband was superior to the president in wisdom, and arguing that this war could not be won by force of arms. Annoyed and offended at her words and demeanor, Lincoln exclaimed, "You are quite a female politician." Lincoln would say later that Mrs. Frémont "taxed me so violently with many things that I had to exercise all the awkward tact I have to avoid quarrelling with her."

Frémont, who had earned his initial fame as the Pathmarker of the physical geography of the West, seemed unable to find his way in the admittedly complicated political geography of Missouri. He stubbornly tried to hang on to his command by finally taking the field. But in a short one hundred days, Lincoln terminated Frémont's appointment as commander of the Department of the West.

Governor John Andrew of Massachusetts voiced the sentiments of many in the North when he declared that Frémont's proclamation offered "an impetus of the grandest character to the whole cause." New England poet and essayist James Russell Lowell asked, "How many times are we to save Kentucky and lose our self-respect?"

Frederick Douglass turned his editorial guns on Lincoln for not supporting Frémont's proclamation. "Slavery is the bulwark of rebellion—the common bond that binds all slaveholding rebel hearts together. Cut that bond, and the rebellion falls asunder. If the Government does this, it will succeed, and if it does not, it will not deserve success."

Lincoln was not surprised by the comments of Andrew and Douglass, but he was astonished at how all of the New York newspaper generals, as well as politicians in his own Republican Party, rallied to

Frémont's proclamation. The proclamation raised Frémont to the stature of an antislavery hero in the eyes of many Republicans, putting Lincoln in an awkward position. Many Republicans were appalled when they learned that he had rescinded Frémont's order. Lincoln's correspondence with his friends demonstrated how divisive Frémont and his proclamation were.

Joshua Speed spoke for many in the border states when he wrote to Lincoln from Kentucky on September 3, 1861, "I have been so distressed since reading . . . that foolish proclamation of Frémont that I have been unable to eat or sleep." Speed voiced his concern that "it will crush out every vestage of a union party in the state—I perhaps & a few others will be left alone."

Illinois senator Orville Browning, usually a conservative on matters of slavery, wrote from his home in Quincy on September 22, "Frémont's proclamation was necessary, and will do good. It has the full approval of all loyal citizens of the west and North West. It was rumored here that the cabinet had disapproved it, but I trust this is not so. Such a step would disappoint and dishearten all loyal men who are fighting for the life of the Government."

Browning's letter caught Lincoln off guard. Had he so misjudged the attitudes of conservative Republicans? Lincoln replied, "Coming from you, I confess it astonishes me." Because of his long friendship with Browning, Lincoln took the time in his response to say, in private, what he never quite said in public. "Genl. Frémont's proclamation, as to the confiscation of property, and the liberation of slaves, is *purely political,* and not within the range of *military* law, or necessity." Lincoln then got to what for him was the nub of the matter. "You speak of it as being the only means of *saving* the government. On the contrary it is itself the surrender of the government. Can it be pretended that it is any longer the government of the U.S.—any government of Constitution and laws—wherein a General, or a President, may make permanent rules of property by proclamation?"

Lincoln's letter to Browning is one of the best indications of his thinking in the fall of 1861. Even as his own power as president and commander in chief was increasing, he articulated his belief that no general, or president, could put himself above or outside the laws embodied in the Constitution in an attempt to deal with the vexing issue of slavery. Bound by the Constitution, he could not envision such a sweeping liberation of slaves at this time.

By the end of 1861, Lincoln had played his first hands in a contest with four border states as the prizes. He stood pat on Delaware. He undertook a high-stakes strategy with Maryland and, by alternating both pressure and passivity, allowed state politics to emerge into a modified Unionist posture. After initially underestimating the complexity of conflicting loyalties in Kentucky, his hands-off posture succeeded not simply because of the wisdom of his policies but because of the misguided hands-on policies of the Confederacy. Missouri, farthest from Washington and closest to Kansas and the frontier, became the most difficult hand for Lincoln to play. His tendency to stay with the leadership he had appointed made it difficult for him to change. But change he did when he nullified Frémont's declaration of emancipation. Lincoln's action cost him dearly in the short run, but he had come to believe that military strategy must grow out of the policies directed by the commander in chief alone.

ON A BALMY SUNDAY AFTERNOON in October 1861, Lincoln welcomed his old friend Edward Dickinson Baker to the White House. As Lincoln leaned against a tree on the lawn, just as he used to do long ago in New Salem, the two old friends talked of their days together as lawyers and politicians in Illinois. Baker had introduced Lincoln at his inauguration, but other than that they had seen little of each other in recent years. He had moved to San Francisco in 1852, ran unsuccessfully for the Senate, and then moved to Oregon in 1859, where he won election to the Senate in 1860. When the war broke out, Baker organized a California regiment. Lincoln offered to appoint him a brigadier general, but he turned it down, saying he would serve as a colonel, which would allow him to retain his Senate seat. As Baker rose to leave, he lifted ten-year-old Willie in his arms. Mary Lincoln gave him a bouquet of autumn flowers as a measure of their affection for him.

All summer, Baker—courageous but impetuous—had had a premonition that he would die in combat. In August, he had prepared a will and put his affairs in order. Before midnight on October 20, 1861, he was ordered to prepare his men for battle. Brigadier General Charles P. Stone, operating under orders from General McClellan, led 2,000 Union troops against 1,600 Confederates in a badly synchronized effort to cross the Potomac and capture Leesburg, Virginia. The Confederates, under the command of General Nathan "Shanks" Evans, counterattacked and forced the Union forces over the bluff and into the Potomac River. Ball's Bluff, although a small battle, was a disaster with large implications. The Union forces suffered a total of 1,070 casualties, including more than 700 captured, compared to only 149 casualties for the Confederates.

As Lincoln was monitoring the progress of the battle in the War Department, a telegram came through announcing the death of Colonel Baker. In scaling Ball's Bluff on the Virginia shore, he and his men were surrounded by Confederate forces and Baker was killed. Lincoln emerged from the telegraph office "with bowed head, and tears rolling down his furrowed cheeks, his face pale and wan."

Of all the tributes to Baker in the Senate, in Washington, and in San Francisco where he was buried, the most touching may have been the one by Willie Lincoln. In what he called his "first attempt at poetry," Willie wrote a poem that he sent to the editor of the *National Republican*.

> *There was no patriot like Baker,*
>> *So noble and so true;*
> *He fell as a soldier on the field,*
>> *His face to the sky of blue.*

BY NOVEMBER 1861, as the leaves began to vanish from the trees in Washington, the aura around McClellan, the summer sunshine soldier, was starting to darken. He was acclaimed in July as the rescuer of the nation, but by the fall critics from all sides—newspaper generals, politicians, and ordinary citizens—were questioning the Young Napoleon's capacity to lead and fight. Lincoln wanted to support McClellan, but he, too, was growing impatient for the army to move south before winter.

On a crisp Wednesday evening, November 13, 1861, Lincoln, accompanied by Secretary of State Seward and Hay, called on McClellan at his home. When they arrived, Ellen McClellan told the president that the general was attending a wedding but would return soon. After about an hour, the general returned. Informed the president was waiting to see him, he "went up stairs, passing the door of the room where the President and Secretary of State were seated." After waiting yet another half hour, the president asked the servant to inform the general, again, that they were waiting to speak with him. Presently the servant returned to announce that "the General had gone to bed." On the walk home, Hay spoke with Lincoln about what had just taken place, "but he seemed not to have noted it specially, saying, it was better at this time not to be making points of etiquette & personal dignity."

Three days later, on November 16, 1861, Lincoln watched McClellan present sixty-five thousand men on parade before thirty thousand spectators. Criticism was mounting. With so many men in uniform, why could they not move from the parade ground to the battleground?

In December, during one of Senator Orville Browning's regular visits to the White House, Lincoln asked the Illinois senator if he would come along with him on another evening visit to McClellan. Lincoln valued Browning's opinion and wanted his judgment on the general. This was Browning's first meeting with McClellan. He wrote later that night in his diary, "I was favourably impressed—like his plain, direct straight forward way of talking and acting. He has brains—looks as if he ought to have courage, and I think, is altogether more than an ordinary man." McClellan once again made a good first impression, and Lincoln took no action.

THE TOPIC OF SLAVERY would not go away, even if Lincoln told Frémont to stop talking about it. Lincoln himself was continually thinking about it and by the end of 1861 began to test ideas and tease out the issue in his varied communications.

Lincoln believed that Delaware, with its less than two thousand slaves, might prove to be the best test case for compensated emancipation. In November, Lincoln presented his idea to Congressman George P. Fisher. They discussed how much compensation to provide for each slave. In the end, they proposed a bill that called for a payment of $400 per slave, or a total of $719,200 to Delaware. The bill called for adult slaves over thirty-five to be freed immediately. In the draft, Lincoln wrote that all remaining slaves would be freed by 1893, but then struck that date and changed it to 1872. The bill would cover 587 slave owners in Delaware. Lincoln told Fisher it was the "cheapest and most human way of ending this war and saving slaves."

When Fisher introduced the bill in the Delaware legislature, the debate quickly turned not on the fate of slaves but on the political loyalties of representatives. Some of the bill's detractors were nonslaveholders who characterized its proponents as "Black Republicans." In the end, the bill was never voted on in the legislature.

Senator Charles Sumner of Massachusetts was determined to keep talking with Lincoln about slavery. Sumner believed the only course for the government was to proclaim a policy of emancipation. He had grown concerned about Lincoln's slowness to act. Yet, Sumner believed Lincoln was "a deeply convinced and faithful anti-slavery man." He was sure that before too long Lincoln would be forced to act.

Sumner, the chairman of the Senate's Foreign Relations Committee, also believed that keeping peace abroad was directly related to freeing the slaves at home. He struggled to get Lincoln to understand that an emancipation edict would cut off any chance for the recognition of the Confederacy by foreign nations. Though Lincoln seemed to be making no movement toward emancipation, Sumner worked hard to win his trust. He refused to attack Lincoln as many of his radical Republican friends were beginning to do.

When Congress reassembled in December, Sumner resumed his conversations with the president. After one particularly long discussion, Lincoln said to Sumner, "Well, Mr. Sumner, the only difference between you and me on this subject is a difference of a month or six weeks in time."

"Mr. President," Sumner responded, "if that is the only difference between us, I will not say another word to you about it till the longest time your name has passed by." Sumner kept his promise to Lincoln in the White House, while in the Senate he kept building support for emancipation.

THE CONVENING OF the Thirty-seventh Congress only one month after the retirement of General Scott quickly became a forum for debate about the progress of the Union war effort. There was restlessness in the air. Lincoln was under obligation to give an annual message to Congress when it assembled on December 2, 1861. He had addressed Congress in special session on July 4, but that was a targeted message asking for support at the beginning of the war. The annual message, by tradition, had become a cobbling together of reports by cabinet secretaries, long on detail and short on eloquence. Lincoln adhered to this tradition in this, his first annual message, but he also offered his perspective on what was important at the close of 1861.

At the center of his address was his report on the border states. "Noble little Delaware led off right from the first. Maryland was made to *seem* against the Union." After recounting the story of the assault on soldiers, bridges, and railroads, he rejoiced in the fact that at a regular election, the people of Maryland "have sustained the Union." He was most pleased to declare, "Kentucky, too, for some time in doubt, is now decidedly, and, I think, unchangeably ranged on the side of the Union." Finally, "Missouri is comparatively quiet; and I believe cannot be over-run by the insurrectionists."

Lincoln was not sure yet how best to use the traditional format, in which his words would be read by someone else. He did not include any of the striking words that marked his formal addresses and many of his letters. But at the end of the speech, as he looked to the future, one could almost hear his voice. He recalled that, from the first census in 1790 to the last in 1860, the nation was "eight times as great as it was at the begin-ning." He then predicted that there would be some "among us" who, "if the Union be preserved," would live to see a nation of 250 million peo-ple. "The struggle of today, is not altogether for today—it is for a vast future also. With a reliance on Providence, all the more firm and earnest, let us proceed in the great task which events have devolved upon us."

The fresh memory of the October defeat at Ball's Bluff, as well as Lincoln's decision to relieve General Frémont of his command, pro-duced determination among returning Congressmen to exercise more congressional oversight over the war. Radical Republicans led the way, establishing a Joint Committee on the Conduct of the War. Republicans controlled the committee 5 to 2.

Under the leadership of Senator Benjamin Wade of Ohio, the com-mittee called General McClellan as their first witness for a meeting scheduled on December 23, 1861. McClellan, in bed with typhoid fever, could not attend. In light of his absence, other witnesses began to paint an unfavorable portrait of Little Mac's inaction.

Lincoln took an initial benign posture to the committee's oversight. He gave the members easy access to himself and the War Department. He chose not to become defensive in response to their inquiries even when it became obvious the committee was pushing him for a more aggressive prosecution of the war. He may have become rankled as the committee started evaluating his generals—especially the Democratic ones—not on their performance in the field but on their political alle-giances. But Lincoln came to the conclusion that the efforts of the Joint Committee on the Conduct of the War, even when noisy or overblown, could be used to support his own positions as commander in chief.

BY THE END OF 1861, Secretary of War Simon Cameron was proving to be the most problematic member of Lincoln's cabinet. Cameron had a

Simon Cameron, former senator from Pennsylvania, served as secretary of war in the first year of the Civil War.

dignified bearing: tall, with a high, broad forehead, abundant gray hair, and intense gray eyes. People sometimes initially regarded him as aloof but changed their minds as he proved himself a person of ability. He had succeeded in business and accumulated a fortune before entering politics and, so his critics said, turned politics into his business, where he made even more money. A man of energy and affability, he had worked with large groups of people in both of his careers, which suggested he could succeed at his admittedly large task of equipping the War Department to be the engine of a new kind of war.

Lincoln quickly recognized that the secretary of war had been handed the most difficult task of all. He inherited a woefully small department that was expected to support a huge and growing army. In April 1861, the War Department consisted of eight bureaus staffed by about ninety employees and used out-of-date systems of record keeping. Cameron, recognizing his own shortcomings as an administrator, welcomed Secretary of the Treasury Salmon Chase's assistance. With Lincoln's blessing, it was Chase who drafted the order on May 3 enlarging the army that was sent out under Lincoln's name.

As the army grew exponentially, Cameron became a tense, perplexed executive who lost command of his own department. Disdaining the use of a clerk or secretary, Cameron seemed to run his growing department with records he kept in his head or his pockets.

Lincoln's leadership style was to offer his colleagues both support and the benefit of the doubt. But by the summer of 1861, Lincoln was hearing grumblings about Cameron and his department from many quarters. He understood that Cameron had many critics for his past actions, but Lincoln was interested only in the present. The president wanted to weigh, not count, the criticism.

Lincoln took his time when it came to people. By the end of 1861, he decided not to simply fire Cameron, but to find another position for him that would save his dignity. Lincoln wrote a brief letter to Cameron on January 11, 1862, informing him that he was nominating him to be minister to Russia. The letter did not include any recognition of Cameron's service as secretary of war. Cameron, expressing his feelings to Chase, his closest cabinet colleague, said he "was quite offended, supposing the letter intended as a dismissal, and therefore discourteous." When Cameron expressed his feelings to Lincoln, he wrote a second letter, which shifted the initiative "to gratify your wish" and to express "my personal regard for you, and my confidence in your ability, patriotism, and fidelity to public trust."

Did Lincoln take too long to remove Cameron? The critics had been nipping at Cameron's heels since the summer. Lincoln's loyalty was a strong character trait that sometimes overrode his judgment. The president refused to discuss his criticisms of Cameron's shortcomings, and now he gave the secretary of war a second letter that could be released to the public. Cameron went to Russia, retaining a deep appreciation for Lincoln.

FOR LINCOLN, the last day of 1861, the coda to a dispiriting fall, symbolized all that was going wrong. The year ended with the central actors he was attempting to direct either unwilling or incapable of receiving direction. George McClellan, his main commander in the East, was temporarily offstage with typhoid fever. On December 31, Lincoln wired his two key commanders in the West, Henry W. Halleck and Don Carlos Buell, encouraging them to act in a "simultaneous movement" to support Unionists in Kentucky and eastern Tennessee. Halleck's reply was not encouraging. "I have never received a word from General Buell." Halleck said he was "not ready to cooperate" with Buell and that "too much haste will ruin everything."

On New Year's Eve, Lincoln received a visit from the entire Joint Committee on the Conduct of the War. The committee, not including members who were familiar with military matters, was eager to strike a blow that would win the war in one grand battle. They looked down their political noses at West Point–trained professional soldiers. At the outset of the meeting, Ohio senator Benjamin Wade aggressively attacked General McClellan. Lincoln was placed in a difficult position. He wanted to be receptive to influential members of Congress, but he was determined to defend McClellan. As Lincoln tried to be a mediator, Wade raged, "Mr. President, you are murdering your country by inches in consequence of the inactivity of the military and the want of a distinct policy in regard to slavery." Wade had succinctly named the two problems confronting Lincoln at the beginning of 1862.

Attorney General Edward Bates, who had grown quite fond of the president, confided to his diary, "For some months past (and lately more pressingly) I have urged upon the President to have some military organization about his own person." Bates believed that if Lincoln had more and better assistants, and was better organized himself, he would be in a better position to command. "I insisted that being 'Commander in chief' by law, he *must* command—especially in a war as this. The Nation requires it, and History will hold him responsible." Bates went on to complain of McClellan that he "is very reticent. Nobody knows his plans." Finally, after an unusually long entry, Bates concluded, "The Prest. is an excellent man, and in the main wise; but he lacks *will* and *purpose,* and, I greatly fear he, has not the *power to command.*"

THE NEW YEAR did not bring any better news. On January 6, 1862, General Halleck wrote the president explaining that because of the state of affairs in Missouri he could not comply with Lincoln's request to cooperate with Buell by ordering a force to Columbus, Kentucky. Four days later, Lincoln passed along the letter to Cameron, writing on it, "It is exceedingly discouraging. As everything else, nothing can be done."

On Friday morning, January 10, 1862, knowing that a recovering McClellan was carrying on business from his bed, Lincoln decided to call on the general. The mild weather of the abnormally lengthy fall of

Montgomery Meigs, a civil engineer, served as quartermaster general of the Union army. He earned Lincoln's respect for his management of the logistical necessities of equipping a huge new volunteer army.

1861 had given way to 1862's snows. The temperatures were not very cold, though, so Lincoln walked through a gloomy fog to McClellan's home. When he arrived he was told that the general could not see him.

A troubled Lincoln then walked to the office of Montgomery C. Meigs, quartermaster general of the army, in the brick Winder Building, which housed the headquarters of the army and navy. Lincoln pulled up a chair before the open fire.

In 1860, Meigs had been a Douglas Democrat, not a Lincoln man. Standing an inch and a half over six feet, Meigs went to Lincoln's inauguration on March 4, 1861, to hear what this new president stood for. He was surprised. As Meigs wrote to his brother, John, that evening, "I feared until last night that some weak shilly shally policy would prevail that we had a chief with no character a buffoon." Meigs told his brother he believed he spoke for many, for he now recognized that Lincoln's inaugural address "put into every patriotic heart new strength and hope."

Lincoln came to Meigs's office that day, as he had on a number of previous days, because he had found new strength and hope in this career West Point professional who had almost single-handedly put in place, after the disastrous summer of 1861, an extensive system of communications, purchases, and transportation to provision an army growing to a million and a half men. Lincoln was both growing in wisdom and suffering some of his most virulent criticism. In the midst of dealing with McClellan and Cameron, he appreciated the opportunity to unburden himself with a military man who talked less and acted more.

Lincoln mournfully asked the trusted Meigs a question he had been asking himself for some time. "General, what shall I do? The people are impatient; Chase has no money and tells he can raise no more; the General of the Army has typhoid fever." Lincoln was despondent. "The bottom is out of the tub. What shall we do?"

Francis Carpenter's famous painting, First Reading of the Emancipation Proclamation of President Lincoln, *grew out of his work in the White House in 1864, where he studied and sketched Lincoln for nearly seven months.*

CHAPTER 20

We Are Coming, Father Abraham
January 1862–July 1862

I EXPECT TO MAINTAIN THIS CONTEST UNTIL SUCCESSFUL, OR TILL I
DIE, OR AM CONQUERED, OR MY TERM EXPIRES OR CONGRESS OR THE
COUNTRY FORSAKES ME.

ABRAHAM LINCOLN TO WILLIAM H. SEWARD
June 28, 1862

*P*RESIDENT LINCOLN'S CHOICE FOR A NEW SECRETARY OF WAR TOOK
everyone by surprise: Edwin M. Stanton, the combative lawyer who
seven years earlier had scorned Lincoln at the "Reaper" trial in Cincinnati.

Lincoln does not tell us why or how he made this decision, but it
may be possible to tease it out. To be sure, Stanton received several recommendations, notably from Treasury Secretary Salmon P. Chase, who
had persuaded the outgoing secretary of war, Simon Cameron, to join
him in doing so. True, Lincoln had already appointed Republican rivals
Seward, Chase, Bates, and Cameron to the cabinet, but the choice of
Stanton, a Democrat, struck political observers as even more startling.
Actually, the fact that Stanton was a Democrat may have worked in his
favor. By January 1862, Lincoln believed that having a Democratic
Unionist in his cabinet could help him persuade other Democrats to support the war more enthusiastically. Lincoln's decision to appoint Stanton would prove to be a turning point in the prosecution of the war.

Edwin Stanton was born in 1814 in Steubenville, Ohio, and attended
Kenyon College, where he was a classmate of Judge David Davis, Lincoln's legal colleague from Bloomington, Illinois. Admitted to the bar in
1836, Stanton moved to Pittsburgh in 1847, where he established an
impressive reputation trying cases before the federal courts. The up-

wardly mobile Stanton settled in Washington in 1856 so that he could practice regularly before the Supreme Court. By the outbreak of the Civil War, Stanton earned fifty thousand dollars a year.

Outwardly successful and gifted with talent and energy, Stanton had a combative manner in pleading cases that may have been due in part to the losses he suffered as a young man, which friends say darkened his personality. His daughter Lucy died in 1841 at one and a half, and his lovely wife, Mary Lamson, died suddenly in 1844, after only seven years of marriage. For the next decade, Stanton buried his grief in his work, establishing a reputation for legal skill and an obstreperous spirit. In 1856, he married Ellen Hutchinson, sixteen years younger, opening a new chapter in his life.

As an antislavery Democrat living in Washington, Stanton had watched President Buchanan stumble as secessionist drums grew noisier in the South. On December 20, 1860, the same day that the U.S. flag was lowered in South Carolina, Stanton accepted an appointment as attorney general in Buchanan's lame-duck cabinet, hoping he could make a difference in preserving the Union.

As a part of the president's inner circle, Stanton concluded that Buchanan's White House was adrift in its policy toward the South. At this critical moment of transition, Stanton reached out to Republicans behind President Buchanan's back as a way to prevent the nation from sliding into collapse. Stanton met almost daily with soon-to-be secretary of state William Seward to keep him abreast of the Buchanan administration's actions and inactions.

When Lincoln finally arrived in Washington in late February 1861, Stanton welcomed the new Republican administration, but he did not have much hope for the Lincoln he remembered from Cincinnati. He attended Lincoln's inauguration on March 4, writing to a friend the same day, "The inauguration is over and whether for good or evil Abraham Lincoln is President of the United States." Stanton would go on to watch the first year of the Lincoln administration with a critical eye.

When George McClellan came to Washington in the summer of 1861 as the savior-general, he and Edwin Stanton, both Democrats, were brought together by mutual friends. A fruitful relationship developed. A few days before being appointed secretary of war, Stanton met with McClellan and promised his support. McClellan, who was increasingly distancing himself from Lincoln, believed he now had an ally in the administration.

*Lincoln appointed Edwin
M. Stanton, the lawyer who
had humiliated him in the
famous "Reaper Case"
in Cincinnati in 1855,
to be his new secretary of war
in January 1862.*

Stanton made a good first impression on many people in his initial
months on the job. The Joint Committee on the Conduct of the War
met with him on his first day in office. Senator Benjamin Wade of Ohio
wrote, "The political horizon has brightened" since Stanton had
assumed his new position. Attorney General Edward Bates wrote in his
diary, "The new Sec.y of War is a man of mind and action. He is well
recd. by all." Joshua Speed, who traveled up from Kentucky to procure
arms for his state, wrote Joseph Holt, the last secretary of war in the
Buchanan administration, that Stanton "accomplished in a few days
what heretofore would have taken as many weeks." Speed believed
Stanton would "infuse into the whole army an energy & activity which
we have not seen heretofore." George Templeton Strong, as treasurer of
the U.S. Sanitary Commission, an agency of the government that coordinated relief efforts in army camps, traveled from New York to visit
with War Department officials at the end of January. Upon meeting
Stanton, Strong was impressed. He was sure Stanton was worth "a
wagon load of Camerons." But Strong, who knew his way around
Washington, confided to his diary, "He is the most popular man in
Washington now, but will it last?"

The president was also impressed by what he saw and heard in Stanton's first weeks. When Lincoln wandered over to the telegraph office in
the War Department in the evening, he saw that Stanton, in his private
office on the second floor that overlooked the White House, worked

many nights until 10 p.m. Lincoln knew that Stanton was strong-minded, and could at any moment unleash his fiery temper, but Lincoln was never defensive around people who knew more than he did and were proficient at getting the job done. Lincoln told Massachusetts congressman Henry L. Dawes that Stanton's energy reminded him of an old Methodist preacher in the West who would become so energetic in the pulpit that a number of parishioners decided to put bricks in his pockets in order to hold him down. "We may be obliged to serve Stanton the same way," Lincoln drawled, "but I guess we'll just let him jump a while first."

Stanton quickly assumed total control of his department. He was everywhere, and he seemed to know everything. He would brook no interference from "Premier" Seward, who outranked him, and treated almost everyone else, including Gideon Welles, secretary of the navy, as beneath him. Treasury Secretary Chase predicted in his diary that the new secretary of war "would be master of his Department, and yield to no one save the President." The developing relationship between Lincoln and Stanton would become one of the most intriguing inner stories of the war.

In the first months of 1862, the president became visibly energized by Stanton's presence. He walked over to the telegraph office at the War Department more frequently. Stanton, whose honeymoon in office was quickly over because of his bearish manner that terrified many around him, treated the president with respect, even deference. Welles sized up Stanton as a person who was "fond of power and its exercise," but this quality never put Lincoln off. Lincoln had observed that Simon Cameron liked to exercise power, too, but often for his own self-aggrandizement. Lincoln saw in Stanton what many others did not. He came to admire his intellect and energy, despite what Gideon Welles called Stanton's "imperious nature," because Lincoln understood that Stanton offered enormous gifts in the service of the army and the Union.

"ALL QUIET ON THE POTOMAC" read the military news bulletins McClellan issued with monotonous predictability from his headquarters in the winter of 1861–62. Politicians in Washington, now that the Thirty-seventh Congress was in session, regularly derided McClellan and his announcement as nothing more than procrastination. All the while, Lincoln was waiting for General McClellan to lead his troops into battle.

On January 12, 1862, Illinois senator Orville Browning stopped by the White House. Browning sensed that Lincoln was caught up in his studies of military theory and wanted to talk at length about military strategy. He told Browning he believed the Union armies "should threaten all [the Confederate] positions at the same time with superior force, and if they weakened one to strengthen another seize and hold the one weakened." Discouraged with his generals, Lincoln told Browning he "was thinking of taking the field himself."

Finally, Lincoln could wait no longer. On January 27, 1862, he issued the President's General Order Number One. He ordered army and navy forces to prepare to move by February 22 against "the insurgent forces." This order, which Lincoln talked through with his new secretary of war, was a bold and curious document. Why February 22? Lincoln never said, but the president, with a penchant for precedents, probably chose it because it was George Washington's birthday. Lincoln's order was ridiculed by his detractors in Congress for its grand simplicity, but no one could miss its larger point—as commander in chief he was ordering McClellan to prepare to march in less than one month.

Four days later, Lincoln followed up his take-charge posture by issuing the President's Special War Order Number One. This brief order demonstrated Lincoln's ability to perform a political high-wire act. On the one hand, Lincoln stated that an "immediate object" should be the "seizing and occupying" of Manassas Junction. At the same time, he deferred "all details to be in the discretion of the general-in-chief." He concluded this second order insisting, once again, that the expedition should move "before, or on, the 22nd of February next."

This time, General McClellan rushed to the White House to object. He asked the president if he could present an alternative plan to Secretary of War Stanton. Lincoln accepted, probably believing that he might at last be able to coax from McClellan an actual battle plan in writing. On February 3, 1862, McClellan presented Stanton a detailed twenty-two-page report that included both his plan and his objections to the president's.

McClellan's plan called for transporting troops by water down the Potomac River and the Chesapeake Bay to little Urbana, Virginia, a tobacco port on the south side of the Rappahannock River. From this base he would advance the nearly sixty miles to Richmond. McClellan's intention was to draw the Confederate forces under Joseph Johnston away from a defensive line around Manassas in a march to protect Richmond. McClellan wrote that his advance "affords the shortest possible land routes to Richmond, & strikes directly at the heart of the enemy's power in the East." With Richmond won, McClellan envisioned a large circle under Union command, from Ambrose Burnside in North Carolina to Don Carlos Buell in Tennessee to Henry Halleck on the Mississippi.

McClellan's Urbana plan had its merits. He believed he could seize the advantage by fighting on the ground of his choosing while using the Union superiority in naval forces. McClellan concluded with a plea and a resolve. "I will stake my life, my reputation on the result—more than that, I will stake upon it the success of our cause."

The plan did not persuade Lincoln. Even if McClellan began his advance in February, the president worried there would be long delays before marching on the Confederate forces. Lincoln also expressed concern that McClellan's plan would leave Washington vulnerable to attack from what he now believed were very capable Southern military leaders.

Lincoln asked five tough questions of McClellan, including, "Does not your plan involve a greatly larger expenditure of *time,* and *money* than mine?" Lincoln also posed, "In case of disaster, would not a safe retreat be more difficult by your plan than by mine?" Although addressed to McClellan, Lincoln's questions were as much to himself, as he worked in his typical logical way to discern the way forward. He told McClellan, "If you will give me satisfactory answers to the following questions, I shall gladly yield my plan to yours."

Lincoln, as commander in chief, in the back-and-forth relationship with his top general, found himself honing the foundations of his evolving military strategy. First, he believed the Confederate armies, not Richmond or any other fixed place, should be his most important military target. Second, he increasingly recognized the risk of overstretched supply lines. And third, he wanted to avoid leaving Washington vulnerable to attack.

In the end, Lincoln signed off on McClellan's plans despite his deep reservations. His respect for professional officers still outweighed Lincoln's growing knowledge about military strategy.

WITH MCCLELLAN'S ARMY of the Potomac still confined to its winter bases in February, Lincoln received some good news from Kentucky. On January 19, 1862, Don Carlos Buell, responding to the president's

This Currier and Ives print depicts the bombardment and capture of Fort Henry and the heroic work of federal gunboats under command of Commodore Andrew H. Foote.

urgent call for action, dispatched General George H. Thomas, a Virginian loyal to the Union, on a risky mission in eastern Kentucky. Thomas, a large, imposing man who expected steeled discipline from his troops, led four thousand men over treacherous, trackless mountains in winter sleet to achieve a victory at Mill Springs, Kentucky.

Lincoln, with his eye turned toward the West, with which he was familiar, began monitoring the movements of General Ulysses S. Grant. On February 4, 1862, Grant attacked Fort Henry, a Confederate earthen fort eighty miles up the Tennessee River from the Union headquarters at Paducah, Kentucky, believing that the fort was the weak point in the Confederacy's line. It was exactly the strategy Lincoln had commended to Browning three weeks earlier. Grant approached Fort Henry from two sides. Supported by Commodore Andrew H. Foote's four ironclad and three wooden gunboats, Grant won a decisive victory on February 6, 1862, dealing the Confederates their first significant defeat of the war.

Some of the Confederates defending Fort Henry retreated to Fort Donelson on the Cumberland River, which became Grant's next objective. General Don Carlos Buell warned that Grant was about to take on a much larger force and should retire after his initial victory. In addition, Buell could send no reinforcements. No matter. Grant, unlike so many other commanders that Lincoln had come to know, never hollered for reinforcements. Instead, he marched his men twelve miles overland and prepared to attack. On February 14, 1862, Foote's gunboats arrived on the Cumberland and began lobbing "iron valentines" at Fort Donelson. Within a short time, however, the Confederate heavy artillery punished Foote's boats, gaining the upper hand. When word came by telegram to the War Department that Foote's boats were absorbing a vicious battering, many were quick to say, "I told you so." Stanton confessed his worry.

Lincoln and the military leaders in Washington knew little about Grant. Refusing to be beaten, Grant pushed on in bitter weather, finally taking Fort Donelson on February 17, 1862, with this famous remark: "No terms except complete and unconditional surrender can be accepted." The Confederates accepted. Grant marched away with thirteen thousand prisoners, giving the Union a second strategic victory in the western theater in less than two weeks.

When Stanton read the "unconditional surrender" dispatch, the secretary of war led three cheers for General Grant. A clerk in Stanton's office recalled that the cheers "shook the old walls, broke the spider's webs, and set the rats scampering." All around Washington, church bells rang and cannons fired.

Grant became an instant hero. Throughout his native Midwest, people started to call him "Unconditional Surrender" Grant. Newspaper stories of Grant at Fort Donelson, chomping on a cigar, prompted grateful citizens to send him hundreds of boxes of cigars. Grant, who began the war smoking his meerschaum pipe, switched full-time to cigars.

Grateful for these victories, Lincoln promptly promoted Grant to major general, second in command only to Halleck in the entire American West.

DURING THE WINTER OF 1862, as Abraham Lincoln worried over his military leadership, his sons Willie and Tad played a game of counting sunny days while stuck inside the White House. Willie had recently received a pony, and despite Washington's cold, wet, and mushy weather, insisted on riding his new horse. Either from exposure or from one of the frequent infections caused by unsanitary Washington conditions,

Willie Lincoln, the third Lincoln son, was a happy, studious, religious boy who enthralled both children and adults.

Willie became sick with what was called "bilious fever," a catchall term that could cover a multitude of illnesses. By the end of January, Willie's condition improved and worsened with frustrating irregularity. His mother frequently stayed up with him all night.

On February 5, 1862, while Grant was engaged in the battle at Fort Henry, the Lincolns hosted an evening reception at the White House that would turn into a nightmare. Continuing to face unfavorable comparisons to Buchanan's stylish niece Harriet Lane, the original First Lady, Mary had planned this party as a model of fine elegance. *Frank Leslie's Illustrated Newspaper* congratulated her for initiating "a social innovation." Heretofore, social events at the White House had either been "state dinners" for the few or a "reception" for the uncontrolled many. Mary Lincoln's event was for a select five hundred guests. The Lincolns' oldest son, Robert, was home from Harvard and stood proudly beside his parents receiving guests in the East Room. Throughout the evening, the marine band "discoursed sweet music," including the new "Mary Lincoln Polka." Mary wore a new dress, jewels, and a headdress of black and white crape myrtle.

Sadly, Abraham and Mary could not enjoy the evening. During the day, Willie's condition had suddenly worsened. Tad also became ill.

First mother, then father left the party, ascending the central staircase to care for Willie, who was burning up with fever.

The party's crowning moment occurred at 11:30 p.m. when servants unveiled beautiful tables of food and pastries prepared by Milliards, an upscale New York caterer. Models of a Union warship and Fort Pickens were depicted in confectioners' art. Dinner lasted until 3 a.m. *Leslie's Illustrated* pronounced the party "a complete success," but guests never knew the anxiety upstairs.

A week later, on Abraham Lincoln's fifty-third birthday, newspapers reported that Willie was recovering and out of danger. But his condition quickly became worse again. Willie asked to see his close friend, Horatio Nelson "Bud" Taft, Jr., who had "been to see him or to enquire about him almost every day," and could always cheer him up.

Mary now stayed beside him day and night.

On Thursday, February 20, 1862, at 5 p.m., Willie Lincoln died. Mary crumpled in a seizure of sobbing. Lizzie Keckley, her African-American seamstress, whose compassion for Mary had become a healing balm in these difficult months, gently led her away.

Only three days after celebrating Grant's second victory in the West, Lincoln was overcome by grief. He spoke softly. "My poor boy. He was too good for this earth . . . but then we loved him so." He walked down the hall to his secretary's office, and "choking with emotion," said, "Well, Nicolay, my boy is gone—actually gone!" Lincoln, "bursting into tears, turned, and went into his own office."

Attorney General Bates wrote in his diary that evening, "A fine boy of 11 years, too much idolized by his parents." The dark cloud of mourning that descended on the White House in February 1862 would never really lift for Mary Lincoln.

The service for Willie Lincoln was held in the East Room on February 24, 1862, at 2 p.m. Phineas Gurley, minister of the New York Avenue Presbyterian Church, conducted the service. Gurley brought a message of consolation and hope. He began by identifying with the grief of the parents over the death of a young child. He then spoke words of comfort. "It is well for us, and very comforting on such an occasion as this, to get a clear and scriptural view of the providence of God."

Gurley was a preacher who anticipated questions in his sermons. In this funeral oration, he addressed the delicate balance between free will and determinism. He told the grieving Abraham and Mary seated before him that sometimes providence appeared as "a mysterious dealing." Gurley's final counsel was to "acknowledge His hand, and hear His voice, and inquire after His will."

Gurley offered Lincoln pastoral care at one of the darkest moments in his life. In less than a year, Lincoln had experienced the death of the charming young Elmer Ellsworth, his close Illinois friend Edward Baker, and now his son.

When the pallbearers carried the casket from the White House, they were followed by a group of children, members of Willie's Sunday school class. Departing the White House, Lincoln rode in a carriage drawn by two black horses, accompanied by his oldest son, Robert, and his Illinois friends Senators Browning and Trumbull, in a procession to the Oak Hill Cemetery in Georgetown.

Life for Tad was now profoundly different without his older brother Willie, who had been his constant companion. He also lost their close friends Bud and Holly Taft. At the time of the funeral, Mary Lincoln wrote to Mary Taft, "Please keep the boys home the day of the funeral; it makes me feel worse to see them." Because the Taft boys reminded her of Willie, they were never again invited to the White House, leaving Tad even more alone.

Mary simply could not deal with the death of a second son. Eddie Lincoln had died at three and a half in 1850. Although extreme public mourning was a custom of the day, the death of Willie left Mary inconsolable. She never again entered the room where he died. She sought to remove from the White House everything and everyone that could remind her of Willie. Her husband felt the loss of his son deeply, too, but as president he knew he had to resume his leadership of a deeply wounded nation. As Lincoln increasingly found himself comfortable with cabinet members William Seward, Edwin Stanton, Gideon Welles, and a few other trusted colleagues, he was less available for the often-painful task of helping Mary cope with her grief.

In the wake of Willie's death, Lincoln forged a new relationship with Tad. He became the boy's chief companion. Tad and Willie had often slept together, but now Tad wanted to sleep with his father. The young Tad would be present at official meetings, sometimes sitting in Lincoln's lap or even perching on his shoulder, to the consternation of some of the president's guests. The hardworking president kept late hours at his

Abraham Lincoln forged a new, special relationship with Tad, the fourth Lincoln son.

desk, and often near midnight, when he had finished his last correspondence or signed his last order, Lincoln would pick up his small son from under the desk or in front of the fireplace and carry him off to bed.

ON MANY EVENINGS, Lincoln would amble across the street to Secretary of State Seward's redbrick three-story mansion on Lafayette Square just north and east of the White House. Living with Seward in Washington was his son, Frederick, and daughter-in-law Anna, who frequently served as hostess because Seward's wife, Frances, preferred to stay in their home in Auburn, New York.

After working with him for almost a year, Lincoln had grown to appreciate the company of the intellectual and witty Seward, a conversationalist with a thousand stories. To the other members of Lincoln's cabinet, and many in Washington, Lincoln and Seward were an odd couple. As the two men lounged in Seward's library, the secretary of state would take pleasure in his Havana cigars, while Lincoln did not smoke; Seward enjoyed vintage wines and brandy, while Lincoln did not drink; Seward was known for his colorful language, whereas Lincoln almost never swore. One day, Lincoln and Seward were on their way to review troops near Arlington. Traveling in an ambulance drawn by four mules over rutted roads, the driver, losing control of his team, began to swear. As the roads became even rougher, the swearing increased. At last Lincoln spoke up. "Driver, my friend, are you an Episcopalian?"

"No, Mr. President, I ain't much of anything; but if I go to church at all, I go to the Methodist Church."

"Oh, excuse me," Lincoln replied, "I thought you must be an Episcopalian for you swear just like Secretary Seward, and he's a churchwarden."

Lincoln enjoyed Seward because they could talk openly about many subjects besides the war. With portraits of George Washington, Andrew Jackson, and Daniel Webster arrayed on the walls of Seward's residence, their conversations turned regularly to the merits of American leaders. Lincoln had idolized Washington as a youth and still revered the nation's first president. He had joined in the Whig excoriation of Jackson as a young man, but with the hindsight of age, and the different chair in which he now sat, Lincoln had come to appreciate Old Hickory. In a conversation about Jackson, the two men discussed how to manage the delicate balance of presidential power. Lincoln had long admired Webster for his eloquent enunciation of American political ideals; he often used Webster's speeches as models for his own. In the course of another conversation, Seward argued that the reputations of neither Clay nor Webster would live "a tithe as long" as that of John Quincy Adams. Lincoln disagreed. He stated that he thought Webster "would be read forever."

Mary became resentful of the time her husband spent with Seward. She still held a grudge against him for the Republican nomination fight in 1860. Even after Seward joined her husband's administration, Mary derided him as that "hypocrite," and a "dirty abolition sneak." After almost a year in the White House, Mary saw her role as confidant and counselor being eclipsed by Seward at the very time she needed her husband more than ever.

LINCOLN'S IMPATIENCE WITH General McClellan increased as February turned into March. The Joint Committee on the Conduct of the War had been complaining about McClellan's lack of response to the Confederate control of the Potomac both above and below Washington. At last McClellan decided to break this grip by sending a Union detachment to the upper Potomac to reopen the Baltimore and Ohio Railroad link to the West. In order to cross the Potomac to rebuild a strategic bridge at Harpers Ferry, McClellan had arranged to bring canal boats up the Chesapeake and Ohio Canal, which paralleled the Potomac River. These boats would serve as platforms for the timbers to build the bridge. Just as they were about to travel from the canal into the river, sailors discovered the boats were six inches too wide to pass through the lock.

When McClellan, who had a reputation as an excellent planner, sent this bad news to Stanton, the secretary of war hurried over to tell Lincoln at the White House. After locking the door, Stanton read to Lincoln two dispatches from McClellan. Exasperated, Lincoln inquired, "What does this mean?" Stanton replied, "It means it is a damned fizzle. It means he does not intend to do anything."

Lincoln, "dejected," sent for Randolph Marcy, McClellan's chief of staff and father-in-law. As Lincoln paced the floor of his office, he may well have thought back to his days on the Eighth Judicial Circuit when he delighted in examining new farm machinery. Always a stickler for quality, Lincoln would lie down under a new machine to "sight" it, to see if it was straight or warped. With Nicolay present, he now asked Marcy, "Why in the —— nation, Gen. Marcy, couldn't the Gen. have known whether a boat would go through that lock before spending a million dollars getting them there? I am no engineer, but it seems to me that if I wished to know whether a boat would go through a hole or a lock, common sense would teach me to go and measure it." Lincoln concluded his remarks by summing up his feelings about more than canal boats. "Everything seems to fail. The general impression is daily gaining ground that the General does not intend to do anything. By a failure like this we lose all the prestige we gained by the capture of Fort Donelson. I am grievously disappointed—almost in despair."

Lincoln met with members of the Joint Committee on the Conduct of the War on the evening of March 3, 1862. Senators Benjamin Wade of Ohio and Zachariah Chandler of Michigan informed Lincoln that reports were circulating that McClellan was secretly in sympathy, if not in league, with the Confederates. This was not news to the president, who held one of these letters accusing McClellan of treason in his vest pocket. McClellan had made no secret of his dislike for abolitionists and radical Republicans who wished to destroy slavery. The meeting quickly degenerated into a heated exchange between the committee and the president about removing McClellan. Lincoln asked Senator Wade if McClellan were to be removed, who would replace him? "Well, anybody!" Wade cried out. "Wade," Lincoln replied, "anybody will do for you, but I must have somebody."

The committee actually had two candidates in mind. They were divided in their opinion between Irvin McDowell and John C. Frémont. Lincoln believed that both of these generals had lost standing with the public by their respective failures at Bull Run and in Missouri. He did agree, however, when the committee recommended that the army modify its command structure to encompass four corps, each with three divisions. Although the Joint Committee on the Conduct of the War was made up of a bunch of military amateurs, Lincoln knew that the professional army in early 1862, far larger than any previous army in America, had become too large to be commanded by one person. The meeting ended inconclusively. Lincoln was not about to be told what to do by a congressional committee, but, in truth, he, too, was also thinking about changing generals.

At half past seven on the morning of March 7, 1862, Lincoln met with McClellan at the White House. After speaking to him about the fiasco with the boats in the canal, he reiterated his concerns about the Urbana plan, which McClellan had yet to implement. The real purpose of Lincoln's summons was to tell McClellan, more than two weeks after his February 22 deadline, that it was time to start his march to Richmond. He also spoke to McClellan about what he called "an ugly matter." The president told McClellan that some members of Congress believed that the lengthened march of the Urbana plan was actually a strategy of "giving over to the enemy the capital and the government, thus left defenseless." McClellan, who had been seated, rose and demanded that the president retract such charges. Lincoln, "much agitated," disclaimed that these were not his ideas and said "he did not believe a word of it."

To set Lincoln's mind at ease, McClellan said he had convened a meeting with his generals to review the options between his Urbana plan and Lincoln's plan to march on Manassas. McClellan, a politician as well as a general, already knew what the result of the discussion would be. His generals voted in favor of his plan 8 to 4, with most of the eight being junior officers appointed by McClellan himself.

Subsequently, the generals reconvened at the White House at the president's request. Lincoln listened to the account of their meeting and their decision. He told the assembled military group that since he was not a military man he would respect the opinion of the majority. He advised Secretary of War Stanton, "We can do nothing else but accept their plan."

Out of respect for the military, Lincoln once again went against his better judgment. But not completely. Without consulting McClellan, on the next day he issued two orders. First, Lincoln commanded that the army be reorganized into four corps with twelve divisions. He appointed four senior generals to lead the new corps. Second, he approved the Urbana plan on the condition that McClellan agree to place "in, and about Washington," a force that would leave the capital "entirely secure." McClellan was furious with the first order. He did not disagree with the concept, but he wanted to handpick his own men.

The next day, March 9, 1862, after all of the debates about Richmond or Manassas, news came that Confederate general Joseph Johnston had evacuated his lines around Manassas and had taken up new defensive positions behind the Rappahannock River. By shifting his line farther to the south, he was now near the position at Urbana where McClellan had intended to begin his advance to Richmond.

In a show of bravado, McClellan immediately dispatched some of his troops south to Manassas, accompanied by a collection of newspaper reporters. Everyone was astounded by what they found. The configuration of the Confederate defenses had space for at most fifty thousand men, only half of the one hundred thousand troops McClellan had long insisted would face him. They also found that some of the enemy artillery were nothing more than painted black logs—"Quaker guns." These simple black logs had effectively deceived McClellan's intelligence service for months. The findings made McClellan look foolish. Never again, so Lincoln and Stanton agreed, would they accept his estimates of the strength of the opposition.

George McClellan finally began to march his army on March 17, 1862. By the beginning of April, a remarkable sight was taking shape at the upper end of the Virginia peninsula. Near the towns of Hampton and Old Point Comfort, baggage wagons, artillery, and shelter tents arrived daily. On Chesapeake Bay, a massive armada of 405 side-wheel steamers, propeller-driven steamers, brigs, and barges was assembling. The ships ferried thousands of supply wagons and hundreds of ambulances. The armies and navies who fought on this same peninsula eighty years before at the battle for Yorktown in the Revolutionary War would have been amazed at the preparation for a military operation far larger than anything ever seen on the American continent. General George B. McClellan was slowly bringing into formation one hundred thousand soldiers for the long-awaited attack on Richmond.

McClellan came to the White House on March 31, 1862, to bid good-bye to the president, but really to seek his approval after so much acrimony between them. The next day, McClellan informed the War Department that he was complying with the president's injunction to ensure that Washington was protected by leaving behind 19,000 troops, augmented by 7,800 at Harpers Ferry and Irvin McDowell's 30,000 troops in the nearby Shenandoah Valley. Lincoln was aghast. He believed the force was too few and too raw and most of them too distant from the capital. On April 3, Lincoln told Stanton he wanted McDowell's corps, slated to join the march to Richmond, to stay behind to protect Washington.

McClellan's plan to lay siege to Richmond was patterned after the siege of Sevastopol in the final battle of the Crimean War in 1855. Just as England and France brought to bear their industrial might on the Russian fortress, he would bring the industrial might of the Union army, including naval power and heavy artillery, to defeat the Confederates in the fortified city.

McClellan's forces advanced with little opposition until they approached Yorktown. Along the march he had encountered an elaborate network of trenches, which convinced him he was facing a large enemy force. The visible maneuvers of Confederate major general John B. Magruder's troops near Yorktown further alarmed McClellan. The Young Napoleon, believing he was outnumbered, decided to dig in and bring up his enormous guns for an assault.

Lincoln, now visiting the War Department telegraph office at all hours of the day and night, attempted to encourage McClellan to move forward. He wired on April 6, 1862, "You now have over one hundred thousand troops. . . . I think you better break the enemy's line from the

York-town to the Warwick River at once." The president, gaining in military knowledge, told McClellan, "They will probably use *time* as advantageously as you can."

McClellan was piqued. He fired off a telegram to Lincoln with the usual litany of complaints—he was outnumbered and the president and Stanton had failed to supply him with enough troops. McClellan later wrote his wife, "I was much tempted to reply that he had better come and do it himself."

Lincoln, not about to be put off by McClellan, raised his own ongoing concern. "After you left, I ascertained that less than twenty thousand unorganized men, without a single field battery, were all that you designed to be left for the defense of Washington, and Manassas Junction." McClellan believed his march to Richmond was the best prevention of an attack on Washington. Lincoln's worry was that, while McClellan was leading his large Union army slowly up the Virginia peninsula to capture a well-defended Richmond, the Confederates could, with a relatively small army, march quickly to capture a thinly defended Washington.

Lincoln and Stanton were so furious with McClellan's dithering that they offered the command of the Army of the Potomac to Ethan Allen Hitchcock, grandson of Revolutionary War hero Ethan Allen. Hitchcock, a curious character with a philosophical mind (he read Immanuel Kant's *Critique of Pure Reason* in German) had become Stanton's adviser in February. Now the president and the secretary of war asked him to assume command of the Army of the Potomac. He said he was too old, nearly sixty-four, and turned them down.

By early May, McClellan finally said he was ready to attack Yorktown with his heavy guns. Vastly overemphasizing the size of the enemy before him, which probably was only eleven thousand when he first approached Yorktown, his dawdling had allowed the Confederates to concentrate their defense. Lincoln wrote to McClellan, "Your call for Parrott guns from Washington alarms me, chiefly because it argues indefinite procrastination. Is anything to be done?"

McClellan now received a surprise. As he prepared to attack with his guns, to be followed by an infantry assault, Confederate general Joseph Johnston, under the cover of darkness on the night of May 3, 1862, executed a strategic retreat with his troops to help defend Richmond. Just like at Manassas, the overly cautious McClellan found no one to fight.

The South laughed that he had been tricked again. The North was not laughing.

On May 6, 1862, Lincoln, with Stanton and Treasury Secretary Chase at his side, decided to travel to Fortress Monroe to discover for himself exactly what General McClellan was or was not doing.

Two months before, a Confederate ironclad ship, the CSS *Virginia,* had steamed down the Elizabeth River into Hampton Roads to attack the wooden-sided Union ships set up there. The *Virginia* had rammed and sunk the twenty-four-gun USS *Cumberland* and then fired on the fifty-gun frigate USS *Congress.* The next day, the Union ironclad USS *Monitor* arrived on the scene. The two slow-moving ships could not damage each other. The dramatic encounter proved in two days the superiority of iron over wood. When Lincoln arrived, the *Virginia* was still lurking inside the Norfolk harbor. When Lincoln discovered the general had still done nothing to remove the *Virginia,* he threw his hat to the ground.

The next day, Lincoln took charge of a plan to capture Norfolk. Soldiers and sailors watched in amazement as Lincoln commandeered a boat to select the best landing site to launch his attack. He ordered gunboats to attack the Confederate shore batteries at Sewall's Point.

On May 9, 1862, the Confederates abandoned Norfolk, blowing up the *Virginia* so that it could not be captured. A soldier aboard one of the navy transports watched Lincoln directing reinforcements to the front. "Abe was rushing about, hollering to someone on the wharf—dressed in a black suit with a very seedy crepe on his hat, and hanging over the railing, he looked like some hoosier just starting for home from California, with store clothes and a biled shirt on." An officer aboard the *Monitor* wrote, "It is extremely fortunate that the President came down as he did—he seems to have infused new life into everything." The president's action began "stirring up dry bones." Salmon Chase wrote to his daughter, "So has ended a brilliant week's campaign of the President; for I think it quite certain that if he had not come down, Norfolk would still have been in possession of the enemy, and the 'Merrimac' as grim and defiant and as much a terror as ever. The whole coast is now virtually ours."

While at Fortress Monroe, Lincoln met Union general Ambrose Burnside, who had come up from North Carolina. On May 11, 1862, Lincoln invited Burnside to sail back with him on the USS *Baltimore.*

Once in Washington, Burnside found himself responding to a whole battery of questions from the president. When the general returned to the Willard Hotel, he offered his initial assessment of the president to members of his staff. "If there is an honest man on the face of the earth, Lincoln is one."

Also on May 11, 1862, Lincoln removed McClellan as general in chief, relieving him of his overall command. Lincoln's rationale was that Little Mac could not do it all. He placed Henry Halleck in charge of the armies in the West, and John C. Frémont in charge of a new Mountain Division, consisting of western Virginia and eastern Tennessee. McClellan retained his command of the Army of the Potomac. Inside the War Department, there was debate about whether Lincoln had gracefully let McClellan down, or challenged him that if he succeeded in taking Richmond his command would be restored.

Even so, Lincoln's orders further strengthened his own role as commander in chief. Henceforth, Halleck, Frémont, and McClellan would be equals reporting through Stanton to the president. Lincoln had come to trust Stanton and could work with him in ways he never could with Cameron. The hospitable Lincoln and his demanding secretary of war became a formidable team.

BY THE MIDDLE OF MAY, under the command of the freshly demoted George McClellan, the Army of the Potomac's 105,000 men could see the church spires of Richmond as they approached the city's gates. Sixty thousand Confederate troops defended Richmond, yet McClellan called for reinforcements, complaining he was fighting twice that number. For a while there was a standoff, but on May 31, 1862, Joseph Johnston unleashed an attack on McClellan south of the Chickahominy River. The ensuing battle of Seven Pines, or Fair Oaks, devolved into chaotic skirmishes in confusing terrain. Johnston was severely wounded and replaced by Robert E. Lee. Two days of blooding fighting resulted in a tactical draw.

McClellan was delighted when Lee, Jefferson Davis's military adviser, replaced the veteran Johnston. McClellan wrote Lincoln, "I prefer Lee to Johnston—the former is *too* cautious & weak under grave responsibility—personally brave & energetic to a fault, he yet is wanting in moral firmness when pressed by heavy responsibility & is likely to be timid and irresolute in action." Lincoln likely wondered whether McClellan had misjudged an opponent once again.

The answer came soon. General Robert E. Lee, whom Lincoln had asked to assume command of the entire Union army at the beginning of the war, was now in charge of the Confederate forces defending Richmond. He quickly proved to be a formidable commander. He directed General Stonewall Jackson into the Shenandoah Valley. Jackson was a risk taker who could move his often-outnumbered troops to take advantage of an opponent's weakness.

Lincoln, sensing the danger of Jackson, implored McClellan to instruct his senior generals to trap the wily Jackson in the valley. At the same time, he sent out his own orders to the division commanders from the telegraph office. But while the Union forces slowly came into position in a pincer move, Jackson's men stayed steps ahead by marching hard to escape the potential trap. Jackson won small battles at Front Royal, Winchester, Cross Keys, and Port Republic, frustrating the Union forces. He then joined Lee in the defense of Richmond.

In June, Lee led a counteroffensive, the Seven Days Battles, in which McClellan was forced to retreat from his position four miles east of Richmond. If McClellan thought he knew Lee, the Virginia general clearly remembered McClellan from Mexico. Convinced that McClellan would be tied to his guns, Lee risked leaving only twenty-five thousand troops to defend Richmond, and prepared to attack McClellan north of the Chickahominy. Not successful the first day, he attacked again and again. In a series of six battles in seven days, McClellan's peninsular campaign came to an end. By July 4, 1862, one year after Lincoln's special message to Congress, it had become clear to the president and the nation that McClellan's grand opportunity had been lost. Richmond had survived, and Lee and Jackson and their armies were on the rise.

Lincoln determined to find out firsthand what went wrong. He arrived by steamer at Fort Harrison, at the eastern tip of the Virginia peninsula, on July 8, 1862. McClellan came on board the steamer *Ariel* at Harrison's Landing and handed Lincoln a long letter, resuming a conversation he had started with the president before the Seven Days Battles. Admitting that he was going beyond his duties as an army commander but believing that the war had reached a crucial stage, McClellan wrote, "The Government must determine upon a civil and military policy, covering the whole ground of our national trouble."

McClellan's letter was partly a response to whispers in Washington debating the need for a second Confiscation Act. The first, signed by

Lincoln on August 6, 1861, permitted the seizure of any property, including slaves, being used by Confederates to support their insurrection. Lincoln, after negotiating with Congress, had signed it because it did not explicitly free all the slaves. The rumored second act would go further. "It should not be a war looking to the subjugation of the [Southern] people," McClellan lectured. "Neither confiscation of property . . . or the forcible abolition of slavery should be contemplated."

Lincoln, who had not met with McClellan in three months, received the letter, thanked him, and said nothing. The next day, discouraged, McClellan wrote his wife, Ellen, of the visit to "His Excellency." He said he doubted Lincoln "profited" from the call. The president "really seems quite incapable of rising to the height of the merits of the question & the magnitude of the crisis," he wrote.

But Lincoln did understand the enormity of the crisis. Whereas he might have agreed with McClellan six months earlier, he had changed his point of view. Three weeks later, Lincoln wrote as much in a letter to Cuthbert Bullitt, a Southern Unionist in New Orleans. He asked a series of rhetorical questions. "What would you do in my position? Would you drop the war where it is? Or, would you prosecute it in the future, with elder-stalk squirts, charged with rose water?" Lincoln strongly implied his answer in asking, "Would you deal lighter blows than heavier ones?" Three days later, in the same spirit, Lincoln wrote August Belmont, a prominent Northern Democrat. "This government cannot much longer play a game in which it stakes all, and its enemies stake nothing." Lincoln had reached a crucial decision in July 1862, about the nature of the war and new means to win the peace.

IN EARLY JUNE, Abraham and Mary Lincoln made an unannounced trip from the White House to a residence known as the Soldiers' Home. Located on shaded hills three miles north of the White House along the road to Silver Spring, Maryland, the Soldiers' Home was only a half-hour carriage ride from the White House. The seclusion of its three hundred acres was a welcome relief from the frenetic pace, humidity, and stench that constantly enveloped the Executive Mansion in Washington. Abraham and Mary would stay until early November, and would return the following two summers, living there a total of thirteen months, or more than one-quarter of Lincoln's presidency.

What came to be called the Soldiers' Home was built in 1842 by Washington banker George W. Riggs. In 1851, it became an asylum for

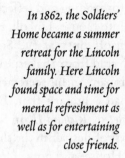

In 1862, the Soldiers' Home became a summer retreat for the Lincoln family. Here Lincoln found space and time for mental refreshment as well as for entertaining close friends.

disabled veterans of previous wars who could not provide for themselves. James Buchanan became the first president to stay at the Soldiers' Home. He probably suggested it to the Lincolns as a retreat. Both Mary and Abraham visited the Soldiers' Home separately in the days immediately following the inauguration on March 4, 1861, but the events leading up to Bull Run postponed a move in 1861 to the summer of 1862. In their summers there, the Lincolns may have stayed in more than one of the cottages, including the Riggs family home, a country house with a large porch built in the English Gothic Revival style whose popularity had begun in England in the 1830s.

After Willie's death, Mary especially enjoyed getting away from busy Washington. Benjamin B. French, commissioner of public buildings, visited the White House on Monday, June 16, 1862, just as Mary was getting ready to depart for the Soldiers' Home. French wrote in his diary, "She seemed to be in excellent spirits, and delighted at getting out of the city." One reason she surely was delighted was that the retreat provided more of an opportunity to be alone with her husband and Tad. Robert joined them from Harvard at the end of June. Mary and Abraham read to each other, and, whenever she could, she encouraged him to accompany her on late-afternoon carriage rides. In July, in a letter to a friend, she wrote, "We are truly delighted, with this retreat, the drives & walks around here are delightful, & each day, brings its visitors. Then, too, our boy Robert, is with us."

As a daily commuter, Lincoln rose early in the summer months and was on his way into Washington well before 8 a.m. One of the soldiers who was responsible for escorting the president, Captain David Derickson, reported that he would arrive at the cottage many days about 6:30 a.m. to find Lincoln "reading the Bible or some work on the art of war."

Although he would accomplish presidential work at the Soldiers' Home, Lincoln also welcomed private time for reading and reflection in this retreat setting. While on duty at the White House, Lincoln regaled visitors with stories and humor, but when off duty at the Soldiers' Home he much preferred, guests recalled, to read from Shakespeare and several of his other favorite poets. In the company of his secretary John Hay, a graduate of Brown College who had a literary flair, Lincoln would read for hours from *Macbeth* or *Hamlet* or *Richard II.* In Springfield, Hay had heard Lincoln read the outburst of despair in the third act of *Richard II;* he heard it again at the White House, and now at the Soldiers' Home.

> *For God's sake, let us sit upon the ground*
> *And tell sad stories of the death of kings;*
> *How some have been deposed; some slain in war,*
> *Some haunted by the ghosts they have deposed;*
> *Some poison'd by their wives: some sleeping kill'd;*
> *All murder'd:*

Lincoln seemed drawn to those plays of Shakespeare that spoke of an England split apart by civil war and of men driven by overwhelming ambition. The president's young assistant reported that Lincoln "read Shakespeare more than all other writers together."

AT THE END OF JUNE 1862, at a time of great Northern discouragement, Lincoln asked his secretary of state to sound out confidentially the state governors about the need to call up more troops. Worried that such a call might produce a panic across the North, Lincoln nonetheless told Seward of his resolve. "I expect to maintain this contest until successful, or till I die, or am conquered, or my term expires or Congress or the country forsakes me." On July 1, a few days before the nation celebrated its eighty-sixth birthday, Lincoln issued a call for another three hundred thousand three-year volunteers.

Quaker abolitionist James Sloan Gibbons, a businessman who was one of the lead supporters of the *National Anti-Slavery Standard,* wrote a poem that was published anonymously in the *New York Evening Post* on

July 16, 1862. The poem struck a chord with the public. No less than eight composers quickly set it to music. By the early fall the poem was being sung by choruses at Union rallies and by the public in town squares. The song expressed the Union's heart in music.

> We are coming, Father Abraham, 300,000 more,
> From Mississippi's winding stream and from New England's shore.
> We leave our plows and workshops, our wives and children dear,
> With hearts too full for utterance, with but a silent tear.
> We dare not look behind us but steadfastly before.
> We are coming, Father Abraham, 300,000 more!
>
> CHORUS: We are coming, we are coming our Union to restore,
> We are coming, Father Abraham, 300,000 more!

The poem elicited such a popular response because it voiced what everyone was saying. The last stanza begins, "You have called us and we're coming." The growing esteem of the Union soldiers and sailors for their commander in chief was spreading to citizens around the country.

Through the years, people had affixed nicknames to Lincoln in admiration. The earliest moniker, "Honest Abe," stuck because it captured the essential character of Lincoln in his midtwenties. Lincoln had endured the constant harangue that he was the "Black Republican" in his debates with Stephen Douglas, and again in the presidential campaign of 1860. This latest name, "Father Abraham," was a signpost that by the middle of 1862, appreciation for Lincoln had moved beyond an admiration reserved for an American president to an unusual affection bestowed upon a loving father figure by his grateful citizens.

IN THE SUMMER quiet at the Soldiers' Home, Lincoln brooded about slavery. Though personally he had long been opposed to slavery, as president he felt that in his oath he was constrained by the Constitution not to interfere with it where it already existed. He understood that taking this principled position had put him at odds with many leaders of his own party.

Lincoln's viewpoint on slavery was not so different from those of his critics, whose passion against slavery he admired. As he had told Massachusetts senator Charles Sumner at the end of 1861, timing was everything. Since signing the original Confiscation Act, he had tried to shift the burden of responsibility from the federal government to the states in a plan of compensated emancipation. He had high hopes for his trial plan in Delaware, but it was not going anywhere. Turning back to the ideas of his mentor, Henry Clay, he had advanced the idea of colonization as a solution to the problem of strife between whites and blacks. Colonization was a plan to settle African-Americans outside the United States. He floated this idea in his December 1861 annual message to Congress, with little response.

In early March 1862, Lincoln sent to Congress a bill providing for a federal-state emancipation plan similar to his Delaware plan. In order to soothe fears of white Northerners, he again coupled emancipation with colonization. Whereas in his annual message he had assured Congress that he would not resort to any "radical" or "revolutionary" measures, this time he warned them that if compensated emancipation did not work, he would be free to use means "such as seem indispensable, or may obviously promise great efficiency towards ending the struggle." This message created an uproar, but Sumner and Greeley praised it. Henry J. Raymond, editor of the *New York Times,* wrote Lincoln to complain that the plan would cost too much. The president replied that the cost of fighting the war for seven to eight days would pay entirely the price of emancipating the slaves in the four border states. On March 10, he met with border state representatives at the White House who, to his discouragement, almost to a person opposed his plan.

On April 16, 1862, Lincoln signed into law a bill abolishing slavery in Washington, D.C. The bill compensated owners and made plans to send slaves, if they so wished, to either Haiti or Liberia. On June 9, he signed a bill outlawing slavery in all the federal territories. This bill effectively reversed the ruling in the Dred Scott decision of 1857.

On July 12, 1862, two days after Lincoln returned from seeing McClellan at Harrison's Landing, Congress passed a second confiscation bill. This bill dealt with a problem that plagued field commanders occupying Southern territory. As troops advanced, slaves sought refuge in Union camps, and federal commanders were confused over their obligations to the refugees. Some freed the slaves, others sent them back to their masters for lack of means to care for them. The Confiscation Act of 1862 declared that all slaves taking refuge behind Union lines were captives of war who were to be set free.

On the same day, Lincoln met, once again, with representatives of the border states. He told them that they must forget their retreat into earlier, quieter times, and face up to "the unprecedentedly stern facts of our case." If they rejected his plan for compensated emancipation, the war would kill off slavery "by mere friction and abrasion," and they would not get a dollar for their slaves. Did not they see that his plan was the best option for them?

They did not. The plan would cost too much. It would only further fan the flames of rebellion.

Lincoln returned to the Soldiers' Home to continue work on a document he had been readying in recent days, perhaps weeks. He had tried his best to move people toward compensated emancipation with colonization. Now he was prepared for a much bolder move.

ON SUNDAY AFTERNOON, July 13, 1862, Lincoln invited Seward and Welles to ride with him to the funeral of Secretary of War Stanton's infant child, James, not quite nine months old. Both his guests were startled when Lincoln informed them that he was thinking of emancipating the slaves. Welles wrote in his diary, "He dwelt earnestly on the gravity, importance, and delicacy of the movement, and said he had given it much thought." Lincoln had come to the conclusion "that we must free the slaves or be ourselves subdued."

Lincoln, as usual, would say nothing more to anyone for more than a week as he continued to mull over his decision. He would later reflect, "Things had gone from bad to worse, until I felt that we had reached the end of our rope on the plan of operations we had been pursuing; that we had about played our last card, and must change our tactics, or lose the game!" Lincoln now decided to convene his cabinet to make his first public disclosure of his momentous decision.

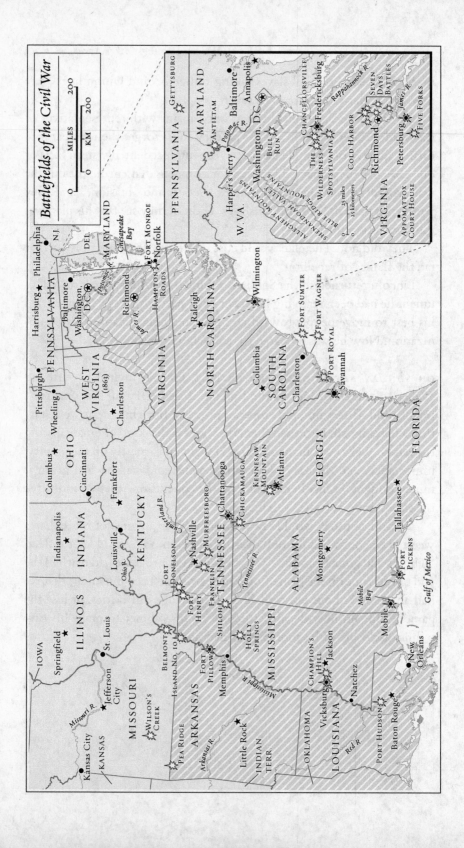

Battlefields of the Civil War

CHAPTER 21

We Must Think Anew
July 1862–December 1862

THE DOGMAS OF THE QUIET PAST, ARE INADEQUATE TO THE STORMY
PRESENT.

ABRAHAM LINCOLN
Second annual message to Congress, December 1, 1862

ON JULY 22, 1862, LINCOLN EMERGED FROM HIS SOLITARY BROODING AND
writing at the Soldiers' Home. "After much anxious thought," he had
come to the conclusion that it was not possible to return to the past, or
even stand in the shifting sands of the present. He determined to step
forward into an unknown future.

For Lincoln, using his largely undefined war powers as commander
in chief to propose emancipation was contrary to much in his personal
makeup. His intellectual roots were planted more in the reasonableness
of the Enlightenment than in the sentiments of Romanticism. As a
lawyer, he had grounded his legal briefs in precedent. In his religious
pilgrimage, he had chosen to attend rational, nonpolitical Old School
Presbyterian congregations over experiential, antislavery New School
congregations in both Springfield and Washington. Although his heart
had long been tormented by the immorality of slavery, his Enlightenment, precedent-based, Old School head had heretofore tethered him to
what he believed to be the Constitution's prohibition against eliminating slavery where it already existed in the South.

Lincoln had not set his sights on emancipation at the beginning of
the war. His single goal was to save the Union. The subject of slavery
was virtually absent in both his inaugural address and his special message to Congress on July 4, 1861. But now, sixteen months later, his
developing ideas, the press of events, the military defeats, and his own

sense of timing coalesced into a determination to redefine the war's purpose.

On July 22, 1862, when Lincoln began to read to his cabinet a preliminary draft of a proclamation promising emancipation, he said he was not asking for their assent but informing them of his plan of action. None were prepared for his final sentence. Lincoln, "as a fit and necessary military measure," declared that on January 1, 1863, "all persons held as slaves within any state or states, wherein the constitutional authority of the United States shall not then be practically recognized . . . shall then, thenceforward, and forever, be free." The members of the cabinet sat stunned.

William Seward, who had known of Lincoln's plan in advance, expressed his strong concern about the timing of Lincoln's proclamation. To issue it at a time of continuing Union defeats might appear to many to be an act of desperation. Why not wait until a significant military victory would place the proclamation in a more positive light? Lincoln would say afterward, "The wisdom of the view of the Secretary of State struck me with very great force."

LINCOLN STARTED THE SECOND SUMMER of the war dealing with a retreating army and a restless public. He had hovered over the telegraph operators on the second floor of the War Department during the anxiety of the Seven Days Battles from June 25 to July 1, 1862. He followed events in Tennessee and Kentucky, where guerrilla attacks by Confederate generals Nathan Bedford Forrest and John Hunt Morgan behind Union lines dispelled any lingering notions that widespread Unionist sentiment remained in the South. The Confederate tactics heightened anger in the North. Lincoln heard that Union soldiers were writing home about "bushwhackers," insurgents hiding behind day jobs as farmers or shopkeepers, but harassing and killing Union bluecoats at night. Soldiers began to protest that what had begun as a "kid glove war" must now give way to a "hard war."

The president decided the time had come to make changes in the military command. Discouraged by the inability of the armies of Irvin McDowell, Nathaniel Banks, and John C. Frémont to trap the wily Stonewall Jackson in the Shenandoah Valley, Lincoln decided to consolidate these forces under a new army led by a new commander. He appointed General John Pope of Illinois to lead a newly designated Army of Virginia on June 26, 1862. Lincoln had practiced law under

Pope's father, Judge Nathaniel Pope, a gruff man appointed by President James Monroe to be the first U.S. district judge for Illinois. John, an 1842 West Point graduate, was a large man with piercing eyes. He had served in the military escort accompanying Lincoln from Springfield to Washington in February 1861, when the two exchanged humorous stories. Pope had served under Henry Halleck in the West and had won fame for his capture of Island Number Ten, fifty miles downriver from Columbus, Kentucky, on April 7, 1862.

Lincoln was just getting started. On July 11, 1862, only two days after his visit with General McClellan at Harrison's Landing, Lincoln appointed Henry W. Halleck as general in chief. Lincoln's decision to change commanding generals was not only a rejection of McClellan as a leader, but a decision to change the political and military strategy of the war.

Henry Halleck was born in 1815 on a farm in the Mohawk Valley of New York, and ranked third in the class of 1839 at West Point. At the military academy, he studied the "art of war" through the writings of Baron Henri Jomini, a Swiss military historian. Taking a different tack from his contemporary Carl von Clausewitz, Jomini argued that Napoleon's success grew from rational principles that stressed movement rather than total destruction. The goal became to inflict damage to the enemy with the least risk to one's own troops.

After serving in California during the Mexican War, Halleck retired from the army in 1854. In 1855, he married Elizabeth Hamilton, granddaughter of Alexander Hamilton. When the Civil War erupted, he left California, where he had accumulated an estate worth $500,000 in quicksilver mines, for an appointment as a major general. Two years later Lincoln named him his top general.

In a war where the public wanted their generals to look like heroes, Halleck did not fit the part. He appeared much older than his forty-seven years. Standing five feet nine inches tall and one hundred ninety pounds, he was paunchy, with flabby cheeks and a double chin. He had an annoying habit of constantly scratching his elbows. Because of his dull, fishlike eyes, some said he was an opium addict. He acquired the nickname "Old Brains," not for his prowess as a military theorist, but for his high forehead and bulging eyes.

Lincoln looked forward to a partnership with a man he had admired from a distance. He had read Halleck's *Elements of Military Art and Science* as part of his early tutorial in military strategy. In Lincoln's recent visit

Lincoln's decision to appoint Henry Halleck, "Old Brains," to replace George McClellan as general in chief was about both a new leader and a new strategy.

to West Point, retired general Scott, who had recommended Halleck over McClellan as his successor in the summer of 1861, commended him to Lincoln once again. Lincoln wrote to Halleck on July 14, 1862, "I am very anxious—almost impatient—to have you here. . . . When can you reach here?"

That Lincoln felt more than anxious had become apparent to those closest to him. Orville Browning saw Lincoln frequently in June and July 1862, often at the Soldiers' Home, where they enjoyed sitting together on the portico's stone steps on summer evenings. On July 15, Browning visited Lincoln at the White House. When he entered the library, he observed that Lincoln "looked weary, care-worn and troubled." They shook hands and Browning asked Lincoln how he was. "Tolerably well," he replied. Browning, concerned, told Lincoln he "feared his health was suffering." At that, Lincoln reached for Browning's hand, "pressed it, and said in a very tender and touching tone—'Browning I must die sometime.' He looked very sad, and there was a cadence of sadness in his voice." The two old friends parted, "both of us with tears in our eyes."

LINCOLN HAD HEARD the snide remarks about Halleck's looks and mannerisms, but he never put stock in outward appearances. When the general finally arrived on July 23, 1862, Halleck and Lincoln traveled to McClellan's headquarters, accompanied by Montgomery Meigs and Ambrose Burnside. Lincoln wanted Halleck's recommendation on whether to retain "Little Mac" as commander of the Army of the Potomac, and whether his battered forces should be withdrawn from the Virginia peninsula.

McClellan told Halleck that he needed more men, because he was certain that Lee's opposing army had 200,000 soldiers. Upon their return, Meigs, whom Lincoln trusted, told the president that by his calculations Lee had only 105,000 men. (The figure was closer to 75,000.)

On Friday evening, July 25, 1862, Orville Browning visited Lincoln at the Soldiers' Home. The Illinois senator confided to his diary that Lincoln told him that McClellan would never fight. It was as "if by magic he could reinforce McClellan with 100,000 men to day he would be in an ecstasy over it, thank him for it, and tell him that he would go to Richmond tomorrow, but that when tomorrow came he would telegraph that he had certain information that the enemy had 400,000 men, and he could not advance without reinforcements."

Tired of McClellan's foot dragging, Lincoln decided to replace him with Ambrose E. Burnside, an Indiana native and a graduate of West Point in the class of 1847, as commander of the Army of the Potomac. On February 7 and 8, 1862, Lincoln had been heartened by Burnside's leadership of an amphibious landing through the Hatteras inlet to attack Roanoke Island off the coast of North Carolina. Supported by gunboats, and fighting the fury of nature as much as the outnumbered Confederate defenders, Burnside secured a vital outpost in the Union's effort to tighten the blockade of the Atlantic Coast.

Everyone who met Burnside liked him at once. Six feet tall and handsome, with a sturdy build and his face partially enclosed by bushy muttonchop whiskers, he was a skilled horseman with long buckskin gloves and a pistol that swung loosely from a holster on his hip. Sometime between July 22 and 27, 1862, Lincoln asked Burnside to relieve McClellan and assume command of the Army of the Potomac. Burnside, surprised, told the president he was not eager to command a large army. He turned down the president's offer to replace his good friend

Lincoln asked Ambrose E. Burnside to become the new commander of the Army of the Potomac in July 1862.

McClellan who, he said, only needed more time to prove his leadership. Lincoln would not forget Burnside's self-effacing manner.

In Henry Halleck, Lincoln believed he had finally found someone who could relieve him of the burden of his responsibility for the supervision of the army. McClellan and Pope, who did not hide their dislike of each other, would now both report to Halleck. Lincoln quickly came to depend on "Old Brains" for technical military advice. A month later, McClellan was surely surprised when Lincoln answered a query by replying, "I wish not to control. That I now leave to Gen. Halleck." With many tough decisions to be made, Lincoln would sometimes feign ignorance of military strategy and let Halleck be the public face of the Union forces. In responding to the multitude of questions coming his way, he began to offer a standard reply, "You must call on General Halleck, who commands."

LONG BEFORE THE ADVENT of televised presidential press conferences, Lincoln mastered a new means of communication developing in the nineteenth century. As he struggled to find his footing in the second year of his presidency, this mastery would become a key to his emerging political leadership.

In his first debate with Stephen Douglas in Ottawa, Illinois, in 1858,

Lincoln offered his insight into the role of public opinion in a democratic society. "Public sentiment is everything. With public sentiment, nothing can fail; without it nothing can succeed. Consequently he who moulds sentiment, goes deeper than he who enacts statutes or pronounces decisions."

But Lincoln offered this comment in an Illinois he knew well. How would he be able to keep his finger on the pulse of public opinion while he lived in Washington, often confined to the White House and consumed by his duties as commander in chief? In 1862, he worked hard to listen to the public and to find more ways to communicate his vision for the Union. He found the answer in newsprint.

Newspapers conveyed the immediacy of daily events to Americans as never before. At the time of Lincoln's birth, there were approximately 250 American newspapers. By the beginning of the Civil War, there were more than 2,500 newspapers, both daily and weekly. In New York, Boston, Philadelphia, and other larger cities, newspapers published multiple editions each day in order to keep up with people's appetite for news. Many more people read newspapers than paid subscribers. At countless general stores and post offices, neighbors gathered to listen to someone read from "Uncle Horace's Weekly Try-bune," or the like.

Lincoln was a newspaper junkie. Francis B. Carpenter, an artist in residence in the White House in 1864, reported that he regularly saw in the secretary's quarters the *New York Tribune, Herald, Evening Post, World, Times,* and *Independent;* the *Boston Advertiser, Journal,* and *Transcript;* the *Philadelphia Press* and *North American;* the *Baltimore American* and *Sun;* the *Cincinnati Gazette* and *Commercial;* the *St. Louis Republican* and *Democrat;* the *Albany Evening Journal;* and the *Chicago Tribune* and *Journal.*

Instead of letters to the editor, editors wrote letters to Lincoln. They offered their counsel on every political issue, but especially the war. More than three hundred letters from newspaper editors were received at the White House during Lincoln's presidency. Editors not only wrote to Lincoln, they also traveled to Washington to speak to him in person.

And Lincoln also wrote letters. After his special message to Congress on March 6, 1862, in which he again advocated compensation to Southern states if they would put an end to slavery, he sent a letter to Henry Raymond to object that the *New York Times* got it wrong about how much the compensation would cost. He told the editor he was "grateful to the New-York Journals, and not less to the Times than to the others, for their kind notices of the late special Message to Congress." Lincoln was not just playing up to Raymond, for he had cut out and saved editorials from six New York newspapers—the *New York Times, Tribune, Evening Bulletin, Herald, World,* and *Evening Post,* all written on March 7, all supporting compensated emancipation.

In the first months of the war, Lincoln had appreciated Horace Greeley's central role among the newspaper generals. "Having him firmly behind me will be as helpful to me as an army of one hundred thousand men." But the *New York Tribune* editor's support for Lincoln began to vacillate in 1862 as he became more and more distressed by Lincoln's silence about slavery. Greeley decided to speak straight to the president through the most public communication he knew—his newspaper.

On August 19, 1862, Greeley wrote a letter to Lincoln that he published the following day in the *Tribune* under the heading "The Prayer of Twenty Millions." Greeley complained that the president was "strangely and disastrously remiss" in not proclaiming emancipation now.

> On the face of this wide earth, Mr. President, there is not one disinterested, determined, intelligent, champion of the Union cause who does not feel that all attempts to put down the Rebellion, and at the same time uphold its inciting cause, are preposterous and futile—that the Rebellion, if crushed out to-morrow, would be renewed within a year if slavery were left in full vigor. . . . I close as I began, with the statement that what an immense majority of the loyal millions of your countrymen require of you is a frank, declared unqualified, ungrudging execution of the laws of the land.

Appearing toward the end of a long summer of Union dissatisfaction, Greeley's letter created a commotion. Newspapers across the North reprinted his protest.

Lincoln notified the Washington *National Intelligencer* that he intended to write a response to Greeley, asking the paper to send one of its editors, James C. Welling, to the White House to assist him. Welling reviewed Lincoln's reply word by word. He proposed one sentence be "erased," in the third paragraph: "Broken eggs can never be mended, and the longer the breaking proceeds the more will be broken." The young literary editor recalled that Lincoln acquiesced "with some reluctance." Welling doesn't expand upon Lincoln's answer but did offer his

Horace Greeley, reforming editor of the New York Tribune, *wrote a letter to Lincoln entitled "The Prayer of Twenty Millions," challenging the president to move faster on emancipation.*

own reason for removing it. This sentence "seemed somewhat exceptional, on rhetorical grounds, in a paper of such dignity."

Welling's response sounded like printer John D. Defrees's response to "sugar-coated" in Lincoln's annual message to Congress in 1861. The editor and the printer wished to correct Lincoln about proper speech. They were telling the president of the United States that his humble American expressions did not fit the rhetorical etiquette of the occasion.

Lincoln's response to Greeley was published in the *National Intelligencer* on August 22, 1862. The president's "public letter," addressed to an individual but understood to be meant for a larger public consumption, was also quickly republished in numerous newspapers. The meaning of the letter has been debated from the moment Lincoln penned it. Although he must have been disconcerted by Greeley's imperious tone, he started his letter with a generosity of spirit.

I have just read yours of the 19th, addressed to myself. . . . If there be in it any statements, or assumptions of fact, which I may know to be erroneous, I do not now and here, controvert them. If there be in it any inferences which I may believe to be falsely drawn, I do not now and here, argue against them. If there be perceptible in it an impatient and dictatorial tone, I waive it in deference to an old friend, whose heart I have always supposed to be right.

That beginning, which is often omitted in reprinting Lincoln's reply, sets the tone for all that follows.

> I would save the Union. I would save it the shortest way under the Constitution. The sooner the national authority can be restored, the nearer the Union will be "the Union as it was." If there be those who would not save the Union, unless they could at the same time save slavery, I do not agree with them. If there be those who would not save the Union unless they could at the same time destroy slavery, I do not agree with them. My paramount object in this struggle is to save the Union, and is not either to save or to destroy slavery. If I could save the Union without freeing any slave I would do it, and if I could save it by freeing all the slaves I would do it; and if I could save it by freeing some and leaving others alone I would also do that. What I do about slavery, and the colored race, I do because it helps to save the Union; and what I forbear, I forbear because I do not believe it would help save the Union. I shall do less whenever I shall believe what I am doing hurts the cause, and I shall do more whenever I shall believe doing more will help the cause. I shall try to correct errors when shown to be errors; I shall adopt new views so fast as they appear to be true views.

At the center of the letter Lincoln offers a thesis sentence that spells out his meaning: "My paramount object in this struggle is to save the Union, and is not either to save or destroy slavery." He then expanded on what he would save and what he would not save. The verb "save" pulsates twelve times through this central paragraph of the letter.

Lincoln wished to speak to three groups. First, most people in the South wanted to save slavery, and Lincoln knew that many Northern Democrats were also opposed to emancipation. In response to this position, Lincoln offered a resonant: "I do not agree with them."

The second group were political abolitionists, represented by Charles Sumner in Congress and Horace Greeley in the press. Greeley presented himself as representing twenty million, which to Lincoln's mind was clearly an overstatement.

Lincoln had become especially sensitive to a third group. Unnamed in his letter, he was thinking of the common soldier. He understood that the majority of soldiers had enlisted to save the Union, not to free the slaves. Even those soldiers who believed that blacks might be able to work at jobs behind the lines did not believe they were capable of fighting on the front lines. An astute Lincoln used his public letter to speak to all these groups at once.

He concluded with a disclaimer: "I have here stated my purpose according to my view of official duty, and I intend no modification of my oft-expressed personal wish that all men everywhere could be free." Understanding this final paragraph is imperative to appreciating the full meaning of Lincoln's reply to Greeley. His final sentiment enunciated the continuing creative tension felt between the obligation of his office to abide by the Constitution and his personal wishes.

What did Lincoln accomplish with his public letter? An impatient Greeley was calling out a patient Lincoln. Lincoln's reply did not really answer Greeley's appeal, but that was not his purpose. The president made his own appeal—to save the Union. He had shrewdly outflanked the leading New York general of opinion, and on his own territory, the newspaper.

The reply to Greeley is misconstrued if interpreted as a simple declaration of support for the Union. As Lincoln crafted his reply, he held in his coat pocket his preliminary Emancipation Proclamation. Lincoln had become adroit at keeping his own counsel and moving forward on his own schedule.

A FEW DAYS AFTER Lincoln's reply to Greeley, Union and Confederate forces fought a second furious battle around Manassas Junction. Thirteen months earlier, the Union army had suffered a devastating defeat at Bull Run. In the summer of 1862, the newly designated Union Army of Virginia, under General John Pope, vowed things would be different.

Pope told everyone who would listen that his headquarters would be in his saddle. His tough talk about leading an offensive war had a positive effect on the many politicians who were tired of McClellan's delays.

Pope's initial letter to the officers and soldiers of the Army of Virginia had the opposite effect. McClellan remained popular with many of the soldiers, but Pope minced no words. "I have come from the West, where we have always seen the backs of our enemies." He told his men "to dismiss from your minds certain phrases, which I am sorry to find so much in vogue amongst you. I hear constantly of 'taking strong positions and holding them,' of 'lines of retreat,' and of 'bases of supplies.' Let us discard such ideas." No one could mistake Pope's words as anything but criticism of McClellan. The new commander's men began calling him "boastful Pope" behind his back.

In the last week of August, Stonewall Jackson, commanding the leading edge of Robert E. Lee's army, marched his "foot cavalry" fifty-six miles in two days on a wide swing around Pope's right flank to attack the Union supplies at Manassas. Jackson could hardly believe what his men found in one hundred freight cars and countless warehouses. His hungry men feasted on the Union's lobster salad and Rhine wine. Men strutted about in new shoes, wore women's hats with elaborate ribbons, and carried off pickled oysters, molds of cheese, and candy. Jackson ordered all the whiskey poured on the ground (an order not completely obeyed). What the soldiers could not eat or carry with them they burned. Lincoln watched from the south lawn of the White House as black smoke rose in the sky above northern Virginia. Then Jackson's troops disappeared.

The next day, August 28, 1862, Jackson's troops drew Pope's army into battle at Brawner Farm near Bull Run. On the following morning, Pope carried out disjointed attacks against Jackson along an uncompleted railroad grade. Although neither side gained an advantage, Pope reported he had Jackson on the run. He failed to recognize that reinforcements led by General James Longstreet's troops had broken through Thoroughfare Gap and were fast arriving to support Jackson. A wary George Templeton Strong in New York wrote in his diary, "I am not prepared to crow quite yet. Pope is an imaginative chieftain and ranks with Cooper as a writer of fiction. Good news from Bull Run is suspicious."

Lincoln, standing beside his new general in chief Henry Halleck, listened to updates helplessly in the telegraph office. McClellan, now at Alexandria, was responsible for reinforcing Pope. Halleck, unsure of himself, called again and again for McClellan to begin sending reinforcements. Over and over, McClellan responded that for one reason or another, the officers in his command could not move. "We are not yet in a condition to move." "It would be a sacrifice to send them now." "I still think that a premature movement in small force will accomplish nothing but the destruction of the troops."

At 2:45 in the afternoon, McClellan telegraphed Lincoln. "I am clear that one of two courses should be adopted—1st To concentrate all our available forces to open communication with Pope—2nd To leave Pope to get out of this scrape & at once use all our means to make the Capital perfectly safe." Lincoln was astonished by McClellan's response. He was also disappointed in Halleck, who, standing beside him as if in shock, seemed unable to exercise command over McClellan.

On August 30, 1862, Pope, believing that Lee's repositioning of forces was actually the beginning of a retreat, attacked, failing to wait until he had fully massed his own forces. Pope's divisions, especially his all-Western "Iron Brigade" from Wisconsin and Indiana, fought bravely. But Longstreet, with twenty-eight thousand men, counterattacked and Pope's troops began to fall back.

That same morning, Lincoln and John Hay had ridden in together from the Soldiers' Home. As they talked about all that had happened in the previous several days, Lincoln "was very outspoken in regard to McClellan's present conduct." He said "it really seemed to him that McC wanted Pope defeated."

At eight o'clock on August 30, 1862, Lincoln came into Hay's room in the White House to say, "Well John we are whipped again." Indeed, Pope's Union troops gave ground in a retreat to Centreville. In the days that followed, beaten Union units fell all the way back to their defenses on the outskirts of Washington. In five days of fighting, the Union forces of 65,000 men suffered 13,830 casualties while Lee and Jackson's 55,000 troops lost 8,350.

AT 7:30 ON TUESDAY MORNING, September 2, 1862, Lincoln and Henry Halleck walked to McClellan's house on H Street. Lincoln knocked on the door, unannounced, and found the general at breakfast. Lincoln told McClellan "that the troubles now impending could be overcome better" by him "than anyone else." Lincoln had decided to keep McClellan. In touch with the sentiment of the soldiers, Lincoln understood that whatever the newspaper generals or the senators might think, Little Mac remained immensely popular with the rank-and-file soldiers. The soldiers believed they had never been outgeneraled, certainly not outfought, but had been defeated by superior numbers.

McClellan told his wife that when Pope's troops fell back to Washington "everything is to come under my command again." McClellan said he was being given "a terrible & thankless task—yet I will do my best with God's blessing to perform it."

When Lincoln walked into the regular Tuesday cabinet meeting, he found the members buzzing with conversation. After Pope's predictions of a Union victory, the Northern press criticized the leadership of "boastful Pope"; of McClellan, for failing to come to Pope's aid; and of the president, who, as commander in chief, allowed this debacle to develop on his watch. The Southern press and people were ecstatic.

Secretary of the Navy Welles captured the mood of the meeting and of the president. "There was a more disturbed and desponding feeling than I have ever witnessed in council; the President was greatly distressed." Attorney General Bates recorded in his diary that the president was deeply discouraged after early predictions of victory had turned into reports of a disastrous defeat. Bates wrote that Lincoln "seemed wrung by the bitterest anguish—said he felt almost ready to hang himself."

Lincoln then stunned the members of his cabinet by informing them that he had decided to place McClellan in charge of an army that would fold in the Army of the Potomac and Pope's Army of Virginia. Secretary of War Stanton, who had prepared a petition already signed by several members of the cabinet, became indignant. Chase argued that McClellan's "experience as a military commander had been little else than a series of failures." Particularly upset with McClellan's failure to come to Pope's aid, Chase believed this "rendered him unworthy of trust."

Later that day, Lincoln's decision to reappoint McClellan was validated, if not by the cabinet, then by the soldiers. On a cold and rainy afternoon, as discouraged soldiers straggled back into Washington, they were met by a lone officer on a black horse, dressed in full military uniform, wearing a general's yellow sash and dress sword. Brigadier General Jacob Cox saw McClellan first.

"Well, General," McClellan said, "I am in command again."

What followed would be talked about for years to come. As McClellan rode forward toward the soldiers, he saluted them with his cap, and they, suddenly encouraged, broke out in shouts and cheers "with wild delight." The word spread along the columns of soldiers, "Little Mac is back!"

—

AS JULY TURNED INTO AUGUST, and then into September, Lincoln waited for the military victory that would allow him to announce his Emancipation Proclamation. For months now, the most furious assault on Lincoln came not from Confederate troops besieging Washington, but from radical Republican senators assailing his leadership. Senators Charles Sumner and Henry Wilson of Massachusetts, along with Congressman Thaddeus Stevens of Pennsylvania, gave Lincoln no respite. Lincoln told a visitor that he would look out the White House window and see them coming, singly, as a pair, or all together to attack him for not making a more frontal assault on slavery. In these dire days, Lincoln often found refuge in his bottomless barrel of humor. He told a friend that the visits of these three reminded him of the boy in Sunday school, who, when asked to read from the Bible the story of the three men in the fiery furnace, struggled over the difficult names of Shadrach, Meshach, and Abednego. The boy read on, mortified, until he looked down the page and saw their names coming again. This time, in agony, he cried out, "Look! Look there! Here comes them same three damn fellers again!"

Lincoln used this time to refine his thinking about emancipation. Sometime in early August, he telegraphed his old friend Leonard Swett in Bloomington, Illinois, asking him to come to Washington immediately. Lincoln ushered the tall, dark-eyed Swett into the cabinet room, where he pulled out several letters from a drawer in his desk. He first read one from William Lloyd Garrison, the New England abolitionist, then one by Garrett Davis, state senator from the border state of Kentucky, followed by one or two more letters about emancipation.

Without commenting on the quite different opinions, Lincoln began to debate the issue. First, he took one side, often using phrases from the letters but adding his own arguments. Then he argued the other side. Swett, who had traveled the Eighth Judicial Circuit with Lincoln, had observed this pattern in countless courtrooms. Lincoln could "state the case of his adversary better and more forcibly than his opponent could state it himself." Lincoln went on for more than an hour with his one-man debate. Swett became impressed that Lincoln's "manner did not indicate that he wished to impress his views *upon* the hearer, but rather to weight and examine them for his own enlightenment *in the presence of* the hearer." Swett, so trusted by Lincoln, believed he was privileged to be "a witness of the President's mental operations."

When Lincoln finished, he asked for no comment from Swett. He thanked him for coming, wished him a pleasant trip home, and sent greetings to "mutual friends." So evenhanded was Lincoln's debate that Swett predicted to his wife, "He will issue no proclamation emancipating negroes."

STILL WRESTLING OVER HOW TO PROCLAIM emancipation, Lincoln sent word to the black leadership in Washington that he wished to speak with them. On the afternoon of August 14, 1862, an American president did something that no one could remember: He welcomed to the White House a committee of five black leaders. The group did not include national figures such as Frederick Douglass. Lincoln told them that money "had been appropriated by Congress, and placed at his disposition" for the purpose of colonization. Lincoln asked, "Why should they leave the country?" He then answered his own question. "You and we are different races. We have between us a broader difference than exists between almost any other two races. Whether it is right or wrong I need not discuss." Lincoln went on to clarify what he meant. "This physical difference is a great disadvantage to us both, as I think your race suffer very greatly, many of them by living among us, while ours suffer from your presence."

Lincoln acknowledged that his guests were free men, probably free their whole lives. "Your race is suffering, in my judgment, the greatest wrong inflicted on any people." He went on to discuss how racial equality did not exist in the United States. "I cannot alter it if I would. It is a fact, about which we all think and feel alike, I and you." With this comment, Lincoln uncharacteristically made an assumption he did not test. He then talked about the evil of slavery, for both blacks and whites. His conclusion: "It is better for us both, therefore, to be separated."

Lincoln hoped these leaders would be the vanguard of a colonization project in Central America. He said he understood that of all the blacks in America these men had made the most of their opportunities, but he urged them to avoid "a selfish view of the case." If they took the lead, he was confident others would follow. He concluded by asking them to study his proposal. "Take your full time—no hurry at all." Lincoln, believing he was taking the lead in appealing to black leaders to think of their future, seemed to be closing the door to a future in the United States precisely at the moment he was revising his Emancipation Proclamation.

This episode is puzzling. Lincoln did not convene a dialogue. He did not say, "This I believe," but rather offered his comments as the accepted thinking about race of the day. It has been suggested that Lincoln's continuing remarks about colonization right up to the moment of his announcement of emancipation were calculated to make this bitter pill easier to swallow for moderates, if not conservatives. But there is no doubt that Lincoln had hit a low point in his public speech about slavery and race just as he was about to reach for the higher ground of emancipation.

Lincoln's comments infuriated Frederick Douglass. In the September issue of *Douglass' Monthly,* the abolitionist editor printed the full text of Lincoln's remarks and offered his most abrasive criticism yet of the president. "Mr. Lincoln assumes the language and arguments of an itinerant Colonization lecturer." He lambasted Lincoln's "contempt for Negroes and his canting hypocrisy." Douglass was at pains to point out that Lincoln, "elected as an anti-slavery man by Republican and Abolition voters . . . is quite a genuine representative of American prejudice and Negro hatred and far more concerned for the preservation of slavery, and the favor of the Border Slave States, than for any sentiment of magnanimity or principles of justice and humanity."

BY 1862, LINCOLN HAD BECOME accustomed to ministers and church officials coming to Washington to offer their advice on the management of the war. On September 13, he welcomed two Chicago ministers, William W. Patton and John Dempster, to the Red Room, one of three public parlors on the first floor of the White House. Mary Lincoln had installed a new red carpet in the room, which the Lincolns used as a family parlor and a place to entertain friends. The ministers from Lincoln's home state represented a "meeting of Christians of all denominations" that had gathered in Bryan Hall in Chicago on September 7 to express their support for emancipation. They came to lobby Lincoln and present him with memorials in English and German.

Lincoln used this occasion to both affirm and question his visitors on the use and misuse of religion. Lincoln spoke of the dilemma he wrestled with day and night, and then spoke of his own desire.

I am approached with the most opposite opinions and advice, and that by religious men, who are equally certain that they represent the Divine will. I am sure that either the one or the other class is mistaken in that belief, and perhaps in some respects both. I hope it will not be irreverent for me to say that if it is probable that God would reveal his will to others, on a point so connected with my duty, it might be supposed he would reveal it directly to me; for, unless I am more deceived in myself than I often am, it is my earnest desire to know the will of Providence in this matter.

Even as Lincoln was increasingly pondering the meaning and purpose of God in the war, he was growing impatient with religious people who came to him regularly to express their certainty that God was on the side of the North: "*And if I can learn what it is I will do it!*" Lincoln underlined his affirmation and then put an exclamation point to underscore his conviction.

Lincoln had been receiving a good deal of mail from church organizations regarding emancipation. He told the ministers from Illinois and others, "The subject is difficult, and good men do not agree." He then asked, "What *good* would a proclamation of emancipation from me do, especially as we are now situated? I do not want to issue a document that the whole world will see must necessarily be inoperative, like the Pope's bull against the comet!" He continued, "Would *my word* free the slaves, when I cannot even enforce the Constitution in the rebel states?" After his long disquisition on slavery, Lincoln concluded, "I can assure you that the subject is on my mind, day and night, more than any other."

Some have commented that Lincoln toyed with these and other petitioners in this time period, fully aware that he intended to issue an Emancipation Proclamation. A better explanation may be, like Lincoln's conversation with Leonard Swett, that he was still mulling over all sides of the issue, as much for his own ears as for the ears of his listeners. As people came to him with their certainties, he responded with his ambiguities. Yet for Lincoln, ambiguity did not mean inaction.

WITH BOTH THE UNION AND THE CONFEDERATE armies exhausted from the second battle of Bull Run, most were resting and resupplying their troops. This wasn't the case for Robert E. Lee. Lee sensed this was the moment not to retreat, but to advance. Fresh from summer victories on the Virginia peninsula, and now at Bull Run, he nonetheless believed the South could never defeat the North in a long, drawn-out war, because it would always be outpaced in men and industrial resources. He understood that the Union's momentary weakness was probably his best opportunity. An insatiable reader of newspapers, Lee read of the despair on the Northern home front and the low morale of Union troops. Back home, it was as if the *Richmond Dispatch* and Lee were reading each other's minds. The *Dispatch* wrote on August 29, 1862, "Now is the time to strike the telling and decisive blows . . . and to bring the war to a close."

Lee gambled he could invade Maryland and catch McClellan's Army of the Potomac by surprise. He believed that in Maryland, a Union state but with slaves making up 35 percent of the population, he would find citizens ready to rally to the Confederate cause. His men would be able to live off the produce of friendly farmers. On the night of September 4, 1862, under the cover of darkness, Lee and his troops crossed the Potomac just forty miles upriver from Washington.

When word of Lee's movements reached Maryland and Pennsylvania, the state leaders panicked. Lee was on Union soil. Pennsylvania governor Andrew Curtin telegraphed Lincoln on September 11, insisting the Confederate army numbered 120,000 men. He requested 80,000 federal troops to protect Philadelphia and Harrisburg. Curtin and McClellan rivaled each other in their estimates, for McClellan estimated that Lee's army was 110,000 men. In fact, Lee's army actually numbered 55,000 men. Losing stragglers by the mile, by the time it would finally engage Union troops, it would be down to 45,000 men.

If Governor Curtin saw Lee's march northward as a danger, Lincoln saw it as an opportunity. Contrary to his leading generals, Lincoln had long believed that the best Union military strategy was not to attack cities or occupy territories but to defeat armies. He now thought that Lee's army, stretched long and thin, in unfamiliar territory without its usual base of supplies, was vulnerable. On September 7, 1862, McClellan's army moved north from Washington, while apprehension riveted the North.

Once in Maryland, the two armies experienced a surprising reversal of fortunes. The Confederate army, expecting that they would be treated as liberators, arrived looking more like beggars. The populace treated them coolly. The Union army began their march with depressed morale due to their recent defeats, but once in Maryland "the friendly, almost tumultuous welcome they received . . . boosted their spirits." As the soldiers passed by farms, the daughters of the farmers greeted them at the roadside with buckets of cold water. In small villages and towns, and finally in Frederick, where McClellan had set up his field headquarters, they were welcomed by hundreds and often thousands of grateful citizens.

As McClellan's reports were sparse in coming in, Lincoln worried in the War Department's telegraph office. He considered traveling up to Frederick, but General in Chief Halleck talked him out it, even going so far as writing down his advice so that it would be part of the official record. He and other military leaders feared that Lincoln could be intercepted by Confederate cavalry.

On the morning of September 13, 1862, Corporal Barton W. Mitchell of the Twenty-seventh Indiana Infantry was relaxing in a field near Frederick when he found a copy of Lee's Special Order Number 191, dated September 9, wrapped in an envelope around three cigars. One of nine copies of Lee's order, this particular one had been mislaid by a never-to-be-identified Confederate courier. Delighted, McClellan telegraphed Lincoln, "I have the plans of the Rebels and will catch them in their own trap if my men are equal to the emergency." The plans in McClellan's hands told him that Lee had adopted the risky strategy of dividing his army into four or five parts, sending several detachments to capture Harpers Ferry and leaving his other divisions positioned several miles from one another.

McClellan waited six hours before issuing his own orders to his commanders. If McClellan had acted within the first hours, he might have exploited these gaps, but he moved warily and lost his advantage.

Within two days, Lee realized that McClellan had his orders and immediately began to reassemble his army. By hard marching and riding, they quickly reached the east side of Antietam Creek near the town of Sharpsburg, Maryland.

All through the day of September 14, 1862, Lincoln, Halleck, and Stanton waited apprehensively for any news. Halleck was suffering from hemorrhoids so painful that he could not even stand. A conventional medical treatment at the time was an opium suppository. This condition contributed to his lethargy, and his overall health was breaking down in the midst of this military crisis. For Lincoln, it seemed like Halleck was falling apart before his eyes in Washington, and he was not at all sure what McClellan was doing in Maryland.

At 9:40 p.m., Lincoln and Halleck received a telegram from McClellan: "It has been a glorious victory." By eight the next morning,

McClellan wired that the enemy had "disappeared during the night." Later in the day, McClellan, euphoric with the prospect of victory over a retreating Confederate army, wired that the enemy is "in a perfect panic," and that "Genl. Lee is reported wounded."

Lincoln immediately wrote back to McClellan, "God bless you, and all with you. Destroy the rebel army, if possible." Fifteen minutes later, departing from his usual skepticism about McClellan's predictions, Lincoln sent an ecstatic telegram to his old friend Jesse Dubois, Illinois state auditor, in Springfield. "I now consider it safe to say that General McClellan has gained a great victory over the great rebel army in Maryland. He is now pursuing the flying foe." Lincoln's words traveled faster and farther than he may have thought possible, for at midnight he received a telegram from Illinois governor Richard Yates, "Your dispatch to Col. Dubois has filled our people with the wildest joy. Salutes are being fired & our citizens are relieved from a fearful state of suspense." But McClellan, with his characteristic hyperbole, had once again misjudged the situation.

Lee was not retreating. Instead, the Confederate general was positioning his forces on a row of hills and ridges that ran through the rural countryside of pasture and farmland between Sharpsburg and Antietam Creek. Lee invited McClellan to attack his smaller but battle-tested veteran army.

McClellan spent much of September 16, 1862, planning his attack, which only allowed more time for Lee to consolidate his forces. In the late afternoon, he finally sent "Fighting Joe" Hooker across Antietam Creek to attack the Confederate left. He ordered Ambrose Burnside to also cross Antietam Creek and attack the Confederate right. These opening maneuvers were probing skirmishes for the fight everyone knew was coming the next day.

McClellan attacked on September 17, 1862, starting what became known as the battle of Antietam. In the most violent day of the whole Civil War, Union and Confederate soldiers attacked, counterattacked, and fought on. It was said that one thirty-acre cornfield was so covered with dead bodies that one could walk across it without ever touching the earth.

"We are in the midst of the most terrible battle of the war, perhaps of history," telegraphed McClellan to Halleck and Lincoln at 1:25 p.m. This was the battle Lincoln had been waiting for. McClellan wrote, "It will be either a great defeat or a most glorious victory."

McClellan ordered 60,000 of his 80,000 troops to assault 37,000 Confederates, but he could not push back an army that he assessed to be over 100,000. McClellan had more than twice as many men as Lee, but by attacking division after division, he afforded Lee the time to shift his troops to meet the Union attacks. McClellan, convinced that Lee had far more troops than he did, was unwilling to commit any of his 20,000 reserves to the battle. At one point, General John Sedgwick marched his division, with sixty-four-year-old E. V. "Bull" Sumner in the lead, through the cornfield, across the Hagerstown Pike, and into the West Woods, only to discover they were being fired upon from the rear. Once again, the Confederates, appearing to retreat, led the Union bluecoats into a trap. By the end of the day, Sedgwick would lose 1,700 men—killed, wounded, or missing.

The next day, September 18, 1862, both sides were exhausted; the battle came to a lull, not to be joined again. McClellan wrote to Halleck on September 19, "Our victory was complete. The enemy is driven back into Virginia."

Lincoln had ordered McClellan to "destroy the rebel army," but he did not. On the evening of September 18, 1862, Lee and his army crossed the Potomac again and returned to the safe haven of Virginia. McClellan sent a small detachment in pursuit, but it came to nothing.

For once, McClellan was not exaggerating the scope of the battle. Almost 6,500 Union and Confederate soldiers were killed in one day at Antietam. This staggering number was four times the number that would be killed in the landings at Normandy on June 6, 1944. The total for this one day was more than the deaths in all of the other wars of the nineteenth century—the War of 1812, the Indian wars, the Mexican War, and the Spanish-American War—combined.

ALTHOUGH THE VICTORY AT ANTIETAM was not decisive, it was enough for Abraham Lincoln. At the Soldiers' Home, Lincoln wrote out a second draft of his Emancipation Proclamation. He returned to the White House, where he refused to meet any visitors. He worked alone in his office, editing the most important statement of his life yet.

Five days after the battle at Antietam, he convened a special cabinet meeting on Monday, September 22, 1862. Lincoln presented to the cabinet a new four-page document of just under one thousand words. What Lincoln said at this momentous cabinet meeting was recorded by both Salmon Chase and Gideon Welles, independently, in their diaries. Chase wrote that Lincoln told them that "when the rebel army was at Frederick," he had "determined" that if they be "driven out of Maryland," he would issue a "Proclamation of Emancipation." Lincoln continued, "I said nothing to any one; but I made the promise to myself, and"—here Chase indicated that Lincoln hesitated a little—"to my Maker. The rebel army is now driven out, and I am going to fulfill that promise."

Welles, who had been writing detailed entries in his diary almost every day since July 1862, recorded that the president began by informing the cabinet that regarding emancipation, "the question was finally decided, the act and the consequences were his," but he wanted to invite the cabinet's "criticism" of the paper he had prepared. In his explanation, Lincoln "remarked that he had made a vow, a covenant, that if God gave us the victory in the approaching battle, he would consider it an indication of Divine will, and that it was his duty to move forward in the cause of emancipation."

Lincoln understood that his explanation of his actions would appear unusual to these shrewd politicians. He admitted as much. "It might be thought strange, he said, that he had in this way submitted the disposal of matters when the way was not clear to his mind what he should do." Welles reported that Lincoln summed up his remarkable discourse by telling them, "God had decided this question in favor of the slaves."

The members of the cabinet sat in silence. Lincoln broke it by picking up the text of the preliminary Emancipation Proclamation and beginning to read it aloud.

> I, Abraham Lincoln, President of the United States of America, and Commander-in-chief of the Army and Navy thereof, do hereby proclaim and declare that hereafter, as heretofore, the war will be prosecuted for the object of practically restoring the constitutional relation between the United States, and each of the states, and the people thereof, in which States that relation is, or may be suspended, or disturbed.

Although the language was still legalistic, the fruit of Lincoln's continual brooding and editing over the long summer of 1862 was evident in this newly revised second proclamation. Unlike the document he had presented in July, Lincoln knew this proclamation would soon become public. With keen insight into the range of possible public reactions, he anticipated and therefore sought to alleviate public criticism. He stressed at the outset that the war remained about preserving the Union, even though he knew that the press would emphasize the freeing of the slaves. He built in precedent with a reminder of two laws passed earlier in the year about the handling of escaped slaves. He had employed scissors and paste to insert these laws into his document.

At the heart of Lincoln's preliminary Emancipation Proclamation, he offered the language that reflected his change of heart. On the first day of January 1863, "all persons held as slaves within any state, or designated part of a state, the people whereof shall then be in rebellion against the United States shall be then, thenceforward, and forever free."

Lincoln concluded with generosity.

> And the executive will in due time recommend that all citizens of the United States who shall have remained loyal thereto throughout the rebellion, shall (upon the restoration of the constitutional relation between the United States, and their respective states, and people, if that relation shall have been suspended or disturbed) be compensated for all losses by acts of the United States, including the loss of slaves.

Lincoln knew he was issuing a strong proclamation, solely based in his military powers as president, but he was determined to be fair and munificent to those who would be affected. Newspapers around the country published the Emancipation Proclamation, announcing that Lincoln would sign it into law on January 1, 1863.

However one might view the concrete results of Lincoln's Emancipation Proclamation—how many people were freed in which areas of the Union—the symbolic significance of Lincoln's act was powerful. He had changed the purpose of the war from restoring the old Union to creating a new Union cleansed of slavery. His old nemesis Horace Greeley spelled it out in large letters in his *Tribune*. "GOD BLESS ABRAHAM LINCOLN!" Greeley predicted, "It is the beginning of the end of the rebellion; the beginning of the new life of the nation."

ON OCTOBER 1, 1862, Lincoln traveled to Sharpsburg, Maryland, to visit McClellan. After the battle of Antietam, many questions remained. Why did McClellan not pursue and defeat Lee's army when he had the opportunity? If McClellan needed time to recover from Antietam, why was he not planning to cross the Potomac and pursue Lee now?

The next day, as Lincoln prepared to review the troops, artillery officer Charles Wainwright observed the president riding in an ambulance wagon. Wainwright was not impressed. "Mr. Lincoln not only is the ugliest man I ever saw, but the most uncouth and gawky in his manners and appearance." McClellan started to explain how the battle took shape, but Lincoln, seemingly not interested, turned away and asked to be driven back to the camp.

The next morning, Lincoln awakened Ozias M. Hatch, the Illinois secretary of state, who had accompanied him on his visit. They walked to an eminence from which they could survey the camp. Lincoln, gesturing with his long arms, asked, "Hatch, what do you suppose all these people are?"

"Why," replied Hatch, "I suppose it be a part of the grand army."

"No," responded the President, "you are mistaken."

"What are they then?" asked Hatch.

Lincoln paused, and then "in a tone of patient but melancholy sarcasm," replied, "*That is General McClellan's body guard.*"

LINCOLN'S PRELIMINARY EMANCIPATION PROCLAMATION did not bring him the full backing of radical Republicans. Believing that he had waited too long already, they were not pleased to be asked to wait an additional one hundred days for the signing of the proclamation. Senators Charles Sumner, Benjamin Wade, Henry Wilson, and Lyman Trumbull welcomed Lincoln's proposal, but also cast a critical eye on what the proclamation did not do. They criticized it as a wartime measure too limited in its scope. The ultimate goal of the radical Republicans, and their abolitionist allies, became a constitutional amendment that would abolish slavery forever.

Meanwhile, many moderate Republicans and border-state Unionists worried about the meaning of the proclamation for Kentucky, Maryland, and Missouri. Democrats, who had opposed Lincoln from the start, were enraged at what they saw as presidential authoritarianism. After a while, however, some of them became convinced that the proclamation provided them with an opening to turn around their political fortunes by appealing to a nation growing weary of war and death.

Lincoln, who always followed election results like an accountant checking financial records, watched the biennial elections in 1862 with concern. Twenty-three states voted in elections held in April, June,

*Lincoln, after the ambiguous victory at Antietam, traveled
to Sharpsburg, Maryland, to confer with General George B. McClellan.*

August, September, October, and November. No national body oversaw
the elections, so voters went to the polls in the spring in New England and
in late summer and fall in the West. The inconclusive course of the war
and the preliminary Emancipation Proclamation figured in differently as
factors in various states according to the timing of their elections.

By November, the election returns had given the Democrats a net
increase of thirty-two seats in the House, reducing the Republican
majority to twenty-five. Five vital states, where Lincoln had won every
electoral vote in 1860—New York, Pennsylvania, Ohio, Indiana, and
Illinois—elected Democratic majorities in Congress. In the Senate,
however, Republicans picked up five seats. Illinois elected nine Democrats and only five Republicans to the House of Representatives. Most
painfully for Lincoln, in his home district, John Todd Stuart, Lincoln's
first law partner, now a Democrat, defeated the Republican candidate,
Leonard Swett, Lincoln's close friend.

In state contests the results were more dismal. New York and New
Jersey elected Democrats as governors. Criticizing Lincoln as an abolitionist dictator, Democrats gained control of the state legislatures in

Pennsylvania, Ohio, and Indiana. The *New York Times,* usually a supporter of the president, summed up the total results as a "vote of want of confidence" in his leadership.

On November 5, the day after New Yorkers voted in the last midterm election, Lincoln asked Halleck to remove McClellan from his command of the Army of the Potomac. The next day Lincoln told Francis P. Blair that he had "tried long enough to bore with an auger too dull to take hold." The president appointed Ambrose P. Burnside as the new commander.

"NEVER HAS SUCH a paper been delivered to the National Legislature under auspices so grave, and rarely, if ever, has one been awaited with equal solicitude by the people of the country." The *National Intelligencer* underlined the import of Lincoln's annual message to Congress on December 1, 1862. After a string of military setbacks, interrupted in September by an ambiguous victory at Antietam, the publication of his preliminary Emancipation Proclamation, and the difficult 1862 elections, Lincoln delivered his annual message.

Listeners of the annual presidential message did not expect, nor did they usually receive, any rhetorical dessert at the end of the standard meat and potatoes of political fare. Lincoln's annual message for 1862 covered a wide range of topics, with reports from a number of departments using words supplied by cabinet members. But unlike his first annual message in 1861, Lincoln decided to use this opportunity to educate citizens and to mobilize public opinion across the North.

One last time he spoke of the benefits of colonization. Next, after reminding Congress of his Emancipation Proclamation of September 22, 1862, he called their attention to "compensated emancipation." He even offered three constitutional amendments to augment his plan, the first amendment calling for each state where slavery existed to have until 1900 to abolish it. Another amendment called on Congress to appropriate money for colonization. Lincoln's goal was to end slavery peacefully even while still in the midst of war. He summarized the meaning of these amendments by stating, "Without slavery the rebellion could never have existed; without slavery it could not continue."

By the end of 1862, Lincoln was speaking openly of slavery as the cause of the war. He recognized, however, that "among the friends of the Union," a diversity of opinion existed. Some would perpetuate slavery; some would abolish it suddenly without compensation; some would abolish it gradually with compensation; some would remove the freed people, and some would retain them. In Lincoln's habit of validating all voices, he listed five options. He did so in the best words their proponents would use. However, Lincoln averred that "because of these diversities, we waste much strength in struggles among ourselves." He then discussed how persons advocating each of the five positions could see strengths and weaknesses in his three amendments.

Lincoln took time toward the end of this second annual message to offer a remarkable tribute to his senior colleagues. "I do not . . . forget that some of you are my seniors, nor that many of you have more experience than I, in the conduct of public affairs." Yet, he said, he hoped that "in view of the great responsibility resting upon me, you will perceive no want of respect to yourselves, in any undue earnestness I may display." Lincoln won the right to be heard about his own ideas by first expressing respect for his audience.

If his message to this point seemed gradualist in tone, his audience was certainly not prepared for his finale. "The dogmas of the quiet past, are inadequate to the stormy present. The occasion is piled high with difficulty, and we must rise with the occasion. As our case is new, so we must think anew, and act anew." Although Lincoln appealed explicitly for support of his proposals, and implicitly for the Emancipation Proclamation, his conclusion expanded his appeal beyond any particular agenda to a willingness to embrace a new and better future.

In contrasting the "quiet past" with the "stormy present," he tapped into his favorite metaphor to describe the Civil War. In this storm, Lincoln once again had been subjected to the voices of those who wished to define him and tell him what he should do.

Lincoln included himself when he said, "We must rise with the occasion." Stung by criticism that he had underestimated the determination of the South to go its own way, he made no such misjudgments now about what was at stake or how long the war might go on. Lincoln replaced the studied, rational argument of his inaugural address with a more evocative rhetoric better able to resonate with the emotional fears and longings of his audience.

"As our case is new, so we must think anew, and act anew." These words have often been mislaid or forgotten because of the dramatic final words that follow. Presidential leadership comes from the ability to articulate a compelling vision for the nation. For the first year and a half of the war, Lincoln's public rhetoric showed him acting with fidelity to the great ideals of the past, especially as they were enshrined in the Declaration of Independence and the Constitution. By the end of 1862, Lincoln became willing to change the definition of the war in terms of the future.

In his concluding appeal, Lincoln joined together history and memory. From his first reading of Parson Mason Locke Weems's biography of George Washington as a boy, to his first major speech, the address to the Young Men's Lyceum in Springfield in 1838 as a young man, we find Lincoln always invoking history. He held himself accountable to the great ideals of both the founding fathers and the primary documents of the nation. Now he wanted Congress to join him in a new accountability, and asked them to unite behind him. He was aware of all the political divisions in Congress. To underscore their unified responsibility, he used the plural pronouns "we" and "us."

> Fellow-citizens, *we* cannot escape history. We of this Congress and this administration, will be remembered in spite of ourselves. No personal significance, or insignificance, can spare one or another of us.
>
> The fiery trial through which we pass, will light us down, in honor or dishonor, to the latest generation.

When Lincoln spoke of a "fiery trial," he borrowed an image from a recent visitor to the White House, Eliza P. Gurney, a Quaker minister from Philadelphia. Ten weeks earlier, Mrs. Gurney and three women had sought a meeting with the president to comfort and encourage him. Following her sermon about the necessity to seek divine guidance, Gurney convened a prayer meeting in the president's office, kneeling and offering a prayer "that light and wisdom might be shed down from on high, to guide our President."

Lincoln, reticent to speak about his deepest feelings, especially religious ones, became surprisingly open in a correspondence he subsequently began with Mrs. Gurney. In his first letter, on October 26, 1862, he thanked her for her "sympathy and prayers." He then declared, "We are indeed going through a great trial—a fiery trial." The "indeed" indicated that he was responding to her sermon, in which she had commended Lincoln for the steadfastness of his leadership in such a difficult time. Lincoln's image of "a fiery trial" was surely drawn from 1 Peter

4:12, a letter written to a people undergoing persecution: "Beloved, think it not strange concerning the fiery trial which is to try you, as though some strange thing happened unto you."

Lincoln now underlined the key words in his concluding sentences, which balanced each other almost musically: "In *giving* freedom to the *slave,* we *assure* freedom to the *free*—honorable alike in what we give, and what we preserve. We shall nobly save, or meanly lose, the last best, hope of earth."

In this remarkable message to Congress, Lincoln was crafting an alternative vision of reality. He asked his listeners to move beyond their limited worldviews and embrace a future that could not be fully known.

LINCOLN'S NEW COMMANDER of the Army of the Potomac, Ambrose Burnside, after so many of McClellan's delays, intended to attack. He set his sights on the well-fortified town of Fredericksburg. The boyhood home of George Washington and a center of activity in the Revolutionary War, Fredericksburg was about to become the site of one of the crucial battles of the Civil War.

Lincoln expressed skepticism of Burnside's operational plans, but on November 14, Halleck wrote Burnside, "The President had just assented to your plan. He thinks it will succeed if you move rapidly; otherwise not." Still not satisfied, Lincoln traveled down the Potomac to meet Burnside for a long conference. The president told Burnside that he needed to be sure his troops could cross the river "free from risk" and be sure that "the enemy . . . be prevented from falling back, accumulating strength as he goes, into his intrenchments at Richmond."

Burnside did not proceed rapidly. A full one month later, at 3 a.m. on the morning of December 11, engineers finally began putting pontoon bridges in place over the frigid waters of the Rappahannock River directly across from the town. Ice glazed the river and fog obscured the view of the historic political and economic center that once numbered five thousand people. Burnside, who knew his army of one hundred fifteen thousand men outnumbered Lee's eighty thousand, believed he would be victorious by sheer force of numbers. With plenty of advance notice of Burnside's intentions, Lee ordered General James Longstreet's forces into place on the heights of the south side of the town.

On December 13, Burnside, turning aside advice from senior officers that he cross the Rappahannock River south and north of Fredericksburg, instead mounted a direct assault on the town. General George G.

Meade made an initial advance against "Stonewall" Jackson's Corp, but when Union forces attempted to storm Mayre's Heights on the south side of the town, they were repelled with heavy losses. By December 15, the Union army was in full retreat back across the pontoon bridges, thereby admitting a devastating defeat. The loss of more than thirteen thousand casualties to the less than five thousand casualties of the Confederates told the grim story.

Many blamed Lincoln for compelling Burnside to fight, but "Old Burn" accepted responsibility for the defeat, something George McClellan would not have done. Lincoln, ever conscious of the morale of the troops, issued a proclamation hoping to take the edge off the defeat. "Although you were not successful, the attempt was not in error," the President stated. "The courage with which you, in an open field, maintained the contest against an entrenched foe . . . shows that you possess all the qualities of a great army."

THE MILITARY DEFEAT at Fredericksburg quickly became a flashpoint for smoldering political grievances. Radical Republicans in Congress believed the administration ought to be pursuing a more vigorous military policy or risk conservative Democratic pleas for a peace that would scuttle Lincoln's plans for emancipation. Unable yet to lay a hand on the president, Radical Republicans took aim at Lincoln's cabinet.

On Tuesday afternoon, December 16, Republican senators caucused for five hours. Illinois senator Lyman Trumbull, once Lincoln's ally but increasingly his critic, started the discussion by arguing that "the recent repulse at Fredericksburg" called for Congressional action. Minnesota senator Morton Wilkinson decried that "the country was ruined and the cause was lost." The agitation of the senators quickly focused on William Henry Seward, secretary of state, who they viewed as "President *de facto*." One senator after another blamed Seward for the postponement in discharging General McClellan, the slowness in making the war a campaign against slavery, and the resurgence of conservatives in the 1862 elections. Tough-talking Maine senator William Pitt Fessenden summarized the sentiment of many when he said he had been informed by a member of the cabinet that "there was a back-stairs influence which often controlled the apparent conclusions of the Cabinet itself." It was common knowledge that the source of Fessenden's remark was Treasury Secretary Salmon P. Chase. Old Ben Wade of Ohio proposed that the Senate "go in a body and demand of the President the dismissal of Mr. Seward." At this point, Iowa Senator James W. Grimes offered a resolution expressing "a want of confidence in the Secretary of State, and that he ought to be removed from the Cabinet."

In the midst of rising emotions, New York senator Preston King left the caucus early to proceed to Seward's home and apprise him of what was afoot. Seward responded to King's news: "They may do as they please about me, but they shall not put the President in a false position on my account." The secretary of state wrote a letter of resignation, and King and Seward's son Frederick walked to the White House to deliver it to the president.

Lincoln read Seward's resignation "with a face full of pain and surprise" as King recounted the charges in the emotional Republican caucus. After reading Seward's letter, Lincoln immediately walked to the secretary of state's home on Lafayette Square. The president exerted all of his persuasion to talk his friend out of resigning. But it was no use. Seward told Lincoln he would be relieved to be freed of the burden and criticism stalking him day and night. Lincoln responded, "Ah, yes, Governor, that will do very well for you, but I am like the [caged] starling in [Laurence] Sterne's story, 'I can't get out.' "

What was Lincoln to do? He understood that he was the real object of the radicals' wrath. He also knew that if Seward's imperious ways could be off-putting, he valued his enormous abilities and steadfast loyalty. Lincoln knew that even though the caucus involved only senators, behind their recriminations darts were being thrown at Seward and himself by Treasury Secretary Chase. Lincoln decided not to be put on the defensive, but to get out front in this cabinet crisis of leadership.

On December 17, the Republican senators met again, passed a slightly revised resolution, appointed a committee of nine, and requested a meeting with the president. Not wishing to cause the wound at the heart of his cabinet to fester, Lincoln did not want delay and proposed that they meet with him the next evening at 7 p.m.

Shortly before the meeting on December 18, Senator Orville Browning, not a member of the committee, called on Lincoln at the White House. "I saw in a moment that he was in distress." When Browning said that things could have been worse, Lincoln replied, "They wish to get rid of me, and I am sometimes half disposed to gratify them."

Lincoln, keeping his distress under his green shawl, received the committee at 7 p.m. "with his usual urbanity" and listened to their litany of complaints. Ohio senator Ben Wade charged that the reason for the recent defeats of Republicans was because "the President had placed the direction of our military affairs in the hands of bitter and malignant Democrats," a reference to George McClellan. But the real target was Seward, who the Committee of Nine impugned "was not in accord with the majority of Cabinet and exerted an injurious influence upon the conduct of the war." Senator Charles Sumner complained about Seward's handling of foreign affairs, singling out one memo where he seemed to put the mentality of the Congress and the Confederates on a similar plane. Lincoln mostly listened for three hours and told the committee he would respond to the paper they prepared which itemized their complaints. Lincoln's goal was to calm some of the irritation which he did by his own open spirit to the senators.

Lincoln now moved to act quickly. He sent notices to each cabinet officer, except Seward, for a special meeting the next morning, December 20, at 10:30 a.m. He told the Cabinet the Senate movement to reconfigure his cabinet "had shocked and grieved him." He informed them of Seward's resignation. He told the cabinet, "While they seemed to believe in my honesty, they also appeared to think that when I had in me any good purpose or intention Seward contrived to suck it out of me unperceived." Lincoln seemed particularly upset at the charge, obviously fomented by Chase that the cabinet did not work well together. Lincoln expressed his belief was that "the members had gone on harmoniously, whatever had been their previous feelings and associations." He told them that in the midst of "the overwhelming troubles of the country, which had borne heavily upon him, he had been sustained and consoled by the good feeling and the mutual and unselfish confidence and zeal that pervaded the Cabinet." Lincoln concluded the meeting by asking the Cabinet to join him for a scheduled meeting with the Committee of Nine that very evening. Everyone assented to his request except Chase, who, telling his colleagues "he had no movement whatever of the movement" against Seward, strongly objected to the joint meeting but reluctantly agreed to attend.

Lincoln's decision to have the Committee of Nine and the Cabinet meet face to face and "discus their mutual misunderstanding under his own eye" exhibited his political genius. It was no longer possible to play the game of "he said," no "he said." Lincoln began this remarkable meeting by reading the resolutions of the Committee. Lincoln acknowledged that perhaps he should have called more cabinet meetings, but parried the charges of the Committee by affirming "the unity of his Cabinet." He declared that "though they could not be expected to think and act alike on all subjects, they acquiesced in measures when decided." The subtext of Lincoln's remarks was that Seward made no decisions without the assent of the president and the Cabinet. The focus of many eyes was on Chase, not long before the haughty accuser of Seward, but now under Lincoln's watchful eye suddenly cowed into silence and embarrassment. In the end Lincoln asked for a vote. "Do you, gentlemen, still think Seward ought to be excused?" Only four Senators—Grimes, Trumbull, Sumner, and Samuel Pomeroy of Kansas—voted yes. Secretary of the Navy Welles captured Lincoln's leadership, confiding to his diary that "the President managed his own case, speaking freely, and showed great tact, shrewdness, and ability." After five hours of discussion lasting until 1 a.m., Lincoln, having confronted the senators with the Cabinet, emerged as the strong conciliator of both groups.

But how was Lincoln to deal with Seward and Chase? The news of Seward's resignation was spreading throughout Washington. The duplicitous behavior of Chase infuriated even those senators who had been his allies.

The next morning, December 20, Lincoln sent for Chase. When the secretary of the treasury arrived, Welles and Stanton were calling upon Lincoln on their own accord. When Chase entered, Lincoln said, "I sent for you, for this matter is giving me great trouble." Chase replied that he "had been painfully affected" by the meeting the previous evening and now told the president he had "prepared his resignation." "Where is it?" Lincoln asked, reaching out his hand to get hold of it. Chase, taken aback by Lincoln's eagerness, held on momentarily to the sealed envelope. He surrendered the resignation, and Lincoln opened the envelope with a pleased expression on his face while Chase, usually filled with self-confidence, left Lincoln's office deeply perplexed.

Later that morning Lincoln met with his Cabinet, minus Seward and Chase. After acknowledging Seward's resignation, he held up Chase's resignation. He then announced, "Now I have the biggest half of the hog. I shall accept neither resignation."

That same day Lincoln wrote a letter to both Cabinet secretaries. He told them that for the sake of "the public interest" he had decided not to accept their resignations and "I therefore have to request that you will resume the duty of your Departments respectively."

Lincoln emerged from this grave crisis in his inner government the conciliatory victor. He had listened with respect to the radicals, he had affirmed his cabinet, and he secured his own presidential prerogative. Welles, whose appreciation of Lincoln was growing, said it well. "Seward comforts him,—Chase he deems a necessity." In the end he decided to continue with the service of two of his most talented cabinet secretaries.

This chromolithograph from 1863 portrays a homespun Lincoln working in an office cluttered with a bust of President James Buchanan and texts of states' rights theories by John C. Calhoun and John Randolph. Lincoln rests his left hand on the Bible while heeding the injunction of President Andrew Jackson: "The Union Must & Shall Be Preserved."

CHAPTER 22

What Will the Country Say?
January 1863 – May 1863

ALL PERSONS HELD AS SLAVES . . . SHALL BE THEN, THENCEFORWARD,
AND FOREVER FREE.

ABRAHAM LINCOLN
Emancipation Proclamation, January 1, 1863

*A*BRAHAM LINCOLN DID NOT GO TO BED ON NEW YEAR'S EVE. AS
revelers celebrated in streets nearby, he paced back and forth on the
White House second floor. For weeks he had been absorbed with finalizing the wording of his Emancipation Proclamation.

In the early hours of January 1, 1863, Lincoln walked from his bedroom in the west end of the White House to his office in the east end.
He sat at the long oak table cluttered with rolled-up maps, newspapers,
letters, and military orders, and reached for the proclamation that had
become the subject of so much debate and controversy in recent
months.

More than anyone, Lincoln understood the implications of the signing to take place that afternoon. The war had now convulsed the nation
for more than two and a half years; some had started calling it "Mr. Lincoln's war." In the spring of 1861, most people in the North had predicted a quick victory, but the question on everyone's mind now was:
How long would this war go on?

As the first rays of sun came through his office's east window, Lincoln reviewed three long pieces of paper, determined to revise the
proclamation one more time before signing it. He studied again the central paragraph.

And by virtue of the power, and for the purpose aforesaid, I do
order and declare that all persons held as slaves within said desig-

nated States, and parts of States, are, and henceforward shall be free, and that the Executive government of the United States, including the military and naval authorities thereof, will recognize and maintain the freedom of said persons.

How long he had brooded over the decision about slavery announced in these words.

IN THE LAST WEEKS OF DECEMBER, critics had besieged Lincoln from all sides. He barely mentioned the proclamation in his annual message to Congress on December 1, 1862, and many wondered whether Lincoln still intended to hold fast to it. Abolitionists were acclaiming Lincoln's initiative but grumbling that it did not go far enough. African-American leader Frederick Douglass wondered aloud, "What if the President fails in this trial hour, what if he now listens to the demon slavery—and rejects the entreaties of the Angel of Liberty?" Old-line Republican supporters were concerned about how the proclamation would affect the morale of troops, who, they repeated, had signed on to save the Union, not to free slaves. Emboldened by Democratic gains in the 1862 elections, Democratic newspapers, such as the *Chicago Times,* predicted that Lincoln would withdraw the final proclamation.

Republican senators Charles Sumner and Orville Browning offered opposite recommendations to Lincoln. On December 27, 1862, Sumner called on the president at the White House. He brought with him a memorial signed by ministers calling for him to "stand by" his proclamation. The Massachusetts senator talked with Lincoln about how many persons were "impatient" that the act be signed. Lincoln responded, he "could not stop the Proclamation if he would, & would not if he could."

Browning, who always had personal access to the president, called at the White House to convey his belief that the proclamation "was fraught with evil . . . and would do much injury." A conservative Republican, Browning had previously told the president that he believed the announcement of the proclamation in September was the main reason behind the disappointing biennial election results. Resigned to the fact that the president intended to sign it, Browning concluded his diary for 1862 with the words, "There is no hope. The proclamation will come—God grant it may not be productive of the mischief I fear." Lincoln and Browning had enjoyed a close relationship in recent years, but their friendship would begin to cool once Lincoln signed the proclamation.

Early Monday morning, December 29, 1862, Lincoln assembled his notes and wrote a draft of the proclamation. He gave it to John Nicolay and asked his secretary to make printed copies for members of the cabinet. Lincoln convened his regular cabinet meeting at 10 a.m. He read aloud the final draft, asking the cabinet to make suggestions to him in writing. Secretary of State Seward expressed concern that the proclamation, which he supported in principle, would lead to a total collapse of order in the South. He recommended language urging the freed slaves "to abstain from all violence unless in necessary self-defense." Treasury Secretary Chase presented a new preamble that was lengthier than Lincoln's whole proclamation. Lincoln's original manuscript copy has not survived, but the copies handed out to Seward, Chase, Edward Bates, and Montgomery Blair do, along with their comments.

On Wednesday, December 31, 1862, Lincoln, having read the cabinet members' written responses, convened a special cabinet meeting to consider the proclamation a final time. Chase proposed adding a "felicitous" concluding sentence. He believed it important for Lincoln to offer justifications for this bold act beyond military necessity. He wanted Lincoln to invoke both the Constitution and God. Lincoln thanked them for their suggestions and told the cabinet "he would complete the document."

After the meeting concluded, Lincoln greeted a committee of New York abolitionist ministers headed by George Cheever, pastor of the Church of the Puritans, who had authored *God Against Slavery* in 1857, and William Goodell, who had helped organize both the American Anti-Slavery Society and the Liberty Party. The ministers wanted some confirmation that Lincoln was actually going to sign the proclamation. Lincoln would only say, "Tomorrow at noon, you shall know—and the country shall know—my decision."

Now, on the morning of January 1, 1863, as he sat alone at his table, he decided to ignore the bulk of his cabinet's recommendations. He did work with Chase's suggestion, which became a new final paragraph: "And upon this act, sincerely believed to be an act of justice, warranted by the Constitution, upon military necessity, I invoke the considerate judgment of mankind, and the gracious favor of Almighty God."

While Lincoln was bent over the table revising, his wife and oldest son appeared in his office. Before retiring the previous evening, Mary had asked her husband, "What do you intend doing?" Now Lincoln looked up, his face worn with lines. Robert Lincoln would comment later that there was a "presence" in his father's manner that silenced both his mother and himself.

Lincoln completed his editing. A clerk was called and asked to carry the document to the State Department where a final copy would be prepared for Lincoln's signature.

At 10:45 a.m. William Seward and his son, Frederick, climbed the stairs to the president's office bearing the newly revised proclamation. While preparing to sign it, the president noticed an error in the transcription. He made the necessary change and asked Seward to have a new copy engrossed, completed in a fine handwriting. By now it was nearly eleven o'clock and Lincoln needed to prepare to meet his New Year's Day guests in the Blue Room.

Outside the White House, the streets of Washington had been thronged with persons eager to welcome in the New Year since early morning. The day had dawned bright and clear. People greeted one another with "warm salutations." Despite the tenseness in the capital in the wake of the demoralizing defeat at Fredericksburg in December, the festivities of New Year's Day seemed to hold out the prospect of a hopeful and better future.

The crowd, larger than usual, knew how special this reception would be. New Year's Day receptions at the White House were a long tradition, and on January 1, 1863, persons of all walks of life wanted to be present when Lincoln signed the Emancipation Proclamation. People lined up two and three abreast along Pennsylvania Avenue stretching back toward Seventeenth Street.

The official guests entered the White House at 11 a.m., beginning with the diplomatic corps arrayed in their best finery from the fashions of the various countries. The nine judges of the Supreme Court came next, led by the aged Roger Taney. Gideon Welles, secretary of the navy, attended, but most cabinet members hosted their own receptions at their residences. A group of army officers, who had assembled at the War Department, arrived together, led by General Henry Halleck.

At twelve noon, the large White House gates were opened and the crowd surged in. Delegations from Maine to California had been waiting in line for hours. The civil and the uncivil pressed and pushed their way the length of the grand portico toward the main entrance. A small detachment of police, backed up by members of a Pennsylvania regiment, tried to maintain some order, but there was little. Visitors were admitted in groups at intervals. As soon as one group had entered, another was passed through. Once inside, the "scuffle" of the annual New Year's Day reception began. The plush carpets had been covered to protect them from the mud.

Abraham and Mary Lincoln stood in the Blue Room in the midst of the melee. This was Mary's first public reception since the death of Willie the previous February. Some of the surviving soldiers of the War of 1812, known as the "old defenders," stood out among the visitors. Lincoln was flanked on his left by his outsized Illinois friend Ward Hill Lamon, acting as marshal for the occasion. Lamon obtained the name of each guest and announced the person to the president. Each person was eager to shake the hand of the "pres," as he was familiarly called. Lincoln pumped each hand in return. After three hours of hand shaking, the president was exhausted and his right hand was swollen. Finally, at shortly after 2 p.m., the last of the crowd exited the White House.

The president returned upstairs to his office. Visibly drooping with fatigue, he prepared to sign the proclamation. As he took up his gold pen and dipped it in ink, "his hand trembled, so that he held the pen with difficulty," Senator Charles Sumner observed. Illinois congressman Isaac Arnold reported that Lincoln told him when he grasped the pen, "My hand and arm trembled so violently, that I could not write." Unusually, Lincoln signed his full name in a slow and careful hand. He looked up and allowed himself a little laugh, exclaiming, "That will do." When it was all over, Lincoln sighed, "I never, in my life, felt more certain that I was doing right, than I do in signing this paper."

EVEN ON THIS DAY OF CELEBRATION, Lincoln's continuing struggle to find competent military leadership intruded. After the Union army's demoralizing defeat at Fredericksburg, General Ambrose Burnside, commander of the Army of the Potomac, traveled to Washington and requested a meeting with the president. They met briefly on December 31, but Lincoln convened a larger meeting on the morning of January 1 that included General in Chief Halleck and Secretary of War Stanton.

Lincoln had developed a strong liking for Burnside, a man with large blue eyes and a winning smile. His regard was only strengthened when the general accepted responsibility for the defeat at Fredericksburg, an attitude so unlike that of the previous commander. When Burnside arrived, he gave the president a letter he had written the night before at Willard's Hotel. "Burn," as his men called him, appeared outwardly strong, but inside self-doubt ate away at his ability to command. In his letter he told Lincoln, "It is of the utmost importance that you be surrounded and supported by men who have the confidence of the people and of the army." Because Burnside believed he no longer retained that confidence, he asked to be relieved so that he might "retire to private life." He went on to say that neither Stanton nor Halleck had the confidence of the army, and they should resign also. Lincoln read the letter, and, without saying a word, returned it to Burnside.

The four men talked about Burnside's plan to cross the Rappahannock again. Burnside, cordial but agitated, did not defend his plan but simply expanded on the reasons for it. Lincoln turned to Halleck and asked for his opinion. Halleck hesitated, hemming and hawing. The tension between Burnside and Halleck was evident. The president, irritated, continued to press Halleck for his recommendation; the general in chief replied that the decision was the prerogative of the field commander. Seeing that he was not getting anywhere, Lincoln concluded the meeting.

After Burnside, Stanton, and Halleck left, Lincoln wrote a letter to Halleck instructing him to go with Burnside, assess the situation, consult with the other officers, and then either approve or disapprove the plan. "If in such a difficulty as this you do not help," Lincoln wrote, "you fail me precisely in the point for which I sought your assistance. Your military skill is useless to me, if you will not do this." Lincoln gave the letter to Stanton to deliver to Halleck.

When Halleck received the letter, he resigned. Lincoln, finding himself caught in an intolerable situation between a man who acted more like a clerk than a commander, but with no one else to take his place, withdrew his letter. He wrote on the bottom, "Withdrawn, because considered harsh by Gen. Halleck."

LINCOLN DID NOT ACCEPT Burnside's resignation. He wished to give him another opportunity to succeed.

Relieved by Lincoln's support, Burnside's spirits were revived. He worked long hours with little sleep in an effort to redeem himself and took advantage of the unusual dry winter weather of the first weeks of January to prepare for battle.

Burnside did not intend to keep his troops cooped up in winter quarters. He was determined to win a victory in January that was denied him in December. On a cold, clear January day he mounted his walleyed gray horse, Major, for "a fine ride of 15 or 18 miles," bound for a personal reconnaissance of the upper fords of the Rappahannock, looking for the best place where his huge army might cross above Fredericksburg.

On Monday morning, January 19, 1863, Burnside gave the orders for his 130,000-man army to begin the march up the Rappahannock. The river, which traversed 184 miles across northern Virginia, had become an unofficial boundary between North and South. The troops initially marched quickly on dry roads. Intelligence, which would later prove faulty, brought news that James Longstreet's corps had departed for Tennessee. Burnside hoped this might be the beginning of a great Union victory.

His hopes were quickly dashed. After three weeks of clear weather, it began to rain heavily, turning the roads into a quagmire. Wagons bogged down. Horses struggled to pull the heavy artillery. After two days, Burnside ordered the troops back to winter camp. What became dubbed derisively the "Mud March" resulted in yet another failure for the Army of the Potomac.

Burnside learned that Joseph Hooker and William B. Franklin, two key senior officers, had openly criticized his plans to their troops. He was determined that there should be accountability for the defeatist chatter. He headed for Washington, and, after considerable difficulty because of the continuing horrendous weather, made it shortly after 7 a.m. on January 24, 1863. He went directly to see Lincoln, carrying Order Number Eight, which outlined his determination to fire or transfer Hooker, William Franklin, and other complainers who he believed had sowed dissension in the ranks, or be himself relieved of command.

The next day, January 25, 1863, Lincoln welcomed Burnside into his office at 10 a.m. The president thanked Burnside for his service and told him he had decided to replace him. Burnside was reassigned to the Department of the Ohio.

WHO WOULD BE BURNSIDE'S REPLACEMENT? At a time of low morale, both in the country and throughout the Army of the Potomac, Lincoln understood how much was riding on making the right appointment. Whoever he chose would be the fourth commander of the Army of the

Potomac in less than two years. Lincoln determined not to consider George McClellan or any of McClellan's partisans, some of whom the president now transferred out of the Army of the Potomac. He may have thought of Western commanders, such as Ulysses S. Grant or William S. Rosecrans, but they were doing well where they were. Besides, Lincoln did not want to antagonize his Eastern soldiers with another imported Western commander, as had happened six months earlier with the appointment of John Pope.

Lincoln offered a surprise when he decided to appoint Joseph Hooker, even after all of Hooker's sniping at Burnside behind his back. Lincoln did not consult Stanton, Halleck, or members of his cabinet. At a White House reception the evening of January 24, 1863, Henry J. Raymond, editor of the New York Times, warned Lincoln about Hooker's loose talk. Lincoln put his hand on Raymond's shoulder and, speaking softly into his ear, not wanting to be overheard, said, "That is all true. Hooker does talk badly, but the trouble is, he is stronger with the country today than any other man." Lincoln's primary priority in early 1863 had become the public and the soldiers.

Born in Hadley, Massachusetts, and a graduate of West Point, "Fighting Joe" Hooker was handsome, with wavy brown hair and blue eyes. He had earned his nickname for his courage at Williamsburg in the battle on the Virginia peninsula in the spring of 1862. Hooker seemed to be everywhere, calmly directing his men from the vantage point of "Colonel," his large white horse. Hooker did not like his nickname because he believed it did him "incalculable injury," leading the public to think "I am a hot headed, furious young fellow" not given to calm and thoughtful military leadership. He earned a reputation for caring about his soldiers during the siege at Yorktown. He commanded a division in the second battle of Bull Run and was wounded in the foot at Antietam in September 1862.

If Lincoln may have earlier overlooked some of the flaws of McClellan, Pope, Halleck, and Burnside, he made the appointment of Hooker with his eyes wide open. Lincoln knew that Hooker came with both assets and liabilities. Hooker's chief assets were that he was an independent and outspoken soldier. Hooker's chief liabilities were the same two qualities. In the Mexican War, he had criticized General Winfield Scott, testifying against him in a court of inquiry. Assigned to command the Center Grand Division under Burnside at Fredericksburg, he was

*Abraham Lincoln made a
surprise appointment in
choosing "Fighting Joe" Hooker
to become the fourth
commander of the Army of the
Potomac in January 1863.*

"incensed" from the start of Burn's much-too-slow strategy to cross the Rappahannock. He tried to persuade Burnside not to continue the suicidal attack on Marye's Heights.

When Lincoln made his decision to appoint Hooker, he summoned him to the White House. The president told him,

> I think it best for you to know that there are some things in regard to which, I am not quite satisfied with you. . . . I think that during Gen. Burnside's command of the Army, you have taken counsel of your ambition, and thwarted him as much as you could, in which you did a great wrong to the country, and to a most meritorious and honorable brother officer.

One can only imagine Hooker's expression when Lincoln then said, "Of course it was not *for* this, but in spite of it, that I have given you the command." Lincoln had heard that among Hooker's headstrong loose talk he had made the suggestion that what the country might need in this crisis was a dictator. Lincoln told Hooker, "Only those generals who gain successes, can set up dictators. What I now ask of you is military success, and I will risk the dictatorship."

Lincoln later wrote what he had said in Hooker's letter of appointment. He mingled affirmation with admonition in the remarkable letter, all in a tone of kindness, even humor. Several months later, Hooker told reporter Noah Brooks, "That is just such a letter as a father might write to a son. It is a beautiful letter, and although I think he was harder on me than I deserved, I will say I love the man who wrote it."

As a part of his appointment, Hooker requested that he report directly to the president, wanting to bypass Henry Halleck. Hooker and Halleck had studied together at West Point, but bad blood had developed in their days in California in the 1850s. Apparently Hooker owed Halleck money, and Halleck had publicly disapproved of Hooker's drinking and carousing. Lincoln, sometimes too willing to oblige, acquiesced to Hooker's request. His decision to bypass the chain of command would pose problems in the future.

With a new commander in place and no immediate advance planned, Lincoln could finally step back from his daily regimen as commander in chief. No president, before or after, ever spent nearly as much time in the day-to-day, hour-by-hour command of the armed forces of the nation. Lincoln's nonstop work was taking a tremendous toll on him.

WHO DID THE EMANCIPATION PROCLAMATION FREE? Critics quickly created an oft-repeated maxim that the only slaves emancipated were outside the reach of the Northern army. The proclamation exempted the border states, as well as Tennessee, plus areas of Virginia and Louisiana occupied by Union troops. The proclamation was not so much a fact accomplished as a promise to be realized.

If the Emancipation Proclamation could be achieved, it would be by the marching feet of a liberating army. But up until now this had been "a white man's war." By the middle of the nineteenth century, most Americans had forgotten that African-Americans fought in both the Revolutionary War and the War of 1812. Blacks had been barred from state militias since 1792. The regular army, including West Point, did not recruit or enroll black soldiers.

If critics pointed to the weaknesses of the proclamation, it contained one potentially large strength: "And I further declare and make known, that such persons of suitable condition, will be received into the armed service of the United States to garrison forts, positions, stations, and other places, and to man vessels of all sorts in said service." But the promise came with a question. Did Lincoln intend that freed slaves join the Union army and navy? If so, in what roles? Even Lincoln's closest colleagues were not sure what he intended at the beginning of 1863.

The second Confiscation Act of July 17, 1862, gave Lincoln the power to employ blacks in any way he chose, but he had been reluctant to use them as soldiers. Since early in the war, slaves had sought refuge in Union camps. Soldiers quickly learned that some slaves were willing bearers of information about Confederate troops and movements.

The overwhelming majority of Northern soldiers did not sign up to free black slaves or fight beside them in the Union army. The attitudes of these soldiers combined a hatred of blacks with a greater hatred of the system of slavery they saw as a foundation of the Confederate states.

Recruitment of slaves for the Union military had taken place piecemeal in South Carolina, Louisiana, and Kansas in 1862, without either Lincoln's affirmation or authorization. In July 1862, days before sharing his plans for an Emancipation Proclamation with his cabinet, Lincoln had told Senator Orville Browning that the arming of black soldiers "would produce dangerous & fatal dissatisfaction in our army, and do more injury than good." After his public announcement of his plans for emancipation in September, the suggestion of arming black soldiers incited as much or more antagonism from Democrats and from Unionists in border states than the idea of emancipation itself.

AFTER MONTHS OF FOREBODING, Frederick Douglass was elated when he heard that Lincoln had signed the Emancipation Proclamation. He had been encouraging the arming of black troops since the start of the war. From his editor's desk in Rochester, and on platforms across the North, Douglass had criticized the president in 1861 and 1862 for fighting a war with his white hand while his black hand was tied behind his back.

Now, at the beginning of 1863, Douglass made plans to act upon the military promise within the civil promise of emancipation. In February, he traveled two thousand miles to encourage black enlistment. In an address delivered at the Cooper Institute in New York, Douglass declared, "The colored man only waits for honorable admission into the service of the country. They know that who would be free, themselves must strike the blow, and they long for the opportunity to strike that blow." On his tour, Douglass was struck by the clash of twin emotions—white Northern discouragement with the war effort and eager-ness on the part of blacks to enlist and serve.

As black leaders, abolitionists, and radical Republicans promoted the deployment of black troops, Lincoln moved, quietly, behind the scenes. All the while he was being encouraged, if not pushed, by Secretary of War Stanton, with whom he had forged a strong working relationship.

When Stanton replaced Simon Cameron in Lincoln's cabinet in Jan-uary 1862, he quickly learned that Treasury Secretary Salmon Chase stood alone in the cabinet in arguing that it made no sense to fight a war while refusing to deal with the underlying cause of the rebellion. Stan-ton had made himself acceptable to the Buchanan-Breckinridge cabinet by muting his own views, and he did the same thing in his first months in the Lincoln cabinet.

In his early work with Lincoln, Stanton recognized in the president a cautious if not apprehensive attitude about the arming of black troops. In Stanton's dealings with Congress, however, he found himself gravi-tating toward the ideas of the Benjamin Wade–Zachariah Chandler–Thaddeus Stevens troika, who were far ahead of Lincoln in seeing the absolute necessity of using black troops to win the war.

After January 1, 1863, Lincoln followed Stanton's lead in the arming of black troops. But moving African-Americans from their role as con-traband laborers in the rear to trained soldiers at the front would require navigating a tricky obstacle course. The initial obstacle was the white mind-set that blacks, after years of plantation life, did not have the courage to step forward and fight, but would melt away at the first sign of struggle. A second obstacle was the deep prejudice of most white officers from the North who were unwilling to see black soldiers fight alongside white ones. The Confederates were the third obstacle as, alert to the problem of runaway slaves, they moved their slaves away from the seacoast, far from Union lines.

On March 25, 1863, Stanton ordered General Lorenzo Thomas, a career officer, to go to the Mississippi Valley to head up recruitment of African-Americans. Thomas, who for most of his career had been a desk general, surprised his colleagues by becoming a military entrepreneur who, with tireless energy, regularized the recruitment of black soldiers. On the day he began his assignment, only five black regiments had been organized. By the end of 1863, twenty regiments would be organized. The day Thomas headed west, Lincoln wrote to Andrew Johnson, the Democratic military governor of Tennessee, "The bare sight of fifty

Artist James Fuller Queen painted these twelve illustrated cards in 1863 depicting the journey of a slave from plantation life to freedom. The culmination of the journey is service in the Union army, where he willingly gives his life for the cause of the Union and liberty.

thousand armed, and drilled black soldiers on the banks of the Mississippi, would end the rebellion at once. And who doubts that we can present that sight, if we but take hold in earnest?"

In these months, Lincoln moved from hesitant consent to eager advocacy of black soldiers. He wrote to Stanton, "I desire that a renewed and vigorous effort be made to raise colored forces along the shores of the

Mississippi." Stanton had kept Lincoln informed of Thomas's success. The president was impressed. "I think the evidence is nearly conclusive that Gen. Thomas is one of the best, if not the very best, instruments for this service."

LINCOLN WATCHED IMPATIENTLY as Joseph Hooker took charge of the Army of the Potomac. Skeptics abounded. Charles Francis Adams, Jr., great-grandson and grandson of presidents, wrote his father, the U.S. minister to England, that the "Army of the Potomac is at present fearfully demoralized." He added, "The Government" took away McClellan and relieved Burnside—"all this that Hooker may be placed in command, a man who has not the confidence of the army and who in private character is well known to be—I need not say what."

Much of the resentment in the initial days of Hooker's command was due to the disheartening condition of the soldiers. Thousands were in poor health, and hundreds were dying from lack of adequate medical care in their winter quarters. The majority opposed Lincoln's Emancipation Proclamation. Desertions numbered two hundred per day.

Ill will turned to goodwill, however, as Hooker initiated changes. New hospitals were built and older ones revamped. Improved rations, especially vegetables, suddenly appeared. Hooker stated, "My men shall be fed before I am fed, and before any of my officers are fed." In March, he instituted insignia badges of different colors, two inches square, which were worn with pride on the caps of the men of each corps. He implemented Lincoln's order of November 15, 1862, wherein the president, as commander in chief, directed "the orderly observance of the Sabbath," as "a becoming deference to the best sentiment of a Christian people, and a due regard for the Divine will."

Hooker was still not without his detractors. Women and whiskey have always followed soldiers, but Hooker's headquarters became a gathering place for female camp followers who acquired a name that stuck long after the Civil War—"hookers." Stanton warned Hooker to prohibit women and liquor from his camps. Young Adams described Hooker's headquarters as "a combination of bar-room and brothel."

Although Hooker was proving to be a good administrator, Lincoln wondered if he was up to the challenge of leading a large army into battle. In February and March, Hooker sent out detachments up and down the Rappahannock, but Robert E. Lee and his troops, in their winter camps south of the river, derided these moves as intended merely to frighten. Southern pickets greeted Union soldiers with derisive cheers. The winter weather was dark, with plenty of snow and sleet, but Halleck and Stanton wondered whether Hooker, despite his earlier criticisms of McClellan, was afflicted with the same disease of inaction. Lincoln decided to see for himself.

On April 4, 1863, Lincoln left the Navy Yard on the steamer *Carrie Martin* at 5 p.m. leading a party that included Mary, Tad, Attorney General Bates, and Noah Brooks, correspondent for the *Sacramento Daily Union,* bound for Hooker's camp at Falmouth, in northern Virginia. On April 6, a blustery day, Lincoln reviewed the cavalry. The president, an excellent horseman, rode using a saddle recently received by Hooker from San Francisco, while little Tad clung to the saddle of his pony, as drums rolled, trumpets blared, and the various regiments dipped their colors. As the president and General Hooker prepared to receive the troops in review, they witnessed a sight never seen before. In the first two years of the war, the Union cavalry were attached to infantry units and generally misused as escort or messenger services. Now, under the leadership of Major General George Stoneman, who had roomed with Stonewall Jackson at West Point, the cavalry had been brought together under a single command. On this day, seventeen thousand cavalry, with horses prancing, the largest cavalry parade ever assembled, with the six-foot-four-inch Stoneman in the lead, marched before the president.

The next day, Lincoln insisted on going through all the hospital tents and talking with countless soldiers. He listened with endless patience to the stories of soldiers and offered kindness and comfort in return. When he left the hospital tents he was greeted by a thunderous cheer.

On April 8, 1863, Lincoln reviewed sixty thousand men in the infantry and artillery. He touched his stovepipe hat in a return salute to the officers, but uncovered his head to the soldiers in the ranks. The review went on, uninterrupted, for five and a half hours.

But Lincoln mainly came to talk with Hooker. From the outset their conversation took the form of an odd call-and-response. Hooker would begin his conversations with, "When I get to Richmond," to which Lincoln would respond, "If you get to Richmond, General," Hooker would then interrupt, "Excuse me, Mr. President, but there is no if in the case. I am going straight to Richmond if I live."

Lincoln, in a final conference, haunted by the misuse of resources by

George McClellan at Antietam and Ambrose Burnside at Fredericks-burg, spoke with both Hooker and Darius N. Couch, the senior corps commander. "Gentlemen, in your next battle, *put in all your men.*"

Lincoln returned to Washington impressed with the changes insti-tuted by Hooker, which had resulted in an obvious upturn of morale, but disturbed by the easy, almost nonchalant attitude he witnessed when he sought to engage Hooker in conversation about the difficult days ahead. Lincoln confided to Brooks, "That is the most depressing thing about Hooker. It seems to me that he is over-confident."

THREE AND A HALF MONTHS after signing the Emancipation Proclama-tion, Lincoln continued to consider its implications, not just for the United States, but for the family of nations. In another of his reflec-tions, this time on the back of Executive Mansion stationery, Lincoln wrote out a resolution on slavery. First, Lincoln stated the problem: "Whereas, while heretofore, States, and Nations, have tolerated slavery, Recently, for the first time in the world, an attempt has been made to construct a new Nation, upon the basis of, and with the primary, and fundamental object to maintain, enlarge, and perpetuate human slavery, therefore, ..."

Then he stated the resolution: "Resolved, That no such embryo State should ever be recognized by, or Admitted into, the family of christian and civilized nations; and that all ch[r]istian and civilized men everywhere should, by all lawful means, resist to the utmost, such recognition or admission."

On April 17, 1863, Lincoln showed this resolution to Senator Charles Sumner. They talked about its use, including publishing it in the English press, to further bolster the cause of the Union there. The resolution was never published, perhaps made unnecessary by events on the battlefield in the next three months. On November 30, Sumner would write to Lincoln encouraging the president to include the resolu-tion in his upcoming annual message to Congress. Lincoln did not do so. Although never to see the public light of day, this private memo is fur-ther evidence that Lincoln's Emancipation Proclamation was not simply a military emergency strategy, but in his mind the conception of the model of a new nation.

ULYSSES S. GRANT was one of the few senior generals Lincoln had never met. The president liked what he first heard of the Illinoisan's unassuming manner. What a contrast after dealing earlier with McClellan and now with Hooker. Lincoln appreciated Grant's spare but concise communications, his lack of concern about rank, and, most of all, that he never asked for reinforcements and was ready every day to fight.

The president had heard all the gossip about Grant—that the general was surprised at Shiloh; that Grant had reverted to old habits and was tippling again. He discovered that whenever a politician or another gen-

Whereas, while heretofore States, and Nations, have tolerated slavery, recently, for the first in the world, an attempt has been made to construct a new Nation, upon the basis of, and with the primary, and fundamental object to maintain, enlarge, and perpetuate human slavery, therefore

Resolved, That no such embryo State should ever be recognized by, or admitted into, the family of Christian and civilized nations; And that all Christian and civilized men everywhere should, by all lawful means resist to the utmost, such recognition or admission.

In April 1863, Lincoln, in a private reflection, continued to think about the wider implications of emancipation for the family of nations.

eral wished to undercut Grant in the field, they resorted to recycling old stories about Grant and liquor. The president quickly learned of the jealousies within the army. He could believe the resentments against Grant were increasing in direct proportion to his rapid rise in rank.

Only once had Lincoln questioned Grant's judgment. In the fall of 1862, frustrated by the illicit cotton trading along the Mississippi that he believed was channeling supplies and money into the Confederacy, Grant took steps to try to stop it. In November, he gave orders to conductors that some of the traders, Jews, could no longer travel south on the railroad into his military department. On December 17, 1862, when Grant believed his order was being evaded, he issued General Order Number Eleven: "The Jews, as a class, violating every regulation of trade established by the Treasury Department, and also Department orders, are hereby expelled from the Department." Some at the time tried to say that Grant's order was issued by his staff, or that the word "Jew" was shorthand for shrewd merchants, but Grant alone was responsible for this sweeping anti-Jewish order.

When it became public, the order produced widespread denunciations of Grant. Cesar J. Kaskel, of Paducah, Kentucky, led a delegation of Jewish leaders who called on Lincoln at the White House. The president, who seven years earlier had expressed his strong disagreement with a nativism that targeted immigrants, especially Catholics, listened respectfully. Kaskel reported that Lincoln defused the tension in the room with a "heartwarming, semi-humorous, Biblical" exchange.

"And so the children of Israel were driven from the happy land of Canaan?"

Kaskel replied, "Yes, and that is why we have come unto Father Abraham's bosom, asking protection."

Lincoln responded, "And this protection they shall have at once." Lincoln told Grant that he was revoking the order immediately.

IN 1863, Lincoln understood that control of the Mississippi River, which he had navigated twice to New Orleans as a youth and young man, could cut the Confederacy in two. Control depended on the strategic Mississippi fortress town of Vicksburg.

With Lincoln unable to bring Grant to Washington or visit him in the field, and with rumors circulating in the steamy political air of Washington, Stanton, with Lincoln's approval, decided to send a personal emissary to be their eyes and ears in Grant's headquarters. Stanton

Lincoln, although he had never met Ulysses S. Grant, took a long-distance liking to this modest, hard-fighting general. Their growing appreciation of each other would become one of the fascinating stories of the Civil War.

tapped Charles A. Dana, who since 1847 had been the managing editor of the *New York Tribune,* to become his assistant secretary of war. He assigned Dana to travel to Grant's headquarters supposedly to investigate the paymaster service in the Western armies, but really to spy for Stanton.

Dana took the measure of Grant and passed on his findings in almost daily secret ciphers to Stanton and Lincoln. Writing later, he described Grant to be "an uncommon fellow—the most modest, the most disinterested, and the most honest man." Dana found him "not an original or brilliant man, but sincere, thoughtful, deep, and gifted with courage that never faltered." Lincoln was strongly inclined to believe in Grant before Dana's visit, but the newspaperman's reports only confirmed his own intuition.

Even so, Lincoln continued to receive charges against the major general. On April 1, 1863, Murat Halstead, editor of the influential *Cincinnati Commercial,* contacted John Nicolay in an effort "to reach the ear of the President through you." Halstead wrote, "Grant's Mississippi opening enterprise is a failure—a total, complete failure." Three days later, Chase wrote to Lincoln, passing on a letter he had received from Halstead. "Genl. Grant, entrusted with our greatest army, is a jackass in the original package. He is a poor drunken imbecile." Halstead asked, "Now are our Western heroes to be sacrificed by the ten thousand by this poor devil? Grant will fail miserably, hopelessly, eternally." Chase added, in an accompanying note, that although he didn't like the tone of Halstead's letter, these comments "are too common to be safely or even prudently disregarded."

Lincoln had been down this road before—with Pope, McClellan, and Burnside. Criticisms would rise up from the public. Complaints would be registered from within the ranks of officers. Would the criticisms of Grant lead to the same unhappy ending? In May, Lincoln admitted, "I have had stronger influence brought against Grant, praying for his removal . . . than for any other object, coming too from good men."

Grant would need all of his military wisdom and courage for a siege against Vicksburg. Sitting atop two-hundred-foot bluffs, the Confederate garrison was commanded by John Pemberton, a forty-eight-year-old native of Philadelphia who, married to a Virginian, was one of the few Northern officers to join the Confederacy. Grant and Pemberton fought alongside each other in Mexico. Now Pemberton's soldiers were positioned on the top and the sides of this Mississippi River fortress, ready to rain down fire upon approaching enemy troops.

Throughout the winter and spring of 1863, Grant pursued option after option. He had his engineers attempt to rechannel the Mississippi River by digging a canal opposite Vicksburg to divert the river, so that he could make an assault from land. Lincoln, with his long-standing fascination with engineering ventures, followed the progress of this project closely. Halleck wrote Grant, "The President attaches much importance to this." After months of hard labor, however, Grant's engineers had to abandon the canal as nature took its course.

In another venture, Admiral David D. Porter sent his ironclad gunboats through Steele's Bayou, twenty-five miles north of Vicksburg, but the boats were almost trapped by Confederates who felled trees to try to block the boats from each end. Reports began to circulate of flagging morale and of spreading sickness among Grant's troops—dysentery, typhoid, and pneumonia. The failed attempts, and the rumors about troop morale, increased the criticism of Grant and the pressure on Lincoln.

Lincoln had his own ideas as to what Grant should do to achieve victory at Vicksburg. Early on, he believed Grant should join forces with General Nathaniel Banks, who became commander of the Department of the Gulf, based in New Orleans, in December 1862. Banks was one of the political generals, having served as Speaker of the House of Representatives and Republican governor of Massachusetts. Lincoln suggested that either Grant move south to help Banks in his attempts to take Port Hudson, Louisiana, or Banks move north to cooperate with Grant in attacking Vicksburg. Grant, however, knew that two hundred treacherous river miles lay between Vicksburg and Port Hudson, and he did not trust Banks's competency. Great respect for Lincoln notwithstanding, Grant rejected the idea. On April 2, 1863, Henry Halleck telegraphed Grant that the president was becoming "impatient" and continually asking "questions" about Grant's progress.

Lincoln put another roadblock in Grant's path to Vicksburg when he allowed himself to be persuaded by another political general, John A. McClernand, who had served with Lincoln in the Illinois legislature. Lincoln appreciated that McClernand, a Democrat, had led the way in damping down secessionist views in southern Illinois. The former congressman commanded a division at Forts Henry and Donelson and also at Shiloh, all under Grant.

McClernand took advantage of his friendship with Lincoln to go outside normal military channels and communicate with him directly. Lincoln, always wishing to see the best qualities in people, was slow to perceive McClernand's shadowy side. Not so, General Grant. "Unconditional Surrender" Grant saw what Lincoln did not see: At Forts Henry and Donelson, McClernand acted without orders and not only claimed far more for himself and his troops than results warranted, but downplayed the actions of fellow officers.

McClernand came to Washington in late September 1862, to lobby the president and members of his cabinet for an independent command of a new force of Midwestern volunteers, many of them democrats, to open up the Mississippi River. He made a favorable impression on Chase, but when the treasury secretary asked the president his opinion of McClernand, Lincoln replied that "he thought him brave and capable, but too desirous to be independent of every body else." Lincoln's comment notwithstanding, the president's largess toward his independent-minded Illinois friend would become Grant's management headache on the Mississippi in the months ahead.

In early May, Grant made his own plans. Instead of marching back to Port Hudson, or moving directly on Vicksburg, he struck out northeast into the Mississippi countryside. After four dreary months of camping in the mud by the Mississippi River, the Army of the Tennessee, with thirty thousand men, left its supply line on the river behind and, determined to live off the land, simply disappeared. Lincoln, anxious for any news, read Grant's spare telegram to Halleck, "You may not hear from me for several days." Grant pressed ahead on an authority based in his own experience.

In the days ahead, Grant marched his men 130 miles, captured Jackson, the capital of Mississippi, and waged five battles against surprised opponents. The Confederate forces, in total, were actually as large as Grant's army, but he was determined to fight their different divisions separately and never let them combine.

Elihu Washburne, Lincoln's friend and the congressman for Grant's district in northwestern Illinois, was traveling with Grant and wrote the president. Washburne and Lincoln had enjoyed many laughs together back in Illinois. The congressman closed with comments sure to bring a smile to the president. "I am afraid Grant will have to be reproved for want to style. On this whole move of five days he had neither a horse nor an orderly or servant, a blanket or overcoat or clean shirt, or even a sword. His entire baggage consists of a tooth brush."

"THE PRESIDENT TELLS ME that he now fears 'the fire in the rear'— meaning the Democracy, especially in the Northwest—more than our military chances." So wrote Senator Charles Sumner to Francis Lieber, German-born professor of law at Columbia College in New York on January 17, 1863. Antiwar protest surged in the winter and spring of 1863, nowhere more than in Lincoln's Midwest. Two years after the start of the war, "Peace Democrats," or "Copperheads," lashed out at the Emancipation Proclamation, which, they said, would produce "nigger equality." Republicans coined the name "Copperheads" in the summer of 1861 when an anonymous writer to the *Cincinnati Commercial* likened the peace faction of the Democratic Party to the snake in Genesis 3:14: "Upon thy belly shalt thou go, and dust shalt thou eat all the days of thy life." Copperheads were poisonous snakes, but like many labels that begin as terms of derision, the disparaged soon wore the term as a badge of honor. They cut the Goddess of Liberty from the head of pennies—"Copperheads"—and wore them in the lapels of their coats. Their efforts were no small sideshow, as has often been suggested, but rather a relentless push by well-organized forces that gathered momentum in 1863. They sought to gain control of all states in the Midwest.

THE COPPERHEAD PARTY.—IN FAVOR OF A *VIGOROUS PROSECUTION OF PEACE!*

This cartoon from the February 28, 1863, issue of Harper's Weekly *depicts three Copperheads advancing on Columbia, who bears a sword and a shield inscribed "Union."*

Lincoln, knowing well the sentiments from which the Copperheads sprung, took the movement seriously.

Lincoln's comment to Sumner was surely a response to a speech in Congress by Congressman Clement L. Vallandigham of Ohio three days earlier. Born in New Lisbon, Ohio, the handsome son of a Presbyterian minister, the self-assured Vallandigham was first elected to the Ohio state legislature in 1845, just months after his twenty-fifth birthday. Elected to Congress in 1858, he became a vigorous states' rights advocate in the tradition of Andrew Jackson. Often caricatured as a wacko, Vallandigham, a conservative Democrat, was actually an effective spokesman for the interests of concerned citizens, especially farmers and immigrants, in the Midwest.

After Republicans had gerrymandered the forty-two-year-old Vallandigham out of a fourth term in Congress in the fall of 1862, he returned to Washington for the final session of the Thirty-seventh Congress determined to make his voice heard before he left office. He had campaigned on the slogan "The Constitution as it is, the Union as it was," stressing that the "arbitrary government" of Lincoln, with its record of unlawful arrests and the Emancipation Proclamation, was changing the Union forever. Vallandigham believed the Confederacy could not be defeated, and that the nation should go forward as it had in the past, with a mixed political system that allowed for slavery. When he listened to the reading of Lincoln's annual message on December 1, 1862, the words that especially piqued him were, "The dogmas of the quiet past are inadequate to the stormy present. . . . As our case is new, we must think anew."

On January 14, 1863, as Vallandigham left his seat and moved to the center of the opposition benches to speak, congressmen laid aside their newspapers and put down their pens. He began by reproaching the Republicans, not the Southern fire-eaters, for the crisis that had erupted into war. He argued that despite the repudiation of Republicans in the fall elections, especially in the Midwest, Lincoln did not withdraw his Emancipation Proclamation, which, he claimed, was a strategy to divert attention from the president's own failures.

Vallandigham asked: What was the result of twenty months of war? His answer: "Defeat, debt, taxation, sepulchers, these are your trophies." Claiming to speak for the greater Midwest, he thundered, "The people of the West demand peace, and they begin to suspect that New England [by which he meant abolitionism] is in the way." Since the war had failed, it was time to give peace a chance. He proposed pulling Northern troops from the South and opening negotiations for an armistice. He concluded, "Let time do his office—drying tears, dispelling sorrows, mellowing passions, and making herb and grass and tree grow again upon the hundred battlefields of this terrible war." Vallandigham, dubbed the apostle of peace, spoke for more than one hour while the packed gallery, including many uniformed soldiers, sat mesmerized.

Peace as well as War Democrats shared an apprehension about the quickly moving developments in the Midwest. John A. McClernand wrote the president on February 14, 1863, "The Peace Party means, as I predicted long since, not only a separation from the New England States, but reunion of the Middle and Northwestern States with the revolted States." Many War Democrats, initially supportive of the war, were becoming increasingly critical of Lincoln because of their disagreement with the Emancipation Proclamation and the continuing price of the war. McClernand put Lincoln on notice. "Unless the war

Clement L. Vallandigham, former Ohio congressman, became the symbol of the "fire in the rear." Lincoln did not underestimate the power the Copperhead, or Peace Democrat, movement had in the Midwest.

shall be brought to a close before the expiration of your Administration, or decisive victories gained, this scheme, in whole or a part, will find authoritative sanction."

Back in Lincoln's Illinois, the bitter fruits of the Democratic victories in 1862 were ripened in the state legislative agenda of 1863. The legislature passed resolutions criticizing the federal administration and calling for an armistice to end the war. A bill to stop the immigration of African-Americans was put on the docket for a vote. Finally, to stop further motions, Republican governor Richard Yates arbitrarily ended the session of the legislature, the first time this had ever happened in Illinois.

As winter gave way to spring, the Copperheads, incited by the March 3, 1863, passage of the Conscription Act, the first federal military draft, which stipulated that every male citizen between the ages of twenty and forty-five would be obligated to serve for three years or until the end of the war, moved from words to deeds. Protesters swiftly denounced the draft as unconstitutional. Recruiting officers were murdered. Young men were encouraged to desert. Violence sometimes erupted when Union army officers tried to round up deserters. African-Americans were attacked when Copperheads promoted the fear that the

Emancipation Proclamation would produce an unwanted influx of blacks from South to North.

When Congress adjourned in March, Vallandigham returned home to a hero's welcome in Dayton, Ohio. In the same month, the new commander of the Department of the Ohio, General Ambrose Burnside, arrived at his headquarters at Cincinnati. Each man had recently endured failures; each man came to Ohio determined to make his mark.

Vallandigham, not one to sit on the sidelines, set about making speeches and announced his plans to run for governor. Burnside, incapable of understanding the disaffection in Ohio and not recognizing the partisan editorial viewpoint in Murat Halstead's attacks on Peace Democrats in the *Cincinnati Commercial,* decided to stamp out tyranny by force. On April 13, 1863, Burnside issued General Order Number Thirty-eight, a military edict aimed at persons who "uttered one word against the government of the United States." Anyone guilty of "acts for the benefit of the enemies of our country" could be liable to execution. Burnside assured Ohio Republicans that he had the power to decide what treason was and what the suitable punishment would be.

Vallandigham saw immediately that Burnside's overreaching offered an opportunity to test the limits of dissent. He became determined to bait Burnside. The commander of the Department of the Ohio proved more than willing to take that bait.

On May 1, 1863, with Vallandigham scheduled to speak at a Democratic rally in Mount Vernon, Ohio, Burnside dispatched two staff members to observe and take notes. A friend of Vallandigham tipped him off to Burnside's intentions. Vallandigham began his speech by pointing to the American flags, with their thirty-four stars, that surrounded the speakers' stands. He told the crowd the flag with all the states would still be united if it were not for Republican treachery. Looking right at one of Burnside's note-taking agents, he said that his right to speak came from a document—the Constitution—that was higher than General Order Number Thirty-eight, which he derided as "a bane usurpation of arbitrary power." "Valiant Val" concluded by saying that the remedy for all "the evils" was the ballot box, by which they could throw "King Lincoln" from his throne.

Burnside heard the applause for Vallandigham in Cincinnati and decided to act. He dispatched Captain Charles G. Hutton and a posse of sixty-seven men to Dayton. They arrived at 323 First Street at 2 a.m.

When Vallandigham refused to come out of his house, Hutton's men attacked the front door with bars and axes.

Union troops transported Vallandigham to Burnside's headquarters in Cincinnati, where a military court tried him. While in custody, Vallandigham wrote an address, "To the Democracy of Ohio," which was smuggled out of his confinement and published in newspapers across the country. "I am here in a military bastile for no other offense than my political opinions." Vallandigham, denied a writ of habeas corpus, was sentenced to confinement in a military prison for the rest of the war.

The two main players in this Ohio melodrama appeared, at first glance, to be Vallandigham and Burnside, but the national audience understood that the lead actor was President Lincoln. All eyes watched to see what action he would take.

Lincoln recognized that both actors, Vallandigham and Burnside, had overplayed their roles. He brought the issue to a cabinet meeting on May 19, 1863, where Welles noted that the arrest was "an error on the part of Burnside." Burnside learned of the cabinet's deliberations and telegraphed Lincoln that he understood his actions were "a source of Embarrassment," and offered to resign his command. Lincoln replied the same day that "being done, all were for seeing you through with it."

Lincoln's generous letter still did not answer the question of what to do. The president did not want to make Vallandigham a martyr, which would happen if he served in a military prison to the end of the war, but he also did not want to publicly reprimand Burnside. The president came up with his own resolution: Release Vallandigham, remove him from the Midwest, where he was becoming a folk hero, and banish him to the Confederacy. Burnside transferred Vallandigham as a prisoner to William Rosecrans's Army of the Cumberland at Murfreesboro, Tennessee. On the morning of May 25, 1863, an Alabama cavalry officer on the Shelbyville Turnpike was surely surprised to be met by Union officers under a flag of truce presenting Clement L. Vallandigham.

BY THE MIDDLE OF APRIL, Joseph Hooker and the Army of the Potomac were finally ready to move. Fighting Joe's army of 133,868 outnumbered Lee's army of 60,892 by more than two to one. On April 12, 1863, Hooker sent Daniel Butterfield, his chief of staff, to the White House to deliver to Lincoln his battle plan, complete with maps. Lincoln wanted to be included. Hooker, on the other hand, was terribly afraid that no one could keep a secret, so that he did not inform his senior commanders of his final plans until the last moment. On April 13, he told his infantry commanders to have their men ready in two days with eight days' rations and 140 rounds of ammunition. On April 14, George Stoneman, with more than 10,000 cavalry, was ready to make the first strike, intending to cross the Rappahannock, move around Lee's left flank, and head for Culpeper Courthouse and Gordonsville, tearing up the railroads and communication lines along the way, with the goal of cutting off Lee's supply line southeast to Richmond. Fighting Joe Hooker's orders were "fight, fight, fight."

As the battle was about to begin, Lincoln was filled with anxiety. He spent long hours at the telegraph office in the War Department. On April 14, 1863, he telegraphed Hooker, "Would like to have a letter from you as soon as convenient." Lincoln became increasingly frustrated with the incomplete information he was receiving.

General Stoneman, so impressive in parading his cavalry before Lincoln on April 6, 1863, now moved unexplainably slowly. Before he could cross the Rappahannock, the rains came. At 11 p.m. Hooker wrote to Lincoln, but was not clear about the progress of his cavalry. Hooker did not like to send the president bad news.

On the morning of April 15, 1863, Hooker telegraphed Lincoln, assuring him that Stoneman would cross the Rappahannock, and "if he should meet with no unusual delay, he will strike the Aquia and Richmond Rail Road on the night of the second day."

Lincoln was not assured. He replied that Hooker's last letters gave him "considerable uneasiness." Lincoln, by now a veteran commander in chief, understood a great deal about tactics and terrain. He wrote, "He has now been out three days without hindrance from the enemy, and yet he is not twenty five miles from where he started." The president was not fooled. "To reach his point, he still has sixty to go; another river, the Rapidan, to cross, and will be hindered by the enemy." Lincoln concluded, "I greatly fear it is another failure already." He closed, "Write me often. I am very anxious."

Weather was always the wild card. The best military plans, long before scientific methods of weather prediction, could be derailed by the sudden appearance of rain that could continue for who knew how long.

Because the Civil War shone a bright light on the inability to predict the weather, many weather "experts" began appearing in Washington. On the morning of April 25, 1863, Lincoln was visited by Francis L. Capen, who described himself as "A Certified Practical Meteorologist & Expert in Computing the Changes in Weather." He wanted Lincoln to recommend him for a job. Three days later, Lincoln wrote to the War Department. "It seems to me Mr. Capen knows nothing about the weather, in advance. He told me three days ago it would not rain till the 30th of April or 1st of May. It is raining now & has been for ten hours. I can not spare any more time to Mr. Capen."

The weather forced Hooker to modify his strategy. Still concerned about secrecy, he sent a message to Lincoln on April 27, 1863, saying, "I fully appreciate the anxiety weighing upon your mind, and hasten to relieve you from so much of it as lies in my power." Hooker told Lincoln he intended to feint a crossing at Fredericksburg, while sending his main force thirty miles north to confront Lee's forces. His ultimate goal was to trap a retreating Lee between two wings of his infantry and Stoneman's cavalry. He would keep more than twenty thousand troops in reserve, able to move to the most urgent battle line.

Lincoln, receiving little communication, remained fretful. At 3:30 p.m. on the same day, he telegraphed Hooker one sentence: "How does it look now?" Hooker replied at 5 p.m. "I am not sufficiently advanced to give an opinion. We are busy. Will tell you all as soon as I can, and have it satisfactory."

Hooker's grand plan began with promise. On April 29, 1863, two infantry corps crossed the Rappahannock below Fredericksburg while five infantry corps marched upriver, crossed the Rappahannock, and moved eastward toward Fredericksburg and Robert E. Lee.

Lee was initially unsure about how to respond to the larger Union forces. He decided to adopt a risky strategy of dividing his outnumbered army and then dividing it again. He audaciously sent Stonewall Jackson to block Hooker's left flank. Because Stoneman's cavalry was in his rear, Jeb Stuart's Confederate cavalry "owned" the spaces between the dueling armies, which Lee now used for reconnaissance between his different units.

On May 1, 1863, a bright and breezy morning, Hooker's seventy thousand troops encountered Lee's twenty-five thousand troops along the Orange Turnpike and Orange Plank Road just east of the hamlet of Chancellorsville, little more than a brick farmhouse occupied by the ten members of the Chancellor family. Suddenly, for reasons never fully explained, Hooker stopped, wavered, and ordered his troops to fall back and take up defensive positions around Chancellorsville.

Hooker lost the initiative. He later suggested that he intended to fight a defensive war and let the enemy attack him. Attack they did. On May 2, 1863, Jackson smashed the Union right flank.

In the late morning of May 3, 1863, just as a careworn Hooker leaned forward to receive a report, a twelve-pound shot fired by Confederate artillery hit a pillar on the south side of the Chancellor house veranda, splitting it in two. One of the beams struck Hooker on his head and side. For some time—a debate would ensue about how much time—the commander of the Army of the Potomac was out of action. By the middle of the day, the center of Hooker's line was pushed back.

Lincoln, pacing back and forth from the White House to the War Department, telegraphed Butterfield:

"Where is General Hooker? Where is Sedgwick? Where is Stoneman?"

On May 4, 1863, the left side of Hooker's forces was forced back across the river. Early in the afternoon, Secretary of the Navy Gideon Welles met Lincoln at the War Department. The president told him "he had a feverish anxiety to get some facts." At 3:10 p.m. Lincoln telegraphed Hooker, "We have news here that the enemy has reoccupied heights above Fredericksburg. Is that so?" Hooker replied, "I am informed that is so, but attach no importance to it." Hooker was by now in almost total denial of what was happening.

On May 6, 1863, Hooker ordered the remaining troops to recross to the north side of the Rappahannock in a heavy rainstorm. The battle was lost. At Chancellorsville, the Union army had had all the advantages on its side—numbers of troops, horses, guns, supplies, telegraph wires, even balloons. The Union had far superior numbers, but once again, even after Lincoln had given him the strongest mandate, Hooker did not put into battle all of his men—he held out his reserves. The Union suffered a terrible loss at Chancellorsville—more than seventeen thousand casualties. Lee won perhaps his greatest victory, but it came at a huge cost: thirteen thousand Confederate casualties, a higher percentage of casualties than the Union forces.

When Lincoln received word at 3 p.m. that Hooker's troops were retreating across the Rappahannock River, he was overcome. Noah Brooks, who was with the president, said his complexion, usually "sallow," turned "ashen in hue." The correspondent for the *Sacramento Daily Union* said he had never seen the president "so broken, so dispirited, and so ghostlike. . . . Clasping his hands behind his back, he walked up and down the room, saying, 'My God! my God! What will the country say! What will the country say!' "

Frenchman Thomas Le Mere, who worked for Mathew Brady, told Lincoln there was "considerable call" for a full-length photograph of the president. Lincoln stood for it at Brady's Washington studio on April 17, 1863.

CHAPTER 23

You Say You Will Not Fight to Free Negroes
May 1863–September 1863

PEACE DOES NOT APPEAR SO DISTANT AS IT DID. I HOPE IT WILL
COME SOON, AND COME TO STAY; AND SO COME AS TO BE WORTH THE
KEEPING IN ALL FUTURE TIME.

ABRAHAM LINCOLN
Speech to the Springfield rally, September 3, 1863

DURING HIS FIRST TWO YEARS AS PRESIDENT, LINCOLN TURNED DOWN
all invitations to speak outside Washington. He believed he could not
spare the time away; as he expanded his role as commander in chief, he
wanted to stay close to the White House and the War Department in
order to communicate with his generals and monitor the ebb and flow
of military battles.

He broke his silence in 1863 in response to a deafening volley of criticism. The contest for public opinion escalated in May as rallies were
organized in Detroit, Indianapolis, New York, and other Northern
cities to protest Lincoln's handling of the arrest and trial of Vallandigham. Copperheads led the way, but conservative Democrats, who
did not approve of the actions of the Ohio congressman, saw this
episode as an opportunity to attack an administration weakened by
defeats at Fredericksburg and Chancellorsville. On May 19, 1863,
Erastus Corning, wealthy iron manufacturer, railroad owner, and conservative Democratic politician, forwarded to Lincoln the "Albany
Resolves," ten resolutions from a boisterous public meeting in Albany,
New York, on May 16. The resolutions called upon the president to "be
true to the Constitution" and "maintain the rights of States and the liberties of the citizen."

Lincoln could easily have been defensive at the tone of the protests but as a political leader, he realized they presented an opportunity for him to make his case, not simply to a local group of New York Democrats, but to a national audience. He replied to Corning on May 28, 1863, that he intended to "make a respectful response."

By the early summer of 1863, Lincoln began to take considerable care in drafting his "public letters." Although he worked hard in the last days of May on his response to Erastus Corning, he told Congressman James F. Wilson of Iowa that when he started to write the letter, "I had it nearly all in there," pointing to the drawer in his desk, "but it was in disconnected thoughts, which I had jotted down from time to time on separate scraps of paper." Lincoln was referring to the notes to himself he had been writing for decades. He told Wilson it was by this method that "I saved my best thoughts on the subject." He added, "Such things often come in a kind of intuitive way more clearly than if one were to sit down and deliberately reason them out."

A measure of Lincoln's seriousness was that he took the unusual step of bringing his letter to a cabinet meeting on June 5, 1863. Lincoln read it in its entirety, which, at more than 3,800 words, would have taken at least twenty-five minutes. Navy Secretary Gideon Welles wrote in his diary, "It has vigor and ability and with some corrections will be a strong paper." One week later, on June 12, Lincoln mailed the letter to Corning, sending it at the same time to Horace Greeley's *New York Tribune,* which published it on June 15.

Lincoln began his letter not with confrontation but with commendation. He lauded those who met in Albany for "doing their part to maintain our common government and country." He described their intention as "eminently patriotic." He sought to stand with them in their commitment to the Union. "My own purpose is the same." Lincoln sounded like he was back in Illinois putting the arguments of the opposing lawyer in their own words. He emphasized their common purpose at the very moment when his opponents were seeking to incite division. He lowered his voice even as his opponents were raising theirs. He finally joined the fray when he said, "The meeting and myself have a common object, and can have no difference, except in the means or measures for effecting that object."

The "except" was the transition to the purpose of the letter. The "means" became the occasion for Lincoln's disquisition on the meaning and proper interpretation of the Constitution. The supplicants "assert and argue, that certain military arrests and proceedings following them for which I am ultimately responsible, are unconstitutional. I think they are not."

Lincoln, in this public letter, did not allow his opponents to set the agenda. Although he had addressed the question of civil liberties in his message to Congress in July 1861, Lincoln now used Corning's complaints to put the issue into a much larger context. He started with what he declared were the real origins of the war. "The insurgents had been preparing for it more than thirty years, while the government had taken no steps to resist them." The South, he argued, had set out on "an unrestricted effort to destroy Union, constitution, and law," whereas the government was "restrained by the same constitution and law, from arresting their progress."

Once the war started, everyone, including the South, knew that there must be detentions to thwart the actions of "a most efficient corps of spies, informers, suppliers, and aiders and abettors." They fully understood, Lincoln said, that habeas corpus would be suspended, and then his opponents would set up a "clamor" of protests. Lincoln's only apology, ironically, was that "thoroughly imbued with a reverence for the guaranteed rights of individuals, I was slow to adopt strong measures."

At this point, Lincoln made a telling comment on the judicial system. He argued that the courts worked well in peacetime for cases involving individuals, but in "a clear, flagrant, and gigantic case of Rebellion," the ordinary courts were often "incompetent" to deal with whole classes or groups of individuals. By way of example, he said it was common knowledge in the first days after his inauguration that many leading officers, including Robert E. Lee, Joseph E. Johnston, and John B. Magruder, were about to defect from their military obligations to the Union. In hindsight, Lincoln said, they could have been arrested as traitors. If this had been done, "the insurgent cause would be much weaker." Lincoln declared, "I think the time not unlikely to come when I shall be blamed for having made too few arrests rather than too many."

When Lincoln turned to the case of Ohio Peace Democrat Clement Vallandigham, he argued that the resolutions from Albany had it all wrong. The former Ohio congressman "was not arrested because he was damaging the political prospects of the administration, or the personal interests of the commanding general; but because he was damaging the army, upon the existence, and vigor of which, the life of the nation

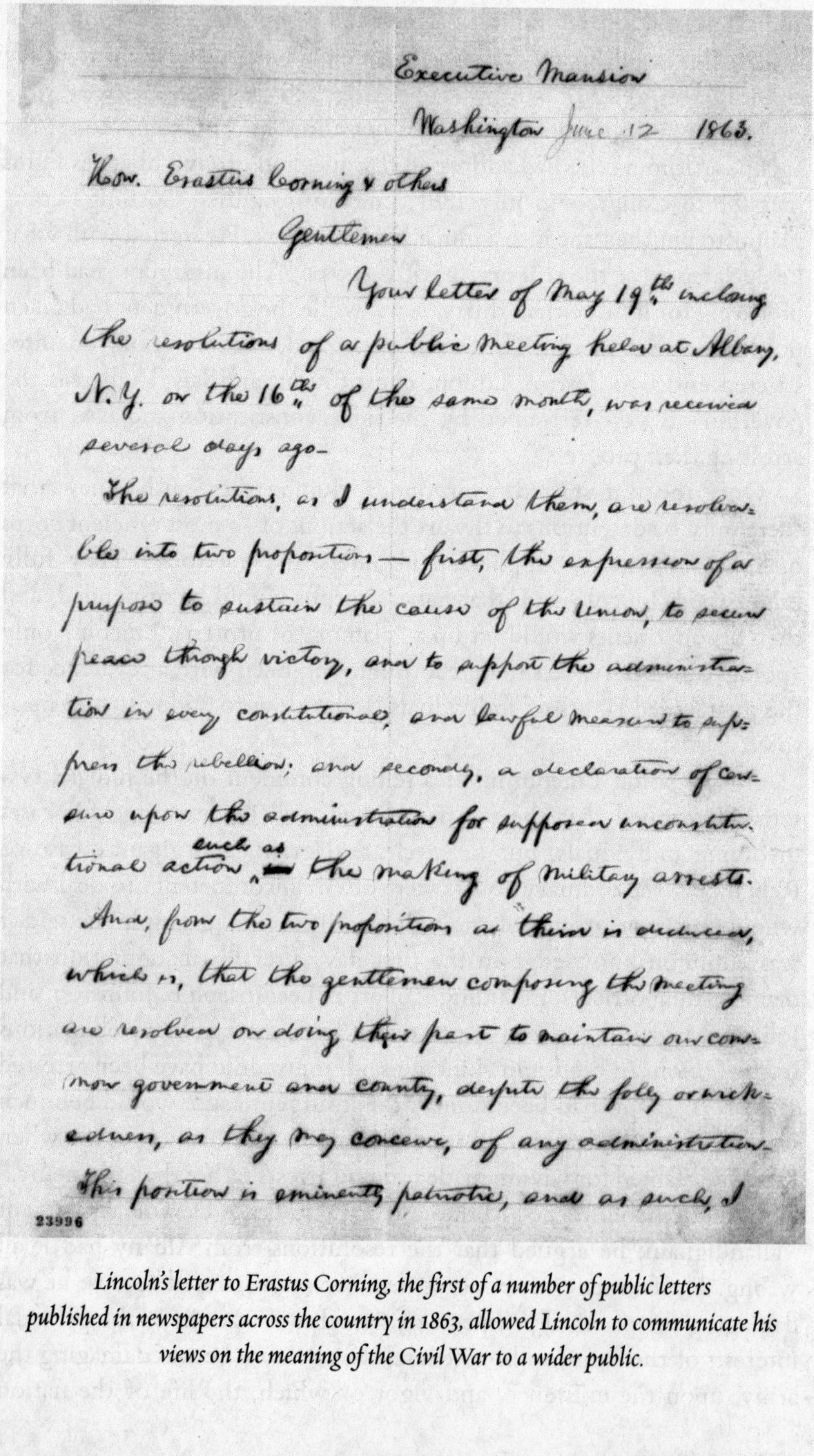

Executive Mansion

Washington June 12 1863.

Hon. Erastus Corning & others

Gentlemen

Your letter of May 19th inclosing the resolutions of a public meeting held at Albany, N.Y. on the 16th of the same month, was received several days ago—

The resolutions, as I understand them, are resolvable into two propositions—first, the expression of a purpose to sustain the cause of the Union, to secure peace through victory, and to support the administration in every constitutional, and lawful measure to suppress the rebellion; and secondly, a declaration of censure upon the administration for supposed unconstitutional action, such as the making of military arrests.

And, from the two propositions a third is deduced, which is, that the gentlemen composing the meeting are resolved on doing their part to maintain our common government and country, despite the folly or wickedness, as they may conceive, of any administration. This position is eminently patriotic, and as such, I

23996

Lincoln's letter to Erastus Corning, the first of a number of public letters published in newspapers across the country in 1863, allowed Lincoln to communicate his views on the meaning of the Civil War to a wider public.

depends." It was his attack on the military that gave the military "constitutional jurisdiction to lay hands on him." Lincoln even offered to review the case if it could be shown that Vallandigham "was not damaging the military power of this country." He knew his opponents had no such proof.

To embody his logic, Lincoln offered one of his favorite literary devices—a dramatic contrast: "Must I shoot a simple-minded soldier boy who deserts, while I must not touch a hair of a wiley agitator who induces him to desert?" One of Lincoln's great agonies in the war was signing off on an execution order as the punishment for desertion. Lincoln brought into sharp focus not simply the sympathetic picture of the "soldier boy," but a portrait of a Copperhead fomenting such desertions. Lincoln's term "wiley agitator" stuck with the public. "I think that in such a case, to silence the agitator, and save the boy, is not only constitutional, but withal, a great mercy." Lincoln's opponents had been arguing for justice for Vallandigham; he inverted their argument by putting the focus on the real victims, young soldiers, and calling for the Christian virtue that was higher than justice—mercy. This empathic figure immediately became the "sound bite" of his public letter.

At this point, Lincoln pasted a scrap of paper to his draft, wanting to use an argument that probably had been sitting as a note in his desk drawer for some time. He invoked Democratic president Andrew Jackson in order to make his case against his Democratic critics. Lincoln grew into political manhood in steadfast opposition to Jackson. He may have chuckled as he brought into his letter an episode that followed Jackson's victory over the British at New Orleans in 1815. Lincoln recounted how, after the battle was over, the hero of New Orleans "maintained martial, or military law" by making a number of crucial arrests.

Lincoln understood that his critics were foisting upon the public the notion that the president was changing the understanding of the Constitution and the rule of law in American society. He was at pains to disabuse them of the notion that "throughout the indefinite peaceful future" the American people will lose the basic freedoms enumerated in the Bill of Rights. Lincoln would not admit this danger because he was not able to believe "that a man could contract so strong an appetite for emetics during temporary illness, as to persist in feeding upon them through the remainder of his healthful life." Where were the government printer, John D. Defrees, and the *National Intelligencer* literary editor, James C. Welling, who both had tried to talk Lincoln out of indelicate language in previous communications? One of the marks of Lincoln's communication skills was his ability to combine in the same speech or public letter various styles of language and analogies that helped him appeal to a wide audience.

Lincoln wrote his letter to Corning at a time of rapidly diminishing confidence in himself and his administration. He knew he needed to calm the fears of the nation. Even though he thought the letter to be one of his best efforts, he must have been surprised by the responses to it. John W. Forney, editor of the *Washington Chronicle*, wrote, "God be praised the right word has at last been spoken by the right man, at the right time, and from the right place. It will thrill the whole land." It was "timely, wise, one of your best State Papers," was the response of New York senator Edwin D. Morgan. Roscoe Conkling, born in Albany, one of the founders of the Republican Party in New York who had been defeated for reelection to Congress in the fall of 1862, wrote to thank Lincoln for a letter that "covered all essential ground in few words, and in a temper as felicitous and timely, as could be." Secretaries Nicolay and Hay recalled, "There are few of the President's state papers which produced a stronger impression upon the public mind."

Wanting this letter to be read by as wide an audience as possible, Lincoln had John Nicolay send it to leading Republicans. Francis Lieber, law professor at Columbia, and president of the recently formed Loyal Publication Society of New York, wrote Lincoln telling him that he was planning to print an initial installment of ten thousand copies. "The Publication Society will do it with great pleasure." At least five hundred thousand copies of the public letter to Corning were read by upward of ten million people. The letter served to damp down, for the moment, the pervasive despair and fear across the North. Most important, it lifted Lincoln's standing among members of his own Republican Party. Comfortable with pen and ink, and perhaps surprised by the results of the letter, Lincoln learned an important lesson about public communication that he would apply again and again in the coming months.

The letter did not, however, put an end to dissent. On June 25, 1863, Lincoln received a delegation from Ohio who came to protest the treatment of Vallandigham. They were coming fresh from a June 11 state Democratic convention where they had nominated Vallandigham, in absentia, for governor. David Tod, the present Republican governor of Ohio, had written Lincoln on June 14, "Allow me to express the hope that you will treat the Vallandigham Committee about to call on you with the contempt they richly merit." Tod did not know Lincoln.

The lobbying group arrived with the advantage of having read the Corning letter. They were more strident in their criticisms of Lincoln than their New York co-belligerents. Cabinet secretaries Chase and Stanton, both Ohioans, having witnessed the positive reactions to Lincoln's public letter to Corning, advised the president not to reply to the committee in person, but to tell them he would write a public letter.

Lincoln, buoyed up by the response to the Corning letter, was much more forceful in his letter to Matthew Birchard and the Ohio delegation. He challenged their misrepresentations of his previous comments on the subject. He disputed their "phraseology calculated to represent me as struggling for an arbitrary personal prerogative." As for Vallandigham, Lincoln went further than he had in the Corning letter, charging that the acts against the military were "due to him personally, in a greater degree than to any other one man." In his conclusion, Lincoln offered to return Vallandigham to Ohio, provided each member of the delegation would sign a pledge "to do all he can to have the officers, soldiers, and seamen of the army and navy, while engaged in the effort to suppress the rebellion, paid, fed, clad, and otherwise well provided and supported."

The delegation would not accept this responsibility. They replied on July 1, 1863, that to do so would be at the "sacrifice of their dignity and self-respect." They offered a defensive response to a president who was now on the offensive. In this second public letter, Lincoln again forcefully enunciated his principles, which began to win the day with Unionists across the North.

IN MAY 1863, Lincoln studied the framed and rolled-up maps in his office. In the East, Joseph Hooker had been beaten at Chancellorsville. In the West, Grant was stalled, and Lincoln did not know where, near Vicksburg. The president knew that Lee's next high-stakes gamble was yet to be revealed.

By the middle of 1863, Lincoln had settled into a pattern of leadership both as commander in chief and, in effect, general in chief. Halleck may have held that title, but Lincoln had decided to ride both horses with a tight rein. As irritated as Lincoln may have been with "Old Brains's" passivity, Halleck's inaction created space for Lincoln's action.

During the next two months, two decisive battles would be fought in the war's eastern and western theaters. In Washington, the gaunt man in the White House often worked eighteen hours a day, walking back and forth to the War Department several times daily.

Lincoln typically downplayed his contribution. He closed a letter to Hooker by recalling the story of Jesus's commendation of the widow who willingly gave out of her poverty an ancient coin called a mite, saying that he, although less qualified than his generals, would continue to contribute "his poor mite."

At each crucial moment of the war, Lincoln sought face-to-face communication with his key generals. On May 6, 1863, within only one hour of learning of the retreat of the Army of the Potomac back across the Rappahannock, Lincoln traveled to Hooker's headquarters at Falmouth. To the surprise of Hooker and his senior officers, Lincoln did not come to question or to criticize. He was sympathetic to the fact that Hooker had been injured and perhaps not able to be in full command of his troops. He was distressed to hear Hooker's criticisms of his key officers—Stoneman, Leftwich, Reynolds—blaming them for missteps in his battle plan. During Lincoln's visit, and in subsequent meetings and letters, he learned that many of the senior officers blamed Hooker for the defeat. "I have some painful intimations that some of your corps and division commanders are not giving you their entire confidence. This would be ruinous, if true." Lincoln was doing his own reconnaissance.

Lincoln always followed up a personal conversation with a letter that usually combined both commendation and questions. On May 7, 1863, the president expressed his confidence in Hooker but encouraged him to plan to move forward. "Have you already in your mind a plan wholly or partially formed?" Lincoln let Hooker know he wanted to stay involved, but he expressed his wish in a winsome self-deprecation. "If you have, prossecute it without interference from me. If you have not, please inform me, so that I, incompetent as I may be, can try [to] assist in the formation of some plan for the Army."

LINCOLN WAS RESTLESS to hear any news about Grant and Vicksburg. Having heard nothing at the telegraph office, and with no news from war correspondents in the Northern newspapers, on May 11, 1863, he telegraphed General John A. Dix at Fortress Monroe, Virginia, "Do the Richmond papers have anything about Grand Gulf or Vicksburg?"

On May 19, 1863, unbeknownst to Lincoln, Grant attacked Confederate general John Pemberton's garrison at Vicksburg. At 2 p.m. Pemberton ordered three volleys fired from each piece of artillery high atop the bluffs. Union forces advanced but, met by an overwhelming barrage of cannon and bullets, fell back.

Three days later, on May 22, 1863, Grant's men mounted a second attack, applying the force of two hundred pieces of artillery plus one hundred guns from Admiral Porter's ironclads, only to be repulsed again. The Union forces sustained almost four thousand casualties in these two days of fighting. Grant, though stymied, knew he was not to be stopped. He prepared to lay siege to Vicksburg. Grant wrote Halleck on May 24, "The fall of Vicksburg, and the capture of most of the garrison, can only be a question of time."

Meanwhile, time was passing slowly for Lincoln in Washington. More oppressive than the onset of warm, humid weather was the sense of despair about Union armies east and west. Finally, word of Grant's advance on Vicksburg began filtering into the capital. Lincoln, who was learning not to make predictions, could not contain his jubilation upon hearing the news that Grant was now investing the Southern Gibraltar. On May 26, 1863, the president replied to a letter from Chicago congressman Isaac Arnold, "Whether Gen. Grant shall or shall not consummate the capture of Vicksburg, his campaign from the beginning of this month to the twenty second day of it, is one of the most brilliant in the world." Lincoln, despite his many misgivings about Grant's strategy, was eager to salute him for his efforts.

WHILE JOSEPH HOOKER STRUGGLED with his own plan, Robert E. Lee was sure of his next move. He determined that he could not remain below the Rappahannock River in Virginia and wait for the Army of the Potomac to attack him yet a third time. Lee regularly scanned Northern newspapers. Heartened by victories at Fredericksburg and Chancellorsville, he became convinced that the way forward against a larger and better-equipped foe was to move north again in another daring military move that might convince the North that they could not win. Lee had come to believe that the more the Confederacy was successful on the battlefield, the greater the chance for anti-Lincoln forces to be successful at the ballot box in the elections of 1863 and 1864. On April 19, 1863, Lee wrote his wife, Mary Anna, "I do not think our enemies are so confident of success as they used to be. . . . If successful this year, next fall there will be a great change in public opinion at the North. The Republicans will be destroyed & I think the friends of peace will become so strong that the next administration will go in on that basis." Lee, always realistic about the odds his smaller armies faced, believed the road to a third morale-crushing victory lay in another invasion of the North.

However, the whole South had heard the story of their greatest loss at Chancellorsville. On the evening of May 2, 1863, just before 9:30 p.m., Stonewall Jackson, with a few of his officers, rode beyond Confederate lines to try to gain information about Union positions. As he and his party rode back toward their lines, in the darkness they were mistaken for Union cavalry and fired upon. Three bullets struck Jackson. Initially there was hope that he would recover, but he died on Sunday, May 10. His death took away Lee's right-hand man and severely tested the South's belief that God was on their side.

Three days later, Lincoln read in the *Washington Chronicle* an appreciative editorial on Jackson. That same day, Lincoln wrote editor John W. Forney, "I wish to lose no time in thanking you for the excellent and manly article in the Chronicle on 'Stonewall Jackson.'" Lincoln's respect for a Christian gentleman and soldier knew no borders.

Lee began his next march north on June 3, 1863. For several days, the Northern intelligence service, the Bureau of Military Information, struggled to discern his intentions. What was his objective? Baltimore? Philadelphia? Harrisburg? Anxious crowds gathered at the Willard Hotel hoping for some credible information.

On the morning of June 5, 1863, Hooker sent a telegram to Lincoln proposing a response. As Lee moved north, Hooker wanted "to pitch into his rear." Lincoln, seeing more clearly than Hooker, believed Lee was "tempting" Hooker and saw this offensive as an opening. After first stating his objection in military language, Lincoln employed a colorful analogy to make his point. "I would not take any risk of being entangled upon the river, like an ox jumped half over a fence, and liable to be torn by dogs, front and rear, without a fair chance to gore one way or kick the other."

Hooker, not convinced that Lee intended to take his whole army on a raid into Maryland or Pennsylvania, presented a plan to Lincoln and Halleck on June 10, 1863. He believed he could strike a mortal blow by crossing the Rappahannock at Fredericksburg and marching directly to Richmond, which he believed was defended by only 1,500 men.

Lincoln replied within ninety minutes. "I would not go South of the Rappahannock upon Lee's moving North of It." Furthermore, "If you had Richmond invested to-day, you would not be able to take it in twenty days; meanwhile, your communications, and with them, your army, would be ruined." The president told Hooker what he had told McClellan and Burnside. "I think *Lee's* Army, and not *Richmond,* is your true objective point." He then offered military advice. "If he comes towards the Upper Potomac, follow on his flank, and on the inside track, shortening your lines, while he lengthens his. Fight him when opportunity affords. If he stays where he is, fret him, and fret him." With his growing sense of military strategy, Lincoln was out-generaling one of his leading generals.

As Lee's divisions moved north down the Shenandoah Valley, Jeb Stuart's cavalry guarded the passes and gaps of the Blue Ridge to screen these movements from federal eyes. Hooker had been instructed by Lincoln and Halleck to keep the bulk of his army between Lee and Washington in order to protect the capital from any sudden Confederate incursion. Lee skillfully had his division commanders move their troops at different times and in different directions.

Lincoln, listening to the chatter at the telegraph office, understood that Lee's line of march must be strung out over many miles. Accordingly, on June 14, 1863, he wrote to Hooker, "If the head of Lee's army is at Martinsburg and the tail of it on the Plank road between Fredericksburg and Chancellorsville, the animal must be very slim somewhere. Could you not break him?"

That same Sunday, Gideon Welles wrote in his diary, "Scary rumors abroad of army operations and a threatened movement of Lee upon Pennsylvania." In the evening, Welles found Lincoln and Halleck at the War Department. The president told Welles "he was feeling very bad." Welles volunteered that if Lee was moving, this could be an opportunity for Hooker to "take advantage and sever his forces." Lincoln agreed, replying that "our folks . . . showed no evidence that they ever availed themselves of any advantage."

The next day, June 15, 1863, Lincoln learned that the Union garrison at Winchester, Virginia, had fallen to Confederate general Richard Ewell's troops. He also received reports that the advance units of Lee's army were beginning to cross the Potomac into Maryland and Pennsylvania.

Growing more upset with Hooker, on June 16, 1863, Lincoln told him that his strategy "looks like defensive merely, and seems to abandon the fair chance now presented of breaking the enemy's long and necessarily thin line." In Lincoln's third communication of the day to Hooker, the president, exasperated, placed Hooker under Halleck's direct command.

This break was the beginning of the end for Hooker. Lincoln made a mistake at the outset in allowing him to go around Halleck and report directly to the president. In the next ten days, Hooker quarreled with Halleck, especially over Hooker's request to have the troops guarding Harpers Ferry transferred to his command. The break was painful. On June 26, 1863, Welles confided in his diary that "the President in a single remark to-day betrayed doubts about Hooker, to whom he is quite partial."

The next evening, Lincoln, Stanton, and Halleck, agreeing that Hooker was no longer the man to face Lee, selected General George Gordon Meade to replace him. A native of Pennsylvania, Meade "would fight well on his own dunghill," Lincoln remarked. The next day, June 28, 1863, Lincoln pulled from his pocket a resignation letter from Hooker that he had accepted and told his cabinet he had "observed in Hooker the same failings that were witnessed in McClellan after the battle of Antietam—a want of alacrity to obey, and a greedy call for more troops which could not, and ought not to be taken from other points." He announced that the new commander would be Meade.

Even before informing the cabinet, Stanton and Lincoln had dispatched Colonel James A. Hardie to Pennsylvania with orders for Meade. Clad in civilian clothes, Hardie persuaded Meade's staff members to let him enter the general's tent at three o'clock in the morning. Waking Meade, Hardie's first words to him were that he had come from the War Department to bring him trouble. Startled out of his sleep, hearing this ill-timed humor, Meade later wrote his wife that his first thought was that Hooker had sent this man to arrest him.

George Meade was born in 1815 in Cadiz, Spain, where his father was an agent for the navy. Young George, tall and slender, graduated from West Point in 1835. At the outbreak of the Civil War, he was appointed brigadier general of the Pennsylvania Reserves. He fought under McClellan on the Virginia peninsula campaign in 1862 and was seriously wounded at Glendale when a musket ball hit him above his hip and just missed his spine. An additional bullet struck his arm, but Meade had stayed on his horse and persisted in commanding his troops until his loss of blood forced him to retire from the field.

After recuperating in a Philadelphia hospital, Meade led his Pennsyl-

Lincoln appointed George Meade to succeed Joseph Hooker as commander of the Army of the Potomac at the end of June 1863.

vania troops at South Mountain and Antietam. As a corps commander at Chancellorsville, he was dismayed by Hooker's defensive tactics, but he led his own troops with great skill. In the aftermath of the battle, when Hooker's leading generals believed their leader had lost his nerve in battle, the talk in the officers' tents was that they wanted Meade to replace Hooker as commander of the Army of the Potomac, but he had refused to be part of any uprising.

Lincoln dealt differently with this new commander. Perhaps learning a lesson after trying to offer fatherly advice to Burnside and Hooker, he let his intentions be communicated through Halleck. Meade, at age forty-seven, was in no danger of being mistaken for a prima donna. Competent, if colorless, he gained the nickname "the Old Snapping Turtle" because he was short-tempered, especially with civilians and newspapermen. Unlike Hooker at Chancellorsville, Meade always led from the front.

AS ROBERT E. LEE invaded Pennsylvania, Lincoln stepped up his monitoring of the telegraph traffic. But he did not simply receive information; he constantly asked for updates. On June 24, 1863, he wired

General Darius N. Couch, in command of the Department of the Susquehanna, "Have you any reports of the enemy moving into Pennsylvania?" On the day that Meade assumed command, he asked Couch, "What news now? What are the enemy firing at four miles from your works?"

Although Lincoln's steady stream of telegrams might sound like he was pushing a panic button along with everyone else in Washington, his true beliefs were revealed in an exchange of letters with Governor Joel Parker of New Jersey. Parker wrote on June 29, 1863, "The people of New Jersey are apprehensive." The governor insisted on telling the president what to do. McClellan should be reinstated as commander of the Army of the Potomac and "the enemy should be driven from Pennsylvania." Lincoln responded on the day before the commencement of the battle at Gettysburg with the exact opposite opinion. "I really think the attitude of the enemies' army in Pennsylvania, presents us the best opportunity we have had since the war began." Lincoln, almost alone, saw Lee's invasion not as a dire tragedy, but as an opportunity. The president was also fully aware that he was placing Meade in command of a recently twice-beaten army whose morale, from fighting for so long in Virginia, was fragile. His basic concern was that Meade's Army of the Potomac needed to fulfill two functions at once: protect Washington and Baltimore and strike at Lee and the Army of Northern Virginia as they entered Pennsylvania.

THE STRIKE CAME SOONER than Meade or Lee or even Lincoln expected. On the morning of June 30, 1863, John Buford, one of the best intelligence men in the Union army, rode into Gettysburg, a market town and county seat of 2,400 residents 75 miles north of Washington, 115 miles west of Philadelphia, and only 8 miles across the Maryland border. Brigadier General Buford rode at the head of 2,950 men in two divisions of the Eighth Illinois Cavalry. At 12:20 p.m. he wrote General Alfred Pleasanton, "I entered this place to-day at 11 a.m. Found everybody in a terrible state of excitement on account of the enemy's advance upon this place." Buford, carefully reconnoitering the countryside, deployed his horse soldiers in ever-wider arcs of defensive pickets seven miles long around the town.

On the morning of July 1, 1863, with a "blood red sunrise" in the east, A. P. Hill, one of Lee's senior commanders, sent one of his divisions led by Major General Henry Heth down the Chambersburg Pike toward Gettysburg, where information said there was a supply of shoes. As his men approached this hub town, where twelve roads converged, the two armies simultaneously spied each other. At 7:30 a.m., Lieutenant Marcellus E. Jones of the Eighth Illinois Cavalry borrowed his sergeant's carbine, steadied it on a fence rail, and fired the first shot of what would become the largest battle ever fought in the Western Hemisphere.

Both sides had stumbled into what the military textbooks called a "meeting engagement." Neither side was prepared to fight at this place at this time; the approaching battle was "unintended"; neither side held an obvious advantage. General Meade, on only the fourth day of his command, would discover that 165,000 soldiers would soon converge on a town of 2,400.

The engagement, like a spontaneous three-act play, grew as more and more actors converged on Gettysburg. Meade, perched on "Old Baldy," his hat pulled low over his face, was by nature a cautious general, and once engaged, fought mostly from a defensive posture. Lee, who had invaded the North to pull the Union troops away from Washington and to relieve the pressure upon Virginia, wanted to fight in Pennsylvania at a time and a place of his own choosing. He did not choose Gettysburg.

Seventy-five miles away, Washington watched and waited. Lincoln now believed a battle was looming. He did not attend the regularly scheduled cabinet meeting on June 30, 1863, but camped out at the War Department with Stanton and Halleck.

Early on the morning of July 2, 1863, Lincoln read the incoming dispatches from General Meade. The Confederate attacks were uncoordinated and disjointed, whereas the Union leaders acted with initiative and self-assurance. Yet there was no clear outcome of the battles on this second day of fighting.

With Lincoln busy at the War Department, word came that Mary Lincoln, while being driven in her carriage from the Soldiers' Home to the White House, had been involved in an accident. The driver's seat became detached from the carriage, frightening the horses; Mary was tossed from the coach and hit her head on a rock. Although injured, Mary would make a full recovery.

On the morning of July 3, 1863, as preparations in Washington for the Independence Day celebration were in full swing, the battle at Gettysburg turned. Lee, against the counsel of his most trusted generals,

decided to attack the center of the Union line. The plan was to over-
whelm the Union artillery with Confederate cannon followed by a
charge of 13,000 soldiers—ever after known as "Pickett's charge." The
advance led to a crushing defeat, with approximately 6,600 Confederate
casualties and half again that number taken prisoner. Meade, with the
advantage shifted to his side, did not counterattack. An evening rain
helped end three of the most deadly days in the war.

*On July 3, 1863, at Gettysburg, Mathew Brady photographed the dead
of the First Minnesota near the Peach Orchard.*

On July 4, 1863, Meade's headquarters issued a congratulatory declaration to the army. He did not write it but must have approved it.
"Our task is not yet accomplished, and the commanding general looks
to the army for greater efforts to drive from our soil every vestige of the
presence of the invader." Lincoln surely winced when he read Meade's
declaration. Once again, a Union commander revealed that he did not
understand that his task was to destroy the army, not drive it from
Union soil, where it could only restore itself once again.

—

BY THE END OF MAY 1863, Lincoln believed that the fall of Vicksburg was just a matter of time. Grant, having suffered more than 3,000 casualties in his initial assaults, and with an overwhelming advantage in manpower, decided to settle into a siege. Confederate general John Pemberton pleaded for relief, but with Sherman guarding the Union rear with six divisions, no relief would be forthcoming.

As the days turned into weeks, Grant's 80,000 men, with limitless ammunition, slowly squeezed the 30,000 defenders of Vicksburg into submission. Finally, on July 3, Pemberton, who had served in the same division with Grant in the Mexican War, sent his aide-de-camp to discuss terms of surrender with Grant. Lincoln's leading general offered his standard reply: unconditional surrender.

After a siege of forty-seven days, as the Confederate soldiers stacked their rifles in defeat, there was no cheering but silent respect by the victors. The unconditional Grant, out of respect for the bravery of the defenders, granted the condition to the defenders not of a Union prison but of parole. On July 4, at 10 a.m., twelve hundred miles from Gettysburg, the Stars and Stripes was raised over Vicksburg.

FOR THREE DAYS, Washington had waited as incomplete reports trickled in about the battle at Gettysburg. Finally, at 10 p.m. on July 3, the *Washington Star* issued a bulletin of Meade's victory. The next day, the Fourth of July, amid firecrackers and rockets, the U.S. Marine Band played "The Star-Spangled Banner" over and over again. At 10 a.m., the president issued an announcement. He wished the nation to know that the victory at Gettysburg "is such to cover that Army with the highest honor, and to promise a success to the cause of the Union." The announcement concluded, "He especially desires that on this day, He whose will, not ours, should ever be done, be everywhere remembered and reverenced with profoundest gratitude."

On July 7, Secretary Welles received word from Admiral Porter that Vicksburg had fallen on July 4, 1863. The celebration started up again. At 8 p.m. on July 7, 1863, a huge throng assembled at the National Hotel and marched up Pennsylvania Avenue to the Executive Mansion. Reaching the White House, the crowd serenaded the president until Lincoln appeared at a window and offered an impromptu response. After thanking both the assemblage and "Almighty God," Lincoln asked a question. "How long ago is it?—eighty odd years—since on the Fourth of July for the first time in the history of the world a nation by its representatives, assembled and declared as a self-evident truth that 'all men are created equal?' " The sentence was too long and complex, but he would tuck the idea away for later use.

UNBEKNOWNST TO THE PUBLIC that festive evening, but known to members of his cabinet who had met earlier that day, Lincoln was deeply disturbed that Meade, flushed with victory and attending to housekeeping duties of his battered troops, had failed to go after Lee. The rains that fell on Gettysburg on the evening of July 3, 1863, kept falling, so Lee was stuck in Pennsylvania, unable to ford the raging Potomac River. Meade's infantry skirmished with some of Lee's rearguard troops on July 11, 12, and 13, more than a week after the victory celebrations in Washington. Finally, on the morning of July 14, at 6 a.m., the Union forces mounted their long-awaited offensive. But when they approached the river, there was no one to fight. The last of Lee's troops had crossed over during the night.

That day, Halleck wrote Meade, "The enemy should be pursued and cut up, wherever he may have gone." He went on to say, "I need hardly say to you that the escape of Lee's army without another battle has created great dissatisfaction in the mind of the President."

Meade could not bear this censure and immediately offered to resign his command. Lincoln took up his pen to reply that very day, although his letter may have taken several days to compose. After thanking Meade for what he did at Gettysburg and recapitulating the strength of Meade's forces and the weakness of Lee's forces, he concluded:

I do not believe you appreciate the magnitude of the misfortune involved in Lee's escape—He was within your easy grasp, and to have closed upon him would, in connection with our other late successes, have ended the war—As it is, the war will be prolonged indefinitely. If you could not safely attack Lee last Monday, how can you possibly do so South of the river, when you can take with you very few more than two thirds of the force you then had in hand? It would be unreasonable to expect, and I do not expect you can now effect much. Your golden opportunity is gone, and I am distressed immeasurably because of it.

This was a strong letter from the commander in chief to the commander of the Army of the Potomac. Too strong. Lincoln never sent it, understanding that if he sent it he would lose the services of a hard-working commander. Lincoln folded the letter and placed it in an envelope, on which he wrote, "To Gen. Meade, never sent, or signed."

Lincoln recognized, even if many did not, that the victory at Vicksburg was at least equal to the accomplishment at Gettysburg.

One day before writing Meade, Lincoln took up his pen to write a very different letter to Grant. On July 13, 1863, he began, "I do not remember that you and I ever met personally." After acknowledging "the almost inestimable service you have done the country," Lincoln said he wished "to say a word further."

> When you first reached the vicinity of Vicksburg, I thought you should do what you finally did—march the troops across the neck, run the batteries with the transports and thus go below; and I never had any faith, except a general hope that you knew better than I, that the Yazoo-Pass expedition, and the like could succeed. When you got below, and took Port Gibson, Grand Gulf and vicinity, I thought you should go down the river and join Gen. Banks; and when you turned Northward, East of the Big Black, I feared it was a mistake.

Lincoln, after this detailed recitation of his disagreements with Grant's strategy, concluded: "I now wish to make the personal acknowledgement that you were right and I was wrong."

In two days, Lincoln wrote two completely different letters to the commanders who had won victories at Gettysburg and Vicksburg. The letters reflected his quite different views of the two generals. Meade had fought well in a defensive posture in a battle he had not sought, but had failed to follow up that victory. Grant had continuously sought the initiative and, in the face of many setbacks, against massive fortifications, determined to achieve nothing but unconditional surrender of the enemy.

The Union victories at Gettysburg and Vicksburg marked a turning point in the war, but Lincoln understood that the South was far from defeated and that there would be much hard fighting ahead. Lincoln, confronting a North tiring of war, had much to do to convince them that the fight to preserve the Union was worth the sacrifice.

—

IN AN AUGUST 9, 1863, letter to Ulysses S. Grant, Lincoln brought up the possibility of the arming of black troops. He noted that General Lorenzo Thomas was recruiting black troops. "I believe it is a resource which if vigourously applied now, will soon close the contest."

Yet, Frederick Douglass was discouraged. He had discovered the Union army was treating black soldiers poorly and not providing equal pay. Draft riots had erupted in New York City in early July. The mostly black victims were beaten to death while their homes and churches were burned. Lincoln had to deploy federal troops to restore order. Major George Luther Stearns, a wealthy Boston abolitionist, had appointed Douglass as an agent for recruitment and now encouraged him to present his concerns to Lincoln.

On August 10, 1863, Douglass arrived at the White House in hopes of seeing Lincoln, but when he entered, he saw a large number of people waiting with the same intent. To his surprise, within minutes, a door opened and Douglass was ushered into Lincoln's office. The president stood to welcome him. Douglass pressed upon Lincoln the need for more official recognition of black troops. They spoke about the troublesome issue of unequal pay for blacks.

Douglass was taken aback by the tone and substance of their conversation. Later, in Philadelphia, he spoke about his meeting with Lincoln. "I never met with a man, who, on the first blush, impressed me more entirely with his sincerity, with his devotion to his country, and with his determination to save it at all hazards."

On August 23, 1863, Grant replied to Lincoln, "I have given the subject of arming the negro my hearty support. This, with the emancipation of the negro, is the heaviest blow yet given the Confederacy." The exchange with Grant and the meeting with Douglass prompted the president to seek out a public opportunity to defend both emancipation and the courage of the black soldiers.

So when he was invited to speak at a "Grand Mass Meeting" in Springfield, Illinois, on September 3, 1863, his heart must surely have leapt.

Lincoln's old Springfield neighbor James C. Conkling had tendered the invitation. He wrote, "It would be gratifying to the many thousands who will be present on that occasion if you will also meet with them." He concluded with a plea, "Can you not give us a favorable reply?"

Conkling made Lincoln a tempting offer. After victories at Gettys-

Frederick Douglass, abolitionist editor and reformer, strongly disapproved of Lincoln's First Inaugural Address. Douglass's meeting with Lincoln at the White House in August 1863 began a series of significant conversations between the two leaders.

burg and Vicksburg, Conkling believed the Springfield meeting offered Lincoln the opportunity to speak about his policies at a crucial moment. Lincoln could expect that vindication would be his traveling companion on the train trip home to Springfield.

Six days later Lincoln replied: "Your letter of the 14th is received. I think I will go, or send a letter—probably the latter."

Lincoln's secretaries, John Nicolay and John Hay, both from Illinois, appreciated the emotional tug-of-war they observed in their boss. "For a moment the President cherished the hope of going to Springfield, and once more in his life renewing the sensation, so dear to politicians, of personal contact with great and enthusiastic masses, and of making one more speech to shouting thousands of his fellow-citizens."

Conkling wrote again on August 21, 1863. "While it would afford the many thousands of loyal men assembled together on that occasion, great pleasure to hear from you, by Letter . . . they would infinitely prefer to see you in person."

With little time before the event, Lincoln had to make a decision. On

August 26, 1863, he gave his answer. "It would be very agreeable to me, to thus meet my old friends, at my own home; but I can not, just now, be absent from here, so long as a visit there, would require."

The next day, Lincoln wrote on War Department stationery, "I cannot leave here now. Herewith is a letter instead. I have but one suggestion—read it very slowly."

William O. Stoddard witnessed the composition of the letter. As a young newspaper editor from Champaign, Illinois, he was one of the first to champion Lincoln for the Republican nomination in 1859. He now served as an additional secretary, assisting Nicolay and Hay, from 1861 to 1864. Stoddard entered Lincoln's office on or about August 23, 1863, and the president asked him if he could read what he was writing aloud, saying, "I can always tell more about a thing after I've heard it read aloud, and know how it sounds."

The September 3, 1863, meeting was in part a response to a large "peace meeting" that had been held in Springfield on June 17. On a warm summer's day, a Democratic antiadministration crowd of upward of forty thousand had listened to heated oratory critical of Lincoln, the Emancipation Proclamation, and the arming of black troops. The culmination of the day's events was the adoption of twenty-four resolutions, highlighted by what became known as the famous twenty-third resolution, declaring, "Further offensive prosecution of this war tends to subvert the constitution and the government, and entail upon this Nation all the disastrous consequences of misrule and anarchy." In Lincoln's hometown, the boisterous assemblage churned out anti-Lincoln sentiment as it called for peace.

Expecting a huge crowd for the September meeting, organizers arranged for speeches to take place into the twilight at a half dozen stands. Conkling drew out Lincoln's letter and started to read—slowly.

Lincoln did not usually respond to critics, especially Peace Democrats or Copperheads, but he began this speech by addressing them as well as his supporters, not simply at Springfield but in the nation. "There are those who are dissatisfied with me. To such I would say: You desire peace; and you blame me that we do not have it."

The victories at Gettysburg and Vicksburg, hailed by most Republicans, were understood quite differently by Peace Democrats, War Democrats, and some conservative Republicans. They greeted these victories as an opportunity to bargain for peace and end the war.

2

There are those who are dissatisfied with me. To such I would say: You desire peace; and you blame me that we do not have it. But how can we attain it? There are but three conceivable ways. First, to suppress the rebellion by force of arms. This I am trying to do. Are you for it? If you are, so far we are agreed. If you are not for it, a second way is to give up the Union. I am against this. Are you for it? If you are, you should say so plainly. If you are not for *force*, nor yet for *dissolution*, there only remains some imaginable *compromise*. I do not believe any compromise, embracing the maintenance of the union, is now possible. All I learn leads to a directly opposite belief. The strength of the rebellion, is its military—its army. That army dominates all the country, and all the people, within its range. Any offer of terms made by any man or men within that range, in opposition to that army, is simply nothing for the present; because such man or men, have no power whatever to enforce their side of a compromise, if one were made with them. To illustrate. Suppose refugees from the South, and peace men of the North, get together in convention, and frame and proclaim a compromise embracing a restoration of the Union; in what way can that compromise be used to keep Lee's army out of Pennsylvania? Meade's army can keep Lee's army out of Pennsylvania; and, I think, can ultimately drive

Lincoln, invited to speak in Springfield on September 3, 1863, sent a letter
read by his friend James Conkling to the largest Union rally of the war.

But, to be plain, you are dissatisfied with me about the negro. Quite likely there is a difference of opinion between you and myself upon that subject. I certainly wish that all men could be free, while I suppose you do not. . . . You dislike the emancipation proclamation; and, perhaps, would have it retracted. You say it is unconstitutional—I think differently, I think the Constitution invests its commander-in-chief, with the law of war, in time of war.

Lincoln recognized that their conflict with him was over African-Americans and slavery. He knew that there were few abolitionists in the West. Most who united with the Republican Party in the 1850s shared his rejection of the expansion of slavery, but were not committed to its obliteration.

Lincoln used here almost the same words with which he had ended his public letter to Horace Greeley: "I certainly wish that all men could be free." In his response to Greeley, written one year before, he had made a distinction between his personal wish and his duty under the Constitution. A year later, this division between personal and public views was no longer present.

> You say you will not fight to free negroes. Some of them seem willing to fight for you; but, no matter. Fight you, then, exclusively to save the Union. I issued the [Emancipation] proclamation on purpose to aid you in saving the Union. Whenever you shall have conquered all resistance to the Union, if I shall urge you to continue fighting, it will be an apt time, then, for you to declare you will not fight to free Negroes.

Lincoln had concluded his letter to Greeley by stating, "I shall adopt new views so fast as they appear to be true views." His affirmation of black soldiers here demonstrates how far he had traveled in the eight months since January 1, 1863.

These fiery words gave the Springfield letter its identity, but nowhere is Lincoln's political and military strategy expressed in more picturesque language. Instead of detailing a list of military battles and victories, Lincoln invited his audience to stand with him on the mighty Mississippi. For Western people whose lives radiated around rivers, Lincoln could not have chosen a more open metaphor. He wanted this Illinois audience to appreciate all the partners in making the Mississippi free again.

> The signs look better. The Father of Waters again goes unvexed to the sea. Thanks to the great North-West for it. Not yet wholly to them. Three hundred miles up, they met New-England, Empire, Keystone, and Jersey, hewing their way right and left.

The Sunny South too, in more colors than one, also lent a hand.
On the spot, their part of the history was jotted down in black
and white.

Lincoln's rhetoric soared when he allowed his imagination free rein. A
sign signifies something that points beyond itself. What did these signs
point toward? The preservation of the Union. If Lincoln told Greeley
he would save the Union, he told Conkling what kind of Union was
worth saving.

Lincoln used images to describe these allies working together. He
also doffed his tall stovepipe hat to the "Sunny South." Up until now,
the images had all been geographical, one kind of diversity. Lincoln
now changed the metaphors of diversity in his word picture: "in more
colors than one." He said to the naysayers and doubters in the audience
that even the South has "lent a hand" and that this part was acted out by
both "black and white."

Douglass had once accused Lincoln of fighting with his white hand
while his black hand was tied behind his back. Lincoln now used the
same metaphor to affirm the black hand and point to the courageous
actions of black soldiers. The great majority of black soldiers who
would fight for the Union were from the South.

In a grand transitional sentence, Lincoln moved from images of space
to images of time.

Peace does not appear so distant as it did. I hope it will come
soon, and come to stay; and so come as to be worth the keeping in
all future time. It will then have been proved that, among free
men, there can be no successful appeal from the ballot to the bullet; and that they who take such appeal are sure to lose their case,
and pay the cost.

Lincoln allowed himself to think in the future tense about the shape of
peace. He expressed his sense of hope by repeating the image of "come"
three times: "come soon," "come to stay"; "come as to be worth keeping in all future time."

This balanced sentence created in the listener a crescendo of expectation toward the future.

Finally, Lincoln presented a contrast between the courage of black
soldiers and the malevolence of some whites. Lincoln had previously

commended the use of black soldiers in private letters, and he now did so, dramatically, in a public letter and speech.

> And then, there will be some black men who can remember that, with silent tongue, and clenched teeth, and steady eye, and well-poised bayonet, they have helped mankind on to this great consummation; while, I fear, there will be some white ones, unable to forget that, with malignant heart, and deceitful speech, they have strove to hinder it.

His words were powerful because he did not rely on analysis but on description. The "black men" that Lincoln extols are portrayed "with silent tongue, and clenched teeth," "and well-poised bayonet." Whereas the white men are pictured "with malignant heart," "and deceitful speech."

Lincoln worked with contrasts to heighten his message. The black men are "silent" whereas the "white ones" are noisy with "deceitful speech." The black soldiers, who had won Lincoln's admiration, he praised because "they have helped mankind on to this great consummation"; whereas some white men "have strove to hinder it."

Lincoln did not just praise the courage of blacks; he did so in contrast to the reticence of whites.

Because Conkling read Lincoln's words, it would seem we cannot know how Lincoln would have spoken these words to a real audience. But we can, through Stoddard's recollections of Lincoln reading the letter aloud in his office.

Stoddard described the metamorphosis in Lincoln when he was roused from writer to speaker. "He is more an orator than a writer, and he is quickly warmed up to the place where his voice rises and his long right arm goes out, and he speaks to you somewhat as if you were a hundred thousand people of an audience, and as if he believes that fifty thousand of you do not at all agree with him. He will convince the half of you, if he can, before he has done with it."

Stoddard "noted the singular emphasis which he put upon the words: 'And there will be some black men who can remember with silent tongue, and clenched teeth, and steady eye, and well poised bayonet, they have helped mankind on to this great consummation.' "

He was a witness to the weight that Lincoln gave to these words— even if he was speaking to an audience of one.

The mass meeting in Springfield was a huge success. Conkling wrote to Lincoln on September 4, 1863, "The Letter was received by the Convention with the greatest enthusiasm."

In the following days a wide circle of people commended the letter. Greeley, one year later, appreciated that Lincoln had used a rally to defend the Emancipation Proclamation. " 'God Bless Abraham Lincoln!' The Promise must be kept!"

Abolitionists offered enthusiastic praise not accorded earlier Lincoln speeches. Senator Charles Sumner wrote from Boston, "Thanks for your true and noble letter. It is an historical document." Sumner's Massachusetts colleague, Senator Henry Wilson, wrote, "God Almighty bless you for your noble, patriotic, and Christian letter." Wilson understood the public letter's importance in the crosscurrents of conversation. "It will be on the lips, and in the hearts of hundreds of thousands this day." John Murray Forbes, a railroad magnate and abolitionist, who had helped to organize African-American troops in Massachusetts, wrote to Lincoln on September 8, 1863. "Your letter to the Springfield Convention . . . will live in history side by side with your [Emancipation] proclamation." Forbes believed Lincoln's letter to Conkling spoke to a wide audience. "It meets the fears of the timid and the doubts of the reformer."

On September 10, 1863, George Opdyke, the mayor of New York, stopped at the White House. Opdyke was a wealthy merchant who had joined the Republican Party in large measure because of its antislavery posture. Only three weeks before, on the evening of August 18, a group of twenty-five radical Republicans had met at Opdyke's home to explore the possibility of convening a convention to nominate a candidate for president in 1864 other than Lincoln. Opdyke now came to thank the president "for his recent admirable letter to the Springfield Convention."

IN SEPTEMBER 1863, Lincoln understood more than ever that his task was to convince more than half of a wearying Northern public that this terrible war was worth fighting. His words at Springfield on September 3 were his pledge that he intended to follow through on the full meaning of the promise of the Emancipation Proclamation. Surprised by the public response to his words, as summer turned into fall, Lincoln was more alert than ever for other occasions where he could convey his vision and influence public opinion about the meaning and purpose of the war.

This photograph by Alexander Gardner was taken on November 8, 1863, ten days before Lincoln traveled to Gettysburg to deliver his address.

CHAPTER 24

A New Birth of Freedom
September 1863–March 1864

NOW WE ARE ENGAGED IN A GREAT CIVIL WAR, TESTING WHETHER
THAT NATION, OR ANY NATION SO CONCEIVED, AND SO DEDICATED,
CAN LONG ENDURE.

ABRAHAM LINCOLN
Gettysburg Address, November 19, 1863

"THE SIGNS LOOK BETTER." SO ABRAHAM LINCOLN HAD DECLARED IN
his letter to the Springfield meeting on September 3, 1863, but not
everyone agreed. Whether the president's confident outlook was justified would become a matter of vigorous debate in the fall of 1863.
Politicians, generals, and preachers all became instant pundits, forecast-
ing the future. How one saw "the signs" depended on where one stood.

With crucial elections in key states coming up in October, Republicans closed ranks—at least on the surface—to express their public support for the president. They feared Democratic election gains of 1862
could be expanded in the state elections of 1863. Meanwhile, Lincoln
found himself damned with faint praise by leaders in Washington. The
president was an honest and good person, so went the conversations in
the congressional corridors of power, but he remained too soft and too
slow. In the barrooms beyond the cloakrooms, radical Republicans
freely voiced their denunciations of the president—he was not up to the
job.

Out in the country, by contrast, people increasingly recognized in
Lincoln a gentle leader, free from the egomania associated with most
political leaders; in short, he was a man they could trust. Lincoln's public letters of 1863 generated an upswing of goodwill. He received a
boost in the fall when *The Letters of President Lincoln on Questions of*

National Policy enjoyed a brisk sale at eight cents a copy. The twenty-two-page pamphlet brought together letters to General George McClellan, Horace Greeley, New York mayor Fernando Wood, the Albany Committee, Governor Horatio Seymour, and the Springfield meeting. Ordinary people, when reading the pamphlet, began to recognize both Lincoln's political genius in dealing with nettlesome questions and his artistry with words.

Henry Ward Beecher spoke for many religious leaders in his estimate of Lincoln. Writing in the *Independent,* an influential weekly founded in 1848 with evangelical and antislavery roots, Beecher declared, "Rising to the dignity of the time, the President during his third year has shown a comprehensive policy and a wisdom in its execution which promise to broaden his sun at its setting."

George Curtis, author of the celebrated "Lounger" column in *Harper's Weekly,* provided the most astute analysis in the fall of 1863. "The conservative Republicans think him too much in the hands of the radicals; while the radical Republicans think him too slow, yielding, and half-hearted." Curtis had come to believe Lincoln knew better than anyone how to play the political game. "Both factions had to accept [Lincoln's] leadership—for the moment."

"FOR THE MOMENT." Time indeed weighed heavily on Lincoln's mind. He said so in a private letter to Governor Andrew Johnson of Tennessee. "It is something on the question of *time,* to remember that it cannot be known who is next to occupy the position I now hold, nor what he will do." He knew party radicals were dissatisfied with him, and that some in his party were casting about for an alternative candidate for 1864. He believed that Democrats thought their chances for victory in 1864 improved the longer the war went on. Aware it had been more than thirty years since a president had been elected to a second term, Lincoln pondered how to improve the Republicans' odds.

Should he assume the mantle of the partisan party leader? He had become a party leader in Illinois by learning how to apply grease to the wheels of party machinery, be they Whig or Republican wheels. In Washington, he had assumed a more independent stance in terms of party organization.

Or should he increase his efforts to reach out beyond his Republican base? From his first political campaign in Illinois to his appointment of his presidential rivals to his cabinet, Lincoln possessed the rare political instinct to move beyond partisanship and bring people of differing viewpoints together.

Lincoln made his decision. He would appeal for a larger loyalty. He had been pleased when the call went out to the Springfield meeting of September 3, 1863, to "Unconditional Union men of the State of Illinois, without regard to former party associations." He now envisioned a new National Union Party to run in the remaining state elections of 1863 and in the national election of 1864. He urged Republicans to run under this banner in the hopes of attracting the votes of Democrats.

LINCOLN QUICKLY LEARNED that battlefield results influenced election results. The battle for the West now shifted from Vicksburg to Chattanooga. Lincoln understood that while Vicksburg had been the key to controlling the Mississippi, whoever controlled Chattanooga, located at the juncture of Tennessee, Alabama, and Georgia, held the keys to the back doors of Virginia to the east and Georgia to the south. Situated in a valley between the Appalachian and the Cumberland mountain ranges, Chattanooga was a hub for rail lines radiating to the Ohio and Mississippi rivers, the Gulf of Mexico, and the Atlantic Ocean. It was second only to Richmond as the prize for federal forces in the fall of 1863. If the Union forces could oust the Confederate forces from the region around Chattanooga, the door could swing wide open to Georgia and ultimately to the Atlantic Ocean. If the Confederate forces could hold this corner of eastern Tennessee, they could keep the door open to supply Virginia from the west.

Lincoln knew that the people of this mountainous region, although living in a seceded state, remained fiercely loyal to the Union. They did not own slaves. Cut off geographically from both middle Tennessee to the west and Georgia to the south, they were an isolated mountain island in the midst of the Confederacy.

Lincoln had been discouraged when General William Rosecrans had stopped at Murfreesboro in middle Tennessee after his victory at Stones River in January 1863. Rosecrans, with a reputation for bold action, inexplicably seemed to give way to caution. Finally, on June 23, after nearly six months of preparation and unrelenting pressure from Lincoln and Secretary of War Stanton, Rosecrans's Army of the Cumberland pushed the Confederate forces under General Braxton Bragg one hundred miles over the Cumberland mountains and across the Tennessee River to the edge of Chattanooga, with a loss of only 560 casualties. Then Rosecrans stopped again.

On July 7, 1863, Stanton, elated by the news of the victories at Gettysburg and Vicksburg, wired Rosecrans, "You and your noble army now have the chance to put the finishing blow to the rebellion. Will you neglect the chance?"

Rosecrans, more than a little annoyed that his army's accomplishments had not been fully acknowledged, wired back, "You do not appear to observe the fact that this noble army has driven the rebels from Middle Tennessee. . . . I beg in behalf of this army that the War Department may not overlook so great an event because it is not written in showers of blood." Old Rosy's final comment was a not-so-subtle reference to his belief that Grant had sacrificed far too many men to achieve victory at Vicksburg.

At Lincoln's urging, Henry Halleck wired Rosecrans on July 24, 1863. "There is great disappointment felt here at the slowness of your advance." Later that day, Halleck wrote again, "The patience of the authorities here has been completely exhausted."

Rosecrans, bypassing Halleck, wrote the principal authority on August 1, 1863. In a long letter to Lincoln he listed nine reasons for his delay. He told Lincoln he had been held up by a torn-up Louisville and Nashville railroad, by a lack of "adequate cavalry," by rains that had rendered the "turnpikes next to impossible," that he needed to draw supplies 260 miles "exposed to hostile cavalry raids," and on and on. Rosecrans concluded, "You will not be surprised if in face of these difficulties it takes time to organize the means of success."

Lincoln, having the same sinking feeling about Rosecrans that he had in the past about too many previous commanders, began his reply with his customary affirmation, expressing his "kind feeling for and confidence in you." Lincoln hoped to calm the agitated Rosecrans, to get him to stop worrying and start fighting. The president concluded, "Do not misunderstand. . . . I am not watching you with an evil eye."

Rosecrans's Army of the Cumberland finally moved on Chattanooga on August 16, 1863. The Confederate Army of Tennessee, under General Braxton Bragg, abandoned the city on September 9. General Ambrose Burnside, in command of the small Army of the Ohio, had captured Knoxville, Tennessee, in a parallel advance a week earlier. Lincoln had hoped to liberate eastern Tennessee in the fall of 1861, but it seemed finally accomplished in the fall of 1863. Or was it? Rosecrans, heading south into Georgia in three columns, believed he had defeated Bragg, but the Confederate general had only engineered a

General William Rosecrans, "Old Rosy," commanded the Army of the Cumberland as it approached Chattanooga, the back door to Virginia and Georgia.

strategic retreat, waiting to fight another day at a time and place of his choosing.

On September 19 and 20, 1863, Bragg hurled his troops at Rosecrans at Chickamauga Creek southeast of Chattanooga. A misguided move by Rosecrans on the second day allowed fifteen thousand Confederate troops to punch through on his right. General James Longstreet, Rosecrans's roommate from the class of 1842 at West Point, arrived on September 20 with two divisions from the Army of Northern Virginia and helped sweep one-third of the Union forces from the field. Rosecrans and part of his army retreated back to Chattanooga, but General George H. Thomas stayed on the field, rallied his men on Snodgrass Hill, and blocked the further movement of the Confederate forces. For his heroism, Thomas earned the nickname "the Rock of Chickamauga."

On September 20, 1863, Charles Dana, assistant secretary of war, but in truth Stanton's spy, wired his boss, "Chickamauga is as fatal a name in our history as Bull Run. . . . [O]ur soldiers turned and fled. It was a wholesale panic."

Lincoln stayed at the telegraph office late into the evening, wiring Burnside at 2 a.m., September 21, 1863, "Go to Rosecrans with your force, without a moments delay." Learning that Burnside had sent troops in the opposite direction to Jonesboro, in pursuit of small guerrilla forces, Lincoln returned to the telegraph office. "Damn Jonesboro!" he exclaimed.

"Well, Rosecrans has been whipped, as I feared." Lincoln walked into John Hay's bedroom in the White House early on the morning of September 21, even before his young secretary was up. Sitting down on Hay's bed, Lincoln continued, "I have feared it for several days. I believe I feel trouble in the air before it comes."

At 11 a.m., Lincoln wrote Burnside again, "If you are to do any good to Rosecrans it will not do to waste time with Jonesboro." Four days later, in exasperation, Lincoln wrote saying that the receipt of Burnside's most recent telegram "makes me doubt whether I am awake or dreaming." Lincoln recounted Burnside's protestations over the many days that he was preparing to move, but never seemed to do so. At one point, Lincoln called Burnside's actions "incomprehensible." Lincoln signed the letter, blotted the ink, endorsed the envelope, struggled to get control of his anger, and decided not to send it.

On the evening of September 23, 1863, shortly after Lincoln had gone to bed at the Soldiers' Home, he was awakened by his secretary John Hay, who had ridden out in "splendid moonlight" to invite the president back to a hastily called midnight meeting convened by Stanton. A "considerably disturbed" Lincoln dressed and returned with Hay, where he found Halleck, Seward, and Chase had joined Stanton. They discussed the options for sending reinforcements to support Rosecrans. Stanton asked Halleck how long it would take for troops from the Army of the Potomac to reach Chattanooga. The general supposed sixty days, perhaps forty. Stanton responded that if traders could ship twenty thousand bales of cotton by railroad to Chattanooga in twenty days, let the Union send twenty thousand soldiers.

Lincoln was skeptical of the whole operation, pointing out that "you can't get one corps into Washington in the time you fix for reaching Nashville." He then proceeded to humorously illustrate this "impossibility," but Stanton interjected that "the danger was too imminent & the occasion too serious for jokes." The conversation continued until almost morning with the president and Halleck, originally opposed, finally offering their support for the plan.

Lincoln was wrong. The troops began moving to the railheads in twelve hours and boarded the trains on the morning of September 25, 1863. In a stunning example of the transportation revolution, Stanton elicited cooperation from railroad men so that five trains, each with thirty cars, left Washington. In the end, five sets of five trains traveled on a route of 1,233 miles. Lincoln had his doubts, but twenty-three thousand men, more than twenty thousand horses, plus artillery and equipment, rolled toward Chattanooga. They traveled on nine independently operated railroads with different gauge tracks over the Appalachians and across the Ohio River, where bridges had to be improvised twice, arriving eleven days later at a railhead near Chattanooga.

All of these reinforcements, including General William Sherman's four divisions from Vicksburg, seemed neither to mollify nor strengthen Rosecrans. His army, back in Chattanooga, found itself besieged, with guns aimed at them from Missionary Ridge on the north and Lookout Mountain on the south. Lincoln wrote to Rosecrans in early October to stress the stakes. "If we can hold Chattanooga, and East Tennessee, I think the rebellion must dwindle and die."

Even the president's encouragement did not work. Charles Dana reported to Lincoln that Old Rosy "was for the present completely broken down." The president, upon receiving this report, told John Hay that Rosecrans was "confused and stunned like a duck hit on the head" ever since the disaster at Chickamauga.

Lincoln now knew he needed to replace Rosecrans. But timing was everything. Lincoln decided to delay doing anything until after the Ohio elections, knowing that Rosecrans and his chief of staff, James Garfield, were both natives of Ohio and enjoyed immense popularity in their home state.

THE ISSUES LINCOLN FACED in the border state of Missouri did not go away, but became even more contentious in the summer and fall of 1863. Lincoln believed he had a friend in Missouri in Hamilton R. Gamble, a conservative former Whig who had been elected as the provisional governor in 1861 and who remained in office. Throughout the Civil War, however, the state was locked in internal warfare and political factionalism exacerbated by continual changes in civilian and military leadership. In 1863, the president became caught between radicals and conservatives battling over emancipation, each attacking him for not taking their side.

Lincoln did not know Missouri well, but the way he dealt with the state's complex problems revealed his political dexterity. When a conflict arose at the end of 1862 over who would appoint and organize Union troops in Missouri, the governor or the War Department, Lincoln told

Attorney General Edward Bates, himself from Missouri, "I therefore think it is safer when a practical question arises, to decide that question directly, and not indirectly, by deciding a general abstraction supposed to include it." This directive lifted up the central core of Lincoln's political philosophy. He embraced a pragmatic approach to politics and had become wary of politicians whose ideology, be it conservative or liberal, blinded them to the practical considerations inherent in local conditions.

In September 1862, General John M. Schofield was replaced by General Samuel R. Curtis as commander of the Department of Missouri. Curtis had achieved fame by leading outnumbered Union forces to victory at Pea Ridge, Arkansas, on the Arkansas-Missouri border on March 7–8, 1862. Curtis soon sided with Missouri's antislavery forces, which led to a clash with Governor Gamble. In December, Curtis arrested the Reverend Samuel B. McPheeters, minister of the Pine Street Presbyterian Church in St. Louis, charging him with sympathy for the enemy and ordering him to stop preaching in his church and leave the state. Lincoln, following a detailed investigation, wrote Curtis informing him that he was suspending his order. He told Curtis that after speaking with McPheeters, "I tell you frankly, I believe he does sympathize with the rebels," but a larger point was at issue. "The U.S. government must not . . . undertake to run the churches." Lincoln then stated a policy that he adhered to all during the war: "Let the churches, as such take care of themselves."

By May 1863, having had enough of Curtis's continuing to side with the radicals, Lincoln decided to reappoint John Schofield, who he believed would be more evenhanded. He told Schofield that the people of Missouri had entered into "a pestilent factional quarrel among themselves." He knew he was handing him "a difficult *role*," so he offered him advice: "If both factions, or neither, shall abuse you, you will probably be about right."

Lincoln's appointment of Schofield brought a testy letter from a group of "Union people" asking Lincoln to "suspend that appointment until you hear from us." The president replied that day. "It is very painful to me that you in Missouri cannot, or will not, settle your factional quarrel among yourselves. I have been tormented with it beyond endurance for months, by both sides." What upset Lincoln the most: "Neither side pays the least respect to my appeals to your reasons."

In the summer and fall of 1863, both sides stepped up their attacks on Lincoln. Although a number of issues were in play, including patronage, the central problem was emancipation. The radicals, called "Charcoals," favored immediate emancipation. The conservatives, known as "Snowflakes," resisted interference with the institution of slavery. The "Claybanks," so called because their position was purportedly colorless, occupied the middle ground, calling for gradual emancipation.

Lincoln tried to distinguish for the combatants the difference between ends and means. He favored emancipation, but in a state long wedded to slavery, he believed that immediate emancipation would produce too much of a backlash. He would have backed a plan for gradual emancipation, but the Snowflakes proposed a plan stating that slavery not end until 1870, and that peonage, a system where blacks would continue to labor in servitude until their debts were paid, could go on from eleven years to life. Lincoln told John Hay that he disliked this proposal because it ended up "*postponing* the benefits of freedom to the slave instead of giving him an immediate vested interest therein."

When the Missourians could not get their way, they traveled to Washington to protest. Governor Gamble called on Lincoln at the White House wishing to enlist Lincoln's support against the radicals' plan for immediate emancipation. When he did not receive that support, he wrote angrily to Attorney General Bates, "I express to you my profound conviction that the President is a mere intriguing, pettifogging, piddling politician."

In late September 1863, Lincoln welcomed a delegation of radicals fresh from an emancipation convention in Jefferson City. Charles D. Drake, their firebrand leader, had been a Whig, a Know-Nothing, and a Democrat; he was now a radical Republican. Lincoln knew that the resolutions passed at their convention included removing both Gamble and Schofield. Lincoln kept them cooling their heels for three days in Washington before meeting them on September 30. Confident that they could pressure the president to remove Schofield and accede to their demands, the group was surprised when he did not. Instead, he told Drake that he had had enough of their tough tactics. Restraining his anger, he told them he would write them his decisions.

On October 5, 1863, he wrote that he would retain Schofield and would instruct him to place Missouri again under martial law. With time to collect his thoughts, Lincoln laid out for them what happens when "all being for the Union. . . . each will prefer a different way of sustaining the Union." A pattern developed: "At once sincerity is questioned, and motives are assailed. Actual war coming, blood grows hot, and blood is spilled. Thought is forced from old channels into confusion. Deception breeds and thrives. Confidence dies, and universal suspicion reigns." No psychologist could have described it better.

Both sides, true to Lincoln's analysis, could not hear. Both Gamble and Drake went home angry. Lincoln, in the fall of 1863, decided, despite his best efforts, he could not solve the problems of Missouri. In late October, he told Missourian Bates, he "had no friends in Missouri."

LINCOLN HAD ONE EYE TRAINED on the military battlefield and another on the election battlefield in the fall of 1863. Although the spring elections in Massachusetts and Connecticut had gone well, he knew the fall elections offered an opportunity for Democrats to vote against his policies. Governors were to be elected in Maine, Massachusetts, Pennsylvania, Ohio, Wisconsin, Minnesota, Iowa, Kentucky, and California. Lincoln understood that Democrats, having scored gains in the 1862 midterm elections, wished to demonstrate that voting in 1863 could set the tone for the national elections of 1864.

The political practice of the day prevented Lincoln from campaigning. He did encourage his close friends, both in Washington and in the states, to campaign vigorously. The president worked closely with Secretary of War Stanton to arrange furloughs for soldiers so they could return home and vote, and, in some instances, vote in the field. Confined to Washington, Lincoln monitored the elections closely from the War Department telegraph office.

In Ohio, John Brough, a tough-talking Republican, was running under a Union ticket against the outspoken Clement Vallandigham, the Democratic peace candidate exiled in Canada. In Pennsylvania, Governor Andrew G. Curtin faced a tough challenger in Democratic Pennsylvania chief justice George W. Woodward, who was holding hearings on the constitutionality of Lincoln's controversial March Conscription Act.

Ohio and Pennsylvania voted on Tuesday, October 13, 1863. During the day, Lincoln told Welles he felt "nervous" about the contests. In the evening, an anxious Lincoln telegraphed Columbus. "Where is John Brough?" Learning that Brough was in the telegraph office, Lincoln asked, "Brough, what is your majority now?" He replied, "Over 30,000." Lincoln requested Brough to remain in the telegraph office in Columbus during the night as would he in Washington. The majority rose to over 50,000 at midnight, and by five o'clock the next morning, over 100,000. Vallandigham had been decisively defeated. Chase, who had used his considerable influence campaigning in his home state, wired Lincoln: "The victory is complete, beyond all hopes." Lincoln, ecstatic, wired back, "Glory to God in the highest. Ohio has saved the Nation."

On election night, Lincoln also heard welcome news from the Keystone State. Even though Curtin won by just twenty thousand votes, an exuberant supporter wrote to Lincoln, "Pennsylvania stands by you, keeping step with Maine and California to the music of the Union." The next day, Welles met the president, "who is in good spirits and greatly relieved from the depression of yesterday." Lincoln told the secretary of the navy "he had more anxiety in regard to the election results of yesterday than he had in 1860 when he was chosen."

James F. Moorhead, a congressman from Pennsylvania, wrote Lincoln to suggest the larger meaning of the election victories. "Let me congratulate you on the glorious result in Ohio & Penna, who now declare for *A Lincoln* in 1864."

THREE DAYS AFTER THE VICTORIES in the crucial fall elections, Lincoln acted to win the victory on the military battlefield. On October 16, 1863, he directed Halleck to inform Grant, "You will receive herewith the orders of the President of the United States placing you in command of the Departments of the Ohio, Cumberland, and Tennessee." Lincoln decided to combine these three separate commands under his best general. He further gave Grant the option of changing the organization of these departments "as you deem most practicable." Grant was told he had the option to keep William Rosecrans or put George Thomas in his place. Thomas became commander of the Army of the Cumberland. Immediately upon receiving his new command, Thomas wrote Grant from Chattanooga, "I will hold the town till we starve."

Lincoln, receiving mail from eastern Tennessee, replied to two concerned citizens of Knoxville, "You do not estimate the holding of East Tennessee more highly than I do."

LINCOLN SURPRISED HIS CABINET when he accepted an invitation to travel to Gettysburg, Pennsylvania, to be the secondary speaker at the dedication of the nation's first national military cemetery. They had watched as Lincoln turned down all invitations to speak outside Washington. When the president had left Washington, he did so only to visit the Army of the Potomac at the front.

In late September, Massachusetts senator Charles Sumner reminded Lincoln of the letter from John Murray Forbes, a Boston industrialist who had written on September 8, 1863, to commend the president for his letter to the Springfield rally. Forbes wrote, "My suggestion then is that you should seize an early opportunity and any subsequent chance to teach your great audience." After a series of successful public letters, Lincoln became more open to opportunities to speak outside Washington.

Within days after the battle of Gettysburg, plans were set in motion that would lead to a national soldiers' cemetery. In previous wars, American soldiers were buried where they fell in battle. This remained the pattern into the first two years of the Civil War. Graves were marked in makeshift ways that too often were not permanent. Everything began to change on the battlefields in 1862, and reached a new dimension at Gettysburg in the fall of 1863.

David Wills, a successful Gettysburg attorney, directed plans for the national cemetery. Wills and his committee made the decision that a national cemetery required a national dedication. The planners set October 23, 1863, for the dedication, a fall day that would still ensure good weather. Exactly one month before, on September 23, Edward Everett, the most celebrated speaker in the United States, was invited to offer the central address. Everett replied immediately that a month would not be sufficient time for the research and preparation of a totally new address. He responded that he would not be ready to deliver such an important address until November 19. Thus, Everett set the date for the dedication ceremonies.

Wills also invited some of the leading literary artists of the day to participate. Henry Wadsworth Longfellow, John Greenleaf Whittier, and William Cullen Bryant were requested to prepare a poem or ode for the occasion. Each declined.

Abraham Lincoln was the last speaker invited. Wills wrote to the president on November 2, 1863, just seventeen days before the event. "I am authorized by the Governors of the different states to invite you to be present, and participate in these ceremonies, which will doubtless be very imposing and solemnly impressive." Wills's invitation included a brief word about the nature of the remarks the president should give. "It is the desire that, after the Oration, You as Chief Executive of the Nation formally set apart these grounds to their Sacred use by a few appropriate remarks."

On Wednesday, November 18, 1863, Lincoln arrived at the little depot on Carlisle Street in Gettysburg at sundown. Stepping from the train, he observed hundreds of coffins lined up on the station platform.

He was met by Wills, Everett, and Ward Hill Lamon, who had been appointed marshal in chief for the dedication.

The president was driven to the Wills residence, the most splendid home on the town square, or "the Diamond," as the locals called it. Lincoln was shown up the steep front stairs to his bedroom on the second floor, where he intended to spend some time finalizing his speech. Lincoln appreciated the hospitality he received that evening, but his heart was back in Washington. Young Tad had fallen seriously ill, and he knew that Mary, never forgetting the death of Willie, would be as deeply fearful as he was.

On November 19, 1863, Ward Hill Lamon, acting as marshal, struggled to assemble the dignitaries outside the Wills home on the Diamond. Lincoln appeared at the appointed hour of 10 a.m. dressed in a black suit with a frock coat. He wore his usual tall silk hat, to which he had added a wide mourning band in memory of Willie. Lincoln was assigned a bay horse so small that the president's long legs nearly touched the ground.

Lincoln rode in a parade along Baltimore Street in Gettysburg
on the morning of November 19, 1863.

American flags could be seen everywhere along the route up Baltimore Street. Buildings were pockmarked with bullet holes, evidence of the battle less than five months before. Children were selling cookies and lemonade, as well as souvenir bullets, and even cannonballs.

At least fifteen thousand people had come from many parts of the country to be present at the dedication. The proceedings began with an invocation and hymn. Edward Everett then stepped forward to deliver his oration. Lincoln respected Everett, protégé of Daniel Webster, because the New England orator had delivered a lecture on George Washington nearly 150 times across the nation, donating close to $100,000 to the restoration of Washington's home at Mount Vernon.

Lincoln followed Everett's address attentively. The president stirred when Everett, losing his footing, spoke of "General Lee"; Lincoln, turning to Seward, whispered a correction—"General Meade." Everett, after speaking for two hours and eight minutes, finally concluded.

Lamon introduced Lincoln. The crowd had become restless after

New England politician Edward Everett was invited to be the featured speaker at Gettysburg.

Lincoln, in this enlarged photograph taken before his address, is in the center, hatless, with part of his face covered by the hat of a soldier.

such a long oration. A photographer who had pitched his equipment directly in front of the platform busily adjusted his camera as he prepared to take a photograph of the president speaking. Lincoln rose, adjusted his spectacles, and took out of the left breast pocket of his coat his dedicatory remarks. Beyond the sprawling crowd, Lincoln could see row upon row of soldiers' graves. He shifted his speaking text to his left hand, and began: "Four score and seven years ago our fathers brought forth, on this continent, a new nation, conceived in Liberty, and dedicated to the proposition that all men are created equal."

In the four and a half months since Lincoln's response to the victories at Gettysburg and Vicksburg, his earlier words at the White House, "eighty odd years," became "Four score and seven years ago" at Gettysburg. This was not a simple way to say "eighty-seven." Lincoln asked his audience to calculate backward to discover that the nation began with the signing of the Declaration of Independence in 1776. Lincoln's opening words found their root in Psalm 90: "The days of our years are threescore years and ten; And if by reason of strength they be fourscore years." Lincoln never named the Bible, or quoted directly from it in his remarks, but the whole of his speech would be suffused with biblical content and cadence.

Lincoln built the architecture of the Gettysburg Address upon a structure of past, present, and future time. He started in the past by placing the dedication of the battlefield in the larger context of American history. His opening words highlighted historical continuity. He began with a biblical allusion that accented permanence, and yet at the same time noted the nation's continuity had already surpassed the biblical time frame for life and death. In speaking of "our fathers" Lincoln invoked a common heritage of the founding fathers, and at the same time identified himself with his audience.

Lincoln's first sentence took flight with the Declaration of Independence's American truth that "all men are created equal." Lincoln had sounded this note in his recent letter to the Springfield meeting. When Lincoln reaffirmed this truth at Gettysburg, he was asserting the war to be about both liberty and union.

"Now we are engaged in a great civil war, testing whether that nation, or any nation so conceived, and so dedicated, can long endure. We are met on a great battle-field of that war. We have come to dedicate a portion of that field, as a final resting-place for those who here gave their lives, that that nation might live." After his long introductory sentence, Lincoln traveled rapidly forward from the Revolution to the Civil War. With quick brushstrokes, he recapitulated the meaning of the war. As a speaker, he was usually spare with his adjectives, but on this occasion he modified both Civil War and battlefield with "great." Unlike Everett, he spent none of his words on the details of the battle. His purpose was to transfigure the dedication with a larger meaning of the purpose of the "nation," a word he would use five times in his address. The Civil War was a "testing" of the founding ideals of the nation to see whether they can "endure."

"It is altogether fitting and proper that we should do this. But, in a larger sense, we can not dedicate—we can not consecrate—we can not hallow—this ground. The brave men, living and dead, who struggled here, have consecrated it far above our poor power to add or detract." His words "but, in a larger sense" were his clue to the audience that he was about to expand the parameters of his intentions for this day. With this transition, he began his appeal from the past battle to the present dedication.

But before he lifted their eyes beyond the battlefield, Lincoln told his audience what they could not do: "we cannot dedicate," "we cannot consecrate," "we cannot hallow." At this point Lincoln employed a dramatic antithesis by contrasting "The brave men" with "our poor power."

In the last three sentences of the address Lincoln shifted the focus a final time.

> The world will little note, nor long remember what we say here, but it cannot forget what they did here. It is for us the living, rather, to be dedicated here to the unfinished work which they who fought here have thus far so nobly advanced. It is rather for us to be here dedicated to the great task remaining before us— that from these honored dead we take increased devotion to that cause for which they gave the last full measure of devotion—that we here highly resolve that these dead shall not have died in vain—that this nation, under God, shall have a new birth of freedom—and that government of the people, by the people, for the people, shall not perish from the earth.

Lincoln now opened out the future and spoke to the responsibility of the hearers. He pointed away from words—there had been more than two hours of words already—to deeds. He contrasted "what we say here" with "what they did here."

Lincoln's concluding paragraph, in a speech known for its brevity, was a surprisingly long, complex sentence of eighty-two words. In his closing paragraph Lincoln continued his use of repetition: "to be dedicated," "to be here dedicated," "we take increased devotion," "the last full measure of devotion." Repetition reiterated the accountability of the audience.

Lincoln, who always took much time in choosing his words, here used religious ones—"dedicate" and "devotion"—which conjured up the call to commitment present in the revival services of the Second Great Awakening and in the Presbyterian and other Protestant churches Lincoln was attending in Washington.

At this point, Lincoln made his only addition to his speaking text. He added the words "under God." This addition was uncharacteristic for a speaker who did not trust extemporaneous speech. It is not known what impelled Lincoln to add these two words, and after the Gettysburg Address there was no apology for this interjection. Lincoln included "under God" in all three copies of the address he prepared at later dates.

Lincoln, the Whig and the Republican, had always insisted that the American nation drew its breath from both political and religious sources. His words were consistent with invocations of God in almost all of his major presidential speeches. Lincoln, as president, walked back and forth across the line between religion and politics.

The phrase "a new birth of freedom" was layered with both political and religious meanings as well. He was no longer, as in his inaugural address, defending an old Union, but proclaiming a new Union. The old Union had attempted to contain slavery. The new Union would fulfill the promise of liberty, the crucial step into the future that the founders had been unwilling to take.

The "new birth" also pointed to a paradox in both politics and religion. Lincoln had come to see the Civil War as a ritual of purification. The old Union had to die. Death became a transition into a new Union and a new humanity.

As Lincoln approached the unexpected climax of his address, he uttered the words that would be most remembered from his address: "and that government of the people, by the people, for the people, shall not perish from the earth."

Investigations to unearth the sources of the Gettysburg Address have centered on similar words by politician Daniel Webster and New England Unitarian minister Theodore Parker. There is no doubt Lincoln knew their earlier words. But this sleuthing has overshadowed the fact that Lincoln built on his own words. In his inaugural address he declared, "The chief Magistrate derives all his authority from the people." In his message to Congress in special session on July 4, 1861, he had asked the question, "Whether a constitutional republic, or a democracy—a government of the people, by the same people—can, or cannot, maintain its territorial integrity against its own domestic foes." As president, Lincoln worked with a definition of democracy that he continued to expand and refine.

Lincoln did not use one first-person singular pronoun in his entire address. It was as if Lincoln disappeared so that transcendent truths could appear.

He concluded his address before the photographer could begin.

Newspapers in the major cities had set up their page forms with type set in advance with Everett's text, which they had had for days. They therefore pasted in Lincoln's words below Everett's address without comment. In the days following, newspapers traditionally supportive of Lincoln found much to praise in his remarks at Gettysburg. The *Chicago Tribune* declared, "Half a century hence, to have lived in this age will be fame. To have served it as well as Lincoln, will be immortality."

One of the first editors to grasp the importance of Lincoln's succinct address was Josiah Holland, associate editor of the *Springfield* (Massachusetts) *Republican*. On November 20, 1863, he wrote, "Surprisingly fine as Mr. Everett's oration was in the Gettysburg consecration, the rhetorical honors of the occasion were won by President Lincoln." He continued, "His little speech is a perfect gem, deep in feeling, compact in thought and expression, and tasteful and elegant in every word and comma."

Criticism from Lincoln's political opponents in the press was instant. The *Chicago Times* responded, "The cheek of every American must tingle with shame as he reads the filly, flat, and dishwatery utterances of a man who has to be pointed out to intelligent foreigners as the President of the United States." Thirty-six miles from Gettysburg, the *Harrisburg Patriot and Union* spoke acrimoniously, "We pass over the silly remarks of the President; for the credit of the nation, we are willing that the veil of oblivion shall be dropped over them and that they shall no more be repeated or thought of."

Far away, the *Times* of London, which did not like much that was American, did not appreciate Lincoln's American eloquence either. The *Times* editorialized, "The ceremony was rendered ludicrous by some of the sallies of that poor President Lincoln."

America's greatest orator, however, did appreciate Lincoln's words. Edward Everett wrote to Lincoln on the following day. "Permit me . . . to express my great admiration of the thoughts expressed by you, with such eloquent simplicity & appropriateness, at the consecration of the Cemetery." Everett, who three years earlier confided to his diary his criticisms of Lincoln's speaking abilities on the president-elect's train trip from Springfield to Washington, now told Lincoln, "I should be glad, if I could flatter myself that I came as near to the central idea of the occasion in two hours, as you did in two minutes."

WITHIN DAYS OF RETURNING FROM GETTYSBURG, Lincoln lay sick in the White House. Doctors diagnosed his illness as varioloid, a mild form of smallpox. Tad remained sick but showed clear signs of getting better.

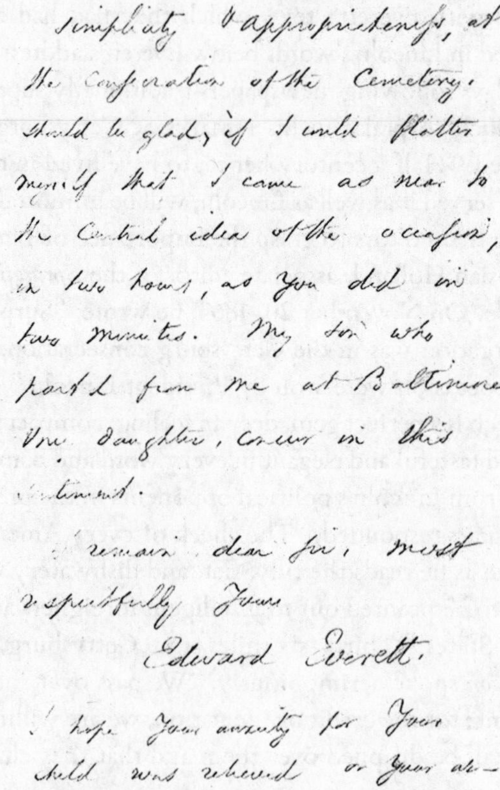

[handwritten letter in cursive]

simplicity & appropriateness, at
the consecration of the Cemetery. I
should be glad, if I could flatter
myself that I came as near to
the central idea of the occasion,
in two hours, as you did in
two minutes. My son who
parted from me at Baltimore
& my daughter, concur in this
sentiment.

I remain, dear sir, most
respectfully yours,

Edward Everett.

I hope your anxiety for your
child was relieved or your —

*Edward Everett, who early in Lincoln's presidency doubted
his abilities as a speaker, wrote a generous letter
commending Lincoln's Gettysburg Address.*

Lincoln used his enforced confinement to work on his third message to
Congress, scheduled to convene on December 8, 1863.

Lincoln could not walk to the telegraph office, but he wanted to
learn all he could about Grant's intentions in the West. In the month following Grant's assumption of command in October, "Fighting Joe"
Hooker arrived with twenty thousand men from the Army of the
Potomac, and William Tecumseh Sherman, Grant's trusted sidekick,
arrived with seventeen thousand troops. Whereas Grant enjoyed the
confidence of his officers and men, Confederate general Braxton
Bragg's effort suffered from bickering within his command, his tenure
continued by the vote of the only man that counted—Jefferson Davis—

who traveled by train to Bragg's headquarters to try to hold things together. Davis, who often acted precipitously as Confederate commander in chief, instructed Bragg to detach James Longstreet's fifteen thousand men in an attempt to recapture Knoxville.

Hooker's men began the campaign to retake Chattanooga on November 24, 1863, with a daring and courageous attack up the northern slope of Lookout Mountain, raising the American flag at the moment of a total eclipse of the moon. The next day, Sherman attacked Missionary Ridge but was stopped by determined Confederate forces. At that point, George Thomas's Army of the Cumberland, which Grant had assigned a secondary role because he believed they still might be shell-shocked from their courageous stand at Chickamauga Creek, crossed an open plain against a murderous barrage and stormed up Missionary Ridge. Grant, crunching his cigar, asked, "Thomas, who ordered those men up the ridge?"

"I don't know," Thomas replied. They both looked on in wonder as Thomas's men continued their victorious charge, regimental flags flying, shouting at the top of their lungs, "Chickamauga, Chickamauga." In less than three days, Grant's army, consisting of three armies that had never fought together before, drove the Confederate army thirty miles south toward Atlanta. The door was opened to Georgia. Then on November 29, 1863, Longstreet was driven off from Knoxville back into Virginia.

"The storming of the Ridge by our troops was one of the greatest miracles in Military history," wrote Charles Dana to Secretary of War Stanton on November 26, 1863. "No man who climbs the ascent, by any of the roads that wind along its front, can believe that eighteen thousand men were moved up its broken and crumbling face, unless it was his fortune to witness the deed."

A grateful president wrote to General Grant on December 8, 1863. "I wish to tender you, and all under your command, my more than thanks—my profoundest gratitude—for the skill, courage, and perseverance, with which you and they, over so great difficulties, have effected that important object. God bless you all. A. Lincoln."

ON THE SAME DAY, December 8, 1863, Lincoln offered his annual message to Congress. Ill and confined to his bedroom during its preparation, he exhibited his political agility if not his literary grace in this third annual message. He sought the advice of Secretary of War Stanton and

Treasury Secretary Chase, but their assistance consisted of information, for Lincoln knew that he needed to assert his authority at a crucial transitional moment in the war.

Victories at Gettysburg and Vicksburg, and now at Chattanooga, sparked a widespread conversation on what politicians had begun to call "Reconstruction." Lincoln took heart in the summer and fall by what informants told him was disaffection with the Confederacy and a resurgent Union spirit. Amistad Burwell, a prominent Mississippi businessman, wrote Lincoln that if one were to walk through Vicksburg, where he once lived, in disguise, one would hear "Jeff Davis . . . cursed from the bottom of the heart, & with the whole soul." Burwell wanted Lincoln to know "there are many bold and talented men, once men of wealth and influence, who at all hazards are willing to raise the old standard, and follow it to the death."

Events in Arkansas and North Carolina offered further encouragement. In September, Lincoln learned, after federal occupation of Little Rock and Fort Smith, a series of Union meetings urged the restoration of a civil government loyal to the Union. A peace movement headed by William Woods Holden, editor of the *Raleigh Standard,* led the way in efforts to disconnect North Carolina from the Confederacy. Many radical Republicans were suspicious of these reports, but Lincoln was not.

Congress, already chafing against what many believed to be Lincoln's expansion of presidential power, determined to assert their right to determine the guidelines for Reconstruction. But they found themselves in escalating disagreement about the purpose and terms of policies that would follow the end of the war.

Conservatives, including Democratic senator Reverdy Johnson of Maryland, wanted Lincoln to withdraw the Emancipation Proclamation as the precursor for a policy of amnesty that would invite Southern states to once again send representatives to Congress in fulfillment of their long-held dictum: "The Union as it was and the Constitution as it was." Lincoln had heard all this before.

The real battle, however, was an intramural family squabble among Republicans. Massachusetts senator Charles Sumner, a spokesman for the radicals, published "Our Domestic Relations" in the *Atlantic Monthly* in October. Though it was unsigned, everyone knew from its content and tone that Sumner had written it to get in a first word that the prerogative for organizing the South after the war belonged solely to Congress, and not the president. Sumner's larger point was that "as a restraint upon the lawless vindictiveness and inhumanity of the Rebel States," Congress should divide the liberated lands "among patriotic soldiers, poor whites, and freedmen."

Postmaster General Montgomery Blair, speaking for the far-flung Blair family who had a foot in all three major border states, Maryland, Kentucky, and Missouri, addressed Sumner and the radicals in a shrill October speech at Rockville, Maryland. Long believing the radicals to be audacious and arrogant, Blair asserted that the imminent peace was "menaced by the ambition of the ultra-Abolitionists, which is equally despotic in its tendencies" to the Southern despotism about to be overthrown. Blair, giving voice to the fears of Republican conservatives, stated that the "abolition party whilst pronouncing philippics against slavery, seek to make a caste of another color by amalgamating the black element with the free white labor of our land." Sumner had spoken of "state suicide" in arguing that Southern states had lost all their rights by rebelling. Blair argued that this notion was absurd, for treason could only apply to individuals. Blair bid his fellow Republicans to trust the course of Reconstruction to the "safe and healing policy of the President."

With this backdrop to his annual message, Lincoln determined not to be drawn into this infighting in his party, and tried to stay above the fray. He recognized the "uneasiness among ourselves" so much in evidence in 1863. He voiced his presidential realism when he stated, "The policy of emancipation, and of employing black soldiers, gave to the future a new aspect, about which hope, and fear, and doubt contended in uncertain conflict." He saluted the fact that "of those who were slaves at the beginning of the rebellion, full one hundred thousand are now in the United States military service." To his critics who wished to return to the Union as it was, Lincoln responded, "I shall not attempt to retract or modify the emancipation proclamation; nor shall I return to slavery any person who is free by the terms of the proclamation, or by any of the acts of Congress."

Lincoln's third annual message summed up where he believed events stood at the end of 1863. It lacked the forward-looking energy of his annual message of 1862. Although he recognized the service of blacks, his affirmation of their contributions lacked the praise for their valor so evident in his message to the Springfield meeting three months earlier.

Lincoln accompanied his third annual message with a Proclamation of Amnesty and Reconstruction, which indicated how much his thinking had changed in the previous two and a half years. At the outset of the war, he had believed there existed in the South a strong if largely silent Unionist sentiment waiting to be encouraged. He began his presidency reiterating his stance that he did not intend to touch slavery where it already existed in the South; he now stated that adherence to the Emancipation Proclamation would be the price of admission to his determination to "think anew" about a newly constituted Union. Lincoln's painful journey into political realism meant that if a small minority, 10 percent, started the process toward Reconstruction, he would consider this an adequate beginning. The alternative, already being voiced in the South, would be that Confederates, realizing the war was a lost cause, would simply try to return to the Union admitting nothing and gaining everything.

The enthusiastic reception to Lincoln's annual message and proclamation testified to the president's dexterity in appealing to all sides in the growing debate over Reconstruction. John Hay, ever alert to responses to his boss, wrote in his diary, "Men acted as if the Millennium had come." He wrote that "Sumner is beaming, while at the other political pole Dixon & Reverdy Johnson said it was highly satisfactory." To top it off, Massachusetts senator "Henry Wilson came to me and laying his broad palms on my shoulders said, 'The President has struck another great blow.' "

AS 1863 TURNED INTO 1864, conversation about the next presidential election picked up. At the end of the year, the *Chicago Tribune* spoke for many when it stated, "Mr. Lincoln has the inside track. He has the confidence of the people, and even the respect and affection of the masses." The president's popularity extended beyond Republicans. Albert Smith, a former Democratic member of Congress, wrote, "You have touched & *taken* the popular heart—and secured your re-election."

Yet for all of Lincoln's growing popularity with the people, politicians continued to question the desirability, if not the electability, of Abraham Lincoln for a second term. He had not been the leading candidate for the Republican nomination in 1860, and a significant number of disparate groups of Republicans were not certain he was the best choice for 1864. The fact that no one had been inaugurated for a second term since President Andrew Jackson in 1832 added some historical bulk as the scales began to be weighed at the beginning of the year.

The question in the minds of the detractors became, who would be the best challenger? In the corridors of power, Republicans talked about a not surprising list of potential candidates, including William Seward and Edward Bates. Some wanted John C. Frémont again, who was known to dislike Lincoln and was popular with radicals. The new military hero, Ulysses S. Grant, brought to mind the election of past generals as president.

One man stepped forward. Talented and experienced as governor, senator, and secretary of the treasury, Salmon P. Chase had long desired the highest office of all. He also chafed in Lincoln's cabinet, especially after his embarrassing defeat as the leader of the mutiny against Secretary of State William Seward in December 1862. Chase would admit that Lincoln treated him with respect, yet he felt that his work as secretary of the treasury went unappreciated. His chief complaint against Lincoln was that he was too cautious. Chase, as president, would have moved more quickly toward emancipation and the use of black troops.

In September 1863, Lincoln read aloud to Chase an unfinished letter explaining why he felt the need to include exceptions in his Emancipation Proclamation. As was Lincoln's style, he then posed for Chase a series of questions to demonstrate the many sides to the question of emancipation. One month later, Chase wrote to an Ohio newspaper editor, "Oh! that the President could be induced to take the positive responsibility of prompt action as readily as he takes the passive responsibility of delay and letting bad enough alone."

As was the custom, Chase campaigned for Lincoln in Ohio and Indiana at the time of the October state elections. His speeches on behalf of the president, however, did not fool Attorney General Edward Bates, who confided to his diary, "That visit to the west is generally understood as Mr. Ch[a]se's opening campaign for the presidency."

Lincoln's response to Chase's ambition was never to join the criticisms of the secretary of the treasury voiced by the president's friends. Lincoln's own secure sense of self meant he did not become defensive against Chase's criticisms. By 1863, John Hay, while barely twenty-five, had become a confidant of the president. The observant Hay complained to the president about the ways Chase undercut Lincoln's leadership. The president responded, "It was in very bad taste, but that he had determined to shut his eyes to all these performances: that Chase made a good secretary and that he would keep him where he is." Lincoln added, "If he becomes Pres all right. I hope we may never have a worse man. I have seen all along clearly his plan of strengthening himself."

By mid-December, Kansas senator Samuel Pomeroy headed up a covert Chase presidential campaign. Prominent supporters included Senators B. Gratz Brown of Missouri and John Sherman of Ohio.

Anthony Berger took this seated portrait on February 9, 1864.

CHAPTER 25

The Will of God Prevails
March 1864–November 1864

IN THE PRESENT CIVIL WAR IT IS QUITE POSSIBLE THAT GOD'S PUR-
POSE IS SOMETHING DIFFERENT FROM THE PURPOSE OF EITHER
PARTY—AND YET THE HUMAN INSTRUMENTALITIES, WORKING JUST
AS THEY DO, ARE OF THE BEST ADAPTATION TO EFFECT HIS PURPOSE.

ABRAHAM LINCOLN
Meditation on the Divine Will [1864]

IN MARCH 1864, ABRAHAM LINCOLN EAGERLY LOOKED FORWARD TO
meeting General Ulysses S. Grant for the first time. Lincoln had long
admired the small man from Galena, Illinois, and could not wait to talk
with him about what he hoped would become the war's decisive campaign in the spring and summer of 1864.

Grant arrived in Washington on the afternoon of March 8, 1864,
accompanied by his thirteen-year-old son, Fred. A planned official welcoming committee to meet him at the Baltimore and Ohio railway station never materialized, so Grant took a carriage with his son to the
Willard Hotel. Dressed in a travel-stained duster that hid his uniform,
he was not recognized by the hotel clerk, who assigned him to a small
room on the top floor. When the clerk turned the register around and
saw the name "U.S. Grant and son, Galena, Illinois," his demeanor suddenly changed. The now-attentive clerk reassigned Grant Parlor Suite
6, the best rooms in the hotel—indeed, the same ones Abraham and
Mary Lincoln had stayed in when they had arrived in Washington in
February 1861.

A message from the president awaited General Grant: Would he join
him that evening for the weekly reception at the White House?

After dinner at the Willard, where other guests gawked and gossiped about the famous general, Grant walked two blocks to the Executive Mansion. Directed through the foyer, he walked down the great corridor. When he entered the brightly decorated East Room, the guests fell silent. Grant saw the tall man at the far side of the room and walked toward him. Lincoln extended his hand. "Why, here is General Grant! Well, this is a great pleasure, I assure you."

Only nine days before, on Leap Year Day, February 29, 1864, the Senate confirmed what the House had already passed: The rank of lieutenant general, last held by General George Washington in 1798, would be conferred upon Grant in grateful recognition of his military accomplishments.

Lincoln turned Grant over to Secretary of State Seward, who introduced him all around. Shouts went up, "Grant, Grant, Grant," accompanied by cheer after cheer. It was one of the few times the president of the United States was not the center of attention, but, smiling, Lincoln seemed perfectly pleased to cede the spotlight. He hoped that the arrival of Grant as the new commander of all the Union armies would mean the beginning of the end of the war. Although quite willing to defer to his new military commander, as commander in chief, Lincoln also relished the opportunity to sit down with Grant to talk together about the upcoming campaigns.

TWO AND A HALF WEEKS LATER, on March 26, 1864, Lincoln received three visitors who had traveled all the way from Kentucky to give the president an earful about growing resentment in their native state over the recent recruiting of African-American troops. Kentucky governor Thomas E. Bramlette, former United States senator Archibald Dixon, and Albert G. Hodges, editor of the *Frankfort Commonwealth,* met with Lincoln for an unusually long Saturday morning interview. At the conclusion, Lincoln asked if he could make "a little speech." He wanted them to understand why he had changed course from the pledge in his inaugural address that he would not interfere with slavery where it already existed, to his decision to issue the Emancipation Proclamation and subsequently deploy black troops.

Lincoln's "little speech" made such an impact on Hodges that the editor came back in the afternoon to ask if he could take a copy of the president's remarks to Kentucky. Lincoln replied that what he had said was extemporaneous, but he told Hodges he would write him a letter re-creating his words.

Lincoln's public letter to Kentucky editor Albert G. Hodges spoke of
his attitude toward slavery and his own "agency" in the Civil War.

On April 4, 1864, Lincoln sent his promised letter, which, in the
intervening nine days, had become a public letter meant for an audience
beyond the three Kentucky leaders. The content and style rose to the
level of the president's best public rhetoric. His letter began forcefully:
"I am naturally anti-slavery. If slavery is not wrong, nothing is wrong. I
cannot remember when I did not so think, and feel." These initial words

were unambiguous. The president, who often acted as a moderator between extremes, now unequivocally owned his personal position as "anti-slavery."

The words achieve additional resonance when we remember to whom Lincoln was speaking. He was not talking with strong abolitionists such as Senators Charles Sumner and Henry Wilson of Massachusetts, but with leaders from a key border state. Next, he spoke about the tension he felt between his loathing for slavery and his duty under the Constitution.

And yet I have never understood that the Presidency conferred upon me an unrestricted right to act officially upon this judgment and feeling. It was in the oath I took that I would, to the best of my ability, preserve, protect, and defend the Constitution of the United States. I could not take the office without taking the oath. Nor was it my view that I might take an oath to get power, and break the oath in using the power. I understood, too, that in ordinary civil administration this oath even forbade me to practically indulge my primary abstract judgment on the moral question of slavery.

He reminded his audience that he had overruled attempts at emancipation by General John C. Frémont, former secretary of war Simon Cameron, and General David Hunter in South Carolina. He recalled his own three appeals for compensated emancipation in 1862, all of which the leaders of the border states rebuffed.

Lincoln reiterated this narrative in some detail so that the Kentuckians might appreciate that, in the latter part of 1862, he had been "driven to the alternative of either surrendering the Union, and with it, the Constitution," or arming Southern slaves. If at the beginning of his letter Lincoln spoke of his antislavery beliefs in moral terms, by the middle of the letter he discussed the arming of black soldiers in strategic terms.

Lincoln was remarkably candid in admitting the uncertainty in his decision. "I hoped for greater gain than loss; but of this, I was not entirely confident." Lincoln's willingness to openly discuss his doubts is a distinguishing characteristic of his political leadership.

As Hodges came to the end of the "little speech," he must have been surprised to see that the letter continued beyond what the president had said in their meeting. "I add a word which was not in the verbal conversation," he wrote.

> In telling this tale I attempt no complement to my own sagacity. I claim not to have controlled events, but confess plainly that events have controlled me. Now, at the end of three years struggle the nation's condition is not what either party, or any man devised, or expected. God alone can claim it. Whither it is tending seems plain. If God now wills the removal of a great wrong, and wills also that we of the North as well as you of the South, shall pay fairly for our complicity in that wrong, impartial history will find therein new cause to attest and revere the justice and goodness of God.

Some observers have used one sentence from this paragraph, "I claim not to have controlled events, but confess plainly that events have controlled me," to emphasize the overall passivity of Lincoln's leadership. They have suggested, with this sentence given as proof, that Lincoln's essential nature was more responsive than initiatory.

But if one reads the whole paragraph, it is clearly not about passivity. Lincoln, as if a lawyer in a courtroom, began his case with three negative statements:

1. "no complement to my own sagacity";
2. "I claim not to have controlled events";
3. "the nation's condition is not what either party, or any man devised or expected."

These negative assertions, building in crescendo from a singular negation of Lincoln himself, to the wider negation of "either party," to a universal negation of "any man," were meant to prompt the question: What was the source of "the nation's condition"?

Lincoln answered in four positive assertions that more than balanced the three negative ones.

1. "God alone can claim it";
2. "If God now wills the removal of a great wrong";

3. "wills that we of the North as well as you of the South, shall
   pay fairly for our complicity in that wrong";
4. "to attest and revere the justice and goodness of God."

The central meaning of the paragraph becomes clear. By employing the verb "devised," Lincoln spoke about the agency—the politicians and generals—responsible for carrying out the war. He did not exempt himself. The trajectory of the paragraph meant to underscore the "agency" of God. Crafted with a lawyer's logic, the letter pointed beyond Lincoln as president to God as the primary actor. Lincoln was quite willing to acknowledge his passivity as a way to emphasize the larger truth of the activity of God.

Hodges received Lincoln's letter with delight. Lincoln, in person and now by letter, made such a strong impression on the influential Kentucky editor that he began to correspond regularly with the president, supplying information and opinions about affairs in Kentucky. Starting on April 22, he would write twelve letters to Lincoln in 1864 and two more in 1865.

The ideas and language of the last paragraph of the letter to Hodges did not stay put. Eleven months later, that final paragraph would become the basis of the opening sentences of the third paragraph of Lincoln's finest speech.

AT SOME POINT during the latter part of his presidency, Lincoln put his pencil to a small piece of lined paper to ruminate on the question of the presence of God in the Civil War.

The will of God prevails. In great contests each party claims to act in accordance with the will of God. Both *may* be, and one *must* be, wrong. God cannot be *for* and *against* the same thing at the same time. In the present civil war it is quite possible that God's purpose is something different from the purpose of either party—and yet the human instrumentalities, working just as they do, are of the best adaptation to effect His purpose. I am almost ready to say that this is probably true—that God wills this contest, and wills that it shall not end yet. By his mere great power, on the minds of the now contestants, He could have either *saved* or *destroyed* the Union without a human contest. Yet

The will of God prevails— In great contests each party claims to act in accordance with the will of God. Both may be, and one must be wrong. God can not be for, and against the same thing at the same time. In the present civil war it is quite possible that God's purpose is something different from the purpose of either party— and yet the human instrumentalities, working just as they do, are of the best adaptation to effect His purpose. I am almost ready to say this is probably true— that God wills this contest, and wills that it shall not end yet— By his mere quiet power, on the minds of the now contestants, He could have either *saved* or *destroyed* the Union without a human contest— Yet the contest began— And having begun He could give the final victory to either side any day— Yet the contest proceeds—

Lincoln's private reflection "Meditation on the Divine Will," unknown during his life, is a signpost revealing his developing beliefs about the activity of God in the Civil War.

the contest began. And, having begun He could give the final victory to either side any day. Yet the contest proceeds.

A question is often asked of Lincoln's speeches: As a shrewd politician, did he use religion in his speeches because he knew it would play well with the largely churchgoing American public? This private reflection is critical in answering that question, for its theological ideas were never meant for public consumption.

As in his letter to Hodges, he started with an unambiguous affirmation. Lincoln brooded here not on an abstract problem in philosophy or theology; the impetus for his musing grew out of the very real forces of war pressing in upon him as president. He had received claims on a regular basis from delegations telling him that "God is on our side."

In this reflection, Lincoln weighed the validity of these claims. His first response: "Both *may* be, and one *must* be wrong." This language is typical of Lincoln as he thinks his way into a problem. At first he is tentative in his judgments. His tendency is to look at all sides of a problem. The rational Lincoln, as if working through the logic of a syllogism, comes to the conclusion that both of the claimants may be wrong and one must be wrong. Why? "God cannot be *for,* and *against* the same thing at the same time." His answer presumed something about the nature and purposes of God. For Lincoln, this God was not the original first cause of Jefferson. Lincoln's meditation is about a God who acts in history.

One sentence may be the best clue to Lincoln's understanding of God's purposes in the Civil War. "In the present civil war it is quite possible that God's purpose is something different from the purpose of either party—and yet the human instrumentalities, working just as they do, are of the best adaptation to effect His purpose." Lincoln appears to be seeking an equilibrium between God's action and human actions. Forced by the war to think more deeply, Lincoln emerged broader than his contemporaries in discerning the ways of God. While nearly everyone else, North and South, was declaring "God is on our side," Lincoln wrote that "God's purpose is something different from the purpose of either party." As the war was beginning to turn in the Union's favor, Lincoln had arrived at a remarkable declaration about God's purposes.

On the trip from Springfield to Washington in 1861, Lincoln had called himself one of those "human instrumentalities" on several occasions. In this reflection, he adds that "human instrumentalities" are "the best adaptation" to do God's work in the world. The noun "adaptation" suggests the act or process of adjustment to external conditions. With the word "almost," Lincoln suggested a point of view to which he was only now arriving. He qualified this affirmation further by the use of the second adverb, "probably."

Even more surprising was his judgment that God "wills that it shall not end yet." In public, Lincoln, as commander in chief, was working night and day to bring the war to an end; in private, he was writing that God seemed to be deciding that the war should continue.

Who, then, is this God of whom Lincoln speaks? Four times, in the brief 147 words of the reflection, Lincoln described God as a God who "wills." Lincoln's repetitive use of that active verb underscored the main point of his meditation: God is the primary if "quiet" actor in the war.

The content of this private reflection illuminates how far Lincoln had traveled on his journey from fatalism to providence. The modern suggestion that fatalism and providence are part of a continuum would have surprised Protestant theologians in the nineteenth century. The two constellations of ideas had different origins and different outcomes. In fatalism, events unfolded according to certain laws of nature. In 1859, Francis Wharton, author of *A Treatise on Theism and Modern Skeptical Theories,* described fatalism as "a distinct scheme of unbelief." Wharton, an Episcopal minister, who after the Civil War would become a professor at the new Episcopal Theological Seminary in Cambridge, Massachusetts, singled out fatalism as an opponent of Christianity because it did not acknowledge a God who acted in history. Wharton contrasted fatalism with the God of Christianity known by "his watchful care and love."

Lincoln's brief contemplation would remain unknown during his lifetime. John Hay would find it after Lincoln's death. In 1872, Hay gave it the title "Meditation on the Divine Will." But in 1865, this private musing, along with the letter to Hodges, would form the core of what would become Lincoln's best address.

WHAT WERE THE SOURCES of Lincoln's thinking about the purposes of God? Phineas Densmore Gurley, the minister of the New York Avenue Presbyterian Church, an often-overlooked person in the Lincoln story, is a chief resource. Lincoln's attendance at New York Avenue Presbyterian coincided with his deepening struggles to understand the meaning of God's activity in the war.

Beginning in March 1861, Abraham and Mary sat in their reserved pew eight rows from the front of the church sanctuary. Attorney General Edward Bates noted their attendance, as did Illinois senator Orville Browning. Noah Brooks, correspondent for the *Sacramento Daily Union,* observed the Lincolns from the gallery at New York Avenue "where they habitually attended." He wrote, "Conspicuous among them all, as the crowd poured out of the ailes, was the tall form of the Father of the Faithful, who is instantly recognizable."

As a young adult, Lincoln had reacted against his father's Baptist tradition with its low tolerance for questions and doubts. As president, he was drawn to Gurley's learned preaching with its steady punctuation of questions. Lincoln's Illinois friend Leonard Swett said of Lincoln, "The whole world to him was a question of cause and effect."

One of Lincoln's requirements for choosing a minister and a church was politics, or the lack thereof. In consulting Montgomery Blair, who may have recommended New York Avenue, Lincoln is reported to have said, "I wish to find a church whose clergyman holds himself aloof from politics." When asked about Gurley and his sermons, Lincoln is said to have replied, "I like Gurley. He don't preach politics. I get enough of that through the week."

Many times Lincoln heard Gurley preach sermons that were both intellectual and theological. Over and over again, Gurley highlighted God's loving providence in the world. Gurley's chief mentor at Princeton Seminary, Professor Charles Hodge, taught that the recognition of the personality of God was the key to the distinction between providence and fatalism. In his three-volume *Systematic Theology,* Hodge said of providence that "an infinitely wise, good, and powerful God is everywhere present, controlling all events great and small, necessary, and free, in a way perfectly consistent with the nature of his creatures and his own infinite excellence." In Christian theology, according to Hodge, God's divine power is able to embrace human freedom and responsibility.

A fellow minister described Gurley's ministry as "Calvinism presented in his beautiful examples and spirit and preaching." In Gurley's Calvinist emphasis on providence, he acknowledged, as Lincoln would increasingly do, elements of ambiguity and mystery. The Presbyterian minister called attention to the potential logical contradiction of free agency and God's governance. By the use of various metaphors, he heightened, not lessened, this paradox. "Man devises; the Lord directs." Or "man *proposes;* God *disposes.*" And, "man's agency, and God's overruling sovereignty." This theme of human agency and God's sovereignty, Gurley said, was the best way to understand "the probable fruits and consequences of the terrible struggle in which the nation has been engaged."

The president was present on August 6, 1863, when Gurley preached a sermon in response to Lincoln's recent call for a national day of public humiliation, prayer, and fasting. Gurley's sermon, "Man Projects and

God Results," was based on a text from Proverbs 16:9: "A man's heart
deviseth his way; but the Lord directs his steps."

"Man is a rational, a free, and, therefore an accountable moral
agent," Gurley preached, adding, "while this is true, it is also true that
God governs the world." Gurley went on to affirm, "He accomplishes
His fixed and eternal purposes through the instrumentality of free, and
accountable, and even *wicked* agents." That these themes in Gurley's
preaching struck a responsive chord in Lincoln would become clear in
the coming months.

IN LINCOLN'S NEWFOUND WILLINGNESS to speak outside Washington, he welcomed the invitation to address a sanitary fair in Baltimore
on April 18, 1864. The Sanitary Commission had become a chief organization aiding soldiers, and Lincoln decided to lend his presidential
hand in raising money for it. The memory of passing through Baltimore
in disguise on his way to Washington in February 1861 remained one of
the lowest moments in his life. He told the crowd he accepted the invitation because "the world moves," and he came to Baltimore to mark
the moving. He reminded his audience that at the beginning of the war
three years ago, Union "soldiers could not so much as pass through Baltimore."

In his speech, Lincoln offered compelling remarks on the meaning of
liberty. "The world has never had a good definition of the word liberty,
and the American people, just now, are in want of one." Lincoln
believed in clear definitions. "We all declare for Liberty; but in using the
same *word* we do not all mean the same *thing*." Lincoln explained: "With
some the word liberty may mean for each man to do as he pleased with
himself, and the product of his labor; while with others the same word
may mean for some men to do as they please with other men, and the
product of other men's labor." Lincoln underlined the tragic truth that
these two "incompatable things" were called by the same name—
liberty."

He drove his point home with a metaphor whose meaning no one
could miss. "The shepherd drives the wolf from the sheep's throat, for
which the sheep thanks the shepherd as a *liberator,* while the wolf
denounces him for the same act as the destroyer of liberty, especially if
the sheep was a black one."

As Lincoln came to the end of his speech he abruptly changed his tone. "A painful rumor, true I fear, has reached us of the massacre, by rebel forces, at Fort Pillow," a fort high above the Mississippi River forty miles north of Memphis.

Everyone in his audience had recently learned about the massacre. Early on the morning of April 14, 1864, Confederate general Nathan Bedford Forrest attacked Fort Pillow. Forrest was a guerrilla fighter revered in the South. Possessing no military education, he despised the West Point doctrine that called for holding one-third of one's forces in reserve. He achieved a reputation as the master of cavalry, using horses for lightning attacks by which his outnumbered troops could suddenly gain the advantage. To General William Sherman he was "that devil Forrest," who should be "hunted down and killed if it costs 10,000 lives and bankrupts the [national] treasury." Union major Lionel F. Booth had defended the fort with 580 troops, 292 of whom were African-American.

What followed became the subject of controversy, not just for weeks, but for years. The surviving Union soldiers reported that as the defenders of the fort were overwhelmed, the soldiers threw up their hands to surrender. They charged that the Confederate troops, disregarding the clear signs of surrender, proceeded to massacre the black soldiers. General Forrest's own report to his superior, General Leonidas Polk, stated, "The river was dyed red with the blood of the slaughtered for 200 yards."

In Baltimore Lincoln announced plans for a congressional investigation. He concluded his speech forcefully. "It will be a matter of grave consideration in what exact course to apply the retribution; but in the supported case, it must come." Lincoln, who up to this point in the war had downplayed all cries for revenge, plainly was caught up in the escalating talk of retribution.

On April 22, 1864, the Joint Committee on the Conduct of the War began public hearings. In a highly charged atmosphere, their report mixed fact-finding and propaganda. The cries to execute Confederate prisoners in eye-for-eye reprisals grew.

On May 3, 1864, Lincoln asked his cabinet "to give me in writing your opinion as to what course the government should take in this case." He received long and quite different replies. Seward, Chase, Stanton, and Welles argued that Confederate troops equal in number to the Union troops massacred should be held as hostages and killed if the

Confederate government admitted the massacre. Bates and John P. Usher, who had succeeded Caleb Smith as secretary of the interior, advocated no retaliation against innocent hostages, but argued execution of the offenders if apprehended.

There is no record of Lincoln's opinion in response to the recommendations of the members of his cabinet. He rarely had a heart for revenge and may have simply allowed the discussion of retaliation for Fort Pillow to be overtaken by more pressing events on the battlefield demanding his attention in the spring of 1864.

MEANWHILE, LINCOLN'S NEW COMMANDER, Ulysses S. Grant, pressed ahead. Grant had told his best friend, General William Sherman, that he feared if he came to Washington he would get stuck behind a desk, so he established his headquarters in the field at Culpeper Court House in Virginia. What a contrast to George McClellan's command from his opulent rented Washington home. Lincoln met with Grant three times at the White House in March and April and anticipated accepting Grant's invitation for a fourth meeting at Grant's Virginia headquarters in April, but the president was unable to keep that date.

Grant's plan for the 1864 spring offensive directed his senior commanders to move simultaneously on five fronts. In the past, Confederate generals, although almost always outnumbered, had shifted their interior lines to meet the often disjointed attacks of the Union forces. In the East, Grant ordered General George Meade's Army of the Potomac to cross the Rapidan River in northern Virginia and attack Robert E. Lee's Army of Northern Virginia without letting up. General Franz Sigel would drive his army south up the Shenandoah Valley and apply pressure on Richmond from the west, while General Benjamin Butler, coming up from Fort Monroe at the tip of the Virginia peninsula, would push toward Richmond from the south. In the West, Grant directed William Tecumseh Sherman, his successor as leader of the armies of the Cumberland, Ohio, and Tennessee, now one hundred thousand strong, to slice southeast through Georgia to capture Atlanta, a valuable railroad center. In a secondary move, Nathaniel Banks would overcome Mobile, Alabama, and push north to unite with Sherman.

Grant told Meade, "Lee's army will be your objective point. . . . Wherever Lee goes, there you will go also." He instructed Sherman "to move against Johnston's army, to break it up." Lincoln backed Grant's plan. Finally, Lincoln had found a commander who believed with him that opposing armies, not Richmond or Atlanta, should be the real focus of the Union armies.

At the end of April, as the military campaign was about to begin, Lincoln wrote Grant, "Not expecting to see you again before the Spring campaign opens." The president expressed "entire satisfaction with what you have done up to this time." He added, "You are vigilant and self-reliant; and pleased with this, I wish not to obtrude any constraints or restraints upon you." Lincoln had waited a long time to be able to declare such confidence in his commanding general. At the beginning of the war, Lincoln had expressed deference to his commanding generals because he recognized what he did not know. Now, after three years during which he taught himself a great deal about military strategy, he gladly expressed a new kind of deference, not because he did not know or have an opinion, but because of his implicit trust in Grant.

IN THE EARLY MORNING HOURS of May 4, 1864, the Army of the Potomac broke their winter camp and crossed the Rapidan River seventeen miles west of Fredericksburg in northern Virginia. The politicians and the public believed that with Grant now in charge, the war would be over by the fall of 1864. Indeed, the Army of the Potomac was confident, well clothed, and equipped with ample ammunition. Days before, Robert E. Lee had withdrawn his army from the Rapidan, ill-clad, ill-equipped, but also confident in themselves and their ability to fight on their home ground, and in their leader. If Grant and Meade's tactics were to press forward at all times, Lee's tactic now was to defend and delay. He hoped to defeat an enemy at least twice his size by exacting such losses that the Northern public and politicians would finally come to believe victory was not worth the cost.

Lee pulled his forces back from the Rapidan River into "the Wilderness," twelve miles wide and six miles deep, a part of the area where the battle of Chancellorsville had been fought a year before. He chose this dense forest of second-growth scrub oak and dwarf pines, interlaced by streams and roads and trails, so that Union superiority in numbers could be neutralized, and Union artillery rendered practically useless. On May 5 and 6, 1864, firefights erupted in the thick undergrowth, often setting it on fire, as both sides gave no quarter in this forbidding landscape.

As Lincoln huddled with Secretary Stanton at the War Department, reports came in from the Wilderness of two days of terrible, confusing fighting. Lee's forces, although outnumbered two to one, believed they won a victory in the Wilderness, but Grant did not consider the battles a defeat. He did not retreat north of the Rapidan as Joe Hooker had done a year earlier after the battle of Chancellorsville. Both sides paid dearly in the battle of the Wilderness as the Union suffered eighteen thousand casualties and the Confederates close to eleven thousand.

In the midst of the battle of the Wilderness a young cub reporter for the *New York Tribune* arrived at the White House with a message from General Grant for the president: "There will be no turning back." Lincoln put his long arm around the young man and "pressed a kiss on his cheek."

The next day, Schuyler Colfax, Speaker of the House of Representatives, called on Lincoln. "I saw [Lincoln] walk up and down the Executive Chamber, his long arms behind his back, his dark features contracted still more with gloom." As they met, "I thought his face the saddest one I had ever seen." Yet Lincoln "quickly recovered" when the conversation turned to General Grant. "Hope beamed on his face."

Grant was now determined to stay on the offensive. He moved his army around Lee's right flank and pushed south toward Richmond. Lincoln told John Hay, "I believe that if any other General had been at the Head of that army it would have been on this side of the Rapidan." Lincoln summed up his confidence in Grant: "It is the dogged pertinacity of Grant that wins."

At Spotsylvania Court House, twelve miles to the southeast of the Wilderness, Union forces ran into a fierce Southern defense: a complex system of breastworks, trenches, and artillery emplacements that allowed the outnumbered Confederates to engage in a strong defensive fight. As the battle was about to begin, Elihu Washburne, the congressman from Grant's home district who sometimes traveled with the general, decided to return to Washington. Washburne asked Grant if he could take a message to Lincoln and Stanton. The general, realizing he was in a much tougher fight than he had imagined, did not want to paint too positive a picture, which could be misinterpreted by a public hungry for news of victories. Chomping on his cigar, he wrote, "I propose to fight it out on this line if it takes all summer."

Nonetheless, the initial reports of Grant's successes at Spotsylvania, including the capture of three thousand prisoners, produced euphoria in the North. Yet subsequent news from Spotsylvania told of twenty consecutive hours of fighting at the Bloody Angle, the top of the U of Lee's defensive formation, in which bodies stacked up five feet deep. Lincoln could see the cost of the battle in the streets of Washington as the wounded arrived throughout the day and night. Attorney General Edward Bates wrote in his diary on May 15, 1864, "For the last 8 or 10 days, the most terrible battles of the war have occurred in Virginia. The carnage has been unexampled." After so much bloodshed, questions began to rise about the price of victory. Grant and Meade had suffered sixty thousand casualties in one month of fighting, almost the size of Lee's entire army.

The carnage increased as Grant attacked the crossroads called Cold Harbor at the beginning of June. Lee, for whom Grant had increasing respect, was turning this war into a war of attrition, and so Grant decided to mount a massive assault. On the morning of June 3, 1864, hundreds of troops pinned their names and addresses to their uniforms in a premonition of what lay ahead. In the next hours, Union soldiers charged forward and were met by a withering hail of bullets. Grant lost 7,000 men, while Lee, fighting from trenches, suffered 1,500 casualties. At the end of the day Grant stopped the attack, admitting defeat. The Union army learned that day what European armies would learn a half century later in World War I: the deadly horrors of trench warfare. General George Meade wrote to his wife, "I think Grant has had his eyes opened, and is willing to admit now that Virginia and Lee's army is not Tennessee and Bragg's army."

The public began to turn against Grant, but Lincoln did not. The president told Noah Brooks, "I wish when you write and speak to people you would do all you can to correct the impression that the war in Virginia will end right off victoriously." He continued, "To me the most trying thing in all this war is that people are too sanguine; they expect too much at once." Lincoln, who would not make predictions, told Brooks, "As God is my judge, I shall be satisfied if we are over with the fight in Virginia within a year."

EVEN WITH SALMON CHASE'S WITHDRAWAL from the Republican field for president in March, the anti-Lincoln sentiment among Republican radicals did not go away. On May 31, 1864, four hundred radicals, in what Henry Raymond of the *New York Times* called "the bolter's convention," gathered in Cleveland's Chapin Hall to nominate an alternative candidate for president. Passionate speeches called for suppressing the South and confiscating all the territory under federal authority. Some speakers called for suffrage to be expanded to blacks. Elizabeth Cady Stanton and other women's rights advocates led a contingent of women to the convention. General John C. Frémont, with a deep personal animus toward Lincoln, was nominated as the presidential candidate on this third-party ticket.

Lincoln, in the telegraph office, received the announcement of Frémont's nomination. He asked for a Bible and fingered through the Old Testament to 1 Samuel 22:2, the story of David standing before the cave of Adullam. "And every one that was discontented, gathered themselves unto him; and he became a captain over them; and there were with him about four hundred men."

In the first week of June, well-wishers and office seekers came through Washington to shake the hand of the president on their way to the National Union Party convention in Baltimore. The distressing news from Cold Harbor blighted what should have been anticipation of Lincoln's nomination, by now a foregone conclusion, for a second term. Lincoln, following nineteenth-century protocol, would not be present in Baltimore, but that did not mean he had not been working behind the scenes to help shape the convention. On June 5, 1864, John Nicolay and Simon Cameron traveled to the convention on behalf of the president. Leonard Swett, always ready to help, traveled in from Illinois. Henry J. Raymond, editor of the *New York Times,* who had become a chief Lincoln supporter among newspaper editors, had been writing a first history of Lincoln's administration, a full 496 pages containing a brief biographical sketch but composed mostly of Lincoln's letters, speeches, and proclamations, which he published on the eve of the convention.

At twelve noon on June 7, 1864, New York senator Edwin G. Morgan, national chairman of the Republican Party, gaveled the convention to order at the Front Street Theatre. Morgan had been a Seward man at Chicago in 1860, but during the past four years his admiration for Lincoln had grown steadily. Now, after huddling with the president in Washington before the convention, he told the delegates what they wanted to hear. "In view of the dread realities of the past . . . and with the knowledge . . . that this has been caused by slavery," Morgan, with Lincoln's strong approval, proposed as the chief plank in the convention platform "an amendment of the Constitution as will positively prohibit African slavery in the United States."

The next day, Raymond presented the planks of the platform. In a convention that Lincoln hoped would bring a National Union Party together, the sixth resolution steered the boat in the other direction. The plank called for a purge of any cabinet member who did not "cordially endorse the principles proclaimed in these resolutions." The plank was clearly aimed at Montgomery Blair, whom the radicals had grown to disdain for his attacks on them. Beneath the formal language, the plank demanded the president fire Blair.

Vice President Hamlin waited to hear news that he, too, would be renominated, but he waited in vain. Over the past four years, Hamlin had moved steadily toward the camp of the radicals. For months, word had been gossiped that Lincoln preferred Andrew Johnson, War Democrat governor of Tennessee. When various emissaries before and during the convention tried to get Lincoln to name his preference, he said he would leave it up to the convention. Hay wired Nicolay that the president wished "not to interfere in the nomination even by a confidential suggestion."

Lincoln and Johnson formed an unlikely duo that elicited much comment after the convention. The *Richmond Examiner* reported that the Union Party had nominated the "Illinois rail-splitter" and the "Tennessee tailor." By contrast, Charles Sumner, representing the sentiment of the convention, called Andrew Johnson the "faithful among the faithless" and "the Abdiel of the South," referencing the figure in the Bible and in John Milton's *Paradise Lost* who denounces Satan. Lincoln appreciated Johnson's courage in standing against his native state in support of the Union. But, as time and different circumstances would reveal later, Lincoln and Johnson were quite different in temperament and perspective on the South.

On June 9, 1864, a committee composed of one delegate from each state present at the convention called on the president at the White House to offer official notification of his nomination. Lincoln replied, "I will neither conceal my gratification, nor restrain the expression of my gratitude, that the Union people . . . in their continued effort to save, and advance the nation, have deemed me not unworthy to remain in my present position." Lincoln then took the unusual step of saying he could "not declare definitely" he would accept the nomination until he read the platform. He took this opportunity to say to the committee that his first priority would be "amending the Constitution as to prohibit slavery throughout the nation." He concluded his acceptance, "In the joint names of Liberty and Union," reflecting how the aim of the war had changed in the space of four years.

FOLLOWING THE CONVENTION, Montgomery Blair offered Lincoln his resignation. The president refused to accept it. He valued Blair's loyalty and was not about to have his advisers prescribed by others. Blair's resignation was undated and he told the president to use it whenever he needed to relieve the pressure from the radicals.

The larger burr under Lincoln's saddle was Salmon Chase. Although Lincoln knew Chase took many opportunities to criticize him behind his back, up until now Lincoln found no fault with how Chase ran the Treasury Department. His ability to raise and manage money lay behind the expansion and mobilization of the Union army. Lincoln was sympathetic to Chase's efforts, often in the face of a Congress that refused to raise adequate taxes to support the war effort. Twice in three years Chase had submitted his resignation, but Lincoln had not accepted it.

In June 1864, Lincoln found himself between the strong-willed Chase and the wishes of New York senator Edwin Morgan over a key appointment. When Chase nominated Maunsell B. Field as assistant treasurer in New York, Lincoln wrote him, "I can not, without much embarrassment, make this appointment, principally because of Senator Morgan's firm opposition to it." Lincoln then proceeded to give Chase three options of qualified persons from which he could choose. These names had been suggested by Morgan, and Chase instantly recognized them as allies of his longtime rival, Seward, and, from his perspective, having little financial experience.

Chase objected. The next day he asked for a private meeting with the president. Lincoln, probably wanting to avert another debate with Chase, replied immediately that he could not meet with him "because the difficulty does not, in the main part, lie within the range of a conversation between you and me." Lincoln was saying, as politely as he could, that the leaders of New York had a right to offer their judgment on whoever would serve as the assistant treasurer of their state.

Chase, acting impulsively and with rising anger, resigned. He wrote Lincoln on June 29, 1864, "I cannot help feeling that my position here is not altogether agreeable to you; and it is certainly too full of embarrassment and difficulty and painful responsibility to allow in me the least desire to retain it."

Lincoln, who usually did not act impulsively, accepted Chase's resignation. Lincoln wrote, "Of all I have said in commendation of your ability and fidelity, I have nothing to unsay; and yet you and I have reached a point of mutual embarrassment in our official relation which it seems can not be overcome, or longer sustained, consistently with the public service."

After writing out his brief letter, Lincoln called for Hay. "When does the Senate meet today?"

"Eleven o'clock."

"I wish you to be there when they meet. It is a big fish. Mr. Chase has resigned & I have accepted his resignation. I thought I could not stand it any longer."

THE NATIONAL UNION PARTY convention had adjourned on an upbeat note in June, but back in Washington everything had seemed to deteriorate. Discontent with Lincoln simmered just below the surface of outward enthusiasm. Discouraging news from Grant and Meade's spring offensive grew apace and began to diminish the earlier optimism about Lincoln's chances for reelection. Sherman seemed stuck in Georgia with little communication about his movements. Lincoln had undergone other seasons of despair—after the first battle of Bull Run in the summer of 1861, the discouraging battles on the Virginia peninsula in the spring and summer of 1862, after Fredericksburg in December 1862, and following the defeat at Chancellorsville in May 1863—but the spirits of Lincoln and the North descended to their lowest point yet in the summer of 1864. Detractors in the North, including one in the White House, Mary Lincoln, began calling Lincoln's commander "Grant the Butcher." The Northern public began to ask if victory was worth the enormous cost in human life.

By the middle of June, Grant's advance corps reached Petersburg, twenty miles southeast of Richmond. After achieving some early success, Meade and Grant expected a breakthrough, but it was not to be. Ending seven weeks of forward movement, they settled in for a long siege. By the time Grant reached Petersburg, he had lost so many officers and troops that he found himself relying on fatigued veterans and inexperienced new volunteers.

Lincoln accepted another invitation to another sanitary fair, this one in Philadelphia, because he knew he needed opportunities to speak to a discouraged public.

On June 16, 1864, he got right to the point. "War, at the best, is terrible, and this war of ours, in its magnitude and duration, is one of the most terrible." He described what his audience was experiencing. "It has damaged business. . . . It has destroyed property, and ruined homes; it has produced a national debt and taxation unprecedented." Most of all, "it has carried mourning to almost every home, until it can almost be said that the 'heavens are hung in black.'" Lincoln declared, "We accepted this war for an object, a worthy object, and the war will end when the object is attained."

In early July, the terror of war came to the front door of Washington. General Jubal Early led fifteen thousand Confederate troops down the Shenandoah Valley and across the Potomac River into Maryland. Pushing aside a Union force east of Frederick on July 9, they set their sights on Washington. The irony of this fourth summer of war was not lost on anyone: Union fear for Washington suddenly replaced Confederate anxiety about Richmond. Lincoln quickly realized that there were few men left to defend Washington. On July 11, Early reached the outskirts of Washington near Silver Spring and burned the home of Postmaster General Montgomery Blair. The next day, as Early's troops came within five miles of the White House, Lincoln traveled to Fort Stevens to see the combat in person. As he peered out over a parapet, a sharpshooter's bullet came perilously close. According to legend, a young army captain, Oliver Wendell Holmes, Jr., who would later serve on the Supreme Court, yelled out, "Get down, you damn fool, before you get shot."

In this summer of despondency, a welcome visitor was Joshua Speed. When Speed arrived at the Soldiers' Home he found Lincoln sitting reading the Bible. Speed said, "I am glad to see you profitably engaged." "Yes," said Lincoln, "I am profitably engaged." "Well," Speed continued, "if you have recovered from your skepticism, I am sorry to say that I have not." Lincoln rose, placed his hand on Speed's shoulder, and said, "You are wrong, Speed. Take all this book upon reason that you can and the balance on faith, and you will live and die a happier and better man." Speed, describing himself as a skeptic, in his recollection of this conversation had little incentive to magnify Lincoln's use of the Bible.

In addition to the bad news from the battlefield, Lincoln began receiving pessimistic reports about his prospects for reelection. Henry B. Raymond, editor of the *New York Times,* wrote Lincoln from the Republican National Committee in New York City on August 22, 1864, with disturbing news, telling Lincoln that New York "would go

50,000 against us tomorrow." Raymond reported that Illinois congressman Elihu Washburne believed that if the election were "to be held now in Illinois we should be beaten." Simon Cameron, Lincoln's former secretary of war, predicted "Pennsylvania is against us."

Why this dismal turn of events? Raymond wrote candidly about Lincoln's difficulty. "The want of military success, and the impression in some minds, the fear and suspicion in others, that we are not to have peace *in any event* under this Administration until Slavery is abandoned." Lincoln, long criticized by abolitionists and radical Republicans for going too slowly on slavery, now was being arraigned for standing his ground on the moral imperative of getting rid of slavery in the new Union. In sum, Raymond told Lincoln, "The tide is setting strongly against us."

By early August, Lincoln was convinced that he could not be reelected. On August 23, 1864, six days before the Democratic convention would select his opponent, Lincoln wrote a private memorandum stating his feelings.

> This morning, as for some days past, it seems exceedingly probable that this administration will not be re-elected. Then it will be my duty to so cooperate with the President-elect as to save the Union between the election and the inauguration; as he will have secured his election on such ground that he cannot possibly save it afterwards.

Lincoln brought his message to that day's cabinet meeting. He presented it to his colleagues, folded so that none of the text was visible, and asked each of them to sign the back of the document. Lincoln never explained why he did not read or show the members of his cabinet the contents of his memo. Lincoln surely believed that if a Democrat was elected president, that person would end the war on the terms that guaranteed Confederate independence.

THE DEMOCRATS HEADED for Chicago at the end of August for their ninth national convention. Eleven railroad lines, each overflowing with delegates, converged on the new capital of the Midwest. Noah Brooks, dispatched by Lincoln to be his observer, caught a train from Washington on August 25, 1864, quickly finding himself "burdened with Copperheads." Before the Sacramento writer departed, Lincoln predicted to Brooks, "They must nominate a Peace Democrat on a war platform, or

Executive Mansion,

Washington, Aug. 23, 1864.

This morning, as for some days past, it seems exceedingly probably that this Administration will not be re-elected. Then it will be my duty to so coöperate with the ~~Government~~ President elect, as to save the Union between the election and the inauguration; as he will have secured his election on such ground that he cannot possibly save it afterwards.

A. Lincoln.

William H. Seward

W.P. Fessenden

Edwin M. Stanton

Gideon Welles

Edward Bates

M. Blair

J.P. Usher

August 23. 1864

On August 23, 1864, Lincoln wrote a memo for his cabinet revealing his belief that he could not be reelected for a second term as president.

a War Democrat on a peace platform; and I personally can't say I care much which they do."

The Democrats fulfilled Lincoln's prediction. They sought to find middle ground between the two wings of their party. The War Democrats succeeded in nominating Lincoln's former top military commander General George B. McClellan for president. The Peace Democrats, most notably Clement Vallandigham, wrote a platform that declared "after four years of failure to restore the Union by the experiment of war, . . . justice, humanity, liberty and the public welfare demand" an end to the war "on the basis of the Federal Union of States." August Belmont, who called the convention to order on August 29, 1864, warned his fellow Democrats that dissension in their ranks had cost them the 1860 election. At the end of the convention the two branches of the Democratic Party had arrived at a compromise. But would it last?

The Democrats had waited to hold their convention until the end of the summer, hoping that the continuing bad news would be good news for their candidate. Now they waited some more. For days, George McClellan, at his home in Orange, New Jersey, struggled to determine

640 / A. Lincoln

how to run as a War Democrat on a peace platform. He stayed out of sight as he worked on draft after draft of an acceptance letter. Advice poured in from every quarter as to how the general could reconcile the war and peace branches of his party and go on the offensive against Lincoln.

But before McClellan would speak, General William Tecumseh Sherman spoke. The fall political campaign had barely begun when, on September 3, 1864, a telegram arrived from General Sherman announcing, "Atlanta is ours, and fairly won." The victory at Atlanta, an important railroad and manufacturing city, against two Confederate armies, was one of the most important military accomplishments of the war. Sherman took Atlanta by surrounding the city with overwhelming force and persuading its defenders to evacuate and retreat rather than fight and risk heavy loss of life, both military and civilian.

Sherman's victory at Atlanta changed everything overnight. "Glorious news this morning—*Atlanta taken at last!!!*" wrote George Templeton Strong in New York. He understood the impact of this event. "It is the greatest event of the war." The mood of pessimism broke immediately. A revival of Unionist fervor began to sweep through the North. Lincoln's spirits were buoyed.

After this turn of events, McClellan released a letter at midnight on September 8, 1854. After declaring he had not sought the nomination, he affirmed, "The preservation of our Union was the sole avowed object for which the war was commenced." What he did not say, loudly, was that the war should never have been fought to overthrow slavery. He obviously struggled over the peace platform and renounced it when he said: "I could not look in the face of my gallant comrades of the army and navy who have survived so many bloody battles, and tell them their labors and the sacrifices of so many of our slain and wounded brethren had been in vain." McClellan was saying for all who would hear that he was not willing to end the war at any price. With these words, he hoped he could garner the large soldiers' vote.

McClellan's published letter both electrified and disappointed Democrats. War Democrats became convinced they had their candidate, a man who could garner the soldiers' votes and push Lincoln out of office. But New York Democratic mayor Fernando Wood was not so sure. Realizing McClellan's no-win position, he suggested reconvening the Democratic convention "either to remodel the platform to suit the nominee, or nominate a candidate to suit the platform." Henry Raymond, discouraged with Lincoln's chances in August, now editorialized in September, "Well, we see at last Gen. McClellan practices his favorite strategy—with bold front he fights shy." Raymond described McClellan as "all ambition and no courage, all desire and no decision."

IN KEEPING WITH CAMPAIGN PROTOCOL, neither Lincoln nor McClellan campaigned in person but left it to surrogates to make their cases to the public. By September, cartoonists disparaged General McClellan in comparison to Lincoln. Frank Bellew, in *Harper's Weekly,* drew a visual contrast between a large Lincoln and a small McClellan. The caption heightened the contrast. A political cartoon portrayed McClellan as the

The illustration "This reminds me of a little joke"
appeared in Harper's Weekly *on September 17, 1864.*

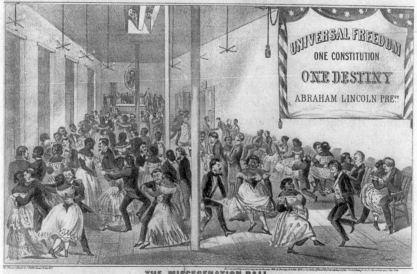

POLITICAL CARICATURE. N⁰4.

UNIVERSAL FREEDOM
ONE CONSTITUTION
ONE DESTINY
ABRAHAM LINCOLN PRE⁵ᵗ

THE MISCEGENATION BALL

at the Headquarters of the Lincoln Central Campaign Club, Corner of Broadway and Twenty Third Street New York Sept. 22ᵈ 1864 being a perfect fac simile of the room &c. &c. (From the New York World Sept. 23ᵈ 1864) No sooner were the formal proceedings and speeches hurried through with, than the room was cleared for a 'negro ball', which then and there took place.' Some members of the Central Lincoln Club 'left the room before the mystical and circling rites of Inodysalung [?] glasses and many dance commenced. But that MANY remained is also true. This fact WE CERTIFY, that on the floor during the progress of the ball were many of the ennobled leaders of the Black Republican party, thus testifying their faith by their works in the hall and headquarters of their political gathering. There were Republican OFFICE-HOLDERS, and prominent men of various degrees, and at least one PRESIDENTIAL ELECTOR ON THE REPUBLICAN TICKET."

This anti-Republican satire, "The Miscegenation Ball," was a campaign cartoon meant to tie Lincoln to radical abolitionism. The artist portrays the fear of racial intermingling—white men are dancing with black women in a large hall. Above the musicians' stage hangs a portrait of Abraham Lincoln.

one man keeping Abraham Lincoln and Jefferson Davis from continuing to attack each other. Another portrayed McClellan as a traitor to the ideals of liberty and yet another showed Lincoln as a dictator. A cartoon popular with Democrats portrayed Lincoln presiding at a ball where white men were dancing with black women. A new word, "miscegenation," had been coined by two reporters for the *New York World* in 1863, and now was used to attack Lincoln. The two Latin roots, *miscere,* to mix, and *genus,* race, replaced the old word, amalgamation, and instantly produced more loathing and disgust. A tract called "The Lincoln Catechism" claimed that Lincoln's ultimate goal was miscegenation.

Lincoln and the Republicans campaigned on a theme of "No Peace Without Victory." Posters, ribbons, ferrotypes, medals, and tokens in the 1864 presidential campaign became visible everywhere. An 1864 campaign ribbon captured the now clearly understood twin goals of the

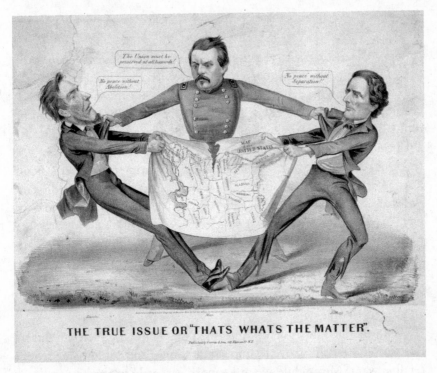

THE TRUE ISSUE OR "THATS WHATS THE MATTER".

This cartoon depicts General George McClellan as the one peace figure who can keep President Abraham Lincoln and President Jefferson Davis apart.

war: "Union and Liberty." Another medal was inscribed: "Freedom to All Men / War for the Union." The theme of human rights was captured in tokens. One side read "Lincoln," while on the other side was inscribed "Proclaim Liberty Throughout the Land." Another read "Lincoln and Liberty" on one side and on the other, "Freedom/Justice/Truth."

The change in the fortunes of battle energized the Lincoln reelection campaign. Ulysses S. Grant and William T. Sherman captured the public's imagination, and both were known to admire Lincoln. But something more began to emerge across the North. Despite the politicians' wariness about Lincoln, the people were not suspicious but enthusiastic. Lincoln had communicated his love for the Union in his public letters and at Gettysburg. They believed in him. The commander in chief, better known to his troops as Father Abraham, found an admiration and affection among the troops that seemed ready to translate into votes on the first Tuesday in November.

JUST AS THE FALL political campaign began, after a lapse of more than a year, Lincoln resumed his correspondence with Mrs. Eliza Gurney, the Quaker leader who had called on him in his office in the fall of 1862. Gurney wrote the president in August 1863, but there is no record of his reply. Lincoln received scores of delegations of religious leaders, but for a reason never explained, he felt free to share his deepest thoughts with this Quaker woman. On September 4, 1864, writing right after Lincoln learned of the capture of Atlanta, he seemed more confident of the purposes of God than he had been two years earlier in his first letter to Gurney. "The purposes of the Almighty are perfect," he now wrote. The president believed these purposes "must prevail, though we erring mortals may fail to accurately perceive them in advance." He expressed to Mrs. Gurney both his hopes and his resignation. "We hoped for a happy termination of this terrible war long before this; but God knows best, and has ruled otherwise."

With the terrible violence unleashed by Grant and Sherman during this period, Lincoln strove to understand how good could come from a terrible war. "Meanwhile we must work earnestly in the best light He gives us, trusting that so working still conduces to the great ends He ordains. Surely He intends some great good to follow this mighty convulsion, which no mortal could make, and no mortal could stay."

ELECTION DAY, November 8, 1864, dawned dark and rainy in Washington. McClellan had been counting on the soldiers' votes, but Republicans, in control of all the state legislatures except New Jersey, Indiana, and Illinois, determined to provide absentee ballots in hopes the soldiers would vote for the commander in chief.

At seven in the evening, Lincoln walked to the telegraph office with John Hay and Noah Brooks to follow the returns. Initial returns from Philadelphia brightened everyone's spirits. Lincoln had the results taken to Mary, who, he acknowledged, "is more anxious than I." The telegraph chatter continued to signal good news. At a midnight supper, Lincoln, in a jubilant mood, passed out oysters to everyone.

The final election results revealed that Lincoln had won an overwhelming victory. He received 2,203,831 votes to McClellan's 1,797,019. He won the electoral vote even more decisively, 221 to 21, winning every state except New Jersey, Delaware, and Kentucky. Lincoln won, but even Republicans admitted that, for many, the vote was against McClellan as much as for Lincoln. The president did feel a sense of relief and pride, however, in the soldiers' vote: 116,887 for him and only 37,748 for General McClellan.

Lincoln would approach his second inauguration vindicated personally and expecting final victory on the field of battle.

Alexander Gardner took this photograph on February 5, 1865, one month before Lincoln's second inaugural address. The photograph shows the tremendous aging that had taken place in just four years.

CHAPTER 26

With Malice Toward None, with Charity for All
December 1864–April 1865

A KING'S CURE FOR ALL THE EVILS.

ABRAHAM LINCOLN
Describing the Thirteenth Amendment, February 1, 1865

ABRAHAM LINCOLN WENT TO BED AFTER MIDNIGHT ON ELECTION night, November 8, 1864. His old friend Ward Hill Lamon, who had always worried about the president's safety more than anyone, gathered some blankets and lay down in front of the president's bedroom door armed with a brace of pistols and a Bowie knife. Knowing Lincoln would have discounted any danger, Lamon left before the president awoke in the morning.

Lamon had been warning the president of danger from the moment he accompanied Lincoln on his midnight train ride through Baltimore to Washington after an assassination plot was uncovered in February 1861. His fears increased when Lincoln started riding back and forth from the White House to the Soldiers' Home in the summer of 1862. At that time, Lamon urged upon him "the necessity of a military escort," but the president waved off the suggestion and persisted in riding alone. One evening at about eleven, a rifle shot rang out as Lincoln rode from the White House to the Soldiers' Home. Lincoln's horse, Old Abe, took off "at a break-neck speed." The next morning Lincoln, minus his eight-dollar plug hat, told Lamon this story but to his surprise, "in a spirit of levity," Lincoln protested that it must have been an accident, but admitted, "I tell you there is no time on record equal to that made by the two Old Abes on that occasion."

The threats to Lincoln multiplied after his reelection when foes, both in the South and North, recognized that the president would be in office for another four years. In December 1864, Lamon put his concerns in writing. "I regret that you do not appreciate what I have repeatedly said to you in regard to proper police arrangements connected with your household and your own personal safety." He added, "You know, or ought to know, that your life is sought after, and will be taken unless you and your friends are cautious; for you have many enemies within our lines." His plea to the president: "*You are in danger.*"

TWO NIGHTS LATER, Lincoln greeted serenaders from a second-floor window at the White House. In prepared remarks he spoke to them not about a Republican triumph, but about the fact "that a people's government can sustain a national election, in the midst of a great civil war." Lincoln said the election affirmed that "he who is most devoted to the Union, and most opposed to treason, can receive most of the people's votes." With the debate over the future of Reconstruction after the war on the lips of politicians, Lincoln signaled his attitude. "For my own part I have striven to avoid placing any obstacle in the way. So long as I have been here I have not willingly planted a thorn in any man's bosom." Many in Lincoln's own party did not appreciate the president's offering of reconciliation.

In the weeks that followed, Lincoln looked toward a second term that would last until March 1869. He busied himself thinking about his staff, cabinet, and an important judicial appointment. In his first term Lincoln had enjoyed the full support of his two loyal secretaries, John Nicolay and John Hay, but he knew they were exhausted. The president intended to reward their service by appointing them to diplomatic positions in France.

He already knew who would take their place. In the last two years of his first term, no one had become closer to Lincoln than Noah Brooks, the politically perceptive correspondent for the *Sacramento Daily Union*. Brooks had become a trusted friend as well as a liaison with the press. Born in Castine, Maine, Brooks moved to Dixon, Illinois, in 1856, where he first became acquainted with Lincoln during John C. Frémont's Republican presidential campaign. Brooks moved to California in 1859, but when his wife died in childbirth in 1862, he accepted an assignment to report for the *Sacramento Daily Union* from Washington. He enjoyed unusual access to the president. When so many around Lincoln constantly pestered him for preferment, Brooks asked nothing for himself.

Lincoln needed to make new cabinet appointments. Attorney General Edward Bates, at seventy-one, had decided to step down. Lincoln asked James Speed, the older brother of Joshua Speed, to accept this important post. Unlike his younger brother, James Speed was an early and strong opponent of slavery. "I am a thorough Constitutional Abolitionist," he had declared in the fall campaign of 1864.

Lincoln appointed Ohioan William Dennison, who had chaired the National Union Party convention in Baltimore in June 1864, to replace Montgomery Blair, who had resigned. Lincoln would also replace the largely ineffectual interior secretary, John P. Usher, with Senator James Harlan of Iowa, a strong supporter of Lincoln. Treasury Secretary William Fessenden told Lincoln he wanted to return to the Senate, so the president selected the competent if colorless Hugh McCullough, comptroller of the currency, for treasury.

Taken together, these appointments signaled the prospect of a quite different leadership style for Lincoln's second term. In his first term he had selected recognized leaders for his cabinet, both Republican and Democratic, arguing that he needed the most capable people around him. What Lincoln didn't say, but implied, was an acknowledgment of his own lack of experience. Lincoln's selections for the second term, on the other hand, represented capable people, but none of them rose to the same level of prominence as party leaders as Seward, Chase, Bates, and Cameron. He gladly continued with William Seward as secretary of state, a recognized but controversial leader who had become his closest political friend. The appointments of Speed and Dennison strengthened the radical side of the Republican Party in his cabinet. All of the new appointees, unlike some of his first-term appointments, had demonstrated their personal loyalty to the president.

LINCOLN'S MOST IMPORTANT APPOINTMENT would be a new chief justice of the United States to succeed Roger Taney, who had died on October 12, 1864. There was no shortage of candidates who stepped forward in self-promotion or were lobbied for by friends. Attorney General Edward Bates wrote Lincoln the day after Taney's death requesting to be appointed "as the crowning, retiring honor of my life." Former Illinois senator Orville Browning encouraged Lincoln to appoint Secretary of War Edwin Stanton. Francis Blair, Sr., wrote Lincoln imploring him to appoint his son, Montgomery, until recently postmaster general, which would "remove the cloud which his ostracism from your Cabinet" brought about by his forced resignation. Charles Sumner recommended Salmon P. Chase, whose candidacy, in a typically clumsy manner, was supported by an overkill of letters to the president. Sumner, who had Lincoln's ear, went so far as to ask Chase to write him a letter that he would then show the president. Chase must have swallowed hard when he penned Sumner before the November election, "Happily it is now certain that the next Administration will be in the hands of Mr. Lincoln from whom the world will expect great things."

Lincoln decided to take his time with this appointment. To the frustration of the many candidates and their supporters, he had not made any decision before the election. Lincoln had already appointed four associate justices—Noah Swayne, Samuel F. Miller, David Davis, and Stephen J. Field—more than any president since Andrew Jackson.

Lincoln, the lawyer in the White House, believed that the validity of the Emancipation Proclamation and other Civil War acts could easily come under the review of the Supreme Court. Weighing this distinctive circumstance, Lincoln believed he should go with a person whose views were known. He told Congressman George S. Boutwell of Massachusetts, "We cannot ask a man what he will do, and if we should, and he should answer us, we should despise him for it. Therefore we must take a man whose opinions are known."

Lincoln chose Salmon P. Chase. The president understood better than anyone that Chase was hugely ambitious, had tried to unseat him for the 1864 Republican nomination, and criticized him behind his back from the beginning of his presidency. But Lincoln also knew Chase's opinions. He knew that he would stand by the Emancipation Proclamation and a hoped-for amendment to outlaw slavery forever. It would be the last time Lincoln would turn to one of his rivals to carry out his policies.

When the new Congress convened on December 5, 1864, Lincoln's choice of Chase proved generally popular. Everyone recognized that the court would far outlast Lincoln in deciding the issues sure to emerge from the Civil War. Chase's huge political ambition, which seemingly could be satisfied only by winning the presidency, would now be put aside forever by appointment to the top judicial post in the country. Lincoln's generosity of spirit, combined with his shrewd political thinking, shone in this strategic choice.

LINCOLN HAD COME TO ADMIRE William Tecumseh Sherman for his pluck and courage, but he was also worried. After his capture of Atlanta, Sherman sought permission for a bold plan to leave his supply lines behind, march 285 miles to the sea, and then turn north to join Grant by attacking Robert E. Lee from the rear. Lincoln and Grant both worried that General John Bell Hood, who had replaced Confederate general Joseph Johnston, would disengage from Sherman and march north and west to reinvade Tennessee. Sherman met these objections by offering to send General George Thomas, "the Rock of Chickamauga," with sixty thousand men to block Hood. Sherman argued that marching through Georgia would impose not simply a military defeat but a psychological blow on Southern morale. He won the argument and received permission for the march.

On November 15, 1864, Sherman departed a smoldering Atlanta to march east to the Atlantic Ocean. Just as Lincoln and Grant had feared, Hood immediately struck out for Tennessee, hoping to draw some of Sherman's army out of Georgia.

In Georgia, the slim, red-bearded Sherman understood the venture before him as not simply the clash of two armies but of two societies. Sherman led a march in which his troops, deployed fifty miles wide, tore up railroad tracks and burned both businesses and homes that lay in their path. His words to his men, veterans of Shiloh, Vicksburg, and Chattanooga: "Forage liberally on the country." Sherman offered his own definition of war: "War is cruelty and you cannot refine it," he declared to the mayor of Atlanta.

For the next month, in November and December 1864, with no telegraphic communication from Sherman, reports of his whereabouts, mostly from hostile Confederate newspaper accounts, were fragmentary. Nevertheless, the Northern public became caught up in the drama of Sherman's march. In New York, George Templeton Strong wrote on November 28, 1864, "He has passed by Macon, has harried Milledgeville, and is threatening Savannah. Rebel editors judiciously keep back most of their information about his movements." On December 8, Strong reflected the mood in the North when he confided to his diary, "Much concern about Sherman. His failure would be a fearful calamity."

No one was more worried about Sherman than Lincoln. Finally, after more than five weeks of waiting, he received a telegram from Sherman that had been carried by ship to the Virginia peninsula for transmittal to Washington. "I beg to present you as a Christmas gift the City of Savannah with 150 heavy guns & plenty of ammunition & also about 25,000 bales of cotton." The ten thousand Confederate defenders of Savannah had evacuated the city before Sherman could launch an attack.

Lincoln answered Sherman immediately. Reminiscent of the spirit of his congratulatory letter to Grant after the victory at Vicksburg, he wrote, "When you were about leaving Atlanta . . . I was *anxious,* if not fearful; but feeling that you were the better judge." Lincoln added, "Now, the undertaking being a success, the honor is all yours; for I believe none of us went farther than to acquiesce." Lincoln, in this Christmas season of 1864, used words from the prophet Isaiah to tell Sherman that his march "brings those who sat in darkness, to see a great light."

THROUGHOUT THE WAR, one of the burdens that Lincoln took upon himself was writing to families who had lost a loved one in battle. In November, Lincoln learned through the War Department that Mrs. Lydia Bixby, a Boston widow, had lost five sons in the war. On November 16, 1864, Lincoln wrote her a heartfelt letter in which he told her, "I feel how weak and fruitless must be any words of mine which should attempt to beguile you from the grief of a loss so overwhelming." Lincoln concluded with a prayer: "that our Heavenly Father may assuage the anguish of your bereavement, and leave you only the cherished memory of the loved and lost, and the solemn pride that must be yours, to have laid so costly a sacrifice upon the altar of Freedom."

An equal or greater burden for the president was reviewing capital sentences of soldiers after court-martial trials. He set aside time each Friday for what he called "butcher's day." He thoroughly disliked this task but knew it had to be done. Lincoln looked for reasons to pardon soldiers accused of falling asleep on sentry duty, going home without leave, fleeing from the battlefront, and desertion. Lincoln was known to be especially amenable to mothers and wives who came to the White House to plead for sons and husbands. He knew in issuing so many pardons he was going against the opinion of commanding officers who worried that the president's penchant for leniency could work against their obligation to establish order and discipline. On the same day Lincoln wrote to Mrs. Bixby, he wrote a letter typical of hundreds he penned during the Civil War. "Upon rejoining his regiment as soon as practicable & faithfully serving out his term, this man is pardoned for any overstaying of time or deserting heretofore committed."

The care that Lincoln devoted to this task was especially reflected in a letter to James Madison Cutts, who was sentenced to dismissal from the army after a series of problems, including peering through a hotel transom at a woman undressing, violence and abuse toward soldiers under his command, and quarreling with other officers. Lincoln knew Cutts was the brother of Adele Cutts Douglas, the widow of Senator Stephen A. Douglas, and now wrote him a fatherly letter. "You have too much of life before you, and have shown too much promise as an officer, for your future to be lightly surrendered." After quoting Shakespeare's *Hamlet,* "Beware of entrance to a quarrel," Lincoln offered his own advice: "Quarrel not at all." Why? "No man resolved to make the most of himself, can spare time for personal contention. Still less can he afford to take all the consequences, including the vitiating of his temper, and the loss of self-control." Lincoln sent him back to serve in the Army of the Potomac. Cutts went on to distinguish himself in the battles at the Wilderness, Spotsylvania, and Petersburg, winning the only triple Medal of Honor in the history of the U.S. military.

AFTER HIS REELECTION, Lincoln, thinking of the future, determined to pass an amendment that would abolish slavery for all time. One of the problems facing any amendment was the fact that the Constitution had been amended only twice since the ratification of the Bill of Rights in 1791. There had been no new amendments for sixty years. Lincoln had remained silent as debates over various proposed amendments on slavery went forward in the winter and spring of 1864. On June 15, 1864, a proposed Thirteenth Amendment failed to receive the necessary two-thirds majority, falling short by thirteen votes in the House.

In November 1864, Republicans generated a strong majority in Congress, but the Thirty-ninth Congress would not convene for four months. Republican leaders counseled Lincoln to be patient and rely on future action by the new Congress. Another option would be to call a special session of Congress, as Lincoln had done in July 1861. He decided against both alternatives.

Rather, with formal debate in the old Congress due to begin in less than two months in January 1865, Lincoln went into action. In his first four years as president, Lincoln had not often become involved in the day-to-day legislative processes of the Congress. But now he turned his full attention to a renewed effort to pass a Thirteenth Amendment. He and Secretary of State Seward selected various Democratic congressmen and lobbied them to change their votes. The fact that Lincoln was not willing to wait a mere four months to pass this antislavery amendment is the best indication of his full commitment to end slavery.

The House of Representatives scheduled a final vote on January 31, 1865. The Thirteenth Amendment read:

Section 1. Neither slavery nor involuntary servitude, except as a punishment for crime whereof the party shall have been duly convicted, shall exist within the United States, or any place subject to their jurisdiction.

Section 2. Congress shall have power to enforce this article by appropriate legislation.

Spectators packed the Capitol's galleries, including African-Americans of all ages. Charles Douglass, Frederick Douglass's oldest son, who had served in the famous Massachusetts Fifty-fourth Infantry, took a seat in the gallery.

The clerk called the roll. The final tally was 119 to 56 in favor, with eight members absent. The House erupted in shouts and cheers. People in the galleries held one another in joy. Both blacks and whites wept. Charles Douglass wrote his father, "I wish that you could have been here, such rejoicing I have never before witnessed (white people I mean)."

Lincoln joined the celebration the next day. Even though the Constitution did not require a president to sign a constitutional amendment, he took great pleasure in signing the Thirteenth Amendment and greeting serenaders at the White House. Immediately, Lincoln was criticized by foes in Congress and the press as wielding unseemly presidential power.

That evening, February 1, 1865, in response to a serenade at the White House, Lincoln spoke with passion. One phrase captured Lincoln's sentiments on this momentous occasion: "This amendment is a King's cure for all the evils."

SCENE IN THE HOUSE ON THE PASSAGE OF THE PROPOSITION TO AMEND THE CONSTITUTION, JANUARY 31, 1865.

This illustration in Harper's Weekly depicts the joyous scene in the House of Representatives at the passage of the Thirteenth Amendment on January 31, 1865.

—

THE CRY FOR PEACE was mounting from all sides. Desertions from Lee's Army of Northern Virginia reached pandemic quantities: fully 8 percent in both January and February. Morale on the Union homefront was not much better. Death and terrible wounds, so often resulting in amputations, were diminishing support for Grant and the Army of the Potomac.

Lincoln was wary of these calls for peace, which he believed would either doom his twin goals of Union and emancipation, or unwittingly prolong the war. In his annual message to Congress on December 5, 1864, Lincoln had stated that Jefferson Davis "would accept nothing short of severance of the Union—precisely what we will not and cannot give. His declarations to this effect are explicit and oft repeated. He does not attempt to deceive us. He affords us no excuse to deceive ourselves." Lincoln told Congress: "Between him and us the issue is distinct, simple, and inflexible. It is an issue which can only be tried by war, and decided by victory."

In early January 1865, sensitive to the charges that he was not making every effort to end the war, Lincoln, against his better judgment, allowed his friend Francis P. Blair to undertake a peace mission to Richmond. The elder Blair, once a friend of Jefferson Davis, arrived in Richmond on January 11 determined to use many keys to open doors to peace. In one scenario, Blair and Davis talked about the possibility of the Union and Confederate armies joining together to drive the French from Mexico, which they had occupied since 1862. In the end, the Confederate president gave Blair a letter to take to Lincoln saying he would appoint commissioners "to secure peace to the two countries."

Davis's letter to Blair confirmed Lincoln's doubts about negotiation. Lincoln sent Blair on a return mission to Richmond armed with his own letter, which stated clearly that he would be willing to receive commissioners to secure peace, but only "to the people of our one common country."

But Davis was also under pressure from Confederate leaders; he agreed to appoint three commissioners who were each advocates of negotiation: Alexander Stephens, vice president of the Confederacy; John A. Campbell, assistant secretary of war; and Robert M. T. Hunter, Confederate senator from Virginia. Davis, however, reduced any possibilities of success by tenaciously insisting on Southern independence.

Lincoln and Stanton initially refused to meet with the Confederate commissioners because of Davis's language about two countries. Lincoln finally agreed that it would look impolite if he did not meet with the three commissioners.

On February 3, 1865, Lincoln and Secretary of State Seward met Stephens, Campbell, and Hunter on Lincoln's steamer, the *River Queen,* at Hampton Roads off the tip of the Virginia peninsula. Lincoln remembered Alexander Stephens fondly from their time together in the Thirtieth Congress, which helped engender an air of cordiality aboard the ship. The participants agreed to keep no notes of the meeting, which lasted four hours.

Stephens took the lead in asking Lincoln, "Well, Mr. President, is there no way of putting an end to the present trouble, and bringing about a restoration of the general feeling and harmony . . . between the different States and Sections of the country?" Stephens carefully avoided Davis's language of two countries. Lincoln replied directly: "There was but one way that he knew of, and that was, for those who were resisting the laws of the Union to cease that resistance." Stephens, the shrewd politician that Lincoln remembered, attempted to change the trajectory of the conversation by speaking of the "Continental question." He referred to Francis Blair's discussion in Richmond about the Union and Confederate armies joining together to force the French from Mexico.

Campbell asked Lincoln what could be the terms of Reconstruction if the Southern states agreed to rejoin the Union. Lincoln replied that once armed resistance ceased, the Southern states "would be immediately restored to their practical relations to the Union." The president told the commissioners that he could not negotiate as long as the South persisted in its armed aggression against the Union. When Hunter tried to counter with a history lesson that Charles I of England had negotiated with enemy forces, Lincoln replied, "I do not profess to be posted in history. On all such matters I will turn over to Seward. All I distinctly recollect about the case of Charles I, is, that he lost his head at the end." The Hampton Roads conference, as Lincoln told Congress a week later, "ended without result."

ON FEBRUARY 1, 1865, General Sherman led his sixty thousand troops north out of Savannah. Slicing up through South Carolina, his veteran soldiers pummeled the state they knew had been the seedbed of secession with even greater destruction than they inflicted on Georgia. Lincoln understood this aggressive military destruction as necessary to end the Confederacy's resistance. To celebrate Sherman's victories in Charleston, South Carolina, and Wilmington, North Carolina, Lincoln, three weeks later, ordered a nighttime illumination in the capital on February 22, George Washington's birthday.

Meanwhile, the Army of the Potomac remained in front of Petersburg, twenty-five miles south of Richmond. Petersburg, with its five railroads and important connecting roads, was the key to sustaining the Confederate capital. In what would become the longest siege in American warfare, Grant slowly cut the rail and roads into Petersburg. The Confederates, reduced to defensive warfare, hung on as Lee, forever reading Northern newspapers, still hoped the Northern population would grow tired of this endless war. The siege had begun in June 1864, and although Grant and Meade had slowly tightened the noose in more than two hundred days of trench warfare, they still remained on the outside looking in. Grant lived in fear that Robert E. Lee would one day disappear and try to link up with General John Bell Hood further south.

At the end of February, Union general Edward Ord and Confederate general James Longstreet talked about possibilities for peace in a conversation during an exchange of prisoners. Longstreet took this conversation back to Lee, who wrote to Grant on March 3, 1865, the day before Lincoln's second inauguration, proposing to meet and enter into "an interchange of views" aimed at "the possibility of arriving at a satisfactory adjustment of the present unhappy difficulties." Lincoln, through Stanton, immediately wrote Grant. "The President directs me to say to you he wishes you to have no conference with General Lee unless it be for the capitulation of Gen. Lee's army, or on some minor, purely military matter." He then articulated Lincoln's political leadership position. "He instructs me to say that you are not to decide, discuss, or confer upon any political question. Such questions the President holds in his own hands; and will submit them to no military conferences or conventions." Despite Lincoln's unbounded confidence in Grant, he reiterated through Stanton what he had determined at the beginning of the war—he alone would decide national policy, which, because he was also commander in chief, encompassed military policy.

WASHINGTON HAD NEVER SEEN so many people, as travelers converged on the capital for Lincoln's second inauguration. With March 4, 1865, approaching, apprehension mingled with hope. Rumors abounded that desperate Confederates, now realizing that defeat was imminent, would attempt to abduct or assassinate the president. Stanton took extraordinary safety measures. Roads leading to Washington had been heavily picketed by Union soldiers for some days. Sharpshooters positioned themselves on the buildings that would ring the inaugural ceremonies.

The president, assaulted by critics for much of the war, was finally receiving recognition for his political leadership. Supporters rejoiced that recent events vindicated him. The *Illinois State Journal* in Springfield declared in its March 4, 1865, editorial, "All honor to Abraham Lincoln through whose honesty, fidelity, and patriotism, those glorious results have been achieved." The *Chicago Tribune* editorialized, "Mr. Lincoln has slowly and steadily risen in the respect, confidence, and admiration of the people." The Washington *Daily Morning Chronicle* urged Mr. Lincoln to crow a bit. "We shall not be surprised if the President does not, in the words he will utter this morning, point to the pledges he gave us in his inaugural of 1861, and claim that he has not departed from them in a single substantial instance."

Inauguration Day dawned with incessant rain. In the early morning, fog continued to hang over the city as the crowd began arriving at the east entrance of the Capitol. The streets oozed with soft mud, described by locals as "black plaster." Gale winds whipped through the city uprooting trees. Police estimates placed the crowd between thirty thousand and forty thousand. The *Philadelphia Inquirer* reported that the arriving throng was present "in force sufficient to have struck terror into the heart of Lee's army (had the umbrellas been muskets)."

The ceremonies would not differ greatly from Lincoln's first inaugural. Yet, there were some differences. Instead of the small clusters of soldiers present in 1861, large numbers of soldiers were present all through the city. Ever-increasing numbers of Confederate deserters were visible. In February alone twelve hundred and thirty-nine disheartened Confederate soldiers had arrived in the capital.

The presence of so many blacks in the inaugural crowd particularly struck the correspondent for the *Times* of London. He estimated that "at least half the multitude were colored people. It was remarked by everybody, stranger as well as natives, that there never had been such crowds of negroes in the capital."

At 11:40, the rain suddenly ceased and rifts in the clouds revealed an azure sky. Washington camera artist Alexander Gardner stood ready to

This photograph, for years mislabeled as the grand review of the army in May 1865, is now understood to be a photo of the crowd at Lincoln's second inaugural. Notice the large presence of soldiers in the crowd.

record the event for posterity. The second inaugural address would be the only occasion in which Lincoln was photographed delivering a speech. Subject to the limitations of a craft and technology still in its young adulthood, the photo shows Lincoln's face but not clearly.

From the podium, the president recognized in the crowd Frederick Douglass. After meetings with the president in 1863 and 1864, Douglass had come to hear what Lincoln would say with the end of the war in view.

Behind Lincoln, only thirty-five feet away, stood the actor John Wilkes Booth. Lincoln had seen Booth perform at Ford's Theatre in *The Marble Heart* on November 9, 1863, a week before he traveled to Gettysburg. The dashing twenty-six-year-old Booth, five feet eight inches tall, with black hair and a black mustache, had first won fame as a Shakespearean actor in Southern theaters, especially Richmond. Booth, seething with hatred, had come to the Second Inaugural with his own dark motives: He had been working on a plan to abduct Lincoln and take him to Richmond.

When Lincoln was introduced, the crowd exploded in expectation. The president rose from his chair and stepped out from beneath the shelter of the Capitol. At fifty-six, he looked much older than his years. Precisely as he began to speak, the sun broke through the clouds. Many persons, at the time and for years after, commented on this celestial phenomenon. Michael Shiner, an African-American mechanic in the naval shipyard in Washington, recorded his awe in his diary entry for March 4, 1865. "As soon as Mr. Lincoln came out the wind ceased blowing and the rain ceased raining and the Sun came out and it became clear as it could be and calm."

In the highly charged atmosphere of wartime Washington, with soldiers everywhere, politicians and newspaper editors had speculated on what Lincoln would say were his latest plans for reconstruction. Would he use his rhetorical skills to hit hard at his opponents in the South and North? Should the Confederate States of America be treated as a conquered nation? How did one distinguish between the innocent and the guilty, between citizens and soldiers? What about the slaves? They had been emancipated, but what about the question of suffrage?

Lincoln began his finest address in a subdued tone.

At this second appearing to take the oath of the Presidential office there is less occasion for an extended address than there was at the first. Then a statement somewhat in detail of a course to be pursued seemed fitting and proper. Now, at the expiration of four years, during which public declarations have been constantly called forth on every point and phase of the great contest which still absorbs the attention and engrosses the energies of the nation, little that is new could be presented. The progress of our arms, upon which all else chiefly depends, is as well known to the public as to myself, and it is, I trust, reasonably satisfactory and encouraging to all. With high hope for the future, no prediction in regard to it is ventured.

In the impersonal language of the first paragraph, Lincoln lowered expectations with the words "less," "little," and "no." He started more like an observer than the main actor and directed the focus of his remarks away from himself by speaking in a passive voice. After the first paragraph he would use no more personal pronouns.

On the occasion corresponding to this four years ago all thoughts were anxiously directed to an impending civil war. All dreaded it, all sought to avert it. While the inaugural address was being delivered from this place, devoted altogether to *saving* the Union without war, urgent agents were in the city seeking to *destroy* it without war—seeking to dissolve the Union and divide effects by negotiation. Both parties deprecated war, but one of them would *make* war rather than let the nation survive, and the other would *accept* war rather than let it perish, and the war came.

In the second paragraph, we first hear Lincoln's political vision. His primary rhetorical strategy was the use of inclusive language. Over and over again in the sentences of the second paragraph, he used the adjectives "all" and "both." How the crowd would have cheered if Lincoln had chosen to demonize the South. Lincoln, instead, imputed the best possible motives to the supposed enemy.

One-eighth of the whole population were colored slaves, not distributed generally over the Union, but localized in the southern part of it. These slaves constituted a peculiar and powerful interest. All knew that this interest was somehow the cause of the war. To strengthen, perpetuate, and extend this interest was the object for which the insurgents would rend the Union even by war, while the Government claimed no right to do more than to restrict the territorial enlargement of it. Neither party expected for the war the magnitude or the duration which it has already attained. Neither anticipated that the *cause* of the conflict might cease with or even before the conflict itself should cease. Each looked for an easier triumph, and a result less fundamental and astounding. Both read the same Bible and pray to the same God, and each invokes His aid against the other. It may seem strange that any men should dare to ask a just God's assistance in wringing their bread from the sweat of other men's faces, but let us judge not, that we be not judged. The prayers of both could not be answered. That of neither has been answered fully. The Almighty has His own purposes. "Woe unto the world because of offenses; for it must needs be that offenses come, but woe to that man by whom the offense cometh." If we shall suppose that American slavery is one of those offenses which, in the providence of God, must needs come, but which, having continued through His appointed time, He now wills to remove, and that He gives to both North and South this terrible war as the woe due to those by whom the offense came, shall we discern therein any departure from those divine attributes which the believers in a living God always ascribe to Him? Fondly do we hope, fervently do we pray, that this mighty scourge of war may speedily pass away. Yet, if God wills that it continue until all the wealth piled by the bondsman's two hundred and fifty years of unrequited toil shall be sunk, and until every drop of blood drawn with the lash shall be paid by another drawn with the sword, as was said three thousand years ago, so still it must be said "the judgments of the Lord are true and righteous altogether."

When Lincoln introduced the Bible in the third paragraph, "Both read the same Bible and pray to the same God," he signaled his intention to speak theologically as well as politically about the meaning of the war. In the 701 words of his second inaugural address, Lincoln mentioned God fourteen times, quoted the Bible four times, and invoked prayer three times. The Bible had been quoted only one time in the previous eighteen addresses, by John Quincy Adams, but the lack of precedent did not deter Lincoln.

This sentence is filled with multiple meanings. First, Lincoln was affirming the use of the Bible and prayer by both Union and Confederate soldiers. He was also probing the appropriate use of the Bible. Throughout the war, Lincoln had hosted delegations of ministers and politicians, most of whom were quite confident that God was on the side of the Union. Lincoln here suggested that the Bible and prayer can be used as weapons to curry God's favor for one side or the other. On one side stood those who read a Bible that they steadfastly believed sanctioned slavery. On the other side were those who understood the Bible as encouraging the abolition of slavery.

Lincoln asked how it was possible for one side to seek God's aid against the other side. He inveighed against a tribal God who took the side of a section or party. But Lincoln seemed to balance judgment from the Old Testament with mercy from the New Testament: "Let us judge not that we be not judged." These words came from the Sermon on the Mount, in which Jesus advocated a new ethic rooted in humility and compassion.

Lincoln, throughout his address, balanced pretension with possibility. The pretension of the misuse of religion provides the transition to Lincoln's major theological affirmation of his address: "The Almighty has His own purposes." It becomes clear here that Lincoln was building on his private "Meditation on the Divine Will," written in 1864. He began that reflection with similar words, "The will of God prevails."

*Alexander Gardner took the only photograph of Lincoln speaking, here
at the second inaugural on March 4, 1865, standing on a platform
in front of the east portico of the Capitol.*

After discussing different players, Lincoln concentrates on God as the
primary actor. He described God's actions: "He now wills to remove,"
"He gives to both North and South, this terrible war," "Yet, if God
wills that it continue."

Though praising the inscrutable intentions of God, Lincoln did not
retreat to agnosticism. He focused on God's purposes by invoking a
fiery biblical quotation from Matthew 18:7: "Woe unto the world
because of offences! For it must needs be that offences come; but woe to
that man by whom the offence cometh!" The purposes of God can also
bring judgment.

Before his election as president, Lincoln had been willing to contain
slavery politically and geographically, but he had since come to the conclusion that its moral implications could not be contained. When he
said, "If we shall suppose that American slavery is one of those
offenses," Lincoln employed the sanction of Scripture to initiate his

indictment of slavery and his formal charge against the American people. He did not say "Southern slavery." By saying "American slavery," Lincoln again used inclusive language to assert that North and South must together own the offense. He was not simply trying to set the historical record straight. He was thinking of the future. Lincoln understood, as the radicals in his party did not, that the Southern people would never be able to take their full places in the Union if they felt that they alone were saddled with the guilt for the national offense of slavery.

Who was this God who "gives to both North and South this terrible war"? Lincoln answered that question by observing that God's activity is no "departure from those divine attributes which the believers in a Living God always ascribe to him." Lincoln heard Phineas Gurley speak of the "divine attributes" of God at New York Avenue Presbyterian Church. Gurley learned this language from Professor Charles Hodge at Princeton Seminary, who titled chapter 5 in his *Systematic Theology* "The Nature and Attributes of God," spending nearly eighty pages making the case that attributes are "essential to the nature of a divine Being" with personality.

As the address built toward its final paragraph, Lincoln made an unexpected political and religious move. Speaking on the eve of military victory, when many expected him to celebrate the successes of the Union, he called upon his audience to recognize a perilous evil in their midst. Instead of self-congratulation, he asked his fellow citizens for self-analysis.

Lincoln's second inaugural resembled a Puritan jeremiad as he combined both criticism and reaffirmation. The task of the preacher was to point out to the congregation the cause of God's anger. Because of the evil of the "offence" of slavery, the nation was deserving of God's punishment. As in a jeremiad, Lincoln prosecuted his case not in generalities but with concrete, visual representations. He reached back beyond the nation's birth as he recalled "two hundred and fifty years of unrequited toil." Lincoln reminded his audience that the stain of slavery was enmeshed in the fabric of American history from its beginnings. His images reached their zenith in "until every drop of blood drawn with the lash, shall be paid by another drawn with the sword." The sword of military battle was the judgment of God. Lincoln drew his confidence in "the judgments of the Lord" from Psalm 19, the fourth biblical passage he cited.

> With malice toward none, with charity for all, with firmness in
> the right as God gives us to see the right, let us strive on to finish
> the work we are in, to bind up the nation's wounds, to care for
> him who shall have borne the battle and for his widow and his
> orphan, to do all which may achieve and cherish a just and lasting
> peace among ourselves and with all nations.

Lincoln now moved quickly from the past to the future, from judgment to hope. In an address filled with surprises, he turned briskly to his unexpected conclusion: "With malice toward none, with charity for all." Lincoln began his final exhortation by asking his audience to enter a new era, armed not with enmity but with forgiveness. He summoned them to overcome the boundary of sectionalism, of North and South, and come together in reconciliation.

In the final paragraph, Lincoln offered an ethical imperative, a response to his political and theological indicative declared in the first three paragraphs. In the Presbyterian sermons that Lincoln heard, the preacher would have spent the majority of the sermon reciting a grand indicative about what God had done. The indicative pattern of Christ's life, teaching, and death led to the imperative for selfless love and reconciliation. This was a frequent motif in Phineas Gurley's sermons.

Lincoln's imperative was ethical in content if pastoral in tone. Lincoln concluded his second inaugural address with a coda of healing: "to bind up," "to care for," "to do all which may achieve and cherish a just and a lasting peace." Portraits of widows and orphans now balanced the images of blood and swords.

To win the peace there must be reconciliation. Lincoln declared that the true test of the aims of war is how the victors treat those who have been defeated. If enmity continued after hostilities ceased, the war would have been in vain. These are no maudlin words crafted for emotional effect. His words describe the tough, practical living actions that must replace retribution with "charity." He set this mandate for himself as he looked forward to his second term.

FREDERICK DOUGLASS, AFTER LISTENING to Lincoln's Second Inaugural Address, was determined to attend the inaugural reception that evening at the White House. Thousands of people crowded the streets outside the White House waiting for the gates to open at 8 p.m. Immediately a free-for-all began. William H. Crook, Lincoln's bodyguard, observed, "The White House looked as if a regiment of rebel troops had been quartered there—with permission to forage." Lincoln, in the East Room, looking exhausted, prepared to shake the hands of the more than six thousand people who would crowd the reception.

Douglass found himself barred at the door by two policemen. When he protested, they informed him that their "directions were to admit no one of color." He understood that the old practices were still in effect. Douglass spoke up that there must be some mistake for "no such order could have emanated from President Lincoln." In order to end the war of words that was blocking the doorway, one officer offered to escort Douglass in. It was not long, however, before Douglass found himself being ushered through a window that had been set up as a short-term exit. Douglass saw the ploy and asked a guest to please tell Mr. Lincoln that he was being held up. The petition reached the president.

All of the handshaking ceased as Frederick Douglass entered the East Room. As he walked in, Lincoln called out, "Here comes my friend Douglass." Lincoln's greeting was said in such a loud voice "that all around could hear him." Taking Douglass by the hand, the president said, "I am glad to see you. I saw you in the crowd today, listening to my inaugural address; how did you like it?"

Douglass replied, "Mr. Lincoln, I must not detain you with my poor opinion, when there are thousands waiting to shake hands with you."

"No, no," Lincoln answered, "you must stop a little Douglass; there is no man in the country whose opinion I value more than yours. I want to know what you think of it?"

"Mr. Lincoln, that was a sacred effort."

SOON AFTER LINCOLN'S INAUGURATION, General Grant invited the president to come down to his headquarters at City Point, Virginia. "I think the rest will do you good." Lincoln arrived on the *River Queen* on March 24, 1865. Always enjoying visiting with the troops, Lincoln spent time talking with wounded soldiers in the hospital tents, making a special point of speaking with wounded Confederates.

Although Lincoln would make no public predictions about the end of the war, privately he knew that Robert E. Lee, for all his deserved renown, could not hold out much longer. Grant and Meade and the Army of the Potomac were slowly closing off both supply routes and escape routes for Lee's Army of Northern Virginia.

With his army down to fifty thousand men, of whom thirty-five thousand were fit to fight, with desertions sapping his strength daily, Lee decided to take one more desperate gamble. He would try to break through the weakest point of the Union line. On the day after Lincoln's arrival at City Point, Lee dispatched General John B. Gordon, who had succeeded Stonewall Jackson, to attempt a breakout against Fort Stedman. Gordon punched open a hole in the Union line, but it was quickly closed as Lincoln watched from a distance. In desperate fighting, the Confederates lost 5,000 men compared to Union losses of 1,500.

On March 28, 1865, Grant arranged a meeting with the president, Admiral David Porter, and General Sherman, who had come up by boat from North Carolina. During the conference, Sherman asked Lincoln: "What is to be done with the rebel armies when defeated?" The president offered a lengthy reply stressing his desire for reconciliation. Lincoln told Sherman he wanted to "get the men comprising the Confederate armies back to their homes, at work on their farms and in their shops." Sherman wanted to know if that generosity would include Jefferson Davis and the top Confederate leaders. Lincoln responded with a story about a teetotaler who when asked whether he wanted his lemonade spiked with whiskey responded that it would be all right if he didn't know about it. Grant, Sherman, and Porter understood the president to say that if Davis and the chief Confederate leaders were to escape it would be all right with him.

As the meeting was about to conclude, Lincoln turned to Sherman. "Do you know why I took a shine to you and Grant?"

"I don't know, Mr. Lincoln. You have been extremely kind to me, far more than I deserve."

"Well," Lincoln replied, "you never found fault with me."

Sherman left immediately to return to his troops and never saw Lincoln again. He wrote later, "Of all the men I have met, he seemed to possess more of the elements of greatness, combined with goodness, than any other."

Grant knew that he now had Lee cornered, having cut off nearly all his escape routes to the south. On April 2, 1865, the Army of the Potomac attacked all along the lines at Petersburg. After a siege of 293 days, the Confederates finally abandoned both Petersburg and Richmond on the same evening.

When Lincoln learned that Confederate forces had left Richmond, he decided he wanted to visit the capital of the Confederacy. Secretary of War Edwin M. Stanton, concerned that snipers might still be in

Richmond, telegraphed Lincoln urging him not to expose himself to great risk. Lincoln replied, "I will take care of myself."

Why did he go? Southerners said, then and later, that he came with a ghoulish desire to gloat over a city still burning. The real reason he went was revealed in his actions and words there.

On the morning of April 4, 1865, Lincoln started up the James River for Richmond on the *River Queen*. Lincoln took Tad with him, who was celebrating his twelfth birthday that day. Admiral Porter had hoped to arrive with a grand display of naval power, but the Confederates had blocked and mined the river. By the time his original flotilla of ships approached Richmond, Lincoln and his entourage—Porter, two officers, and a guard of twelve sailors in blue jackets and round blue hats—were reduced to travel in what amounted to a large rowboat. As the boat docked at Richmond's Rocket's Landing, the president could see smoke rising from the burning city. General Godfrey Weitzel, the new Union commander of the Army of the James, had been alerted to Lincoln's plans, but since the president was not expected until the afternoon, no honor guard was present to meet him.

Although Lincoln entered Richmond unannounced, the tall man with the silk hat did not go far before the city's black residents recognized him. A woman greeted him. "I know that I am free, for I have seen Father Abraham." Lincoln said to a black man who dropped to his knees, "Don't kneel to me. That is not right. You must kneel to God only, and thank Him for the liberty you will enjoy hereafter." With each block, more black residents joined the parade, many coming up to the president to shake his hand or simply touch him. White residents observed the pageant from the steps of their homes or stayed behind locked doors.

Lincoln's destination was General Weitzel's headquarters at Jefferson Davis's house, three blocks from Richmond's Capitol Square. As the president arrived, the crowd broke into cheers. Lincoln turned and bowed in response. He entered the house and sat at the departed Davis's desk. While soldiers were taking everything that was not bolted down in the White House of the Confederacy, Lincoln took only a glass of water.

In the afternoon, Lincoln toured the burned district of the city and the prisons, the conditions of which had long been a source of anger in the North. Now the prisons were filled with Confederates, but the evidence of years of inhumane conditions prompted a Union officer to exclaim, "Jefferson Davis should be hanged." Lincoln replied quietly, "Judge not, that ye be not judged."

Lincoln left Richmond late in the afternoon. As he was departing, General Weitzel asked for his counsel in dealing with the proud but frightened people of the Confederate capital as well as the prisoners. Lincoln replied, "If I were in your place, I'd let 'em up easy, let 'em up easy."

WHEN RICHMOND FELL, Lee led his exhausted troops toward the last rail link to North Carolina and a hoped-for meeting with General Joseph Johnston's troops. General Philip Sheridan's cavalry raced to cut off Lee's supplies at Amelia Court House. On the night of April 7, 1865, Grant passed on to Lincoln a note from Sheridan: "If the thing is pressed I think Lee will surrender." Lincoln replied: "Let the thing be pressed."

Early on Palm Sunday, April 9, 1865, Lee asked for an interview with Grant for the purposes of surrender. An aide of Grant was sent to find a suitable meeting place and secured a first-floor parlor in Wilmer McLean's house in the little town of Appomattox Court House, Virginia. McLean had owned a farm at Manassas in 1861, but when a shell came through his window in the first battle of Bull Run he decided to move to this small town in isolated southern Virginia to escape the war.

Lee arrived first, in full dress uniform, with saber at his side. Grant arrived at 1:30 in a mud-spattered private's uniform. Grant wished to preserve Lee's dignity even as he asked for the surrender of his army. If Lincoln had been firm that he wanted Grant to accept only unconditional surrender, now Grant, with Lincoln's full backing, offered a generous peace. Each Confederate soldier would be allowed to return to his home and a normal life, and he could take his horse and mule with him. Lee was grateful. "This will have the best possible effect upon the men. It will be very gratifying and will do much toward conciliating our people."

LINCOLN DECIDED TO RETURN from Virginia to Washington on the morning of April 9, 1865, when he was informed that William Seward had been seriously injured in a carriage accident. Upon his return on the *River Queen,* he was informed by Secretary of War Stanton that Lee had surrendered to Grant earlier in the day. Lincoln made his way through surging crowds to visit Seward, who had suffered a fractured jaw, a broken arm, and facial lacerations.

On the morning of April 10, 1865, all of Washington learned the war was over when Secretary of War Stanton ordered the firing of five hundred cannons, which broke windows on Lafayette Square. In the afternoon, three thousand people marched to the White House to serenade the president. They called for a speech. He thanked them for coming, but unprepared to speak spontaneously, asked them to return the following evening. He asked the military band to play "Dixie," a song he said that now belonged to the whole country.

April 11, 1865, became an official day of celebration. Government offices closed. Across the Potomac in Arlington, thousands of African-Americans gathered on the lawn of Robert E. Lee's former home to sing "The Year of Jubilee." In the evening, public buildings and private homes were illuminated.

An even larger crowd walked to the White House to hear the president speak. Noah Brooks stood behind the president with a candle to help illuminate the pages from Lincoln's prepared remarks. Tad, crouching below the window, delighted in picking up the pages as they fell from his father's hands. Lincoln focused his remarks not on the past but on the future. Avoiding the contentious debate about whether the seceded states had been in or out of the Union the past four years, Lincoln declared, "Let us all join in doing the acts necessary to restoring the proper relations between these states and the Union." He devoted the bulk of his speech to speaking about Louisiana, admitting that he had been severely criticized for his Reconstruction plan for the state. Secretary of War Stanton, Chief Justice Chase, and Republican Senate radicals complained that without granting Southern blacks suffrage, they would remain under the control of their former masters. Lincoln, who was not yet certain of his ideas on suffrage, said he preferred that "very intelligent blacks," and the nearly two hundred thousand who had served in the military, be granted the right to vote.

Lincoln called for everyone to exercise flexibility in navigating the whole new territory of Reconstruction. He tipped his hat to Congress, saying they had a rightful role to play, but declared that "no exclusive, and inflexible plan can safely be prescribed as to details and collaterals" at this time. Lincoln concluded, "In the present '*situation*,' as the phrase goes, it may be my duty to make some new announcement to the people of the South. I am considering, and shall not fail to act, when satisfied that action will be proper."

The response to Lincoln's address was polite but muted. The crowd came expecting a rousing speech praising the Union and the courageous efforts of soldiers, not a rather technical defense of Lincoln's Reconstruction policies. Some people, disappointed, left before Lincoln finished his remarks. The president sensed the cool response of the crowd.

The response of one man, however, was far from muted. When the Civil War had first erupted, John Wilkes Booth continued to work in the North, making no effort to cover up his Southern sympathies, including his support for slavery. Booth, taking pride in himself as a cultured actor, held Lincoln in disdain as a man of low culture and coarse jokes.

Booth had become despondent when Lincoln was reelected in November and the fortunes of the South shrank in the winter and early spring of 1865. Now that the war was over, he resolved that stronger measures were needed. He was in touch with the Southern secret service as he sought to do something "heroic" for the South. When Lincoln spoke about the possibility of voting rights for some African-Americans, Booth turned to a friend and snapped, "That means nigger citizenship. Now, by God, I'll put him through. That is the last speech he will ever make."

ON GOOD FRIDAY MORNING, April 14, 1865, Lincoln arose feeling well. He had enjoyed a good night's sleep after many nights of restlessness. He had had once again a recurrent dream. He found himself on a ship traveling to a distant, unknown shore. He told Mary of the dream, but said he was not concerned because he had experienced a similar dream several times before, always before a significant Union victory, at Antietam, Gettysburg, and Vicksburg. He hoped that the dream meant favorable news this day. Perhaps Johnston, in North Carolina, had surrendered to Sherman.

He enjoyed breakfast with Mary and Tad; Robert arrived later. He had invited Mary for a carriage ride in the afternoon. In the evening he was looking forward to going to Ford's Theatre to see *Our American Cousin,* an English comedy starring the celebrated English actress Laura Keene. Lincoln invited Ulysses and Julia Grant to join them.

At 11 a.m. Grant, who had arrived in the city the night before, joined Lincoln for a cabinet meeting. Grant shared news of the last drive in Virginia and the surrender of Lee at Appomattox Court House. Lincoln asked about news from Sherman in North Carolina. He told everyone that the news would surely be that Johnston had surrendered because he had had a dream the night before that had always preceded military victories. When the discussion turned to how to deal with the defeated South, Lincoln spoke sympathetically of Lee. The president then spoke with discouragement that men in his own party "possess feelings of hate and vindictiveness in which I do not sympathize and cannot participate."

Grant lingered after the cabinet meeting to tell Lincoln that they would not be accompanying him that evening to Ford's Theatre. The Grants were going to take the evening train to Philadelphia as they were anxious to see their sons in Long Branch, New Jersey.

Lincoln ate an apple for lunch and, back at his office, signed another pardon, this time for a man accused as a Confederate spy. "Well, I think the boy can do us more good above ground than under ground." After dealing patiently with a number of callers, Lincoln went to get Mary for their four o'clock carriage ride.

Lincoln did his best to try to calm Mary. At City Point she had embarrassed him by claiming loudly that he was flirting with an officer's wife. She had even accosted Julia Grant and upbraided her for wanting to succeed her in the White House. Now, on this Good Friday afternoon, he told Mary, "We must *both* be more cheerful in the future." He acknowledged that "between the war & the loss of our darling Willie— we have both been very miserable." But the conversation turned happier when they spoke of the future. Lincoln said he wanted to visit Europe, perhaps even Jerusalem. One day he wanted to travel out west—to California.

Returning to the White House, Lincoln endured more callers. Mary, who complained of a headache, said she would rather stay home. Lincoln knew their plan had been announced in the newspapers and said they must attend, and so they dressed for the evening. She wore a lovely gray silk dress and he a black suit, overcoat, white kid gloves, and top hat. As they were about to go, Congressman Isaac Arnold came by to see Lincoln. The president told him, "I am going to the theatre. Come by and see me in the morning."

Finally, after a quick walk to the War Department, Abraham and Mary prepared to leave. William H. Crook, a White House guard, wanted to accompany the president, but Lincoln told Crook he knew he had had a long day and he should take the night off. On their way to the theater, they stopped at Senator Ira Harris's house to pick up Major

Henry R. Rathbone and Harris's daughter Clara, whom Lincoln invited when the Grants declined. On a foggy Washington evening, the Lincolns finally arrived at Ford's at eight-thirty, late for the play.

When the Lincolns entered their flag-draped box, the play stopped and the audience cheered. Major Rathbone and Miss Harris took the front seats while Abraham and Mary sat in the rear. John F. Parker, another White House guard, who was to stand in front of the door to the Lincolns' box, instead decided to find a seat in order to see the play.

As the farcical comedy rollicked forward, Mary had to point out to her exhausted husband what was happening onstage. Lincoln found it difficult to get his mind off the myriad of problems with Reconstruction. Mary slipped her hand into his.

During the third act, John Wilkes Booth entered the unguarded box. He aimed a small derringer pistol at the back of Lincoln's head, and, from a distance of six inches, fired one shot. Lincoln slumped ahead in his chair. Mary screamed in terror. Rathbone rose to confront the intruder, but Booth, dagger in hand, slashed the young major before leaping from the box to the stage. He yelled in defiance, *"Sic semper tyrannis!"* ("Thus ever to tyrants.")

The audience was stunned. Bedlam erupted and people rushed for the exits. Lincoln's limp body was carried across the street to the modest home of William Peterson, a tailor. The doctor who examined the president knew that he could not live. The bullet had entered his head on the left side and lodged near his right eye.

As Mary Lincoln sobbed inconsolably, Secretary of War Stanton took charge. Welles arrived and observed, "The giant sufferer lay extended diagonally across the bed, which was not long enough for him." House Speaker Colfax, Senator Sumner, and prominent members of the cabinet gathered in the small back room of the Peterson home. Lincoln's pastor, Phineas Gurley, arrived. Rumors circulated that assassins had also attacked Vice President Johnson and General Grant. A further report said Secretary of State Seward was assaulted but survived.

Throughout the long night, Washington officials came and went. Robert Lincoln arrived and broke down when he saw his father. Mary tried to speak to her husband, kissed his face, and told him to speak to their departed children. She recalled his dream he told her of the phantom ship traveling to the distant shore.

Finally, Lincoln's pulse weakened, and he died at 7:22 a.m. on Saturday, April 15, 1865. Stanton asked Pastor Gurley to offer a prayer. Then the secretary of war, who had come to such a deep appreciation of Lincoln, said simply, "Now, he belongs to the ages."

GRIEF FOR THE DEAD PRESIDENT spread quickly across the country. Many well-known people spoke in impromptu meetings in cities large and small. In Rochester, New York, Mayor Daniel David Tompkins hastily called a meeting at the city hall. He invited three of the leading citizens of Rochester to speak of their appreciation for Abraham Lincoln. Frederick Douglass took a seat toward the back of the auditorium. After the scheduled speakers delivered their eulogies, attendees called for Douglass to speak. He walked to the platform to offer his spontaneous eulogy, focusing his remarks on words from Lincoln's second inaugural address. He quoted two sentences from the address.

> Fondly do we hope, fervently do we pray that this mighty scourge of war may speedily pass away. Yet if God wills that it continue until all the wealth piled by the bond-man's two hundred and fifty years of unrequited toil shall be sunk, and until every drop of blood drawn with the lash shall be paid by another, drawn with the sword, as was said three thousand years ago, so still must it be said, that the judgments of the Lord are righteous altogether.

Douglass spoke the words from memory, declaring that "those memorable words—words which will live immortal in history," will "be read with increasing admiration from age to age."

The day after Lincoln's death, Easter Sunday, hundreds of ministers and preachers offered a new definition of Abraham Lincoln. In sermons across the North they interpreted the president's death as a sacrifice for the nation's sins. They declared him the Civil War's final casualty.

In the subsequent days and weeks, in general stores and schools and churches across the country, others attempted to define the meaning of Lincoln's life. Their first instinct was to look backward, from the vantage point of the end of the Civil War, to see with new appreciation what Lincoln had accomplished in holding the Union together and declaring freedom for the slaves. Some pondered what might have been in Lincoln's second term as the nation suddenly faced the uncertainty of reconciliation and reconstruction. They wondered what role Lincoln might have played in healing the country after so many years of violence. They wondered what new designation he might have earned.

In the years that have followed, each generation of Americans, indeed citizens around the world, has attempted to define and redefine Lincoln from their own historical vantage point, asking new questions relevant to their day. One reason we have never settled on one definition of Lincoln, and, indeed, never will, is that Lincoln never stopped asking questions of himself. Painfully aware of the shortcomings of his early education, Lincoln—whether as schoolboy, Illinois legislator, prairie lawyer, or as president—always continued his self-study, growing in wisdom and self-knowledge with each passing year. He read, discussed, and pondered the great ideas not only of his time, but of those of the generations before him. He also thought into the future, anticipating the moral questions of subsequent generations. And Lincoln underwent a religious odyssey that deepened as he aged, inquiring about everlasting truths until his last day.

In the days after Lincoln's death, preparations began for a vast public mourning. Arrangements were made for the long train ride home to the prairies of Illinois. Lincoln's casket would retrace the exact route where cheering crowds had greeted the president-elect on his way to Washington four years before. On Tuesday, April 18, it seemed that all of Washington stood in line outside the White House to pay their respects to the dead president. After waiting hours they entered the East Room to pass the president's open casket, finding him dressed in the black suit he had worn at his Second Inaugural. Three days after the assassination, some of the mourners may have offered the most accurate characterization of the man behind the signature "A. Lincoln." As was the custom of the time, many people wore silk mourning badges. One badge, seen everywhere in Washington during those sad days, said what was in people's hearts: "With malice toward none; with charity for all."

Acknowledgments

In writing a biography of Abraham Lincoln, I have been conscious at every moment of being supported by a community of scholars, friends, and institutions. I am privileged to do research and writing as a Fellow at the incomparable Huntington Library in San Marino, California. I wish to thank Steven Koblik, president; Robert C. Ritchie, W. M. Keck director of research; and David S. Zeidberg, Avery director of the library. Special thanks go to the Readers Services Department, especially Christopher J. S. Adde, Jill Cogan, and Barbara Quinn.

The Abraham Lincoln Presidential Library and Museum in Springfield, Illinois, is a treasure trove of manuscripts and people. From the beginning of my journey with Mr. Lincoln, Illinois state historian Tom Schwartz, always willing to answer any query, has generously shared his vast knowledge of Lincoln. Daniel W. Stowell, director and editor of the Lincoln Papers, has offered his friendship and counsel, as well as early admission to the manuscript versions of the Lincoln Legal Papers published by the University of Virginia Press in 2008. Stowell and his excellent team of editors also provided access to their massive project of collecting and annotating the Abraham Lincoln Papers, which, unlike the *Collected Works of Abraham Lincoln* published in the 1950s, will include all of the incoming correspondence to Lincoln. I also thank James M. Cornelius, curator of the Henry Hoerner Lincoln Collection, and Cheryl Schnirring, director of the Manuscripts Division. Tim Townsend, National Park Service historian for the Abraham Lincoln home in Springfield, guided me through the home and answered innumerable questions in succeeding years.

At the Library of Congress, John Sellers, historical specialist for the Civil War and Reconstruction, has been a resource and sounding board for all things Lincoln. Clark Evans, director, Rare Books Division, and Mary Ison, head of the Photography and Prints Division, have, again, rendered valuable assistance.

I wish to thank the staffs of the John Hay Collection at Brown University, the Chicago History Museum, and the Lincoln Museum in Fort Wayne, Indiana, for their help during research visits.

I am grateful to President George W. Bush for his invitation to Cynthia and me to meet with him and to explore firsthand Lincoln's White House. Mr. Peter Wehner, deputy assistant to the president and director of the Office of Strategic Initiatives, coordinated our visit. William G. Allman, White House curator, provided us an extensive tour of the White House, including the upstairs living quarters, and spoke with us about how this great house functioned in Lincoln's time. It is one thing to read about the White House; it is another to meander through its rooms and imagine where Abraham, Mary, Tad, Willie, and secretaries John Nicolay and John Hay lived and worked. We appreciated seeing the marvelous George P. A. Healey portrait of Lincoln in the White House state dining room.

Jim McPherson generously shared with me *Tried by War: Abraham Lincoln as Commander in Chief* while still in manuscript form. Catherine Clinton kindly allowed me to read an early draft of her new book, *Mrs. Lincoln: A Life*.

I am indebted to friends who read parts or all of the manuscript. Tom Schwartz read an early version of the Illinois portion of the manuscript. Huntington colleagues Jack Rogers and Paul Zall provided me their seasoned insights. Douglas Wilson and Daniel Howe read parts of the manuscript and offered both critical questions and critical insights. Gary Gallagher, Jim McPherson, and Richard Wightman Fox deserve full thanks for reading the full manuscript.

Karen Needles, director of the Lincolnarchives Digital Project (www .lincolnarchives.us), tirelessly assisted me in searching the Library of Congress, National Archives, and other repositories for texts, photographs, illustrations, and cartoons. Annie Russell, a former Ph.D. student, both offered her own critical reading of the manuscript and helped organize the notes and the bibliography. Nancy Macky, a dear friend and Huntington reader, offered her enthusiastic help at a timely moment toward the end of the project.

So many friends, old and new, have offered encouragement, hospitality, and insight along this journey. I can only mention a few: Herb and Roberta Ludwig, Gordon and Sandy Hess, Don and Deanda Roberts, John and Lois Harrison, and Dale Soden.

Mary Evans, my literary agent, has once again been a thoughtful editor, counselor, and cheerleader for this, our third book together.

The greatest privilege and joy has been working with my editor, David Ebershoff, at Random House. A brilliant novelist, David worked with me chapter by chapter as he brought his perceptive counsel and penetrating questions, always ending every interchange with encouragement. I thank Lindsey Schwoeri and many others at Random House for their support. I am grateful to Michelle Daniel for her excellent skills in copy editing.

Finally, and foremost, my best reader has been my wife, Cynthia, who read every page, in many versions, with wisdom and questions born of her own love of reading. Her good humor in relation to my insatiable curiosity about Mr. Lincoln became more than matched by her affirmation of every facet of the long-distance journey of writing this biography. I dedicate this book to Cynthia.

Notes

ABBREVIATIONS AND SHORT TITLES EMPLOYED IN NOTES

AL   Abraham Lincoln

ALPLC   Available at *Abraham Lincoln Papers at the Library of Congress,* Manuscript Division (Washington, D.C.: American Memory Project, 2000), http://memory.loc.gov/ammem/alhtml/alhome.html, accessed 2002.

ALPLM   Abraham Lincoln Presidential Library and Museum, Springfield, Illinois

ALQ   *Abraham Lincoln Quarterly*

Baker, *Mary Todd Lincoln*   Jean H. Baker, *Mary Todd Lincoln: A Biography* (New York: W. W. Norton and Company, 1987).

Bates, *Diary*   *The Diary of Edward Bates, 1859–1866,* ed. Howard K. Beale (Washington, D.C.: Government Printing Office, 1933).

Beveridge, *Abraham Lincoln*   Albert J. Beveridge, *Abraham Lincoln 1809–1858,* 2 vols. (Boston: Houghton Mifflin Company, 1928).

Browning, *Diary*   *The Diary of Orville Hickman Browning,* Vol. 20, ed. Theodore C. Pease and James G. Randall (Springfield: Illinois State Historical Library, 1925).

Chase, *Diaries*   *Inside Lincoln's Cabinet: The Civil War Diaries of Salmon P. Chase,* ed. David Donald (New York: Longmans, Green and Company, 1954).

CW   *The Collected Works of Abraham Lincoln,* 9 vols., ed. Roy P. Basler (New Brunswick, N.J.: Rutgers University Press, 1953–55) and *Supplement, 1832–1865,* 2 vols. (Westport, Conn.: Greenwood Press, 1974).

Day by Day   Early Schenk Miers, ed. *Lincoln Day by Day,* 3 vols. (Washington, D.C.: Lincoln Sesquicentennial Commission, 1960).

Donald, *Lincoln*   David Herbert Donald, *Lincoln* (New York: Simon & Schuster, 1995).

Fehrenbacher, *Recollected Words*   Don E. Fehrenbacher and Virginia Fehrenbacher, eds., *Recollected Words of Abraham Lincoln* (Stanford, Calif.: Stanford University Press, 1996).

Frederick Douglass   John W. Blasingame et al., eds., *The Frederick Douglass Papers,* 5 vols. (New Haven, Conn.: Yale University Press, 1979–1992).

Hay, *Inside*   *Inside Lincoln's White House: The Complete Civil War Diary of John Hay,* ed. Michael Burlingame and John R. Turner Ettlinger (Carbondale: Southern Illinois University Press, 1997).

HEH   Huntington Library, San Marino, California

HI   Douglas L. Wilson and Rodney O. Davis, eds., *Herndon's Informants: Letters, Interviews, and Statements about Abraham Lincoln* (Urbana: University of Illinois Press, 1998).

HL   William H. Herndon and Jesse W. Weik, *Herndon's Lincoln,* ed. Douglas L. Wilson and Rodney O. Davis (Urbana: University of Illinois Press, 2006).

JISHS   *Journal of the Illinois State Historical Society*

Johannsen, *Douglas*   Robert W. Johannsen, *Stephen A. Douglas* (Urbana: University of Illinois Press, 1973).

LEGAL   Daniel W. Stowell, ed., *The Papers of Abraham Lincoln: Legal Documents and Cases,* 4 vols. (Charlottesville: University of Virginia Press, 2008).

McClellan, *Civil War Papers*   Stephen W. Sears, ed. *The Civil War Papers of George B. McClellan* (New York: Ticknor and Fields, 1989).

MTL   Justin G. Turner and Linda Levitt Turner, eds., *Mary Todd Lincoln: Her Life and Letters* (New York: Alfred A. Knopf, 1972).

Nicolay and Hay   *Complete Works of Abraham Lincoln,* 10 vols., ed. John G. Nicolay and John Hay (New York: Francis D. Tandy Company, 1905).

OR   *Official Records of the Union and Confederate Armies,* 128 vols. (Washington D.C.: Government Printing Office, 1880–1901).

PUSG   John Y. Simon et al., eds., *Papers of Ulysses S. Grant,* 28 vols. (Carbondale: Southern Illinois University Press, 1967–).

Strong, *Diary*   *The Diary of George Templeton Strong,* vol. 2, *1850–59,* and vol. 3, *1860–65,* ed. Allan Nevins and Milton Halsey Thomas (New York: The Macmillan Company, 1952).

Taft, *Diary*   *Washington During the Civil War: The Diary of Horatio Nelson Taft,* vol. 1, *1861–1865* (Washington, D.C.: Library of Congress, Manuscript Division).

Welles, *Diary*   *Diary of Gideon Welles, Secretary of the Navy Under Lincoln and Johnson,* 3 vols., ed. Howard K. Beale and Alan W. Brownsword (New York: W. W. Norton and Company, 1960).

The original spelling and punctuation are used in quotations without adding the intrustive "[sic]."

CHAPTER 1. *A. Lincoln and the Promise of America*

3   **"so awful ugly"** Walt Whitman to Nathaniel Bloom and John F. S. Gray, March 19–20, 1863, in *Walt Whitman: The Correspondence,* vol. 1, *1842–1867,* ed. Edwin Haviland Miller (New York: New York University Press, 1961), 81.

3   **"The first task"** G. Vann Woodward, "The Great Prop," *Time* LXIII, no. 13 (March 29, 1954), 52.

4   **"He was the most ... shut-mouthed man"** *Brief Analysis of Lincoln's Character: A Letter to J. E. Remsburg from W. H. Herndon, September 10, 1887,* (Springfield: H. E. Barker, 1917), 3.

4   **Lincoln's "diary" consists of hundreds** Roy P. Basler and the editors of *The Collected Works of Abraham Lincoln* (New Brunswick, N.J.: Rutgers University Press, 1953–55) called "fragments." These fragments in *The Collected Works,* arranged chronologically, are thus kept separate from one another.

6   **"The dogmas of the quiet past"** AL, "Annual Message to Congress," December 1, 1862, *CW,* 5:537.

CHAPTER 2. *Undistinguished Families: 1809–16*

7   **"A. now thinks"** AL, "Autobiography," *CW,* 4:62.

7   **referring to himself as "A"** Ibid., 61–62.

8   **Lincoln's spare account** John Locke Scripps, *Life of Abraham Lincoln,* ed. Roy P. Basler and Lloyd A. Dunlop (Bloomington: Indiana University Press, 1961).

8   **"to induce [Lincoln]"** John L. Scripps to WHH, June 24, 1865, *HI,* 57–58.

8   **"It is a great piece of folly"** Scripps, *Life of Abraham Lincoln,* 13.

8   **portrait of himself** See Daniel Walker Howe, *Making the American Self: Jonathan Edwards to Abraham Lincoln* (Cambridge, Mass.: Harvard University Press, 1997), 108–14.

8   **"My parents were both born"** AL to Jesse W. Fell, "Enclosing Autobiography," December 20, 1859, *CW,* 3:511.

9   **"the Great Migration"** For a description of the migration to New England, see Virginia D. Anderson, *New England's Generation: The Great Migration and the Formation of Society and Culture in the Seventeenth Century* (Cambridge: Cambridge University Press, 1991), 22.

9   **these emigrants had given up hope** David Hackett Fischer, *Albion's Seed: Four British Folkways in America* (New York: Oxford University Press, 1989) discusses the religious, social, and regional origins of the migration from England to New England, 13–36.

9   **Like many of his fellow immigrants** For the story of Samuel Lincoln, see Ida M. Tarbell, *In the Footsteps of the Lincolns* (New York: Harper and Brothers, 1924), 1–16, and William E. Barton, *The Lineage of Lincoln* (Indianapolis: The Bobbs-Merrill Company, 1929), 20–40.

9   **Samuel Lincoln landed in Salem** See Tarbell, *In the Footsteps of the Lincolns,* 2.

9   **church membership provided** Barton, *The Lineage of Lincoln,* 35–36.

9   **next generations of American Lincolns** Kenneth J. Winkle places the story of young Abraham Lincoln in the context of his larger family; see *The Young Eagle: The Rise of Abraham Lincoln* (Dallas: Taylor Trade Publishing, 2001), 1–9.

10   **new immigrants were Quaker farmers** Tarbell, *In the Footsteps of the Lincolns,* 45–48. Abraham Lincoln believed his ancestors at one time were Quakers, a fact difficult to prove or disprove since Quaker meetings did not keep lists of members for their first two hundred years in the United States. See David S. Keiser, "Quaker Ancestors for Lincoln," *Lincoln Herald* 63 (Fall 1961), 134–37.

10   **the grandfather of Abraham Lincoln** For the story of Abraham Lincoln, grandfather of Abraham Lincoln, see Tarbell, *In the Footsteps of the Lincolns,* 53–63, and Barton, *The Lineage of Lincoln,* 51–62.

11   **"Eden of the West"** Steven A. Channing, *Kentucky: A Bicentennial History* (New York: Norton, 1977), 4.

12   **Lincoln built his family** Barton, *The Lineage of Lincoln,* 58–59.

12   **the future president's grandfather** Louis A. Warren, *Lincoln's Parentage and Childhood: A History of the Kentucky Lincolns Supported by Documentary Evidence* (New York: The Century Company, 1926), 4–5; Tarbell, *In the Footsteps of the Lincolns,* 62–65.

13   **"legend more strongly"** AL to Jesse Lincoln, April 1, 1854, *CW,* 2:217.

13   **the future president's father** For the story of the young Thomas Lincoln, see Tarbell, *In the Footsteps of the Lincolns,* 53–63, and Barton, *The Lineage of Lincoln,* 51–62.

13   **"Even in childhood"** AL, "Autobiography," *CW,* 4:61.

13   **"grew up literally"** Ibid.

14   **"He was a man who took"** Dennis F. Hanks (Erastus Wright interview), June 8, 1865, *HI,* 27.

14   **"plain unpretending plodding man"** Samuel Haycraft to WHH, [June 1865], *HI,* 67.

14   **"good quiet citizen"** John Hanks (John Miles interview), May 25, 1865, *HI,* 5.

14   **"accumulated considerable property"** A. H. Chapman (written statement), [September 8, 1865], *HI,* 97.

14   **Nancy Hanks's ancestry** On Nancy Hanks see Tarbell, *In the Footsteps of the Lincolns,* 78–89; and Paul H. Verduin, "New Evidence Suggests Lincoln's Mother Born in Richmond County, Virginia, Giving Credibility to Planter-Grandfather Legend," *Northern Neck of Virginia Historical Magazine* 38 (December 1988), 4354–389.

14   **Thomas Lincoln and Nancy Hanks probably met** William E. Barton, *The Women Lincoln Loved* (Indianapolis: The Bobbs-Merrill Company, 1927), 73–77.

16   **Thomas and Nancy Lincoln moved again** E. R. Burba to WHH, May 25, 1866, *HI,* 257.

17   **"Slavery Inconsistent with Justice"** John B. Boles, *Religion in Antebellum Kentucky* (Lexington: The University Press of Kentucky, 1976), 101–3.

17   **experienced slavery everywhere they lived** Louis A. Warren, *The Slavery Atmosphere of Lincoln's Youth* (Fort Wayne, Ind.: Lincolniana Publishers, 1933), 4–5.

17   **Baptists in Kentucky were divided** John B. Boles, *The Great Revival, 1787–1805: The Origins of the Southern Evangelical Mind* (Lexington: The University Press of Kentucky, 1972), 3–4.

18   **"amansapator"** Warren, *The Slavery Atmosphere of Lincoln's Youth,* 8.

18   **"My earliest recollection"** Warren, *Lincoln's Parentage and Childhood,* 143.

18   **"He married Nancy Hanks"** A. H. Chapman (written statement), [September 8, 1865], *HI,* 97.

18   **"quiet and amiable"** John Hanks (John Miles interview), May 25, 1865, *HI,* 5.

18 **"a Kind disposition"** Dennis F. Hanks (Erastus Wright interview), June 8, 1865, *HI*, 27.

18 **his "angel mother"** Joshua F. Speed, *Reminiscences of Abraham Lincoln and Notes of a Visit to California: Two Lectures* (Louisville, Ky.: John P. Morton and Company, 1884), 19.

20 **No Man may put off** Thomas A. Dilworth, *A New Guide to the English Tongue* (London: W. Osborne and T. Griffin, 1786), 5, 7.

20 **"could perhaps teach spelling"** Samuel Haycraft to WHH, [June 1865], *HI*, 67.

20 **instructions for teachers** Gerald R. McMurtry, *A Series of Monographs Concerning the Lincolns and Hardin County, Kentucky* (Elizabethtown, Ky.: Enterprise Press, 1938), 25.

21 **"partly on account of slavery"** AL, "Autobiography," *CW,* 4:61–62.

21 **"There shall be neither slavery"** Robert M. Taylor, Jr., ed., *The Northwest Ordinance 1787: A Bicentennial Handbook* (Indianapolis: Indiana Historical Society, 1987), 72.

21 **the American Lincolns migrated** Winkle, *Young Eagle,* 2–8, tells the story of the Lincoln family migration with maps and graphs.

CHAPTER 3. *Persistent in Learning: 1816–30*

23 **In the fall of 1816** Beveridge, *Abraham Lincoln* 1:37. Beveridge is the most reliable guide to Lincoln's early years.

24 **Coming ashore in Indiana** Ibid., 41–42.

24 **"a vast forest"** Elias Pym Fordham, *Personal Narrative of Travels in Virginia, Maryland, Pennsylvania, Ohio, Indiana, Kentucky, and of a Residence in the Illinois Territory, 1817–1818,* ed. Frederic Austin Ogg (Cleveland, Ohio: The Arthur H. Clark Company, 1906), 96.

25 **Stepping onto Indiana soil** Beveridge, *Abraham Lincoln,* 1:38–42.

25 **"A., though very young"** AL, "Autobiography," *CW,* 4:62. Lincoln's Indiana years are not easy to track, because much of our information comes from persons remembering back thirty-five to fifty years to the young Abraham.

25 **An ax in Lincoln's day** For a discussion of the ax in pioneer America, see R. Carlyle Buley, *The Old Northwest: Pioneer Period 1815–1840* (Indianapolis: Indiana Historical Society, 1950), 159–62.

26 **When first my father** AL, "The Bear Hunt" [September 6, 1846?], *CW,* 1:386.

26 **"a few days before"** AL, "Autobiography," *CW,* 4:62.

26 **"[I have] never"** Ibid.

27 **She died seven days later** Dennis F. Hanks to WHH (interview), June 13, 1865, *HI*, 40.

28 **"Her good humored laugh"** Nathaniel Grigsby (WHH interview), September 12, 1865, *HI*, 113.

28 **Each had lost a spouse** Beveridge, *Abraham Lincoln,* 57–58.

28 **"She Soaped—rubbed"** Dennis F. Hanks to WHH (interview), June 13, 1865, *HI*, 41.

28 **"She proved a good and kind mother"** AL, "Autobiography," *CW,* 4:62.

29 **"In [my] tenth year"** Ibid.

29 **"the Old Man Loved"** Dennis F. Hanks to WHH, January 26, 1866, *HI,* 176.

30 **"Thos. Lincoln never showed"** A. H. Chapman to WHH, September 28, 1865, *HI,* 134.

30 **"Owing to my father"** AL to Solomon Lincoln, March 6, 1848, *CW,* 1:455–56.

30 **Abraham showed little empathy** See the perceptive book by John Y. Simon, *House Divided: Lincoln and His Father* (Fort Wayne, Ind.: Lincoln Library and Museum, 1987).

30 **"I can say what scarcely"** Sarah Bush Johnson, interview by WHH, September 8, 1865, *HI,* 107.

30 **"God bless my mother"** *HL,* 3–4. There is some dispute about the year Lincoln made this statement. Simon, *House Divided,* 23–24 n. 5.

30 **"didn't like physical labor"** Sarah Bush Lincoln (WHH interview), September 8, 1865, *HI,* 107.

30 **"Abe was not Energetic"** Matilda Johnston Moore (WHH interview), September 8, 1865, *HI,* 109.

31 **Abraham's first teacher** Beveridge, *Abraham Lincoln,* 1:55–56.

31 **"There were some schools"** AL to Jesse W. Fell, "Enclosing Autobiography," December 19, 1859, *CW,* 3:511.

31 **"Whilst other boys were idling"** Nathaniel Grigsby (WHH interview), September 12, 1865, *HI,* 113.

31 **"What Lincoln read"** David Turnham (HH interview), September 15, 1865, *HI,* 121.

31 **"What he has in the way"** AL, "Autobiography," *CW* 4:62.

31 **"Abe was getting hungry"** Dennis F. Hanks to WHH (interview), June 13, 1865, *HI,* 41.

32 **Lincoln read the King James Version** Beveridge, *Abraham Lincoln,* 10–12.

33 **"a difficulty"** *Aesop's Fables: With Upwards of One Hundred and Fifty Emblematical Devices* (Philadelphia: John Locken, 1821?), 5–6.

33 **According to Grigsby and Turnham** Nathaniel Grigsby (WHH interview), September 12, 1865, *HI,* 112; David Turnham (WHH interview), September 15, 1865, *HI,* 121; and David Turnham to WHH, December 30, 1865, *HI,* 148.

33 **young Abraham did not have a voice** *HL,* 49.

33 **John Bunyan's** *Pilgrims Progress* Beveridge, *Abraham Lincoln,* 70, 72; and Warren, *Lincoln's Youth,* 49.

33 **Lincoln read William Grimshaw's** Matilda Johnston Moore (WHH interview), September 8, 1865, *HI,* 109.

33 **"What a climax of human cupidity"** William Grimshaw, *History of the United States* (Philadelphia: Grigg and Elliott, 1820), cited in Beveridge, *Abraham Lincoln,* 73–74.

34 **"he would write it down"** Sara Bush Lincoln (WHH interview), September 8, 1865, *HI,* 107.

34 **Abraham Lincoln is my nam** AL, "Copy-Book Verses," [1824–26], *CW,* 1:1.

34 **Abraham realized that he was different** Douglas L. Wilson, "Young Man Lin-

coln," in *The Lincoln Enigma: The Changing Focus of an American Icon,* ed. Gabor Boritt (New York: Oxford University Press, 2001), 35.

34   **"His mind soared"** Nathaniel Grigsby (WHH interview), September 12, 1865, *HI,* 114.

35   **"We saw something laying"** David Turnham (WHH interview), September 15, 1865, *HI,* 122.

35   **"A devout Christian"** Nathaniel Grigsby to WHH, September 4, 1865, *HI,* 94.

35   **asked Thomas Lincoln to oversee** Beveridge, *Abraham Lincoln,* 71.

36   **"by Experience"** Minute Book, Little Pigeon Baptist Church, June 7, 1823, and April 8, 1826, ALPLM.

36   **"He sometimes attended Church"** Sara Bush Lincoln (WHH interview), September 8, 1865, *HI,* 108.

36   **"call the children"** Matilda Johnston Moore (WHH interview), September 8, 1865, *HI,* 110.

36   **the need for fences grew** Warren, *Lincoln's Youth,* 142–44.

38   **"Gentleman, you may think"** Francis Bicknell Carpenter, *The Inner Life of Abraham Lincoln: Six Months at the White House* (New York: Hurd and Houghton, 1866), 97–98.

38   **he had not violated any law** Beveridge, *Abraham Lincoln,* 85.

39   **"One night they were attacked"** AL, "Autobiography," *CW,* 4:62.

40   **Men, women, and children** Years later, John Hanks reported that Lincoln, deeply troubled by what he saw at the slave auction, exclaimed, "If I ever get a chance to hit that thing, I'll hit it hard." Hanks's recollections, however, were often not reliable.

40   **he decided to help his father move** David Turnham (WHH interview), September 15, 1865, *HI,* 121.

40   **Lincoln family camped in the village square** John Hanks (WHH interview) [1865–66], *HI,* 456.

41   **Lincoln made his first political speech** Jane Martin Johns, *Personal Recollections of Early Decatur, Abraham Lincoln, Richard J. Oglesby and the Civil War,* ed. Howard C. Schaub (Decatur, Ill.: Decatur Chapter Daughters of the American Revolution, 1912), 60–61.

CHAPTER 4. *Rendering Myself Worthy of Their Esteem: 1831–34*

43   **a long flatboat** John Hanks reported that the flatboat was eighty feet long and eighteen feet wide. John Hanks to WHH (interview), June 13, 1865, *HI,* 44.

44   **community of New Salem first met** This story was remembered by many of the residents of New Salem. William G. Greene to WHH (interview), May 30, 1865, *HI,* 17.

44   **"A stopped indefinitely"** AL, "Autobiography," *CW,* 4:64.

45   **first farmers called** The story of the early settlers on the prairies is told by John Mack Faragher, *Sugar Creek: Life on the Illinois Prairie* (New Haven, Conn.: Yale University Press, 1986), 62–63.

45   **"Camp meetings are all the rage"** Charles James Fox Clarke to Mary Clarke, August 22, 1836, ALPLM.

46 **"slept on the same cott"** William G. Greene to WHH (interview), May 30, 1865, *HI,* 17–18.

46 **into a contest he didn't choose** Douglas L. Wilson has researched the conflicting tales of the wrestling match in his chapter, "Wrestling with the Evidence," in *Honor's Voice: The Transformation of Abraham Lincoln* (New York: Alfred A. Knopf, 1999), 19–51.

48 **"Frequently when Mr. L"** James Short to WHH, July 7, 1865, *HI,* 73–74.

48 **"I foxed his pants"** Hannah Armstrong (WHH interview), [1866], *HI,* 525–526.

48 **"blue round about coat"** Robert Rutledge to WHH, November 1, 1865; *HI,* 382.

48 **"I am well aware"** *Sangamo Journal,* January 26, 1832.

48 **"Springfield can no longer"** Ibid.

49 FELLOW-CITIZENS *Sangamo Journal,* March 15, 1832.

50 **Indians had left their settlements** See prologue, *The Black Hawk War, 1831–1832,* ed. Ellen M. Whitney (Springfield: Illinois State Historical Library, 1970), 1:1–51.

50 **Black Hawk** See Roger L. Nichols, *Black Hawk and the Warrior's Path* (Arlington Heights, Ill.: Harlan Davidson, 1992).

50 **Lincoln promptly volunteered** Harry E. Pratt, "Lincoln in the Black Hawk War," *Bulletin of the Abraham Lincoln Association* 54 (December 1938): 4.

50 **put forward Lincoln's name** William G. Greene to WHH (interview), May 30, 1865, *HI,* 18; William G. Green (WHH interview), October 9, 1865, *HI,* 368.

51 **"to his own surprise"** AL, Autobiography, *CW,* 4:64.

51 **"a good and true man"** William G. Greene to WHH (interview), *HI,* 18–19.

51 **"This is cowardly"** Royal Clary (WHH interview), [October 1866?], *HI,* 372.

52 **"He says he has not"** AL, "Autobiography," *CW,* 4:64.

52 **Fellow Citizens, I presume** *HL,* 75.

53 **"As he rose to speak"** Robert B. Rutledge to WHH, [ca. November 1, 1866], *HI,* 384.

53 **"After he was twenty-three"** AL, "Autobiography," *CW,* 4:62.

53 **Kirkham's *Grammar*** Samuel Kirkham, *English Grammar in Familiar Lectures* (Rochester, N.Y.: Marshall and Dan, 1829), 8. A Kirkham grammar, one Lincoln owned and gave to Ann Rutledge, is now in the Library of Congress. This copy was handed down through the family of Ann Rutledge, a young woman Lincoln courted in New Salem. There is no evidence that this was the grammar Lincoln acquired from the farmer Vance.

54 **"read by fire light"** J. Rowan Herndon to WHH, July 3, 1865, *HI,* 69.

54 **"His mind was full"** Isaac Cogdal (WHH Interview), [1865–66], *HI,* 441.

54 **"read some"** Abner Y. Ellis (statement for WHH), January 23, 1866, *HI,* 171–72.

54 **while in prison** Eric Foner, *Tom Paine and Revolutionary America* (New York: Oxford University Press, 1976), 211.

55 **"Burns helped Lincoln"** James H. Matheny (WHH Interview), March 2, 1870, *HI,* 577.

55 **a paper read one evening** John Hill to WHH, June 27, 1865, *HI,* 61.

55 **"He studied"** AL, "Autobiography," *CW,* 4:65.

56   **"Of course they did nothing"** Ibid.

56   **"The store winked out"** Ibid.

56   **"too insignificant"** Ibid.

56   **the mail came** Benjamin P. Thomas, *Abraham Lincoln: A Biography* (New York: Alfred A. Knopf, 1952), 38.

56   **As postmaster** See Benjamin Thomas, "Lincoln the Postmaster," *Bulletin of the Abraham Lincoln Association* 31 (June 1933): 3–9.

57   **"generally Read for the By standers"** J. Rowan Herndon to WHH, August 16, 1865, *HI*, 92.

57   **Lincoln began reading** See Thomas, "Lincoln the Postmaster," 7.

57   **"His text book"** Mentor Graham to WHH (interview), May 29, 1865, *HI*, 10.

57   **"[I] accepted"** AL, "Autobiography," *CW*, 4:65.

57   **as his deputy** Wilson, *Honor's Voice*, 148.

57   **he would not compromise** John Moore Fisk (WHH interview), February 18, 1887, *HI*, 715.

57   **knew nothing about surveying** Adin Baber, *A. Lincoln with Compass and Chain* (Kansas, Ill.: Privately printed, 1968), 11.

58   **Godbey employed Lincoln** "Certificate of Survey for Russell Godbey," January 14, 1834, *CW*, 1:20–21.

58   **"staid with me all night"** Russell Godbey (WHH interview), [1865–66], *HI*, 449.

58   **"This procured bread"** AL, "Autobiography," *CW*, 4:65.

59   **"Every one knew him"** Robert L. Wilson to WHH, February 10, 1866, *HI*, 201.

59   **build national party machinery** Michael Holt, *The Rise and Fall of the American Whig Party: Jacksonian Politics and the Onset of the Civil War* (New York: Oxford University Press, 1999), 35.

59   **"they could not vote"** J. Rowan Herndon to WHH, May 28, 1865, *HI*, 8.

59   **"I voted for Lincoln"** Russell Godbey (WHH Interview), [1865–66], *HI*, 449.

CHAPTER 5. *The Whole People of Sangamon: 1834–37*

61   **"Did you vote for me?"** Coleman Smoot to WHH, May 7, 1866, *HI*, 254.

62   **a capital invented by politicians** See William E. Baringer, *Lincoln's Vandalia: A Pioneer Portrait* (New Brunswick, N.J.: Rutgers University Press, 1949), 12–14.

63   **Farmers constituted the largest group** Ibid., 40.

63   **writing for them** Baringer, Ibid., 62–63.

64   **a brief letter** *Sangamo Journal*, December 13, 1834; January 31, 1835; and February 7, 1835.

64   **"There was no danger"** AL, "Speech in Illinois Legislature Concerning the Surveyor of Schuyler County," January 6, 1835, *CW*, 1:31.

65   **"I always thought"** Abner Y. Ellis to WHH, December 6, 1866, *HI*, 500.

65   **creditors pressed various judgments** A fresh reading calls into question the traditional assumption that Lincoln spent his entire time boarding with families. When the village of New Salem was reconstructed in the 1930s, the planners used a plat from 1829 that did not show the additional homes and businesses built in the 1830s. Furthermore, the execution of judgment in

March 1835 of Lincoln's personal property has always been read that Lincoln owned two horses, but new digital technology has shown the document actually reads a "horse" and a "house." Recent historical and archaeological investigation suggests Lincoln was the owner of "the undivided half of lots 16 & 17 north of Main Street New Salem." These findings show that Lincoln, by 1835, was already a responsible property owner. See Thomas Schwartz, "Finding the Missing Link: A Promissory Note and the Lost Town of Pappsville," Historical Bulletin Number 51 (The Lincoln Fellowship of Wisconsin, 1996), pp. 10-11, and Robert Mazrim, "Magnificent Storehouse and Forgotten Lot Lines: New Light on Lincoln and Storekeeping in New Salem." *Archival Studies Bulletin* 4 (Sangamo Archaeological Center, 2005), pp. 11–12.

65 **common for debtors** Winkle, *Young Eagle,* 99.

65 **Lincoln's first employer** J. Rowan Herndon, October 26, 1866, *HI,* 378.

65 **earned a nickname** On Lincoln's nickname "Honest Abe," see Donald, *Lincoln,* 149, 244.

66 **tract of land** "Document Drawn for James Eastep," November 12, 1831, *CW,* 1:3–4.

66 **"right and title"** "Bill of Sale Drawn for John Ferguson," January 25, 1832, *CW,* 1:4.

66 **"as there [were] no Attorneys"** Jason Duncan to WHH [late 1866–early 1867], *HI,* 540.

66 **"he thought of trying"** *CW,* 4:65.

66 **Stuart was from Kentucky** Paul M. Angle, *One Hundred Years of Law: An Account of the Law Office Which John T. Stuart Founded in Springfield, Illinois, a Century Ago* (Springfield, Ill.: Brown, Hay and Stephens, 1928).

66 **"Regular instruction"** Josiah Quincy, "An Address Delivered at the Dedication of the Dane Law College in Harvard University, October 23, 1832," in *The Legal Mind in America: From Independence to the Civil War,* ed. Perry Miller (Garden City, N.Y.: Doubleday, 1962), 210–11.

67 **"uncouth looking man"** H. E. Dummer (WHH interview), [1865–66], *HI,* 442.

67 **"seemed to have but little to say"** Paul M. Angle, "The Record of a Friendship—A Series of Letters from Lincoln to Henry E. Dummer," *JISHS* 31 (June 1938): 125–27.

67 **"went at it"** AL, "Autobiography," *CW,* 4:65.

67 **"on a goods box"** Henry McHenry to WHH (interview), May 29, 1865, *HI,* 14.

67 **His favorite place of study** William Dean Howells, *Lives and Speeches of Abraham Lincoln and Hannibal Hamlin* (Columbus, Ohio: Follett, Foster and Company, 1860), 31.

68 **"While acting as their representative"** *Sangamo Journal,* June 13, 1836

68 **Andrew Jackson . . . declined** See Richard P. McCormick, "Was There a 'Whig Strategy' in 1836?" *Journal of Early Republic* 4 (Spring 1984): 47–70; Glyndon G. Van Deusen, "The Whig Party," in Arthur M. Schlesinger, Jr., ed., *History of U.S. Political Parties* (New York: Chelsea House, 1973), 333–493.

68   **"If alive"** *Sangamo Journal,* June 13, 1836.

68   **nothing about presidential politics** Winkle, *Young Eagle,* 118.

69   **"Mr. Lincoln took"** Robert L. Wilson to WHH, February 10, 1866, *HI,* 202–3.

70   **"The present legislature"** *Sangamo Journal,* January 6, 1837.

70   **three future governors** Paul Simon, *Lincoln's Preparation for Greatness: The Illinois Legislative Years* (Urbana: University of Illinois Press, 1971), 49–50.

70   **a twenty-three-year-old attorney** See Johannsen, *Douglas,* 24–25.

72   **Politics became his passion** Ibid., 24–25.

72   **"It is now time"** *Sangamo Journal,* November 19, 1836.

74   **Lincoln was adamant** Simon, *Lincoln's Preparation for Greatness,* 52.

74   **"never for one moment"** Robert L. Wilson to WHH, February 10, 1866, *HI,* 204.

75   **"the unfortunate condition"** *House Journal,* Tenth General Assembly, First Session, 243–44.

76   **"They believe that"** "Protest in Illinois Legislature on Slavery," *CW,* 1:74–75.

76   **called "cautious"** Donald, *Lincoln,* 63.

76   **paused to recall his protest** AL, "Autobiography," *CW,* 4:65.

CHAPTER 6. *Without Contemplating Consequences: 1837–42*

79   **walked about the store with Lincoln** Joshua F. Speed (statement for WHH), [by 1882], *HI,* 590.

79   **"J. T. Stuart and A. Lincoln"** *Sangamo Journal,* April 15, 1837.

80   **"It is probably cheap"** Speed, *Reminiscences of Abraham Lincoln,* 21–22.

80   **"I never saw so gloomy"** Joshua Speed (statement for WHH), [by 1882] *HI,* 590.

80   **an unprepossessing town** Paul Angle, *"Here I Have Lived": A History of Lincoln's Springfield, 1821–1865* (New Brunswick, N.J.: Rutgers University Press, 1935), 45–46.

81   **"The owner of real estate"** *Sangamo Journal,* February 20, 1837.

82   **his first criminal case** Harry E. Pratt, "Abraham Lincoln's First Murder Trial," *JISHS* 37 (September 1944): 242–49; and John J. Duff, *A. Lincoln: Prairie Lawyer* (New York: Rinehart, 1960), 53–61.

83   **entrusted with the closing argument** Pratt, "Abraham Lincoln's First Murder Trial," 247. Criminal cases would represent only 5.6 percent of the cases in Lincoln's law practice; of these, murder represented only 9 percent, LEGAL, 2:338–39.

83   **"I have received five dollars"** Fee Book of Stuart and Lincoln, ALPLM.

84   **contest between Stuart and Douglas** Johannsen, *Douglas,* 63–68.

84   **"Commencement of Lincoln's administration"** Fee Book of Stuart and Lincoln, ALPLM.

84   **"The rooms were generally crowded"** James C. Conkling, "Recollections of the Bench and Bar of Central Illinois," *Fergus Historical Series* 22 (Chicago: Fergus Printing Company, 1882), 51–53.

86   **Speed was born** Speed, *Reminiscences,* 3–4.

86   **"almost without friends"** Ibid., 23.

86 **"I've never been"** AL to Mary S. Owens, May 7, 1837, *CW,* 1:78.

86 **"choice spirits,"** Speed, *Reminiscences,* 4.

87 **"We find ourselves"** AL, "Address Before the Young Men's Lyceum of Springfield, Illinois," January 27, 1838, *CW,* 1:108. This speech has captivated historians in search of the ideas of the young Lincoln. See Thomas F. Schwartz, "The Springfield Lyceums and Lincoln's 1838 Speech," *Illinois Historical Journal* 83 (1990): 41–49; and Mark E. Neeley, Jr., "Lincoln's Lyceum Speech and the Origins of a Modern Myth," *Lincoln Lore* (1987), 1776 (February 1987), 1–3, 1777 (March 1987), 1.

87 **"mobocratic spirit"** AL, "Address Before the Young Men's Lyceum," 109, 111.

87 **immediate occasion of the address** See Paul Simon, *Freedom's Champion: Elijah Lovejoy* (Carbondale: Southern Illinois University Press, 1994).

87 **"some transatlantic military giant"** AL, "Address Before the Young Men's Lyceum," 109.

88 **"his own course"** "Remarks in Illinois Legislature Concerning Resolutions Asking Information on Railroad and Fund Commissioners," December 8, 1838, *CW,* 1:122–23.

88 **"We are now so far advanced"** "Report and Resolutions Introduced in Illinois Legislature in Relation to Purchase of Public Lands," January 17, 1839, *CW,* 1:135.

90 **accused Lincoln** *Illinois State Register,* November 23, 1839.

90 **"He was conscious"** Joseph Gillespie to WHH, January 31, 1866, *HI,* 181.

90 **"peculiarly embarrassing"** AL, "Speech on the Sub-Treasury," December [26], 1839, *CW,* 1:159.

90 **"Many free countries"** Ibid., 178.

91 **"fearlessly and eloquently exposing"** *Peoria Register,* February 15, 1840.

92 **"appoint one person"** "Lincoln's Plan of Campaign in 1840," [ca. January 1840], *CW,* 1:180–81.

92 **"Our intention is"** "Campaign Circular from Whig Committee," January [31?], 1840, *CW,* 1:201–3.

92 **whirlwind speaking campaign** Simon, *Lincoln's Preparation for Greatness,* 216–17.

92 **extolled the Second Bank** *Alton Telegraph,* April 11, 1840.

92 **"have not been able"** *Quincy Whig,* May 25, 1840.

93 **"listened to"** *Illinois State Register,* October 16, 1840.

93 **"reviewed the political course"** *Sangamo Journal,* May 15, 1840.

94 **became antagonistic** Wilson, *Honor's Voice,* 206–9.

94 **"He imitated Thomas"** *HL,* 130.

94 **"the skinning of Thomas"** Ibid., 130.

94 **the 1840 presidential election** Richard P. McCormick, "New Perspectives on Jacksonian Politics," *American Historical Review* 65 (1960), 288–301.

94 **the most esteemed jurist** Duff, *A. Lincoln,* 79.

95 **had gone head-to-head** Albert A. Woldman, *Lawyer Lincoln* (Boston: Houghton Mifflin, 1936), 39.

95 **"*just now*"** AL, "Temperance Address," February 22, 1842, *CW,* 1:271–72.

96 **"But," say some,** Ibid., 275, 278.

CHAPTER 7. *A Matter of Profound Wonder: 1831–42*

99   **"He was not very fond"** Sarah Bush Lincoln (WHH interview), September 8, 1865, *HI,* 108.

99   **"did not go much"** Anna Caroline Gentry (WHH interview), September 17, *HI,* 131.

99   **"Lincoln loved my Mother"** Elizabeth Herndon Bell (WHH interview), [March 1887?], *HI,* 606.

99   **"Abe's son"** Hannah Armstrong (WHH interview), [1865–66], *HI,* 527.

99   **court the young Ann Rutledge** In the first half of the twentieth century, several leading Lincoln scholars attacked the legitimacy of the Ann Rutledge story. For recent evaluations, see John Evangelist Walsh, *The Shadows Rise: Abraham Lincoln and the Ann Rutledge Legend* (Urbana: University of Illinois Press, 1993); and Douglas L. Wilson, *Lincoln Before Washington: New Perspectives on the Illinois Years* (Urbana: University of Illinois Press, 1997), 74–98.

100   **"a young lady"** William G. Greene to WHH (interview), May 30, 1865, *HI,* 21.

100   **"My sister was"** Robert B. Rutledge to WHH, [ca. November 1, 1866], *HI,* 383.

100   **"became deeply in love"** James McGrady Rutledge (WHH interview), [March 1887], *HI,* 607–8.

100   **"Had she lived"** Fern Nance Pond, ed., "The Memoirs of James McGrady Rutledge 1814–1899," *JISHS* 29 (April 1936): 80–88.

101   **"It was a great shock"** Elizabeth Abell to WHH, February 15, 1867, *HI,* 556–57.

101   **"The effect upon"** Robert B. Rutledge to WHH, [ca. November 1, 1866], *HI,* 382.

101   **"The other gentlemen"** Mary Owens Vineyard to WHH, July 22, 1866, *HI,* 262.

102   **"With other things"** AL to Mary S. Owens, December 13, 1836, *CW,* 1:54.

103   **"This thing of living"** AL to Mary S. Owens, May 7, 1837, *CW,* 1:78.

103   **"I want in all cases"** AL to Mary S. Owens, August 16, 1837, *CW,* 1:94–95.

105   **"for her skin"** AL to Mrs. Orville H. Browning, April 1, 1838, *CW,* 1:117–19.

105   **"deficient in those little links"** Mary Owens Vineyard to WHH, May 23, 1866, *HI,* 256.

105   **had helped settle** Stephen Berry, *House of Abraham: Lincoln and the Todds, a Family Divided by War* (Boston: Houghton Mifflin, 2007), 6–8.

105   **Mary, their fourth child** Catherine Clinton, *Mrs. Lincoln: A Life,* forthcoming.

106   **her father married** Ibid.

106   **"Mary was far in advance"** Katherine Helm, *The True Story of Mary, Wife of Lincoln* (New York: Harper, 1928), 21.

107   **she spoke up** Baker, *Mary Todd Lincoln,* 60.

107   **observed slave auctions** Ibid., 68.

108   **"her temper and tongue"** Clinton, *Mrs. Lincoln: A Life,* forthcoming.

108 **"the very creature"** James C. Conkling to Mercy Ann Levering, September 21, 1840, ALPLM.

108 **"Mary could make"** Helm, *True Story of Mary, Wife of Lincoln*, 81.

109 **Mary's dearest friend** Baker, *Mary Todd Lincoln*, 80–82.

109 **"a widower"** Mary Todd to Mercy Ann Levering, December [15?], 1840, and June 1841, *MTL*, 20, 26.

110 **"And he certainly did"** Helm, *True Story of Mary, Wife of Lincoln*, 74.

110 **"Mary led"** Elizabeth Todd Edwards (WHH interview), [1865–66], *HI*, 443.

110 **"This fall I became"** Mary Todd to Mercy Ann Levering, December [15?], 1840, *MTL*, 13, 21.

110 **many young men of his time** Baker, *Mary Todd Lincoln*, puts Lincoln's questions and doubts in the context of his time.

111 **"I warned Mary"** Baker, *Mary Todd Lincoln*, 89.

111 **sexually segregated Victorian society** Karen Lystra, *Searching the Heart: Women, Men, and Romantic Love in Nineteenth-Century America* (New York: Oxford University Press, 1989), 157, 179.

111 **"a great sharpener"** Junior Theocritus (pseudonym), *Dictionary of Love* (New York: Dick and Fitzgerald, 1858), cited in Lystra, *Searching the Heart*, 179.

111 **relationship advanced** Baker, *Mary Todd Lincoln*, 85.

111 **their relationship suddenly fell apart** For an analysis of the multiple strands of the breaking of the engagement, see "Abraham Lincoln and 'That Fatal First of January,' " in Wilson, *Lincoln Before Washington*, 99–132.

111 **"a most interesting"** Mary Todd to Mercy Ann Levering, December [15] 1840, *MTL*, 20.

112 **"went to see"** Joshua F. Speed (WHH interview), [1865–66], *HI*, 475.

112 **"emaciated in appearance"** James C. Conkling to Mercy Ann Levering, January 24, 1841, ALPLM.

112 **"moody and hypochondriac"** Joshua F. Speed to WHH, January 12, 1866, *HI*, 158.

112 **"pained at his deep"** Joshua F. Speed to WHH, September 17, 1866, *HI*, 342.

113 **"I am now"** AL to John T. Stuart, January 23, 1841, *CW*, 1:229.

113 **"[Lincoln] deems me"** *MTL*, 159.

113 **an odd allusion** Baker, *Mary Todd Lincoln*, 91.

114 **"Shields is a fool"** "The 'Rebecca' Letter," *Sangamo Journal*, September 2, 1842, *CW*, 1:295.

116 **the dueling ground** For a vivid account of the duel, see James E. Myers, *The Astonishing Saber Duel of Abraham Lincoln* (Springfield, Ill.: Lincoln-Herndon Building Publishers, 1968).

116 **"Are you now"** AL to Joshua Speed, October 5, 1842, *CW*, 1:302–3.

116 **"One thing is plainly discernable"** Joshua F. Speed to WHH, November 30, 1866, *HI*, 431.

116 **they intended to marry** Clinton, *Mrs. Lincoln*, 68–70.

117 **"With this ring"** William Jayne to WHH, August 17, 1887, *HI*, 624. Reports of the wedding, most given many years after, vary about what took place on that day and evening.

117 **"Nothing new here"** AL to Samuel D. Marshall, November 11, 1842, *CW*, 1:305.

CHAPTER 8. *The Truth Is, I Would Like to Go Very Much: 1843–46*

120 **Baker, two years younger** Harry C. Blair and Rebecca Tarshis, *The Life of Colonel Edward D. Baker, Lincoln's Constant Ally, Together with Four of His Great Orations* (Portland: Oregon Historical Society, 1960); and Winfred Ernest Garrison, *Religion Follows the Frontier: A History of the Disciples of Christ* (New York: Harper and Brothers, 1931).

121 **"Now if you should hear"** AL to Richard S. Thomas, February 14, 1843, *CW,* 1:307.

122 **"that great fabulist"** Campaign Circular from Whig Committee, March 4, 1843, *CW,* 1:309–18.

122 **"It would astonish"** AL to Martin S. Morris, March 26, 1843, *CW,* 1:320.

122 **"There was the strangest"** Ibid.

123 **"I only mean"** Ibid.

123 **"In getting Baker"** AL to Joshua Speed, March 24, 1843, *CW,* 1:270.

123 **"a suitable person"** "Resolution Adopted at Whig Convention at Pekin, Illinois," May 1, 1843, *CW,* 1:322.

124 **"whether the Whigs"** AL to John J. Hardin, May 11, 1843, *CW,* 1:322–23.

124 **Lincoln voted** Thomas, *Abraham Lincoln,* 104.

124 **started their married life** Clinton, *Mrs. Lincoln,* 70–73; and Daniel Mark Epstein, *The Lincolns: Portrait of a Marriage* (New York: Ballantine Books, 2008), 54–55.

125 **Abraham and Mary purchased** "Sale Contract by Charles Dresser and Abraham Lincoln," January 16, 1844, *CW,* 1:331.

126 **"turn a Chair down"** Harriet A. Chapman to WHH, December 10, 1866, *HI,* 512.

126 **" 'This rock' "** Helm, *The True Story of Mary, Wife of Lincoln,* 108.

127 **A fresh opportunity** John A. Lupton, "A. Lincoln, Esquire: The Evolution of a Lawyer," in Allen D. Spiegel, *A. Lincoln, Esquire: A Shrewd, Sophisticated Lawyer in His Time* (Macon, Ga.: Mercer University Press, 2002), 26.

127 **"I have seen him"** *Lincoln Centennial Association Bulletin,* September 1928, 5.

127 **Lincoln selected an unlikely** David H. Donald, in *Lincoln's Herndon: A Biography* (New York: Alfred A. Knopf, 1948), 19–21, discusses the various reasons proposed as to why Lincoln chose Herndon.

128 **he sent Billy** Ibid., 8–14. For a discussion of Herndon's year at Illinois College, see 8–14.

129 **"There is Nat"** Nathaniel Grigsby (WHH interview), September 16, 1865, *HI,* 127–28.

129 **"walked over"** (*Rockport*) *Indiana Herald,* November 1, 1844, *CW,* 1:341–42.

129 **"I went into the neighborhood"** AL to Andrew Johnston, April 18, 1846, *CW,* 1:378.

130 *My childhood's home* AL to Andrew Johnston, April 18, 1846, *CW,* 1:377–79.

130 **publish these words** *Quincy Whig,* May 5, 1847.

130 **"If the whig abolitionists"** AL to Williamson Durley, October 3, 1845, *CW,* 1:347.

131 **"We are not to do *evil*"** Ibid.

131 **"I strongly suspect"** AL to Henry E. Dummer, November 18, 1845, *CW,* 1:350.

131 **"I know of no argument"** Ibid.; *CW,* 1:350.

131 **"That Hardin is"** AL to Robert Boal, January 7, 1846, *CW,* 1:352.

131 **"I do not well see"** Robert Boal to John J. Hardin, January 10, 1846, Hardin MSS, Chicago History Museum.

132 **"He never overlooked"** *HL,* 304.

132 **"In doing this"** AL to Benjamin F. James, December 6, 1845, *CW,* 1:351.

132 **"It is my intention"** AL to Benjamin F. James, January 14, 1846, *CW,* 1:354.

132 **"spins a good yarn"** John Morrison to John J. Hardin, February 3, 1846, Hardin MSS, Chicago History Museum.

132 **"I am entirely satisfied"** AL to John J. Hardin, January 19, 1846, *CW,* 1:356–57.

133 **"I believe you"** AL to John J. Hardin, February 7, 1846, *CW,* 1:360–65.

133 **he sent** *Sangamo Journal,* February 26, 1846.

133 **Committee on Nominations** Donald W. Riddle, *Lincoln Runs for Congress* (New Brunswick, N.J.: Rutgers University Press, 1948), 156–59.

133 **"prompt and united action"** *Sangamo Journal,* June 4, 1846.

134 **Cartwright was born** For the story of Cartwright, see Robert Bray, *Peter Cartwright: Legendary Frontier Preacher* (Urbana: University of Illinois Press, 2005).

134 **"I would get"** Peter Cartwright, *Autobiography of Peter Cartwright: The Backwoods Preacher,* ed. W. P. Strickland (New York: Carlton and Porter, 1856), 165.

135 **"Mr. Cartwright was whispering"** *CW,* 1:384 n. 3; Bray, *Peter Cartwright,* 210.

135 **"Cartwright, never heard"** AL to Allen N. Ford, August 11, 1846, *CW,* 1:383–84.

135 **"an open scoffer"** AL, "Handbill Replying to Charges of Infidelity," July 31, 1846, *CW,* 1:382.

135 **"Being elected"** AL to Joshua F. Speed, October 22, 1846, *CW,* 1:391.

136 **"at the terminus"** *Chicago Journal,* November 16, 1846; and July 5–6, 1847.

136 **July 6** Robert Fergus et al., *Chicago River-And-Harbor Convention: An Account of Its Origin and Proceedings* (Chicago: Fergus Printing Company, 1882), 80–81; Mentor L. Williams, "The Chicago River and Harbor Convention, 1847," *Mississippi Valley Historical Review* 35, no. 4 (March 1949), 607–26.

136 **"how many States"** J. James Shaw, "A Neglected Episode in the Life of Abraham Lincoln," *Transactions of the Illinois State Historical Society* 29 (1922), 56.

136 **"Hon. Abraham Lincoln"** *New York Tribune,* July 14, 1847.

137 **He first advertised** *Sangamo Journal,* October 30, 1845.

CHAPTER 9. *My Best Impression of the Truth: 1847–49*

139 **"Success to our talented member"** *Illinois State Journal,* October 28, 1847.

139 **leased their family home** Lease Contract Between Abraham Lincoln and Cornelius Ludlum, October 23, 1847, *CW,* 1:406.

139 **four Lincolns continued** Ruth Painter Randall, *Mary Lincoln: Biography of a Marriage* (Boston: Little, Brown, 1953), 104–5.

140 **Negroes for sale** *Lexington Observer and Reporter,* November 20, 1847.

140 **"who is slow"** Ibid., November 3, 1847.

141 **"dark and gloomy"** Henry Clay, "Speech at Lexington, KY, November 13, 1847," *The Papers of Henry Clay,* ed. Melba Porter Hay (Lexington: The University Press of Kentucky, 1991), 10:361–64.

141 **Clay laid the blame** Robert V. Remini, *Henry Clay: Statesman for the Union* (New York: W. W. Norton and Company, 1991), 692–93.

142 **"to disavow"** Henry Clay, "Speech at Lexington, KY," 372.

142 **"noted for his hostility"** James Freeman Clarke, *Anti-slavery Days: A Sketch of the Struggle Which Ended in the Abolition of Slavery in the United States* (New York: R. Worthington, 1884), 27.

142 **"A. Lincoln & Lady"** Ibid., 8.

142 **which had a population** Wilhelmus Bogart Bryan, *A History of the National Capital,* vol. 2, *1815–1878* (New York: The Macmillan Company, 1916), 420.

143 **"the City of Magnificent Intentions"** Charles Dickens, *American Notes* (London: Chapman and Hall, 1842), 281.

143 **"Washington may be called"** Ibid., 272.

144 **Lincoln drew seat 191** Donald W. Riddle, *Congressman Abraham Lincoln* (Urbana: University of Illinois Press, 1957), 12–13.

145 **"mileage-elongators"** Glyndon G. Van Deusen, *Horace Greeley: Nineteenth-Century Crusader* (Philadelphia: University of Pennsylvania Press, 1953), 127.

145 **"a wanton outrage"** *Congressional Globe,* 30th Cong., 1st sess., 61, appendix, 159–63.

146 **"wonderful earnestness"** Charles Lanman, *Haphazard Personalities Chiefly of Noted Americans* (Boston: Lee and Shepard, 1886), 342.

146 **"Mr. Stephens of Georgia"** AL to William H. Herndon, February 2, 1848, *CW,* 2:448.

146 **splendid oratory** See Thomas E. Schott, *Alexander H. Stephens of Georgia: A Biography* (Baton Rouge: Louisiana State University Press, 1988).

147 **"As soon as the Congressional"** AL to William H. Herndon, December 12, 1847, *CW,* 1:419.

148 **sent out 7,080 copies** Riddle, *Congressman Abraham Lincoln,* 74.

148 **"When about to tell"** Samuel C. Busey, *Personal Reminiscences and Recollections* (Washington, D.C. [Philadelphia: Dornan, printer], 1895), 25.

149 **"They would have been laughed"** Nathan Sargent, *Public Men and Events* (Philadelphia: J. B. Lippincott and Co., 1875).

149 **"The confusion and noise"** Private letters quoted by Paul Findley, *A Lincoln: The Crucible of Congress* (New York: Crown Publishers, 1979), 97.

149 **"the aggrieved nation"** "Message of the President of the United States" [James K. Polk], *Congressional Globe,* 30th Cong., 1st sess. appendix (December 7, 1847), http://memory.loc.gov/ammem/amlaw/lwcg.html, "Presidential Messages" (accessed 8/7/08).

149 **"of a portion"** Ibid.

150 **"As you are all so anxious"** AL to William H. Herndon, December 13, 1847, *CW,* 1:420.

150 **"This House desires"** AL, "Spot Resolutions in the U.S. House of Representatives," December 22, 1847, *CW,* 1:420–21.

150 **"unnecessarily and unconstitutionally begun"** *Congressional Globe,* 30th Cong., 1st sess., 1848, 9.

150 **"as citizens and patriots"** AL, "Speech in United States House of Representatives: The War with Mexico," January 12, 1848, *CW,* 1:432.

151 **"Now I propose"** Ibid., 439.

152 **"I more than suspect"** Ibid., 439, 441–42.

152 **"Thank heaven"** *Springfield Register,* January 16, 1848.

152 **"If you misunderstand"** AL to William H. Herndon, February 1, 1848, *CW,* 1:446–47.

153 **"I have always intended"** Ibid., 447.

153 **"provision of the Constitution"** AL to William H. Herndon, February 15, 1848, *CW,* 1:451. The two Herndon letters to Lincoln do not exist today.

153 **"We have a vague"** AL to Solomon Lincoln, March 6 and 24, 1848, *CW,* 1:455–56, 459–60.

153 **"There is no longer"** AL to David Lincoln, April 2, 1848, *CW,* 1:461–62.

154 **"In this troublesome"** AL to Mary Todd Lincoln, April 16, 1848, *CW,* 1:465–66.

154 **"Will you be a *good girl"*** AL to Mary Todd Lincoln, June 12, 1848, *CW,* 1:477–78.

155 **Library began** For the story of the Library of Congress, see James Conway, *America's Library: The Story of the Library of Congress 1800–2000* (New Haven, Conn.: Yale University Press, 2000); and William Dawson Johnston, *History of the Library of Congress,* vol. 1, *1800–1864* (Washington: Government Printing Office, 1904).

155 **"a puzzle"** This account is from Hubert M. Skinner, *The Lincoln–Douglas Debate* (Lincoln-Jefferson University, 1909), 7, but the trustworthiness of his account is not supported by footnotes; Findley, *A. Lincoln: The Crucible of Congress,* 100.

155 **served in the military** See "The Soldier Becomes a Politician," in K. Jack Bauer, *Zachary Taylor: Soldier, Planter, Statesman of the Old Southwest* (Baton Rouge: Louisiana State University Press, 1985), 215–38.

156 **"I am in favor"** AL to Thomas S. Flournoy, February 17, 1848, *CW,* 1:452. Flournoy was a Whig member of Congress from Virginia.

156 **"Our only chance"** AL to Jesse Lynch, April 10, 1848, *CW,* 1:463.

157 **"Like a horde of hungry ticks"** AL, "Speech in the U.S. House of Representatives on the Presidential Question," July 27, 1848, *CW,* 1:508.

157 **"By the way"** Ibid., 509–10.

158 **"was so good natured"** *Baltimore American,* July 29, 1848.

158 **campaign tour in Massachusetts** William F. Hanna, *Abraham Among the Yankees: Abraham Lincoln's 1848 Visit to Massachusetts* (Taunton, Mass.: The Old Colony Historical Society, 1983), 30–34; and Sheldon H. Harris, "Abraham Lincoln Stumps a Yankee Audience," *New England Quarterly* 38 (June 1865), 227–33.

159 **"frequently interrupted"** *Springfield* (Massachusetts) *Republican,* September 14, 1848.

159 **"Mr. Lincoln has"** *Boston Daily Advertiser,* September 13, 1848.

159 **"It was an altogether new show"** *Old Colony Republican* (Taunton, Massachusetts), September 23, 1848.

160 **"in a most forcible"** *Boston Courier,* September 23, 1848.

160 **"We spent the greater part"** Frederick Seward, *Seward at Washington as Senator and Secretary of State* (New York: Derby and Miller, 1861), 79–80.

160 **"overwhelmed in the contemplation"** AL, Fragment: Niagara Falls [ca. September 25–30, 1848], *CW,* 2:10.

160 **traveled on the steamer** *HL,* 188.

161 **"Lincoln has made nothing"** *Springfield Register,* n.d., ca. 1848 (as quoted in Thomas, *Abraham Lincoln,* 125).

161 **Lincoln showed it to** Findley, *A. Lincoln: The Crucible of Congress,* 138

161 **"No person within the District"** AL, Remarks and Resolution Introduced in United States House of Representatives Concerning Abolition in the District of Columbia, January 10, 1862, *CW,* 2:20–22.

162 **"I believed it as good"** Findley, *A. Lincoln: The Crucible of Congress,* 139.

163 **first and only case** See "Attorney's Notes," March 1849, LEGAL, 1:415–28, 430–31.

163 **"the threatened revolution"** *HL,* 188.

164 **"Not one man"** AL to George W. Rives, May 7, 1849, *CW,* 2:46.

164 **"I must not only"** AL to William B. Warren and others, April 7, 1849, *CW,* 2:41.

164 **return was not greeted** Willard L. King, *Lincoln's Manager, David Davis* (Cambridge, Mass.: Harvard University Press, 1960), 62.

164 **"He is my personal"** Riddle, *Congressman Abraham Lincoln,* 122.

165 **"I opposed"** Donald, *Lincoln,* 140.

165 **"determined to eschew"** *HL,* 193.

CHAPTER 10. *As a Peacemaker the Lawyer Has a Superior Opportunity: 1849–52*

167 **"If [I] went"** David Davis (WHH interview), September 20, 1866, *HI,* 349.

167 **"From 1849 to 1854"** AL to Jesse W. Fell, "Enclosing Autobiography," December 20, 1859, *CW,* 3:512.

167 **"These cases attended"** Lincoln Fee Book, ALPLM.

168 **"How hard"** WHH to WHL, March 6, 1870, The Papers of Ward Hill Lamon, HEH.

168 **"It went below"** *HL,* 193.

168 **discarded fruit seeds** Ibid., 198.

168 **"innocent of water"** Woldman, *Lawyer Lincoln,* 83.

168 **"When I read aloud"** *HL,* 207.

169 **"Let us have both sides"** Woldman, *Lawyer Lincoln,* 55.

170 **The best lawyers** Robert A. Ferguson, *Law and Letters in American Culture* (Cambridge, Mass.: Harvard University Press, 1984), 87.

171 **"Lincoln's knowledge"** Quoted in Mark E. Steiner, *An Honest Calling: The Law Practice of Abraham Lincoln* (Dekalb: Northern Illinois University Press, 40–42.

171 **"Sometimes Lincoln studied"** David Davis (WHH interview), [1866], *HI,* 529.

171 **Lincoln approached the practice of law** Emanuel Hertz, ed., *The Hidden Lincoln: From the Papers of William H. Herndon* (New York: H. Liveright, 1931), 176.

171 **relied on published digests** Steiner, *Honest Calling,* 49.

172 **legislature had elected Davis** For the biography of David Davis, see King, *Lincoln's Manager.*

173 **"Lincoln is the best"** David Davis to William P. Walker, May 4, 1844, Davis Papers, ALPML.

175 **"an amicable arrangement"** Remini, *Henry Clay,* 732.

175 **"How can the Union be preserved?"** Irving Bartlett, *Calhoun: A Biography* (New York: W. W. Norton and Company, 1993), 371–72.

175 **"I wish to speak"** Merrill D. Peterson, *The Great Triumvirate: Webster, Clay, and Calhoun* (New York: Oxford University Press, 1987), 462–63.

176 **"I am not an accomplished lawyer"** AL, "Fragment: Notes for a Law Lecture," [July 1, 1850?], *CW,* 2:81.

177 **"the leading rule"** Ibid.

177 **"I sincerely hope"** AL to Abram Bale, February 22, 1850, LEGAL, 1:4–5.

178 **In his examination** (Danville) *Illinois Citizen,* May 29, 1850.

179 **Mary bore these absences** Baker, *Mary Todd Lincoln,* 125–28.

180 **"Eat, Mary"** Ibid., 126.

180 **"We miss him"** AL to John D. Johnston, February 23, 1850, *CW,* 2:76–77.

180 **Mary joined First Presbyterian** Wayne C. Temple, *Abraham Lincoln: From Skeptic to Prophet* (Mahomet, Ill.: Mayhaven Publishing, 1995), 47–48.

180 **"the exercises"** James Smith, *The Christian's Defence, Containing a Fair Statement, and Impartial Examination of the Leading Objections Urged by Infidels Against the Antiquity, Genuineness, Credibility, and Inspiration of the Holy Scriptures* (Cincinnati, Ohio: J. A. James, 1843), 1:4.

181 **"the mind must"** Robert T. Lincoln to Isaac Markens, November 4, 1917, Robert Todd Lincoln MSS, Chicago History Museum; Temple, *Abraham Lincoln,* 72.

181 **"everything must be given up"** Smith, *Christian's Defence,* 1:4.

181 **Lincoln accepted an invitation** "On motion, Abraham Lincoln, Henry Van Huff and Thomas Lewis were appointed a committee to aid the Rev. James Smith in a suit pending in Presbytery against this church." *Minutes of the Board of Trustees,* First Presbyterian Church, 1829–1866, April 26, 1853, ALPLM.

181 **Lincoln began to attend** John T. Stuart to J. A. Reed, December 17, 1872, in *Scribner's Monthly* 6 (July 1873): 336.

181 **"could thunder out"** Elizabeth Todd Grimsley, "Six Months in the White House," *JISHS* 19, nos. 3–4 (October 1926–January 1927): 64.

182 **Lincolns were becoming fond** Temple, *Abraham Lincoln,* 60.

182 **continued to lobby** AL to the Editors of the *Illinois Journal,* June 5, 1850, *CW,* 2:79.

182 **"The want of time"** AL to Lewis C. Kercheval and Others, July 24, 1850, *CW,* 2:82–83.

182 **"I fear"** AL, "Eulogy on Zachary Taylor," July 25, 1850, *CW,* 2:89–90.

183 **"it is no[t because]"** AL to John D. Johnston, January 12, 1851, *CW,* 2:96–97.

184 **"Say to him"** Ibid., 97; and Donald, *Lincoln,* 153.

184 **"I have been thinking"** AL to John D. Johnston, November 4, 1851, *CW,* 2:111.

185 **"The infant nation"** "Eulogy on Henry Clay," July 6, 1852, *CW,* 2:121–32.

CHAPTER 11. *Let No One Be Deceived: 1852–56*

187 **"We were thunderstruck"** AL, "Speech at Peoria, Illinois," October 16, 1854, *CW,* 2:282.

188 **"all questions"** Johannsen, *Douglas,* 408.

188 **"outSouthernized the South"** John Niven, *Salmon P. Chase: A Biography* (New York: Oxford University Press, 1995), 237–38.

188 **"destroy all sectional parties"** Johannsen, *Douglas,* 409, 431, 439–445.

191 **"We arraign this bill"** "An Appeal of Independent Democrats," *Congressional Globe,* 33 Cong., 1st sess., 280–82.

192 **popularly known as Know-Nothings** See Douglas M. Strong, *Perfectionist Politics: Abolitionism and the Religious Tensions in American Democracy* (Syracuse, N.Y.: Syracuse University Press, 1999); David M. Potter, *The Impending Crisis: 1848–1861,* ed. Don E. Fehrenbacher (New York: Harper and Row, 1976), 250–53.

192 **"I do not perceive"** AL to Owen Lovejoy, August 11, 1855, *CW,* 2:316.

194 **"I am not a Know-Nothing"** AL to Joshua Speed, August 24, 1855, *CW,* 2:323.

194 **"Although volume upon volume"** AL, "Fragment on Slavery," [July 1, 1854?], *CW,* 2:222.

194 **"but a grown up"** See Harvey Wish, *George Fitzhugh: Propagandist of the Old South* (Baton Rouge: Louisiana State University Press, 1943), especially 82–93.

195 **"If A. can prove"** AL, "Fragment on Slavery," [July 1, 1854?], *CW,* 2:222.

195 **ideas in these notes** "Fragment: Notes for Law Lecture," [July 1, 1850], *CW,* 2:81–82; "Fragment on Government," [July 1, 1854], *CW,* 2:221; "Fragment on Slavery," [July 1, 1854?], *CW,* 2:222; "Fragment on Slavery," [July 1, 1854], *CW,* 2:222–23; "Fragment on Sectionalism," [July 23, 1856], *CW,* 2:349–53; "Fragment on Stephen A. Douglas," [December 1856?], *CW,* 2:382–83; "Fragment on the Dred Scott Case," [January 1857], *CW,* 2:387–88; "Fragment on the Formation of the Republican Party," [February 28, 1857], *CW,* 2:391.

195 **"whittling sticks"** Donald, *Lincoln,* 170.

195 **"The Declaration of Independence"** *Illinois Journal,* July 11, 1854.

196 **"the great wrong"** AL, "Speech at Winchester, Illinois," August 26, 1854, *CW,* 2:226.

196 **"If we were situated"** AL, "Speech at Bloomington, Illinois," September 12, 1854, *CW,* 2:230–32.

197 **Douglas prepared to speak** Johannsen, *Douglas,* 453–54; James W. Sheahan, *The Life of Stephen A. Douglas* (New York: Harper and Brothers, 1860), 271–73.

198 **"had been nosing"** *Illinois State Register,* September 27, 1854.

198 **"pander to prejudice"** AL, "Speech at Bloomington, Illinois," September 26, 1854, *CW,* 2:234, 236, 240.

199 **"a thin, high-pitched falsetto"** Horace White, "Abraham Lincoln in 1854," *Transactions of the Illinois State Historical Society, 1908* 13 (1909): 32.

199 **"I do not propose"** Lincoln made much the same speech at Springfield on October 4, 1854, and again on October 16. The Springfield speech exists only in brief summary, thus the text employed here is of the later Peoria speech. AL, "Speech at Peoria, Illinois," October 16, 1854, *CW*, 2:248–49, 255, 265–66, 275–76. For an excellent examination of Lincoln's Peoria speech in its historical context, see Lewis E. Lehrman, *Lincoln at Peoria: The Turning Point* (Mechanicsburg, PA: Stackpole Books, 2008).

202 **It reentered the national dialogue** Philip F. Detweiler, "The Changing Reputation of the Declaration of Independence: The First Fifty Years," *The William and Mary Quarterly*, 3rd Series 19, no. 4 (October 1962): 557–74.

202 **"The Declaration of Independence"** Jean V. Matthews, *Rufus Choate: The Law and Civic Virtue* (Philadelphia: Temple University Press, 1980), 99.

202 **a historical signpost** Pauline Maier, *American Scripture: Making the Declaration of Independence* (New York: Alfred A. Knopf, 1997), 160–208.

202 **"false and dangerous assumption"** John C. Calhoun, "Speech on the Oregon Bill," June 27, 1848, *The Papers of John C. Calhoun*, ed. Clyde N. Wilson and Shirley Bright Cook (Columbia: University of South Carolina Press, 1999), 534–35.

203 **"The anti-Nebraska speech"** *Illinois Journal*, October 5, 1854.

203 **"under the pretense"** Donald, *Lincoln's Herndon*, 77–78.

203 **"I have been perplexed"** AL to Ichabod Codding, November 27, 1854, *CW*, 2:288.

204 **"he took the stump"** AL, "Autobiography," *CW*, 4:67.

204 **"No—I can't"** William Jayne (WHH interview), August 15, 1866, *HI*, 266.

204 **"What would have happened"** AL, "Speech at Chicago, Illinois," October 27, 1854, *CW*, 2:283–84.

205 **wrote to ask** AL to Charles Hoyt, November 10, 1854, *CW*, 2:286.

205 **"I do not ask"** AL to Joseph Gillespie, December 1, 1854, *CW*, 2:290.

206 **"the names"** AL to Hugh Lemaster, November 29, 1854, *CW*, 2:289.

206 **"It will give me pleasure"** Charles Hoyt to AL, November 20, 1854, ALPLC.

206 **"We want some one"** Hugh Lemaster to AL, December 11, 1854, ALPLC.

207 **"a total stranger"** AL to Elihu Washburne, December 11, 14, 1854, *CW*, 2:292, 293.

207 **wrote the names** "List of Members of the Illinois Legislature in 1855," [January 1, 1855?], *CW*, 2:296–98.

207 **"I cannot doubt"** AL to Elihu B. Washburne, January 6, 1855, *CW*, 2:303–4.

208 **"You ought to drop"** Joseph Gillespie to WHH, January 31, 1866, *HI*, 183.

208 **BALLOTS FOR UNITED STATES SENATE** Fehrenbacher, *Prelude*, 175.

208 **"I regret my defeat"** AL to Elihu B. Washburne, February 9, 1854, *CW*, 2:306.

208 **broke off her long friendship** Baker, *Mary Todd Lincoln*, 150.

208 **"he would never strive"** Joseph Gillespie, memorandum, April 22, 1880, Gillespie MSS, Chicago Historical Society.

209 **"his defeat now gives me"** AL to Elihu B. Washburne, February 9, 1854, *CW*, 2:1855, 307.

209 **"Not *too* disappointed"** Horace White, *The Life of Lyman Trumbull* (Boston: Houghton Mifflin Company, 1913), 45.

209 **"I was dabbling"** AL to James Sandford, Mortimer Porter, and Ambrose K. Striker, March 10, 1855, *CW*, 2:308.

209 **"No other improvement"** AL, "Communication to the People of Sangamo County," March 9, 1832, *CW*, 1:5.

209 **problems and roadblocks** George Rogers Taylor, *The Transportation Revolution, 1815–1860* (New York: Rinehart, 1951), 79.

210 **represent the railroads** Steiner, *Honest Calling*, 138; in Lincoln's debates with Stephen A. Douglas in 1858, the senator from Illinois tried to make an issue of Lincoln's associations with the railroads. On October 22, 1858, Lincoln gave a speech clarifying his relationship with the Illinois Central Railroad. *Chicago Press and Tribune*, October 27, 1858, in LEGAL, 2:412–14.

210 **"A stitch in time"** AL to Milton Brayman, March 31, 1854, *LPAL, 1:8*.

210 **The railroad protested** For *Illinois Central Railroad v. the County of McLean*, see "Illinois Central Railroad v. McClean County, Illinois, and Parke" in LEGAL, 2:373–415; Steiner, *Honest Calling*, 150–54; and Duff, *A. Lincoln*, 312–17.

211 **"is the largest law"** AL to Thompson R. Webber, September 12, 1853, LEGAL, 2:376–77.

211 **Lincoln argued** Steiner, *Honest Calling*, 153–54.

211 **Lincoln brought suit** "Illinois Central Railroad v. the County of McClean," in LEGAL, 2:404–12.

212 **a rising Illinois lawyer** Benjamin P. Thomas and Harold M. Hyman, *Stanton: The Life and Times of Lincoln's Secretary of War* (New York: Alfred A. Knopf, 1962), 63–64.

213 **"During August"** AL to Peter H. Watson, July 23, 1855, *CW*, 2:314–15.

213 **Lincoln finally wrote** AL to John H. Manny and Company, September 1, 1855, *CW*, 2:325.

213 **"a tall rawly boned"** Robert Henry Parkinson, "The Patent Case That Lifted Lincoln into a Presidential Candidate," *ALQ* 4, no. 3 (September 1946): 114–15.

213 **"roughly handled"** HL, 220.

214 **"Since then we have had thirty six"** AL to George Robertson, August 15, 1855, *CW*, 2:318.

215 **"You say that sooner"** AL to Joshua F. Speed, August 24, 1855, *CW*, 2:320–23.

216 **"Revolutionize through the ballot box"** Herndon and Weik, *Abraham Lincoln*, 2:49.

216 **"as the warm and consistent"** Mark A. Plummer, *Lincoln's Rail-Splitter: Governor Richard J. Oglesby* (Urbana: University of Illinois Press, 2001), 18–19.

216 **"The latter part"** Beveridge, *Abraham Lincoln*, 2:359.

217 **"buckle on his armor"** AL, "Speech at Decatur, Illinois," February 22, 1856, *CW*, 2:333.

217 **"Did Lincoln authorize you"** Herndon and Weik, *Abraham Lincoln*, 2:51–52.

218 **"he had got to be"** Henry C. Whitney, *Life on the Circuit with Lincoln* (Boston: Estes and Lauriat, 1892), 75.

218 **"A man couldn't think"** AL, "Speech at Bloomington, Illinois," May 28, 1856, *CW*, 2:340–41.

219 **"proscribe no one"** William E. Gienapp, *The Origins of the Republican Party, 1852–1856* (New York: Oxford University Press, 1987), 294–95.

220 **"The Union must be preserved"** AL, "Speech at Bloomington," May 31, 1856, *CW,* 2:341.

220 **"I have heard or read"** *HL,* 236.

CHAPTER 12. *A House Divided: 1856–58*

223 **"secreted"** Henry C. Whitney (JWW interview), [1887–89], *HI,* 733–34.

224 **"as pure a patriot"** Jesse W. Weik, "Lincoln's Vote for Vice-President in the Philadelphia Convention of 1856," *Century Magazine* 76 (June 1908): 186–89.

224 **received votes from eleven states** *Proceedings of the First Three Republican National Conventions of 1856, 1860, and 1864* (Minneapolis, Minn.: Charles W. Johnson, 1893), 61–62.

225 **"When you meet Judge Dayton"** AL to John Van Dyke, June 27, 1856, *CW,* 2:346.

225 **"the gallant Fremont"** *Urbana Union,* June 26, *Day by Day,* 2:172.

227 **"It is constantly objected"** AL, "Fragment on Sectionalism," [ca. July 23, 1856], *CW,* 2:349–53.

228 **"showed how the South"** AL, "Speech at Princeton," July 4, 1856, *CW,* 2:346–47.

228 **"demonstrated in the strongest manner"** AL, "Speech at Chicago, Illinois," July 19, 1856, *CW,* 2:348–49.

228 **"All this talk about the dissolution"** AL, "Speech at Galena, Illinois," July 23, 1856, *CW,* 2:353–55.

228 **"to learn what people differ"** AL, "Speech at Kalamazoo, Michigan," August 27, 1856, *CW,* 2:361–66.

229 **"His language is pure"** *Amboy* (Illinois) *Times,* July 24, 1856.

229 **"Altho' Mr L is"** Mary Lincoln to Emilie Todd Helm, November 23, 1856, *MTL,* 46.

230 **"The storm of abolition"** George Ticknor Curtis, *Life of James Buchanan: Fifteenth President of the United States* (New York: Harper and Brothers, 1883), 2:176.

231 **"assailed as the enemies"** AL, "Speech at a Republican Banquet, Chicago, Illinois," December 10, 1856, *CW,* 2:383–85.

231 **"Twenty-two years ago"** AL, "Fragment on Stephen A. Douglas," [December 1856], *CW,* 2:382–83.

232 **"Do you know where Lincoln lives?"** Wayne C. Temple, *By Square and Compasses: The Building of Lincoln's Home and Its Saga* (Bloomington, Ill.: Ashlar Press, 1984), 41.

232 **a sharp comment** Baker, *Mary Todd Lincoln,* 116.

232 **"commenced raising"** Mrs. John Todd Stuart to Betty Stuart, April 3, 1856, John T. Stuart–Milton Hay Collection, ALPLM.

232 **The final cost** Richard S. Hagen, "What a Pleasant Home Abe Lincoln Has," *JISHS* 48, no. 1 (Spring 1955): 5–27.

233 **"A more immense judicial power"** Alexis de Tocqueville, *Democracy in Amer-*

ica, ed. Harvey C. Mansfield and Debra Winthrop (Chicago: University of Chicago Press, 2000), 141.

234 **he petitioned the Missouri Circuit Court** See Don E. Fehrenbacher, *The Dred Scott Case: Its Significance in American Law and Politics* (New York: Oxford University Press, 1978), 285–334.

235 **"The decision will be"** Richard Malcolm Johnston and William Hand Browne, *Life of Alexander H. Stephens* (Philadelphia: J. B. Lippincott and Company, 1884), 318, 141; and *New York Courier,* December 18, 1856.

235 **"What would be the effect"** AL, "Fragment on the Dred Scott Case," [January 1857?], *CW,* 2:387–88.

235 **"blacks are not citizens"** James F. Simon, *Lincoln and Chief Justice Taney: Slavery, Secession, and the President's War Powers* (New York: Simon & Schuster, 2006), 115–16.

236 **"it is understood"** James Buchanan, "Inaugural Address, March 4, 1857," *Inaugural Addresses of the Presidents of the United States* (Washington, D.C.: Government Printing Office, 1961), 112.

236 **"been regarded as beings"** Simon, *Lincoln and Chief Justice Taney,* 122.

237 **"main proposition"** Johannsen, *Douglas,* 569–71.

238 **"The curtain of 1860"** *New York Herald,* June 23, 24, 1857.

238 **"But we think the Dred Scott"** Fehrenbacher, *Dred Scott Case,* 351.

240 **"I think the authors"** AL, "Speech at Springfield, Illinois," June 26, 1857, *CW,* 2:398–410.

240 **"too much on the old"** Johannsen, *Douglas,* 573.

241 **"an intolerable nuisance"** *St. Louis Republican,* August 24, 1856.

241 **"do not warrant"** *Chicago Tribune,* September 26, 1856.

242 **wanted the best lawyer** For an excellent discussion of the case, see "Hurd Et Al. V. Rock Island Bridge Company," in LEGAL, 3:308–83.

242 **preparation for the trial** Ibid., 326–27.

243 **resumed his closing argument** See the long excerpt of a newspaper report of Lincoln's closing argument, ibid., 359–65.

244 **a case growing out** For a full description of the Duff Armstrong case, see "People V. Armstrong," in LEGAL, 4:1–45.

245 **Lincoln's cross-examination** Hannah Armstrong (WHH interview), [1866], *HI,* 526.

245 **"The almanac floored"** Duff, *A. Lincoln,* 350–55.

245 **"of his kind feelings"** William Walker to WHH, June 3, 1865, *HI,* 22; "People V. Armstrong," 23–26.

245 **"It was generally admitted"** J. Henry Shaw to WHH, August 22, 1866, *HI,* 316; and J. Henry Shaw to WHH, September 5, 1866, *HI,* 332–34.

245 **"Why—Hannah, I shant"** Hannah Armstrong (WHH interview), 1866, *HI,* 526.

246 **"altogether the most exquisite"** AL, Speech at Springfield, June 26, 1857, *CW,* 2:400.

246 **The meeting at Lecompton** For a discussion of the controversial Lecompton Convention, see Johannsen, *Douglas,* 576–84.

246 **"I have spent too much"** Ibid., 590.

246 **"bring more weight"** Potter, *Impending Crisis,* 320–21.

247   **"your general view"** AL to Lyman Trumbull, November 30, December 18, 28, 1857, *CW,* 2:427, 428, 430.

247   **"the unexpected course"** Lyman Trumbull to AL, January 3, 1858, Lyman Trumbull Papers, Library of Congress.

247   **"of that *Friend"* ** Ibid.

248   **"There seems to be"** *Chicago Press & Tribune,* April 21, 1858.

248   **"Let us have a state convention"** AL to Ozias M. Hatch, March 24, 1858, *CW,* First Supplement, 29–30.

249   **"is the only one who *improves"* ** The *Collected Works* prints two separate lectures, but they may well have been two parts of a single lecture. AL, "First Lecture on Discoveries and Inventions," [April 6, 1858], 2:437; "Second Lecture on Discoveries and Inventions," [February 11, 1859], 3:356–62.

250   **"too far in advance"** John Armstrong (WHH interview), [February 1870], *HI,* 574–75; *HL,* 2:68–69.

250   **"Cook County Is for"** Donald, *Lincoln,* 205.

251   **If we could first know** AL, "A House Divided: Speech at Springfield, Illinois," June 16, 1858, *CW,* 2:461.

252   **use of a biblical metaphor** The metaphor "A house divided against itself" appears in Matthew 12:25, Mark 3:25, and Luke 11:17.

252   **Whatever its past use** Campaign Circular from Whig Committee, March 4, 1843, *CW,* 1:315; AL to George Robertson, August 15, 1855, *CW,* 2:318; T. Lyle Dickey to WHH, December 8, 1866, *HI,* 504.

253   **"angry agitation"** AL, "Fragment of a Speech" [ca. May 18, 1858], *CW,* 2:452–53. The *Collected Works of Abraham Lincoln,* edited in the 1950s, dated this "Fragment of a Speech" to May 1858, but a close examination reveals that Lincoln wrote it seven months earlier, in December 1857.

254   **"*working* points of that machinery"** AL, "A House Divided," 462–67.

254   **"*softly,* that Douglas is"** Ibid., 467.

CHAPTER 13. *The Eternal Struggle Between These Two Principles: 1858*

257   **Lincoln had defeated himself** Leonard Swett to WHH, January 17, 1866, *HI,* 163.

257   **"some of my Kentucky friends"** John L. Scripps to AL, June 22, 1858, ALPLC.

258   **"and yet I am mortified"** AL to John L. Scripps, June 23, 1858, *CW,* 2:471.

258   **"I shall have my hands full"** John W. Forney, *Anecdotes of Public Men* (New York: Harper and Brothers, 1881), 2:179.

258   **"that great principle"** Johannsen, *Douglas,* 641–42.

260   **"provided I can find it"** AL, "Speech at Chicago, Illinois," July 10, 1858, *CW,* 2:485.

260   **"I did not say"** Ibid., 491, 501.

261   **"a kind-hearted, amiable"** Johannsen, *Douglas,* 657.

261   **"having been a party"** AL, "Speech at Springfield, Illinois," July 17, 1858, *CW,* 2:519–20.

262   **"I should be at your town"** AL to Joseph T. Eccles, August 2, 1858, *CW,* 2:533.

262   **"Will it be agreeable"** AL to Stephen A. Douglas, July 24, 1858, *CW,* 2:522.

263   **"I accede"** AL to Stephen A. Douglas, July 31, 1858, *CW,* 2:531. For the story

of the debates, see Allen G. Guelzo's new book, *Lincoln and Douglas: The Debates That Defined America* (New York: Simon & Schuster, 2008).

264 **"It is astonishing"** *New York Post,* September 24, 1858.

265 **"Ottawa was deluged in dust"** *New York Evening Post,* August 27, 1858.

265 **"to connect the members"** The new authoritative version of the debates, *The Lincoln-Douglas Debates,* ed. Rodney O. Davis and Douglas L. Wilson (Urbana: The University of Illinois, 2008). "First Debate at Ottawa, Illinois," August 21, 1858, 8–9.

266 **"I mean nothing personally"** Ibid., 6, 9.

266 **"Are you in favor of"** *Ibid.,* 14.

266 **"He had a lean"** Henry Villard, *Memoirs of Henry Villard: Journalist and Financier, 1835–1900* (Boston: Houghton, Mifflin and Company, 1904), 1:93.

267 **"I must confess"** *New York Evening Post,* quoted in King, *Lincoln's Manager,* 122.

268 **"When a man hears"** "First Debate with Stephen A. Douglas at Ottawa, Illinois," August 21, 1858, *CW,* 3:13.

268 **reported two different debates** Harold Holzer tells the story of these two texts in *The Lincoln-Douglas Debates: The First Complete, Unexpurgated Text* (New York: HarperCollins, 1993).

268 **"Everybody here"** David Davis to AL, August 25, 1858, ALPLC.

268 **"We were *well satisfied"*** Richard Yates to AL, August 26, 1858, ALPLC.

268 **"Douglas and I"** AL to Joseph O. Cunningham, August 22, 1858, *CW,* 3:37.

269 **advisers were not so pleased** Holzer, *Lincoln-Douglas Debates,* 89; David Zarefsky, *Lincoln, Douglas and Slavery: In the Crucible of Public Debate* (Chicago: University of Chicago Press, 1990), 56.

269 **"Don't act"** Norman B. Judd (WHH interview), October 2, 1890, *HI,* 723.

269 **attire of the debaters** *The Lincoln-Douglas Debates of 1858,* ed. Edwin E. Sparks (Springfield: Illinois State Historical Library, 1908), 207.

269 **"I shall be exceedingly glad"** "Second Debate at Freeport, Illinois," August 27, 1858, *The Lincoln-Douglas Debates,* 48.

270 **"Q.2. Can the people"** Ibid., 50.

270 **"It is *most extraordinary"*** Ibid., 51.

271 **"It matters not"** Ibid., 58.

271 **"think that Fred. Douglass"** Ibid., 62.

272 **"the popular sympathy"** Joseph Medill to John A. Gurley, August 28, 1858, cited in Zarefsky, *Lincoln, Douglas and Slavery,* 58.

272 **"the contest going on"** Frederick Douglass, "Freedom in the West Indies: Address Delivered in Poughkeepsie, NY," August 2, 1858, *Frederick Douglass,* 3:233, 236–37.

273 **The debates were only** A strength of Allen Guelzo's book, *Lincoln and Douglas: The Debates That Defined America,* is his attention to the many facets of the Lincoln-Douglas campaign beyond the debates.

273 **"Little Egypt"** For a description of the context of the debate in "Egypt," see John Y. Simon, "Union County in 1858 and the Lincoln-Douglas Debate," *JISHS* 62 (Autumn 1969): 267–92.

274 **"If the slaveholding"** AL, "Third Debate at Jonesboro, Illinois," September 15, 1858, *The Lincoln-Douglas Debates,* 115.

275   **old-line Whig district** Charles H. Coleman, *Abraham Lincoln and Coles County, Illinois* (New Brunswick, N.J.: Scarecrow Press, 1955), 173–75.

275   **"I was really in favor"** AL, "Fourth Debate at Charleston, Illinois," September 18, 1858, *The Lincoln-Douglas Debates,* 131.

276   **"Race prejudice"** Tocqueville, *Democracy in America,* 329.

277   **"great apprehension"** AL, "Fourth Debate," September 18, 1858, *The Lincoln-Douglas Debates,* 132.

277   **"Allow me to suggest"** Norman B. Judd to AL, September? 1858, ALPLC.

277   **"I am amazed"** *The Lincoln-Douglas Debates,* 145.

278   **the nineteen days** A. H. Chapman to WHH, October 18, 1865, *HI,* 139.

278   **"Suppose it is true"** AL, "Fragment on Pro-slavery Theology," [October 1, 1858], *CW,* 3:204–5.

279   **"But there is a larger issue"** AL, "Fragment: Notes for Speeches," [October 1, 1858], *CW,* 3:205.

280   **"Well, at last"** Holzer, *Lincoln-Douglas Debates,* 234–35.

280   **"In the extreme northern"** "Fifth Debate at Galesburg, Illinois," October 7, 1858, *The Lincoln-Douglas Debates,* 181.

280   **"I believe that the entire"** Ibid., 220–25.

281   **"When Douglas concluded"** *Quincy Whig,* October 9, 1858.

281   **"blowing out the moral lights"** *The Lincoln-Douglas Debates,* 201.

281   **labeled "Constitution"** Allen Guelzo, *Lincoln and Douglas: The Debates That Defined America,* 241.

282   **charm did not** Carl Schurz, *Abraham Lincoln: A Biographical Essay* (Boston: Houghton Mifflin and Company, 1907), 68–69.

283   **"When Judge Douglas says"** "Sixth Debate at Quincy, Illinois," October 13, 1858, *The Lincoln-Douglas Debates,* 224–25.

283   **"I tell you why"** Ibid., 233.

283   **"We are getting"** Ibid., 242.

284   **"of carrying the State"** Gustave Koerner, *Memoirs of Gustave Koerner, 1809–1896: Life-Sketches Written at the Suggestion of His Children,* ed. Thomas J. McCormack (Cedar Rapids, Iowa: The Torch Press, 1909), 2:66–67.

284   **"I hold that the signers"** "Seventh Debate at Alton, Illinois," October 15, 1858, *The Lincoln-Douglas Debates,* 266.

284   **"strong sympathies"** Ibid., 269.

285   **"fundamental principle"** Ibid., 273.

285   **"That is the issue"** Ibid., 284–85.

286   **"I now have a high degree"** AL to Norman Judd, October 20, 1858, *CW,* 3:329–30.

286   **"Outside Republicans"** King, *Lincoln's Manager,* 125.

287   **"that you are anxious"** AL to John J. Crittenden, July 7, 1858, *CW,* 3:483–84.

287   **"Ambition has been"** AL, "Fragment, Last Speech of the Campaign at Springfield, Illinois," October 30, 1858, *CW,* 3:334.

287   **"Street fights"** *Illinois State Journal,* November 3, 1858.

288   **"but I recovered"** Nicolay and Hay, 9:377.

288   **"the causes of our defeat"** Joseph Fort Newton, *Lincoln and Herndon* (Cedar Rapids, Iowa: The Torch Press, 1910), 234–35.

288   **"unauthorized"** John L. Crittenden to AL, October 27, 1858, ALPLC.

288   **"was handed me"** AL to John J. Crittenden, November 4, 1858, *CW,* 3:335–36.

289   **"Mr. Lincoln is beaten"** *Chicago Press & Tribune,* November 10, 1858.

289   **"I am glad"** AL to Anson G. Henry, November 19, 1858, *CW,* 3:339.

CHAPTER 14. *The Taste* Is *in My Mouth, a Little: 1858–60*

291   **"What man now fills"** Jeriah Bonham, *Fifty Years' Recollections: With Observations and Reflections on Historical Events, Giving Sketches on Eminent Citizens—Their Lives and Public Services* (Peoria, Ill.: J. W. Franks and Sons, 1883), 528–30.

291   **"An enthusiastic meeting"** Allen T. Rice, ed., *Reminiscences of Abraham Lincoln by Distinguished Men of His Time* (New York: North American Publishing Company, 1886), 441–42.

291   **"present his [Lincoln's] name"** William Baringer, *Lincoln's Rise to Power* (Boston: Little, Brown, and Company, 1937), 51–58.

292   **"Who is this man?"** Statement of Jesse Fell, "Story of the Lincoln Biography," Bloomington, Illinois, March 1872, in the Oldroyd Lincoln Memorial Collection.

293   **in a two-hundred-page scrapbook** AL to Charles H. Ray, November 20, 1858, *CW,* 3:341.

293   **"There is some probability"** AL to Henry C. Whitney, December 15, 1858, *CW,* 3:347.

293   **"I have been on expenses"** AL to Norman B. Judd, November 16, 1858, *CW,* 3:337.

294   **"personally engaged"** AL to Samuel C. Davis and Company, November 17, 1858, *CW,* 3:338.

294   **"we have performed no service"** AL to Joel A. Matteson, November 25, 1858.

294   **"I wish you would return"** AL to William M. Fishback, December 19, 1858, *CW,* 3:346.

294   **"It annoys me"** AL to Maria Bullock, January 3, 1859, *CW,* 3:348.

294   **"In that day"** AL to Norman B. Judd, November 15, 1858, *CW,* 3:36–337.

295   **"I look upon"** Wentworth is quoted in a letter from David Davis to AL, January 1, 1859 (misdated 1858), ALPLC.

295   **"the Republican editors"** Thomas J. Pickett to AL, April 13, 1858, ALPLC.

295   **"I must in candor"** AL to Thomas J. Pickett, April 16, 1858, *CW,* 3:377.

296   **"All honor to Jefferson"** AL to Henry L. Pierce and Others, April 6, 1859, *CW,* 3:374–76.

296   **"The only danger"** AL to Mark W. Delahay, May 14, 1859, *CW,* 3:378–79.

297   **met in a convention** Salmon P. Chase to AL, April 14, 1858, ALPLC.

297   **"one of the very few"** AL to Salmon P. Chase, April 30, 1859, *CW,* 3:378.

297   **"I hope you can"** AL to Salmon P. Chase, June 9, 1859, *CW,* 3:384.

297   **"avowal of our great principles"** Salmon P. Chase to AL, June 13, 1859, ALPLC.

297   **"to enact a Fugitive Slave"** AL to Salmon P. Chase, June 20, 1859, *CW,* 3:386.

297   **"As I understand"** AL to Theodore Canisius, May 17, 1859, *CW,* 3:380.

298   **"hedge against divisions"** AL to Schuyler Colfax, July 6, 1859, *CW,* 3:390.

299   **"We desire to head off"** William T. Bascom to AL, September 1, 1859, ALPLC.

299   **"Douglasism"** *Chicago Press & Tribune,* November 9, 1858; and Johannsen, *Douglas,* 682–86.

300   **"there can be no peace"** See Stephen A. Douglas, "The Dividing Line Between Federal and Local Authority: Popular Sovereignty in the Territories," *Harper's Magazine* 14 (September 1859): 519–37.

300   **"Now, what is Judge Douglas'"** AL, "Speech at Columbus, Ohio," September 16, 1859, *CW,* 3:405.

301   **"I am what they call"** AL, "Speech at Cincinnati, Ohio," September 17, 1859, *CW,* 3:440–41.

301   **"Our fathers"** AL, "Speech at Indianapolis, Indiana," September 19, 1859, *CW,* 3:465–66.

301   **requested the assistance** "AL to George M. Parsons and Others," December 19, 1859, *CW,* 3:510.

302   **"will make the contest in 1860"** Thomas Corwin to AL, September 25, 1859, ALPLC.

302   **"What brought these Democrats with us!"** In 2004, a member of the Corwin family of Ohio brought the supposedly lost letter to Daniel Weinberg, proprietor of the Abraham Lincoln Book Shop in Chicago. I am grateful to Harold Holzer, who writes about the import of the letter in the Preface to the paperback edition of *Lincoln at Cooper Union* (New York: Simon & Schuster, 2006) xviii–xix

302   **"Six months hence"** Thomas Corwin to AL, October 17, 1859, ALPLC.

303   **"Mr. Lincoln, the 'giant' "** *Illinois State Journal,* October 17, 1859.

303   **Hon A. Lincoln** James A. Briggs to AL, October 12, 1859, ALPLC.

303   **eager to accept** See Harold Holzer, *Lincoln at Cooper Union: The Speech That Made Abraham Lincoln President* (New York: Simon and Schuster, 2004) for the address and its impact; Angle, *"Here I Have Lived,"* 231.

304   **"painstaking and thorough"** *HL,* 273–74.

304   **"violation of law"** AL, "Speech at Ellwood, Kansas," December 1 [November 30?], 1859, *CW,* 3:496.

304   **"the slavery question"** Ibid., *CW,* 3:499, 502.

304   **"Old John Brown,"** AL, "Speech at Leavenworth, Kansas," December 3, 1859, *CW,* 3:502.

305   **Judd was secretly** Norman B. Judd to AL, December 1, 1859, ALPLC.

305   **"I would rather have"** AL to Norman B. Judd, December 9, 1859, *CW,* 3:505.

305   **"I find some of our friends"** AL to Norman B. Judd, December 14, 1859, *CW,* 3:509.

305   **Judd understood the importance** Reinhard H. Luthin, *The First Lincoln Campaign* (Gloucester, Mass.: P. Smith, 1944), 20–21.

305   **"Herewith is a little"** AL to Jesse W. Fell, "Enclosing Autobiography," Dec. 20, 1859, *CW,* 3:511–12.

305   **I was born Feb. 12, 1809** Ibid.

307   **wrote his own biography** William E. Barton, *President Lincoln* (Indianapolis: The Bobbs-Merrill Company, 1933), 63–64.

308   **"if his name"** Jackson Grimshaw to WHH, April 28, 1866, *HI,* 247; and Lamon, *Life,* 424 (Lamon is incorrect about the year of the meeting).

308   **"It is not improbable"** Browning, *Diary,* February 8, 1860, 395.

308 **"the nomination of Lincoln"** *Chicago Press & Tribune,* February 16, 1860.

309 **endorsement of Lincoln** Philip Kinsley, *The Chicago Tribune: Its First Hundred Years,* vol. I, *1847–1865* (New York: Alfred A. Knopf, 1943), 105–7.

309 **"No former effort"** *HL,* 2:165.

309 **SIGNIFICANT.—The Hon.** *Illinois State Register,* February 23, 1860.

309 **at the Cooper Union** For the complete story of the Cooper Union Address, see Holzer, *Lincoln at Cooper Union.*

310 **"I am on my way"** Francis Fisher Browne, *The Every-Day Life of Abraham Lincoln: A Narrative and Descriptive Biography* (Chicago: Browne and Howell Company, 1913), 1:217.

310 **"I see you want"** Roy Meredith, *Mr. Lincoln's Camera Man, Mathew B. Brady* (New York: Dover Publications, 1946), 59.

311 **"a gallant soldier"** Holzer, *Lincoln at Cooper Union,* 107.

311 **The first impression** Rufus Rockwell Wilson, ed., *Intimate Memories of Lincoln* (Elmira, N.Y.: Primavera Press, 1945), 258.

311 **"Mr. Cheerman"** Holzer, *Lincoln at Cooper Union,* 114.

314 **"Mr. Lincoln is one of Nature's"** *New York Tribune,* February 28, 1860.

314 **"somewhat funny, to see"** Mayson Brayman to William H. Bailhache, February 28, 1860, ALPLM, quoted in Holzer, *Lincoln at Cooper Union,* 145.

315 **"according to Bob's orders"** AL to Mary Lincoln, March 4, 1860, *CW,* 3:555.

315 **"Enclosed please find"** James A. Briggs to AL, February 29, 1860, ALPLC.

315 **"I have been unable"** AL to Mary Lincoln, March 4, 1860, *CW,* 3:555.

316 **Welles, an ex-Democrat** John Niven, *Gideon Welles: Lincoln's Secretary of the Navy* (New York: Oxford University Press, 1973), 283, 288–89.

316 **"I am glad to know"** AL, "Speech at Hartford, Connecticut, March 5, 1860," *CW,* 4:7.

317 **"recent success had stimulated"** *HL,* 2:275.

317 **"there will be but little"** Samuel Galloway to AL, March 15, 1860, ALPLC.

318 **"My name is new"** AL to Samuel Galloway, March 24, 1860, *CW,* 4:33–34.

318 **"I have heard your name"** James F. Babcock to AL, April 9, 1860, ALPLC.

318 **"As to the Presidential"** AL to James F. Babcock, April 14, 1860, *CW,* 4:43.

318 **"to be put fully"** AL to Lyman Trumbull, April 29, 1860, *CW,* 4:45.

319 **"I keep no secrets"** Mark E. Neely, Jr., *The Abraham Lincoln Encyclopedia* (New York: McGraw-Hill, 1982), 299.

320 **"I am informed"** ____ Johnson to WHH, [1865–1866], *HI,* 463.

320 **old John Hanks** Ibid.

321 **"prominent candidates"** *Harper's Weekly,* May 12, 1860.

323 **receiving reports** King, *Lincoln's Manager,* 135–36.

324 **"He was almost too much"** Wilson, *Intimate Memories of Lincoln,* 294.

324 **"We are here"** Jesse K. Dubois to AL, May 13, 1860, ALPLC.

324 **"Things are working"** Nathan M. Knapp to AL, May 14, 1860.

324 **"We are laboring"** Nathan M. Knapp to Ozias M. Hatch, May 12, 1860, in "Praise for the 'Most Available Candidate,' " *JISHS* 71, no. 1 (February 1978): 72.

324 **"Dont come"** Jesse K. Dubois and David Davis to AL, May 14, 1860, ALPLC.

324 **"Don't be too sanguine"** Charles H. Ray to AL, May 14, 1860, ALPLC.

325 **"Make no contracts"** "Endorsement on the Margin of the *Missouri Democrat,*" [May 17, 1860], *CW,* 4:50.

326 **"he hardly thought this"** Clinton L. Conkling, "How Mr. Lincoln Received the News of His First Nomination," *Transactions of the Illinois State Historical Society* (1909):64–65.

326 **Judd stood second** *Proceedings of the First Three Republican National Conventions,* 151–54.

328 **"I-I a-a-rise"** Charles H. Workman, "Tablet to Abraham Lincoln at Mansfield," *Ohio Archaeological and Historical Publications* 34 (1925) 519–20.

329 **"Well gentlemen there is"** Charles S. Zane (statement for WHH), [1865–66], *HI,* 491.

CHAPTER 15. *Justice and Fairness to All: May 1860–November 1860*

331 **"did not suppose"** AL, "Response to a Serenade," May 18, 1860, *CW,* 4:50.

331 **"Write no letters"** David Davis to AL, May 18, 1860, ALPLC.

332 **"his modest frame house"** Carl Schurz, *The Reminiscences of Carl Schurz* (New York: The McClure Company, 1908), 2:188.

332 **"Justice and fairness"** AL, *CW,* 4:94.

332 **"such intuitive knowledge"** *Life of Thurlow Weed: Including His Autobiography and a Memoir,* vol. 1: Weed (Boston: Houghton, Mifflin and Company, 1883), 602.

333 **met with Edward Bates** Browning, *Diary,* May 24, 1860, 410–11.

333 **"Holding myself"** AL to Salmon P. Chase, May 26, 1860, *CW,* 4:53.

333 **"You distinguish between yourself"** AL to Schuyler Colfax, May 26, 1860, *CW,* 4:54.

333 **"We know not"** AL to Anson G. Henry, July 4, 1860, *CW,* 4:82.

335 **"I missed the greatest chance"** William Dean Howells, *Life of Abraham Lincoln* (Springfield, Ill.: The Abraham Lincoln Association, 1938), vii.

336 **"I believe the biography"** John L. Scripps to AL, July 17, 1860, ALPLC.

336 **"made frequent humorous"** John L. Scripps to WHH, June 24, 1865, *HI,* 57.

337 **became his one-man** Helen Nicolay, *Lincoln's Secretary: A Biography of John G. Nicolay* (New York: Longmans, Green and Company, 1949), 6–7, 84.

338 **"Lincoln bears his honors"** Browning, *Diary,* June 12, 1860, 415.

338 **"That looks better"** Lloyd Ostendorf, *Lincoln's Photographs: A Complete Album* (Dayton, Ohio: Rockywood Press, 1998), 46–48.

339 **"I think there"** AL to Thurlow Weed, August 17, 1860, *CW,* 4:98.

340 **"I am slow"** AL to John M. Pomeroy, August 31, 1860, *CW,* 4:103.

340 **"amiable and accomplished"** *New York Tribune,* May 25, 1860.

340 **"a sparkling talker"** Baker, *Mary Todd Lincoln,* 160.

341 **"Mr. Lincoln has never been"** Mary Lincoln to Dyer Burgess, October 29, 1860, *MTL,* 67.

341 **"You are an ambitious"** "William M. Dickson to AL, with Note from Annie M. Dickson to Mary Todd Lincoln," May 21, 1860, ALPLC.

341 **"You used to be worried"** Mary Lincoln to Hannah Shearer, October 20, 1860, *MTL,* 63–64.

341 **"warmly welcomed"** Frank Fuller, *A Day with the Lincoln Family* (New York: n.d.).

342 **"a man of unblemished"** *Douglass' Monthly,* June 1860.

343 **"On Monday night"** *Illinois State Journal,* August 8, 1860.

343 **Westward the star** Stephen B. Oates, *With Malice Toward None: A Life of Abraham Lincoln* (New York: Harper and Row, 1977), 185.

343 **"The Prairies on Fire"** *Illinois State Journal,* August 9, 1860.

344 **"It has been my purpose"** AL, "Remarks at a Springfield Rally, Springfield, Illinois," August 8, 1860, *CW,* 4:91.

344 **"slipped him over"** George Brinkerhoff (WHH interview), [1865–1866], *HI,* 437.

344 **"The reward that fidelity"** Edward D. Baker to AL, August 1, 1860, ALPLOC.

344 **"such a result"** AL to Hannibal Hamlin, September 4, 1860, *CW,* 4:110.

345 **"The people of the South"** AL to John B. Fry, August 15, 1860, *CW,* 4:95.

346 **a sense of relief** WHL to AL, October 10, 1860, ALPLC.

346 **"It now looks"** AL to William H. Seward, October 12, 1860, *CW,* 4:126.

347 **"a very happy man"** Henry C. Bowen, "Recollections of Abraham Lincoln," *Independent,* April 4, 1895, 4.

CHAPTER 16. *An Humble Instrument in the Hands of the Almighty:*
November 1860–February 1861

349 **"Well, boys"** Oates, *With Malice Toward None,* 195.

350 **"I then felt"** Lincoln spoke about this evening in 1862 with Gideon Welles; Welles, *Diary,* August 15, 1862, 1:82.

351 **Public exigencies may** Truman Smith to AL, November 7, 1860, ALPLC.

351 **"It is with the most profound"** AL to Truman Smith, November 10, 1860, *CW,* 4:138.

352 **"You would look"** AL to Grace Bedell, October 19, 1860, *CW,* 4:129–30 n. 1.

352 **"He sits or stands"** *New York Herald,* November 11, 14, 20, 1860.

352 **"He is precisely the same man"** *Lincoln on the Eve of '61: A Journalist's Story by Henry Villard* (New York: Alfred A. Knopf, 1941), 20.

352 **"each and all of the States"** "Passage Written for Lyman Trumbull's Speech at Springfield, Illinois," November 20, 1860, *CW,* 4:141–42.

353 **"all knowledge of the Southern"** *New York Herald,* November 22, 1860.

354 **"would lean heavily"** Mark M. Krug, *Lyman Trumbull: Conservative Radical* (New York: A. S. Barnes, 1965), 165.

354 **"The long continued"** James Buchanan, "Fourth Annual Message," December 3, 1860, *The Works of James Buchanan: Comprising His Speeches, State Papers, and Private Correspondence,* ed., John Bassett Moore (Philadelphia: J. B. Lippincott Company, 1910), 11:7–9.

355 **written to urge Lincoln** Henry J. Raymond to AL, November 14, 1860, ALPLC.

355 **"a demonstration in favor"** AL to Henry J. Raymond, November 28, 1860, *CW,* 4:145–46.

355 **reaching for a way** Francis Brown, *Raymond of the Times* (New York: W. W. Norton and Company, 1951), 197.

355 **"They seek a sign"** Matt. 12:39, 16:4.

356 **"delayed so long"** AL to William H. Seward, December 8, 1860, *CW,* 4:148.

356   "free in his communications" Bates, *Diary,* December 16, 1860, 164.

356   at least one Southerner David M. Potter, *Lincoln and His Party in the Secession Crisis* (New Haven, Conn.: Yale University Press, 1942), 151.

356   Lincoln sent Speed Joshua F. Speed (WHH interview), [1865–66], 475.

357   "Don't give up the ship" Schott, *Alexander Stephens of Georgia,* 306.

357   "The country is certainly" Alexander H. Stephens to AL, December 14, 1860, ALPLC.

357   "Do the people of the South" AL to Alexander H. Stephens, December 22, 1860, *CW,* 4:160.

357   "In addressing you thus" Alexander H. Stephens to AL, December 30, 1860, *CW,* 4:160–61 n.1.

357   "frequent allusion" "Editorial in the *Illinois State Journal,*" December 12, 1860, *CW,* 4:150.

358   "While Mr. Lincoln" Weed, *Autobiography,* 606–11.

358   "For one politically" John A. Gilmer to AL, December 10, 1860, ALPLC.

358   "May I be pardoned" AL to John A. Gilmer, December 15, *CW,* 4:151–53.

358   "consent to take" AL to William H. Seward, January 12, 1861, *CW,* 4:173.

359   "But why do you assume" Weed, *Autobiography,* 610.

360   offered compromise legislation Albert Dennis Kirwan, *John J. Crittenden: The Struggle for the Union* (Lexington: University of Kentucky Press, 1962), 373ff.

361   "The secession feeling" Elihu Washburne to AL, December 9, 1860, ALPLC.

361   "Let there be no compromise" AL to Lyman Trumbull, December 10, 1860, *CW,* 4:149–50.

361   "Prevent, as far as possible" AL to Elihu B. Washburne, December 13, 1860, *CW,* 4:151.

361   "The election of Lincoln" Robert S. Harper, *Lincoln and the Press* (New York: McGraw-Hill, 1951), 67–70.

362   "If she violates" *Illinois State Journal,* December 20, 1860.

362   begun his research Amy Louise Sutton, "Lincoln and Son Borrow Books," *Illinois Libraries,* June 1966, 443–44.

363   accepted an invitation Harry E. Pratt, *Lincoln's Springfield* (Springfield: Illinois State Historical Society, 1955), 12; Harry B. Rankin, *Intimate Character Sketches of Abraham Lincoln* (Philadelphia: J. B. Lippincott and Company, 1924), 146–47.

363   copies of two speeches *HL,* 287.

364   Clay's memorable speech AL, "Eulogy on Henry Clay," July 6, 1852, *CW,* 2:126; Remini, *Henry Clay,* 733–38.

364   she feared Sarah Bush Lincoln elaborated on these sentiments in her interview with William Herndon on September 8, 1865. "I did not want Abe to run for Presdt—did not want him Elected—was afraid Somehow or other—felt it in my heart that Something would happen to him and when he came down to see me after he was Elected Presdt I still felt that Something told me that Something would befall Abe and that I should see him no more." *HI,* 108.

365   "Let it hang there" *HL,* 290.

365   "The President elect" *New York Tribune,* February 11, 1861.

365   "face was pale" Villard, *Memoirs,* 1:149.

365 **"My friends—No one"** AL, "Farewell Address at Springfield, Illinois," February 11, 1861, *CW,* 4:190.

366 **"silent artillery of time"** AL, "Address Before the Young Men's Lyceum of Springfield, Illinois," January 27, 1836, *CW,* I, 115.

366 **capacity to connect** *New York Tribune,* February 12, 1861.

366 **"We will do it"** *Harper's Weekly,* February 23, 1861, 119.

368 **"Many eyes"** James C. Conkling to Clinton Conkling, February 12, 1861, in Pratt, *Lincoln's Springfield,* 50.

368 **"We have known Mr. Lincoln"** *Illinois State Journal,* February 12, 1861.

368 **The twelve-day trip** Much of the detail of the journey to Washington is taken from local newspapers. The standard account of the train trip to Washington is Victor Searcher, *Lincoln's Journey to Greatness: A Factual Account of the Twelve-Day Inaugural Trip* (Philadelphia: John C. Winston Company, 1960), but it contains no footnotes. Harold Holzer's new book, *Lincoln President-Elect: Abraham Lincoln and the Great Secession Winter* (New York: Simon & Schuster, 2008) challenges the traditional story of a weak and vacillating Lincoln in the four months between his election and inauguration and instead shows his political dexterity in facing the emerging crisis.

369 **"I therefore renew"** William H. Seward to AL, December 29, 1860, quoted in *CW,* 4:170 n. 1. The letter, highly secret, was unsigned; Nicolay and Hay, 3:289.

369 **carried by boat** The description of Jefferson Davis's train trip can be found in William Cooper, *Jefferson Davis, American* (New York: Alfred A. Knopf, 2000), 328–29; and William C. Davis, *Jefferson Davis: The Man and His Hour* (New York: HarperCollins, 1991), 304–6; *New York Times,* February 11, 1861.

370 **"I do not expect"** AL, "Reply to Oliver P. Morton at Indianapolis, Indiana," February 11, 1861, *CW,* 4:193.

370 **"temporary" and "for a limited"** Ibid.

370 **left the oilcloth bag** Searcher, *Lincoln's Journey,* 29–31.

370 **"All the power"** This copy, with Browning's comment, is in the Huntington Library, San Marino, California.

371 **"occupied every available"** *New Orleans Daily Delta,* February 14, 17, 1861.

371 **"with stern serenity"** *Papers of Jefferson Davis,* ed. Lynda Lasswell Crist and Mary Seaton Dix (Baton Rouge: Louisiana State University Press, 1992), 7:38, 41.

371 **"go forward"** Davis, *Jefferson Davis,* 304–5.

371 **"I have not maintained"** AL, "Address to the Ohio legislature, Columbus, Ohio," February 13, 1861, *CW,* 4:204.

371 **"England will recognize"** *Memphis Daily Appeal,* February 19, 1861, quoted in *Papers of Jefferson Davis,* 7:42–43.

372 **"The tariff is"** AL, "Speech at Pittsburgh, Pennsylvania," February 15, 1861, *CW,* 4:211–12.

372 **"the least creditable"** Villard, *Memoirs,* 1:152.

372 **"Frequent allusion"** AL, "Speech at Cleveland, Ohio," February 15, 1861, *CW,* 4:215.

372 **"These speeches thus far"** Paul Revere Frothingham, *Edward Everett: Orator and Statesman* (Port Washington, N.Y.: Kennikat Press, 1925), 415.

373   **"let his whiskers"** AL, "Remarks at Westfield, New York," February 16, *CW,* 4:219.

373   **"We Will Pray"** Searcher, *Lincoln's Journey,* 129.

374   **"its systematic aggression"** *Atlanta Intelligencer,* February 18, 1861; *Papers of Jefferson Davis,* 7:44–45.

374   **of the same speech** *New York Tribune,* March 5, 1861.

374   **Looking forward to** Jefferson Davis, "Inaugural Address," February 18, 1861, *Papers of Jefferson Davis,* 7:45–50.

375   **I had, I say** Walt Whitman, *Prose Works 1892,* ed. Floyd Stovall (New York: New York University Press, 1963–64), 2:499–501.

375   **"Many an assassin's"** *The Complete Writings of Walt Whitman,* ed. Richard Maurice Bucke, Thomas B. Harned, and Horace L. Traubel (New York: G. P. Putnam's Sons, 1902), 15:243–44.

375   **"Lincoln is making"** Strong, *Diary,* February 18, 1861, 3:100.

376   **"the great rail-splitter's face"** Ibid., 101.

376   **"He approaches the capital"** "Lincoln and His Wayside Speeches," *Baltimore Sun,* reprinted in the *Crisis* (Columbus, Ohio), February 21, 1861.

376   **"The wiseacres"** *Chicago Tribune,* February 21, 1861.

376   **some pro-Lincoln editors** Stephen G. Weisner, *Embattled Editor: The Life of Samuel Bowles* (Lanham, Md.: University Press of America, 1986), 27.

376   **"Lincoln is a 'simple Susan' "** George Merriam, *The Life and Times of Samuel Bowles* (New York: The Century Company, 1885), 1:318.

376   **"[Lincoln's speeches]"** Charles Francis Adams Diary, February 20, 1861, cited in Martin B. Duberman, *Charles Francis Adams, 1807–1886* (Boston: Houghton Mifflin Company, 1961), 253–54.

377   **"struggles for"** AL, "Address to the New Jersey Senate at Trenton, New Jersey," February 21, 1861, *CW,* 4:235.

377   **"I shall be most happy"** Ibid., 236.

377   **"All my political"** AL, "Reply to Mayor Alexander Henry at Philadelphia, Pennsylvania," February 21, 1861, *CW,* 4:238–39; Psalms 137:5–6.

378   **"I have never had"** AL, "Speech in Independence Hall, Philadelphia, Pennsylvania," February 22, 1861, *CW,* 4:240.

378   **"I would rather be assassinated"** Ibid.

379   **"could not lay straight"** Norma B. Cuthbert, ed., *Lincoln and the Baltimore Plot, 1861* (San Marino, Calif.: Huntington Library, 1949), xx, 80–81.

CHAPTER 17. *We Must Not Be Enemies: February 1861–April 1861*

381   **the plot to smuggle the president** Cuthbert, *Lincoln and the Baltimore Plot,* utilizes the Pinkerton documents, including his record book, at the Huntington Library, 15–16, 82.

382   **Seward informed Lincoln** *Charles Francis Adams, 1835–1915: An Autobiography* (Boston: Houghton Mifflin Company, 1916), 64.

382   **"This surreptitious nocturnal"** Strong, *Diary,* February 23, 1861, 3:102.

382   **"He reached the Capital"** *Douglass' Monthly,* April 1861, in *The Life and Writings of Frederick Douglass,* vol. 3, *The Civil War, 1861–1865,* ed. Philip S. Foner (New York: International Publishers, 1952), 71.

382 **speak with Senator Stephen Douglas** Johannsen, *Douglas,* 840–41.

383 **"He is very cordial"** William H. Seward to Frances Seward, February 23, 1861, Seward, *Seward at Washington,* 511.

383 **"Your case is quite like"** William H. Seward to AL, February 24, 1861, in Nicolay and Hay, 3:312–20.

384 **"You are about to assume"** Francis P. Blair to AL, January 14, 1861, ALPLC.

386 **"A host of ravenous partisans"** Muriel Burnitt, ed., "Two Manuscripts of Gideon Welles," *The New England Quarterly 11,* no. 3 (September 1938): 594.

386 **"It was bad enough"** Villard, *Memoirs,* 1:156.

387 **"When you were brought forward"** AL to Schuyler Colfax, March 8, 1861, ALPLC.

387 **"Circumstances which have occurred"** William H. Seward to AL, March 2, ALPLC.

387 **"I can't afford"** John G. Nicolay, *An Oral History of Abraham Lincoln: John G. Nicolay's Interviews and Essays,* ed. Michael Burlingame (Carbondale: Southern Illinois University Press, 1996), 154.

387 **"I feel constrained"** AL to William Seward, March 4, 1861, *CW,* 4:273.

387 **"had a long and confidential"** William H. Seward to AL, March 5, 1861, ALPLC.

387 **"more intent on the distribution"** Charles Francis Adams, *Autobiography,* 126.

387 **"was accused of wasting"** Burnitt, "Two Manuscripts of Gideon Welles," 594.

388 **"appeared pale"** Philip Shriver Klein, *President James Buchanan: A Biography* (University Park: Pennsylvania State University Press, 1962), 402.

388 **"If you are as happy"** Jean H. Baker, *James Buchanan* (New York: Times Books, 2004), 140.

389 **"Fellow citizens of the United States,"** AL, First Inaugural Address, March 4, 1861, *CW,* 4:262–268.

389 **"Apprehension seems to exist,"** Ibid., 262.

391 **he almost expected to hear** Horace Greeley, *Recollections of a Busy Life* (New York: J. B. Ford and Company, 1868), 404.

391 **"I hold, that in contemplation"** AL, First Inaugural Address, 264.

392 **"Good," "That's so"** Johannsen, *Stephen A. Douglas,* 844.

393 **"I am loathe to close"** All of William H. Seward's suggestions are included in the footnotes to the text in *CW,* 4:249–71, and in Nicolay and Hay, 3:27–44.

394 **"The avowal"** *New York Tribune,* March 6, 1861.

394 **"conservative people"** *New York Times,* March 5, 1861.

394 **"No document"** *Chicago Tribune,* March 5, 1861.

394 **"The Inaugural Address"** *Illinois State Journal,* March 6, 1861.

394 **"a loose, disjointed"** *Chicago Times,* March 6, 1861.

394 **"neither candid nor statesmanlike"** *New York Herald,* March 6, 1861.

394 **"the cool, unimpassioned"** *Richmond Enquirer,* March 5, 1861.

394 **"lamentable display"** *Charleston Mercury,* March 5, 1861.

395 **"Before the Inaugural"** *New York Times,* March 6, 1861.

395 **"news from Washington"** Strong, *Diary,* March 4, 1861, 3:105–6.

395 **"result in Civil War"** Frothingham, *Edward Everett,* 414–15.

395 **"tension and frustration"** *Douglass' Monthly,* April 1861; and *The Life and Writings of Frederick Douglass,* 3:72–74.

396   **"Some thought we had"** David Blight, *Frederick Douglass' Civil War: Keeping Faith with Jubilee* (Baton Rouge: Louisiana State University Press, 1989), 78–79.

396   **supplies to last** Browning, *Diary,* July 3, 1861, 476.

396   **Absent from the floor** Niven, *Salmon P. Chase,* 237–38.

397   **"I accept the post"** Salmon P. Chase to AL, March 6, 1861, ALPLC.

397   **Bates confided** Bates, *Diary,* March 6, 1861, 177.

397   **large walnut table** William O. Stoddard, *Inside the White House in War Times: Memoirs and Reports of Lincoln's Secretary,* ed. Michael Burlingame (Lincoln: University of Nebraska Press, 2000), 11.

398   **"he had no administrative"** David Davis (WHH Interview), September 20, 1866, *HI,* 351.

398   **"When [I] first commenced"** Robert L. Wilson to WHH, February 10, 1866, *HI,* 207.

398   **"There was little order"** John Hay, *Addresses of John Hay* (New York: The Century Company, 1906), 323–24.

399   **"He was disinclined"** Welles, *Diary,* March 30, 1861, 1:4, 6. Welles, although referring to events by date, often entered his comments days or weeks after events and conversations.

399   **wrote out three questions** AL to Winfield Scott, March 9, 1861, *CW,* 4:279.

399   **"To raise, organize"** Winfield Scott to AL, March 11, 1861, ALPLC.

400   **"I may have said"** Francis P. Blair, Sr., to Montgomery Blair, March 12, 1861, ALPLC.

400   **"Assuming it to be possible"** AL to William H. Seward, March 15, 1861, *CW,* 4:284.

401   **"the Sentiment of National Patriotism"** Stephen A. Hurlbut, March 27, 1861, ALPLC.

401   **There entered** William Howard Russell, *My Diary North and South,* ed. Eugene H. Berwanger (New York: Alfred A. Knopf, 1988), 44–45.

402   **"Resolved, the opinion"** Krug, *Lyman Trumbull,* 183.

402   **"ambitious, but indecisive"** Ibid., 171, 183.

403   **"but he took care"** Richard N. Current, *Lincoln and the First Shot* (Philadelphia: J. B. Lippincott Company, 1963), 188.

403   **"If to be the head of Hell"** Nicolay, *Lincoln's Secretary,* 101.

403   **" 'Abe' is getting heartily sick"** Sam Ward to Samuel L. M. Barlow, March 31, 1861, in Samuel L. M. Barlow Papers, Huntington Library.

404   **"Wanted—A Policy"** *New York Times,* April 3, 1861.

404   **"We are at the end"** William H. Seward to AL, April 1, 1861, ALPLC.

404   **"It must be somebody's business"** John M. Taylor, *William Henry Seward: Lincoln's Right Hand* (New York: HarperCollins, 1991), 150–54.

405   **"This had your distinct"** AL to William H. Seward, *CW,* 4:316. The exchange between Seward and Lincoln did not become known for thirty years after Lincoln's death. The fact that Lincoln's letter is not to be found in Seward's papers is a strong indication it was never sent.

405   **"Would it impose"** AL to Winfield Scott, April 1, 1861, *CW,* 4:316.

405   **"No report"** "Memorandum," April 19, 1861, *CW,* 4:338.

405 **"An attempt will be made"** War Department to Robert S. Chew, April 6, 1861, *CW,* 4:323.

406 **Beauregard ordered a Confederate battery** For a description of the attack on Fort Sumter, see James M. McPherson, *Battle Cry of Freedom: The Civil War Era* (New York: Oxford University Press, 2002), 264–74.

407 **"Everybody much excited"** Taft, *Diary,* April 13, 1861.

407 **"God, in his merciful"** David Rankin Barbee, "President Lincoln and Doctor Gurley," *ALQ* 5, no. 1 (March 1948): 5.

407 **"I would make it 200,000"** Stephen A. Douglas, *Letters,* ed. Robert W. Johannsen (Urbana: University of Illinois, 1961), 509–10.

407 **"spoke of the present"** Johannsen, *Douglas,* 859–60.

408 **"I've known Mr. Lincoln"** Forney, *Anecdotes of Public Men,* 1:224–25.

408 **critics have scrutinized** Richard N. Current offers an admirable summary of the historiographical debate about Lincoln's actions in the crisis of Fort Sumter, as well as its larger implications for the movement for secession, in the "Afterthoughts" of *Lincoln and the First Shot,* 182–208.

408 **"You and I both anticipated"** AL to Gustavus V. Fox, May 1, 1861, *CW,* 4:350; for an excellent account, see Ari Hoogenboom, "Gustavus Fox and the Relief of Fort Sumter," *Civil War History* 9 (December 1963): 383–98.

408 **"The plan succeeded"** Browning, *Diary,* July 3, 1861, 476.

CHAPTER 18. *A People's Contest: April 1861–July 1861*

411 **"nervous tension"** Nicolay and Hay, 3:151.

412 **"We are in a beleaguered City"** Taft, *Diary,* April 13, 1861.

412 **Lee, the son of** Mary M. Thomas, *Robert E. Lee: A Biography* (New York: W. W. Norton and Company, 1995), 147–49.

413 **"by combinations too powerful"** "Proclamation Calling Militia and Convening Congress," April 15, 1861, *CW,* 4:331–32.

413 **"The people of Maine"** Reinhard H. Luthin, *The Real Abraham Lincoln* (Englewood Cliffs, N.J.: Prentice-Hall, 1960), 279–80.

413 **"Kentucky will furnish"** William Best Hesseltine, *Lincoln and the War Governors* (New York: Alfred A. Knopf, 1948), 147–48.

413 **"Dispatch received"** Ibid., 146–48.

414 **"Send no more troops"** George W. Brown and Thomas H. Hicks to AL, April 20, 1861, ALPLC.

414 **"Now, and ever,"** AL to Thomas H. Hicks, April 20, 1861, *CW,* 4:340.

414 **"The streets were full"** John Hay, *Lincoln and the Civil War in the Diaries and Letters of John Hay,* ed. Tyler Dennett (New York: Dodd, Mead and Company, 1939), 4–5.

414 **"Your citizens attack"** AL, Reply to Baltimore Committee, April 22, 1861, *CW,* 4:341–42.

415 **"I began to believe"** Nicolay and Hay, 4:153.

415 **"created much enthusiasm"** Taft, *Diary,* April 25, 1861.

415 **"In every great crisis"** *New York Times,* April 25, 1861.

416 **"suspend the writ"** AL to Winfield Scott, April 25, 27, 1861, *CW,* 4:344, 347.

416   **suspension of habeas corpus** Mark E. Neely, Jr., *The Fate of Liberty: Abraham Lincoln and Civil Liberties* (New York: Oxford University Press, 1991), xiv–xvii; Daniel Farber, *Lincoln's Constitution* (Chicago: University of Chicago Press, 2003), 157–58.

417   **reorganized the Sixtieth Regiment** Ruth Painter Randall, *Colonel Elmer Ellsworth: A Biography of Lincoln's Friend and First Hero of the Civil War* (Boston: Little, Brown and Company, 1960), 3–6. In the early summer of 1860, Ellsworth published a *Manual of Arms for the U.S. Zouave Cadets.*

420   **"Excuse me"** Randall, *Colonel Elmer Ellsworth,* 262.

420   **"In the untimely loss"** AL to Ephraim D. and Phoebe Ellsworth, May 25, 1861, *CW,* 4:385–86.

422   **Mary decided to restore** Baker, *Mary Todd Lincoln,* 184–85.

423   **"For all the detestable places"** Strong, *Diary,* July 15, 1861, 3:164.

424   **"the Washington National Monument Cattle Yard"** Mark E. Ruane, "Smithsonian Dig Unearths Quirky Traces of History," *Washington Post,* August 30, 2007.

424   **"softening the expression"** Douglas L. Wilson, *Lincoln's Sword: The Presidency and the Power of Words* (New York: Alfred A. Knopf, 2006), 94–95.

425   **"all peaceful measures"** AL, "Message to Congress in Special Session," July 4, 1861, *CW,* 4:425–26.

426   **"the attention of the country"** Ibid., 429–31. Mark E. Neely, Jr., asserts that Lincoln's discussion of habeas corpus revealed "the work of a fledgling president, uncertain of his legal ground and his audience." See Neely, *Fate of Liberty,* 11–13.

427   **"they commenced by an insidious debauching"** Paul M. Angle, "Lincoln's Power with Words," *Abraham Lincoln Association Papers* (Springfield, Ill.: The Abraham Lincoln Association, 1935), 80.

427   **"lacked the dignity"** Roy Basler, "Lincoln's Development as a Writer," *A Touchstone for Greatness: Essays, Addresses, and Occasional Pieces About Abraham Lincoln* (Westport, Conn.: Greenwood Press, 1973), 90.

428   **"message was the most truly"** Edward Cary, *George William Curtis* (Boston: Houghton, Mifflin and Company, 1894), 147.

428   **"In the late Message"** *Douglass' Monthly,* August 1861, 497.

429   **"When would the army"** Van Deusen, *Horace Greeley,* 276–78.

429   *Forward to Richmond!* Henry Luther Stoddard, *Horace Greeley: Printer, Editor, Crusader* (New York: G. P. Putnam's Sons, 1946), 213–14.

429   **the army was unprepared for war** McPherson, *Battle Cry of Freedom,* 313.

431   **"You are green"** William C. Davis, *Battle at Bull Run: A History of the First Major Campaign* (Garden City, N.Y.: Doubleday, 1977), 77.

432   **"Look, men, there is Jackson"** For Bull Run and the role of Thomas "Stonewall" Jackson, see James I. Robertson, *Stonewall Jackson: The Man, The Soldier, The Legend* (New York: The Macmillan Company, 1997), 259–68.

433   **"Our army is retreating"** David Homer Bates, *Lincoln in the Telegraph Office: Recollections of the United States Military Telegraph Corps During the Civil War* (New York: The Century Company, 1907), 91.

433   **"The day is lost"** Ibid., 251.

433 **"Boys, we will stop"** Hans L. Trefousse, *Benjamin Franklin Wade: Radical Republican from Ohio* (New York: Twayne Publishers, 1963), 150–51.

434 **Yankee Doodle, near Bull Run** Burton E. Stevenson, ed., *Poems of American History* (Boston: Houghton Mifflin Company, 1922), 425.

434 **"which gave expression"** *Congressional Globe,* 37th Cong., 1st sess., 222–23, 258–62.

434 **"Today will be known"** Strong, *Diary,* July 22, 1861, 4:169.

435 **"Sir, I am the greatest coward"** Nicolay and Hay, 4:358–59.

CHAPTER 19. *The Bottom Is Out of the Tub: July 1861–January 1862*

438 **Lincoln challenged** Hay, *Inside,* April 21, 1861, 5.

438 **attention to military strategy** I am grateful to James McPherson, who allowed me to see his book *Tried by War: Abraham Lincoln as Commander in Chief* (New York: Penguin Press, 2008), in manuscript form. McPherson makes the case, "In the vast literature on our sixteenth president, the amount of attention devoted to his role as commander in chief is disproportionately far less than the actual percentage of time that he spent on that task."

438 **"Wars, commotions, and revolutions"** Julian M. Sturtevant, "The Lessons of our National Conflict," *New Englander* 19 (October 1861): 894.

438 **"Circumstances make your presence"** General Lorenzo Thomas to George B. McClellan, July 22, 1861, McClellan, *Civil War Papers,* 66.

439 **"seemed more amused"** George B. McClellan, *McClellan's Own Story: The War for the Union, the Soldiers Who Fought It, the Civilians Who Directed It, and His Relations to It and to Them* (New York: Charles L. Webster and Company, 1887), 55.

439 **"I find myself"** George B. McClellan to Ellen McClellan, July 27, July 30, 1861, McClellan, *Civil War Papers,* 70, 71.

439 **"quite overwhelmed"** McClellan, *McClellan's Own Story,* 66.

439 **"It is an immense task"** Stephen W. Sears, *George B. McClellan: The Young Napoleon* (New York: Ticknor and Fields, 1988), 44–47.

440 **tactics used in the Crimean War** Ibid.

441 **seeds of future difficulties** Sears makes this suggestion, but there is nothing in the record to support this interpretation.

441 **"Young Napoleon"** Sears, *George B. McClellan,* 101.

441 **"Little Mac"** *New York Tribune,* August 1, 1861.

441 **pledged no more retreats** Sears, *George B. McClellan,* 97.

441 **"to move into the heart"** George B. McClellan to AL, August 2, 1861, McClellan, *Civil War Papers,* 74.

442 **"making the Blockade effective"** "Memoranda of Military Policy Suggested by the Bull Run Defeat," July 23, 27, 1861, *CW,* 4:457–58.

442 **"The President is himself"** *Lincoln's Journalist: John Hay's Anonymous Writings for the Press, 1860–1864,* ed. Michael Burlingame (Carbondale: Southern Illinois University Press, 1998), November 2, 1861, 130.

442 **"gave himself"** Nicolay and Hay, 5:155–56.

442 **"The poor President!"** Russell, *My Diary, North and South,* October 9, 1861, 317.

442 "**The political objective**" Carl von Clausewitz, *On War,* cited in McPherson, *Tried by War,* forthcoming.

444 "**If the Secretary of War**" AL to Simon Cameron, May 13, 14, 16, 20, 21, 24 [26?], 1861, *CW,* 4:367, 369, 370, 374, 380–81; 384.

445 "**quite independent**" AL to Edwin D. Morgan, May 20, 1861, *CW,* 4:375.

445 "**I am for it**" AL to Simon Cameron, May 13, 21, 1861, *CW,* 4:367, 380.

446 "**information from spies**" McPherson, *Tried by War,* 73–74.

446 "**I feel confident**" Sears, *George B. McClellan,* 104.

447 "**I yield**" George McClellan to AL, August 10, 1861, McClellan, *Civil War Papers,* 82–83.

447 "**patriotic purpose**" McPherson, *Tried by War,* 73–74; Sears, *George B. McClellan,* 104.

447 "**The Presdt is an idiot**" George McClellan to Ellen McClellan, August 16, October 11, 1861, McClellan, *Civil War Papers,* 85.

447 "**I found**" George B. McClellan to Ellen McClellan, October 16, November 17, 1861, McClellan, *Civil War Papers,* 107, 135.

447 "**Draw on me**" Hay, *Inside,* [November 1861], 30.

448 "**As Delaware was the first**" Patience Essah, *A House Divided: Slavery and Emancipation in Delaware, 1638–1865* (Charlottesville: University Press of Virginia, 1996), 161.

449 "**that if quiet was kept**" Hay, *Inside,* May 1, 1861, 16.

449 "**the Stars and Stripes**" *Kentucky Statesman,* June 14, 1861, cited in Townsend, *Lincoln and the Bluegrass,* 281.

450 **Lincoln had stayed in touch** Townsend, *Lincoln and the Bluegrass,* 273–74.

450 "**he contemplated**" Garrett Davis, April 23, 1861, Fehrenbacher, *Recollected Words,* 133–34.

450 "**We have beaten them**" Joshua Speed to AL, May 27, 1861, ALPLC.

452 "**I have given you**" Allan Nevins, *Frémont: Pathmarker of the West* (New York: D. Appleton-Century, 1939), 477.

452 "**I think there is great danger**" AL to John C. Frémont, September 2, 1861, *CW,* 4:506–7.

454 "**Now, at once**" AL to Mrs. John C. Frémont, September 10, 1861, *CW,* 4:515.

454 "**It was a war**" Nevins, *Frémont,* 515–19.

454 "**taxed me so violently**" Hay, *Inside,* December 9, 1863, 123.

454 "**an impetus**" Nevins, *Frémont,* 507.

454 "**How many times are we**" Ibid.

454 "**Slavery is the bulwark**" *Douglass' Monthly,* September 1861.

455 **raised Frémont** James M. McPherson, *The Struggle for Equality: Abolitionists and the Negro in the Civil War and Reconstruction* (Princeton, N.J.: Princeton University Press, 1964), 72–73.

455 "**I have been so distressed**" Joshua Speed to AL, September 3, 1861, ALPLC.

455 "**Frémont's proclamation**" Orville Browning to AL, September 11, 1861, ALPLC.

455 "**Coming from you**" AL to Orville Browning, September 22, 1861, *CW,* 4:531–33.

457 "**with bowed head**" Charles Carlton Coffin, in Rice, *Reminiscences of Lincoln,* 172–73.

457 **There was no patriot like Baker** Blair and Tarshis, *Colonel Edward D. Baker,* 167.

457 **"went up stairs"** Hay, *Inside,* November 13, 1861, 32.

458 **"I was favourably impressed"** Browning, *Diary,* December 19, 1861, 515–16.

458 **compensated emancipation** Essah, *House Divided,* 162–72.

458 **"cheapest and most human"** H. Clay Reed, "Lincoln's Compensated Emancipation Plan," *Delaware Notes* (Newark: University of Delaware, 1931), 65.

459 **"deeply convinced and faithful"** David Donald, *Charles Sumner and the Rights of Man* (New York: Alfred A. Knopf, 1970), 17.

459 **"Mr. President"** Ibid., 48.

459 **"Noble little Delaware"** AL, "Annual Message to Congress," December 3, 1861, *CW,* 5:50.

460 **"eight times as great"** Ibid., 53.

460 **most problematic member of Lincoln's cabinet** Fred A. Shannon, *The Organization and Administration of the Union Army, 1861–1865* (Cleveland, Ohio: Arthur H. Clark Company, 1928), 26.

462 **"was quite offended"** Chase, *Diaries,* January 12, 1862, 61.

462 **"to gratify your wish"** Erwin Stanley Bradley, *Simon Cameron: Lincoln's Secretary of War* (Philadelphia: University of Pennsylvania Press, 1966), 205–9.

462 **"simultaneous movement"** AL to Henry W. Halleck and Don C. Buell, December 31, 1861, *CW,* 5:84.

463 **"I have never received"** Henry W. Halleck to AL, January 1, 1862, *CW,* 5:84.

463 **"Mr. President, you are murdering"** Trefousse, *Benjamin Franklin Wade,* 159.

463 **"For some months"** Bates, *Diary,* December 31, 1861, 218–20.

463 **"It is exceedingly discouraging"** AL to Simon Cameron, January 10, 1862, *CW,* 5:95.

464 **"I feared"** Russell Frank Weigley, *Quartermaster General of the Union Army: A Biography of M. C. Meigs* (New York: Columbia University Press, 1959), 131–32.

465 **"General, what shall I do?"** "General M. C. Meigs on the Civil War," *The American Historical Review* 26, no. 2 (January 1921): 292.

CHAPTER 20. *We Are Coming, Father Abraham: January 1862–July 1862*

468 **"The inauguration is over"** Thomas and Hyman, *Stanton,* 118.

469 **"The political horizon"** Ibid., 149.

469 **"The new Sec.y of War"** Bates, *Diary,* February 2, 1862, 228.

469 **"accomplished in a few days"** Speed's letter to Joseph Holt cited in Thomas and Hyman, *Stanton,* 161.

469 **"a wagon load"** Strong, *Diary,* January 29, 1862, 3:203.

470 **"We may be obliged"** Thomas, *Abraham Lincoln,* 296.

470 **"would be master"** Chase, *Diary,* January 28, 1862, 64–65.

470 **"fond of power"** Welles, *Diary,* 67. Welles's observation, written sometime later, needs to be refracted through his strained relationship with Stanton. Thomas and Hyman, *Stanton,* 151.

471 **"should threaten all"** Browning, *Diary,* January 12, 1862, 523.

471 **"the insurgent forces"** AL, "President's General War Order No. 1," January 27, 1862, *CW*, 5:111–12.

471 **"immediate object"** AL, "President's Special War Order No. 1," January 31, 1862, *CW*, 5:115.

472 **"affords the shortest"** George B. McClellan to Edwin M. Stanton, February 3, 1862, McClellan, *Civil War Papers*, 167, 170.

472 **"I will stake my life"** Joseph T. Glatthaar, *Partners in Command: The Relationship Between Leaders in the Civil War* (New York: The Free Press, 1994), 69–70.

472 **"Does not your plan"** AL to George B. McClellan, February 3, 1862, *CW*, 4:118–19.

474 **"I told you so"** Bates, *Lincoln in the Telegraph Office*, 113.

474 **"No terms except"** Jean Edward Smith, *Grant* (New York: Simon & Schuster, 2001), 162–63.

474 **"shook the old walls"** Brooks Simpson, *Ulysses S. Grant: Triumph over Adversity, 1822–1865* (Boston: Houghton Mifflin Company, 2000), 119.

474 **instant hero** McPherson, *Battle Cry of Freedom*, 394–402; Thomas and Hyman, *Stanton*, 172–73.

475 **Willie became sick** Ruth Painter Randall, *Lincoln's Sons* (Boston: Little, Brown and Company, 1956), 128–30.

475 **"a social innovation"** "The President's Party," *Frank Leslie's Illustrated Newspaper* 13 (February 22, 1862).

475 **could not enjoy the evening** David H. Donald, *Lincoln at Home: Two Glimpses of Abraham Lincoln's Family Life* (New York: Simon & Schuster, 2000), 37–38.

476 **"been to see him"** Taft, *Diary*, February 20, 1862.

476 **Willie Lincoln died** Ruth Painter Randall, *Lincoln's Sons*, 102 ff.

476 **"My poor boy"** John Nicolay, *With Lincoln Inside the White House: Letters, Memoranda, and Other Writings of John G. Nicolay, 1860–1865,* ed. Michael Burlingame (Carbondale: Southern Illinois University Press, 2000), 71.

476 **"A fine boy"** Bates, *Diary*, February 20, 1862, 235.

476 **dark cloud of mourning** Nicolay, *With Lincoln Inside the White House*, 131.

476 **"It is well for us"** Phineas D. Gurley, "Funeral Address on the Occasion of the Death of William Wallace Lincoln" (Washington: n.p., 1862), 3–4.

477 **"Please keep the boys"** Baker, *Mary Todd Lincoln*, 213.

479 **"Driver, my friend"** Wilson, *Intimate Memories of Lincoln*, 422.

479 **Lincoln enjoyed Seward** Burton Jesse Hendrick, *Lincoln's War Cabinet* (Boston: Little, Brown and Company, 1946), 186; Hay, *Inside*, October 12, 1861, 26; Doris Kearns Goodwin, *Team of Rivals: the Political Genius of Abraham Lincoln* (New York: Simon & Schuster, 2005), 387–88.

480 **"What does this mean?"** Nicolay, *With Lincoln in the White House*, February 27, 1862, 72.

481 **"Well, anybody!"** There are a number of versions of this story. See Bruce Tap, *Over Lincoln's Shoulder: The Committee on the Conduct of the War* (Lawrence: University of Kansas Press, 1998), 113.

481 **"giving over to the enemy"** The only account of this conversation is in McClellan, *McClellan's Own Story*, 195–96.

482 **"We can do nothing else"** T. Harry Williams, *Lincoln and His Generals* (New York: Alfred A. Knopf, 1952), 67.

482   **"in, and about Washington"** AL, "President's General War Order No. 2," "President's General War Order No. 3," March 8, 1862, *CW,* 5:149–51.

483   **"You now have over one hundred"** AL to George B. McClellan, April 6, 1862, *CW,* 5:182.

484   **fired off a telegram** George B. McClellan to AL, April 7, 1862, McClellan, *Civil War Papers,* 233.

484   **"I was much tempted"** George B. McClellan to Ellen McClellan, April 8, 1862, McClellan, *Civil War Papers,* 234.

484   **"After you left"** AL to George B. McClellan, April 9, 1862, *CW,* 5:184.

484   **"Your call for Parrott guns"** AL to George B. McClellan, May 1, 1862, *CW,* 5:203.

485   **"Abe was rushing about"** Henry Williams to parents, May 6, 1862, in Stephen Sears, *To the Gates of Richmond: The Peninsula Campaign* (New York: Ticknor and Fields, 1992), 90.

485   **"It is extremely fortunate"** William Keeler to his wife, May 9, 1862, cited in William Frederick Keeler, *Aboard the USS Monitor, 1862: The Letters of Acting Paymaster William Frederick Keeler,* ed. Robert W. Daly (Annapolis: U.S. Naval Institute, 1964), 113, 115.

485   **"So has ended a brilliant week's"** Salmon P. Chase to Janet Chase, May 11, 1862, *The Salmon P. Chase Papers,* ed. John Niven (Kent, Ohio: Kent State University Press, 1996), 3:197.

486   **"If there is an honest man"** William Marvel, *Burnside* (Chapel Hill: The University of North Carolina Press, 1991), 93.

486   **"I prefer Lee to Johnston"** George B. McClellan to AL, July 7, 1862, McClellan, *Civil War Papers,* 344–45.

488   **"It should not be a war"** Sears, *George B. McClellan,* 227–29.

488   **"really seems quite incapable"** George B. McClellan to Ellen McClellan, July 9, 1862, McClellan, *Civil War Papers,* 348.

488   **"What would you do"** AL to Cuthbert Bullitt, July 28, 1862, *CW,* 5:344–46.

488   **"This government cannot much longer"** AL to August Belmont, July 31, 1862, *CW,* 5:350.

488   **a crucial decision** McPherson, *Battle Cry of Freedom,* 502–3.

488   **the Soldier's Home** For the story of the Soldiers' Home, see Matthew Pinsker, *Lincoln's Sanctuary: Abraham Lincoln and the Soldiers' Home* (New York: Oxford University Press, 2003); and Elizabeth Smith Brownstein, *Lincoln's Other White House: The Untold Story of the Man and His Presidency* (New York: John Wiley and Sons, 2005).

489   **"She seemed to be in excellent"** Benjamin B. French, *Witness to the Young Republic: A Yankee's Journal, 1828–1870* (Hanover, N.H.: University Press of New England), diary entry, June 16, 1862, 399–400.

489   **"We are truly delighted"** Mary Lincoln to Mrs. Charles [Fanny] Eames, July 26 [1862], in *MTL,* 130–31.

490   **"reading the Bible"** David V. Derickson, "The President's Guard," a recollection cited in Pinsker, *Lincoln's Sanctuary,* 5, 205.

490   **"read Shakespeare more"** John Hay, "Life in the White House in the Time of Lincoln," *Century Magazine* 90 (November 1890): 35–36.

490 **"I expect to maintain"** AL to William H. Seward, June 28, 1862, *CW,* 5:291–92.

493 **"He dwelt earnestly"** Welles, *Diary,* July 13, 1862, 70.

493 **"Things had gone from bad"** Carpenter, *Inner Life of Abraham Lincoln,* 21–22.

CHAPTER 21. *We Must Think Anew: July 1862–December 1862*

495 **"After much anxious thought"** This comes from Lincoln's later words to Francis Carpenter, *Inner Life of Abraham Lincoln,* 21.

495 **not set his sights on emancipation** I am indebted to the insights of Allen C. Guelzo's excellent study, *Lincoln's Emancipation Proclamation: The End of Slavery in America* (New York: Simon & Schuster, 2004), but I do not agree with his viewpoint, "The most salient feature to emerge from the sixteen months between his inauguration and the first presentation of the Proclamation to his cabinet on July 22, is the consistency with which Lincoln's face was set toward the goal of emancipation from the day he first took the presidential oath" (page 4). Lincoln's path to his Emancipation Proclamation was not consistent. See the essay "Review of *Lincoln's Emancipation Proclamation*" by Michael P. Johnson, *Journal of the Abraham Lincoln Association* 26, no. 2 (Summer 2005): 75–81; and George M. Fredrickson, *Big Enough to Be Inconsistent: Abraham Lincoln Confronts Slavery and Race* (Cambridge, Mass.: Harvard University Press, 2008).

496 **"as a fit and necessary"** "Emancipation Proclamation—First Draft," July 22, 1862, *CW,* 5:336–38.

496 **"The wisdom of the view"** Carpenter, *Inner Life of Abraham Lincoln,* 22.

496 **"kid glove war"** McPherson, *Tried by War,* forthcoming.

497 **"Old Brains"** Stephen E. Ambrose, *Halleck: Lincoln's Chief of Staff* (Baton Rouge: Louisiana State University Press, 1967), 5–6, 47.

498 **"I am very anxious"** AL to Henry W. Halleck, July 14, 1862, *CW,* 5:323.

498 **"looked weary"** Browning, *Diary,* July 15, 1862, 559–60.

499 **"if by magic"** Browning, *Diary,* July 25, 1862, 563.

499 **asked Burnside to relieve McClellan** Marvel, *Burnside,* 99–100.

500 **"I wish not to control"** AL to George B. McClellan, August 29, 1862, *CW,* 5:399.

500 **"You must call on General Halleck"** Ambrose, *Halleck,* 65.

501 **"Public sentiment is everything"** AL, "First Debate with Stephen A. Douglas at Ottawa, Illinois," August 21, 1858, *CW,* 3:13–14, 27.

501 **he regularly saw** Carpenter, *Inner Life of Abraham Lincoln,* 154.

501 **"grateful to the New-York Journals"** AL to Henry J. Raymond, March 9, 1862, *CW,* 5:152–53. Attached to Lincoln's letter to Raymond in the Lincoln Papers in the Library of Congress are all the editorials.

502 **"Having him firmly"** AL to Robert J. Walker, November 21, 1861, Nicolay and Hay, 11:121.

502 **"strangely and disastrously remiss"** Horace Greeley, "The Prayer of Twenty Millions," *New York Tribune,* August 20, 1862.

502 **"Broken eggs can never be mended"** James C. Welling, in Rice, *Reminiscences of Abraham Lincoln,* 525–26.

503 **I have just read yours** AL to Horace Greeley, August 22, 1862, *CW,* 5:388–89, n. 2.

504 **I would save the Union** Ibid., 388.

505 **"I have come from the West"** John Pope to Officers and Soldiers of the Army of Virginia, *OR,* vol. 12, pt. 3, 473–74.

506 **attack the Union supplies** Robertson, *Stonewall Jackson,* 556–57.

506 **"I am not prepared to crow"** Strong, *Diary,* August 30, 1862, 3:249.

506 **"We are not yet in a condition"** George B. McClellan to Henry W. Halleck, August 28 and 29, 1862, McClellan, *Civil War Papers,* 412.

507 **"I am clear"** McClellan to AL, August 29, 1862, McClellan, *Civil War Papers,* 413, 416.

507 **astonished by McClellan's response** John F. Marszalek, *Commander of All Lincoln's Armies: A Life of General Henry W. Halleck* (Cambridge, Mass.: Harvard University Press, 2004), 144–47.

507 **"was very outspoken"** Hay, *Inside,* September 1, 1862, 36–38.

507 **beaten Union units** For a description of the second battle of Manassas (Bull Run), see McPherson, *Battle Cry of Freedom,* 526–33.

507 **"that the troubles now pending"** Thomas and Hyman, *Stanton,* 2.

508 **"everything is to come"** George B. McClellan to Ellen McClellan, September 2, 1862, McClellan, *Civil War Papers,* 428.

508 **"There was a more disturbed"** Welles, *Diary,* September 2, 1862, 105.

508 **"seemed wrung by the bitterest anguish"** Bates's observation is found in footnote 1 in AL, "Meditation on the Divine Will," September [2?], 1862, *CW,* 5:404.

508 **"experience as a military commander"** Chase, *Diaries,* September 2, 1862, 119.

508 **"Well, General"** Sears, *George B. McClellan,* 261–62.

509 **found refuge in his bottomless barrel** Thomas, *Abraham Lincoln,* 343.

509 **"state the case of his adversary"** Tarbell, *The Life of Abraham Lincoln* (New York: The Macmillan Company, 1923), 2:113–15.

509 **"manner did not indicate"** Leonard Swett to WHH, January 17, 1866, *HI,* 167.

510 **"He will issue no proclamation"** Leonard Swett to Laura Swett, August 10, 1862, David Davis MSS, ALPLM, cited in Donald, *Lincoln,* 366.

510 **"had been appropriated"** James Oakes, *The Radical and the Republican: Frederick Douglass, Abraham Lincoln, and the Triumph of Antislavery Politics* (New York: W. W. Norton and Company, 2007), 191–94.

510 **"Your race is suffering"** AL, "Address on Colonization to a Deputation of Negroes," August 14, 1862, *CW,* 5:370–75.

511 **seemed to be closing the door** Blight, *Frederick Douglass' Civil War,* 137–39.

511 **calculated to make this bitter pill** Oakes, *Radical and the Republican,* 191–94.

511 **"Mr. Lincoln assumes"** Frederick Douglass, "The President and His Speeches," *Douglass' Monthly,* September 1862, in *Life and Writings,* 3:267–70.

511 **"meeting of Christians"** *Chicago Tribune,* September 5 and 8, 1862.

512 **I am approached** AL, "Reply to Emancipation Memorial Presented by Chicago Christians of All Denominations," September 13, 1862, *CW,* 5:419–20.

512 **"The subject is difficult"** Ibid., 425.

512 **the moment not to retreat** James M. McPherson, *Crossroads of Freedom: Antietam* (New York: Oxford University Press, 2002), 88–89.

513 **"Now is the time"** *Richmond Dispatch,* August 29, 1862.

513 **Lee was on Union soil** McPherson, *Tried by War,* forthcoming.

513 **"the friendly, almost tumultuous"** McPherson, *Antietam,* 98–105.

514 **Halleck talked him out of it** Henry W. Halleck to AL, September 12, 1862; and Nathaniel B. Banks to AL, September 12, 1862, ALPLC.

514 **"I have the plans"** George B. McClellan to AL, September 13, 1862, ALPLC.

514 **east side of Antietam Creek** The Union and the Confederacy conferred different names to a number of battles.

Union Designation	Confederate Designation	Date
Bull Run	Manassas	July 21, 1861
Logan's Cross Roads	Mill Springs	January 19, 1862
Pittsburg Landing	Shiloh	April 6–7, 1862
Second Bull Run	Second Manassas	August 29–30, 1862
Antietam	Sharpsburg	September 17, 1862

The Union usually named the battle after a landmark adjacent to it, usually a stream or river, such as Bull Run. The Confederates normally named the battle for the town associated with its base of operations, such as Manassas. For many of the battles, the names were often used interchangeably. An exception was the battle in southwestern Tennessee in April 1862. The North originally designated it Pittsburg Landing, after the landing on the Tennessee River they were determined to hold, while the Confederates named it after a church near where the battle began. The North quickly recognized Shiloh as the name of this bloody battle. For an extended discussion, see McPherson, *Battle Cry of Freedom,* 346.

514 **Halleck was suffering** Marszalek, *Commander of All Lincoln's Armies,* 148.

514 **"It has been a glorious victory"** George B. McClellan to Henry W. Halleck, September 14, 15, 1862, McClellan, *Civil War Papers,* 461–63.

515 **"God bless you"** AL to George B. McClellan, September 15, 1862.

515 **"I now consider it safe"** AL to Jesse K. Dubois, September 15, 1862, *CW,* 5:425–26.

515 **"Your dispatch"** Richard Yates to AL, September 15, 1862, ALPLC.

515 **the most violent day** For a description of the battle see McPherson, *Crossroads of Freedom.*

515 **"We are in the midst"** George B. McClellan to Henry W. Halleck, September 17, 1862, McClellan, *Civil War Papers,* 464.

516 **would lose 1,700 men** McPherson, *Crossroads of Freedom,* 119–20.

516 **"Our victory was complete"** George B. McClellan to Henry W. Halleck, September 17, 19, 1862, McPherson, *Crossroads of Freedom,* 467, 470.

516 **the scope of the battle** McPherson, *Crossroads of Freedom,* 3.

517 **"when the rebel army"** *The Salmon P. Chase Papers,* ed. John Niven (Kent, Ohio: Kent State University Press, 1993), 1:149–50.

517 **"the question was finally decided"** Welles, *Diary,* 1:143.

517 **I, Abraham Lincoln,** AL, "Preliminary Emancipation Proclamation" [September 22, 1862], *CW,* 5:433–34.

518   **At the heart of** Ibid., 434.

518   **"GOD BLESS ABRAHAM LINCOLN!"** *New York Tribune,* September 23, 24, 1862.

519   **"Mr. Lincoln not only"** Charles S. Wainwright, *A Diary of Battle: The Personal Journals of Colonel Charles S. Wainwright, 1861–1865,* ed. Allan Nevins (New York: Harcourt, Brace and World, 1962), October 2, 1862, 109–10.

519   **"Hatch, what do you suppose"** Nicolay, *Oral History of Abraham Lincoln,* 16.

519   **watched the biennial elections** Mark E. Neely, Jr., *The Union Divided: Party Conflict in the Civil War North* (Cambridge, Mass.: Harvard University Press, 2002), 37–38.

521   **"vote of want"** *New York Times,* November 7, 1862. The traditional viewpoint has been that the 1862 elections, at both the national and state levels, were a disaster for the Republicans. James M. McPherson argues, "But a closer look at the results challenges the conclusion." See *Battle Cry of Freedom,* 561–62.

521   **On November 5** AL to Henry W. Halleck, November 5, 1862, *CW,* 5:485; Sears, *George B. McClellan,* 337–39; Smith, *The Francis Preston Blair Family in Politics,* II, 144.

521   **"Never has such a paper"** *National Intelligencer,* December 2, 1862.

521   **"Without slavery"** AL, "Annual Message to Congress," December 1, 1862, *CW,* 5:536–37.

522   **"The dogmas of the quiet past,"** Ibid., 537.

522   **"As our case is new"** Ibid.

523   **Fellow-citizens** Ibid., 537.

523   **"that light and wisdom"** See Richard F. Mott, ed., *Memoirs and Correspondence of Eliza P. Gurney* (Philadelphia: J. B. Lippincott Company, 1884), 307–13.

523   **"sympathy and prayers"** AL, "Reply to Eliza P. Gurney," October 26, 1862, *CW,* 5:478 n. 1.

524   **an alternative vision of reality** David Zarefsky, "Lincoln's 1862 Annual Message: A Paradigm of Rhetorical Leadership," *Rhetoric and Public Affairs* 3, (2000) no. 1: 5, 12–13.

524   **Lincoln expressed skepticism** For the story of the Battle of Fredericksburg, see Marvel, *Burnside,* 175–200. For Lincoln's cautions, see his letter to Henry W. Halleck, November 27, 1862, ALPLC.

525   **Many blamed Lincoln** AL, Proclamation to the Army of the Potomac, December 22, 1862, *CW,* 6:13.

525   **On Tuesday afternoon** The best account of the Senate caucus is by Francis Fessenden, *Life and Public Services of William Pitt Fessendent,* Vol. 1 (Boston: Houghton Mifflin, 1907) I, 231–38. See also, Browning, *Diary,* I, December 16–18, 596–98.

526   **Lincoln read Seward's resignation** See Doris Kearns Goodwin's fine narrative of these events in *Team of Rivals,* 486–495.

526   **"I saw in a moment he was in distress."** Browning, *Diary,* December 18, 1862, 600.

526   **"with his usual urbanity"** Fessenden, *Life and Public Services,* 240; Welles, *Diary,* I, December 19, 1862, 194–96.

527   **Lincoln now moved to act quickly** Welles, *Diary,* December 20, 1862, 197.

527   **Lincoln's decision to have the Committee** Fessenden, 246–48.

528   **"I sent for you"** Welles, *Diary,* December 20, 201.

528   **for the sake of "the public interest"** AL to William H. Seward and Salmon P. Chase, December 20, 1862, *CW*, 6:12.

CHAPTER 22. *What Will the Country Say: January 1863–May 1863*

531   **And by virtue** AL, "Emancipation Proclamation," January 1, 1863, *CW*, 6:28–31.

532   **"What if the President fails"** Douglass, *Douglass' Monthly,* January 1863, in *Life and Writings of Frederick Douglass,* 3:307.

532   **"could not stop the Proclamation"** Charles Sumner to John Murray Forbes, December 28, 1862, *The Selected Letters of Charles Sumner,* ed. Beverly Wilson Palmer (Boston: Northeastern University Press, 1990), 2:135–36.

533   **"to abstain from all violence"** Guelzo, *Lincoln's Emancipation Proclamation,* 178.

533   **"he would complete"** Welles, *Diary,* December 31, 1862, 210–11. Senator Charles Sumner of Massachusetts took credit for suggesting the idea to both Chase and the president. See Charles Sumner to George Livermore, January 9, 1863, *Selected Letters of Charles Sumner,* 2:139–40.

533   **"Tomorrow at noon"** Guelzo, *Lincoln's Emancipation Proclamation,* 177–78.

534   **"What do you intend"** Florence W. Stanley, "Emancipation Proclamation: Lincoln's Own Story Retold," *Christian Science Monitor,* September 22, 1937.

534   **"warm salutations"** "New Year's Day in Washington," *Washington Republican,* January 2, 1863.

535   **New Year's Day reception** *Mr. Lincoln's Washington: Selections from the Writings of Noah Brooks, Civil War Correspondent,* ed. P. J. Staudenraus (South Brunswick, N.J.: Thomas Yoseloff, 1967), 57–60.

535   **"his hand trembled"** Charles Sumner to George Livermore, January 9, 1863, *Selected Letters of Charles Sumner,* 2:139–40. See also Guelzo, *Lincoln's Emancipation Proclamation,* 182–83.

535   **"My hand and arm trembled"** Isaac Newton Arnold, *The History of Abraham Lincoln and the Overthrow of Slavery* (Chicago: Clarke and Company, 1866), 304.

535   **"I never, in my life"** Seward, *Seward at Washington,* 2:151.

536   **"It is of the utmost importance"** Ambrose Burnside to AL, January 1, 1863, *CW,* 6:32.

536   **"retire to private life"** Marvel, *Burnside,* 209–11.

536   **confidence of the army** Marszalek, *Commander of All Lincoln's Armies,* 163–64.

536   **tension between Burnside and Halleck** Marvel, *Burnside,* 210–11.

536   **"If in such a difficulty"** AL to Henry W. Halleck, January 1, 1863, *CW,* 6:31–32.

537   **"a fine ride"** Marvel, *Burnside,* 212.

537   **"Mud March"** Ibid., 212–14.

538   **warned Lincoln** Brown, *Raymond of the Times,* 223–24.

538   **"That is all true"** Fehrenbacher, *Recollected Words,* 375.

538   **"I am a hot headed"** Walter H. Hebert, *Fighting Joe Hooker* (Indianapolis: Bobbs-Merrill Company, 1944), 65, 91, 153–61.

540   **"That is just such a letter"** Noah Brooks, *Washington in Lincoln's Time* (New York: The Century Company, 1895), 52–53.

540 **report directly to the president** Marszalek, *Commander of All Lincoln's Armies,* 166.

540 **"a white man's war"** McPherson, *Battle Cry of Freedom,* 563.

540 **"And I further declare"** AL, "Emancipation Proclamation," January 1, 1863, *CW,* 6:30.

541 **"would produce dangerous & fatal"** Browning, *Diary,* July 1, 1862, 555.

541 **"The colored man only waits"** Frederick Douglass, "The Proclamation and a Negro Army," *Douglass' Monthly,* March 1863.

541 **clash of twin emotions** Blight, *Frederick Douglass' Civil War,* 156–57.

542 **gravitating toward the ideas** Thomas and Hyman, *Stanton,* 229–31.

542 **recruitment of African-Americans** Dudley Taylor Cornish, *The Sable Arm: Negro Troops in the Union Army, 1861–1865* (New York: Longmans, Green and Company, 1956), 112–26.

542 **"The bare sight"** AL to Andrew Johnson, March 26, 1863, *CW,* 6:149.

543 **"I desire that a renewed"** AL to Edwin M. Stanton, July 21, 1863, *CW,* 6:342.

544 **"Army of the Potomac"** Charles Francis Adams, Jr., to Charles Francis Adams, January 30, 1863, *A Cycle of Adams Letters 1860–1865,* ed. Worthington C. Ford (Boston: Houghton Mifflin Company, 1920), 1:250.

544 **"My men shall be fed"** Hebert, *Fighting Joe Hooker,* 178–80.

544 **"orderly observance"** AL, "Order for Sabbath Observance," November 15, 1862, *CW,* 5:497–98.

544 **"a combination of bar-room"** *Charles Francis Adams, 1835–1915,* 161.

545 **Lincoln reviewed the cavalry** *Mr. Lincoln's Washington,* 151–54.

545 **"When I get to Richmond,"** Hebert, *Fighting Joe Hooker,* 183.

546 **"Gentlemen, in your next battle"** Darius N. Couch, "The Chancellorsville Campaign," *Battles and Leaders of the Civil War,* ed. Clarence C. Buel and Robert U. Johnson (New York: The Century Company, 1884–88), 3:155.

546 **"That is the most depressing"** Brooks, *Washington in Lincoln's Time,* 52.

546 **"Whereas, while heretofore"** AL, "Resolution on Slavery," April 15, 1863, *CW,* 6:176.

546 **"Resolved, That no such embryo"** Ibid., 177.

548 **"The Jews, as a class"** Smith, *Grant,* 225–26.

548 **Grant alone was responsible** Simpson, *Ulysses S. Grant,* 163–65.

548 **"And so the children of Israel"** Bertram Wallace Korn, *American Jewry and the Civil War* (Philadelphia: Jewish Publication Society of America, 1951), 121–25. Lincoln sent the order through Halleck.

549 **"an uncommon fellow"** Charles A. Dana, *Recollections of the Civil War* (New York: D. Appleton and Company, 1898), 61.

549 **"to reach the ear of the President"** Murat Halstead to John Nicolay, April 1, 1863.

550 **"are too common"** Salmon P. Chase to AL, April 4, 1863, ALPLC. Chase enclosed the letter from Halstead.

550 **"I have had stronger influence"** *Philadelphia Enquirer,* May 15, 1863, verified in Fehrenbacher, *Recollected Words,* 11.

550 **"The President attaches"** OR, vol. 17, pt. 1, 10.

550 **rumors about troop morale** McPherson, *Tried by War,* forthcoming.

551   **"impatient"** Henry Halleck to Ulysses S. Grant, April 2, 1863, cited in McPherson, *Tired by War,* forthcoming.

551   **damping down secessionist views** See Richard L. Kiper, *Major General John Alexander McClernand: Politician in Uniform* (Kent, Ohio: Kent State University Press, 1999); and the treatment of McClernand in Steven E. Woodworth, *Nothing but Victory: The Army of the Tennessee, 1861–1865* (New York: Vintage, 2006).

551   **McClernand took advantage** McClernand wrote to Lincoln on March 31, June 20, and September 28, 1863.

551   **Grant saw** *OR,* vol. 17, pt. 1, 113–14.

551   **"he thought him brave"** Chase, *Diaries,* September 27, 1862, 161.

552   **"You may not hear from me"** Ulysses S. Grant to Henry W. Halleck, *PUSG,* 7:196.

552   **"I am afraid Grant"** Elihu Washburne to AL, May 1, 1863, ALPLC.

552   **"The President tells me"** Charles Sumner to Francis Lieber, January 17, 1863, *Memoir and Letters of Charles Sumner,* ed. Edward L. Pierce (Boston: Roberts Brothers, 1877–93), 4:114.

552   **"Peace Democrats," or "Copperheads"** Jennifer L. Weber's *Copperheads: The Rise and Fall of Lincoln's Opponents in the North* (New York: Oxford University Press, 2006) shows the power and range of the effort of Copperheads to challenge the Union war effort.

553   **caricatured as a wacko** Frank L. Klement, *The Limits of Dissent: Clement L. Vallandigham and the Civil War* (Lexington: The University Press of Kentucky, 1970), paints a more sympathetic portrait of Vallandigham, 102–11, 123–25.

553   **"The Constitution as it is"** Ibid., 116–17.

554   **"Defeat, debt, taxation"** Ibid., 124–25.

554   **"The Peace Party means"** John A. McClernand to AL, February 14, 1863, ALPLC.

555   **bitter fruits of the Democratic victories** Arthur Charles Cole, *The Era of the Civil War, 1848–1870* (Chicago: A. C. McClurg and Company, 1922), 298–99.

556   **"uttered one word"** Marvel, *Burnside,* 231–32.

556   **"a bane usurpation"** Klement, *The Limits of Dissent,* 152–54.

557   **"I am here in a military bastile"** Ibid., 163–64.

557   **"an error on the part"** Welles, *Diary,* May 19, 1863, 306.

557   **"source of Embarrassment"** Ambrose Burnside to AL, May 29, 1863, ALPLC.

557   **"being done, all were"** AL to Ambrose Burnside, May 29, 1863, *CW,* 6:237.

557   **his own resolution** Vallandigham was taken by Confederate authorities to Wilmington, North Carolina, and finally made his way to Canada in July. Nominated by the Democrats of Ohio for governor on June 11, he ran his campaign in exile, represented by surrogates. In the election on October 13, 1863, he was defeated by Republican John Brough 288,000 to 187,000.

558   **"fight, fight, fight"** Hebert, *Fighting Joe Hooker,* 188.

558   **"Would like to have a letter"** AL to Joseph Hooker, April 15, 1863, *CW,* 6:175.

558   **"if he should meet"** Joseph Hooker to AL, April 15, 1863, *CW,* 6:175.

559   **"It seems to me Mr. Capen knows nothing"** "Memorandum Concerning Francis L. Capen's Weather Forecasts," April 28, 1863, *CW,* 6:190–91.

559   **"I fully appreciate the anxiety"** Joseph Hooker to AL, April 27, 1863, ALPLC.

559 **"How does it look now?"** AL to Joseph Hooker, April 27, 1863, *CW*, 6:188.

559 **"I am not sufficiently advanced"** Joseph Hooker to AL, April 27, 1863, *CW*, 6:188.

560 **"Where is General Hooker?"** AL to Daniel Butterfield, May 3, 1863, ALPLC.

560 **"he had a feverish anxiety"** Welles, *Diary*, May 4, 1863, 291.

560 **"We have news here"** AL to Joseph Hooker, May 4, 1863, *CW*, 6:196.

560 **"I am informed"** Joseph Hooker to AL, May 4, 1863, *CW*, 6:196.

561 **"ashen in hue"** Brooks, *Washington in Lincoln's Time*, 57–58.

CHAPTER 23. *You Say You Will Not Fight to Free Negroes: May 1863–September 1863*

563 **"be true to the Constitution"** Klement, *Limits of Dissent*, 178–81.

564 **"make a respectful response"** AL to Erastus Corning, May 28, 1863, *CW*, 6:235.

564 **"I had it nearly all"** James F. Wilson, "Some Memories of Lincoln," *North American Review* 163 (December 1896): 670–71. Although this reminiscence by Wilson was written years later, it rings true with Lincoln's conversations with others about his methods of thinking, retrieving, and writing. See Wilson, *Lincoln's Sword*, for an excellent discussion of the Corning letter, 165–77. See also Neely, *Fate of Liberty*, 66–68.

564 **"It has vigor"** Welles, *Diary*, June 5, 1863, 323.

564 **"doing their part"** AL to Erastus Corning and Others [June 12], 1863, *CW*, 6:261.

564 **"assert and argue"** Ibid.

565 **"was not arrested"** Ibid., 263–66.

567 **"I think that in such a case"** Ibid., 266–67.

567 **"maintained martial, or military law"** Ibid., 268.

567 **"throughout the indefinite peaceful"** Ibid., 267.

568 **"God be praised"** John W. Forney to AL, June 14, 1863, ALPLC.

568 **"timely, wise"** Edwin D. Morgan to AL, June 15, 1863, ALPLC.

568 **"covered all essential ground"** Roscoe Conkling to AL, June 16, 1863, ALPLC.

568 **"There are few"** Nicolay and Hay, 7:349.

568 **"The Publication Society"** Francis Lieber to AL, June 16, 1863, ALPLC.

568 **"Allow me to express"** David Tod to AL, June 14, 1863, ALPLC.

569 **"phraseology calculated"** AL to Matthew Birchard and Others, June 29, 1863, *CW*, 3:303–05. For a discussion of Lincoln's "public persuasion" in the Corning and Birchard public letters, see Philip Shaw Paludan, *The Presidency of Abraham Lincoln* (Lawrence: University Press of Kansas, 1994), 199–202.

569 **"sacrifice of their dignity"** Matthew Birchard to AL, July 1, 1863, ALPLC.

570 **"his poor mite"** AL to Joseph Hooker, June 16, 1863, *CW*, 6:281.

570 **"I have some painful intimations"** AL to Joseph Hooker, May 14, 1863, *CW*, 6:217.

570 **"Have you already"** AL to Joseph Hooker, May 7, 1863, *CW*, 6:201.

570 **"Do the Richmond papers"** AL to John A. Dix, May 11, 1863, *CW*, 6:210.

571 **"The fall of Vicksburg"** Ulysses S. Grant to Halleck, May 24, 1863, cited in Smith, *Grant*, 252–53.

571 **"Whether Gen. Grant shall"** AL to Isaac N. Arnold, May 26, 1863, *CW*, 6:230.

571 **"I do not think our enemies"** Thomas, *Robert E. Lee,* 279.

572 **always realistic** Stephen W. Sears, *Gettysburg* (Boston: Houghton Mifflin Company, 2003), 12–14.

572 **their greatest loss** Robertson, *Stonewall Jackson,* 727–36.

572 **South's belief that God** Daniel W. Stowell, "Stonewall Jackson and the Providence of God," *Religion and the American Civil War,* ed. Randall M. Miller, Harry S. Stout, and Charles Reagan Wilson (New York: Oxford University Press, 1998), 187–207.

572 **"I wish to lose no time"** AL to John W. Forney, May 13, 1863, *CW,* 6:214.

572 **"to pitch into his rear"** Joseph Hooker to AL, June 5, 1863, ALPLC.

572 **"I would not take any risk"** AL to Joseph Hooker, June 5, *CW,* 6:249.

572 **"I would not go South"** AL to Joseph Hooker, June 10, 1863, *CW,* 6:257.

573 **"If the head of Lee's army"** AL to Joseph Hooker, June 14, 1863, *CW,* 6:273.

573 **"Scary rumors abroad"** Welles, *Diary,* June 14, 1863, 328.

573 **"looks like defensive merely"** AL to Joseph Hooker, June 16, June 16, 1863, *CW,* 6:280, 282.

574 **Lincoln made a mistake** Thomas and Hyman, *Stanton,* 273.

574 **"the President in a single remark"** Welles, *Diary,* June 26, 1863, 348.

574 **"observed in Hooker"** Welles, *Diary,* June 28, 1863, 351.

574 **Meade later wrote his wife** Freeman Cleaves, *Meade of Gettysburg* (Norman: University of Oklahoma Press, 1960), 123–24.

574 **Meade led his Pennsylvania troops** Ibid., 103–15.

576 **"Have you any reports"** AL to Darius N. Couch, June 24, 28, *CW,* 6:293, 299.

576 **"The people of New Jersey"** Joel Parker to AL, June 29, 1863 *CW,* 6:311–12.

576 **"I really think the attitude"** AL to Joel Parker, June 30, 1863, *CW,* 6:311–12.

576 **The strike came sooner** Sears, *Gettysburg,* 142–44, 162–63.

576 **"I entered this place"** John Buford to Alfred Pleasanton, June 30, 1863, *OR,* vol. 27, pt. 1, 923.

576 **deployed his horse soldiers** James M. McPherson, *Hallowed Ground: A Walk at Gettysburg* (New York: Crown Journeys, 2003), 18–21.

577 **"meeting engagement"** Sears speaks of the meeting engagement; see *Gettysburg,* 168.

577 **had been involved in an accident** Randall, *Mary Lincoln,* 324.

578 **"Our task is not yet"** George G. Meade to Army of the Potomac, July 7, 1863, *CW,* 6:318.

579 **By the end of May 1863** For a description of the siege and surrender of Vicksburg, see Smith, *Grant,* 252–56.

579 **"is such to cover that Army"** AL, "Announcement of News from Gettysburg," July 4, 1863, *CW,* 6:314.

580 **"How long ago is it"** AL, "Response to a Serenade," July 7, 1863, *CW,* 6:319–20.

580 **"The enemy should be pursued"** Henry C. Halleck to George G. Meade, July 14, 1863, *CW,* 6:328.

580 **I do not believe** AL to George G. Meade, July 14, 1863, *CW,* 6:327.

581 **"I do not remember"** AL to Ulysses S. Grant, July 13, 1863, *CW,* 6:326.

582 **"I believe it is a resource"** AL to Ulysses S. Grant, August 9, 1863, *CW,* 6:374.

582 **"I never met with a man"** Frederick Douglass, "Emancipation, Racism, and the Work Before Us: An Address Delivered in Philadelphia, Pennsylvania," December 4, 1863, *Frederick Douglass* 3:606–7.

582 **"I have given the subject"** Ulysses S. Grant to AL, August 23, 1863, ALPLC. Grant's reply probably did not reach Lincoln before he had sent off his letter to Conkling on August 27. He determined to add the insights from Grant to the letter he had already sent to Conkling. Thus, on August 31, Lincoln wrote to Conkling yet again, asking that he insert the following paragraph.

> I know, as fully as one can know the opinions of others, that some of the commanders of our armies in the field, who have given us our most important successes, believe the emancipation policy, and the use of colored troops, constitute the heaviest blow yet dealt to the rebellion; and that at least some of those important successes could not have been achieved when it was, but for the aid of black soldiers. Among the commanders holding these views are some who have never had any affinity with what is called abolitionism.

582 **"It would be gratifying"** James C. Conkling to AL, August 14, 1863, ALPLC.

583 **"Your letter of the 14th"** AL to James C. Conkling, August 20, 1863, *CW,* 6:399 n. 1. At the lower left-hand corner of the telegram was a note, "Mr. C—Mr. Wilson got this in cipher." Mr. Wilson was the superintendent of the Eastern Division of the Illinois and Mississippi Telegraph Company. The note was signed simply "Operator." This notation suggested the desire to keep the movements of the president secret.

583 **"For a moment the President"** Nicolay and Hay, 7:379–380.

583 **"While it would afford"** James C. Conkling to AL, August 21, 1863, ALPLC.

584 **"It would be very agreeable"** AL to James C. Conkling, August 26, 1863, *CW,* 6:406.

584 **"I cannot leave here"** AL to James C. Conkling, August 27, 1863, *CW,* 6:414. Word of the Conkling invitation triggered a similar invitation from New York. Benjamin Field, secretary of the Union State Committee of New York, telegraphed Lincoln on August 26 telling him of plans to hold "a mass convention" in Syracuse, also on September 3. Field asked that Lincoln send the New York convention "the same address" that he was sending to Illinois. Lincoln wrote to Field on August 29 telling him that he was sending by mail a copy of "the Springfield letter." *CW,* 6:420.

584 **"I can always tell more"** Stoddard, *Inside the White House in War Times,* 129–30.

584 **"Further offensive prosecution"** Ibid., 299.

584 **"There are those who"** AL to James C. Conkling, *CW,* 6:415.

588 **"He is more an orator"** Stoddard, *Inside the White House in War Times,* 130.

589 **"The Letter was received"** James C. Conkling to AL, September 4, 1863, ALPLC.

589 **" 'God Bless Abraham Lincoln!' "** *New York Tribune,* September 3, 1863.

589 **"Thanks for your true"** Charles Sumner to AL, September 7, 1863, ALPLC.

589 **"God Almighty bless you"** Henry Wilson to AL, September 3, 1863, ALPLC.

589 **"Your letter to the Springfield Convention"** John Murray Forbes to AL, September 7, 1863, *Letters and Recollections of John Murray Forbes,* ed. Sarah Forbes Hughes (Boston: Houghton, Mifflin and Company, 1899), 2:73.

589 **"for his recent admirable letter"** Hay, *Inside,* September 10, 1863, 81.

589 **understood more than ever** Donald, *Lincoln,* 458.

CHAPTER 24. *A New Birth of Freedom: September 1863–March 1864*

591 **Lincoln's public letters of 1863** AL, *The Letters of President Lincoln on Questions of National Policy* (New York: H. H. Lloyd and Company, 1863).

592 **"Rising to the dignity"** Henry Ward Beecher, *Independent,* September 17, 1863.

592 **"The conservative Republicans"** "The Lounger," *Harper's Weekly,* August 29, 1863.

592 **"It is something on the question"** AL to Andrew Johnson, September 11, 1863, *CW,* 6:440.

593 **"Unconditional Union men"** Nicolay and Hay, 7:378.

594 **"You and your noble army"** Edwin M. Stanton to William S. Rosecrans, July 7, 1863, *OR,* vol. 23, pt. 2, 518.

594 **"You do not appear"** William S. Rosecrans to Edwin M. Stanton, July 7, 1863, *OR,* vol. 23, pt. 2, 518.

594 **"There is great disappointment"** Henry W. Halleck to William S. Rosecrans, July 24, 1863, *OR,* vol. 23 pt. 2, 552.

594 **"turnpikes next to impossible"** William S. Rosecrans to AL, August 1, 1863, ALPLC.

594 **"kind feeling for and confidence"** AL to William S. Rosecrans, August 10, 1863, *CW,* 6:377–78.

595 **"Chickamauga is as fatal"** Charles H. Dana to Edwin M. Stanton, September 20, 1863, in John E. Clark, Jr., *Railroads in the Civil War: The Impact of Management on Victory and Defeat* (Baton Rouge: Louisiana State University Press, 2001), 142.

595 **"Go to Rosecrans"** AL to Ambrose E. Burnside, September 21, 2 a.m., 11 a.m., *CW,* 6:469, 470.

596 **"Well, Rosecrans has been whipped"** Hay, *Inside,* September 27, 1863, 85.

596 **"If you are to do"** September 25, 1863, *CW,* 6:480–81.

596 **Lincoln signed the letter** Bates, *Lincoln in the Telegraph Office,* 202.

596 **hastily called midnight meeting** Clark, *Railroads in the Civil War,* 146–47.

596 **"you can't get one corps"** Niven, *Salmon P. Chase Papers,* 1:450–54.

596 **began moving to the railheads** Clark tells this story well in *Railroads in the Civil War,* 141–212.

597 **"If we can hold Chattanooga"** AL to William S. Rosecrans, October 4, 1863, *CW,* 6:498.

597 **"confused and stunned"** Hay, *Inside,* October 24, 1863, 99.

598 **"I therefore think it is safer"** AL to Edward Bates, November 29, 1862, *CW,* 5:515–16.

598 **"I tell you frankly"** AL to Samuel R. Curtis, January 2, 1863, *CW,* 6:33–34.

598   **"a pestilent factional quarrel"** AL to John M. Schofield, May 27, 1863, *CW,* 6:234.

598   **"It is very painful to me"** AL to Charles D. Drake, et al., May 15, 1863, ALPLC.

598   **"Neither side pays"** AL to Henry T. Blow, Charles D. Drake, and Others, May 15, 1863, *CW,* 6:218.

598   **a number of issues** David Donald, *Lincoln,* has an excellent discussion of the complicated Missouri story, 451–54.

598   **central problem was emancipation** William E. Gienapp, "Abraham Lincoln and the Border States," *Journal of the Abraham Lincoln Association* 13 (1992): 36–37.

599   **"*postponing* the benefits"** Hay, *Inside,* July 31, 1863, 68.

599   **"I express to you my profound conviction"** William Parrish, *Turbulent Partnership: Missouri and the Union, 1861–1865* (Columbia: University of Missouri Press, 1963), 160.

599   **"all being for the Union"** AL to Charles Drake and Others, October 5, 1863, *CW,* 6:500.

600   **"had no friends"** Edward Bates to AL, October 22, 1863, ALPLC. Bates is making reference to a conversation "the other day" between him and Lincoln.

600   **arrange furloughs** Thomas and Hyman, *Stanton,* 292–95.

600   **he felt "nervous"** Welles, *Diary,* October 13, 1863, 469.

600   **"Where is John Brough?"** Emanuel Hertz, *Abraham Lincoln: A New Portrait* (New York: H. Liveright, 1931), 2:914.

600   **"The victory is complete"** Salmon P. Chase to AL, October 14, 1863, ALPLC.

601   **"Glory to God"** AL to Salmon P. Chase, October 14, 1863, ALPLC.

601   **"Pennsylvania stands by you"** James M. Scovel to AL, October 11, 1863, ALPLC.

601   **"who is in good spirits"** Welles, *Diary,* October 15, 1863, 470.

601   **"Let me congratulate you"** James F. Moorhead to AL, October 15, 1863, ALPLC.

601   **"You will receive herewith"** Henry W. Halleck to Ulysses S. Grant, October 16, 1863, *OR,* vol. 30, pt. 4, 404, 479.

601   **"I will hold the town"** George H. Thomas to Ulysses S. Grant, October 19, 1863, *OR,* vol. 30, pt. 4, 404, 479.

601   **"You do not estimate"** AL to John Williams and Nathaniel G. Taylor, October 17, 1863, *CW,* 6:525.

602   **"My suggestion then"** J. M. Forbes to AL, September 8, 1863, *Letters and Recollections of John Murray Forbes,* 2:76.

602   **In previous wars American soldiers were buried** Drew Gilpin Faust, in *This Republic of Suffering: Death and the American Civil War* (New York: Alfred A. Knopf, 2008), offers a distinctive angle of vision on the changing understandings of death and dying provoked by the massive deaths of the Civil War.

602   **plans for a national cemetery** Kathleen R. Georg, "This Grand National Enterprise: The Origins of Gettysburg's Soldiers National Cemetery and Gettysburg Battlefield Memorial Association" (Gettysburg National Military Park Library, 1982), 82.

602   **Everett set the date** Frothingham, *Edward Everett,* 393.

602   **"I am authorized"** David Wills to AL, November 2, 1863, ALPLC. Gabor Borritt, in *The Gettysburg Gospel: The Lincoln Speech That Nobody Knows* (New York: Simon & Schuster, 2006), offers a fresh and comprehensive examination of Lincoln's Gettysburg Address in its broad historical context.

605   **"Four score and seven"** AL, Gettysburg Address, November 19, 1863, *CW,* 7:23.

606   **"The days of our years"** Psalms 90:10 (King James Version).

607   **In the last three sentences** Ibid.

608   **Investigations to unearth** On Lincoln's awareness of the ideas of Daniel Webster and Theodore Parker, see Garry Wills's suggestive book, *Lincoln at Gettysburg: Words That Remade America* (New York: Simon & Schuster, 1992).

609   **"Half a century hence"** *Chicago Tribune,* November 20, 1863.

609   **"Surprisingly fine as Mr. Everett's oration"** *Springfield* (Massachusetts) *Republican,* November 20, 1863.

609   **"The cheek of every American"** *Chicago Times,* November 21, 1863.

609   **"We pass over"** *Harrisburg Patriot and Union,* November 20, 1863.

609   **"The ceremony was rendered"** *Times* (London), December 4, 1863.

609   **"Permit me . . . to express"** Edward Everett to AL, November 20, 1863, ALPLC.

610   **Braxton Bragg's effort** McPherson, *Battle Cry of Freedom,* 676–77.

611   **"Thomas, who ordered those men"** Ibid., 677–80.

611   **"The storming of the Ridge"** Charles A. Dana to Edwin M. Stanton, November 26, 1863, ALPLC.

611   **"I wish to tender you"** AL to Ulysses S. Grant, December 8, 1863, *CW,* 7:53.

612   **"Jeff Davis . . . cursed"** Amistad Burwell to AL, August 28, 1863, ALPLC.

612   **government loyal to the Union** The story of Southern disaffection and a resurgent Unionist spirit is told well by William C. Harris, *With Charity for All: Lincoln and the Restoration of the Union* (Lexington: The University Press of Kentucky, 1997), 123ff.

612   **"as a restraint"** Donald, *Charles Sumner and the Rights of Man,* 121–22.

613   **"menaced by the ambition"** William E. Smith, *The Francis Preston Blair Family in Politics* (New York, The Macmillan Company, 1933), 2:237–40.

613   **"The policy of emancipation"** AL, "Annual Message to Congress," December 8, 1863, *CW,* 7:49–52.

613   **how much his thinking had changed** AL, "Proclamation of Amnesty and Reconstruction," December 8, 1863, *CW,* 7:53–57.

614   **"Men acted as if the Millennium"** Hay, *Inside,* December 9, 1863, 121–22. Dixon was James Dixon, Republican senator from Connecticut.

614   **"Mr. Lincoln has the inside track"** *Chicago Tribune,* December 30, 1863.

614   **"You have touched"** Albert Smith to AL, December 12, 1863, ALPLC.

615   **"Oh! that the President"** Niven, *Salmon P. Chase: A Biography,* gives a full treatment of Chase's bid for the Republican nomination in 1864.

615   **"That visit to the west"** Bates, *Diary,* October 20, 1863, 311.

615   **"It was in very bad taste"** Hay, *Inside,* October 18, 1863, 93.

CHAPTER 25. *The Will of God Prevails: March 1864–November 1864*

617 **Grant arrived in Washington** Simpson, *Ulysses S. Grant,* 258–59.

618 **"Why, here is General Grant!"** Smith, *Grant,* 289–90.

619 **"I am naturally anti-slavery"** Guelzo, *Lincoln's Emancipation Proclamation,* 44–47, 70–73.

621 **emphasize the overall passivity** See Donald, *Lincoln,* 10, 14.

622 **he began to correspond regularly** Albert G. Hodges to AL, April 22, 1864, ALPLC; Hodges also wrote to Lincoln on April 25, May 27, July 19, August 11, September 15, September 29, October 24, November 1, November 12, December 1, and December 9, 1864, and March 1 and April 1, 1865, ALPLC.

622 **The will of God prevails** AL, "Meditation on the Divine Will," *CW,* 4:404. Roy P. Basler, editor of *The Collected Works of Abraham Lincoln,* calculated the date of this reflection as September 2, 1862, after the discouraging defeat at the second battle of Bull Run, but placed a question mark after the date. Douglas L. Wilson, in *Lincoln's Sword,* offers persuasive evidence that Lincoln's meditation was written sometime in 1864. See 255–56.

625 **"a distinct scheme of unbelief"** Francis Wharton, *A Treatise on Theism and Modern Skeptical Theories* (Philadelphia: J. B. Lippincott and Company, 1859), 147, 152.

625 **Bates noted their attendance** Bates, *Diary,* March 3, 1861, 176.

625 **as did Illinois senator Orville Browning** Browning, *Diary,* December 22, 1861, 517.

625 **"where they habitually attended"** *Lincoln Observed: Civil War Dispatches of Noah Brooks,* ed. Michael Burlingame (Baltimore: Johns Hopkins University Press, 1998), 13.

626 **"The whole world to him"** Leonard Swett to WHH, July 17, 1866, *HI,* 162.

626 **"I wish to find a church"** E. Frank Eddington, *A History of the New York Avenue Presbyterian Church: One Hundred Fifty-Seven Years, 1803–1961* (Washington, D.C.: New York Avenue Presbyterian Church, 1962), 57–58.

626 **"I like Gurley"** David Rankin Barbee, "President Lincoln and Doctor Gurley," *ALQ* 5 (March 1948): 3.

626 **"an infinitely wise"** Charles Hodge, *Systematic Theology* (New York: Charles Scribner and Company, 1871), 1:583, 616. I am grateful to Donald K. McKim for his help in thinking through the issue of fatalism and providence in the Reformed tradition.

626 **"Calvinism presented in his beautiful examples"** William E. Schenck, *A Memorial Sermon on the Life, Labours, and Christian Character of Phineas D. Gurley* (Washington, D.C.: n.p., 1869), 42. I have examined more than thirty sermons by Gurley at the Presbyterian Historical Society in Philadelphia. Although handwritten and undated, they are consistent in their presentation of typical themes of nineteenth-century Old School Presbyterian preaching, especially his emphasis on providence.

627 **"Man is a rational"** Phineas D. Gurley, *Man's Projects and God's Results* (Washington, D.C.: n.p., 1863), 7.

627   **"the world moves"** AL, "Address at Sanitary Fair," April 18, 1864, *CW,* 7:301.

627   **"The world has never had"** Ibid., 301–2.

627   **"The shepherd drives the wolf"** Ibid., 302.

628   **"A painful rumor"** Ibid.

628   **attacked Fort Pillow** The story of Fort Pillow, and what did and did not happen, is best captured in two articles: Albert Castel, "The Fort Pillow Massacre: A Fresh Examination of the Evidence," *Civil War History* 4 (1959): 37–50; and John Cimprich and Robert C. Mainfort, Jr., "Fort Pillow Revisited: New Evidence about an Old Controversy," *Civil War History* 28 (1982): 293–306.

628   **"that devil Forrest"** Sherman's assessment is in *OR,* vol. 39, pt. 2, 121, 142.

628   **"The river was dyed red"** For biographical information on Forrest, see Jack Hurst, *Nathan Bedford Forrest: A Biography* (New York: Alfred A. Knopf, 1993).

628   **"to give me in writing"** Abraham Lincoln, "To Cabinet Members," May 3, 1864, *CW,* 7:328–29.

628   **Seward, Chase, Stanton, and Welles argued** A summary of the cabinet responses is found in Nicolay and Hay, 6:478ff.

629   **"Lee's army will be your objective"** Ulysses S. Grant to George G. Meade, April 9, 1864, *OR,* vol. 33, 27–28.

629   **"to move against Johnston's army"** Ulysses S. Grant to William T. Sherman, April 4, 1864, *OR,* vol. 32, pt. 3, 246, cited in McPherson, *Tried by War,* 205.

630   **"Not expecting to see you again"** AL to Ulysses S. Grant, April 30, 1864, *CW,* 7:324.

630   **two days of terrible, confusing fighting** McPherson, *Tried by War,* 210–11.

631   **"There will be no turning back"** Henry E. Wing, *When Lincoln Kissed Me: A Story of the Wilderness Campaign* (New York: Eaton and Main, 1913), 13.

631   **"I saw [Lincoln]"** Schuyler Colfax, in Rice, *Reminiscences of Abraham Lincoln,* 337–38.

631   **"I believe that if any other"** Hay, *Inside,* May 9, 1864, 195.

631   **"I propose to fight it out"** Ulysses S. Grant to Henry Halleck, May 11, 1864, *PUSG,* 10: 422–23.

632   **"for the last 8 or 10 days"** Bates, *Diary,* May 15, 1864, 366.

632   **"I think Grant"** *The Life and Letters of George Gordon Meade: Major-General, United States Army* (New York: Charles Scribner's Sons, 1913), 2:201.

632   **"I wish when you write"** Brooks, *Lincoln Observed,* 113.

632   **the anti-Lincoln sentiment** John C. Waugh, *Reelecting Lincoln: The Battle for the 1864 Presidency* (New York: Crown Publishers, 1997), 172–81.

633   **Lincoln, in the telegraph office** Bates, *Lincoln in the Telegraph Office,* 195.

633   **writing a first history** Henry J. Raymond, *History of the Administration of President Lincoln* (New York: J. N. Derby and N. C. Miller, 1864).

633   **"In view of the dread realities"** Waugh, *Reelecting Lincoln,* 188–89.

634   **"cordially endorse the principles"** *CW,* 7:382, n. 1.

634   **"not to interfere"** [June 6, 1864], *CW,* 7:377 n. 1.

634   **Lincoln and Johnson formed an unlikely duo** Waugh, *Reelecting Lincoln,* 198–201; *Richmond Examiner,* quoted in *New York Tribune,* June 24, 1864.

634   **"I will neither conceal"** AL, "Reply to Committee Notifying Lincoln of His Renomination," June 9, 1864, *CW,* 7:380.

635   **"I can not"** AL to Salmon P. Chase, June 28, 1864, *CW,* 7:412–13.

635 **give Chase three options** See Niven, *Salmon P. Chase,* 364–66.

635 **"because the difficulty"** AL to Salmon P. Chase, June 28, 1864, *CW,* 7:413.

635 **"I cannot help feeling"** Salmon P. Chase to AL, June 29, 1864, ALPLC.

636 **"Of all I have said"** AL to Salmon P. Chase, June 30, 1864, *CW,* 7:419.

636 **"When does the Senate meet"** Hay, *Inside,* June 30, 1864, 212.

636 **"War, at the best,"** AL, "Speech at Great Central Sanitary Fair, Philadelphia, Pennsylvania," June 16, 1864, *CW,* 7:394–96.

637 **"I am glad"** Joshua F. Speed, *Reminiscences of Abraham Lincoln and Notes of a Visit to California* (Louisville: John P. Morton, 1884), 32–33.

637 **"Get down, you damn fool,"** McPherson, *Battle Cry of Freedom,* 756–57.

638 **"would go 50,000 against us"** Brown, *Raymond of the Times,* 260. Raymond's entire letter is in *CW,* 7:517–18.

638 **"The want of military success"** Henry B. Raymond to AL, *CW,* 7:518.

638 **This morning** AL, "Memorandum Concerning His Probable Failure of Re-election," August 23, 1864, *CW,* 7:514–15.

639 **"They must nominate"** Brooks, *Washington in Lincoln's Time,* 164.

639 **"after four years of failure"** Donald, *Lincoln,* 530.

640 **"Atlanta is ours"** John F. Marszalek, *Sherman: A Soldier's Passion for Order* (New York: The Free Press, 1993), 282–84.

640 **"Glorious news this morning"** Strong, *Diary,* September 3, 1864, 480–81.

640 **"The preservation of"** George B. McClellan to the Democratic Nominating Committee, September 4, 1864, McClellan, *Civil War Papers,* 590–92.

640 **electrified and disappointed Democrats** Waugh, *Reelecting Lincoln,* 298–302.

641 **"Well, we see at last"** *New York Times,* September 10, 1864.

641 **neither Lincoln nor McClellan campaigned** Waugh, *Reelecting Lincoln,* 317–21.

642 **campaigned on a theme** Roger A. Fischer, *Tippecanoe and Trinkets Too: The Material Culture of American Presidential Campaigns, 1828–1984* (Urbana: University of Illinois Press, 1988), 94–96.

644 **"The purposes of the Almighty"** AL to Eliza P. Gurney, September 4, 1864, *CW,* 7:535.

CHAPTER 26. *With Malice Toward None, with Charity for All:*
December 1864–April 1865

647 **"the necessity of a military escort"** Ward Hill Lamon, *Recollections of Abraham Lincoln, 1847–1865* (Chicago: A. C. McClurg and Company, 1895), 265–68.

648 **"I regret"** Ibid., 275.

648 **"that a people's government"** AL, "Response to a Serenade," November 10, 1864, *CW,* 8:100–1.

648 **Brooks had become a trusted friend** Wayne C. Temple and Justin G. Turner, "Lincoln's 'Castine': Noah Brooks," *Lincoln Herald* 94 (Fall 1970), 113–15. Temple wrote a number of articles for the *Lincoln Herald* from 1970 to 1972 based on his doctoral dissertation on Noah Brooks at the University of Illinois (1956). See also Michael Burlingame's introduction in *Lincoln Observed: Civil War Dispatches of Noah Brooks,* 1–12.

649 **"I am a thorough Constitutional Abolitionist"** Goodwin, *Team of Rivals,* 676.

649   **most important appointment** For a discussion of the storm over the selection of a new chief justice, see David M. Silver, *Lincoln's Supreme Court* (Urbana: University of Illinois Press, 1956), especially chapters 15 and 16.

649   **"as the crowning"** Edward G. Bates to AL, October 13, 1864, ALPLC.

649   **"remove the cloud"** Francis P. Blair, Sr., to AL, October 20, 1864, ALPLC.

650   **"Happily it is now certain"** Salmon P. Chase to Charles Sumner, October 19, 1864, ALPLC.

650   **"We cannot ask a man"** Silver, *Lincoln's Supreme Court,* 207–8.

651   **"Forage liberally on the country."** Marszalek, *Sherman,* xv.

651   **"He has passed by Macon"** Strong, *Diary,* November 28, 1864, 522.

651   **"Much concern about Sherman"** Strong, *Diary,* December 8, 1864, 526.

652   **"I beg to present you"** William T. Sherman to AL, December 22, 1864, ALPLC.

652   **"When you were about leaving Atlanta"** AL to William T. Sherman, December 26, 1864, *CW,* 7:181–82.

652   **"I feel how weak"** AL to Mrs. Lydia Bixby, November 21, 1864, *CW,* 8:116–17. The later finding that two of Mrs. Bixby's sons were not killed does not take away from Lincoln's letter. See F. Lauriston Bullard, *Abraham Lincoln and the Widow Bixby* (New Brunswick, N.J.: Rutgers University Press, 1946). John Hay, who wrote some letters for Lincoln, claimed he wrote the letter to Mrs. Bixby. Michael Burlingame supports this claim in "New Light on the Bixby Letter," *Journal of the Abraham Lincoln Association* 16 (1995), 59–71, but the evidence is inconclusive at best.

653   **"Upon rejoining his regiment"** AL, "Pardon," November 16, 1964, *CW,* 8:112. The name of the soldier was not identified.

653   **"You have too much"** AL to James Madison Cutts, Jr., October 26, 1863. *CW,* 6:538.

653   **amendment that would abolish slavery** For a fine treatment of the story of the passage of the Thirteenth Amendment see Michael Vorenberg, *Final Freedom: The Civil War, the Abolition of Slavery, and the Thirteenth Amendment* (Cambridge, England: Cambridge University Press, 2001).

654   **"I wish that you could have been"** Charles R. Douglass to Frederick Douglass, February 9, 1865, quoted in Vorenberg, *Final Freedom,* 207–8.

654   **"This amendment"** AL, "Response to a Serenade," February 1, 1865, *CW,* 8:254.

656   **"would accept nothing short"** AL, "Annual Message to Congress," December 6, 1864, *CW,* 8:151.

656   **"to secure peace"** Jefferson Davis to Francis P. Blair, January 12, 1865, *CW,* 8:275.

656   **"to the people"** AL to Francis P. Blair, January 18, 1865, *CW,* 8:275–76.

657   **"Well, Mr. President"** Although no notes were taken at the Hampton Roads conference, participants did write of the conversations, sometimes years later. Stephens rendered a full account in his *Constitutional View of the Late War Between the States: Its Causes, Character, Conduct, and Results* (Philadelphia: National Publishing Company, 1870), 2:599–619.

657   **"would be immediately restored"** Campbell's report is found in his *Reminiscences and Documents Relating to the Civil War During the Year 1865* (Baltimore: John Murphy and Company, 1887), 8–19.

657 **"ended without result"** Lincoln reported to the Congress on February 10, 1865. AL, "To the House of Representatives," February 10, 1865, *CW*, 8:274–85. Lincoln, who often wished to keep strategic negotiations in his own hands, in this case provided materials from the Blair mission and the Hampton Roads conference to Congress.

658 **"The President directs me"** Edwin M. Stanton to Ulysses S. Grant, March 3, 1865, *CW*, 8:330–31.

659 **"All honor to Abraham Lincoln"** *Illinois State Journal,* March 4, 1865.

659 **"Mr. Lincoln has slowly"** *Chicago Tribune,* March 3, 1865.

659 **"We shall not be surprised"** *Daily Morning Chronicle,* March 4, 1865.

659 **"in force sufficient"** *Philadelphia Inquirer,* March 6, 1865.

659 **"at least half the multitude"** "From Our Correspondent," *Times* (London), March 20, 1865.

660 **Lincoln was photographed delivering a speech** Gardner focused this photograph on the president just as the ceremonies were about to begin. He is seated with his hands folded. Modern technology so restores the image that we can see that Lincoln had what for him was relatively close-cropped and well-managed hair and beard. Visible on the president's right are Vice President Hamlin and Vice President–Elect Andrew Johnson. On the other side, Chief Justice Chase chats amiably with Associate Justice Noah H. Swayne. Behind the president are his two secretaries, John Hay and John G. Nicolay.

661 **"As soon as Mr. Lincoln came out"** Michael Shiner, *Diary,* 1813–1865, Library of Congress, 182.

661 **"At this second appearing"** AL, Second Inaugural Address, March 4, 1865, *CW*, 8:332.

662 **"one-eighth of the whole population"** Ibid.

665 **"essential to the nature"** Charles Hodge, *Systematic Theology* (New York: Charles Scribner, 1871), 1:368. Gurley would have heard Hodge's thinking on "divine attributes" in lectures. Hodge made the decision not to publish his lectures in book form until the end of his career.

666 **response to his political and theological indicative** In the collection of Phineas Gurley sermons at the Presbyterian Historical Society, one hears a consistent indicative/imperative refrain. Gurley first speaks about the indicative of the love of Christ, manifest in Christ's death on the cross. He then calls for a selfless love as the response to Christ's love. Because these eighteen sermons are undated, I could not connect them with Lincoln and the 1860s. Nevertheless, this was a consistent theme in Gurley's sermons.

667 **"The White House looked"** *Through Five Administrations: Reminiscences of Colonel H. Crook,* compiled and edited by Margarita Spalding Gerry (New York: Harper, 1907), 26.

667 **"Here comes my friend Douglass."** Frederick Douglass, *Life and Times of Frederick Douglass* (Hartford, CT: Park Publishing Company, 1882), 402.

668 **"What is to be done"** Shelby Foote, *The Civil War: A Narrative* (New York: Random House, 1974), 3:857.

668 **"Of all the men"** William Tecumseh Sherman, *Memoirs of General W. T. Sherman* (New York: The Century Company, 1893), 327.

669 **"I will take care"** AL to Edwin M. Stanton, April 3, 1865, *CW*, 8:385.

669 **started up the James River** For the story of Lincoln's visit to Richmond, see Nelson Lankford, *Richmond Burning: The Last Days of the Confederate Capital* (New York: Viking, 2002), 156–67.

670 **"Jefferson Davis should be hanged"** Thomas, *Abraham Lincoln,* 512.

670 **"If I were in your place"** Ibid., 166.

671 **"Let us all join"** AL, "Last Public Address," April 11, 1865, *CW,* 8:402–4.

671 **"no exclusive"** Ibid.

672 **"That means nigger citizenship"** Michael W. Kauffman, *American Brutus: John Wilkes Booth and the Lincoln Conspiracies* (New York: Random House, 2004), 210.

673 **"possess feelings of hate"** Thomas, *Abraham Lincoln,* 517.

673 **"We must *both* be more cheerful"** Mary Todd Lincoln (WHH interview), September 5, 1866, *HI,* 273.

673 **they spoke of the future** Turner, *Mary Todd Lincoln,* 283–85.

673 **"I am going"** Isaac N. Arnold, *The Life of Abraham Lincoln* (Chicago: Jansen, McClurg, and Company, 1885), 431.

674 **"The giant sufferer"** Welles, *Diary,* April 14, 1865, 2:286.

675 **"Now, he belongs to the ages."** A long-running debate arose over what Stanton actually said. Did he say "ages" or "angels"? To appreciate the import of this debate, see Adam Gopnik, "Angels and Ages: Lincoln's Language and It's Legacy," *The New Yorker,* May 28, 2007, 30–37.

675 **"those memorable words"** "Our Martyred President: An Address Delivered in Rochester, New York, on 15 April 1865, *The Frederick Douglass Papers,* ed. John W. Blasingame and John R. McKivigan (New Haven: Yale University Press, 1991), 74–77.

Selected Bibliography

CHAPTERS IN BOOKS AND JOURNAL ARTICLES

Angle, Paul M. "The Record of a Friendship—A Series of Letters from Lincoln to Henry E. Dummer." *Journal of the Illinois State Historical Society* 31 (June 1938): 125–37.

Appleby, Joyce. "New Cultural Heroes in the Early National Period." In *The Culture of the Market: Historical Essays,* edited by Thomas L. Haskell and Richard F. Teichgraeber III. Cambridge: Cambridge University Press, 1993.

Atkinson, Betty J. "Some Thoughts on Nancy Hanks." *Lincoln Herald* 73 (Fall 1971): 127–37.

Barbee, David Rankin. "President Lincoln and Doctor Gurley." *The Abraham Lincoln Quarterly* 5, no. 1 (March 1948): 5.

Brown, Caroline Owsley. "Springfield Society Before the Civil War." *Journal of the Illinois State Historical Society* 15: 477–500.

Burnitt, Muriel, ed. "Two Manuscripts of Gideon Welles." *The New England Quarterly* 11, no. 3 (September 1938): 576–605.

Congleton, Betty Carolyn. "George D. Prentice: Nineteenth Century Southern Editor." *Register of the Kentucky Historical Society* 65 (April 1967): 94–119.

Conkling, Clinton L. "How Mr. Lincoln Received the News of His First Nomination." *Transactions of the Illinois State Historical Society* 14 (1909): 63–66.

Detweiler, Philip F. "The Changing Reputation of the Declaration of Independence: The First Fifty Years." *The William and Mary Quarterly, 3rd Series* 19, no. 4 (October 1962): 557–74.

Douglas, Stephen. "The Dividing Line Between Federal and Local Authority: Popular Sovereignty in the Territories." *Harper's Magazine* 14 (September 1859): 519–37.

Eckley, Robert S. *For the People: A Newsletter of the Abraham Lincoln Association* 4, nos. 3, 2, and 8 (Autumn 2002).

———. "Leonard Swett: Lincoln's Legacy to the Chicago Bar." *Journal of the Illinois State Historical Society* 92, no. 1 (Spring 1999): 30–43.

Elizor, Daniel. "The Constitution, the Union, and the Liberties of the People." *Publius: The Journal of Federalism* 8, no. 3 (Summer 1978): 141–75.

Ewing, Thomas. "Lincoln and the General Land Office, 1849." *Journal of the Illinois State Historical Society* 25 (October 1932): 139–52.

Futrell, Roger H. "Zachariah Riney: Lincoln's First Schoolmaster." *Lincoln Herald* 74 (Fall 1972): 136–42.

"General M. C. Meigs on the Civil War." *The American Historical Review* 26, no. 2 (January 1921): 285–303.

Gienapp, William E. "Abraham Lincoln and the Border States." *Journal of the Abraham Lincoln Association* 13 (1992): 1–46.

———. " 'Politics Seem to Enter into Everything': Political Culture in the North, 1840–1860," in *Essays on American Antebellum Politics, 1840–1860,* edited by Stephen E. Maizlish and John J. Kushma. College Station: Texas A&M University Press, 1982.

Grimsley, Elizabeth Todd. "Six Months in the White House." *Journal of the Illinois State Historical Society* 19, nos. 3–4 (October 1926–January 1927): 43–73.

Hagan, Richard S. "What a Pleasant Home Abe Lincoln Has." *Journal of the Illinois State Historical Society* 48, no. 1 (Spring 1955): 5–27.

Hamand, Lavern M. "Lincoln's Particular Friend," in *Essays in Illinois History,* edited by Donald F. Tingley. Carbondale: Southern Illinois University Press, 1968, 18–36.

Harkness, David J. "Lincoln and Byron: Lovers of Liberty." *Lincoln Herald* (December 1941): 2–13.

Harris, Sheldon H. "Abraham Lincoln Stumps a Yankee Audience." *New England Quarterly* 38 (June 1865): 227–33.

Hart, Richard E. "Lincoln's Springfield: The Public Square (1823–1865)." Springfield, Ill.: Elijah Hess House Foundation, 2004, 1–34.

Havlik, Robert J. "Abraham Lincoln and the Reverend James Smith: Lincoln's Presbyterian Experience in Springfield." *Journal of the Illinois State Historical Society* 92, no. 3 (Autumn 1999): 222–37.

[Hawthorne, Nathaniel]. "Chiefly About War Matters, by a Peaceable Man." *Atlantic Monthly* 10, no. 57 (July 1862): 43–61.

Heathcote, Charles William. "Early Lincolns in Pennsylvania." *Lincoln Herald* (February 1944): 18–19.

Hickey, James. "The Lincoln's Globe Tavern: A Study in Tracing the History of a Nineteenth Century Building." *Journal of the Illinois State Historical Society* 56 (Winter 1963): 629–53.

Hoogenboom, Ari. "Gustavus Fox and the Relief of Fort Sumter." *Civil War History* 9 (December 1963): 383–98.

Hyman, Harold M. "Abraham Lincoln, Legal Positivism, and Constitutional History." *Journal of the Abraham Lincoln Association* 13 (1992): 1–11.

Laslett, Barbara. "The Family as a Public and Private Institution: An Historical Perspective." *Journal of Marriage and the Family* 35 (August 1973): 480–92.

McCormick, Richard P. "New Perspectives on Jacksonian Politics." *American Historical Review* 65 (1960): 288–301.

———. "Was There a 'Whig Strategy' in 1836?" *Journal of Early Republic* 4 (Spring 1984): 47–70.

Meigs, M. C. "The Relations of President Lincoln and Secretary Stanton to the Military Commanders in the Civil War." *American Historical Review* 26, no. 2 (January 1921): 285–303.

Menz, Katherine B. *Historic Furnishings Report: The Lincoln Home* (U.S. Department of the Interior, National Park Service, Harpers Ferry Center, 1983), 5–43.

Morsman, Jenry. "Collision of Interests: The *Effie Afton,* the Rock Island Bridge, and the Making of America." *Common-Place* 6, no. 4 (July 2006): 1–12.

Neeley, Mark E., Jr. "Lincoln's Lyceum Speech and the Origins of a Modern Myth." *Lincoln Lore,* nos. 1776–77 (1987): 1–4.

Nicolay, Helen. "The Education of an Historian." *The Abraham Lincoln Quarterly* 2, no. 3 (September 1944): 107–37.

Pratt, Harry E. "Abraham Lincoln's First Murder Trial." *Journal of the Illinois State Historical Society* 37 (September 1944): 242–49.

———. "Lincoln and the Black Hawk War." *Bulletin of the Abraham Lincoln Association,* no. 54 (December 1938): 3–13.

———. "Lincoln Pilots the Talisman." *The Abraham Lincoln Quarterly* 2 (September 1943): 319–29.

Purvis, Thomas L. "The Making of a Myth: Abraham Lincoln's Family Background in the Perspective of Jacksonian Politics." *Journal of the Illinois State Historical Society* 75 (Summer 1982): 148–60.

Robertson, James I. "Revelry and Religion in Frontier Kentucky." *Register of the Kentucky Historical Society* 79 (Autumn 1981): 354–68.

Schurz, Carl. "Reminiscences of a Long Life." *McClure's Magazine* 28 (January 1907): 408–23.

Schwartz, Earl. " 'A Poor Hand to Quote Scripture': Lincoln and Genesis 3:19." *Journal of the Abraham Lincoln Association* 23, no. 2 (2002): 37–49.

Schwartz, Thomas. "An Egregious Political Blunder: Justin Butterfield, Lincoln, and Illinois Whiggery." *Journal of the Abraham Lincoln Association Papers* 8 (1986): 9–19.

———. "The Springfield Lyceums and Lincoln's 1838 Speech." *Illinois Historical Journal* 83, no. 1 (1990): 45–49.

Shaw, James. "A Neglected Episode in the Life of Abraham Lincoln." *Transactions of the Illinois State Historical Society* 29 (1922): 5–58.

Simon, John Y. "Union County in 1858 and the Lincoln-Douglas Debate." *Journal of the Illinois State Historical Society* 62 (Autumn 1969): 267–92.

Snay, Mitchell. "Abraham Lincoln, Owen Lovejoy, and the Emergence of the Republican Party in Illinois." *Journal of the Abraham Lincoln Association* 22, no. 1 (2001): 83–99.

Strouse, Jean. "Semi-Private Lives," in *Studies in Biography,* edited by Daniel Aaron. Cambridge, Mass.: Harvard University Press, 1978.

Sturtevant, Julian M. "The Lessons of Our National Conflict." *New Englander* 19 (October 1861): 894–913.

Swett, Leonard Herbert. "A Memorial of Leonard Swett." *Transactions, McLean County Historical Society* 2: 5–78.

Temple, Wayne C. "Mrs. Frances Wallace Describes Lincoln's Wedding," edited by Wayne C. Temple. Harrogate, Tenn.: Lincoln Memorial University, 1960.

Thomas, Benjamin. "Lincoln the Postmaster." *Bulletin of the Abraham Lincoln Association,* no. 31 (June 1933): 3–9.

Trefousse, Hans. "The Joint Committee on the Conduct of the War: A Reassessment." *Civil War History* 10 (March 1964): 5–19.

Van Deusen, Glyndon G. "The Whig Party," in *History of US Political Parties, Vol. I,* edited by Arthur M. Schlesinger, Jr. New York: Chelsea House, 1973, 333–493.

Vorenberg, Michael. "Abraham Lincoln and the Politics of Black Colonization." *Journal of the Abraham Lincoln Association* 14 (Summer 1993): 23–45.

Washington, Patricia. "Discontent in Frontier Kentucky." *Register of the Kentucky Historical Society* 65 (April 1967): 77–93.

Weik, Jesse W. "Lincoln's Vote for Vice-President in the Philadelphia Convention of 1856." *Century Magazine* 76 (June 1908): 186–89.

White, Horace. "Abraham Lincoln in 1854." *Transactions of the Illinois State Historical Society 1908,* no. 13 (1909): 25–47.

Wilentz, Sean. "Society, Politics, and the Market Revolution, 1815–1848," in *The New American History,* edited by Eric Foner. Philadelphia: Temple University Press, 1990, 51–72.

Williams, Mentor L. "The Chicago River and Harbor Convention, 1847." *Mississippi Valley Historical Review* 35, no. 4 (March 1949): 607–26.

Wilson, Douglas. "The Unfinished Text of the Lincoln-Douglas Debates." *Journal of the Abraham Lincoln Association* 15, no. 1 (Winter 1994): 70–84.

Wilson, James F. "Some Memories of Lincoln." *North American Review* 163 (December 1896): 667–75.

Winger, Stewart. "Lincoln's Economics and the American Dream: A Reappraisal." *Journal of the Abraham Lincoln Association* 22, no. 1 (2001): 51–80.

———. " 'To the Latest Generations': Lincoln's Use of Time, History, and the End of Time in Historical Context." *Journal of the Abraham Lincoln Association* 23, no. 2 (2002): 19–36.

Zarefsky, David. "Lincoln's 1862 Annual Message: A Paradigm of Rhetorical Leadership." *Rhetoric and Public Affairs* 3, no. 1 (2000): 5–14.

BOOKS, LETTERS, DIARIES

Adams, Charles Francis. *Charles Francis Adams by His Son, Charles Francis Adams.* Boston: Houghton Mifflin, 1900.

———. *Charles Francis Adams, 1835–1915: An Autobiography.* Boston: Houghton, Mifflin and Company, 1916.

———. *Richard Henry Dana: A Biography.* 2 vols. Boston: Houghton, Mifflin and Company, 1890.

Adams, Henry. *The Great Secession Winter of 1860–61.* Edited by George Hochfield. New York: A. S. Barnes, 1963.

Allen, John W. *Legends and Lore of Southern Illinois.* Carbondale: Southern Illinois University Press, 1963.

Altschuler, Glenn C., and Stuart M. Blumin. *Rude Republic: Americans and Their Politics in the Nineteenth Century.* Princeton, N.J.: Princeton University Press, 2000.

Ambrose, Stephen E. *Halleck: Lincoln's Chief of Staff.* Baton Rouge: Louisiana State University Press, 1962.

Anderson, Virginia DeJohn. *New England's Generation: The Great Migration and the Formation of Society and Culture in the Seventeenth Century.* Cambridge, England, New York: Cambridge University Press, 1991.

Angle, Paul M. *"Here I Have Lived": A History of Lincoln's Springfield, 1821–1865.* New Brunswick, N.J.: Rutgers University Press, 1935.

———. *Lincoln 1854–1861.* Springfield, Ill.: The Abraham Lincoln Association, 1933.

———. *One Hundred Years of Law: An Account of the Law Office Which John T. Stuart*

Founded in Springfield, Illinois, a Century Ago. Springfield, Ill.: Brown, Hay and Stephens, 1928.

Appleby, Joyce Oldham. *Inheriting the Revolution: The First Generation of Americans*. Cambridge, Mass.: Belknap Press of Harvard University Press, 2000.

Arnold, Isaac Newton. *The History of Abraham Lincoln and the Overthrow of Slavery*. Chicago: Clarke and Company, 1866.

———. *The Life of Abraham Lincoln*. Chicago: Jansen, McClurg, and Company, 1884.

———. *Reminiscences of the Illinois Bar Forty Years Ago: Lincoln and Douglas as Orators and Lawyers*. Chicago: Fergus Printing Company, 1881.

Baber, Adin. *A. Lincoln with Compass and Chain*. Kansas, Ill.: Privately Printed, 1968.

Baker, Jean H. *Affairs of Party: The Political Culture of Northern Democrats in the Mid-Nineteenth Century*. New York: Fordham University Press, 1998.

———. *James Buchanan*. New York: Times Books, 2004.

———. *Mary Todd Lincoln: A Biography*. New York: W. W. Norton and Company, 1987.

———. *"Not Much of Me": Abraham Lincoln as a Typical American*. Fort Wayne, Ind.: Lincoln Library and Museum, 1988.

Baringer, William E. *A House Dividing: Lincoln as President Elect*. Springfield, Ill.: The Abraham Lincoln Association, 1945.

———. *Lincoln's Rise to Power*. Boston: Little, Brown and Company, 1937.

———. *Lincoln's Vandalia: A Pioneer Portrait*. New Brunswick, N.J.: Rutgers University Press, 1949.

Bartlett, Irving H. *Calhoun: A Biography*. New York: W. W. Norton and Company, 1993.

Barton, William E. *The Lineage of Lincoln*. Indianapolis: The Bobbs-Merrill Company, 1929.

———. *President Lincoln*. Indianapolis: The Bobbs-Merrill Company, 1933.

———. *The Women Lincoln Loved*. Indianapolis: The Bobbs-Merrill Company, 1927.

Bates, David Homer. *Lincoln in the Telegraph Office: Recollections of the United States Military Corps During the Civil War*. New York: The Century Company, 1907.

Baxter, Maurice G. *Henry Clay and the American System*. Lexington: University Press of Kentucky, 1995.

Belz, Herman. *Abraham Lincoln, Constitutionalism, and Equal Rights in the Civil War Era*. New York: Fordham University Press, 1998.

———. *Lincoln and the Constitution: The Dictatorship Question Reconsidered*. Fort Wayne, Ind.: Louis A. Warren Library and Museum, 1984.

Bennett, James O'Donnell. *Joseph Medill*. Chicago: Reprinted from *Chicago Tribune*, 1947.

Berry, Stephen. *House of Abraham: Lincoln and the Todds, a Family Divided by War*. Boston: Houghton Mifflin Company, 2007.

Beveridge, Albert J. *Abraham Lincoln 1809–1858*. 2 vols. Boston: Houghton Mifflin Company, 1928.

Blair, Harry C., and Rebecca Tarshis. *The Life of Colonel Edward D. Baker, Lincoln's Constant Ally, Together with Four of His Great Orations*. Portland: Oregon Historical Society, 1960.

Blasingame, John W., et al., eds. *The Frederick Douglass Papers*. 5 vols. New Haven, Conn.: Yale University Press, 1979–92.

Blight, David W. *Frederick Douglass' Civil War: Keeping Faith in Jubilee*. Baton Rouge: Louisiana State University Press, 1989.

Bogue, Allan G. *The Congressman's Civil War*. New York: Cambridge University Press, 1989.

Boles, John B. *The Great Revival, 1787–1805: The Origins of the Southern Evangelical Mind*. Lexington: The University Press of Kentucky, 1972.

———. *Religion in Antebellum Kentucky*. Lexington: The University Press of Kentucky, 1976.

Boman, Dennis K. *Lincoln's Resolute Unionist: Hamilton Gamble*. Baton Rouge: Louisiana State University Press, 2006.

Bonham, Jeriah. *Fifty Years' Recollections: With Observations and Reflections on Historical Events, Giving Sketches on Eminent Citizens—Their Lives and Public Service*. Peoria, Ill.: J. W. Franks and Sons, 1883.

Boritt, Gabor S. *Lincoln and the Economics of the American Dream*. Memphis, Tenn.: Memphis State University Press, 1978.

———, ed. *The Lincoln Enigma: The Changing Faces of an American Icon*. New York: Oxford University Press, 2001.

———, ed. *Lincoln's Generals*. New York: Oxford University Press, 1994.

Bradley, Erwin Stanley. *Simon Cameron: Lincoln's Secretary of War*. Philadelphia: University of Pennsylvania Press, 1966.

Briggs, Harold E., and Ernestine B. Briggs. *Nancy Hanks Lincoln: A Frontier Portrait*. New York: Bookman Associates, 1952.

Brooks, Noah. *Lincoln Observed: Civil War Dispatches of Noah Brooks*. Edited by Michael Burlingame. Baltimore: Johns Hopkins University Press, 1998.

———. *Washington in Lincoln's Time*. New York: The Century Company, 1895.

Brown, Francis. *Raymond of the Times*. New York: W. W. Norton and Company, 1951.

Brown, William Burlie. *The People's Choice: The Presidential Image in the Campaign Biography*. Baton Rouge: Louisiana State University Press, 1960.

Browne, Francis F. *The Every-day Life of Abraham Lincoln: A Narrative and Descriptive Biography*. Chicago: Browne and Howell Company, 1913.

Bruce, Robert V. *Lincoln and the Tools of War*. Indianapolis: The Bobbs-Merrill Company, 1956.

Bryant, William Cullen. *Prose Writings of William Cullen Bryant,* vol. 2. Edited by Parke Godwin. New York: D. Appleton and Company, 1884.

Buchanan, James. *The Works of James Buchanan,* vol. 11. Edited by John Bassett Moore. Philadelphia: J. B. Lippincott Company, 1910.

Buley, R. Carlyle. *The Old Northwest: Pioneer Period 1815–1840*. Indianapolis: Indiana Historical Society, 1950.

Burns, Jeremiah. *The Patriot's Offering*. New York: Baker and Godwin, 1862.

Busey, Samuel C. *Personal Reminiscences and Recollections*. Washington, D.C. [Philadelphia: Dornan, printer], 1895.

Butler, Benjamin F. *Butler's Book*. Boston: A. M. Thayer, 1892.

Cadwallader, Sylvanus. *Three Years with Grant*. Edited by Benjamin P. Thomas. New York: Alfred A. Knopf, 1955.

Calhoun, John C. *The Papers of John C. Calhoun*. Edited by Clyde N. Wilson and Shirley Bright Cook. Columbia: University of South Carolina Press, 1959, 2003.

Carman, Harry J., and Reinhard H. Luthin. *Lincoln and the Patronage*. New York: Columbia University Press, 1943.

Carpenter, Francis Bicknell. *Six Months at the White House with Abraham Lincoln: The Story of a Picture*. New York: Hurd and Houghton, 1866.

Cartwright, Peter. *Autobiography of Peter Cartwright: The Backwoods Preacher*. Edited by W. P. Strickland. New York: Carlton and Porter, 1856.

Carwardine, Richard J. *Evangelicals and Politics in Antebellum America*. New Haven, Conn.: Yale University Press, 1993.

———. *Lincoln: A Life of Purpose and Power*. New York: Alfred A. Knopf, 2006.

Channing, Steven A. *Kentucky: A Bicentennial History*. New York: W. W. Norton and Company, 1977.

Charnwood, Lord. *Abraham Lincoln*. New York: Henry Holt and Company, 1917.

Chicago Bar Association. *Chicago Bar Association Lectures*. Chicago: Fergus Printing Company, 1882.

Clarke, James Freeman. *Anti-slavery Days: A Sketch of the Struggle Which Ended in the Abolition of Slavery in the United States*. New York: R. Worthington, 1884.

Cleaves, Freeman. *Meade of Gettysburg*. Norman: University of Oklahoma Press, 1960.

Clinton, Catherine. *Mrs. Lincoln: A Life*. New York: Harper, 2009.

Cole, Arthur Charles. *The Era of the Civil War, 1848–1870*. Chicago: A. C. McClurg and Company, 1922.

Coleman, Charles H. *Abraham Lincoln and Coles County, Illinois*. New Brunswick, N.J.: Scarecrow Press, 1955.

Colfax, Schuyler. *Life and Principles of Abraham Lincoln, Delivered in the Court House Square, at South Bend*. Philadelphia: James B. Rodgers, 1865.

The Collected Works of Abraham Lincoln. 9 vols. Edited by Roy P. Basler. New Brunswick, N.J.: Rutgers University Press, 1953–55; and *Supplement, 1832–1865*, 2 vols. Westport, Conn.: Greenwood Press, 1974.

Complete Works of Abraham Lincoln. 10 vols. Edited by John G. Nicolay and John Hay. New York: Francis D. Tandy Company, 1905.

Confidential Correspondence of Gustavus Vasa Fox. Edited by Robert Means Thompson and Richard Wainwright. Freeport, N.Y.: Books for Libraries Press, 1972.

Conkin, Paul. *Cane Ridge: America's Pentecost*. Madison: University of Wisconsin Press, 1991.

Conway, James. *America's Library: The Story of the Library of Congress, 1800–2000*. New Haven, Conn.: Yale University Press, 2000.

Cowley, Robert, ed. *With My Face to the Enemy: Perspectives on the Civil War*. New York: G. P. Putnam's Sons, 2001.

Current, Richard N. *Lincoln and the First Shot*. Philadelphia: Lippincott, 1963.

———. *The Lincoln Nobody Knows*. New York: Hill and Wang, 1958.

Curtis, George Ticknor. *Life of James Buchanan: Fifteenth President of the United States*. 2 vols. New York: Harper and Brothers, 1883.

Cuthbert, Norma B., ed. *Lincoln and the Baltimore Plot*. San Marino, Calif.: Huntington Library, 1949.

A Cycle of Adams Letters. 2 vols. Edited by Worthington Chauncey Ford. Boston: Houghton Mifflin Company, 1920.

Dahlgren, Madeleine Vinton. *Memoir of John A. Dahlgren*. Boston: James R. Osgood and Company, 1882.

Dana, Charles A. *Lincoln and His Cabinet*. Cleveland, Ohio: The De Vinne Press, 1896.

———. *Recollections of the Civil War*. New York: D. Appleton and Company, 1898.

Davis, James E. *Frontier Illinois*. Bloomington: Indiana University Press, 1998.

Davis, Martha W., and Cullom Benner, eds. *The Law Practice of Abraham Lincoln: Complete Documentary Edition*. Electronic resource, 3 vols. Urbana: University of Illinois Press, 2000.

Davis, William C. *Battle at Bull Run: A History of the First Major Campaign*. Garden City, N.Y.: Doubleday, 1977.

———. *First Blood: Fort Sumter to Bull Run*. Alexandria, Va.: Time-Life Books, 1983.

———. *Lincoln's Men: How President Lincoln Became Father to an Army and a Nation*. New York: The Free Press, 1999.

Dell, Christopher. *Lincoln and the War Democrats: The Grand Erosion of Conservative Tradition*. Rutherford, N.J.: Fairleigh Dickinson University Press, 1975.

Diary of Edward Bates, 1859–1866. Edited by Howard K. Beale. Washington, D.C.: United States Government Printing Office, 1933.

The Diary of George Templeton Strong, vol. 2, *1850–59,* and vol. 3, *1860–65*. Edited by Allan Nevins and Milton Halsey Thomas. New York: The Macmillan Company, 1952.

Diary of Gideon Welles, Secretary of the Navy Under Lincoln and Johnson. 3 vols. Edited by Howard K. Beale and Alan W. Brownsword. New York: W. W. Norton and Company, 1960.

Diary of Orville Hickman Browning, vol. 20. Edited by Theodore C. Pease and James G. Randall. Springfield: Illinois State Historical Society, 1925.

Dilworth, Thomas. *A New Guide to the English Tongue*. London: W. Osborne and T. Griffin, 1786.

Dixon, Archibald, Mrs. *The True Story of the Missouri Compromise and Its Repeal*. Cincinnati, Ohio: Robert Clarke and Company, 1899.

Donald, David Herbert. *Charles Sumner and the Rights of Man*. New York: Alfred A. Knopf, 1970.

———. *Lincoln*. New York: Simon and Schuster, 1995.

———. *Lincoln at Home: Two Glimpses of Abraham Lincoln's Family Life*. New York: Simon and Schuster, 2000.

———. *We Are Lincoln Men: Abraham Lincoln and His Friends*. New York: Simon and Schuster, 2004.

Douglas, Stephen A. *Letters*. Edited by Robert W. Johannsen. Urbana: University of Illinois Press, 1961.

Douglass, Frederick. *The Life and Writings of Frederick Douglass*. 5 vols. Edited by Philip S. Foner. New York: International Books, 1950, 1975.

Duff, John J. *A. Lincoln: Prairie Lawyer*. New York: Rinehart, 1960.

Earle, Jonathan. *Jackson Antislavery and the Politics of Free Soil, 1824–1854*. Chapel Hill: University of North Carolina Press, 2004.

Engle, Stephen Douglas. *Don Carlos Buell: Most Promising of All*. Chapel Hill: University of North Carolina Press, 1999.

Epstein, Daniel Mark. *Lincoln and Whitman: Parallel Lives in Civil War Washington*. New York: Random House, 2004.

————. *The Lincolns: Portrait of a Marriage*. New York: Ballantine Books, 2008.

Essah, Patience. *A House Divided: Slavery and Emancipation in Delaware, 1638–1865*. Charlottesville: University Press of Virginia, 1996.

Faragher, John Mack. *Daniel Boone: The Life and Legend of an American Pioneer*. New York: Henry Holt and Company, 1992.

————. *Sugar Creek, Life on the Illinois Prairie*. New Haven, Conn.: Yale University Press, 1986.

Farber, Daniel. *Lincoln's Constitution*. Chicago: University of Chicago Press, 2003.

Fehrenbacher, Don E. *Chicago Giant: A Biography of "Long John" Wentworth*. Madison, Wis.: American History Research Center, 1957.

————. *The Dred Scott Case: Its Significance in American Law and Politics*. New York: Oxford University Press, 1978.

————. *Prelude to Greatness: Lincoln in the 1850's*. Stanford, Calif.: Stanford University Press, 1962.

Fehrenbacher, Don E., and Virginia Fehrenbacher, eds. *Recollected Words of Abraham Lincoln*. Stanford, Calif.: Stanford University Press, 1962.

Fellman, Michael. *Inside War: The Guerrilla Conflict in Missouri During the American Civil War*. New York: Oxford University Press, 1989.

Fermer, Douglas. *James Gordon Bennett and the New York Herald: A Study of Editorial Opinion in the Civil War Era, 1854–1867*. New York: St. Martin's Press, 1986.

Fessenden, Francis. *Life and Public Services of William Pitt Fessenden*. 2 vols. Boston: Houghton, Mifflin and Company, 1907.

Field, Henry M. *The Life of David Dudley Field*. New York: Charles Scribner's Sons, 1898.

Fischer, David Hackett. *Albion's Seed: Four British Folkways in America*. New York: Oxford University Press, 1989.

Fisher, Sidney George. *A Philadelphia Perspective: The Civil War Diary of Sidney George Fisher*. Edited by Jonathan White. Bronx, N.Y.: Fordham University Press, 2007.

————. *The Trial of the Constitution*. Philadelphia: J. B. Lippincott and Company, 1862.

Fordham, Elias Pym. *Personal Narrative of Travels in Virginia, Maryland, Pennsylvania, Ohio, Indiana, Kentucky, and of a Residence in the Illinois Territory, 1817–1818*. Edited by Frederic Austin Ogg. Cleveland, Ohio: The Arthur H. Clark Company, 1906.

Forney, John W. *Anecdotes of Public Men,* vol. 2. New York: Harper and Brothers, 1881.

Frank, John Paul. *Lincoln as Lawyer*. Urbana: University of Illinois Press, 1961.

Fredrickson, George M. *The Inner Civil War: Northern Intellectuals and the Crisis of the Union*. New York: Harper and Row, 1965.

French, Benjamin Brown. *Witness to the Young Republic: A Yankee's Journal, 1828–1870*. Hanover, N.H.: University Press of New England, 1989.

Friedman, Lawrence M. *A History of American Law*. Revised edition. New York: Simon and Schuster, 2005.

Fritz, Karen E. *Voices in the Storm: Confederate Rhetoric, 1861–1865*. Denton: University of North Texas Press, 1999.

Furgurson, Ernest B. *Freedom Rising: Washington in the Civil War*. New York: Alfred A. Knopf, 2004.

Gallagher, Gary W., ed. *The Richmond Campaign of 1862: The Peninsular and the Seven Days*. Chapel Hill: University of North Carolina Press, 2000.

Gienapp, William E. *Abraham Lincoln and Civil War America*. New York: Oxford University Press, 2002.

———. *The Origins of the Republican Party, 1852–1856*. New York: Oxford University Press, 1987.

Glatthaar, Joseph T. *Partners in Command: The Relationships Between Leaders in the Civil War*. New York: The Free Press, 1994.

Goodwin, Doris Kearns. *Team of Rivals: The Political Genius of Abraham Lincoln*. New York: Simon and Schuster, 2005.

Gouverneur, Marian Campbell. *As I Remember: Recollections of American Society During the Nineteenth Century*. New York: D. Appleton and Company, 1911.

Graff, Harvey J. *Conflicting Paths: Growing Up in America*. Cambridge, Mass.: Harvard University Press, 1995.

Greeley, Horace. *Recollections of a Busy Life*. New York: J. B. Ford and Company, 1868.

Green, Constance McLaughlin. *Washington*. Princeton, N.J.: Princeton University Press, 1962.

Guelzo, Allen. *Abraham Lincoln: Redeemer President*. Grand Rapids, Mich.: W. B. Eerdmans, 1999.

———. *Lincoln and Douglas: The Debates That Defined America*. New York: Simon and Schuster, 2008.

———. *Lincoln's Emancipation Proclamation: The End of Slavery in America*. New York: Simon and Schuster, 2004.

Halstead, Murat. *Caucuses of 1860: A History of National Political Conventions*. Columbus, Ohio: Follett, Foster and Company, 1860.

Hamlin, Charles Eugene. *The Life and Times of Hannibal Hamlin*. Cambridge, Mass.: Riverside Press, 1899.

Harkness, David J., and Gerald R. McMurtry. *Lincoln's Favorite Poets*. Knoxville: University of Tennessee Press, 1959.

Harper, Robert S. *Lincoln and the Press*. New York: McGraw-Hill, 1951.

Harris, William C. *Lincoln's Last Months*. Cambridge, Mass.: Harvard University Press, 2004.

———. *Lincoln's Rise to the Presidency*. Lawrence: University Press of Kansas, 2007.

Harrison, Lowell H. *The Civil War in Kentucky*. Lexington: The University Press of Kentucky, 1975.

———. *Lincoln of Kentucky*. Lexington: The University Press of Kentucky, 2000.

Harrison, Lowell H., and James C. Klotter. *A New History of Kentucky*. Lexington: The University Press of Kentucky, 1997.

Howe, Daniel Walker, ed. *Victorian America*. Philadelphia: University of Pennsylvania Press, 1976.

Hay, John. *Inside Lincoln's White House: The Complete Civil War Diary of John Hay*. Edited by Michael Burlingame and John R. Turner Ettlinger. Carbondale: Southern Illinois University Press, 1997.

———. *Lincoln and the Civil War in the Diaries and Letters of John Hay*. Edited by Tyler Dennett. New York: Dodd, Mead and Company, 1939.

———. *Lincoln's Journalist: John Hay's Anonymous Writings for the Press, 1860–1864*. Edited by Michael Burlingame. Carbondale: Southern Illinois University Press, 1998.

Hebert, Walker H. *Fighting Joe Hooker.* Indianapolis: The Bobbs-Merrill Company, 1944.

Helm, Katharine. *The True Story of Mary, Wife of Lincoln.* New York: Harper, 1928.

Hendrick, Burton Jesse. *Lincoln's War Cabinet.* Boston: Little, Brown and Company, 1946.

Herndon, William H., and Jesse W. Weik. *Herndon's Lincoln: The True Story of a Great Life.* 3 vols. Edited by Douglas L. Wilson and Rodney O. Davis. Urbana: University of Illinois Press, 2006.

Herr, Pamela. *Jessie Benton Frémont.* New York: Franklin Watts, 1987.

Hertz, Emanuel. *Abraham Lincoln: A New Portrait.* 2 vols. New York: H. Liveright, 1931.

Hesseltine, William Best. *Lincoln and the War Governors.* New York: Alfred A. Knopf, 1948.

Hofstra, Warren R. *The Planting of New Virginia: Settlement and Landscape in the Shenandoah Valley.* Baltimore: The Johns Hopkins University Press, 2004.

Holt, Michael. *The Rise and Fall of the American Whig Party: Jacksonian Politics and the Onset of the Civil War.* New York: Oxford University Press, 1999.

Holzer, Harold, ed. *The Lincoln-Douglas Debates: The First Complete Unexpurgated Text.* New York: HarperCollins, 1993.

Horan, James D. *Mathew Brady: Historian with a Camera.* New York: Crown Publishers, 1955.

Howard, James Quay. *The Life of Abraham Lincoln.* Columbus, Ohio: Follett, Foster and Company, 1860.

Howard, Robert P. *Illinois: A History of the Prairie State.* Grand Rapids, Mich.: W. B. Eerdmans, 1972.

Howe, Daniel Walker. *Making the American Self: Jonathan Edwards to Abraham Lincoln.* Cambridge, Mass.: Harvard University Press, 1997.

———. *The Political Culture of the American Whigs.* Chicago: University of Chicago Press, 1979.

———. *What Hath God Wrought: The Transformation of America, 1815–1848.* New York: Oxford University Press, 2007.

Howells, William Dean. *Life of Abraham Lincoln.* Springfield, Ill.: The Abraham Lincoln Association, 1938.

Hyman, Harold M. *American Singularity: The 1787 Northwest Ordinance, the 1862 Homestead and Morrill Acts, and the 1944 G.I. Bill.* Athens: University of Georgia Press, 1986.

———. *A More Perfect Union: The Impact of the Civil War and Reconstruction on the Constitution.* New York: Alfred A. Knopf, 1973.

Inside Lincoln's Cabinet: The Civil War Diaries of Salmon P. Chase. Edited by David Donald. New York: Longmans, Green and Company, 1954.

Jaffa, Harry V. *Crisis of the House Divided: An Interpretation of the Lincoln-Douglas Debates.* Seattle: University of Washington Press, 1959.

Jaffa, Harry V., and Robert W. Johannsen, eds. *In the Name of the People: Speeches and Writings of Lincoln and Douglas in the Ohio Campaign of 1859.* Columbus: Ohio State University Press, 1959.

Johannsen, Robert W. *The Frontier, the Union, and Stephen A. Douglas.* Urbana: University of Illinois Press, 1989.

————. *Stephen A. Douglas*. Urbana: University of Illinois Press, 1973.

Johnson, Robert Underwood, and Clarence Clough Buel, eds. *Battles and Leaders of the Civil War: Being for the Most Part Contributions by Union and Confederate Officers*. 4 vols. New York: The Century Company, 1887–88.

Kincaid, Robert L. *Joshua Fry Speed: Lincoln's Most Intimate Friend*. Harrogate, Tenn.: Lincoln Memorial University, 1943.

Kinsley, Philip. *The Chicago Tribune: Its First Hundred Years*, vol. 1, *1847–1865*. New York: Alfred A. Knopf, 1943.

Kirkham, Samuel. *English Grammar in Familiar Lectures*. Rochester, N.Y.: Marshal and Dan, 1829.

Kirwan, Albert Dennis. *John J. Crittenden: The Struggle for the Union*. Lexington: University of Kentucky Press, 1962.

Klein, Philip Shriver. *President James Buchanan: A Biography*. University Park: Pennsylvania State University Press, 1962.

Klement, Frank L. *The Limits of Dissent: Clement L. Vallandigham and the Civil War*. Lexington: University of Kentucky Press, 1970.

Korn, Bertram Wallace. *American Jewry and the Civil War*. Philadelphia: Jewish Publication Society of America, 1951.

Kreidberg, Marvin A., and Merton G. Henry. *History of Military Mobilization in the United States Army, 1775–1945*. Westport, Conn.: Greenwood Press, 1975.

Lamers, William M. *The Edge of Glory: A Biography of William S. Rosecrans*. New York: Harcourt, Brace, 1961.

Lamon, Ward Hill. *The Life of Abraham Lincoln*. Boston: James R. Osgood and Company, 1872.

————. *Recollections of Abraham Lincoln, 1847–1865*. Chicago: A. C. McClurg and Company, 1895.

Lanman, Charles. *Haphazard Personalities Chiefly of Noted Americans*. Boston: Lee and Shepard, 1886.

Leech, Margaret. *Reveille in Washington, 1860–1865*. New York: Harper and Brothers, 1941.

Levine, Bruce. *Half-Slave and Half Free: The Roots of the Civil War*. New York: Hill and Wang, 1992.

Lincoln, Abraham. *The Letters of President Lincoln on Questions of National Policy*. New York: H. H. Lloyd and Company, 1863.

Lincoln, Waldo. *History of the Lincoln Family: An Account of the Descendents of Samuel Lincoln of Hingham, Massachusetts, 1637–1920*. Worcester, Mass.: Commonwealth Press, 1923.

Lincoln on the Eve of '61: A Journalist's Story by Henry Villard. New York: Alfred A. Knopf, 1941.

Linder, Usher F. *Reminiscences of the Early Bench and Bar in Illinois*. Chicago: Chicago Legal News Company, 1879.

Luthin, Reinhard H. *The First Lincoln Campaign*. Gloucester, Mass.: P. Smith, 1944.

————. *Lincoln and Patronage*. New York: Columbia University Press, 1943.

————. *The Real Abraham Lincoln*. Englewood Cliffs, N.J.: Prentice-Hall, 1960.

Lystra, Karen. *Searching the Heart: Women, Men, and Romantic Love in Nineteenth-Century America*. New York: Oxford University Press, 1989.

Magdol, Edward. *Owen Lovejoy: Abolitionist in Congress.* New Brunswick, N.J.: Rutgers University Press, 1967.

Manakee, Harold R. *Maryland in the Civil War.* Baltimore: Maryland Historical Society, 1961.

Marvel, William. *Burnside.* Chapel Hill: University of North Carolina Press, 1991.

Masters, Frank Mariro. *A History of Baptists in Kentucky.* Louisville: Kentucky Baptist Historical Society, 1953.

Mazrim, Robert. *Magnificent Storehouses and Forgotten Lot Lines: New Light on Lincoln and Shopkeeping at New Salem.* Elkhart, Ill.: Sangamo Archaeological Center, 2005.

McClellan, George Brinton. *McClellan's Own Story: The War for the Union, the Soldiers Who Fought It, the Civilians Who Directed It, and His Relations to Them.* New York: Charles L. Webster and Company, 1887.

McFeely, William S. *Frederick Douglass.* New York: W. W. Norton and Company, 1991.

McLoughlin, William Gerald. *The Meaning of Henry Ward Beecher.* New York: Alfred A. Knopf, 1970.

McMurtry, R. Gerald. *The Lincoln Migration from Kentucky to Indiana, 1816.* Fort Wayne, Ind.: Lincolniana Publishers, 1938.

———. *A Series of Monographs Concerning the Lincolns and Hardin County, Kentucky.* Elizabethtown, Ky.: Enterprise Press, 1938.

McPherson, James M. *Abraham Lincoln and the Second American Revolution.* New York: Oxford University Press, 1990.

———. *Battle Cry of Freedom: The Civil War Era.* New York: Oxford University Press, 1988.

———. *Crossroads of Freedom: Antietam.* New York: Oxford University Press, 2002.

———. *Drawn with the Sword: Reflections on the American Civil War.* New York: Oxford University Press, 1996.

———. *For Cause and Comrades: Why Men Fought in the Civil War.* New York: Oxford University Press, 1997.

———. *The Negro's Civil War.* New York: Pantheon Books, 1965.

———. *The Struggle for Equality: Abolitionists and the Negro in the Civil War and Reconstruction.* Princeton, N.J.: Princeton University Press, 1964.

———. *Tried by War: Abraham Lincoln as Commander in Chief.* New York: Penguin Press, 2008.

———, ed. *"We Cannot Escape History": Lincoln and the Last Best Hope of Earth.* Urbana: University of Illinois Press, 1995.

Meredith, Roy. *Mr. Lincoln's Camera Man, Mathew B. Brady.* New York: Dover Publications, 1946.

Miers, Early Schenk, ed., *Lincoln Day by Day.* 3 vols. Washington, D.C.: Lincoln Sesquicentennial Commission, 1960.

Miller, Perry, ed. *The Legal Mind in America: From Independence to the Civil War.* Garden City, N.Y.: Doubleday, 1962.

Milton, George Fort. *Abraham Lincoln and the Fifth Column.* New York: Vanguard Press, 1942.

Mitchell, Robert D. *Commercialism and Frontier: Perspectives on the Early Shenandoah Valley*. Charlottesville: University Press of Virginia, 1977.

Mitgang, Herbert. *Abraham Lincoln: A Press Portrait*. New York: Fordham University Press, 2000.

Monkman, Betty C. *The White House: Its Historic Furnishings and First Families*. New York: Abbeville Press, 2000.

Morehouse, Frances, M. *The Life of Jesse W. Fell*. Urbana: University of Illinois Press, 1916.

Myers, James E. *The Astonishing Saber Duel of Abraham Lincoln*. Springfield, Ill.: Lincoln-Herndon Building Publishers, 1968.

Neely, Mark E., Jr. *The Abraham Lincoln Encyclopedia*. New York: McGraw-Hill, 1982.

———. *The Fate of Liberty: Abraham Lincoln and Civil Liberties*. New York: Oxford University Press, 1991.

———. *The Last Best Hope of Earth: Abraham Lincoln and the Promise of America*. Cambridge, Mass.: Harvard University Press, 1995.

———. *The Union Divided: Party Conflict in the Civil War North*. Cambridge, Mass.: Harvard University Press, 2002.

Nevins, Allan. *American Press Opinion, Washington to Coolidge: A Documentary Record of Editorial Leadership and Criticism*. Boston: D. C. Heath, 1928.

———. *The Emergence of Lincoln*. New York: Scribner, 1950.

———. *Frémont, Pathmarker of the West*. New York: D. Appleton-Century, 1939.

———. *Ordeal of the Union*. 2 vols. New York: Scribner, 1947.

———. *The War for the Union*. New York: Scribner, 1959–71.

Newton, Joseph Fort. *Lincoln and Herndon*. Cedar Rapids, Iowa: The Torch Press, 1910.

Nichols, David A. *Lincoln and the Indians: Civil War Policy and Politics*. Columbia: University of Missouri Press, 1978.

Nichols, Roger L. *Black Hawk and the Warrior's Path*. Arlington Heights, Ill.: Harlan Davidson, 1992.

Nicolay, John. *An Oral History of Abraham Lincoln: John Nicolay's Interviews and Essays*. Edited by Michael Burlingame. Carbondale: Southern Illinois University Press, 1996.

Niven, John. *Gideon Welles: Lincoln's Secretary of the Navy*. New York: Oxford University Press, 1973.

———. *John C. Calhoun and the Price of Union*. Baton Rouge: Louisiana State University Press, 1988.

———. *Salmon P. Chase: A Biography*. New York: Oxford University Press, 1995.

Oakes, James. *The Radical and the Republican: Frederick Douglass, Abraham Lincoln, and the Triumph of Antislavery Politics*. New York: W. W. Norton and Company, 2007.

Oates, Stephen B. *With Malice Toward None: A Life of Abraham Lincoln*. New York: Harper and Row, 1977.

Official Records of the Union and Confederate Armies. 128 vols. Washington D.C.: Government Printing Office, 1880–1901.

Parrish, William E. *Turbulent Partnership: Missouri and the Union, 1861–1865*. Columbia: University of Missouri Press, 1963.

Peterson, Merrill D. *The Great Triumvirate: Webster, Clay, and Calhoun*. New York: Oxford University Press, 1987.

————. *Lincoln in American Memory,* New York: Oxford University Press, 1994.

Plummer, Mark A. *Lincoln's Rail-Splitter: Governor Richard J. Oglesby.* Urbana: University of Illinois Press, 2001.

Political Debates Between Hon. Abraham Lincoln and Hon. Stephen A. Douglas, in the Celebrated Campaign of 1858. Columbus, Ohio: Follett, Foster and Company, 1860.

Poore, Benjamin Perley. *Perley's Reminiscences of Sixty Years in the National Metropolis.* Philadelphia: Hubbard Brothers, 1886.

Posey, Walter Brownlow. *Frontier Mission: A History of Religion West of the Southern Appalachians to 1861.* Lexington: The University Press of Kentucky, 1966.

Potter, David M. *The Impending Crisis, 1848–1861.* Edited by Don E. Fehrenbacher. New York: Harper and Row, 1976.

————. *Lincoln and His Party in the Secession Crisis.* New Haven, Conn.: Yale University Press, 1942.

Pratt, Harry E. *Dr. Anson G. Henry: Lincoln's Physician and Friend.* Harrogate, Tenn.: Lincoln Memorial University, 1944.

————. *The Great Debates of 1858.* Springfield: Illinois State Historical Library, 1955.

————. *Lincoln 1809–1839.* Springfield, Ill.: The Abraham Lincoln Association, 1941.

————. *The Personal Finances of Abraham Lincoln.* Springfield, Ill.: The Abraham Lincoln Association, 1943.

Proceedings of the First Three Republican National Conventions of 1856, 1860, and 1864. Minneapolis, Minn.: Charles W. Johnson, 1893.

Rafuse, Ethan S. *McClellan's War: The Failure of Moderation in the Struggle for the Union.* Bloomington: Indiana University Press, 2005.

Randall, James Garfield. *Lincoln, The President.* 3 vols. New York: Dodd, Mead and Company, 1945–55.

Randall, Ruth Painter. *Colonel Elmer Ellsworth: A Biography of Lincoln's Friend and First Hero of the Civil War.* Boston: Little, Brown and Company, 1960.

————. *I Jessie.* Boston: Little, Brown and Company, 1963.

————. *Lincoln's Sons.* Boston: Little, Brown and Company, 1956.

————. *Mary Lincoln: Biography of a Marriage.* Boston: Little, Brown and Company, 1953.

Raymond, Henry J. *The Life and Public Services of Abraham Lincoln.* New York: Derby and Miller, 1865.

Remini, Robert V. *Henry Clay: Statesman for the Union.* New York: W. W. Norton and Company, 1991.

————. *The House: The History of the House of Representatives.* New York: HarperCollins, 2006.

Rice, Allen T., ed. *Reminiscences of Abraham Lincoln by Distinguished Men of His Time.* New York: North American Publishing Company, 1886.

Rice, Otis K. *Frontier Kentucky.* Lexington: The University Press of Kentucky, 1975.

Riddle, Donald W. *Lincoln Runs for Congress.* New Brunswick, N.J.: Rutgers University Press, 1948.

Robertson, George. *Scrap Book on Law and Politics, Men and Times.* Lexington, Ky.: A. W. Elder, 1855.

Robertson, James I., Jr. *Stonewall Jackson: The Man, the Soldier, the Legend.* New York: The Macmillan Company, 1997.

Ross, Frederick A. *Slavery Ordained of God*. Philadelphia: J. B. Lippincott and Company, 1857.

Russell, A. P. *Thomas Corwin*. Cincinnati, Ohio: Robert Clarke and Company, 1882.

Russell, William H. *My Diary, North and South*. Edited by Eugene H. Berwanger. New York: Alfred A. Knopf, 1988.

Schott, Thomas Edwin. *Alexander H. Stephens of Georgia: A Biography*. Baton Rouge: Louisiana State University Press, 1988.

Schurz, Carl. *Abraham Lincoln: A Biographical Essay*. Boston: Houghton, Mifflin and Company, 1907.

———. *The Reminiscences of Carl Schurz*. New York: The McClure Company, 1907–8.

Scripps, John Locke. *Life of Abraham Lincoln*. Edited by Roy P. Basler and Lloyd A. Dunlap. Bloomington: Indiana University Press, 1961.

Seale, William. *The White House: The History of an American Idea*. Washington, D.C.: American Institute of Architects Press, 1992.

Sealsfield, Charles. *The Americans As They Are: Described in a Tour Through the Valley of Mississippi*. London: Hurst, Chance, and Company, 1828.

Sears, Stephen W., ed. *The Civil War Papers of George B. McClellan*. New York: Ticknor and Fields, 1989.

———. *George B. McClellan: The Young Napoleon*. New York: Ticknor and Fields, 1988.

———. *Gettysburg*. Boston: Houghton Mifflin Company, 2003.

———. *Landscape Turned Red: The Battle of Antietam*. New York: Ticknor and Fields, 1983.

———. *To the Gates of Richmond: The Peninsula Campaign*. New York: Ticknor and Fields, 1992.

Sellers, Charles. *The Market Revolution: Jacksonian America, 1815–1846*. New York: Oxford University Press, 1991.

Seward, William H. *An Autobiography from 1801 to 1834*. Edited by Frederick W. Seward. New York: Derby and Miller, 1891.

———. *The Works of William H. Seward*. 5 vols. Edited by George E. Baker. Boston: Houghton, Mifflin and Company, 1884.

Shannon, Fred A. *The Organization and Administration of the Union Army, 1861–1865*. Cleveland, Ohio: The Arthur H. Clark Company, 1928.

Sheahan, James W. *The Life of Stephen A. Douglas*. New York: Harper and Brothers, 1860.

Silbey, Joel H. *A Respectable Minority: The Democratic Party in the Civil War Era, 1860–1869*. New York: W. W. Norton and Company, 1977.

Simon, John Y. *House Divided: Lincoln and His Father*. Fort Wayne, Ind.: Lincoln Library and Museum, 1987.

Simon, John Y., et al. *Papers of Ulysses S. Grant*. 28 vols. Carbondale: Southern Illinois University Press, 1967–.

Simon, Paul. *Freedom's Champion: Elijah Lovejoy*. Carbondale: Southern Illinois University Press, 1994.

———. *Lincoln's Preparation for Greatness: The Illinois Legislative Years*. Urbana: University of Illinois Press, 1971.

Smiley, David L. *Lion of White Hall: The Life of Cassius M. Clay*. Madison: University of Wisconsin Press, 1962.

Smith, William E. *The Francis Preston Blair Family in Politics*. 2 vols. New York: The Macmillan Company, 1933.

Speed, Joshua F. *Reminiscences of Abraham Lincoln and Notes of a Visit to California: Two Lectures*. Louisville, Ky: John P. Morton and Company, 1884.

Spiegel, Allen D. *A. Lincoln, Esquire: A Shrewd, Sophisticated Lawyer in His Time*. Macon, Ga.: Mercer University Press, 2002.

Stampp, Kenneth M. *And the War Came: The North and the Secession Crisis, 1860–1861*. Baton Rouge: Louisiana State University Press, 1950.

Starr, John W. *Lincoln and the Railroads: A Biographical Study*. New York: Dodd, Mead and Company, 1927.

Steiner, Mark E. *An Honest Calling: The Law Practice of Abraham Lincoln*. Dekalb: Northern Illinois University Press, 2006.

Stewart, James Brewer. *Joshua R. Giddings and the Tactics of Radical Politics*. Cleveland, Ohio: Press of Case Western Reserve University, 1970.

———. *Wendell Phillips: Liberty's Hero*. Baton Rouge: Louisiana State University Press, 1986.

Stoddard, William O. *Abraham Lincoln: The True Story of a Great Life*. New York: Fords, Howard, and Hulbert, 1884.

———. *Dispatches from Lincoln's White House: The Anonymous Civil War Journalism of Presidential Secretary William O. Stoddard*. Edited by Michael Burlingame. Lincoln: University of Nebraska Press, 2002.

———. *Inside the White House in War Times: Memoirs and Reports of Lincoln's Secretary*. Edited by Michael Burlingame. Lincoln: University of Nebraska Press, 2000.

———. *Lincoln's Third Secretary: The Memoirs of William O. Stoddard*. Edited by William O. Stoddard, Jr. New York: Exposition Press, 1955.

Stowell, Daniel W., ed. *The Papers of Abraham Lincoln: Legal Documents and Cases*. 4 vols. Charlottesville: University of Virginia Press, 2008.

Striner, Richard. *Father Abraham: Lincoln's Relentless Struggle to End Slavery*. New York: Oxford University Press, 2006.

Strozier, Charles B. *Lincoln's Quest for Union: Public and Private Meanings*. New York: Basic Books, 1982.

Sturtevant, Julian M. *Julian M. Sturtevant: An Autobiography*. Edited by J. M. Sturtevant, Jr. New York: Fleming H. Revell Company, 1896.

———. *Three Months in Great Britain: A Lecture on the Present Attitude of England Towards the United States*. Chicago: John A. Norton, 1864.

Sumner, Charles. *Memoir and Letters of Charles Sumner*. 4 vols. Edited by Edward L. Pierce. Boston: Roberts Brothers, 1877–93.

———. *The Selected Letters of Charles Sumner*, vol. 2. Edited by Beverly Wilson Palmer. Boston: Northeastern University Press, 1990.

Swinton, William. *Campaigns of the Army of the Potomac*. New York: C. B. Richardson, 1866.

Tap, Bruce. *Over Lincoln's Shoulder: The Committee on the Conduct of the War*. Lawrence: University of Kansas Press, 1998.

Tarbell, Ida M. *The Early Life of Abraham Lincoln*. New York: S. S. McClure, 1896.

————. *In the Footsteps of the Lincolns*. New York: Harper and Brothers, 1924.

————. *The Life of Abraham Lincoln*. 2 vols. New York: S. S. McClure, 1895.

Taylor, George Rogers. *The Transportation Revolution, 1815–1860*. New York: Rinehart, 1951.

Taylor, John M. *William Henry Seward: Lincoln's Right Hand*. New York: Harper-Collins, 1991.

Temple, Wayne C. *Abraham Lincoln: From Skeptic to Prophet*. Mahomet, Ill.: Mayhaven Publishing, 1995.

————. *By Square and Compasses: The Building of Lincoln's Home and Its Saga*. Bloomington, Ill.: Ashlar Press, 1984.

————. *Lincoln's Connections with the Illinois and Michigan Canal, His Return from Congress in '48, and His Invention*. Springfield: Illinois Bell, 1986.

Thomas, Benjamin P. *Abraham Lincoln: A Biography*. New York: Alfred A. Knopf, 1952.

————. *Lincoln's New Salem*. Springfield, Ill.: The Abraham Lincoln Association, 1934.

Thomas, Benjamin P., and Harold M. Hyman. *Stanton: The Life and Times of Lincoln's Secretary of War*. New York: Alfred A. Knopf, 1962.

Thomas, Emory M. *Robert E. Lee: A Biography*. New York: W. W. Norton and Company, 1995.

Toqueville, Alexis de. *Democracy in America*. Edited by Harvey C. Mansfield and Delba Winthrop. Chicago: University of Chicago Press, 2000.

Townsend, William H. *Lincoln and His Wife's Home Town*. Indianapolis: The Bobbs-Merrill Company, 1929.

————. *Lincoln and the Bluegrass: Slavery and the Civil War in Kentucky*. Lexington: University of Kentucky Press, 1955.

Trefousse, Hans Louis. *Benjamin Franklin Wade: Radical Republican from Ohio*. New York: Twayne Publishers, 1963.

————. *First Among Equals: Abraham Lincoln's Reputation During His Administration*. New York: Fordham University Press, 2005.

————. *The Radical Republicans: Lincoln's Vanguard for Racial Justice*. New York: Alfred A. Knopf, 1969.

Tripp, C. A. *The Intimate World of Abraham Lincoln*. New York: The Free Press, 2005.

Trollope, Frances Milton. *Domestic Manners of the Americans*. New York: Whittaker, Treacher, and Company 1832.

Turner, Justin G., and Linda Levitt Turner. *Mary Todd Lincoln: Her Life and Letters*. New York: Alfred A. Knopf, 1972.

Vallandigham, Clement L. *The Great Civil War in America*. New York: J. Walter, 1864.

Van Deusen, Glyndon G. *Horace Greeley: Nineteenth-Century Crusader*. Philadelphia: University of Pennsylvania Press, 1953.

————. *Thurlow Weed: Wizard of the Lobby*. Boston: Little, Brown and Company, 1947.

————. *William Henry Seward*. New York: Oxford University Press, 1967.

Walsh, John Evangelist. *The Shadows Rise: Abraham Lincoln and the Ann Rutledge Legend*. Urbana: University of Illinois Press, 1993.

Walters, Ronald G. *American Reformers 1815–1860*. New York: Hill and Wang, 1978.

Walt Whitman: The Correspondence, vol. 1, *1842–1867.* Edited by Edwin Haviland Miller. New York: New York University Press, 1961.

Ward, Geoffrey C. *Lincoln and the Right to Rise.* Springfield, Ill.: Sangamon State University, 1978.

Warren, Louis A. *Lincoln's Parentage and Childhood: A History of the Kentucky Lincolns Supported by Documentary Evidence.* New York: The Century Company, 1926.

———. *Lincoln's Youth: Indiana Years Seven to Twenty-One, 1816–1830.* Indianapolis: Indiana Historical Society, 1959.

Washington During the Civil War: The Diary of Horatio Nelson Taft, vol. 1, *1861–1865.* Washington, D.C.: Library of Congress, Manuscript Division.

Waugh, John. *One Man Great Enough.* New York: Harcourt, 2007.

———. *Reelecting Lincoln: The Battle for the 1864 Presidency.* New York: Crown Publishers, 1997.

Wayland, John W. *The Lincolns in Virginia.* Staunton, Va.: McClure Printing Company, 1946.

Weed, Thurlow. *Life of Thurlow Weed: Including His Autobiography and a Memoir.* 2 vols. Boston: Houghton Mifflin Company, 1883–84.

Weigley, Russell Frank. *Quartermaster General of the Union Army: A Biography of M. C. Meigs.* New York: Columbia University Press, 1959.

Weik, Jesse W. *The Real Lincoln: A Portrait.* Boston: Houghton Mifflin Company, 1922.

Welles, Gideon. *Diary of Gideon Welles,* vol. 1, *1861–March 1864.* Boston: Houghton Mifflin Company, 1911.

White, Horace. *The Life of Lyman Trumbull.* Boston: Houghton Mifflin Company, 1913.

Whitney, Ellen M., ed. *The Black Hawk War, 1831–1832.* 2 vols. Springfield: Illinois State Historical Library, 1970, 1973.

Whitney, Henry C. *Life on the Circuit with Lincoln.* Boston: Estes and Lauriat, 1892.

———. *The Slavery Atmosphere of Lincoln's Youth.* Fort Wayne, Ind.: Lincolniana Publishers, 1933.

Williams, T. Harry. *Lincoln and His Generals.* New York: Alfred A. Knopf, 1952.

———. *Lincoln and the Radicals.* Madison: University of Wisconsin Press, 1941.

Wilson, Douglas L. *Honor's Voice: The Transformation of Abraham Lincoln.* New York: Alfred A. Knopf, 1998.

———. *Lincoln Before Washington: New Perspectives on the Illinois Years.* Urbana: University of Illinois Press, 1997.

———. *Lincoln's Sword: The Presidency and the Power of Words.* New York: Alfred A. Knopf, 2006.

Wilson, Douglas L., and Rodney O. Davis, eds. *Herndon's Informants: Letters, Interviews, and Statements about Abraham Lincoln.* Urbana: University of Illinois Press, 1998.

Wilson, Edmund. *Patriotic Gore: Studies in the Literature of the Civil War.* New York: Oxford University Press, 1962.

Wilson, Rufus Rockwell. *Intimate Memories of Lincoln.* Elmira, N.Y.: Primavera Press, 1945.

Winkle, Kenneth J. *The Young Eagle: The Rise of Abraham Lincoln.* Dallas: Taylor Trade Publishing, 2001.

Wish, Harvey. *George Fitzhugh: Propagandist of the Old South*. Baton Rouge: Louisiana State University Press, 1943.

Woldman, Albert A. *Lawyer Lincoln*. Boston: Houghton Mifflin Company, 1936.

Villard, Henry. *Memoirs of Henry Villard: Journalist and Financier 1835–1900*. 2 vols. Boston: Houghton Mifflin Company, 1904.

Yates, Richard, and Catharine Yates Pickering. *Richard Yates: Civil War Governor*. Danville, Ill.: Interstate Printers and Publishers, [1966].

Zarefsky, David. *Lincoln Douglas and Slavery: In the Crucible of Debate*. Chicago: University of Chicago Press, 1990.

Zornow, William Frank. *Lincoln and the Party Divided*. Norman: University of Oklahoma Press, 1954.

Illustration Credits

138   LIBRARY OF CONGRESS, PRINTS AND PHOTOGRAPHS DIVISION, WASHINGTON, D.C.

141   LIBRARY OF CONGRESS, PRINTS AND PHOTOGRAPHS DIVISION, WASHINGTON, D.C.

144   LIBRARY OF CONGRESS, PRINTS AND PHOTOGRAPHS DIVISION, WASHINGTON, D.C.

145   NATIONAL ARCHIVES AND RECORDS ADMINISTRATION, STILL PICTURE DIVISION, COLLEGE PARK, MARYLAND

146   LIBRARY OF CONGRESS, PRINTS AND PHOTOGRAPHS DIVISION, WASHINGTON, D.C.

151   NATIONAL ARCHIVES AND RECORDS ADMINISTRATION

156   LIBRARY OF CONGRESS, PRINTS AND PHOTOGRAPHS DIVISION, WASHINGTON, D.C.

162   U.S. PATENT OFFICE

170   LIBRARY OF CONGRESS, PRINTS AND PHOTOGRAPHS DIVISION, WASHINGTON, D.C.

173   LIBRARY OF CONGRESS, PRINTS AND PHOTOGRAPHS DIVISION, WASHINGTON, D.C.

186   LIBRARY OF CONGRESS, PRINTS AND PHOTOGRAPHS DIVISION, WASHINGTON, D.C.

191   LIBRARY OF CONGRESS, PRINTS AND PHOTOGRAPHS DIVISION, WASHINGTON, D.C.

193   LIBRARY OF CONGRESS, PRINTS AND PHOTOGRAPHS DIVISION, WASHINGTON, D.C.

206   NATIONAL ARCHIVES AND RECORDS ADMINISTRATION, STILL PICTURE DIVISION, COLLEGE PARK, MARYLAND

219   LIBRARY OF CONGRESS, PRINTS AND PHOTOGRAPHS DIVISION, WASHINGTON, D.C.

222   LIBRARY OF CONGRESS, PRINTS AND PHOTOGRAPHS DIVISION, WASHINGTON, D.C.

225   LIBRARY OF CONGRESS, PRINTS AND PHOTOGRAPHS DIVISION, WASHINGTON, D.C., AND HERITAGE AUCTION GALLERIES, DALLAS, TEXAS

233   LIBRARY OF CONGRESS, PRINTS AND PHOTOGRAPHS DIVISION, WASHINGTON, D.C.

235   LIBRARY OF CONGRESS, PRINTS AND PHOTOGRAPHS DIVISION, WASHINGTON, D.C.

237   LIBRARY OF CONGRESS, PRINTS AND PHOTOGRAPHS DIVISION, WASHINGTON, D.C.

244   FROM THE COLLECTION OF LINCOLN FINANCIAL FOUNDATION

256   LIBRARY OF CONGRESS, PRINTS AND PHOTOGRAPHS DIVISION, WASHINGTON, D.C.

259   NATIONAL ARCHIVES AND RECORDS ADMINISTRATION, STILL PICTURE DIVISION, COLLEGE PARK, MARYLAND

263   KAREN NEEDLES, LINCOLNARCHIVES DIGITAL PROJECT, COLLEGE PARK, MARYLAND

267   LIBRARY OF CONGRESS, RARE BOOK DIVISION, WASHINGTON, D.C.

282   LIBRARY OF CONGRESS, PRINTS AND PHOTOGRAPHS DIVISION, WASHINGTON, D.C.

290   LIBRARY OF CONGRESS, PRINTS AND PHOTOGRAPHS DIVISION, WASHINGTON, D.C.

298   NATIONAL ARCHIVES AND RECORDS ADMINISTRATION, STILL PICTURE DIVISION, COLLEGE PARK, MARYLAND

310   LIBRARY OF CONGRESS, PRINTS AND PHOTOGRAPHS DIVISION, WASHINGTON, D.C.

315   LIBRARY OF CONGRESS, PRINTS AND PHOTOGRAPHS DIVISION, WASHINGTON, D.C.

321   LIBRARY OF CONGRESS, PRINTS AND PHOTOGRAPHS DIVISION, WASHINGTON, D.C.

323   LIBRARY OF CONGRESS, PRINTS AND PHOTOGRAPHS DIVISION, WASHINGTON, D.C.

327   NATIONAL ARCHIVES AND RECORDS ADMINISTRATION, STILL PICTURE DIVISION, COLLEGE PARK, MARYLAND

330   LIBRARY OF CONGRESS, PRINTS AND PHOTOGRAPHS DIVISION, WASHINGTON, D.C.

334   HERITAGE AUCTION GALLERIES, DALLAS, TEXAS

335   HERITAGE AUCTION GALLERIES, DALLAS, TEXAS

336 HERITAGE AUCTION GALLERIES, DALLAS, TEXAS

337 LIBRARY OF CONGRESS, PRINTS AND PHOTOGRAPHS DIVISION, WASHINGTON, D.C.

339 HERITAGE AUCTION GALLERIES, DALLAS, TEXAS

348 LIBRARY OF CONGRESS, PRINTS AND PHOTOGRAPHS DIVISION, WASHINGTON, D.C.

354 LIBRARY OF CONGRESS, PRINTS AND PHOTOGRAPHS DIVISION, WASHINGTON, D.C.

363 LIBRARY OF CONGRESS, PRINTS AND PHOTOGRAPHS DIVISION, WASHINGTON, D.C.

367 LIBRARY OF CONGRESS, MANUSCRIPT DIVISION, WASHINGTON, D.C.

373 GRACE BEDELL FOUNDATION, DELPHOS, KANSAS

378 LIBRARY OF CONGRESS, PRINTS AND PHOTOGRAPHS DIVISION, WASHINGTON, D.C.

379 LIBRARY OF CONGRESS, PRINTS AND PHOTOGRAPHS DIVISION, WASHINGTON, D.C.

380 LIBRARY OF CONGRESS, PRINTS AND PHOTOGRAPHS DIVISION, WASHINGTON, D.C.

389 LIBRARY OF CONGRESS, PRINTS AND PHOTOGRAPHS DIVISION, WASHINGTON, D.C.

390 LIBRARY OF CONGRESS, PRINTS AND PHOTOGRAPHS DIVISION, WASHINGTON, D.C.

406 LIBRARY OF CONGRESS, PRINTS AND PHOTOGRAPHS DIVISION, WASHINGTON, D.C.

410 LIBRARY OF CONGRESS, PRINTS AND PHOTOGRAPHS DIVISION, WASHINGTON, D.C.

419 LIBRARY OF CONGRESS, PRINTS AND PHOTOGRAPHS DIVISION, WASHINGTON, D.C.

421 LIBRARY OF CONGRESS, PRINTS AND PHOTOGRAPHS DIVISION, WASHINGTON, D.C.

424 LIBRARY OF CONGRESS, PRINTS AND PHOTOGRAPHS DIVISION, WASHINGTON, D.C.

431 LIBRARY OF CONGRESS, PRINTS AND PHOTOGRAPHS DIVISION, WASHINGTON, D.C.

436 LIBRARY OF CONGRESS, PRINTS AND PHOTOGRAPHS DIVISION, WASHINGTON, D.C.

439 LIBRARY OF CONGRESS, PRINTS AND PHOTOGRAPHS DIVISION, WASHINGTON, D.C.

453 LIBRARY OF CONGRESS, MANUSCRIPTS DIVISION, WASHINGTON, D.C.

461 LIBRARY OF CONGRESS, PRINTS AND PHOTOGRAPHS DIVISION, WASHINGTON, D.C.

464 LIBRARY OF CONGRESS, PRINTS AND PHOTOGRAPHS DIVISION, WASHINGTON, D.C.

466 LIBRARY OF CONGRESS, PRINTS AND PHOTOGRAPHS DIVISION, WASHINGTON, D.C.

469 LIBRARY OF CONGRESS, PRINTS AND PHOTOGRAPHS DIVISION, WASHINGTON, D.C.

473 LIBRARY OF CONGRESS, PRINTS AND PHOTOGRAPHS DIVISION, WASHINGTON, D.C.

475 LIBRARY OF CONGRESS, PRINTS AND PHOTOGRAPHS DIVISION, WASHINGTON, D.C.

478 LIBRARY OF CONGRESS, PRINTS AND PHOTOGRAPHS DIVISION, WASHINGTON, D.C.

489 LIBRARY OF CONGRESS, PRINTS AND PHOTOGRAPHS DIVISION, WASHINGTON, D.C.

498 LIBRARY OF CONGRESS, PRINTS AND PHOTOGRAPHS DIVISION, WASHINGTON, D.C.

500 LIBRARY OF CONGRESS, PRINTS AND PHOTOGRAPHS DIVISION, WASHINGTON, D.C.

503 LIBRARY OF CONGRESS, PRINTS AND PHOTOGRAPHS DIVISION, WASHINGTON, D.C.

520 LIBRARY OF CONGRESS, PRINTS AND PHOTOGRAPHS DIVISION, WASHINGTON, D.C.

530 LIBRARY OF CONGRESS, PRINTS AND PHOTOGRAPHS DIVISION, WASHINGTON, D.C.

539 LIBRARY OF CONGRESS, PRINTS AND PHOTOGRAPHS DIVISION, WASHINGTON, D.C.

543 LIBRARY OF CONGRESS, PRINTS AND PHOTOGRAPHS DIVISION, WASHINGTON, D.C.

547 LIBRARY OF CONGRESS, MANUSCRIPTS DIVISION, WASHINGTON, D.C.

549 LIBRARY OF CONGRESS, PRINTS AND PHOTOGRAPHS DIVISION, WASHINGTON, D.C.

553 LIBRARY OF CONGRESS, PRINTS AND PHOTOGRAPHS DIVISION, WASHINGTON, D.C.

555 LIBRARY OF CONGRESS, PRINTS AND PHOTOGRAPHS DIVISION, WASHINGTON, D.C.

562 LIBRARY OF CONGRESS, PRINTS AND PHOTOGRAPHS DIVISION, WASHINGTON, D.C.

Index

Page numbers in *italics* refer to illustrations.

RONALD C. WHITE, JR., is the author of *Lincoln's Greatest Speech,* a *New York Times* Notable Book and a *Washington Post* and *San Francisco Chronicle* bestseller, and *The Eloquent President,* a Book-of-the-Month Club selection and a *Los Angeles Times* bestseller. White earned his Ph.D. at Princeton and has taught at UCLA, Princeton Theological Seminary, Whitworth University, Colorado College, and San Francisco Theological Seminary. He is currently a Fellow at the Huntington Library in San Marino, California, and a visiting professor at UCLA. He has lectured at the White House, the Library of Congress, and Gettysburg. He lives with his wife, Cynthia, in La Cañada, California.